CW01184538

SOPHOCLES

TRACHINIAE

SOPHOCLES

TRACHINIAE

With introduction and commentary by
MALCOLM DAVIES

CLARENDON PRESS · OXFORD

Oxford University Press, Great Clarendon Street, Oxford OX2 6DP
Oxford New York
Athens Auckland Bangkok Bogota Bombay
Buenos Aires Calcutta Cape Town Dar es Salaam
Delhi Florence Hong Kong Istanbul Karachi
Kuala Lumpur Madras Madrid Melbourne
Mexico City Nairobi Paris Singapore
Taipei Tokyo Toronto
and associated companies in
Berlin Ibadan

Oxford is a trade mark of Oxford University Press

First published by Oxford University Press 1991
Special edition for Sandpiper Books Ltd., 1996

Text © Oxford University Press 1991
Introduction and Commentary © Malcolm Davies 1991

All rights reserved. No part of this publication may be reproduced,
stored in a retrieval system, or transmitted, in any form or by any means,
without the prior permission in writing of Oxford University Press.
Within the UK, exceptions are allowed in respect of any fair dealing for the
purpose of research or private study, or criticism or review, as permitted
under the Copyright, Designs and Patents Act, 1988, or in the case of
reprographic reproduction in accordance with the terms of the licences
issued by the Copyright Licensing Agency. Enquiries concerning
reproduction outside these terms and in other countries should be
sent to the Rights Department, Oxford University Press,
at the address above

British Library Cataloguing in Publication Data
Data available

Library of Congress Cataloging in Publication Data
Trachiniae/Sophocles: with introduction and commentary
by Malcolm Davies.
Text in Greek; introduction and commentary in English.
Includes bibliographical references and index.
1. Heracles (Greek mythology)—Drama. I. Davies, Malcolm D.
Phil. II. Title.
PA4413.T7   1990   882'.001—dc20   90-7726
ISBN 0-19-814899-2

Printed in Great Britain by
Bookcraft Ltd., Midsomer Norton

PREFACE

PREFACES (especially of academic works) are not always read through thoroughly, do not, perhaps, always deserve a thorough inspection. But the reader who, expecting to find badinage about the last letter of the alphabet, feels predisposed to skip in this case too, is strongly advised to make this book the exception, since the author freely confesses its contents to require careful and elaborate justifying: there is much in the way of both commission and omission that demands explanation.

Its origins are fairly conventional for a work of this type, since it is the end-product of a seminar held in Oxford over the years up until 1987 when the textual criticism of Sophocles' *Trachiniae* was a special subject in 'Literary Greats'. The seminar was supervised by myself and (before his lamented death in 1985) the late T. C. W. Stinton. The publication of Mrs (now Professor) Easterling's commentary on the play (Cambridge, 1982) sharpened our perceptions of the numerous problems posed by this drama, and clarified our minds as to how these should be approached, but left us convinced that there was room for another commentary, one which would (for instance) devote a larger space to consideration of textual problems. However, the premature death of Mr Stinton prevented his participation in the writing of this commentary. I am obliged to his kindness and learning for numerous discussions of the play's difficulties (and, of course, to his published contributions mentioned in the commentary) but it is only right that I should take total and unconditional personal responsibility for the finished product.

It follows that I must accept responsibility for the perhaps controversial decision not to mention Mrs Easterling's commentary (as opposed to her various relevant articles) through the whole

PREFACE

course of the book.[1] This is partly because much of my own commentary had already been provisionally blocked out by the time hers appeared. It then became clear that the disagreements between the two commentaries over the play's many problems were sufficiently numerous to justify publication of a second, more detailed, commentary. But it also became clear that this more detailed commentary would be still further expanded were I to take issue with Mrs Easterling on each (or even every significant) item of disagreement. My verdict (which I stand by) was that the consequent increase in size and polemical content could not be justified. I feel easier on this matter because I have publicly stated my opinion of Mrs Easterling's book in my review (*CR* 33 (1983), 7–9). It seemed to me then (and still seems) that it primarily appealed to sixth-form and University students. My own commentary originates from work on the play with the second category of readers, but hopes to interest professional scholars and colleagues as well.

The latter, though, have every right to query the absence of any section on textual transmission of the type traditionally supplied in works of this sort. But this omission too can be at least explained; also, I hope, justified. The publication, almost simultaneously with the present commentary, of the new Oxford text of Sophocles by Hugh Lloyd-Jones and Nigel Wilson, and their companion volume *Sophoclea*, with full and up-to-date sections on transmission and history of criticism, seemed to me to render any comments from me on this subject superfluous. The work of these scholars must also be cited in mitigation (partial or full, as the reader thinks fit) of my own failure to have collated or even handled a single manuscript of Sophocles in preparation of the book now published. Even though I could not but find this removal of a burden from my shoulders congenial, I trust the impartial judge will agree that reduplication of scholarly effort is senseless and to be avoided if at all possible.

As is now more or less traditional in such cases, the OCT and its apparatus (where 'nos' = Lloyd-Jones and Wilson) are printed with

---

[1] With the exception of a suggestion by L. P. E. Parker recorded in Mrs Easterling's commentary and cited by me on ll. 967 ff.

PREFACE

my commentary, and the latter's lemmata and metrical analyses derive from the former. He who has done no work on the manuscripts has no right to complain at such an arrangement. Besides, I think it is generally conceded that the obvious benefits of such a scheme outweigh the obvious disadvantages. Among these last, disagreement over the preferred reading or conjecture between editor and commentator is likely to loom larger with Sophocles than with Euripides, not least because, as one of his new editors has observed, 'No other author reveals such subtle nuances and no other goes so far in bending language' (Lloyd-Jones, *CR* 33 (1983), 171).

That Lloyd-Jones himself was kind enough to read through and annotate first the manuscript and later the typescript of my commentary has certainly improved it, may conceivably have improved the relevant portions of the OCT, and has inevitably reduced cases of irremediable disagreement. A last-minute view of copy and then proofs for both OCT and *Sophoclea* as they touch on all the plays allowed me to reduce these cases of disagreement still further: they must now be at the barest minimum that can be reasonably expected. I have tried to ensure that my commentary mentions every substantive variant and every conjecture in the OCT's apparatus criticus that I judged significant. On the other hand, I have not confined my discussion of either variants or conjectures to those appearing there, but have also selected for discussion what seemed of interest in the apparatus of Dawe's Teubner, and have ranged further afield in the citation of thought-provoking conjectures and deletions.

My copy-editor Dr John Was expended a great deal of time and intelligence upon the final improvement of my manuscript, in particular upon the elimination of inadvertent discrepancies between my commentary and the OCT (no easy task when even the latter had yet to be published). Dr James Diggle kindly read the first proofs. His great learning effected many improvements and drew to my attention much relevant matter overlooked. It is largely due to him that the Addenda repay a careful reading.

M.D.

CONTENTS

ABBREVIATIONS	xi
METRICAL ABBREVIATIONS	xv
INTRODUCTION	xvii
SIGLA	xl
TEXT	1
COMMENTARY	55
APPENDICES	268
A. The Flexibility of the Oracle in the *Trachiniae*	268
B. Interlinear Hiatus in the *Trachiniae*	270
ADDENDA	273
INDEX OF GREEK WORDS	279
INDEX OF PASSAGES DISCUSSED	281
GENERAL INDEX	283

ABBREVIATIONS

This is not a bibliography, but an explanation of the abbreviations used for the most frequently cited works. Otherwise, Greek authors are generally referred to as in LSJ, periodicals as in *L'Année philologique*: sometimes I have expanded these for greater clarity. The name of Wilamowitz followed by an asterisk refers to unpublished suggestions which this scholar made in lecture or seminar and which were recorded by Eduard Fraenkel in the margins of his copy of Radermacher's commentary on *Trachiniae*, now in the Ashmolean Museum Library, Oxford.

ABV	J. D. Beazley, *Attic Black-Figure Vase-Painters* (Oxford 1956)
*ARV*²	J. D. Beazley, *Attic Red-Figure Vase-Painters*, 2nd edn. (Oxford 1963)
Bers	V. Bers, *Greek Poetic Syntax in the Classical Age* (Yale 1984)
Brommer, *Vasenlisten*³	F. Brommer, *Vasenlisten zur griechischen Heldensage* (Marburg 1973)
Bruhn, *Anhang*	E. Bruhn, *Sophokles*, comm. by F. W. Schneidewin and A. Nauck, viii. *Anhang* (Berlin 1899)
Burkert, *Gr. Relig.*	W. Burkert, *Griechische Religion der archaischen und klassischen Epoche* (Berlin 1977), transl. as *Greek Religion* (Oxford 1985)
Burton	R. W. B. Burton, *The Chorus in Sophocles' Tragedies* (Oxford 1980)
Dale, *MATC*	A. M. Dale, *Metrical Analyses of Tragic Choruses* (BICS suppl. 21. 1–3; 1971–83).
Dawe, *Studies*	R. D. Dawe, *Studies on the Text of Sophocles* i–ii (Leiden 1973); iii (Leiden 1978)
Denniston, *GP*²	J. D. Denniston, *The Greek Particles*, 2nd edn. (Oxford 1954)

ABBREVIATIONS

Diggle, *STE*	J. Diggle, *Studies on the Text of Euripides* (Oxford 1981)
Ellendt–Genthe	*Lexicon Sophocleum* ... by F. Ellendt, 2nd rev. edn. by H. Genthe (Berlin 1872)
Fehling, *Wiederholungsfiguren*	D. Fehling, *Die Wiederholungsfiguren und ihr Gebrauch bei den Griechen vor Gorgias* (Berlin 1969)
Fraenkel, *Beob. zu Aristoph.*	Ed. Fraenkel, *Beobachtungen zu Aristophanes* (Rome 1962)
GP	A. S. F. Gow and D. L. Page, *The Greek Anthology: The Garland of Philip and some Contemporary Epigrams* (Cambridge 1977)
Griffith, *Authenticity of PV*	M. Griffith, *The Authenticity of 'Prometheus Bound'* (Cambridge 1977)
HE	A. S. F. Gow and D. L. Page, *The Greek Anthology: Hellenistic Epigrams* (Cambridge 1965)
Jackson, *MS*	J. Jackson, *Marginalia Scaenica* (Oxford 1955)
KB, KG	R. Kühner, *Ausführliche Grammatik der griechischen Sprache*, 3rd edn., pt. I, by F. Blass; pt. II, by B. Gerth (Hanover 1890–1940)
Kranz, *Stasimon*	W. Kranz, *Stasimon: Untersuchungen zu Form und Gestalt der griechischen Tragödie* (Berlin 1933)
LIMC	*Lexicon Iconographicum Mythorum Classicorum* (Zurich 1981–)
Lloyd-Jones	H. Lloyd-Jones, *CR* 31 (1981), 167–73 (review of Dawe, *Studies*, and of Dawe's Teubner text)
Long, *Language and Thought*	A. A. Long, *Language and Thought in Sophocles: A Study of Abstract Nouns and Poetic Technique* (London 1968)
LSJ	H. G. Liddell and R. Scott, *A Greek–English Lexicon*, 9th edn., rev. H. Stuart-Jones (Oxford 1940; suppl. 1968)
Maas, *GM*	P. Maas, *Greek Metre*, trans. H. Lloyd-Jones (Oxford 1962)

ABBREVIATIONS

March, *The Creative Poet*	J. R. March, *The Creative Poet* (*BICS* suppl. 49; 1987)
Moorhouse	A. C. Moorhouse, *The Syntax of Sophocles* (*Mnem.* suppl. 75; 1982)
Rau, *Paratragodia*	P. Rau, *Paratragodia* (Zetemata 45; 1967)
Reinhardt	K. Reinhardt, *Sophokles*, 4th edn. (Frankfurt 1976), trans. as *Sophocles* (Oxford 1979)
Schuursma	J. A. Schuursma, *De Poetica Vocabulorum Abusione apud Aeschylum* (Amsterdam 1932)
Schwinge	E.-R. Schwinge, *Die Stellung der Trachinierinnen im Werk des Sophokles* (Hypomnemata 1; 1962)
Schwyzer, *Gr. Gr.*	E. Schwyzer, *Griechische Grammatik* (Munich 1939–53)
Sideras, *Aeschylus Homericus*	A. Sideras, *Aeschylus Homericus* (Hypomnemata 31; 1971)
Stinton	T. C. W. Stinton, 'Notes on Greek Tragedy, I', *JHS* 96 (1976), 121–45 (= *Collected Papers on Greek Tragedy*, Oxford 1990, pp. 197–22) [cited by *JHS* pagination]
Taplin, *Stagecraft*	O. Taplin, *The Stagecraft of Aeschylus* (Oxford 1977)
Tycho	Tycho von Wilamowitz, *Die dramatische Technik des Sophokles* (Berlin 1917)
Wackernagel, *Spr. Unt. zu Hom.*	J. W. Wackernagel, *Sprachliche Untersuchungen zu Homer* (Göttingen 1916)
West (1)	M. L. West, *CP* 75 (1980), 364–7 (review of Dawe, *Studies*)
West (2)	M. L. West, *Gnomon* 53 (1981), 522–8 (review of Dawe's Teubner text)
West, *GM*	M. L. West, *Greek Metre* (Oxford 1982)
Zieliński	Th. Zieliński, 'Excurse zu den Trachinierinnen des Sophokles', *Philologus* 9 (1896), 491–540, 577–633, repr. in *Iresione* 1 (1931), 260–391

ABBREVIATIONS

The following editions of and/or commentaries on the *Trachiniae* are referred to in the commentary by their author's names alone:

Hermann	G. Hermann, Berlin 1830
Wunder	Ed. Wunder, Gotha 1844
Nauck–Schneidewin	F. W. Schneidewin, substantially revised by A. Nauck, Berlin 1857
Bergk	Th. Bergk, Leipzig 1858
Campbell	L. Campbell, Oxford 1881 (note also the same scholar's *Paralipomena Sophoclea*, London 1907)
Jebb	R. C. Jebb, Cambridge 1908
Radermacher	L. Radermacher, Berlin 1914 (revision of Nauck–Schneidewin)
Pearson	A. C. Pearson, Oxford Classical Text, 1924
Dain–Mazon	A. Dain (ed.) and P. Mazon (trans.), Budé text, 1955
Kamerbeek	J. C. Kamerbeek, Leiden 1959
Dawe, Dawe[2]	R. D. Dawe, Teubner text, 1979; 2nd edn. 1985

On Easterling's text and commentary see the Preface. The new Oxford text of Sophocles (1990) by Lloyd-Jones and Wilson is referred to as 'the OCT', their accompanying volume of notes (Oxford 1990) as *Sophoclea*.

Fragmentarily preserved authors are cited from the editions mentioned in *A Canon of Greek Authors and Works*, ed. L. Berkowitz and K. A. Squiter, 2nd edn. (Oxford 1986), except that Aeschylus' dramas are cited from Radt's edition (*Tragicorum Graecorum Fragmenta*, 3; Göttingen 1985) and epic fragments from Davies, *Epicorum Graecorum Fragmenta* (Göttingen 1988); and that the fragments of Aristophanes, and comic poets in alphabetical order from Aristophon to Magnes, are quoted from Kassel–Austin's *Poetae Comici Graeci* (Berlin 1983–). The *Greek tragedians* are cited from the latest Oxford texts: Aeschylus: Page (1972). Sophocles: Lloyd-Jones and Wilson (see above); Euripides: Diggle (*Cyclops–Hecuba*, 1984; *Supplices–Ion*, 1981) and Murray, 2nd edn. (*Helen–Rhesus*, 1913). 'Sophocles' is usually shortened to 'S' and 'fr.' *tout court* means a fragment of this author, in cases where no ambiguity results. Σ means 'scholion'.

METRICAL ABBREVIATIONS

⏑		position occupied by a short syllable
–		position occupied by a long syllable
⏒		position occupied by a short or a long syllable (anceps)
‖		verse-end
‖‖		strophe-end
H		hiatus at verse-end
D	– ⏑ ⏑ – ⏑ ⏑ –	in dactylo-epitrite notation
e	– ⏑ –	

anacr.	anacreontic
anap.	anapaest(ic)
aristoph.	aristophanean
bacch.	baccheus
chor.	choriamb(ic)
cr.	cretic
dact.	dactyl(ic)
doch.	dochmiac
enop.	enoplian
glyc.	glyconic
hippon.	hipponacteum
hypodoch.	hypodochmiac
ia.	iamb(ic)
ithyph.	ithyphallic
lec.	lecythion
mol.	molossus
pher.	pherecratean
sp.	spondee
tel.	telesillean
tr.	trochee

METRICAL ABBREVIATIONS

cat.	catalectic
chor. dim. A and B	in A the choriamb comes first
	in B the choriamb comes second
dim.	dimeter
enneasyll.	enneasyllable
hem.	hemiepes
heptasyll.	heptasyllable
hexam.	hexameter
sync.	syncopated
tetram.	tetrameter
trim.	trimeter

For a detailed definition of the above terms and an index to fuller discussion see West, *GM*, pp. 191 ff.

INTRODUCTION

The *Trachiniae* appears to me so very inferior to the other pieces of Sophocles which have reached us, that I could wish there were some warrant for supposing that this tragedy was composed in the age, indeed, and in the school of Sophocles, perhaps by his son Iophon, and that it was by mistake attributed to the father. There is much both in the structure and plan, and in the style of the piece, calculated to excite suspicion; and many critics have remarked that the introductory soliloquy of Deianeira, which is wholly uncalled-for, is very unlike the general character of Sophocles' prologues: and although this poet's usual rules of art are observed on the whole, yet it is very superficially; nowhere can we discern in it the profound mind of Sophocles. But as no writer of antiquity appears to have doubted its authenticity, while Cicero even quotes from it the complaint of Hercules, as from an indisputable work of Sophocles, we are compelled to content ourselves with the remark, that in this one instance the tragedian has failed to reach his usual elevation.

A. W. SCHLEGEL[1]

THE rehabilitation of the *Trachiniae*'s reputation is one of the more impressive achievements of twentieth-century classical scholarship.[2] Closely bound up with it is a changed attitude to two problems: the question of the play's dating; and the issue of characterization, both in general terms and as it effects Deianeira and

---

[1] *A Course of Lectures on Dramatic Art and Literature* (trans. London 1846), 109.
[2] Zieliński, in reprinting 'a once influential, but now deservedly forgotten treatment' (Lloyd-Jones, *CQ* 22 (1972), 221 = *Blood for the Ghosts*, p. 228) in *Iresione* 1 (1931), 260, declared the *Trachiniae* his 'Lieblingstragödie'; but perhaps the manifold eccentricities of his approach delayed rather than accelerated appreciation of the play.

INTRODUCTION

Heracles, the drama's supposed hero and heroine. Whether one approves or not, critical interpretation of the play and the problem of its date have been, as a matter of historical fact, intimately associated. While the *Trachiniae* found little favour with scholars, the urge to prove it an early, perhaps the earliest, extant Sophoclean tragedy was almost irresistible: the numerous perceived faults could then be put down to the dramatist's inexperience and immaturity. And most conspicuous of these faults was the alleged discontinuity of both structure and characterization: as D. L. Page put it with characteristic clarity and incisiveness:[3] 'the action of the play [is] disjointed, and the beauty of the play about Deianeira tarnished by the incomprehensible appendix about Heracles.' It is no coincidence that disillusionment with the notion that the play can be at all closely dated,[4] and enhanced appreciation of the play as a work of

---

[3] *Gnomon* 32 (1960), 317.

[4] For the most recent survey of attempts to date the undatable see T. F. Hoey, *Phoenix* 33 (1979), 210ff. Perhaps the least unsatisfactory criterion advanced is that of interlinear hiatus (see Appendix B below). Here are two examples of the shortcomings that so often characterize attempts to find dating criteria; they come from Schwinge (see Abbreviations), whose approach is more sensitive than most. (1) *Die Entwicklung des Dreigesprächs* (p. 73): absence of a three-cornered dialogue is seen as a sign of earliness. (Therefore, incidentally, all Sophoclean trilogies must have originally lacked such dialogue, and once achieved the three-cornered dialogue can never have failed to feature at least once in a play.) The *Trachiniae* lacks it even at 385 ff., where Deianeira's intervention would effortlessly have produced it, and is therefore early. The possibility of stylistic or other explanations for this failure is dismissed (p. 73 n. 2): one might think that Deianeira's silence at 402–35 is dramatically effective, but would a *brief* intervention from Deianeira have made much difference? But why should Sophocles have risked so dissipating an effective device by trivial tampering (unless to convince a critic twenty-five centuries away that he was the master, not the slave, of the three-cornered dialogue)? (2) *Die Diptychon-Form* (pp. 75–6): this too is seen as a sign of earliness. But again we must infer that at first *all* Sophocles' trilogies were diptych and progressively lost that form—and indeed (p. 76) we are offered the naïve and simplistic statement that the *Antigone* shows partial advance over the diptych form and therefore belongs bang in the middle of *Aj.* and *Tr.* (diptych) and *OT* (non-diptych). The possibility of stylistic or other advantage behind a temporary adaptation of the form is again overlooked.

INTRODUCTION

art, begin to be manifested at roughly the same time: they are negative and positive sides of the same coin. If the play's date of production cannot be firmly fixed, we must finally try to evaluate it on its own terms. And such an evaluation will be easier if we unburden ourselves of the idea that every Greek tragedy must revolve around one central figure.[5] If the Attic tragedians were more interested in unity of theme than the persistence throughout of a single hero or heroine, then the central theme of the *Trachiniae* may be seen[6] as the working out (largely through the agency of Deianeira) of Zeus' plan for his son Heracles. The Iliadic phrase Διὸς δ' ἐτελείετο βουλή might almost serve as the play's subtitle. Of course Sophocles has other, ancillary, concerns: the power of love (as it affects Heracles, Deianeira, Achelous, and Nessus); the late (too late) movement from ignorance to knowledge (as manifested in Heracles, Deianeira, and Hyllus); the ambiguous oracle which, despite the shift in its sense and meaning from scene to scene, runs like a thread through the play, supplying much of its unity; the contrast and balance between the introverted feminine world of the wife at home and the extrovert hero-husband abroad. And of course Sophocles is interested in both Deianeira and Heracles as individuals: but we must not sentimentalize the former or exaggerate the brutality of the latter,[7] in whom may be

---

[5] Against which see e.g. J. Jones, *On Aristotle and Greek Tragedy* (London 1962), 11 ff., with the comments of Lloyd-Jones, *Review of Engl. Studies* 15 (1964), 221 ff. = *Classical Survivals*, pp. 111 ff. For more recent discussion of the relationship between character and action in Greek tragedy see J. Gould, *PCPS* 24 (1978), 43 ff., S. Halliwell, *Aristotle's Poetics* (London 1987), 138 ff., esp. 164 ff.

[6] So e.g. Lloyd-Jones, *CQ* 22 (1972), 223 = *Blood for the Ghosts*, p. 230, arguing against Tycho von Wilamowitz's attitude to Deianeira and Heracles: 'need either be the central figure? The play is about the events that led to the death of Heracles: it shows the fulfilment of the plan of Zeus.'

[7] As Gilbert Murray memorably did in his essay 'Heracles, "The Best of Men"' (cf. *Greek Studies* (Oxford 1946), 122 = *Sophokles* (Wege der Forschung 95; 1967, 342) with his picture of Deianeira as 'womanly in the last degree, tender, chaste, devoted, living for others, and therefore the more battered and broken amid the lusts of a brutish world' and Heracles 'the all-admired grabber, smiter and conqueror, who is stronger, harder, greedier than other men'. Murray's piece

INTRODUCTION

recognized most of the uncompromising and egotistical traits that, for good and ill, characterize the typical Sophoclean hero.[8] And we must recognize that Sophocles' interest in them is subordinated, even more markedly in this play than in others, to the drama's overriding theme.[9]

If the play's central concern, then, is with the working out of Zeus' plan for his heroic son, attention becomes centred on the precise details of that plan. Hence the particular interest shown during recent years[10] in the very end of the play and whether it contains any hint as to the apotheosis of Heracles from the pyre. Just how benevolent Zeus' plan is becomes a question very materially affected by the likelihood or not of allusion to this ultimate deification. Concerning this, external evidence is inexplicit,[11] and the issue is best discussed in the context of a consideration of those similar allusions to events lying beyond the scope of the drama itself which

---

is, indeed, 'one of his most disappointing productions, showing utter inability to understand Sophocles' conception of the great hero' (Lloyd-Jones, CR 19 (1969), 33). But its errors are instructive. For a balanced treatment of the contrast see Easterling, ICS 6 (1981), 56 ff., esp. 63.

[8] In the sense of Bernard Knox's book (see next n.)

[9] To this extent the *Trachiniae* may still prove disappointing to those primarily concerned with the archetypal Sophoclean hero as described by Knox: witness its almost total absence from the text and indexes of *The Sophoclean Hero* (Berkeley and Los Angeles (1966).

[10] See esp. Lloyd-Jones, *The Justice of Zeus* (Sather Class. Lect. 41; Berkeley etc. 1971), 126 ff. (and p. 199), following Bowra, *Sophoclean Tragedy* (Oxford 1944), 159–60 in accepting such an allusion. A subtle treatment from Easterling, ICS 6 (1981), 64 ff., argued (p. 69) against any *compulsory* allusions: 'Sophocles leaves a gap' and is content with ambiguous clues.

[11] For recent surveys of the relevant evidence, literary and artistic, see Stinton, in *Papers Given at a Colloquium . . . in Honour of R. P. Winnington-Ingram* (London 1987), 1 ff., Boardman, in *Studien zur Mythologie und Vasenmalerei* (Schauenburg Festschrift; Mainz 1986), 127 ff. The notion of the hero's apotheosis is relatively early and possibly a 6th-cent. Attic invention (cf. West, *The Hesiodic Catalogue of Women*, p. 169 and n. 91): the pyre can be traced back no earlier than the 460s; the link between the two motifs is first attested in Eur. *Hcld.* 910 ff. and Soph. *Phil.* 727 ff.

INTRODUCTION

have been alleged for other plays of Sophocles. Such is the context chosen by the late T. C. W. Stinton for his treatment of the problem in a posthumously published paper,[12] where an allusion to Heracles' apotheosis is rejected. His approach is characteristically sensitive and tactful: yet one may finally doubt whether limits for allusion in Greek literature can be firmly prescribed even by so sympathetic a judge as Stinton. Perhaps too the context for discussion might be widened still further to include other genres. When Agamemnon in *Il.* 1. 105 ff. rounds on Calchas with the complaint μάντι κακῶν, οὐ πώ ποτέ μοι τὸ κρήγυον εἶπας· | αἰεί τοι τὰ κάκ' ἐστὶ φίλα φρεςὶ μαντεύεςθαι, | ἐςθλὸν δ' οὔτε τί πω εἶπας ἔπος οὐδ' ἐτέλεςςας, the hyperbole is fully explicable in terms of the rhetoric[13] of argument and invective. Need we look further? Evidence that some ancient critics did is afforded by a scholion on the Homeric passage which presupposes an interpretation of the remark in terms of Calchas' earlier recommendation of the sacrifice of Iphigenia at Aulis.[14] Dogmatism either way is undesirable: but it is hard to see how such an allusion could be totally denied now; still less how the poet could originally have precluded any such mental appeal to this legend lying outside the poem's scope by, say, one or two members of the audience. So too for Sophocles: Apollo and the curse on the house of Labdacus with *Antigone* and the *OT*; the pursuit of Orestes by the Erinyes with the *Electra*; and the final catastrophe that overwhelms Antigone with the *OC*. Could Sophocles have prevented recourse by some of his audience to some or any of these sequels and explanations? Should we leave them out of account? The contrast between divine knowledge and mortal ignorance is a central Sophoclean preoccupation: most conspicuously exploited in the *OT*, it undoubtedly permeates the *Trachiniae*

---

[12] 'The Scope and Limits of Allusion in Greek Tragedy', in *Greek Tragedy and its Legacy* (Conacher Festschrift; 1986), 67 ff., esp. 84 ff. = *Collected Papers on Greek Tragedy* (Oxford 1990), 454 ff., esp. 479 ff.

[13] For 'the typical "you always ..." of quarrels, which Homer, as a keen student of life, reproduces' see Macleod on *Il.* 24. 62–3.

[14] Erbse, *Scholia Graeca in Homeri Iliadem*, i. 40.

INTRODUCTION

too. In seeking to exclude allusion to Heracles' apotheosis as a possible justification for some of the seemingly inexplicable human suffering presented in that play, we are also defining, perhaps too rigidly, the limits of mortal ignorance and knowledge. Sophocles may have preferred to keep the question open[15] in this play and elsewhere. See now the detailed argument of P. Holt, *JHS* 109 (1989), 69 ff.

The Story before Sophocles:[16] *'The Sack of Oechalia'*

The contribution to the pre-Sophoclean tradition made by the Hesiodic *Catalogue of Women* has been reassessed by March, *The Creative Poet*, pp. 49 ff. For relatively recent studies of the Οἰχαλίας ἅλωσις note in particular Paul Friedländer's *Herakles* (Berlin 1907), 65 ff., Bethe's vigorous critique thereof (*GGA* 169 (1907), 697 ff.), and Friedländer's restatement, modification, and defence of his original case—in reply to Bethe—at *Rh. Mus.* 69 (1914), 335 ff. = *Studien zur antiken Literatur und Kunst*, 48 ff.[17] See

---

[15] This is very similar to phrasing used by T. F. Hoey (*Arethusa* 10 (1977), 272–3). But perhaps we should not proceed to suggest (as he does) that 'the play... felt itself unable to decide' (against this notion see Easterling, art. cit. (n. 10), 68). That 'to Sophocles' audience Heracles must have been seen as approaching his apotheosis, since his becoming a god was the familiar and fully-accepted ending to the legend of his life on earth' has now been eloquently argued by March, *The Creative Poet*, pp. 49 ff. (I quote from p. 72).

[16] There is no need or space here for a full survey of the numerous treatments of the Heracles myth. Two up-to-date syntheses in English: G. S. Kirk, *The Nature of Greek Myths* (Harmondsworth 1974), 176 ff., and W. Burkert, *Structure and History in Greek Mythology and Ritual* (Berkeley and Los Angeles 1979), 78 ff., with bibliography at p. 176 n. 1.

[17] Friedländer's works try to 'reconstruct and localise early archaic poems about Heracles, creations of Greek poets in special circumstances'. The description is Burkert's (*Structure and History*, p. 79), and he supplies a handy critique of the presuppositions of such an approach. Note in particular his conclusion that 'it is true that myth may reflect certain historical situations to which the traditional tale had been applied, but it is wrong to conclude that if a myth is used and makes sense in a certain situation, it has been invented or "created" expressly for this purpose'.

INTRODUCTION

too Tycho von Wilamowitz, pp. 98 ff., 106 ff.[18] Further bibliography in Burkert, *Mus. Helv.* 29 (1972), 80 n. 27, whose own treatment of the epic (pp. 80 ff.) is very important.

It will be best if we begin with a consideration of the events which must—as the work's very title suggests—have formed the core and kernel of the poem. The testimonia concerning the actual sack of Oechalia[19] and its causes may most conveniently be consulted as they are excerpted and written out on one page of Schwartz's edn. of the Euripidean scholia (ii. 71). The greater part of them are to be found in other scholia and the mythographers; note too the evidence of Pherecydes, *FGrH* 3 F 82, Herodorus, ibid. 31 F 37, and Lysimachus, ibid. 382 F 3. See in general Robert, *Heldensage* ii. 567 ff., 579 ff.

The basis of the story is a folk-tale motif which we also encounter in, for instance, the legend of Oenomaus and Hippodameia: the bride as contest-prize (cf. Stith Thompson, *Motif-Index of Folk-Literature* H 310, H 326. 1. 2, H 335, etc.). Omitting minor variants, we may sketch a general picture of how Heracles, having variously disposed of Megara, is in search of another wife, and is thus led to visit Oechalia, whose king, Eurytus, is offering the hand of his daughter Iole to whoever should vanquish him and—in some versions or—his sons at archery. Heracles duly wins but is refused the bride (the reason for refusal usually given is fear that Iole's offspring might meet the fate suffered by Megara's). In revenge, Heracles musters an army against Oechalia, sacks the city, kills Eurytus and his sons, and drags Iole away by force.

This must have been the original form of the legend, the most basic state of the tale.[20] Only one scholar has taken the extreme view

---

[18] For criticism of this section of Tycho's book see Fraenkel *ap.* Lloyd-Jones, *CQ* 22 (1972), 221 n. 4 = *Blood for the Ghosts*, p. 228 n. 27.

[19] On the disputed locale of the city, see Jacoby on Hecataeus *FGrH* 1 F 28.

[20] Tycho von Wilamowitz (pp. 112–13) excogitates an even more elementary and primary form of the story, in which Heracles overcomes Eurytus in a contest of bow and arrow and Iole plays no role: the motif of Heracles' love for her is taken to be a later embellishment. There is no support for this theory in the passage where Tycho seeks support for it, Eur. *Her.* 472–3, for, in spite of the

INTRODUCTION

that this and this alone formed the subject-matter of the *Oechalias Halosis*, and that scholar is Tycho von Wilamowitz (p. 99). His grounds for this belief are certainly inadequate: even if κλείω δ' Εὔρυτον ὅσσ' ἔπαθεν, | καὶ ξανθὴν Ἰόλειαν were the actual opening words of the poem rather than Callimachus' own summary of it at *Epigr.* 6, it would be unreasonable to infer that its contents were strictly limited to 'die Geschichte der Eurytiden, die Zerstörung Oichalias und Gewinnung Ioles'. Nor should the two words that comprise the epic's title be taken as preserving the truth, the whole truth, and nothing but the truth as to the entire contents of the poem.

The majority of scholars are probably right, then, to assume that the above tradition of Heracles' revenge on Oechalia was already connected by the *Oechalias Halosis* with other details in the way that Sophocles' *Trachiniae* or the late mythographers exhibit. Difficulties arise, of course, as soon as we try to specify precisely which details, or the mode of connection. In the mythographer Apollodorus, for instance, the refusal of Iole's hand and her final abduction are separated from each other by a number of incidents: Heracles exacts the first instalment of his revenge by treacherously throwing Eurytus' son Iphitus from the walls of Tiryns. He is punished for this crime by a year's enslavement to Omphale and upon being released from servitude he wins the hand of Deianeira. Did these details occur in our epic, and if so do they further imply the appearance of Heracles' death and his pyre on Mt. Oeta? An already difficult problem is rendered more hazardous still by the distortions which Sophocles' dramatic technique has imposed on the narrative of events given in the *Trachiniae*, our earliest source to be both detailed and extant.

The dramatic considerations that have warped the *Trachiniae*'s account fall under two heads (see Friedländer, pp. 65–6 n. 2, p. 66

---

elder Wilamowitz ad loc., Megara's reference to the sack of Oechalia does not presuppose any such ancient tradition. The Euripidean verses certainly fail to mention Iole, but that is because Euripides has reworked the legend and omitted Iole as incompatible with his καινοτομία.

INTRODUCTION

n. 2, Tycho, pp. 100 ff., 106 ff., 142 ff.): (1) Heracles' marriage to Deianeira is brought forward in time and made to precede the murder of Iphitus and the consequent servitude so that Heracles' long absence from home creates a great deal of suspense; (2) Lichas' account of the sack of Oechalia and its motives (260 ff.) must conceal Iole's role, the truth about which only emerges in dribbles (351 ff., 379 ff., 475 ff.). I believe that Lichas' fib (265 ff.) about a Heracles who seeks vengeance for Eurytus' insult (the Eurytids surpass Heracles in archery) and injury (the drunken Heracles thrust out of doors) is Sophocles' own invention (see ad loc.). In spite of Robert and Burkert, the same detail is not implied by Euphronius' red-figure vase-painting of Heracles and the Eurytids (see below, p. xxxv). Heracles' exile and association with Omphale stem from his treacherous killing of Iphitus, and that was connected with his love for Iole which in turn led to his death. To what extent these details were already to be found in our epic is impossible to say, but the question is important enough to justify a detailed examination of earlier hypotheses. Our findings will be almost entirely negative, but that too is significant enough.

Let us examine the various elements just listed. We shall endeavour not only to decide how likely it is that they featured in the lost epic but also to throw as much light as possible on the question whether they were invented by that poem's author or instead formed part of a pre-existing tradition. We had best begin with the sack itself.

Friedländer (pp. 73-4) argues that the tradition of Oechalia's sack must be a post-Homeric invention, because it is inconsistent with the scheme of things adumbrated in the *Odyssey*. That poem has its hero relate (8. 224 ff.) how Eurytus was killed by Apollo for his presumption in challenging the god to an archery contest. And at a later stage in the narrative (21. 3 ff.) we learn that Odysseus' bow was a gift from Iphitus made on the occasion of their meeting in Messene, when the latter hero was engaged upon the fatal search for his steeds. Iphitus in turn had received the bow from Eurytus.

The two passages are certainly consistent with each other, and as

INTRODUCTION

certainly incompatible with the familiar tradition outlined above, in which Eurytus meets his end at the hands of Heracles while his city blazes about him, and is predeceased by his son Iphitus, whom Heracles has already separately dispatched. The tradition is therefore un-Homeric. But does it follow that the tradition is post-Homeric too? If this were the case, the author of an epic entitled *The Sack of Oechalia* would come near the top of any list of likely inventors. However, to equate un- and post-Homeric in this way is to underestimate Homer's own amply documented addiction to idiosyncratic innovations in myth. Friedländer himself plausibly identifies Odysseus' encounter with Iphitus in the second passage as a Homeric addition to the story of the latter's death.[21] But he supposes that the *Oechalias Halosis* substituted Heracles for the Apollo of the first passage. A god is certainly more natural than a mortal in this motif of punishment for boasting. But the picture of a bride won in a contest is another common folk-tale motif which could easily be older than Homer's alternative. The latter may be the merest *ad hoc* invention to allow Odysseus a bow of sufficiently glorious descent.[22] The smoothness with which Agamemnon's sceptre passes from hand to hand in *Il.* 2. 101 ff. is achieved by a calculated silence about family strife, and a comparable reworking may be at the bottom of *Od.* 8 and 21.

Unlike Friedländer, we now know that the sack of Oechalia appeared (with Heracles' passion for Iole its immediate inspiration) as early as the Hesiodic *Catalogue*. See Hes. fr. 26. 31 ff. MW: τοὺς δὲ μέθ' ὁπλοτάτην τέκετο ξανθὴν Ἰόλειαν, | τ[ῆς ἕ]νεκ' Οἰχ[αλ]ίη[ν . . . | Ἀμφι]τρυωνιάδης—also Hes. fr. 229 with Merkelbach and West's app. crit. ad loc. The relationship between these lines and the *Oechalias Halosis* is quite uncertain, of course: on the likely dating and place of origin of the Hesiodic *Catalogue* see now West, *The Hesiodic Catalogue of Women* (Oxford 1985), 164 ff., and March, pp. 157 ff.

[21] Thus discounting Gercke's idea (*Neue Jhb.* 8 (1905), 408–9) that the feature derived from the Οἰχαλίας ἅλωςις.

[22] So e.g. Van der Valk *ap.* Stanford, *The Ulysses Theme* (Oxford 1954), 257 n. 2.

INTRODUCTION

Iole

Her appearance in the *Oechalias Halosis* is guaranteed by the testimony of fr. 1, Callimachus' Sixth Epigram, and the dictates of common sense. But how far did her activities extend? Essential for an answer to this question is Carl Robert's observation (*Heldensage* ii. 584 n. 3) that no offspring are anywhere attested for Iole and Heracles.[23] It does not seem too rash an inference from this negative fact that, in Burkert's words (p. 84), 'Iole ist von Anfang an und stets nur der Anlaß für Herakles' Tod.' To object that Iole is reserved by tradition for the role of mother to Hyllus' children is merely to make the same statement in different words, since Hyllus and Iole cannot be united until the death of Heracles.

Ancient scholarship was concerned to stress Homer's ignorance of this particular heroine (Σ *Od.* 21. 22 τὸν γὰρ Ἰόλης ἔρωτα οὐκ οἶδεν ὁ ποιητής; cf. Eust. 1899. 38).[24] As early as Hes. fr. 229 Iole and the sack of her city are immediately followed by Heracles' reception on Olympus. Again the connection between this literary treatment and the *Oechalias Halosis* is unascertainable. On the evidence of 'Hesiod' see now March, pp. 59 ff.

Iphitus' Death and the Enslavement to Omphale

As we have seen (above, p. xxv), Heracles' murder of this son of Eurytus occurs as early as *Od.* 21. 31 ff., where, in a passage whose harsh stance towards Heracles has long been recognized,[25] we are told how Iphitus was entertained by that hero while searching for some stolen horses. Heracles killed him and kept the horses himself:

---

[23] The observation rules out the notion (Tycho, p. 99 n. 1) that Iole was originally conceived as Heracles' wife. Tycho claims that Sophocles 'heißt sie immer Gattin', but this is a misleading statement. The play as a whole treats her as a slave, a piece of war-booty: see J. K. MacKinnon, *CQ* 21 (1971), 33 ff.

[24] The formulation is, of course, Aristarchus': see Séveryns, *Le Cycle épique dans l'école d'Aristarque* (Liège and Paris 1928), 191.

[25] e.g. Robert, *Heldensage*, ii. 581, G. K. Galinsky, *The Heracles Theme* (Oxford 1972), 12, Kirk, *Nature of Greek Myths*, 194.

INTRODUCTION

could it be more strongly implied that he had stolen them in the first place? The stolen horses recur in Sophocles' *Trachiniae* (270 ff.), but there for the first time we encounter an additional motive for the murder: Heracles' grudge against his victim's father.[26]

In Sophocles (as in later authors) the murder of Iphitus and the year's servitude to Omphale are linked to each other in a tight nexus of crime and punishment. In Sophocles they are both associated, chronologically and causally, with the sack of Oechalia. Did such an association find mention in the epic named after that event? The murder certainly, and the servitude very probably, existed in tradition before the time of Sophocles, but Tycho von Wilamowitz (pp. 101 ff. and 106 ff.) vigorously argued that their connection with the sack is the invention of the author of the *Trachiniae*, and he has convinced, among others, Walter Burkert (art. cit., p. 81 n. 31).

Tycho alleged that Sophocles' insertion of the murder and enslavement motifs into the story of Heracles' revenge against the city of Oechalia leaves certain striking anomalies in its wake: it is odd that, after the insults received from Eurytus, Heracles should go straight home and wait until his return from enslavement in Lydia before getting round to the task of raising an army against his enemy (p. 108). If one retorts that Heracles does at least exact a first instalment of his revenge by murdering Iphitus, one must expect the answer that it is no less odd to find the unsuspecting Iphitus prepared to be entertained by his father's enemy (p. 107).

These are serious objections[27] requiring a serious response. But

---

[26] Friedländer (pp. 74–5) observes that the whole tradition of Iphitus' murder contains an odd contradiction: if, as Apollod. 2. 6. 1 has it, Iphitus alone of the Eurytids spoke out for giving Iole to Heracles, why should he be treated so villainously? If, on the other hand, he was as ill-disposed to Heracles as his brothers and father, why should he lodge with him in this foolhardy manner? Friedländer supposed the explanation to lie in the relatively late origin of the tradition regarding Oechalia's sack (so that the murder of Iphitus predated the hostility to Eurytus).

[27] Not so a third raised by Tycho (p. 108): 'der Meuchelmord des Iphitos ist ein eigentümliches Mittel, die Schwester zur Gattin zu gewinnen.' So is the

INTRODUCTION

that response should surely consist in the observation that the oddities are due to the overlaying of the original tradition with the lies of Lichas. The inconsistencies may even be intended to alert the audience to the herald's mendacity. And those of us who believe that Sophocles himself invented the erroneous portions of Lichas' narrative will see in the inconsistencies sketched above further justification for their viewpoint.

Tycho, who refuses to accept that Sophocles did invent those portions, will not accept either (pp. 111–12) that the oddities noted above could be deliberate. He persists in his notion that they are caused by Sophocles' interpolating into the expedition against Oechalia the story of Iphitus' death and the consequent enslavement. This theory is strengthened, he supposes, by the inconsistencies—attributable to the same process—which still remain if we accept the messenger's account as preserving the truth. Here, however, I feel that the anomalies are significantly less real. The supposed difficulty of cramming Heracles' return from Lydia, his mustering of an army, and the capture of Oechalia[28] into the space of three months is not very great at all. Nor am I particularly disturbed by the way in which Heracles at once proceeds to attack the very father and abduct the very sister of the man whose murder Zeus has just finished punishing by a year's exile. The open assault upon them is very different from the underhand treachery against a guest which Zeus abhorred in the case of Iphitus' death. The remaining inconsistencies as to whether Heracles regularly resides in Trachis or has never before clapped eyes on the place are caused, as Tycho himself is well aware (pp. 101–2), by Sophocles' bringing forward in time Heracles' marriage to Deianeira (see above, p. xxv).

I am therefore unconvinced by the argument that Sophocles must have been the first to unite Iphitus' death and the servitude to

murder of the rest of her brothers and her father; but that is how Heracles chose to proceed on this particular occasion.

[28] Tycho adds to this list of events 'Besuch und Werbung des Eurytos' (p. 111), with what justification I do not see. Tycho himself admits (pp. 114ff.) the triviality of other comparable chronological difficulties in the play.

INTRODUCTION

Omphale with the story of Oechalia's destruction. The possibility that these mythical events were already linked in an earlier epic must remain open.[29]

Robert (*Heldensage* ii. 583-4) argues that Omphale must have played a part in the epic *Oechalias Halosis*, because an interval is required between Heracles' killing of the Eurytids at the archery contest and the sack of their city, an interval in which the hero will be cleansed of blood-guilt and seek the help of Ceyx. But again the grounds for the assumption are inadequate: that Heracles first killed Iole's brothers at the actual competition where she was refused him is based solely on the two hypotheses that such a scene is depicted on Greek vases and that these are inspired by the *Oechalias Halosis*. Neither hypothesis is in fact necessary (see below, pp. xxxiv-vii).

Deianeira and the Death of Heracles

On these see in particular F. Stoessl, *Der Tod des Herakles* (Zurich 1945), 16 ff., and March, pp. 49 ff.

Scholars have held the most diverse views concerning the presence or absence of these features in the now lost *Oechalias Halosis*. According to Tycho von Wilamowitz (p. 99), in the light of Callimachus' Sixth Epigram 'wird man die Figur Deianeiras und den Konflikt der zwei Frauen mit seinen Folgen von dem Gedichte des Kreophylos ganz fernhalten müssen'. Friedländer, on the other hand (p. 71), thought that the author of our epic must have practically invented the story of Deianeira ('wenn nicht ihre Gestaltung, so doch ihre maßgebende Fassung'). And Stoessl (p. 17) brings the wheel full circle by asserting that the conflict of the two women for Heracles' affections must have taken up much of the poem. In this composition, he continues, 'Herakles erscheint als Opfer seiner Begehrlichkeit nach Frauen' (p. 19).

Deianeira and the poisoned robe appear as early in literature as

[29] The absence of Iphitus' death from the *Oechalias Halosis* is assumed (on no very good grounds) by Bethe, *GGA* 169 (1907), 704, Robert, *Heldensage*, ii. 586, and, by implication, Merkelbach and West on Hes. fr. 26. 31^.

INTRODUCTION

Hes. fr. 25. 20 ff., and Nessus ferries Deianeira over the river and is killed by Heracles as early as Archil. frr. 286–8 W (on which see Stoessl, pp. 22 ff., March, p. 55). The very name $\Delta\eta\iota\acute{a}\nu\epsilon\iota\rho\alpha$ is often taken to imply 'Töterin des Mannes' (Stoessl, p. 17: cf. F. Errandonea, *Mnem.* 55 (1927), 145 ff.), but the reference to Medea which Stoessl (and March, p. 57) found so very suggestive is, as likely as not, irrelevant (the fragment of the *Oechalias Halosis* which supposedly mentioned her is probably spurious: see my remarks in *Mnem.* 42 (1989), 469). Nevertheless, March is right to stress that (for all we know) the pre-Sophoclean Deianeira may have been 'a boldhearted and courageous woman ... more likely to kill from rage rather than mistakenly from love'.

Heracles' Death and Apotheosis

Here too scholars have regularly drawn conclusions from totally inadequate evidence. Thus, when F. G. Welcker (*Ep. Cycl.* i. 218) argues that the *Oechalias Halosis* is likely to have ended with pyre and apotheosis because several other epics ended with the similar transfiguration of a hero (Amphiaraus in the *Thebais*, Menelaus in the *Nostoi*, Odysseus in the *Telegony*, Achilles in the *Aethiopis*) there is a ready answer: that these epics did so end is, in every instance but the last, based on nothing more substantial than Welcker's own surmise and speculation. And even the *Aethiopis* did not actually *end* with Achilles' transference to Leuce but continued at least as far as Ajax's suicide, as we know from fr. 1 of the poem. Burkert (p. 84) rightly notes that the epic would be more 'Homeric' if it said nothing of immortality and ended with the sombre fact of Heracles' death (cf. *Il.* 18. 117–18). How impressed one is by this observation will depend upon how eager one is to suppose that the ancient attribution of the poem to Homer (and Callimachus' admiration of it) must have had some justification on grounds of style and content.

INTRODUCTION

Sophocles' Trachiniae *and* Bacchylides, Dithyramb 16

The *Oechalias Halosis* has been assumed as the source of the first of these works by, for instance, Wilamowitz, *Sitzb. d. Preuß. Akad. d. Wiss.* (1925), 57 = *Kl. Schr.* v/2. 78. Tycho von Wilamowitz (p. 99) was perfectly prepared to posit *an* epic as the source for much of the content of Sophocles' play (and Bacchylides' poem) but supposed (see above, p. xxviii) that the *Oechalias Halosis* could be excluded from consideration. Those of us who are not prepared to dogmatize about that poem's contents on such slender evidence (see p. xxix) may be readier to identify Sophocles' source with the *Sack of Oechalia*, as long as we remember how far such a hypothesis must remain from certainty.

The similarities between the two extant compositions are often very striking. For instance, both authors connect Deianeira, Iole, and Nessus, and both have Heracles march from Oechalia to Κηναῖον (*Dith.* 16, *Tr.* 238), there to sacrifice to Zeus. The majority of scholars have seen fit to seek an explanation of the undeniable similarities by recourse to the hypothesis of mutual dependence upon a lost epic.[30] The alternative possibility of the indebtedness of the dramatist to the lyric (or vice versa) has appealed to fewer minds, though Stoessl's comparison of the two accounts (pp. 58 ff.) culminates in the conclusion (p. 63) that Bacchylides models himself on the Sophoclean lines, an opinion also put forward by E.-R. Schwinge[31] on the ground that Bacchylides' telling of the story is so elliptical that it must presuppose the fuller account in the *Trachiniae*, especially since it gives a tragic interpretation to the story. I feel this underestimates the tendency of

---

[30] So e.g. Tycho, p. 111, Friedländer, p. 68, Jebb in his commentary on Bacchylides (p. 371), Kamerbeck in his commentary on the *Trachiniae* (pp. 6–7). For other scholars who take the same view (and for the most part take the epic to be the *Oechalias Halosis*), see Schwinge, p. 128 n. 3. Schwinge, pp. 132 ff., gives a detailed account of the similarities between Bacchylides' and Sophocles' versions of the story.

[31] pp. 128 ff. This view has gained recent support from March, *Creative Poet*, pp. 62–3.

INTRODUCTION

much lyric narrative to be allusive,[32] as well as the difficulty of giving the tale a colouring anything other than tragic. Other attempts to identify cases where our epic is the alleged 'common source' of two or more later accounts are largely unsatisfactory. Friedländer (pp. 71–2), for instance, suggested that Bacchylides (5. 56ff.) and Pindar (fr. 249A Sn.; cf. fr. dub. 346) derived their respective pictures of the encounter between Heracles and Meleager in Hades from the *Oechalias Halosis*, where it will have served as προπαρασκευή for the main events. But even if the joint source of the two lyric poets could be firmly established as epic, our poem is by no means the only candidate. Recent scholars have preferred to think in terms of a *Katabasis* of Heracles (see Lloyd-Jones, *Maia* 19 (1967), 206ff., etc.).

However, the resemblance of *Tr.* 856ff. ἰὼ κελαινὰ λόγχα προμάχου δορός, | ἃ τότε θοὰν νύμφαν | ἄγαγες ἀπ' αἰπεινᾶς | τάνδ' Οἰχαλίας αἰχμᾶι to Eur. *Hipp.* 545ff. τὰν μὲν Οἰχαλίαι | πῶλον ἄζυγα λέκτρων | ... | ... | δρομάδα ναΐδ' ὅπως τε βάκχαν ... | ... | Ἀλκμήνας τόκωι Κύπρις ἐξέδωκεν κτλ. may best be explained by the hypothesis of a common epic source: see ad loc.

Other Possible Sources for the Lost Epic

Two specific sets of details from Apollodorus' account of the sack have seemed to some (in particular Burkert, pp. 83–4) to have an epic, indeed a Homeric, ring to them: ἀφικόμενος δὲ εἰς Τραχῖνα στρατιὰν ἐπ' Οἰχαλίαν συνήθροισεν, Εὔρυτον τιμωρήσασθαι θέλων. συμμαχούντων δὲ αὐτῶι Ἀρκάδων καὶ Μηλιέων τῶν ἐκ Τραχῖνος καὶ Λοκρῶν τῶν Ἐπικνημιδίων, κτείνας μετὰ τῶν παίδων Εὔρυτον αἱρεῖ τὴν πόλιν. καὶ θάψας τῶν σὺν αὐτῶι στρατευσαμένων τοὺς ἀποθανόντας, Ἱππασόν τε τὸν Κήυκος καὶ Ἀργεῖον καὶ Μέλανα τοὺς Λικυμνίου παῖδας, καὶ λαφυραγωγήσας τὴν

---

[32] A point noted (but not adequately answered) by Schwinge, p. 131 n. 1.

INTRODUCTION

πόλιν, ἦγεν Ἰόλην αἰχμάλωτον (2. 7. 7). Some sort of catalogue of Heracles' allies and an account of the burial of the slain on Heracles' side would indeed be appropriate for an epic.

The Evidence of Art[33]

A small group of vases variously depict some of the encounters which occurred between Heracles and Eurytus and his offspring. Most of them are listed and discussed by Gisela Richter in *AJA* 20 (1916), 125 ff. Sufficient care has not always been taken in relating some of these artefacts to supposedly relevant literary texts. The *Oechalias Halosis* is one of these texts.

Some of these vases allow of a fairly easy and immediate interpretation, as with a red-figured vase in Palermo (V653: ARV^2 73, 30 = *LIMC* s.v. Eurytus 4) which depicts the archery contest of Heracles and the Eurytids ('anger over the contest' according to Robert, *Heldensage* ii. 582). Others, however, show a conflict between Heracles and the Eurytids which scholars have found difficult to characterize: part of the representation seems appropriate to the archery contest, part to a martial conflict such as we would expect at the sack of Oechalia. Thus, on a vase now in Madrid (10916: *ABV* 508 = *LIMC* s.v. Antiphonus i I. 861 = *LIMC* s.v. Eurytus 3) the painter shows Heracles engaged in killing Eurytus and his sons: three of the latter are labelled Iphitus, Antiphonus, and *TIONO*. Iphitus and another son (unlabelled) lie fatally wounded upon the ground. Eurytus and Antiphonus advance towards Heracles with arms outstretched in supplication. Iole looks on.

This scene has been variously interpreted as (1) the archery contest (Robert, *Heldensage* ii. 583; Furtwängler, *Roscher* i. 2206), (2) Heracles killing the Eurytids (Bieńkowski, *Jhb. Öst. Arch.* 3 (1900), 64; Richter, *AJA* 20 (1916), 130); (3) a combination of (1) and (2) (Hartwig, *JHS* 12 (1891), 338); Robert (loc. cit.), assuming that the vase derives its version from the *Oechalias Halosis*, and that it shows

---

[33] The evidence of art is considered by R. Olmos in *LIMC* iv s.v. Eurytus I (pp. 117 ff.).

INTRODUCTION

the killing of the Eurytids in the context of the archery contest, proceeded to draw important conclusions about our poem's contents (see above, p. xxx). A telescoping of the two events seems the likeliest solution, precisely the sort of technique we have come to expect from visual (as opposed to literary) representations of myth.

A red-figure vase by Euphronius (c.500) (New York 12.231.2: ARV^2 319. 6 = *Vasenlisten*[3] 55. B2) has attracted a particularly damaging misinterpretation which we may briefly dispose of, though it is not directly relevant to the epic which concerns us here. The contents are fully described by Miss Richter (art. cit., pp. 128–9), some of whose remarks I here excerpt. She denotes its subject-matter as the strife of Heracles and the sons of Eurytus 'at a banquet, as is indicated by the two couches, on which the sons of Eurytus were probably reclining when Heracles began his attack'. In the centre we see a Heracles, naked except for his lion's skin and equipped with no weapons, about to punch the labelled Cl(ytius) with his right fist. A Eurytid comes to the rescue from behind, swinging a club and using a panther-skin for a shield. To the other side of Heracles, Iphit(us) strides with bow in right hand towards the hero, while behind Iphitus looms a fourth brother.

The setting is a banquet and Heracles is nude and weaponless. But this hardly justifies Robert's inference (*Heldensage* ii. 585, followed by Burkert, p. 81 n. 33)[34] that the scene represents the expulsion of a drunken Heracles, as described at *Tr.* 261 ff., especially when independent considerations lead us to identify that passage as an *ad hoc* Sophoclean invention (see commentary ad loc.). Miss Richter (p. 129) concludes that the scene 'apparently follows' the tradition of Heracles' murder of the sons of Eurytus on the occasion when he was refused Iole. But (see above) there is no secure evidence for any such tradition.

Also problematic are several vases showing Eurytus or his sons having their feasting disturbed by the entrance of Heracles. An Attic

---

[34] So too Gercke, *Neue Jhb.* 8 (1905), 403.

INTRODUCTION

red-figure cup by the Brygos painter (Acrop. 288: *ARV*² 370. 7 = *LIMC* s.v. Eurytus 2) displays, in Beazley's words, 'Eurytus reclining, Heracles arriving breezily' on one side, and on the other 'Heracles in the house of Eurytus'. A black-figure scyphos in the Louvre (M11: MNC 661: *Vasenlisten*³ 55. A3) has on one side the arrival of Heracles, Iolaus, and Hyllus at the banquet of Eurytus and his sons, on the other Heracles and his companions forcing their way into Eurytus' palace. Heracles in the house of Eurytus is also the subject of a cup by the Brygos painter (Cab. Méd. L243 etc.: *ARV*² 370. 8 = *LIMC* s.v. Eurytus 6). Slightly different is a white-figure cylix in the Louvre (G109: cf. *Vasenlisten*³ 489. B4; A. Waiblinger, *Rev. Arch.* 1 (1972), 233 ff.), allegedly depicting Heracles' murder of an Iphitus reclining on a couch. Miss Richter (p. 130) sees this as compatible with the *Odyssey*'s description of Iphitus' murder, but when we remember the above discussion of that passage (p. xxv) we must conclude that the very existence of such a tradition is highly dubious. And it is a sort of confirmation of this scepticism that A. Waiblinger, in the article cited above, has recently reinterpreted the vase-painting as Tydeus' murder of Ismene.[35]

A final scene of banqueting is mercifully free from such controversy and disagreement: a Corinthian crater to be dated to c.590 and now in the Louvre (E365: *LIMC* s.v. Eurytus 1; cf. K. Schefold, *Mus. Helv.* 19 (1962), 131–2). We see Heracles, Eurytus, Iphitus, and Iole (all securely identified by labels) reclining on couches. As Miss Richter observes (p. 130): 'the scene is entirely peaceful in character and must refer to a banquet held before any trouble arose, before the contest in archery.' The glances exchanged by Heracles and Iole seem to me indicative of nascent love: compare the famous exchanged looks between Achilles and Penthesileia on the Munich vase. Any attempt to come to a conclusion over the question of literary inspiration for this scene must start from the fact that the vase presents us with four sons of Eurytus who bear labels equivalent to

---

[35] Time has removed that section of the victim's body which would at least allow us to determine its sex ... Waiblinger's interpretation is accepted by Brommer's *Vasenlisten*³.

INTRODUCTION

the names of the four Eurytids listed in the Hesiodic *Catalogue* (fr. 26. 29–30 MW): Didaeon,[36] Clytius, Toxeus, and Iphitus. The *Oechalias Halosis* named only two, but Burkert (art. cit., pp. 81–2) would nevertheless derive the 'lively action' from our epic rather than mere Catalogue Poetry, especially since the two middle names are very obviously appropriate for sons of the famed master of the bow. They require no literary inspiration, but the scene depicted does. The first part of the argument is surely right; the second is a little more open to doubt, and it would certainly be rash to follow Burkert in using this vase as a *terminus ad quem* for the *Oechalias Halosis*. See further R. Olmos, *Madrid. Mitteilungen* 18 (1977), 130 ff., esp. 142 ff.

Production

As if in compensation for the multiplicity of other types of problem it provides, the *Trachiniae* is relatively free from difficulties when we come to reconstruct its original production. We do not encounter here the obstacles that arise with the representation of Philoctetes' cave in the play of that name, or the change of scene and suicide of the hero in Sophocles' *Ajax*. No tombs (cf. Aeschylus' *Persae* and *Choephori*) require to be integrated into the staging; there are no skulking or lurking characters whose concealment has to be catered for. Exits and entrances are not so complex that we need ever postulate the existence of more than one door, and there is no sophisticated interplay between the concepts of 'in' and 'out' of doors. 'Extras' (in the form of children, etc.) pose no problems.

Indeed the postulates of this play's production are so simple that I have dealt with them piecemeal throughout the commentary. It will be useful, however, to summarize here the production-schedule, as it were. The cκηνή [37] represents the front of a palace belonging to

---

[36] So the vase (ΔΙΔΑΙΩΝ): Δηϊων the text of Hesiod accepted by Merkelbach and West; Διδαίων *coni.* Rzach (*WS* 21 (1899), 215), *prob.* Burkert (p. 81 n. 33).

[37] On this entity ('a building with a large central door, flanked by a wooden façade') see e.g. Dover's edn. of Aristophanes' *Clouds*, pp. lxx ff.

INTRODUCTION

Ceyx king of Trachis (cf. nn. on vv. 35 and 39). Only one door is required for the play's action,[38] which takes place on 'the acting-area in front of the cκηνή'.[39]

1: Deianeira enters from palace (probably (see n. on 50) accompanied by Nurse; otherwise Nurse enters from palace at v. 49).

58: Hyllus makes a timely entrace via one of the *parodoi* and moves towards or near the palace (see n. ad loc.).

93: Hyllus exits (see n. on 86) through one of the *parodoi* and Nurse exits into palace. D possibly (see nn. on 93 and 141) stays on stage.

94: enter chorus through one of the *parodoi*.

[141: D re-enters from palace if (see above on 93) she is not already on stage.]

180: Messenger enters (see n. on 178–9) via one of the *parodoi*. At end of scene he remains on stage (see n. on 199). D too is on stage during the choral song (cf. 222 ~ 225).

229: Lichas enters via one of the *parodoi* with cτόλoc (see n. on 226) of female prisoners (extras) including Iole (κωφὸν πρόcωπον: see n. on 205).

335 ff.: cτόλoc exits with Iole into palace (see n. ad loc.). Iole does not thereafter reappear (see nn. on 1222 and 1275).

496: D and Lichas exeunt into palace, Messenger (see ad loc.) exits via one of the *parodoi*.

531: D enters from palace, carrying (see vv. 580, 602) the *peplos*.

594: Lichas makes a timely entrance (see n. ad loc.) from palace.

632: D exits into palace, Lichas via one of the *parodoi*, carrying away the *peplos*.

663: D enters from palace.

---

[38] For a bibliography of the controversy on how many doors were required for the production of Attic tragedy and comedy see Garvie's edn. of Aeschylus' *Choephori*, p. xlvii n. 111.

[39] For this definition of the 'stage' and for its relationship to the ὀρχήcτρα see Garvie, op. cit., p. xliv n. 104.

INTRODUCTION

733: Hyllus enters via one of the *parodoi*.

813: D makes a silent exit (see n. ad loc.) into palace.

820: Hyllus exits into palace (see n. on 903).

870: Nurse enters from palace.

946: Nurse exits into palace.

964 ff.: Heracles carried on bier by extras representing strangers (see n. ad loc.), accompanied by old man, enters via one of the *parodoi*. Simultaneously, Hyllus enters from palace (see n. ad loc.).

1264: Heracles exits carried on bier by extras (see n. ad loc.) down one of the *parodoi*.

1274: Hyllus exits down one of the *parodoi*.

1278: chorus exit (see n. on 1275 ff.) down one of the *parodoi*.

The play is performed by three actors; indeed only two scenes (vv. 58–93 and 229–496) require the simultaneous presence of all three. The roles of Deianeira and Heracles are traditionally assigned to the πρωταγωνιcτήc, to the δευτεραγωνιcτήc Hyllus and Lichas, leaving to the τριταγωνιcτήc the parts of Nurse, Messenger and Old Man.[40] For other material relating to Production see General Index s.v.

---

[40] But for the 'possibility ... that the allocation of roles was not solely determined by their importance' see Dover, edn. of Ar. *Clouds*, pp. lxxix f.

SIGLA

L   Laur. 32. 9, saec. x^2
Λ   Lugd. Bat. BPG 60A, saec. x^2
K   Laur. 31. 10, e quo saepius licet lectionem codicis L nondum correcti divinare, saec xii^2
R   Vat gr. 2291, saec. xv (vv. 1–372)
A   Paris. gr. 2712, scriptus fere anno 1300
U   Marc. gr. 467, saec. xiv
Y   Vindob. phil. gr. 48, saec. xiv^2
V   Venet. Marc. gr. 468, scriptus fere anno 1300
Zg   Laur. 32. 2, saec. xiv^1
Zo   Vat. Pal. gr. 287, saec. xv
T   Paris. gr. 2711, saec. xiv
Ta   Marc. gr. 470, saec. xv

l   fons codicum LΛK
a   fons codicum AUY
    V (vv. 1–18)
z   fons codicum ZgZo, qui olim recensionem Thomae Magistri praebere credebantur
t   Demetrius Triclinius, cuius recensio in TTa exstat

Papyri
P.Oxy. 1805 + 3687, saec. ii–iii
P.Oxy. 3688, saec. v–vi
P.Amst. inv. 68, saec. iii

ΣΟΦΟΚΛΕΟΥΣ
ΤΡΑΧΙΝΙΑΙ

ΤΑ ΤΟΥ ΔΡΑΜΑΤΟΣ ΠΡΟΣΩΠΑ

Δηάνειρα
Δούλη τροφός
Ὕλλος
Χορὸς γυναικῶν Τραχινίων
Ἄγγελος
Λίχας
Πρέσβυς
Ἡρακλῆς

ΤΡΑΧΙΝΙΑΙ

ΔΗΙΑΝΕΙΡΑ
Λόγος μὲν ἔστ' ἀρχαῖος ἀνθρώπων φανεὶς
ὡς οὐκ ἂν αἰῶν' ἐκμάθοις βροτῶν, πρὶν ἂν
θάνῃ τις, οὔτ' εἰ χρηστὸς οὔτ' εἴ τῳ κακός·
ἐγὼ δὲ τὸν ἐμόν, καὶ πρὶν εἰς Ἅιδου μολεῖν,
ἔξοιδ' ἔχουσα δυστυχῆ τε καὶ βαρύν, 5
ἥτις πατρὸς μὲν ἐν δόμοισιν Οἰνέως
ναίους' ἔτ' ἐν Πλευρῶνι νυμφείων ὄτλον
ἄλγιστον ἔςχον, εἴ τις Αἰτωλὶς γυνή.
μνηστὴρ γὰρ ἦν μοι ποταμός, Ἀχελῷον λέγω,
ὅς μ' ἐν τρισὶν μορφαῖσιν ἐξῄτει πατρός, 10
φοιτῶν ἐναργὴς ταῦρος, ἄλλοτ' αἰόλος
δράκων ἑλικτός, ἄλλοτ' ἀνδρείῳ κύτει
βούπρῳρος· ἐκ δὲ δαςκίου γενειάδος
κρουνοὶ διερραίνοντο κρηναίου ποτοῦ.
τοιόνδ' ἐγὼ μνηστῆρα προςδεδεγμένη 15
δύστηνος ἀεὶ κατθανεῖν ἐπηυχόμην,
πρὶν τῆςδε κοίτης ἐμπελασθῆναί ποτε.
χρόνῳ δ' ἐν ὑστέρῳ μέν, ἀσμένῃ δέ μοι,
ὁ κλεινὸς ἦλθε Ζηνὸς Ἀλκμήνης τε παῖς·

---

1 ἀνθρώπων] -οις grammaticus ap. Cramer, *Anec. Oxon.* iv. 328
2 ἐκμάθοις LVt: -ης Zo: -οι cett.   βροτῶν post ἂν praebent VRZg
3 θάνῃ lZo, Stobaeus 5. 41. 38: -ει R: -οι cett.   7 ἔτ' ἐν Vitus
Winshemius: ἐν L: ἐνὶ VRa: γ' ἐν z: om. t, qui Πλευρῶνι ναίουςα
praebet   νυμφείων] -φίων lZoTa   ὄτλον Lγρ: ὄγκον Zo: ὄκνον cett.
8 Αἰτωλὶς] -λὴ KR: -λὸς v.l. ap. z et t   10 ἐξῄτει LVRat: ἐζῄτει Kz
12–13 κύτει βούπρῳρος Strabo 10. 458, et vox βούπρῳρα occurrit ap.
Philostr. jun. *Imag.* 4. 1: τύπῳ βούκρανος codd.   16 ἐπηυχόμην AU:
ἐπευ- cett.   17 τῆςδε κοίτης] τοῦδε κοίτης Wunder: ταῖςδε
κοίταις Schneidewin   18 δέ μοι] δ' ἐμοὶ Zot

ϹΟΦΟΚΛΕΟΥϹ

ὃς εἰς ἀγῶνα τῷδε ϲυμπεϲὼν μάχης 20
ἐκλύεταί με. καὶ τρόπον μὲν ἂν πόνων
οὐκ ἂν διείποιμ'· οὐ γὰρ οἶδ'· ἀλλ' ὅϲτις ἦν
θακῶν ἀταρβὴς τῆς θέας, ὅδ' ἂν λέγοι.
ἐγὼ γὰρ ἤμην ἐκπεπληγμένη φόβῳ
μή μοι τὸ κάλλος ἄλγος ἐξεύροι ποτέ. 25
τέλος δ' ἔθηκε Ζεὺς ἀγώνιος καλῶς,
εἰ δὴ καλῶς. λέχος γὰρ Ἡρακλεῖ κριτὸν
ξυϲτᾶϲ' ἀεί τιν' ἐκ φόβου φόβον τρέφω,
κείνου προκηραίνουϲα. νὺξ γὰρ εἰϲάγει
καὶ νὺξ ἀπωθεῖ διαδεδεγμένη πόνον. 30
κἀφύϲαμεν δὴ παῖδας, οὓς κεῖνός ποτε,
γῄτης ὅπως ἄρουραν ἔκτοπον λαβών,
ϲπείρων μόνον προϲεῖδε κἀξαμῶν ἅπαξ·
τοιοῦτος αἰὼν εἰς δόμους τε κἀκ δόμων
ἀεὶ τὸν ἄνδρ' ἔπεμπε λατρεύοντά τῳ. 35
νῦν δ' ἡνίκ' ἄθλων τῶνδ' ὑπερτελὴς ἔφυ,
ἐνταῦθα δὴ μάλιϲτα ταρβήϲαϲ' ἔχω.
ἐξ οὗ γὰρ ἔκτα κεῖνος Ἰφίτου βίαν,
ἡμεῖς μὲν ἐν Τραχῖνι τῇδ' ἀνάϲτατοι
ξένῳ παρ' ἀνδρὶ ναίομεν, κεῖνος δ' ὅπου 40
βέβηκεν οὐδεὶς οἶδε· πλὴν ἐμοὶ πικρὰς
ὠδῖνας αὐτοῦ προϲβαλὼν ἀποίχεται.
ϲχεδὸν δ' ἐπίϲταμαί τι πῆμ' ἔχοντά νιν·
χρόνον γὰρ οὐχὶ βαιόν, ἀλλ' ἤδη δέκα
μῆνας πρὸς ἄλλοις πέντ' ἀκήρυκτος μένει. 45

20–1 μάχης et πόνων permutavit Herwerden   23 θακῶν L^(ac)KRZo: θώκων L^(pc): θακῶν cett.   24 ἤμην L s.l.: ἤμην cett.
26 ἔθηκε] -εν L   27 λέχος] λάχος Harleianus 5743
28 ξυϲτᾶϲ'] ξυνϲτᾶϲ' Lt   30 ἀπωθεῖ διαδεδεγμένη] ἀπωθεῖται δεδεγμένον Suda s.v. πόνος πόνῳ πόνον φέρει   31 κἀφύϲαμεν LRa: κάφυϲα μὲν zt   32 γῄτης L: γῆ- cett.   34 εἰς ... δόμων] ἐκ δόμων τε κεἰς δόμους Zn, probat Brunck   40 ὅπου] ὅποι Brunck   42 αὐτοῦ] αὑ- Hermann   43–8 del. Reeve (43 iam Dindorf, 44–8 Wunder)

4

ΤΡΑΧΙΝΙΑΙ

κἄςτιν τι δεινὸν πῆμα· τοιαύτην ἐμοὶ
δέλτον λιπὼν ἔςτειχε· τὴν ἐγὼ θαμὰ
θεοῖς ἀρῶμαι πημονῆς ἄτερ λαβεῖν.

ΤΡΟΦΟΣ
δέςποινα Δῃάνειρα, πολλὰ μέν ς' ἐγὼ
κατεῖδον ἤδη πανδάκρυτ' ὀδύρματα   50
τὴν Ἡράκλειον ἔξοδον γοωμένην·
νῦν δ', εἰ δίκαιον τοὺς ἐλευθέρους φρενοῦν
γνώμαιςι δούλαις, κἀμὲ χρὴ φράςαι τὸ ςόν·
πῶς παιςὶ μὲν τοςοῖςδε πληθύεις, ἀτὰρ
ἀνδρὸς κατὰ ζήτηςιν οὐ πέμπεις τινά,   55
μάλιςτα δ' ὅνπερ εἰκὸς Ὕλλον, εἰ πατρὸς
νέμοι τιν' ὥραν τοῦ καλῶς πράςςειν δοκεῖν;
ἐγγὺς δ' ὅδ' αὐτὸς ἀρτίπους θρῴςκει δόμοις,
ὥςτ' εἴ τί ςοι πρὸς καιρὸν ἐννέπειν δοκῶ,
πάρεςτι χρῆςθαι τἀνδρὶ τοῖς τ' ἐμοῖς λόγοις.   60

Δῃ. ὦ τέκνον, ὦ παῖ, κἀξ ἀγεννήτων ἄρα
μῦθοι καλῶς πίπτουςιν· ἥδε γὰρ γυνὴ
δούλη μέν, εἴρηκεν δ' ἐλεύθερον λόγον.

ΥΛΛΟΣ
ποῖον; δίδαξον, μῆτερ, εἰ διδακτά μοι.

Δῃ. ςὲ πατρὸς οὕτω δαρὸν ἐξενωμένου   65
τὸ μὴ πυθέςθαι ποῦ 'ςτιν αἰςχύνην φέρειν.

Υλ. ἀλλ' οἶδα, μύθοις γ' εἴ τι πιςτεύειν χρεών.

Δῃ. καὶ ποῦ κλύεις νιν, τέκνον, ἱδρῦςθαι χθονός;

---

46 πῆμα] χρῆμα Wilamowitz   47 ἔςτειχε τὴν] ἔςτειχεν ἣν Dindorf   51 Ἡράκλειον] -είαν Hermann   53 τὸ ςόν LRUz: τόςον AYt, novit sch. L   55 ἀνδρὸς] τἀνδρὸς Wecklein   57 νέμοι] -ει Zo   ὥραν L: ὥραν cett.   καλῶς] κακῶς Roscher   δοκεῖν] -εῖ z   58 fort. interpungendum post αὐτός   ἀρτίπους θρῴςκει] ἄρτι που 'ςθρῴςκει Shilleto et Westcott   δόμοις Wakefield: -ους codd.   60 τ' LRa: om. zt: γ' Hermann   66 φέρειν Valckenaer: -εν Zo: -ει cett.   67 γ' Ra: om. cett.   68 νιν post τέκνον praebent zt

ΣΟΦΟΚΛΕΟΥΣ

Υλ. τὸν μὲν παρελθόντ' ἄροτον ἐν μήκει χρόνου
   Λυδῇ γυναικί φαcί νιν λάτριν πονεῖν. 70
Δη. πᾶν τοίνυν, εἰ καὶ τοῦτ' ἔτλη, κλύοι τιc ἄν.
Υλ. ἀλλ' ἐξαφεῖται τοῦδέ γ', ὡc ἐγὼ κλύω.
Δη. ποῦ δῆτα νῦν ζῶν ἢ θανὼν ἀγγέλλεται;
Υλ. Εὐβοῖδα χώραν φαcίν, Εὐρύτου πόλιν,
   ἐπιcτρατεύειν αὐτόν, ἢ μέλλειν ἔτι. 75
Δη. ἆρ' οἶcθα δῆτ', ὦ τέκνον, ὡc ἔλειπέ μοι
   μαντεῖα πιcτὰ τῆcδε τῆc χρείαc πέρι;
Υλ. τὰ ποῖα, μῆτερ; τὸν λόγον γὰρ ἀγνοῶ.
Δη. ὡc ἢ τελευτὴν τοῦ βίου μέλλει τελεῖν,
   ἢ τοῦτον ἄραc ἆθλον εἰc τό γ' ὕcτερον 80
   τὸν λοιπὸν ἤδη βίοτον εὐαίων' ἔχειν.
   ἐν οὖν ῥοπῇ τοιᾷδε κειμένῳ, τέκνον,
   οὐκ εἶ ξυνέρξων, ἡνίκ' ἢ cεcώμεθα
   [ἢ πίπτομεν cοῦ πατρὸc ἐξολωλότοc]
   κείνου βίον cώcαντοc, ἢ οἰχόμεcθ' ἅμα; 85
Υλ. ἀλλ' εἶμι, μῆτερ· εἰ δὲ θεcφάτων ἐγὼ
   βάξιν κατῄδη τῶνδε, κἂν πάλαι παρῆ.
   ἀλλ' ὁ ξυνήθηc πότμοc οὐκ εἴα πατρὸc
   ἡμᾶc προταρβεῖν οὐδὲ δειμαίνειν ἄγαν.
   νῦν δ' ὡc ξυνίημ', οὐδὲν ἐλλείψω τὸ μὴ 90
   πᾶcαν πυθέcθαι τῶνδ' ἀλήθειαν πέρι.
Δη. χώρει νυν, ὦ παῖ· καὶ γὰρ ὑcτέρῳ, τό γ' εὖ
   πράccειν ἐπεὶ πύθοιτο, κέρδοc ἐμπολᾷ.

69 ἄροτον] ἄροτρον L   71 κλύοι] τλαίη K. Walter
73 post θανὼν add. γ' z   76 ὦ LRaz: om. t   77 χρείαc
Hense: χώραc codd.: ὥραc Dronke   79 ἢ] οἱ L: οἵ R   μέλλει]
μέλλοι Blaydes   80 τό γ' Reiske: τὸν codd.   81 τὸν La: τὸ Rz:
utrumque novit t   83 cεcώμεθα Wecklein: -ὡcμεθα codd.
84 del. Bentley, 85 Vauvilliers   87 κατῄδη Brunck: -δην L: -δειν cett.
παρῇ Elmsley: -ῆν codd.   88-9 del. Hermann, post 91 traiecit Brunck
88 ἀλλ' Brunck: νῦν δ' codd.: πρὶν δ' Wakefield   εἴα Vauvilliers: ἐᾷ codd.
90-1 del. Dindorf   90 μὴ ⟨οὐ⟩ Brunck   93 πύθοιτο] πύθοιο
Earle

6

ΤΡΑΧΙΝΙΑΙ

ΧΟΡΟΣ

ὃν αἰόλα νὺξ ἐναριζομένα   στρ. α'
τίκτει κατευνάζει τε φλογιζόμενον,   95
Ἅλιον Ἅλιον αἰτῶ
τοῦτο, καρῦξαι τὸν Ἀλκμή-
νας· πόθι μοι πόθι μοι
ναίει ποτ', ὦ λαμπρᾷ στεροπᾷ φλεγέθων;
ἢ Ποντίας αὐλῶνας, ἢ   100
διccαῖcιν ἀπείροις κλιθείς;
εἴπ', ὦ κρατιστεύων κατ' ὄμμα.

ποθουμένᾳ γὰρ φρενὶ πυνθάνομαι   ἀντ. α'
τὰν ἀμφινεικῆ Δηιάνειραν ἀεί,
οἷά τιν' ἄθλιον ὄρνιν,   105
οὔποτ' εὐνάζειν ἀδάκρυ-
τον βλεφάρων πόθον, ἀλλ'
εὔμναcτον ἀνδρὸς δεῖμα τρέφουcαν ὁδοῦ
ἐνθυμίοις εὐναῖς ἀναν-
δρώτοιcι τρύχεcθαι, κακὰν   110
δύcτανον ἐλπίζουcαν αἶcαν.

πολλὰ γὰρ ὥστ' ἀκάμαντος   στρ. β'
ἢ νότου ἢ βορέα τις
κύματ' ⟨ἂν⟩ εὐρέι πόντῳ
βάντ' ἐπιόντα τ' ἴδοι,   115
οὕτω δὲ τὸν Καδμογενῆ
τρέφει, τὸ δ' αὔξει βιότου

---

97 τοῦτο Rzt: τούτῳ La   97–8 sic interpunximus post Dover
98 μοι Wunder: μοι παῖc LRaz: παῖc t: γᾶc Schneidewin
100 Ποντίας Lloyd-Jones (cf. sch. ἢ πρὸς τὰ ἑῷα ἢ πρὸς τὰ δυτικά):
ποντίας L: -ίους L s.l., -ίος R: -ίους cett.   αὐλῶνας] -ος Margoliouth
105 ἄθλιον] ἅλιον Lγρ   106 ἀδάκρυτον Dawe: -ύτων codd.
108 τρέφουcαν Casaubon: φέρουcαν codd.   109 post εὐναῖς add. τ'
zt   113 βορέα LRa: βορέου z, v.l. in a   114 ⟨ἂν⟩ Wakefield:
⟨ἐν⟩ Erfurdt: om. codd.   116 post Καδμογενῆ add. τὸ μὲν z
117 τρέφει] cτρέφει Reiske

7

ΣΟΦΟΚΛΕΟΥΣ

πολύπονον, ὥσπερ πέλαγος
Κρήσιον· ἀλλά τις θεῶν
αἰὲν ἀναμπλάκητον Ἅι-   120
δα σφε δόμων ἐρύκει.

ὧν ἐπιμεμφομένας ἀ-   ἀντ. β'
δεῖα μέν, ἀντία δ' οἴσω.
φαμὶ γὰρ οὐκ ἀποτρύειν
ἐλπίδα τὰν ἀγαθὰν   125
χρῆναί σ'· ἀνάλγητα γὰρ οὐδ'
ὁ πάντα κραίνων βασιλεὺς
ἐπέβαλε θνατοῖς Κρονίδας·
ἀλλ' ἐπὶ πῆμα καὶ χαρὰν
πᾶσι κυκλοῦσιν οἷον ἄρ-   130
κτου στροφάδες κέλευθοι.

μένει γὰρ οὔτ' αἰόλα   ἐπ.
νὺξ βροτοῖσιν οὔτε κῆ-
ρες οὔτε πλοῦτος, ἀλλ' ἄφαρ
βέβακε, τῷ δ' ἐπέρχεται   134
χαίρειν τε καὶ στέρεσθαι.
ἃ καὶ σὲ τὰν ἄνασσαν ἐλπίσιν λέγω
τάδ' αἰὲν ἴσχειν· ἐπεὶ τίς ὧδε
τέκνοισι Ζῆν' ἄβουλον εἶδεν;   140

Δη. πεπυσμένη μέν, ὡς ἀπεικάσαι, πάρει
πάθημα τοὐμόν· ὡς δ' ἐγὼ θυμοφθορῶ
μήτ' ἐκμάθοις παθοῦσα, νῦν δ' ἄπειρος εἶ.

---

118 ὥσπερ **a**: ὥστε codd. plerique   120 ἀναμπλάκητον sch. L^pc: ἀμπλάκητον codd.   Ἅιδα Zn: Ἀΐδα cett.   121 ἐρύκει] -οι t   122 ἐπιμεμφομένας LRaZg: -μένας γ' Zo: -μέναι σ' T (σοι T^gl): -μένα σ' Ta   ἀδεῖα] αἰδοῖα Musgrave   128 ἐπέβαλε UZgt: -αλλε cett.   129 ἐπὶ] ἔτι Pearson   πῆμα] πήματι sch. L; de L^ac non liquet   χαρὰν K: de L^ac non liquet: χαρὰ vel χαρᾷ fere cett.   134 βέβακε **a**: βέβηκε cett.   140 εἶδεν LaZo: οἶδε(ν) cett.   141 ἀπεικάσαι] ἐπεικάσαι Hermann: σάφ' εἰκάσαι Wunder   143 δ'] τ' Harleianus 5743 et coni. Dobree

ΤΡΑΧΙΝΙΑΙ

τὸ γὰρ νεάζον ἐν τοιοῖcδε βόcκεται
χώροιcιν αὑτοῦ, καί νιν οὐ θάλποc θεοῦ, 145
οὐδ' ὄμβροc, οὐδὲ πνευμάτων οὐδὲν κλονεῖ,
ἀλλ' ἡδοναῖc ἄμοχθον ἐξαίρει βίον
ἐc τοῦθ', ἕωc τιc ἀντὶ παρθένου γυνὴ
κληθῇ, λάβῃ τ' ἐν νυκτὶ φροντίδων μέροc,
ἤτοι πρὸc ἀνδρὸc ἢ τέκνων φοβουμένη. 150
τότ' ἄν τιc εἰcίδοιτο, τὴν αὑτοῦ cκοπῶν
πρᾶξιν, κακοῖcιν οἷc ἐγὼ βαρύνομαι.
πάθη μὲν οὖν δὴ πόλλ' ἔγωγ' ἐκλαυcάμην·
ἓν δ', οἷον οὔπω πρόcθεν, αὐτίκ' ἐξερῶ.
ὁδὸν γὰρ ἦμοc τὴν τελευταίαν ἄναξ 155
ὡρμᾶτ' ἀπ' οἴκων Ἡρακλῆc, τότ' ἐν δόμοιc
λείπει παλαιὰν δέλτον ἐγγεγραμμένην
ξυνθήμαθ', ἁμοὶ πρόcθεν οὐκ ἔτλη ποτέ,
πολλοὺc ἀγῶναc ἐξιών, οὕτω φράcαι,
ἀλλ' ὥc τι δράcων εἷρπε κοὐ θανούμενοc. 160
νῦν δ' ὡc ἔτ' οὐκ ὢν εἶπε μὲν λέχουc ὅ τι
χρείη μ' ἑλέcθαι κτῆcιν, εἶπε δ' ἣν τέκνοιc
μοῖραν πατρῴαc γῆc διαίρετον νέμοι,
χρόνον προτάξαc ὡc τρίμηνοc ἡνίκ' ἂν
χώραc ἀπείη κἀνιαύcιοc βεβώc, 165
τότ' ἢ θανεῖν χρείη cφε τῷδε τῷ χρόνῳ,
ἢ τοῦθ' ὑπεκδραμόντα τοῦ χρόνου τέλοc
τὸ λοιπὸν ἤδη ζῆν ἀλυπήτῳ βίῳ.

145 χώροιcιν αὑτοῦ] verba frustra vexata   148 τιc] ἄν Blaydes
150 del. Dindorf   151 αὑτοῦ Y et fort. T: αὐτοῦ cett.
158 ἁμοὶ edd.: ἅ μοι codd.   159 οὕτω Harleianus 5743, coni.
Tournier: οὔπω LRU: οὔπω cett.   161 λέχουc] λάχουc Naber
162 χρείη Brunck: χρειὴ K: χρεί' ἤ vel sim. cett.   163 πατρῴαc]
-αν Zot   διαίρετον hoc accentu Hermann et Lobeck: oxytone codd.: -ἢν v.l.
in a   νέμοι] μένειν a   164 τρίμηνοc Wakefield: -ον codd.   ἄν
codd.: del. Dawes   165 ἀπείη L s.l., z: ἀπῄει LRt: ἀπίη a
κἀνιαύcιοc] -ιον Brunck   166-8 del. Dobree   166 χρείη
Brunck: χρεί' ἤ vel sim. codd.   167 τοῦθ'] τοῦδ' Wunder   ὑπεκ-
δραμόντα] ὑπερ- Burges

ΣΟΦΟΚΛΕΟΥΣ

τοιαῦτ᾽ ἔφραζε πρὸς θεῶν εἱμαρμένα
τῶν Ἡρακλείων ἐκτελευτᾶσθαι πόνων,   170
ὡς τὴν παλαιὰν φηγὸν αὐδῆσαί ποτε
Δωδῶνι διccῶν ἐκ πελειάδων ἔφη.
καὶ τῶνδε ναμέρτεια cυμβαίνει χρόνου
τοῦ νῦν παρόντοc ὡc τελεcθῆναι χρεών·
ὥcθ᾽ ἡδέωc εὕδουcαν ἐκπηδᾶν ἐμὲ   175
φόβῳ, φίλαι, ταρβοῦcαν, εἴ με χρὴ μένειν
πάντων ἀρίcτου φωτὸc ἐcτερημένην.
Χο. εὐφημίαν νῦν ἴcχ᾽· ἐπεὶ καταcτεφῆ
cτείχονθ᾽ ὁρῶ τιν᾽ ἄνδρα πρὸc χάριν λόγων.

ΑΓΓΕΛΟΣ
δέcποινα Δῃάνειρα, πρῶτοc ἀγγέλων   180
ὄκνου cε λύcω· τὸν γὰρ Ἀλκμήνηc τόκον
καὶ ζῶντ᾽ ἐπίcτω καὶ κρατοῦντα κἀκ μάχηc
ἄγοντ᾽ ἀπαρχὰc θεοῖcι τοῖc ἐγχωρίοιc.
Δῃ. τίν᾽ εἶπαc, ὦ γεραιέ, τόνδε μοι λόγον;
Αγ. τάχ᾽ ἐc δόμουc cοὺc τὸν πολύζηλον πόcιν   185
ἥξειν, φανέντα cὺν κράτει νικηφόρῳ.
Δῃ. καὶ τοῦ τόδ᾽ ἀcτῶν ἢ ξένων μαθὼν λέγειc;
Αγ. ἐν βουθερεῖ λειμῶνι πρὸc πολλοὺc θροεῖ
Λίχαc ὁ κῆρυξ ταῦτα· τοῦ δ᾽ ἐγὼ κλυὼν
ἀπῇξ᾽, ὅπωc cοι πρῶτοc ἀγγείλαc τάδε   190
πρὸc cοῦ τι κερδάναιμι καὶ κτώμην χάριν.
Δῃ. αὐτὸc δὲ πῶc ἄπεcτιν, εἴπερ εὐτυχεῖ;

169–70 del. Bergk, 170 Wunder   169 an θείμαρμένα?
170 τῶν Ἡρακλείων ... πόνων] τὸν -ειον ... πόνον Hense   171 ὡc]
ὣc Blaydes   174 ὡc] ᾧ Hense   178 νῦν] νυν Blaydes
179 χάριν KR: χαρὰν cett.: χρείαν Margoliouth   181 τόκον] γόνον
RZg   182 κἀκ] καὶ R   184 γεραιέ] γηραιέ ZoT
185 τὸν] cὸν Blaydes   187 τοῦ τόδ᾽ Brunck: ποῦ τόδ᾽ R: τοῦτο δ᾽
cett.   λέγειc] ἔχειc Zo, coni. Blaydes   188 πρὸc πολλοὺc Hermann: πρόcπολοc codd.   189 κλυὼν West: κλύων codd.
190 cοι Brunck: τοι codd.   191 πρὸc cοῦ τι] πρόc cού τι Blaydes

ΤΡΑΧΙΝΙΑΙ

Αγ. οὐκ εὐμαρείᾳ χρώμενος πολλῇ, γύναι.
κύκλῳ γὰρ αὐτὸν Μηλιεὺς ἅπας λεὼς
κρίνει περιστάς, οὐδ' ἔχει βῆναι πρόσω. 195
†τὸ γὰρ ποθοῦντ† ἕκαστος ἐκμαθεῖν θέλων
οὐκ ἂν μεθεῖτο, πρὶν καθ' ἡδονὴν κλύειν.
οὕτως ἐκεῖνος οὐχ ἑκὼν ἑκουσίοις
ξύνεστιν· ὄψῃ δ' αὐτὸν αὐτίκ' ἐμφανῆ.

Δη. ὦ Ζεῦ, τὸν Οἴτης ἄτομον ὃς λειμῶν' ἔχεις, 200
ἔδωκας ἡμῖν ἀλλὰ σὺν χρόνῳ χαράν.
φωνήσατ', ὦ γυναῖκες, αἵ τ' εἴσω στέγης
αἵ τ' ἐκτὸς αὐλῆς, ὡς ἄελπτον ὄμμ' ἐμοὶ
φήμης ἀνασχὸν τῆσδε νῦν καρπούμεθα.

Χο. ἀνολολυξάτω δόμος 205
ἐφεστίοις ἀλαλαγαῖς
ὁ μελλόνυμφος· ἐν δὲ κοινὸς ἀρσένων
ἴτω κλαγγὰ τὸν εὐφαρέτραν
Ἀπόλλω προστάταν,
ὁμοῦ δὲ παιᾶνα παι- 210
ᾶν' ἀνάγετ', ὦ παρθένοι,
βοᾶτε τὰν ὁμόσπορον
Ἄρτεμιν Ὀρτυγίαν, ἐλαφαβόλον, ἀμφίπυρον,
γείτονάς τε Νύμφας. 215

195 περιστὰς Paley: παραστὰς codd.   196 τὸ γὰρ ποθοῦν codd.:
ὃ γὰρ ποθοῦς' Jebb: τοῦ γὰρ ποθῶν J. Král: an πόθῳ γὰρ εἷς?
198 ἐκεῖνος] ἐκείνοις M. Schmidt   ἑκουσίοις Nauck: ἑκοῦσι δὲ codd.
199 αὐτὸν post αὐτίκ' traiecit t   204 ἀνασχὸν] -ὼν L in linea, R
καρπούμεθα] -ώμεθα Margoliouth   205 ἀνολολυξάτω Burges:
ἀνολολύξετε LRa: -ξατε KZg: -ζετε Ζo: -ξον t   δόμος Burges (cf. sch. L
ὁ πᾶς οἶκος κτλ.): δόμοις codd.   206 ἀλαλαγαῖς z: ἀλλαλαγαῖς t:
ἀλαλαῖς LRa, quo recepto ἐφεστίοισιν Blaydes   207 ὁ] ἁ Erfurdt
209 Ἀπόλλω Dindorf: -ωνα codd.   παιᾶνα utrubique codd.: an -ῶνα?
210 post δὲ add. καὶ t   212 τὰν ⟨θ'⟩ Musgrave   213 ἐλαφαβόλον LZo: -ηβόλον KRZg: -οβόλον at

ΣΟΦΟΚΛΕΟΥΣ

αἴρομαι οὐδ' ἀπώσομαι
τὸν αὐλόν, ὦ τύραννε τᾶc ἐμᾶc φρενόc.
ἰδού μ' ἀναταράccει,
εὐοῖ,
ὁ κιccὸc ἄρτι Βακχίαν
ὑποcτρέφων ἅμιλλαν. 220
ἰὼ ἰὼ Παιάν·
ἴδε ἴδ', ὦ φίλα γύναι·
τάδ' ἀντίπρωρα δή coι
βλέπειν πάρεcτ' ἐναργῆ.

Δη. ὁρῶ, φίλαι γυναῖκεc, οὐδέ μ' ὄμματοc 225
φρουρὰν παρῆλθε, τόνδε μὴ λεύccειν cτόλον·
χαίρειν δὲ τὸν κήρυκα προὐννέπω, χρόνῳ
πολλῷ φανέντα, χαρτὸν εἴ τι καὶ φέρειc.

ΛΙΧΑΣ
ἀλλ' εὖ μὲν ἵγμεθ', εὖ δὲ προcφωνούμεθα,
γύναι, κατ' ἔργου κτῆcιν· ἄνδρα γὰρ καλῶc 230
πράccοντ' ἀνάγκη χρηcτὰ κερδαίνειν ἔπη.
Δη. ὦ φίλτατ' ἀνδρῶν, πρῶθ' ἃ πρῶτα βούλομαι
δίδαξον, εἰ ζῶνθ' Ἡρακλῆ προcδέξομαι.
Λι. ἔγωγέ τοί cφ' ἔλειπον ἰcχύοντά τε
καὶ ζῶντα καὶ θάλλοντα κοὐ νόcῳ βαρύν. 235
Δη. ποῦ γῆc; πατρῴαc, εἴτε βαρβάρου, λέγε.
Λι. ἀκτή τιc ἔcτ' Εὐβοιίc, ἔνθ' ὁρίζεται
βωμοὺc τέλη τ' ἔγκαρπα Κηναίῳ Διί.

216 αἴρομαι οὐδ' Lloyd-Jones: ἀείρομ' οὐδ' codd.: ἀείρομαι, οὐδ' Erfurdt: ἄειρέ μ', οὐκ Margoliouth   219 εὐοῖ Wilamowitz: εὐοῖ μ' codd.: εὐοῖ εὐοῖ Dindorf   Βακχίαν Dindorf: -είαν codd.   221 an Παιών (cf. ad 210)?   222 ἴδε ἴδ' ὦ] ἴδ' ἴδε Schütz: ἰδού ἴδ' ὦ Schroeder   226 φρουρὰν Musgrave: -ρὰ codd.   post παρῆλθε add. ἐc Zot   μὴ ⟨οὐ⟩ Hermann   228 φέρειc lR Suda s.v. χαρτόν: -ει cett.   233 Ἡρακλῆ Dindorf: -κλέα codd.   235 καὶ ζῶντα] χλωρόν τε Housman   237 Εὐβοιίc UYZot: Εὐβοῖc cett.
238 τέλη lRzt: τελεῖ a

12

ΤΡΑΧΙΝΙΑΙ

Δη. εὐκταῖα φαίνων, ἢ 'πὸ μαντείας τινός;
Λι. εὐχαῖς, ὅθ' ᾕρει τῶνδ' ἀνάστατον δορὶ 240
 χώραν γυναικῶν ὧν ὁρᾷς ἐν ὄμμασιν.
Δη. αὗται δέ, πρὸς θεῶν, τοῦ ποτ' εἰςὶ καὶ τίνες;
 οἰκτραὶ γάρ, εἰ μὴ ξυμφοραὶ κλέπτουςί με.
Λι. ταύτας ἐκεῖνος Εὐρύτου πέρςας πόλιν
 ἐξείλεθ' αὑτῷ κτῆμα καὶ θεοῖς κριτόν. 245
Δη. ἢ κἀπὶ ταύτῃ τῇ πόλει τὸν ἄσκοπον
 χρόνον βεβὼς ἦν ἡμερῶν ἀνήριθμον;
Λι. οὔκ, ἀλλὰ τὸν μὲν πλεῖστον ἐν Λυδοῖς χρόνον
 κατείχεθ', ὥς φησ' αὐτός, οὐκ ἐλεύθερος,
 ἀλλ' ἐμποληθείς. τῷ λόγῳ δ' οὐ χρὴ φθόνον, 250
 γύναι, προςεῖναι, Ζεὺς ὅτου πράκτωρ φανῇ.
 κεῖνος δὲ πραθεὶς Ὀμφάλῃ τῇ βαρβάρῳ
 ἐνιαυτὸν ἐξέπληςεν, ὡς αὐτὸς λέγει,
 χοὔτως ἐδήχθη τοῦτο τοὔνειδος λαβὼν
 ὥςθ' ὅρκον αὑτῷ προσβαλὼν διώμοσεν, 255
 ἦ μὴν τὸν ἀγχιστῆρα τοῦδε τοῦ πάθους
 ξὺν παιδὶ καὶ γυναικὶ δουλώσειν ἔτι.
 κοὐχ ἡλίωςε τοὔπος, ἀλλ' ὅθ' ἁγνὸς ἦν,
 στρατὸν λαβὼν ἐπακτὸν ἔρχεται πόλιν
 τὴν Εὐρυτείαν. τόνδε γὰρ μεταίτιον 260
 μόνον βροτῶν ἔφαςκε τοῦδ' εἶναι πάθους·
 ὃς αὐτὸν ἐλθόντ' ἐς δόμους ἐφέστιον,
 ξένον παλαιὸν ὄντα, πολλὰ μὲν λόγοις
 ἐπερρόθηςε, πολλὰ δ' ἀτηρᾷ φρενί,
 λέγων χεροῖν μὲν ὡς ἄφυκτ' ἔχων βέλη 265
 τῶν ὧν τέκνων λείποιτο πρὸς τόξου κρίσιν,

239 φαίνων] κραίνων Nauck   240 εὐχαῖς Lzt: εὐχ' R: εὐκταῖ' a
243 ξυμφοραὶ a: -ᾷ cett.   247 ἀνήριθμον a: ἀρίθμιον cett. et γρ in
a: ἀνηρίθμων Wakefield   250 τῷ λόγῳ Margoliouth: τοῦ λόγου
codd.   251 ὅτου] ὅταν Margoliouth   252–3 del. Wunder
254 ἐδήχθη Kazt: ἐδείχθη LR   257 παιδὶ] παιςὶ Turnebus
264 φρενί] χερί Blaydes: post hunc v. lacunam statuit Bergk   266 λείποιτο Kat: λίποιτο cett.

13

ΣΟΦΟΚΛΕΟΥΣ

†φώνει δέ, δοῦλος ἀνδρὸς ὡς ἐλευθέρου,
ῥαίοιτο·† δείπνοις δ' ἡνίκ' ἦν ὠνωμένος,
ἔρριψεν ἐκτὸς αὐτόν. ὧν ἔχων χόλον,
ὡς ἵκετ' αὖθις Ἴφιτος Τιρυνθίαν   270
πρὸς κλειτύν, ἵππους νομάδας ἐξιχνοσκοπῶν,
τότ' ἄλλοσ' αὐτὸν ὄμμα, θητέρᾳ δὲ νοῦν
ἔχοντ', ἀπ' ἄκρας ἧκε πυργώδους πλακός.
ἔργου δ' ἕκατι τοῦδε μηνίσας ἄναξ,
ὁ τῶν ἁπάντων Ζεὺς πατὴρ Ὀλύμπιος,   275
πρατόν νιν ἐξέπεμψεν, οὐδ' ἠνέσχετο,
ὁθούνεκ' αὐτὸν μοῦνον ἀνθρώπων δόλῳ
ἔκτεινεν. εἰ γὰρ ἐμφανῶς ἠμύνατο,
Ζεύς τἂν συνέγνω ξὺν δίκῃ χειρουμένῳ.
ὕβριν γὰρ οὐ στέργουσιν οὐδὲ δαίμονες.   280
κεῖνοι δ' ὑπερχλίοντες ἐκ γλώσσης κακῆς
αὐτοὶ μὲν Ἅιδου πάντες εἰσ' οἰκήτορες,
πόλις δὲ δούλη· τάσδε δ' ἅσπερ εἰσορᾷς
ἐξ ὀλβίων ἄζηλον εὑροῦσαι βίον
χωροῦσι πρὸς σέ· ταῦτα γὰρ πόσις τε σὸς   285
ἐφεῖτ', ἐγὼ δέ, πιστὸς ὢν κείνῳ, τελῶ.
αὐτὸν δ' ἐκεῖνον, εὖτ' ἂν ἁγνὰ θύματα
ῥέξῃ πατρῴῳ Ζηνὶ τῆς ἁλώσεως,
φρόνει νιν ὡς ἥξοντα· τοῦτο γὰρ λόγου
πολλοῦ καλῶς λεχθέντος ἥδιστον κλύειν.   290

Χο. ἄνασσα, νῦν σοι τέρψις ἐμφανὴς κυρεῖ,

267 φώνει] φωνεῖ Vat. Pal. gr. 287, coni. Koechly: φωνῇ Conradt: φανεὶς Hermann   ὡς] ἀντ' Wunder: ἐξ Nauck   268 ὠνωμένος Porson: οἰν- codd.   269 ἐκτὸς αὐτόν] αὐτὸν ἐκτός Zot   271 κλειτύν edd.: κλιτύν codd.   272 θητέρᾳ LRa: θατέρᾳ zt   273 ἧκε] ἔδικε Meineke (ἐδίσκευσε sch.)   274–5 an ἄναξ et πατὴρ permutanda?   275 Ὀλύμπιος Laz: Οὐλ- Rt: Ὀλυμπίων P.Oxy. 1805[ac]   280 del. van Deventer   281 ὑπερχλίοντες L[ac]KR, lm. sch. L: -χλιδῶντες cett.   283 δούλη·τάσδε] δούλη 'σθ' αἵδε Blaydes   286 δέ] τε P.Amst. inv. 68 s.l., coni. Turnebus   289 φρόνει] φρονεῖν Pap., L[ac]

14

ΤΡΑΧΙΝΙΑΙ

  τῶν μὲν παρόντων, τὰ δὲ πεπυςμένῃ λόγῳ.
Δη. πῶς δ' οὐκ ἐγὼ χαίροιμ' ἄν, ἀνδρὸς εὐτυχῆ
  κλύουςα πρᾶξιν τήνδε, πανδίκῳ φρενί;
  πολλή 'cτ' ἀνάγκη τῇδε τοῦτο cυντρέχειν. 295
  ὅμως δ' ἔνεcτι τοῖcιν εὖ cκοπουμένοις
  ταρβεῖν τὸν εὖ πράccοντα, μὴ cφαλῇ ποτε.
  ἐμοὶ γὰρ οἶκτος δεινὸς εἰcέβη, φίλαι,
  ταύτας ὁρώcῃ δυcπότμους ἐπὶ ξένης
  χώρας ἀοίκους ἀπάτοράς τ' ἀλωμένας, 300
  αἳ πρὶν μὲν ἦcαν ἐξ ἐλευθέρων ἴcως
  ἀνδρῶν, τανῦν δὲ δοῦλον ἴcχουcιν βίον.
  ὦ Ζεῦ τροπαῖε, μή ποτ' εἰcίδοιμί cε
  πρὸς τοὐμὸν οὕτω cπέρμα χωρήcαντά ποι,
  μηδ', εἴ τι δράcεις, τῆcδέ γε ζώcης ἔτι. 305
  οὕτως ἐγὼ δέδοικα τάcδ' ὁρωμένη.
  ὦ δυcτάλαινα, τίς ποτ' εἶ νεανίδων;
  ἄνανδρος, ἢ τεκνοῦccα; πρὸς μὲν γὰρ φύcιν
  πάντων ἄπειρος τῶνδε, γενναία δέ τις.
  Λίχα, τίνος ποτ' ἐcτὶν ἡ ξένη βροτῶν; 310
  τίς ἡ τεκοῦcα, τίς δ' ὁ φιτύcας πατήρ;
  ἔξειπ'· ἐπεί νιν τῶνδε πλεῖcτον ᾤκτιcα
  βλέπους', ὅcωπερ καὶ φρονεῖν οἶδεν μόνη.
Λι. τί δ' οἶδ' ἐγώ; τί δ' ἄν με καὶ κρίνοις; ἴcως
  γέννημα τῶν ἐκεῖθεν οὐκ ἐν ὑcτάτοις. 315
Δη. μὴ τῶν τυράννων; Εὐρύτου cπορά τις ἦν;
Λι. οὐκ οἶδα· καὶ γὰρ οὐδ' ἀνιcτόρουν μακράν.
Δη. οὐδ' ὄνομα πρός του τῶν ξυνεμπόρων ἔχεις;
Λι. ἥκιcτα· cιγῇ τοὐμὸν ἔργον ἤνυτον.

292 τὰ Scaliger: τῶν codd. λόγῳ La: -ων cett. 295 del.
Wunder πολλή 'cτ' a, Sudae cod. G s.v. ταρβεῖ: πολλῆcτ' L: πολλή τ'
fere cett. 296 ὅμως δ'] καὶ μὴν Suda τοῖcιν] τοῖcί γ' Dawe
301 ἐλευθέρων] ἀριcτέων Schubert 308 τεκνοῦccα Brunck:
τεκνοῦcα v.l. in L et a: τεκοῦcα codd. 311 post prius τίς add. δ' Zgt
313 οἶδεν μόνη] an εἶδον μόνην? 316 τῶν LRaZo: του Zgt, coni.
Dobree Εὐρύτου] τῶν ἐκεῖ Heimsoeth, puncto post τυράννων deleto
317 οὐδ' Laz: οὐκ Rt

15

ΣΟΦΟΚΛΕΟΥΣ

Δη. εἴπ', ὦ τάλαιν', ἀλλ' ἡμῖν ἐκ σαυτῆς· ἐπεὶ 320
 καὶ ξυμφορά τοι μὴ εἰδέναι σέ γ' ἥτις εἶ.
Λι. οὔ τἆρα τῷ γε πρόσθεν οὐδὲν ἐξ ἴσου
 χρόνῳ διήσει γλῶσσαν, ἥτις οὐδαμὰ
 προὔφηνεν οὔτε μεῖζον· οὔτ' ἐλάσσονα,
 ἀλλ' αἰὲν ὠδίνουσα συμφορᾶς βάρος 325
 δακρυρροεῖ δύστηνος, ἐξ ὅτου πάτραν
 διήνεμον λέλοιπεν. ἡ δέ τοι τύχη
 κακὴ μὲν αὐτή γ', ἀλλὰ συγγνώμην ἔχει.
Δη. ἡ δ' οὖν ἐάσθω, καὶ πορευέσθω στέγας
 οὕτως ὅπως ἥδιστα, μηδὲ πρὸς κακοῖς 330
 τοῖς οὖσιν ἄλλην πρός γ' ἐμοῦ λύπην λάβοι·
 ἅλις γὰρ ἡ παροῦσα. πρὸς δὲ δώματα
 χωρῶμεν ἤδη πάντες, ὡς σύ θ' οἷ θέλεις
 σπεύδῃς, ἐγὼ δὲ τἄνδον ἐξαρκῆ τιθῶ.
Αγ. αὐτοῦ γε πρῶτον βαιὸν ἀμμείνας', ὅπως 335
 μάθῃς, ἄνευ τῶνδ', οὕστινάς γ' ἄγεις ἔσω
 ὧν τ' οὐδὲν εἰσήκουσας ἐκμάθῃς ἃ δεῖ.
 τούτων—ἔχω γὰρ πάντ'—ἐπιστήμων ἐγώ.
Δη. τί δ' ἔστι; τοῦ με τήνδ' ἐφίστασαι βάσιν;
Αγ. σταθεῖσ' ἄκουσον· καὶ γὰρ οὐδὲ τὸν πάρος 340

320 ἡμὶν at: ἡμῖν L: ἡμῖν cett.   321 ξυμφορά τοι μὴ] ξύμφορόν σοί μ' Madvig post Roscher   323 διήσει Wakefield: διοίσει codd. οὐδαμὰ Hermann: οὐδαμᾶ(ι) codd. plerique   326 δακρυρροεῖ K et fort. L^ac: -ρόει cett.   328 αὐτή KZg: αὕτη Zo: αὐτῇ cett.   γ', ἀλλὰ] τἆλλα Reiske, quem secutus κακὴ μὲν αὐτῇ τἆλλα, συγγνώμην ⟨δ'⟩ ἔχει temptavit Stinton   ἔχει] ἔχοι K: ἔχε Hilberg   331 οὖσιν] οἴσιν R   ἄλλην Zo: λύπην LRa: λοιπὴν Zgt, γρ in a: καινὴν C. Schenkl λύπην] διπλῆν F. W. Schmidt   λάβῃ Blaydes: λάβοι codd. 334 δὲ] τε Turnebus   335 ἀμμείνασ'] ἐμμείνασ' a   336 γ' a: τ' t: om. cett.   337 ἃ t: γ' ἃ a: θ' ἃ cett.   338 ἐπιστήμων post Herwerden Jackson, qui v. sic interpunxit: ἐπιστήμην codd.   339 τί δ' ἔστι; τοῦ codd.: τί δ'; ἀντὶ τοῦ Hartung post Wunder (τίνος ἕνεκα sch.) με] μοι Madvig   ἐφίστασαι L^pcK, v.l. in a: ἐπίστασαι cett.: ὑφίστασαι Dobree   340–1 οὐδὲ ... οὐδὲ codd.: οὔτε ... οὔτε Blaydes

16

ΤΡΑΧΙΝΙΑΙ

   μῦθον μάτην ἤκουςας, οὐδὲ νῦν δοκῶ.
Δη. πότερον ἐκείνους δῆτα δεῦρ' αὖθις πάλιν
   καλῶμεν, ἢ 'μοὶ ταῖςδέ τ' ἐξειπεῖν θέλεις;
Αγ. coὶ ταῖςδέ τ' οὐδὲν εἴργεται, τούτους δ' ἔα.
Δη. καὶ δὴ βεβᾶςι, χὠ λόγος ςημαινέτω.   345
Αγ. ἀνὴρ ὅδ' οὐδὲν ὧν ἔλεξεν ἀρτίως
   φωνεῖ δίκης ἐς ὀρθόν, ἀλλ' ἢ νῦν κακός,
   ἢ πρόςθεν οὐ δίκαιος ἄγγελος παρῆν.
Δη. τί φής; ςαφῶς μοι φράζε πᾶν ὅςον νοεῖς·
   ἃ μὲν γὰρ ἐξείρηκας ἀγνοία μ' ἔχει.   350
Αγ. τούτου λέγοντος τἀνδρὸς εἰςήκους' ἐγώ,
   πολλῶν παρόντων μαρτύρων, ὡς τῆς κόρης
   ταύτης ἕκατι κεῖνος Εὔρυτόν θ' ἕλοι
   τήν θ' ὑψίπυργον Οἰχαλίαν, Ἔρως δέ νιν
   μόνος θεῶν θέλξειεν αἰχμάςαι τάδε,   355
   οὐ τἀπὶ Λυδοῖς οὐδ' ὑπ' Ὀμφάλῃ πόνων
   λατρεύματ', οὐδ' ὁ ριπτὸς Ἰφίτου μόρος·
   ὃν νῦν παρώςας οὗτος ἔμπαλιν λέγει.
   ἀλλ' ἡνίκ' οὐκ ἔπειθε τὸν φυτοςπόρον
   τὴν παῖδα δοῦναι, κρύφιον ὡς ἔχοι λέχος,   360
   ἔγκλημα μικρὸν αἰτίαν θ' ἑτοιμάςας
   ἐπιστρατεύει πατρίδα [τὴν ταύτης, ἐν ᾗ
   τὸν Εὔρυτον τόνδ' εἶπε δεςπόζειν θρόνων,
   κτείνει τ' ἄνακτα πατέρα] τῆςδε καὶ πόλιν
   ἔπερςε. καὶ νῦν, ὡς ὁρᾷς, ἥκει δόμους   365

343 ἢ 'μοὶ Groddeck: ἢ μοι codd. 344 εἴργεται] εἴργομαι Hense 346 ἀνὴρ Hermann: ἀνὴρ codd. 347 φωνεῖ] φώνει K et sch. L δίκης ἐς] δικαίως Blaydes, coll. OT 853 350 ἀγνοία A et fort. **t**: ἄγνοια codd. plerique 356–7 del. Wunder 356 οὐδ' ὑπ' Herwerden: οὐδ' ἐπ' **a**Zo: οὔτ' ἐπ' L: οὔτ' ἀπ' RZgt 358 ὃν] ὃ Erfurdt: ἃ Koechly 360 ἔχοι P.Oxy.1805 et **a**: ἔχει L^(ac)R: ἔχῃ cett. 362–4 τὴν ... πατέρα del. Dobree 362–3 del. Wunder 363 τὸν Εὔρυτον] τὸν ἐργάτην Wecklein: ἀναξίως Dawe τόνδ' Zg: τῶνδ' cett. 365 νῦν] νιν Brunck: νῦν γ' Zn: νῦν ⟨ςφ'⟩ Blaydes

17

ϹΟΦΟΚΛΕΟΥϹ

ἐς τούσδε πέμπων οὐκ ἀφροντίστως, γύναι,
οὐδ' ὥστε δούλην· μηδὲ προσδόκα τόδε·
οὐδ' εἰκός, εἴπερ ἐντεθέρμανται πόθῳ.
ἔδοξεν οὖν μοι πρὸς cὲ δηλῶcαι τὸ πᾶν,
δέσποιν', ὃ τοῦδε τυγχάνω μαθὼν πάρα. 370
καὶ ταῦτα πολλοὶ πρὸς μέcῃ Τραχινίων
ἀγορᾷ cυνεξήκουον ὡcαύτως ἐμοί,
ὥcτ' ἐξελέγχειν· εἰ δὲ μὴ λέγω φίλα,
οὐχ ἥδομαι, τὸ δ' ὀρθὸν ἐξείρηχ' ὅμως.

Δη. οἴμοι τάλαινα, ποῦ ποτ' εἰμὶ πράγματος; 375
τίν' ἐcδέδεγμαι πημονὴν ὑπόcτεγον
λαθραῖον; ὢ δύcτηνος· ἆρ' ἀνώνυμος
πέφυκεν, ὥσπερ οὑπάγων διώμνυτο,
ἡ κάρτα λαμπρὰ καὶ κατ' ὄμμα καὶ φύcιν;

Αγ. πατρὸς μὲν οὖσα γένεcιν Εὐρύτου †ποτὲ† 380
Ἰόλη 'καλεῖτο, τῆς ἐκεῖνος οὐδαμὰ
βλάcτας ἐφώνει δῆθεν οὐδὲν ἱστορῶν.

Χο. ὄλοιντο μή τι πάντες οἱ κακοί, τὰ δὲ
λαθραῖ' ὃς ἀσκεῖ μὴ πρέπονθ' αὑτῷ κακά.

Δη. τί χρὴ ποεῖν, γυναῖκες; ὡς ἐγὼ λόγοις 385
τοῖς νῦν παροῦσιν ἐκπεπληγμένη κυρῶ.

Χο. πεύθου μολοῦσα τἀνδρός, ὡς τάχ' ἂν σαφῆ
λέξειεν, εἴ νιν πρὸς βίαν κρίνειν θέλοις.

366 ἐς τούσδε Brunck: ὡς τούσδε codd.: πρὸς τούσδε Schneidewin: cοὺς τήνδε Blaydes   367 τόδε La: τάδε Rzt   368 ἐντεθέρμανται] ἐκ- Dindorf (ἐκκέκαυται interpretatio in L)   370 ὃ] ἃ P.Oxy. 1805 et U   372 post hunc v. deficit R   373 ὥcτ' ἐξελέγχειν] οὓς ἔcτ' ἐλέγχειν Tournier   377 ὢ Zo et corr. Matthiae: ὦ cett.   379 hunc v. nuntio tribuit a   ἡ κάρτα Heath: ἢ καὶ τὰ codd.: ἢ κάρτα Canter: ἣν κάρτα Wilamowitz   ὄμμα] ὄνομα Fröhlich   380 γένεcιν La: -cις zt   ποτὲ] cπορᾷ Blaydes   post hunc v. lacunam statuit Radermacher   381 'καλεῖτο edd.: καλεῖτο codd.   οὐδαμὰ Hermann: -ᾷ(ι) codd.   383 τι] τοι Zg^{ac}t   384 πρέπονθ' αὑτῷ Harleianus 5743: -όντ' αὐτῷ codd.   385 ποεῖν L: ποιεῖν cett.   387 πεύθου] πυθοῦ Nauck   388 νιν Brunck: μιν codd.

18

ΤΡΑΧΙΝΙΑΙ

Δη. ἀλλ' εἶμι· καὶ γὰρ οὐκ ἀπὸ γνώμης λέγεις.
Αγ. ἡμεῖς δὲ προςμένωμεν; ἢ τί χρὴ ποεῖν; 390
Δη. μίμν', ὡς ὅδ' ἀνὴρ οὐκ ἐμῶν ὑπ' ἀγγέλων
      ἀλλ' αὐτόκλητος ἐκ δόμων πορεύεται.
Λι. τί χρή, γύναι, μολόντα μ' Ἡρακλεῖ λέγειν;
      δίδαξον, ὡς ἕρποντος, εἰςορᾷς, ἐμοῦ.
Δη. ὡς ἐκ ταχείας ςὺν χρόνῳ βραδεῖ μολὼν 395
      ᾄςςεις, πρὶν ἡμᾶς κἀννεώςαςθαι λόγους.
Λι. ἀλλ' εἴ τι χρῄζεις ἱςτορεῖν, πάρειμ' ἐγώ.
Δη. ἦ καὶ τὸ πιςτὸν τῆς ἀληθείας νεμεῖς;
Λι. ἴςτω μέγας Ζεύς, ὧν γ' ἂν ἐξειδὼς κυρῶ.
Δη. τίς ἡ γυνὴ δῆτ' ἐςτὶν ἣν ἥκεις ἄγων; 400
Λι. Εὐβοιίς· ὧν δ' ἔβλαςτεν οὐκ ἔχω λέγειν.
Αγ. οὗτος, βλέφ' ὧδε. πρὸς τίν' ἐννέπειν δοκεῖς;
Λι. ςὺ δ' ἐς τί δή με τοῦτ' ἐρωτήςας ἔχεις;
Αγ. τόλμηςον εἰπεῖν, εἰ φρονεῖς, ὅ ς' ἱςτορῶ.
Λι. πρὸς τὴν κρατοῦςαν Δῃάνειραν, Οἰνέως 405
      κόρην, δάμαρτά θ' Ἡρακλέους, εἰ μὴ κυρῶ
      λεύςςων μάταια, δεςπότιν τε τὴν ἐμήν.
Αγ. τοῦτ' αὖτ' ἔχρῃζον, τοῦτό ςου μαθεῖν. λέγεις
      δέςποιναν εἶναι τήνδε ςήν; Λι. δίκαια γάρ.
Αγ. τί δῆτα; ποίαν ἀξιοῖς δοῦναι δίκην, 410
      ἢν εὑρεθῇς ἐς τήνδε μὴ δίκαιος ὤν;
Λι. πῶς μὴ δίκαιος; τί ποτε ποικίλας ἔχεις;
Αγ. οὐδέν. ςὺ μέντοι κάρτα τοῦτο δρῶν κυρεῖς.
Λι. ἄπειμι. μῶρος δ' ἦ πάλαι κλύων ςέθεν.

389 οὐκ] οὖν Viketos   ἀπό Kz: ἄπο cett.   390 nuntio tribuit Hermann, Deianirae a: choro cett.   ποεῖν L: ποιεῖν cett.   391 ἀνήρ Hermann: ἀνὴρ codd.   393 μολόντα Lzt: μολοῦντά a   394 εἰςορᾷς] ὡς ὁρᾷς Wakefield   396 κἀννεώςαςθαι Hermann: καὶ νεώςαςθαι codd.: ἀνανεώςαςθαι testatur Eustathius 811. 20, novit sch. ut videtur: κἀνακοινοῦςθαι Blaydes   397–433 personarum vices in codd. varie turbatas restituit Tyrwhitt   398 νεμεῖς Nauck e sch.: νέμεις codd.   403 ἐρωτήςας Tyrwhitt: -ήςας' codd.   404 ὅ ς' Ka: ὃς L: ἅ ς' zt   412 ποικίλας Tyrwhitt: -ίλας' LZg^{ac}: -ίλλας' cett.   414 ἦ Elmsley: ἢν codd.

19

ϹΟΦΟΚΛΕΟΥϹ

Αγ. οὔ, πρίν γ' ἂν εἴπῃς ἱϲτορούμενοϲ βραχύ. 415
Λι. λέγ' εἴ τι χρῄζειϲ· καὶ γὰρ οὐ ϲιγηλὸϲ εἶ.
Αγ. τὴν αἰχμάλωτον, ἣν ἔπεμψαϲ ἐϲ δόμουϲ,
κάτοιϲθα δήπου; Λι. φημί· πρὸϲ τί δ' ἱϲτορεῖϲ;
Αγ. οὔκουν ϲὺ ταύτην, ἣν ὑπ' ἀγνοίαϲ ὁρᾷϲ,
Ἰόλην ἔφαϲκεϲ Εὐρύτου ϲπορὰν ἄγειν; 420
Λι. ποίοιϲ ἐν ἀνθρώποιϲι; τίϲ πόθεν μολὼν
ϲοὶ μαρτυρήϲει ταῦτ' ἐμοῦ κλυεῖν παρών;
Αγ. πολλοῖϲιν ἀϲτῶν. ἐν μέϲῃ Τραχινίων
ἀγορᾷ πολύϲ ϲου ταῦτά γ' εἰϲήκουϲ' ὄχλοϲ.
Λι. ναί·
κλυεῖν γ' ἔφαϲκον. ταὐτὸ δ' οὐχὶ γίγνεται 425
δόκηϲιν εἰπεῖν κἀξακριβῶϲαι λόγον.
Αγ. ποίαν δόκηϲιν; οὐκ ἐπώμοτοϲ λέγων
δάμαρτ' ἔφαϲκεϲ Ἡρακλεῖ ταύτην ἄγειν;
Λι. ἐγὼ δάμαρτα; πρὸϲ θεῶν, φράϲον, φίλη
δέϲποινα, τόνδε τίϲ ποτ' ἐϲτὶν ὁ ξένοϲ. 430
Αγ. ὃϲ ϲοῦ παρὼν ἤκουϲεν ὡϲ ταύτηϲ πόθῳ
πόλιϲ δαμείη πᾶϲα, κοὐχ ἡ Λυδία
πέρϲειεν αὐτήν, ἀλλ' ὁ τῆϲδ' ἔρωϲ φανείϲ.
Λι. ἄνθρωποϲ, ὦ δέϲποιν', ἀποϲτήτω· τὸ γὰρ
νοϲοῦντι ληρεῖν ἀνδρὸϲ οὐχὶ ϲώφρονοϲ. 435
Δη. μή, πρόϲ ϲε τοῦ κατ' ἄκρον Οἰταῖον νάποϲ
Διὸϲ καταϲτράπτοντοϲ, ἐκκλέψῃϲ λόγον.
οὐ γὰρ γυναικὶ τοὺϲ λόγουϲ ἐρεῖϲ κακῇ,
οὐδ' ἥτιϲ οὐ κάτοιδε τἀνθρώπων, ὅτι

418 δήπου] δῆτ'; *ΛΙ.* οὔ Turnebus   419 ἣν ὑπ' ἀγνοίαϲ ὁρᾷϲ] ἧϲ ϲύ γ' ἀγνοεῖϲ ϲποράϲ Wecklein post Schneidewin: μή μ' ὑπ' ἀγνοίαϲ ὅρα Jackson   422 κλυεῖν West: κλύειν codd.   παρών] πάρα Bothe   424 γ' at: om. **lz**   425 ναί codd.: del. Dindorf   κλυεῖν West: κλύειν codd.   427 οὐκ LaZo: οὐδ' KZgt   432 κοὐχ ἡ **a**: κοὐχὶ cett.   434 ἄνθρωποϲ Brunck: ἄ- codd.   435 νοϲοῦντι] -τα Heath: νοϲοῦν τι H. Stephanus   ληρεῖν suspectum: (νοϲοῦντ') ἐλέγχειν Heimsoeth   436 ϲε Hermann: ϲὲ **lzt**: ϲὺ **a**

20

ΤΡΑΧΙΝΙΑΙ

χαίρειν πέφυκεν οὐχὶ τοῖc αὐτοῖc ἀεί. 440
Ἔρωτι μέν νυν ὅcτιc ἀντανίcταται
πύκτηc ὅπωc ἐc χεῖραc, οὐ καλῶc φρονεῖ.
οὗτοc γὰρ ἄρχει καὶ θεῶν ὅπωc θέλει,
κἀμοῦ γε· πῶc δ' οὐ χἀτέραc οἵαc γ' ἐμοῦ;
ὥcτ' εἴ τι τὠμῷ γ' ἀνδρὶ τῇδε τῇ νόcῳ 445
ληφθέντι μεμπτόc εἰμι, κάρτα μαίνομαι,
ἢ τῇδε τῇ γυναικί, τῇ μεταιτίᾳ
τοῦ μηδὲν αἰcχροῦ μηδ' ἐμοὶ κακοῦ τινοc.
οὐκ ἔcτι ταῦτ'. ἀλλ' εἰ μὲν ἐκ κείνου μαθὼν
ψεύδῃ, μάθηcιν οὐ καλὴν ἐκμανθάνειc· 450
εἰ δ' αὐτὸc αὑτὸν ὧδε παιδεύειc, ὅταν
θέλῃc λέγεcθαι χρηcτόc, ὀφθήcῃ κακόc.
ἀλλ' εἰπὲ πᾶν τἀληθέc· ὡc ἐλευθέρῳ
ψευδεῖ καλεῖcθαι κὴρ πρόcεcτιν οὐ καλή.
ὅπωc δὲ λήcειc, οὐδὲ τοῦτο γίγνεται· 455
πολλοὶ γὰρ οἷc εἴρηκαc, οἳ φράcουc' ἐμοί.
κεἰ μὲν δέδοικαc, οὐ καλῶc ταρβεῖc, ἐπεὶ
τὸ μὴ πυθέcθαι, τοῦτό μ' ἀλγύνειεν ἄν·
τὸ δ' εἰδέναι τί δεινόν; οὐχὶ χἀτέραc
πλείcταc ἀνὴρ εἷc Ἡρακλῆc ἔγημε δή; 460
κοὔπω τιc αὐτῶν ἔκ γ' ἐμοῦ λόγον κακὸν
ἠνέγκατ' οὐδ' ὄνειδοc· ἥδε τ' οὐδ' ἂν εἰ
κάρτ' ἐντακείη τῷ φιλεῖν, ἐπεί cφ' ἐγὼ
ᾤκτιρα δὴ μάλιcτα προcβλέψαc', ὅτι
τὸ κάλλοc αὐτῆc τὸν βίον διώλεcεν, 465
καὶ γῆν πατρῴαν οὐχ ἑκοῦcα δύcμοροc

---

440 πέφυκεν] πεφύκαc' Nauck   441 νυν edd.: νῦν La: οὖν zt et Stobaei codd. MA 4. 20. 23   444 del. Wunder   γ' Laz: om. t   445 γ' ἀνδρὶ Schaefer: τἀνδρὶ codd.: τ' ἀνδρὶ edd. plerique   447 μεταιτίᾳ a: μετ' αἰτίᾳ l: μετ' αἰτίῳ L s.l., K: μήτ' αἰτίῳ zt   451 αὐτὸν L: αὑ- cett.   452 λέγεcθαι nos: γενέcθαι codd.: νέμεcθαι Blaydes   455–6 del. Eva Eicken-Iselin, probante Fraenkel   455 λήcειc] -ῃc l   460 ἀνὴρ εἷc codd.: ἀνάνδρουc interpretabantur quidam teste sch., unde ἀνήρειc Bergk

21

ϹΟΦΟΚΛΕΟΥϹ

ἔπερϲε κἀδούλωϲεν. ἀλλὰ ταῦτα μὲν
ῥείτω κατ' οὖρον· ϲοὶ δ' ἐγὼ φράζω κακὸν
πρὸϲ ἄλλον εἶναι, πρὸϲ δ' ἔμ' ἀψευδεῖν ἀεί.
Χο. πείθου λεγούϲῃ χρηϲτά, κοὐ μέμψῃ χρόνῳ   470
γυναικὶ τῇδε, κἀπ' ἐμοῦ κτήϲῃ χάριν.
Λι. ἀλλ', ὦ φίλη δέϲποιν', ἐπεί ϲε μανθάνω
θνητὴν φρονοῦϲαν θνητὰ κοὐκ ἀγνώμονα,
πᾶν ϲοι φράϲω τἀληθὲϲ οὐδὲ κρύψομαι.
ἔϲτιν γὰρ οὕτωϲ ὥϲπερ οὗτοϲ ἐννέπει.   475
ταύτηϲ ὁ δεινὸϲ ἵμερόϲ ποθ' Ἡρακλῆ
διῆλθε, καὶ τῆϲδ' οὕνεχ' ἡ πολύφθοροϲ
καθῃρέθη πατρῷοϲ Οἰχαλία δορί.
καὶ ταῦτα, δεῖ γὰρ καὶ τὸ πρὸϲ κείνου λέγειν,
οὔτ' εἶπε κρύπτειν οὔτ' ἀπηρνήθη ποτέ,   480
ἀλλ' αὐτόϲ, ὦ δέϲποινα, δειμαίνων τὸ ϲὸν
μὴ ϲτέρνον ἀλγύνοιμι τοῖϲδε τοῖϲ λόγοιϲ,
ἥμαρτον, εἴ τι τῶνδ' ἁμαρτίαν νέμειϲ.
ἐπεί γε μὲν δὴ πάντ' ἐπίϲταϲαι λόγον,
κείνου τε καὶ ϲὴν ἐξ ἴϲου κοινὴν χάριν   485
καὶ ϲτέργε τὴν γυναῖκα καὶ βούλου λόγουϲ
οὓϲ εἶπαϲ ἐϲ τήνδ' ἐμπέδωϲ εἰρηκέναι.
ὡϲ τἄλλ' ἐκεῖνοϲ πάντ' ἀριϲτεύων χεροῖν
τοῦ τῆϲδ' ἔρωτοϲ εἰϲ ἅπανθ' ἥϲϲων ἔφυ.
Δη. ἀλλ' ὧδε καὶ φρονοῦμεν ὥϲτε ταῦτα δρᾶν,   490
κοὔτοι νόϲον γ' ἐπακτὸν ἐξαρούμεθα,
θεοῖϲι δυϲμαχοῦντεϲ. ἀλλ' εἴϲω ϲτέγηϲ
χωρῶμεν, ὡϲ λόγων τ' ἐπιϲτολὰϲ φέρῃϲ,
ἅ τ' ἀντὶ δώρων δῶρα χρὴ προϲαρμόϲαι,
καὶ ταῦτ' ἄγῃϲ. κενὸν γὰρ οὐ δίκαιά ϲε   495
χωρεῖν προϲελθόνθ' ὧδε ϲὺν πολλῷ ϲτόλῳ.

468 φράζω] φράϲω K   470 πείθου] πιθοῦ Dindorf   472 μαν-
θάνω] ἐκμανθάνω t   476 Ἡρακλῆ Ka: -εῖ cett.   483 τῶνδ'
Dawe: τήνδ' codd.   487 ἐμπέδωϲ] -ουϲ Nauck   488–9 post 478
traiecit Bergk, del. alii   491 γ' **azt**: om. **l**   ἐξαρούμεθα Zot:
ἐξαιρούμεθα cett.   495 κενὸν L s.l., UZg: κεινὸν vel κείνον cett.

22

ΤΡΑΧΙΝΙΑΙ

Χο. μέγα τι cθένoc ἁ Κύπριc· ἐκφέρεται νίκαc
 ἀεί. cτρ.
 καὶ τὰ μὲν θεῶν
 παρέβαν, καὶ ὅπωc Κρονίδαν ἀπάταcεν οὐ
  λέγω 500
 οὐδὲ τὸν ἔννυχον Ἅιδαν,
 ἢ Ποcειδάωνα τινάκτορα γαίαc·
 ἀλλ' ἐπὶ τάνδ' ἄρ' ἄκοιτιν
 ⟨τίνεc⟩ ἀμφίγυοι κατέβαν πρὸ γάμων,
 τίνεc πάμπληκτα παγκόνιτά τ' ἐξ- 505
 ῆλθον ἄεθλ' ἀγώνων;

 ὁ μὲν ἦν ποταμοῦ cθένοc, ὑψίκερω
  τετραόρου ἀντ.
 φάcμα ταύρου,
 Ἀχελῷοc ἀπ' Οἰνιαδᾶν, ὁ δὲ Βακχίαc ἄπο 510
 ἦλθε παλίντονα Θήβαc
 τόξα καὶ λόγχαc ῥόπαλόν τε τινάccων,
 παῖc Διόc· οἳ τότ' ἀολλεῖc
 ἴcαν ἐc μέcον ἱέμενοι λεχέων·
 μόνα δ' εὔλεκτροc ἐν μέcῳ Κύπριc 515
 ῥαβδονόμει ξυνοῦcα.

 τότ' ἦν χερόc, ἦν δὲ τό- ἐπ.
 ξων πάταγοc,
 ταυρείων τ' ἀνάμιγδα κεράτων·
 ἦν δ' ἀμφίπλεκτοι κλίμακεc, ἦν δὲ μετώ- 520
 πων ὀλόεντα
 πλήγματα καὶ cτόνοc ἀμφοῖν.

497 post Κύπριc interpunxit Wakefield, qui etiam νικῶc' pro νίκαc coniecit   501 Ἅιδαν edd.: Ἀΐδαν codd.   502 Ποcειδάωνα a: -δῶνα LZg: -δάονα Zot   504 suppl. Hermann   505 τίνεc] τίνων Zieliński   ἐξῆλθον] ἐξῆνον Wakefield   507 τετραόρου Lat: -αώρου z: -άορον Eustathius 573. 27 (recte alibi)   510 Βακχίαc Brunck: -είαc codd.   520 ἀμφίπλεκτοι] -πλικτοι Headlam (πλίγματα in 521 iam Wunder)

23

ϹΟΦΟΚΛΕΟΥϹ

ἁ δ' εὐῶπιϲ ἁβρὰ
τηλαυγεῖ παρ' ὄχθῳ
ἧϲτο τὸν ὃν προϲμένουϲ' ἀκοίταν.   525
†ἐγὼ δὲ μάτηρ μὲν οἷα φράζω·†
τὸ δ' ἀμφινείκητον ὄμμα νύμφαϲ
ἐλεινὸν ἀμμένει ⟨τέλοϲ⟩·
κἀπὸ ματρὸϲ ἄφαρ βέβαχ',
ὥϲτε πόρτιϲ ἐρήμα.   530

Δη.   ἦμοϲ, φίλαι, κατ' οἶκον ὁ ξένοϲ θροεῖ
ταῖϲ αἰχμαλώτοιϲ παιϲὶν ὡϲ ἐπ' ἐξόδῳ,
τῆμοϲ θυραῖοϲ ἦλθον ὡϲ ὑμᾶϲ λάθρᾳ,
τὰ μὲν φράϲουϲα χερϲὶν ἀτεχνηϲάμην,
τὰ δ' οἷα πάϲχω ϲυγκατοικτιουμένη.   535
κόρην γάρ, οἶμαι δ' οὐκέτ', ἀλλ' ἐζευγμένην,
παρεϲδέδεγμαι, φόρτον ὥϲτε ναυτίλοϲ,
λωβητὸν ἐμπόλημα τῆϲ ἐμῆϲ φρενόϲ.
καὶ νῦν δύ' οὖϲαι μίμνομεν μιᾶϲ ὑπὸ
χλαίνηϲ ὑπαγκάλιϲμα. τοιάδ' Ἡρακλῆϲ,   540
ὁ πιϲτὸϲ ἡμῖν κἀγαθὸϲ καλούμενοϲ,
οἰκούρι' ἀντέπεμψε τοῦ μακροῦ χρόνου.
ἐγὼ δὲ θυμοῦϲθαι μὲν οὐκ ἐπίϲταμαι
νοϲοῦντι κείνῳ πολλὰ τῇδε τῇ νόϲῳ,
τὸ δ' αὖ ξυνοικεῖν τῇδ' ὁμοῦ τίϲ ἂν γυνὴ   545
δύναιτο, κοινωνοῦϲα τῶν αὐτῶν γάμων;
ὁρῶ γὰρ ἥβην τὴν μὲν ἕρπουϲαν πρόϲω,
τὴν δὲ φθίνουϲαν· ὧν ⟨δ'⟩ ἀφαρπάζειν φιλεῖ

526–30 del. Wunder   526 μάτηρ] θατὴρ Zieliński suspicionem movent et sensus et collocatio verborum; exspectares ut de pugna adhuc ancipiti diceretur   527 ἀμφινείκητον] -νίκητον LZg   528 ἐλεινὸν Porson: ἐλεεινὸν codd.   ⟨τέλοϲ⟩ suppl. Gleditsch: ⟨λάχοϲ⟩ olim Gleditsch   529 βέβαχ' Dobree: βέβακεν codd.   530 ὥϲτε] ὥϲπερ LZg   ἐρήμα] -αϲ Meineke   531 θροεῖ L^pc zt: θρόει L^ac Ka   539 οὖϲαι] οὖϲα Blaydes   ὑπὸ Brunck: ὕπο codd.   541 καλούμενοϲ] τελούμενοϲ t   547–8 τὴν ... τὴν] τῇ ... τῇ Musgrave: τῆϲ ... τῆϲ Nauck   548 suppl. Zippmann

24

ΤΡΑΧΙΝΙΑΙ

ὀφθαλμὸс ἄνθοс, τῶνδ' ὑπεκτρέπει πόδα.
ταῦτ' οὖν φοβοῦμαι μὴ πόcιc μὲν Ἡρακλῆс   550
ἐμὸc καλῆται, τῆc νεωτέραc δ' ἀνήρ.
ἀλλ' οὐ γάρ, ὥcπερ εἶπον, ὀργαίνειν καλὸν
γυναῖκα νοῦν ἔχουcαν· ᾗ δ' ἔχω, φίλαι,
λυτήριον λύπημα, τῇδ' ὑμῖν φράcω.
ἦν μοι παλαιὸν δῶρον ἀρχαίου ποτὲ   555
θηρόc, λέβητι χαλκέῳ κεκρυμμένον,
ὃ παῖc ἔτ' οὖcα τοῦ δαcυcτέρνου παρὰ
Νέccου φθίνοντοc ἐκ φονῶν ἀνειλόμην,
ὃc τὸν βαθύρρουν ποταμὸν Εὔηνον βροτοὺc
μιcθοῦ 'πόρευε χερcίν, οὔτε πομπίμοιc   560
κώπαιc ἐρέccων οὔτε λαίφεcιν νεώc.
ὃc κἀμέ, τὸν πατρῷον ἡνίκα cτόλον
ξὺν Ἡρακλεῖ τὸ πρῶτον εὖνιc ἑcπόμην,
φέρων ἐπ' ὤμοιc, ἡνίκ' ἦ 'ν μέcῳ πόρῳ,
ψαύει ματαίαιc χερcίν· ἐκ δ' ἤυc' ἐγώ,   565
χὠ Ζηνὸc εὐθὺc παῖc ἐπιcτρέψαc χεροῖν
ἧκεν κομήτην ἰόν· ἐc δὲ πλεύμοναc
cτέρνων διερροίζηcεν. ἐκθνῄcκων δ' ὁ θὴρ
τοcοῦτον εἶπε· "παῖ γέροντοc Οἰνέωc,
τοcόνδ' ὀνήcῃ τῶν ἐμῶν, ἐὰν πίθῃ,   570
πορθμῶν, ὁθούνεχ' ὑcτάτην c' ἔπεμψ' ἐγώ·
ἐὰν γὰρ ἀμφίθρεπτον αἷμα τῶν ἐμῶν
cφαγῶν ἐνέγκῃ χερcίν, ᾗ μελάγχολοc

549 τῶνδ' Zippmann: τῶν δ' codd.   ὑπεκτρέπει l: -ειν cett.
551 καλῆται A^(pc)YZg^(pc): -εῖται cett.   553 ἔχω] ἔχει Wratislaw
554 λύπημα] λώφημα Jebb   555 et 557 ποτὲ et παρὰ permutavit
Kayser   557 παρὰ Brunck: πάρα codd.   558 Νέccου az:
Νέcου Lt   φονῶν Bergk: φόνων codd.   560 'πόρευε edd.:
πόρευε codd.   562 τὸν πατρῷον cτόλον: i.e. ὑπὸ τοῦ πατρὸc
ἐcταλμένη   564 ἦ 'ν Cobet: ἦν fere codd.: ᾖ Dindorf
567 πλεύμοναc Lat: πν- L s.l. z   570 πίθῃ Colinaeus: πιθῇ Lγρa:
πυθῇ L: πύθῃ cett.   571 c' zt: om. La   573 ᾗ] ᾧ Page
573-4 μελάγχολοc ... ἰὸc Dobree: -οὐc ... ἰοὺc codd.: -ου ... ἰοῦ
Wunder

ΣΟΦΟΚΛΕΟΥΣ

ἔβαψεν ἰὸς θρέμμα Λερναίας ὕδρας,
ἔσται φρενός σοι τοῦτο κηλητήριον 575
τῆς Ἡρακλείας, ὥστε μήτιν' εἰσιδὼν
στέρξει γυναῖκα κεῖνος ἀντὶ σοῦ πλέον."
τοῦτ' ἐννοήσασ', ὦ φίλαι, δόμοις γὰρ ἦν
κείνου θανόντος ἐγκεκλῃμένον καλῶς,
χιτῶνα τόνδ' ἔβαψα, προσβαλοῦσ' ὅσα 580
ζῶν κεῖνος εἶπε· καὶ πεπείρανται τάδε.
κακὰς δὲ τόλμας μήτ' ἐπισταίμην ἐγὼ
μήτ' ἐκμάθοιμι, τάς τε τολμώσας στυγῶ.
φίλτροις δ' ἐάν πως τήνδ' ὑπερβαλώμεθα
τὴν παῖδα καὶ θέλκτροισι τοῖς ἐφ' Ἡρακλεῖ, 585
μεμηχάνηται τοὔργον, εἴ τι μὴ δοκῶ
πράσσειν μάταιον· εἰ δὲ μή, πεπαύσομαι.

Χο. ἀλλ' εἴ τις ἐστὶ πίστις ἐν τοῖς δρωμένοις,
δοκεῖς παρ' ἡμῖν οὐ βεβουλεῦσθαι κακῶς.
Δη. οὕτως ἔχει γ' ἡ πίστις, ὡς τὸ μὲν δοκεῖν 590
ἔνεστι, πείρᾳ δ' οὐ προσωμίλησά πω.
Χο. ἀλλ' εἰδέναι χρὴ δρῶσαν· ὡς οὐδ' εἰ δοκεῖς
ἔχειν, ἔχοις ἂν γνῶμα, μὴ πειρωμένη.
Δη. ἀλλ' αὐτίκ' εἰσόμεσθα· τόνδε γὰρ βλέπω
θυραῖον ἤδη· διὰ τάχους δ' ἐλεύσεται. 595
μόνον παρ' ὑμῶν εὖ στεγοίμεθ'· ὡς σκότῳ
κἂν αἰσχρὰ πράσσῃς, οὔποτ' αἰσχύνῃ πεσῇ.
Λι. τί χρὴ ποεῖν; σήμαινε, τέκνον Οἰνέως·
ὡς ἐσμὲν ἤδη τῷ μακρῷ χρόνῳ βραδεῖς.
Δη. ἀλλ' αὐτὰ δή σοι ταῦτα καὶ πράσσω, Λίχα, 600
ἕως σὺ ταῖς ἔσωθεν ἠγορῶ ξέναις,

577 στέρξει] στέρξαι a in linea   579 θανόντος] τὸ δῶρον Hense   ἐγκεκλῃμένον P.Oxy. 1805, coni. Dindorf: -ειμένον L: -εισμένον cett. 581 πεπείρανται La: -αται zt   585 om. Eustathius 799. 4, del. Wunder   587 πεπαύσομαι] -σεται v.l. in a   591 πω] που Zgt 592 οὐδ' εἰ] οὐ l   596 ὑμῶν] ὑμῖν Zg, t s.l.   στεγοίμεθ'] -ώμεθ' Blaydes   598 ποιεῖν L: ποεῖν cett.   601 post hunc v. lacunam statuit Dawe: del. Nauck

ΤΡΑΧΙΝΙΑΙ

ὅπως φέρῃς μοι τόνδε ταναϋφῆ πέπλον,
δώρημ' ἐκείνῳ τἀνδρὶ τῆς ἐμῆς χερός.
διδοὺς δὲ τόνδε φράζ' ὅπως μηδεὶς βροτῶν
κείνου πάροιθεν ἀμφιδύσεται χροΐ, 605
μηδ' ὄψεταί νιν μήτε φέγγος ἡλίου
μήθ' ἕρκος ἱρὸν μήτ' ἐφέςτιον ςέλας,
πρὶν κεῖνος αὐτὸν φανερὸς ἐμφανῶς ςταθεὶς
δείξῃ θεοῖςιν ἡμέρᾳ ταυροςφάγῳ.
οὕτω γὰρ ηὔγμην, εἴ ποτ' αὐτὸν ἐς δόμους 610
ἴδοιμι ςωθέντ' ἢ κλύοιμι, πανδίκως
ςτελεῖν χιτῶνι τῷδε, καὶ φανεῖν θεοῖς
θυτῆρα καινῷ καινὸν ἐν πεπλώματι.
καὶ τῶνδ' ἀποίςεις ςῆμ', ὃ κεῖνος εὐμαθὲς
ςφραγῖδος ἕρκει τῷδ' ἐπὸν μαθήςεται. 615
ἀλλ' ἕρπε, καὶ φύλαςςε πρῶτα μὲν νόμον,
τὸ μὴ 'πιθυμεῖν πομπὸς ὢν περιςςὰ δρᾶν·
ἔπειθ' ὅπως ἂν ἡ χάρις κείνου τέ ςοι
κἀμοῦ ξυνελθοῦς' ἐξ ἁπλῆς διπλῆ φανῇ.
Λι. ἀλλ' εἴπερ Ἑρμοῦ τήνδε πομπεύω τέχνην 620
βέβαιον, οὔ τι μὴ ςφαλῶ γ' ἐν ςοί ποτε,
τὸ μὴ οὐ τόδ' ἄγγος ὡς ἔχει δεῖξαι φέρων,
λόγων τε πίςτιν ὧν λέγεις ἐφαρμόςαι.
Δη. ςτείχοις ἂν ἤδη. καὶ γὰρ ἐξεπίςταςαι
τά γ' ἐν δόμοιςιν ὡς ἔχοντα τυγχάνει. 625
Λι. ἐπίςταμαί τε καὶ φράςω ςεςωμένα.
Δη. ἀλλ' οἶςθα μὲν δὴ καὶ τὰ τῆς ξένης ὁρῶν

602 φέρῃς] -εις a   ταναϋφῆ Wunder: γ' εὐϋφῆ codd. plerique (etiam Λ): γρ(άφεται) δὲ ἀϋφῆ ἀντὶ τοῦ λεπτοϋφῆ sch. L   605 ἀμφιδύςεται] -ηται t   608 φανερὸς] -ὼς UZg: -ὸν t   ἐμφανῶς] -ῆς t (sed -ὼς T s.l.): -ῇ Brunck   611 sunt qui post πανδίκως interpungant   613 ἐν] ἐμ L   615 ἐπὸν μαθήςεται Billerbeck: ἐπ' ὄμμα θήςεται codd.   620 πομπεύω] πρεςβεύω Nauck: ἐγὼ ςπεύδω Hense   621 τι a: τοι cett. (etiam Λ)   622 οὐ La: om. zt   623 λέγεις Wunder: ἔχεις fere codd.   624–32 post 615 traiecit Nauck   626 ςεςωμένα edd.: ςεςωςμένα codd.

27

ΣΟΦΟΚΛΕΟΥΣ

      προσδέγματ' αὐτός, ὥς cφ' ἐδεξάμην φίλως.
Λι. ὥcτ' ἐκπλαγῆναι τοὐμὸν ἡδονῇ κέαρ.
Δη. τί δῆτ' ἂν ἄλλο γ' ἐννέποις; δέδοικα γὰρ   630
      μὴ πρῷ λέγοις ἂν τὸν πόθον τὸν ἐξ ἐμοῦ,
      πρὶν εἰδέναι τἀκεῖθεν εἰ ποθούμεθα.

Χο. ὦ ναύλοχα καὶ πετραῖα θερμὰ λουτρὰ καὶ
          πάγους   cτρ. α'
      Οἴτας παραναιετάοντες, οἵ τε μέccαν   635
      Μηλίδα πὰρ λίμναν
      χρυcαλακάτου τ' ἀκτὰν κόραc,
      ἔνθ' Ἑλλάνων ἀγοραὶ Πυλάτιδεc κλέονται,   639

      ὁ καλλιβόας τάχ' ὑμὶν αὐλὸc οὐκ ἀναρcίαν   ἀντ. α'
      ἀχῶν καναχὰν ἐπάνειcιν, ἀλλὰ θείαc
      ἀντίλυρον μούcαc.
      ὁ γὰρ Διὸc Ἀλκμήναc κόροc
      cοῦται πάcαc ἀρετᾶc λάφυρ' ἔχων ἐπ' οἴκουc· 645

      ὃν ἀπόπτολιν εἴχομεν πάντα   cτρ. β'
      δυοκαιδεκάμηνον ἀμμένουcαι
      χρόνον, πελάγιον, ἴδριεc οὐ-
      δέν· ἁ δέ οἱ φίλα δάμαρ τάλαιναν   650
      δυcτάλαινα καρδίαν
      πάγκλαυτοc αἰὲν ὤλλυτο·

628 αὐτόc Bergk, Patakis: αὐτὴν codd.: αὐτή Koechly   ὥc cφ' Dawe: ὥc θ' lzt: ὡc a   631 πρῷ L^ac a: πρὶν zt   635 παραναιετάοντεc LaZo, t s.l.: πέρι ναιετάοντεc Zg: περιν- t in linea   μέccαν Lt: μέcαν az   636 Μηλίδα] Μα- Blaydes   πὰρ t: παρὰ cett. 639 κλέονται Musgrave: καλέονται codd.   640 ὑμὶν Itsumi: ὑμῖν codd.   642 ἀχῶν Elmsley: ἰάχων codd.   644 post Ἀλκμήναc add. τε Laz: del. t   κόροc Lzt: κοῦροc a   645 cοῦται Elmsley: cεῦται codd.   647 πάντα] πάντᾳ Bothe   650 ἁ δέ οἱ at et fortasse voluit z: ᾶ δέοι L   τάλαιναν Dindorf: -να codd.: fortasse τάλαιν', ἁ,

ΤΡΑΧΙΝΙΑΙ

νῦν δ' Ἄρης οἰςτρηθεὶς
ἐξέλυς' ἐπιπόνων ἀμερᾶν.

ἀφίκοιτ' ἀφίκοιτο· μὴ cταίη   ἀντ. β'
πολύκωπον ὄχημα ναὸς αὐτῷ,   656
πρὶν τάνδε πρὸς πόλιν ἀνύcει-
ε, ναcιῶτιν ἑcτίαν ἀμείψας,
ἔνθα κλῄζεται θυτήρ·
ὅθεν μόλοι †πανάμερος,   660
τᾶς Πειθοῦς παγχρίcτῳ
cυγκραθεὶς ἐπὶ προφάcει θηρόc†.

Δη. γυναῖκες, ὡς δέδοικα μὴ περαιτέρω
     πεπραγμέν' ᾖ μοι πάνθ' ὅc' ἀρτίως ἔδρων.
Χο. τί δ' ἔcτι, Δῃάνειρα, τέκνον Οἰνέως;   665
Δη. οὐκ οἶδ'· ἀθυμῶ δ' εἰ φανήcομαι τάχα
     κακὸν μέγ' ἐκπράξας' ἀπ' ἐλπίδος καλῆς.
Χο. οὐ δή τι τῶν cῶν Ἡρακλεῖ δωρημάτων;
Δη. μάλιcτά γ'· ὥcτε μήποτ' ἂν προθυμίαν
     ἄδηλον ἔργου τῳ παραινέcαι λαβεῖν.   670
Χο. δίδαξον, εἰ διδακτόν, ἐξ ὅτου φοβῇ.
Δη. τοιοῦτον ἐκβέβηκεν, οἷον, ἢν φράcω,
     γυναῖκες, ὑμῖν θαῦμ' ἀνέλπιcτον βαλεῖν.
     ᾧ γὰρ τὸν ἐνδυτῆρα πέπλον ἀρτίως
     ἔχριον, ἀργῆς οἰὸς εὐείρῳ πόκῳ,   675
     τοῦτ' ἠφάνιcται διάβορον πρὸς οὐδενὸς

---

653 οἰcτρηθεὶς codd. plerique: -ωθεὶς Zo, T s.l.: αὖ cτρωθεὶς Musgrave: οἱ cτρωθεὶς Hermann   654 ἐξέλυς'] -cεν Pearson   ἐπιπόνων ἀμερᾶν Erfurdt: -ον -αν codd.   657 ἀνύcειε az: -ειεν t: -εις L^{ac}K   659 κλῄζεται Ka: κληΐζεται cett.   660 πανάμερος] πανίμερος Mudge   662 cυγκραθεὶς] cυντακεὶς Paley, quo recepto θηρὸς ὕπο παρφάcει Pearson   θηρός] φάρους Haupt: alii alia temptaverunt   670 τῳ] του Blaydes   672 ἢν Erfurdt (et Paris. gr. 2886 teste Subkoff): ἂν codd.   673 βαλεῖν nos: λαβεῖν l: παθεῖν Kzt: μαθεῖν a, s.l. in L et Zo   675 ἀργῆς Bergk: ἀργῆτ' codd.   εὐείρῳ] -είρου Valckenaer: -έρου Lobeck   676 ἠφάνιcται La: -το zt

29

ϹΟΦΟΚΛΕΟΥϹ

τῶν ἔνδον, ἀλλ' ἐδεϲτὸν ἐξ αὐτοῦ φθίνει,
καὶ ψῇ κατ' ἄκραϲ ϲπιλάδοϲ. ὡϲ δ' εἰδῇϲ ἅπαν,
ᾖ τοῦτ' ἐπράχθη, μεῖζον' ἐκτενῶ λόγον.
ἐγὼ γὰρ ὧν ὁ θήρ με Κένταυροϲ, πονῶν   680
πλευρὰν πικρᾷ γλωχῖνι, προὐδιδάξατο
παρῆκα θεϲμῶν οὐδέν, ἀλλ' ἐϲῳζόμην,
χαλκῆϲ ὅπωϲ δύϲνιπτον ἐκ δέλτου γραφήν·
[καί μοι τάδ' ἦν πόρρητα καὶ τοιαῦτ' ἔδρων·]
τὸ φάρμακον τοῦτ' ἄπυρον ἀκτῖνόϲ τ' ἀεὶ   685
θερμῆϲ ἄθικτον ἐν μυχοῖϲ ϲῴζειν ἐμέ,
ἕωϲ ἂν ἀρτίχριϲτον ἁρμόϲαιμί που.
κἄδρων τοιαῦτα. νῦν δ', ὅτ' ἦν ἐργαϲτέον,
ἔχριϲα μὲν κατ' οἶκον ἐν δόμοιϲ κρυφῇ
μαλλῷ, ϲπάϲαϲα κτηϲίου βοτοῦ λάχνην,   690
κἄθηκα ϲυμπτύξαϲ' ἀλαμπὲϲ ἡλίου
κοίλῳ ζυγάϲτρῳ δῶρον, ὥϲπερ εἴδετε.
εἴϲω δ' ἀποϲτείχουϲα δέρκομαι φάτιν
ἄφραϲτον, ἀξύμβλητον ἀνθρώπῳ μαθεῖν.
τὸ γὰρ κάταγμα τυγχάνω ῥίψαϲά πωϲ   695
[τῆϲ οἰόϲ, ᾧ προὔχριον, ἐϲ μέϲην φλόγα,]
ἀκτῖν' ἐϲ ἡλιῶτιν· ὡϲ δ' ἐθάλπετο,
ῥεῖ πᾶν ἄδηλον καὶ κατέψηκται χθονί,
μορφῇ μάλιϲτ' εἰκαϲτὸν ὥϲτε πρίονοϲ
ἐκβρώμαθ' ἂν βλέψειαϲ ἐν τομῇ ξύλου.   700
τοιόνδε κεῖται προπετέϲ. ἐκ δὲ γῆϲ, ὅθεν
προὔκειτ', ἀναζέουϲι θρομβώδειϲ ἀφροί,
γλαυκῆϲ ὀπώραϲ ὥϲτε πίονοϲ ποτοῦ
χυθέντοϲ ἐϲ γῆν Βακχίαϲ ἀπ' ἀμπέλου.

677 ἔνδον] ἐκτόϲ Herwerden   678 v. fortasse corruptus   καὶ
ψῇ] ψηκτὸν Wecklein   682 οὐδέν] οὐδέν' Wakefield
684 del. Wunder   685 τ' azt: om. l   686 θερμῆϲ zt: θέρμηϲ
La   687 ἂν] νιν Elmsley   692 ὥϲπερ] ᾧπερ Herwerden,
Blaydes   693 φάτιν] θέαν Blaydes (φάϲμα interpretatio in l)
696 del. Dobree   φλόγα] πλάκα G. Wolff   700 -αθ' ἂν βλέψειαϲ
Dawe: -ατ' ἂν βλέψειαϲ a: -ατ' ἐκβλέψειαϲ Lt: -ατ' ἐμβλέψειαϲ z
704 Βακχίαϲ t et v.l. in a: -είαϲ cett.

30

ΤΡΑΧΙΝΙΑΙ

ὥστ' οὐκ ἔχω τάλαινα ποῖ γνώμης πέςω· 705
ὁρῶ δέ μ' ἔργον δεινὸν ἐξειργαςμένην.
πόθεν γὰρ ἄν ποτ', ἀντὶ τοῦ θνῄςκων ὁ θὴρ
ἐμοὶ παρέςχ' εὔνοιαν, ἧς ἔθνῃςχ' ὕπερ;
οὐκ ἔςτιν, ἀλλὰ τὸν βαλόντ' ἀποφθίςαι
χρῄζων ἔθελγέ μ'· ὧν ἐγὼ μεθύςτερον, 710
ὅτ' οὐκέτ' ἀρκεῖ, τὴν μάθηςιν ἄρνυμαι.
μόνη γὰρ αὐτόν, εἴ τι μὴ ψευςθήςομαι
γνώμης, ἐγὼ δύςτηνος ἐξαποφθερῶ·
τὸν γὰρ βαλόντ' ἄτρακτον οἶδα καὶ θεὸν
Χείρωνα πημήναντα, χὦνπερ ἂν θίγῃ, 715
φθείρει τὰ πάντα κνώδαλ'· ἐκ δὲ τοῦδ' ὅδε
ςφαγῶν διελθὼν ἰὸς αἵματος μέλας
πῶς οὐκ ὀλεῖ καὶ τόνδε; δόξῃ γοῦν ἐμῇ.
καίτοι δέδοκται, κεῖνος εἰ ςφαλήςεται,
ταὐτῇ ςὺν ὁρμῇ κἀμὲ ςυνθανεῖν ἅμα. 720
ζῆν γὰρ κακῶς κλύουςαν οὐκ ἀναςχετόν,
ἥτις προτιμᾷ μὴ κακὴ πεφυκέναι.
Χο. ταρβεῖν μὲν ἔργα δείν' ἀναγκαίως ἔχει,
τὴν δ' ἐλπίδ' οὐ χρὴ τῆς τύχης κρίνειν πάρος.
Δη. οὐκ ἔςτιν ἐν τοῖς μὴ καλοῖς βουλεύμαςιν 725
οὐδ' ἐλπίς, ἥτις καὶ θράςος τι προξενεῖ.
Χο. ἀλλ' ἀμφὶ τοῖς ςφαλεῖςι μὴ 'ξ ἑκουςίας
ὀργὴ πέπειρα, τῆς ςε τυγχάνειν πρέπει.
Δη. τοιαῦτά τἂν λέξειεν οὐχ ὁ τοῦ κακοῦ
κοινωνός, ἀλλ' ᾧ μηδὲν ἔςτ' οἴκοι βαρύ. 730

707 θνῄςκων] θνῄςκειν Wakefield   708 ἧς ⟨γ'⟩ Blaydes
710 ἔθελγέ μ'] -γεν a   715 χὦνπερ Wakefield: χὦςπερ La:
χὦςαπερ zt   716 φθείρει τὰ] φθείροντα Faehse   πάντα
κνώδαλ'· ἐκ] πάντα· κνωδάλου δὲ Hense   τοῦδ' ὅδε] τοῦδε δὴ
Meineke   717 αἵματος] αἱματοῦς Wunder   718 δόξῃ ...
ἐμῇ Lt: δόξει ... ἐμοί fere cett.   720 ταὐτῇ H. Stephanus: ταύτῃ
codd.   ὁρμῇ Lzt: ὀργῇ L s.l. et lm. sch., a   723 ἔργα δείν'] ἔργ'
ἄδηλ' Tournier   729 τἂν Blaydes: δ' ἂν codd.   730 ἔςτ' aZg:
ἐςτιν cett.   οἴκοι Wakefield: οἴκοις codd.

31

ΣΟΦΟΚΛΕΟΥΣ

Χο. cιγᾶν ἂν ἁρμόζοι cε τὸν πλείω λόγον,
 εἰ μή τι λέξεις παιδὶ τῷ cαυτῆς· ἐπεὶ
 πάρεcτι, μαcτὴρ πατρὸc ὃc πρὶν ᾤχετο.
Υλ. ὦ μῆτερ, ὥc ἂν ἐκ τριῶν c' ἓν εἱλόμην,
 ἢ μηκέτ' εἶναι ζῶcαν, ἢ cεcωμένην   735
 ἄλλου κεκλῆcθαι μητέρ', ἢ λῴουc φρέναc
 τῶν νῦν παρουcῶν τῶνδ' ἀμείψαcθαί ποθεν.
Δη. τί δ' ἔcτιν, ὦ παῖ, πρόc γ' ἐμοῦ cτυγούμενον;
Υλ. τὸν ἄνδρα τὸν cὸν ἴcθι, τὸν δ' ἐμὸν λέγω
 πατέρα, κατακτείναcα τῇδ' ἐν ἡμέρᾳ.   740
Δη. οἴμοι, τίν' ἐξήνεγκαc, ὦ τέκνον, λόγον;
Υλ. ὃν οὐχ οἷόν τε μὴ τελεcθῆναι· τὸ γὰρ
 φανθὲν τίc ἂν δύναιτ' ⟨ἂν⟩ ἀγένητον ποεῖν;
Δη. πῶc εἶπαc, ὦ παῖ; τοῦ παρ' ἀνθρώπων μαθὼν
 ἄζηλον οὕτωc ἔργον εἰργάcθαι με φῄc;   745
Υλ. αὐτὸc βαρεῖαν ξυμφορὰν ἐν ὄμμαcιν
 πατρὸc δεδορκὼc κοὐ κατὰ γλῶccαν κλυών.
Δη. ποῦ δ' ἐμπελάζειc τἀνδρὶ καὶ παρίcταcαι;
Υλ. εἰ χρὴ μαθεῖν cε, πάντα δὴ φωνεῖν χρεών.
 ὅθ' εἷρπε κλεινὴν Εὐρύτου πέρcαc πόλιν, 750
 νίκηc ἄγων τροπαῖα κἀκροθίνια,
 ἀκτή τιc ἀμφίκλυcτοc Εὐβοίαc ἄκρον
 Κήναιόν ἐcτιν, ἔνθα πατρῴῳ Διὶ
 βωμοὺc ὁρίζει τεμενίαν τε φυλλάδα·

---

731 λόγον Lγρ: χρόνον codd.   735 cεcωμένην edd.: cεcωc- cett.
736 μητέρ' aZg: μητέρα c' cett.   737 τῶνδ' ἀμείψαcθαι] ἀντα-
μείψαcθαι Nauck   739 δ'] γ' Wakefield   742 μὴ ⟨οὐ⟩ Nauck
743 alterum ἂν suppl. edd., licet Suda s.v. οἴμοι (Υ 101) perperam freti
ἀγένητον L, Sudae codd. AGM: ἀγένν- cett.   ποεῖν L: ποιεῖν cett.
744 ἀνθρώπων] ἀνθρώπου P.Oxy. 1805 in margine   μαθὼν] παρὼν
P.Oxy. 1805ᵃᶜ   746-7 αὐτὸc et πατρὸc permutavit Nauck
747 κοὐ Zg et manus recentior in L: καὶ cett.   κλυών West: κλύων codd.
748 ἐμπελάζειc] -ῃc Lᵃᶜ K: -ῃ Bergk   749 χρὴ μαθεῖν cε] χρῇc
μαθεῖν cύ Bergk   751 τροπαῖα hoc accentu Dindorf: proparoxytone
codd.   753 Κήναιόν] Κηναῖον LZo

32

ΤΡΑΧΙΝΙΑΙ

οὔ νιν τὰ πρῶτ' ἐϲεῖδον ἄϲμενοϲ πόθῳ. 755
μέλλοντι δ' αὐτῷ πολυθύτουϲ τεύχειν ϲφαγὰϲ
κῆρυξ ἀπ' οἴκων ἵκετ' οἰκεῖοϲ Λίχαϲ,
τὸ cὸν φέρων δώρημα, θανάϲιμον πέπλον·
ὃν κεῖνοϲ ἐνδύϲ, ὡϲ cὺ προὐξεφίεϲο,
ταυροκτονεῖ μὲν δώδεκ' ἐντελεῖϲ ἔχων 760
λείαϲ ἀπαρχὴν βοῦϲ· ἀτὰρ τὰ πάνθ' ὁμοῦ
ἑκατὸν προϲῆγε ϲυμμιγῆ βοϲκήματα.
καὶ πρῶτα μὲν δείλαιοϲ ἵλεῳ φρενὶ
κόϲμῳ τε χαίρων καὶ ϲτολῇ κατηύχετο·
ὅπωϲ δὲ ϲεμνῶν ὀργίων ἐδαίετο 765
φλὸξ αἱματηρὰ κἀπὸ πιείραϲ δρυόϲ,
ἱδρὼϲ ἀνῄει χρωτί, καὶ προϲπτύϲϲεται
πλευραῖϲιν ἀρτίκολλοϲ, ὥϲτε τέκτονοϲ
χιτών, ἅπαν κατ' ἄρθρον· ἦλθε δ' ὀϲτέων
ὀδαγμὸϲ ἀντίϲπαϲτοϲ· εἶτα φοίνιοϲ 770
ἐχθρᾶϲ ἐχίδνηϲ ἰὸϲ ὣϲ ἐδαίνυτο.
ἐνταῦθα δὴ 'βόηϲε τὸν δυϲδαίμονα
Λίχαν, τὸν οὐδὲν αἴτιον τοῦ ϲοῦ κακοῦ,
ποίαιϲ ἐνέγκοι τόνδε μηχαναῖϲ πέπλον·
ὁ δ' οὐδὲν εἰδὼϲ δύϲμοροϲ τὸ ϲὸν μόνηϲ 775
δώρημ' ἔλεξεν, ὥϲπερ ἦν ἐϲταλμένον.
κἀκεῖνοϲ ὡϲ ἤκουϲε καὶ διώδυνοϲ
ϲπαραγμὸϲ αὐτοῦ πλευμόνων ἀνθήψατο,
μάρψαϲ ποδόϲ νιν, ἄρθρον ᾗ λυγίζεται,
ῥίπτει πρὸϲ ἀμφίκλυϲτον ἐκ πόντου πέτραν· 780

757 κῆρυξ L: paroxytone cett. οἰκεῖοϲ] οὐ κενὸϲ F. W. Schmidt
760 ἔχων] ἄγων Blaydes: an ἐλὼν? 764 κατηύχετο] κατήρχετο
Meineke 767 ἀνῄει a, T s.l.: ἂν ᾔει L: ἀνίει KZgt
προϲπτύϲϲεται Musgrave: -ετο codd. 768-9 sic interpunxit
Zijderveld 770 ὀδαγμὸϲ] ἀδαγμὸϲ Brunck ex Photio φοίνιοϲ
Pierson: -ίαϲ codd. 771 ὣϲ Wakefield: ὡϲ codd. (etiam K)
772 'βόηϲε Harleianus 5743, Brunck: βόηϲε codd. 774 ἐνέγκοι lt:
-αι a: -αιϲ Zg: -οιϲ Zo 778 αὐτοῦ] αὐτῶν Wille πλευμόνων
Ka: πν- lzt 780 ῥίπτει Elmsley: ῥιπτεῖ codd.

33

ϹΟΦΟΚΛΕΟΥϹ

κόμης δὲ λευκὸν μυελὸν ἐκραίνει, μέϲου
κρατὸϲ διαϲπαρέντοϲ αἵματόϲ θ' ὁμοῦ.
ἅπαϲ δ' ἀνηυφήμηϲεν οἰμωγῇ λεώϲ,
τοῦ μὲν νοϲοῦντοϲ, τοῦ δὲ διαπεπραγμένου·
κοὐδεὶϲ ἐτόλμα τἀνδρὸϲ ἀντίον μολεῖν. 785
ἐϲπᾶτο γὰρ πέδονδε καὶ μετάρϲιοϲ,
βοῶν, ἰύζων· ἀμφὶ δ' ἐκτύπουν πέτραι,
Λοκρῶν τ' ὄρειοι πρῶνεϲ Εὐβοίαϲ τ' ἄκραι.
ἐπεὶ δ' ἀπεῖπε, πολλὰ μὲν τάλαϲ χθονὶ
ῥίπτων ἑαυτόν, πολλὰ δ' οἰμωγῇ βοῶν, 790
τὸ δυϲπάρευνον λέκτρον ἐνδατούμενοϲ
ϲοῦ τῆϲ ταλαίνηϲ καὶ τὸν Οἰνέωϲ γάμον
οἷον κατακτήϲαιτο λυμαντὴν βίου,
τότ' ἐκ προϲέδρου λιγνύοϲ διάϲτροφον
ὀφθαλμὸν ἄραϲ εἶδέ μ' ἐν πολλῷ ϲτρατῷ 795
δακρυρροοῦντα, καί με προϲβλέψαϲ καλεῖ·
"ὦ παῖ, πρόϲελθε, μὴ φύγῃϲ τοὐμὸν κακόν,
μηδ' εἴ ϲε χρὴ θανόντι ϲυνθανεῖν ἐμοί·
ἀλλ' ἆρον ἔξω, καὶ μάλιϲτα μέν με θὲϲ
ἐνταῦθ' ὅπου με μή τιϲ ὄψεται βροτῶν· 800
εἰ δ' οἶκτον ἴϲχειϲ, ἀλλά μ' ἔκ γε τῆϲδε γῆϲ
πόρθμευϲον ὡϲ τάχιϲτα, μηδ' αὐτοῦ θάνω."
τοϲαῦτ' ἐπιϲκήψαντοϲ, ἐν μέϲῳ ϲκάφει
θέντεϲ ϲφε πρὸϲ γῆν τήνδ' ἐκέλϲαμεν μόλιϲ
βρυχώμενον ϲπαϲμοῖϲι. καί νιν αὐτίκα 805

781 κόμηϲ] κομη P.Oxy. 1805 783 δ' Lazt: om. K et P.Oxy.
1805ᵃᶜ ἀνηυφήμηϲεν Dindorf: ἄνευ- P.Oxy. 1805, sch. E. Tro.
573: ἀνευφημήϲει Hesychius: ἀνευφώνηϲεν KA: ἄνευ φωνῆϲ ἐν Lt:
ἀνεφώνηϲεν UYz 787 βοῶν] δάκνων Diog. Laert. 10. 137, unde
λάϲκων Dobree ἐκτύπουν] ἔϲτενον Diog. Laert. 788 prius τ'
Diog. Laert.: om. codd. ἄκραι] ἄκρα Diog. cod. F 790 ῥίπτων]
ῥιπτῶν P.Oxy. 1805 791 ἐνδατούμενοϲ] ἐμματούμενοϲ γρ ap. sch.
L 793 οἷον] οἵαν P.Oxy. 1805 s.l. 796 καλεῖ H. Stephanus:
κάλει codd. 798 θανόντι] θνήϲκοντι Herwerden 799 ἆρον]
αἶρον L με θὲϲ Wakefield: μέθεϲ codd. 801 οἶκτον ἴϲχειϲ]
οἶκτοϲ ἴϲχει ϲ' Kuiper

34

ΤΡΑΧΙΝΙΑΙ

ἢ ζῶντ' ἐcόψεcθ' ἢ τεθνηκότ' ἀρτίωc.
τοιαῦτα, μῆτερ, πατρὶ βουλεύcαc· ἐμῷ
καὶ δρῶc· ἐλήφθηc, ὧν cε ποίνιμοc Δίκη
τείcαιτ' Ἐρινύc τ'. εἰ θέμιc δ', ἐπεύχομαι·
θέμιc δ', ἐπεί μοι τὴν θέμιν cὺ προὔβαλεc,   810
πάντων ἄριcτον ἄνδρα τῶν ἐπὶ χθονὶ
κτείναc', ὁποῖον ἄλλον οὐκ ὄψῃ ποτέ.

Χο. τί cῖγ' ἀφέρπειc; οὐ κάτοιcθ' ὁθούνεκα
ξυνηγορεῖc cιγῶcα τῷ κατηγόρῳ;
Υλ. ἐᾶτ' ἀφέρπειν. οὖροc ὀφθαλμῶν ἐμῶν   815
αὐτῇ γένοιτ' ἄπωθεν ἑρπούcῃ καλόc.
ὄγκον γὰρ ἄλλωc ὀνόματοc τί δεῖ τρέφειν
μητρῷον, ἥτιc μηδὲν ὡc τεκοῦcα δρᾷ;
ἀλλ' ἑρπέτω χαίρουcα· τὴν δὲ τέρψιν ἣν
τὠμῷ δίδωcι πατρί, τήνδ' αὐτὴ λάβοι.   820

Χο. ἴδ' οἷον, ὦ παῖδεc, προcέμειξεν ἄφαρ   cτρ. α'
τοὔποc τὸ θεοπρόπον ἡμῖν
τᾶc παλαιφάτου προνοίαc,
ὅ τ' ἔλακεν, ὁπότε τελεόμηνοc ἐκφέροι
δωδέκατοc ἄροτοc, ἀναδοχὰν τελεῖν πόνων   825
τῷ Διὸc αὐτόπαιδι·
καὶ τάδ' ὀρθῶc
ἔμπεδα κατουρίζει.
πῶc γὰρ ἂν ὁ μὴ λεύccων
ἔτι ποτ' ἔτ' ἐπίπονον
ἔχοι θανὼν λατρείαν;   830

806 ἐcόψεcθ'] ἔτ' ὄψεcθ' Meineke   809 Ἐρινύc L: -ιννύc azt: -ινύεc K   δ' Lat: om. z: γ' Wakefield   v. varie temptatus: ἐπεύχομαι=glorior, ut ap. A. Ag. 1394   810 προὔβαλεc az: -λαβεc lt   816 καλόc t et sch. L: καλῶc cett.   823 παλαιφάτου] παλαιφοίβου γρ ap. sch.   825 ἄροτοc az: ἄροτροc L: τ' ἄροτοc t   ἀναδοχὰν] ἀνοκωχὰν Zg: ἀναπνοὰν Meineke   829 ἐπίπονόν ⟨γ'⟩ Brunck   830 ἔχοι post θανὼν traiecit Wilamowitz, nimirum lapsu memoriae

35

ΣΟΦΟΚΛΕΟΥΣ

εἰ γάρ σφε Κενταύρου φονίᾳ νεφέλᾳ   ἀντ. α'
χρίει δολοποιὸς ἀνάγκα
πλευρά, προστακέντος ἰοῦ,
ὃν τέκετο θάνατος, ἔτεκε δ' αἰόλος δράκων,
πῶς ὅδ' ἂν ἀέλιον ἕτερον ἢ τανῦν ἴδοι,   835
δεινοτέρῳ μὲν ὕδρας
προστετακὼς
φάσματι; μελαγχαίτα τ'
ἄμμιγά νιν αἰκίζει
ὑπόφονα δολόμυ-
θα κέντρ' ἐπιζέσαντα.   840

ὧν ἅδ' ἁ τλάμων ἄοκνος   στρ. β'
μεγάλαν προσορῶσα δόμοισι
βλάβαν νέων ἀΐσσου-
σαν γάμων τὰ μὲν αὐτὰ
προσέβαλεν, τὰ δ' ἀπ' ἀλλόθρου
γνώμας μολόντ' ὀλεθρίαισι συναλλαγαῖς   845
ἦ που ὀλοὰ στένει,
ἦ που ἀδινῶν χλωρὰν
τέγγει δακρύων ἄχναν.
ἁ δ' ἐρχομένα μοῖρα προφαίνει δολίαν
καὶ μεγάλαν ἄταν.   850

831 φονίᾳ A^ac t: φοινίᾳ codd. plerique   833 πλευρὰ t: -ρᾷ cett.
834 ἔτεκε] ἔτρεφε Lobeck   835 ἀέλιον] ἅλιον L: post ἕτερον
traiecit Seidler   836 δεινοτέρῳ Lloyd-Jones: -τάτῳ codd.
837 φάσματι multis suspectum   μελαγχαίτα Lat: -ας z: -ου a s.l., T s.l.
τ'] δ' Wakefield   838 post αἰκίζει add. Νές(ς)ου θ' codd.: del. Erfurdt
839 ὑπόφονα Hermann: ὕπο φοίνια Laz: ὕπο t   841 ἄοκνος
Musgrave: -ον codd.   842 προσορῶσα] προο- Blaydes   δόμοισι t:
-οις cett.   843 ἀΐσσουσαν Nauck: ἀισσόντων codd.   αὐτὰ Blaydes
post Nauck: οὔ τι codd.   844 προσέβαλεν L^pc: -έβαλλεν L^ac K:
-έβαλε cett.   ἀπ' L s.l., aZo: ἐπ' LZgt   ἀλλόθρου Erfurdt: -θρόου
codd.   845 ὀλεθρίαισι t: -ίαις cett.: οὐλίαισι Wunder   συναλλαγαῖς t: ξυν- cett.   846 ὀλοὰ στένει] ὀλό' αἰάζει Blaydes; cf. ad 857

36

ΤΡΑΧΙΝΙΑΙ

ἔρρωγεν παγὰ δακρύων,   ἀντ. β'
κέχυται νόcoc, ὦ πόποι, οἷον
ἀναρcίων ⟨ὕπ'⟩ οὔπω
⟨τοῦδε cῶμ'⟩ ἀγακλειτὸν
ἐπέμολεν πάθος οἰκτίcαι.   855
ἰὼ κελαινὰ λόγχα προμάχου δορόc,
ἃ τότε θοὰν νύμφαν
ἄγαγες ἀπ' αἰπεινᾶc
τάνδ' Οἰχαλίαc αἰχμᾷ·
ἁ δ' ἀμφίπολος Κύπριc ἄναυδος φανερὰ   860
τῶνδ' ἐφάνη πράκτωρ.

⟨Τρ.   ἰώ μοι.⟩
Χο.   πότερον ἐγὼ μάταιος, ἦ κλύω τινὸς
      οἴκτου δι' οἴκων ἀρτίως ὁρμωμένου;
      τί φημι;   865
      ἠχεῖ τις οὐκ ἄcημον, ἀλλὰ δυcτυχῆ
      κωκυτὸν εἴcω, καί τι καινίζει cτέγη.
      ξύνες δὲ
      τήνδ' ὡc ἀγηθὴc καὶ cυνωφρυωμένη
      χωρεῖ πρὸς ἡμᾶc γραῖα cημανοῦcά τι.   870
Τρ.   ὦ παῖδες, ὡc ἄρ' ἡμὶν οὐ cμικρῶν κακῶν
      ἦρξεν τὸ δῶρον Ἡρακλεῖ τὸ πόμπιμον.
Χο.   τί δ', ὦ γεραιά, καινοποιηθὲν λέγειc;
Τρ.   βέβηκε Δηάνειρα τὴν πανυcτάτην
      ὁδῶν ἁπαcῶν ἐξ ἀκινήτου ποδόc.   875
Χο.   οὐ δή ποθ' ὡς θανοῦcα;   Τρ. πάντ' ἀκήκοαc.

---

854 ⟨ὕπ'⟩ et ⟨τοῦδε cῶμ'⟩ suppl. Jebb: οὐπώ⟨ποτ' ἄνδρ'⟩ G. H. Müller post ἀγάκλειτον add. Ἡρακλέουc codd. (-κλέ' t): del. Dindorf   855 ἐπέμολεν Wunder: ἐπέμολε t: ἀπέ- cett.   post πάθοc add. ὥcτ' t   857 νύμφαν] κόραν Blaydes (cτένει in 846 servato)   862 suppl. Meineke   865 φημι] φῶμεν Nauck   866 δυcτυχῆ] an δύcτονον?   869 ἀγηθὴς M. Schmidt: ἀήθηc codd.: ἀηδὴς ed. Londiniensis a. 1722: κατηφὴς Blaydes e Choric. Gaz. 1. 93   870 cημανοῦcα t: cημαίνουcα cett.   871 ἡμὶν aZo[pc]t: -ῖν cett.

ΣΟΦΟΚΛΕΟΥΣ

Χο. τέθνηκεν ἡ τάλαινα; Τρ. δεύτερον κλύεις.
Χο. τάλαιν᾽· ὀλέθρου τίνι τρόπῳ θανεῖν σφε φῄς;
Τρ. σχετλίῳ τὰ πρός γε πρᾶξιν. Χο. εἰπέ, τῷ
     μόρῳ,
     γύναι, ξυντρέχει;   880
Τρ. ταύτην διηίστωσεν ⟨ἄμφηκες ξίφος⟩.
Χο. τίς θυμός, ἢ τίνες νόσοι,
     τάνδ᾽ αἰχμᾷ βέλεος κακοῦ
     ξυνεῖλε; πῶς ἐμήσατο
     πρὸς θανάτῳ θάνατον   885
     ἀνύσασα μόνα στονόεντος
     ἐν τομᾷ σιδάρου;
     ἐπεῖδες—ὦ μάταια—τάνδε ⟨τὰν⟩ ὕβριν;
Τρ. ἐπεῖδον, ὡς δὴ πλησία παραστάτις.
Χο. τίς ἦνεν; φέρ᾽ εἰπέ.   890
Τρ. αὐτὴ πρὸς αὑτῆς χειροποιεῖται τάδε.
Χο. τί φωνεῖς; Τρ. σαφηνῆ.
Χο. ἔτεκ᾽ ἔτεκε μεγάλαν
     ἀνέορτος ἅδε νύμφα
     δόμοισι τοῖσδ᾽ Ἐρινύν.   895
Τρ. ἄγαν γε· μᾶλλον δ᾽ εἰ παροῦσα πλησία
     ἔλευσσες οἷ᾽ ἔδρασε, κάρτ᾽ ἂν ᾤκτισας.
Χο. καὶ ταῦτ᾽ ἔτλη τις χεὶρ γυναικεία κτίσαι;

878 ὀλέθρου Blaydes: ὀλεθρία codd.   879 σχετλίῳ τὰ Hermann: σχετλιώτατα codd.   πρός γε πρᾶξιν] ἐξέπραξεν Nauck: ἅπερ ἔπραξεν L. D. J. Henderson   881 ταύτην nos: αὐτὴν codd.   ⟨ἄμφηκες ξίφος⟩ nos (iam temptaverat ⟨ἀμφήκει ξίφει⟩ L. D. J. Henderson)   883 αἰχμᾷ Hermann: -ᾷ t, qui τάνδ᾽ . . . ξυνεῖλε nutrici tribuit: -ὰν cett.   886–7 στονόεντος . . . σιδάρου choro tribuit Maas, nutrici codd.   887 σιδάρου Erfurdt: σιδήρου codd.   888 ὦ μάταια Dawe: ὦ ματαία L: ὦ ματαία cett.: ὦ μαῖα Conington   ⟨τὰν⟩ suppl. Blaydes   890 τίς ἦνεν; Wunder: τίς ἦν; πῶς; codd.   891 αὐτῆς Uz: αὑ- cett.   894 ἀνέορτος codd.: ἁ νέορτος sch.   895 Ἐρινύν K: -ινῦν L: -ιννῦν cett.   897 ἔλευσσες a: ἔλευσας t: ἔλευσες cett.   898 τις Laz: om. t

ΤΡΑΧΙΝΙΑΙ

Τρ. δεινῶς γε· πεύςῃ δ', ὥςτε μαρτυρεῖν ἐμοί.
ἐπεὶ παρῆλθε δωμάτων εἴςω μόνη, 900
καὶ παῖδ' ἐν αὐλαῖς εἶδε κοῖλα δέμνια
ςτορνύνθ', ὅπως ἄψορρον ἀντῴη πατρί,
κρύψας' ἑαυτὴν ἔνθα μή τις εἰςίδοι,
βρυχᾶτο μὲν βωμοῖςι προςπίπτους' ὅτι
γένοιντ' ἐρῆμοι, κλαῖε δ' ὀργάνων ὅτου 905
ψαύςειεν οἷς ἐχρῆτο δειλαία πάρος·
ἄλλῃ δὲ κἄλλῃ δωμάτων ςτρωφωμένη,
εἴ του φίλων βλέψειεν οἰκετῶν δέμας,
ἔκλαιεν ἡ δύςτηνος εἰςορωμένη,
αὐτὴ τὸν αὑτῆς δαίμον' ἀνακαλουμένη. 910
[καὶ τὰς ἄπαιδας ἐς τὸ λοιπὸν οὐςίας.]
ἐπεὶ δὲ τῶνδ' ἔληξεν, ἐξαίφνης ςφ' ὁρῶ
τὸν Ἡράκλειον θάλαμον εἰςορμωμένην.
κἀγὼ λαθραῖον ὄμμ' ἐπεςκιαςμένη
φρούρουν· ὁρῶ δὲ τὴν γυναῖκα δεμνίοις 915
τοῖς Ἡρακλείοις ςτρωτὰ βάλλουςαν φάρη.
ὅπως δ' ἐτέλεςε τοῦτ', ἐπενθοροῦς' ἄνω
καθέζετ' ἐν μέςοιςιν εὐνατηρίοις,
καὶ δακρύων ῥήξαςα θερμὰ νάματα
ἔλεξεν, "ὦ λέχη τε καὶ νυμφεῖ' ἐμά, 920
τὸ λοιπὸν ἤδη χαίρεθ', ὡς ἔμ' οὔποτε
δέξεςθ' ἔτ' ἐν κοίταιςι ταῖςδ' εὐνάτριαν."
τοςαῦτα φωνήςαςα ςυντόνῳ χερὶ

---

900 παρῆλθε] γὰρ ἦλθε Schaefer   901–3 del. T. von Wilamowitz-Moellendorff, 903 Meineke   901 κοῖλα codd. (etiam Λ): κοινὰ γρ ap. T et sch.   902 ςτορνύνθ' LaZo: ςτρωννύνθ' KZgt   ἄψορρον] -ος Zo, coni. Blaydes   ἀντῴη Zgt: ἀντοίη cett.   903 del. Meineke   905 γένοιντ' ἐρῆμοι Nauck: γένοιτ' ἐρήμη codd.   907–11 del. Wecklein   908 του Lzt: που **a**   910 αὑτῆς Lzt: αὐ- **a**   911 del. L. Dindorf   ἄπαιδας] ἀνάνδρους Blaydes   οὐςίας] ἑςτίας Reiske   914 ὄμμ'] ςῶμ' Meineke   918 εὐνατηρίοις Dindorf: εὐναςτ- codd.   922 εὐνάτριαν Nauck: εὐνη- codd.

ΣΟΦΟΚΛΕΟΥΣ

λύει τὸν αὑτῆς πέπλον, οὗ χρυσήλατος
προὔκειτο μαςτῶν περονίς, ἐκ δ' ἐλώπιςεν   925
πλευρὰν ἅπαςαν ὠλένην τ' εὐώνυμον.
κἀγὼ δρομαία βᾶς', ὅσονπερ ἔσθενον,
τῷ παιδὶ φράζω τῆς τεχνωμένης τάδε.
κἀν ᾧ τὸ κεῖσε δεῦρό τ' ἐξορμώμεθα,
ὁρῶμεν αὐτὴν ἀμφιπλῆγι φασγάνῳ   930
πλευρὰν ὑφ' ἧπαρ καὶ φρένας πεπληγμένην.
ἰδὼν δ' ὁ παῖς ᾤμωξεν· ἔγνω γὰρ τάλας
τοὔργον κατ' ὀργὴν ὡς ἐφάψειεν τόδε,
ὄψ' ἐκδιδαχθεὶς τῶν κατ' οἶκον οὕνεκα
ἄκουςα πρὸς τοῦ θηρὸς ἔρξειεν τάδε.   935
κἀνταῦθ' ὁ παῖς δύστηνος οὔτ' ὀδυρμάτων
ἐλείπετ' οὐδέν, ἀμφί νιν γοώμενος,
οὔτ' ἀμφιπίπτων ςτόμαςιν, ἀλλὰ πλευρόθεν
πλευρὰν παρεὶς ἔκειτο πόλλ' ἀναστένων,
ὥς νιν ματαίως αἰτίᾳ βάλοι κακῇ,   940
κλαίων ὁθούνεχ' εἰς δυοῖν ἔσοιθ' ἅμα,
πατρός τ' ἐκείνης τ', ὠρφανισμένος βίον.
τοιαῦτα τἀνθάδ' ἐστίν. ὥστ' εἴ τις δύο
ἢ κἀπὶ πλείους ἡμέρας λογίζεται,
μάταιός ἐστιν· οὐ γὰρ ἔσθ' ἥ γ' αὔριον   945
πρὶν εὖ πάθῃ τις τὴν παροῦσαν ἡμέραν.

Χο.   πότερα πρότερον ἐπιστένω,   στρ. α'

924 αὑτῆς a: αὐ- cett.   οὗ Schaefer: ᾧ codd.: ᾗ Wakefield
927 δρομαία Zot: -αῖος Zg: -αῖα cett.   928 τῆς τεχνωμένης]
τῆςδε μωμένης Meineke   931 πλευρὰν] -ὰς sch. A in A 103
932 ὁ παῖς azt: om. l   932–5 del. Jernstedt   935 ἄκουσα]
ἁλοῦσα Heimreich   ἔρξειεν LZot: ἔρ- Zga   941 κλαίων ⟨θ'⟩
Wakefield   εἰς Nauck: ἐκ codd.   942 βίον Wakefield: βίου codd.
943 εἴ τις] εἴπερ t   944 κἀπὶ West: καὶ codd. et Eustathius 801. 1:
κἄτι Herwerden   post πλείους add. τις codd. (etiam Λ) et Eust. ibid.: del.
edd.   946 πάθῃ] παρῇ Tournier   947 πότερα πρότερον
Dindorf: πότερ' ἂν πρότερα fere codd.

40

ΤΡΑΧΙΝΙΑΙ

πότερα μέλεα περαιτέρω,
δύcκριτ' ἔμοιγε δυcτάνῳ.

τάδε μὲν ἔχομεν ὁρᾶν δόμοιc, ἀντ. α'
τάδε δὲ μένομεν ἐν ἐλπίcιν· 951
κοινὰ δ' ἔχειν τε καὶ μέλλειν.

εἴθ' ἀνεμόεccά τιc γένοιτ' ἔπουροc ἑcτιῶτιc
αὔρα, cτρ. β'
ἥτιc μ' ἀποικίcειεν ἐκ τόπων, ὅπωc 955
τὸν Ζηνὸc ἄλκιμον γόνον
μὴ ταρβαλέα θάνοιμι
μοῦνον εἰcιδοῦc' ἄφαρ·
ἐπεὶ ἐν δυcαπαλλάκτοιc ὀδύναιc
χωρεῖν πρὸ δόμων λέγουcιν, 960
ἄcπετον θέαμα.

ἀγχοῦ δ' ἄρα κοὐ μακρὰν προὔκλαιον,
ὀξύφωνοc ὡc ἀηδών. ἀντ. β'
ξένων γὰρ ἐξόμιλοc ἅδε τιc cτάcιc.
πᾷ δ' αὖ φορεῖ νιν; ὡc φίλου 965
προκηδομένα βαρεῖαν
ἄψοφον φέρει βάcιν.
αἰαῖ ὅδ' ἀναύδατοc φέρεται.
τί χρή, φθίμενόν νιν, ἢ καθ'
ὕπνον ὄντα κρῖναι; 970

---

948 μέλεα Musgrave: τέλεα Lazt: τὰ τελευταῖα K   951 τάδε δὲ]
τὰ δ' ἔτι Gleditsch   μένομεν Erfurdt: μέλλομεν codd.: μελόμεν'
Hermann   ἐν Blaydes: ἐπ' codd.: ἔτ' Dawe   954 ἑcτιῶτιc]
Ἱcτιῶτιc Blaydes   αὔρα t: αὖρα cett.   955 ἐκ τόπων] ἐκποδών
Herwerden: ἐκτόπιον Postgate   956 Ζηνὸc t: Διὸc cett.: Δίον Nauck
960 πρὸ La: πρὸc Kzt   δόμων] δῶμα t   961 θέαμα C. Schenkl:
τι θαῦμα codd.   963 προὔκλαιον] ἔκλαιον t   post ἀηδὼν add.
ξένοι Laz: del. t   964 ἅδε Blaydes: ἥδε codd.   cτάcιc Meineke:
βάcιc codd.   966 προκηδομένα a: -αν cett. (etiam Λ) (προc- t)
968 αἰαῖ Erfurdt: αἴ vel αἲ quater codd.   ἀναύδατοc Erfurdt: ἄναυδοc
codd.   969 φθίμενον Hermann: θανόντα codd.: θάνατον Bothe

41

ΣΟΦΟΚΛΕΟΥΣ

Υλ.   οἴμοι ἐγὼ coῦ, πάτερ, ὦ μέλεος,
      τί πάθω; τί δὲ μήcομαι; οἴμοι.

ΠΡΕϹΒΥϹ
      cίγα, τέκνον, μὴ κινήcῃc
      ἀγρίαν ὀδύνην πατρὸc ὠμόφρονοc.   975
      ζῇ γὰρ προπετήc. ἀλλ' ἴcχε δακὼν
      cτόμα cόν.   Υλ. πῶc φήc, γέρον; ἦ ζῇ;
Πρ.   οὐ μὴ 'ξεγερεῖc τὸν ὕπνῳ κάτοχον
      κἀκκινήcειc κἀναcτήcειc
      φοιτάδα δεινὴν   980
      νόcον, ὦ τέκνον.   Υλ. ἀλλ' ἐπί μοι μελέῳ
      βάροc ἄπλετον· ἐμμέμονεν φρήν.

ΗΡΑΚΛΗϹ
      ὦ Ζεῦ,
      ποῖ γᾶc ἥκω; παρὰ τοῖcι βροτῶν
      κεῖμαι πεπονημένοc ἀλλήκτοιc   985
      ὀδύναιc; οἴμοι ⟨μοι⟩ ἐγὼ τλάμων·
      ἁ δ' αὖ μιαρὰ βρύκει. φεῦ.
Πρ.   ἆρ' ἐξῄδη c' ὅcον ἦν κέρδοc
      cιγῇ κεύθειν καὶ μὴ cκεδάcαι
      τῷδ' ἀπὸ κρατὸc   990
      βλεφάρων θ' ὕπνον;   Υλ. οὐ γὰρ ἔχω πῶc ἂν
      cτέρξαιμι κακὸν τόδε λεύccων.
Ηρ.   ὦ Κηναία κρηπὶc βωμῶν,

---

971 et 972 οἴμοι Dindorf: ὤιμοι LUY: ὤμοι Azt   971 coῦ KZo: cου cett.   972 ὦ μέλεοc Dindorf: οἴμοι ἐγὼ coῦ (Zo: cου cett.) μέλεοc codd.: οἴμοι ἐγώ, πάτερ, ὦ μέλεοc dubitanter Jebb   977 γέρον a: γέρων LZo: ὦ γέρον KZgt   978 'ξεγερεῖc Dawes: 'ξεγείρειc L: 'ξεγείρῃc L s.l., cett.   979 κἀκκινήcειc κἀναcτήcειc LZo: -ῃc -ῃc cett.   982 interpunxit Vauvilliers   ἐμμέμονεν edd.: -ονε codd.   984 τοῖcι] τέοιcι H. Müller   986 οἴμοι LaZo: ὤμοι Zgt   ⟨μοι⟩ suppl. Brunck   987 ἁ δ' Dindorf: ἡ δ' codd.   988 ἐξῄδη c' Wecklein: ἐξῄδηc La: ἐξῄδειc Kzt: ἐξῄδηcθ' Cobet: ἐξηύδηc' Blaydes   991 θ' codd.: del. Wecklein

42

ΤΡΑΧΙΝΙΑΙ

ἣν μή ποτ' ἐγὼ προcιδεῖν ὁ τάλαc 997
ὤφελον ὅccοιc, ἱερῶν οἵαν 998a/994a
οἵων ἐπί μοι 994b
μελέῳ χάριν ἤνύcω, ὦ Ζεῦ· 995
οἵαν μ' ἄρ' ἔθου λώβαν, οἵαν,
τόδ' ἀκήλητον 998b
μανίαc ἄνθοc καταδερχθῆναι.
τίc γὰρ ἀοιδόc, τίc ὁ χειροτέχναc 1000
ἰατορίαc, ὃc τάνδ' ἄταν
χωρὶc Ζηνὸc κατακηλήcει;
θαῦμ' ἂν πόρρωθεν ἰδοίμαν.

ἒ ἔ, cτρ.
⟨- - - ⏑ -⟩
ἐᾶτέ μ' ἐᾶτέ με
δύcμορον εὐνᾶcθαι, 1005
ἐᾶτέ με δύcτανον.
πᾷ ⟨πᾷ⟩ μου ψαύειc; ποῖ κλίνειc;
ἀπολεῖc μ', ἀπολεῖc.
ἀνατέτροφαc ὅ τι καὶ μύcῃ.
ἧπταί μου, τοτοτοῖ, ἅδ' αὖθ' ἕρπει. πόθεν
ἔcτ', ὦ 1010

994a–6 post 998 ὅccοιc traiecit Wunder, deletis τόδ'. . . καταδερχθῆναι 994b οἵων J. F. Martin: ἀνθ' ὧν θυμάτων codd. 995 ἤνύcω] ἤνυcαc Wakefield 999 καταδερχθῆναι] καταφλεχθῆναι Wakefield 1000 ὁ codd.: del. Erfurdt χειροτέχναc Barrett: -ηc codd. 1001 τάνδ' ἄταν Blaydes: τήνδ' ἄτην codd. 1003 ἰδοίμαν t: -ην L s.l., cett.: ἴδοιμ' ἄν L 1004 lacunam indicavit Coxon 1005 alterum ἐᾶτέ μ' om. t δύcμορον] ὕcτατον Lγρ εὐνᾶcθαι Ellendt: εὐνάcαι az: εὐνᾶcαι Lt 1006 om. zt post δύcτανον add. εὐνᾶcαι vel εὐνάcαι La: del. Dain 1007 ⟨πᾷ⟩ suppl. Seidler ποῖ Laz: ποῖ δὲ t: ποῖ καὶ Wakefield 1009 ἀνατέτροφαc Erfurdt: ἀντέτροφαc La: de z non liquet: ἀντέcτρωφάc θ' t 1010 ἅδ' edd.: ἧδ' codd. αὖθ' ἕρπει] αὖ 'φέρπει Blaydes

ΣΟΦΟΚΛΕΟΥΣ

Ἕλλανες πάντων ἀδικώτατοι ἀνέρες, οἷς δὴ
πολλὰ μὲν ἐν πόντῳ, κατά τε δρία πάντα
 καθαίρων,
ὠλεκόμαν ὁ τάλας, καὶ νῦν ἐπὶ τῷδε νοσοῦντι
οὐ πῦρ, οὐκ ἔγχος τις ὀνήσιμον οὔ ποτε τρέψει;
ἐέ,
οὐδ' ἀπαράξαι ⟨μου⟩ κρᾶτα βίου θέλει   1015
⟨- ‿ ‿ -⟩ μολὼν τοῦ ϲτυγεροῦ; φεῦ φεῦ.

Πρ. ὦ παῖ τοῦδ' ἀνδρόϲ, τοὔργον τόδε μεῖζον ἀνήκει
ἢ κατ' ἐμὰν ῥώμαν· ϲὺ δὲ ϲύλλαβε. †ϲοί τε γὰρ
 ὄμμα
ἔμπλεον ἢ δι' ἐμοῦ† ϲῴζειν.   Υλ. ψαύω μὲν
 ἔγωγε,   1020
λαθίπονον δ' ὀδύναν οὔτ' ἔνδοθεν οὔτε θύραθεν
ἔϲτι μοι ἐξανύϲαι βιότου· τοιαῦτα νέμει Ζεύϲ.

Ηρ. ⟨ἒ ἔ.⟩   ἀντ.
ὦ παῖ, ποῦ ποτ' εἶ;
τᾷδέ με τᾷδέ με
πρόϲλαβε κουφίϲαϲ.   1025
ἒ ἔ, ἰὼ δαῖμον.
θρῴϲκει δ' αὖ, θρῴϲκει δειλαία
διολοῦϲ' ἡμᾶϲ
ἀποτίβατοϲ ἀγρία νόϲοϲ.   1030

1011 Ἕλλανες πάντων Koechly: πάντων Ἑλλάνων codd.: πάντων ἀνθρώπων Wunder   οἷϲ Wakefield: οὖϲ codd.   1012 ἐν] ἐνὶ L 1014 οὔ ποτε τρέψει nos: ἀποτρέψει laZg: ἐπιτρέψει Zo: ἀνϲτρέψει t: οὐ ποτιτρέψει Hense   1015 ⟨μου⟩ suppl. Blaydes   βίου] βίᾳ Wakefield   1017 ⟨παυϲίπονοϲ⟩ vel ⟨λυϲίπονοϲ⟩ ex. gr. Lloyd-Jones 1018 ἀνήκει] ἀνείκει L in linea, Λ: ἂν εἴη Nauck   1019 ϲοί . . . ὄμμα] ϲοὶ γὰρ ἑτοῖμα Jebb   1020 ἔμπλεον] ἐϲ πλέον J. F. Martin 1021 ὀδύναν] ὀδυνᾶν Musgrave   θύραθεν L s.l.: θύραζ' vel θύραζε(ν) cett.   1022 ἔϲτι zt: ἔνεϲτι cett.   βιότου] βίοτον Musgrave 1023 ⟨ἒ ἔ⟩ suppl. Dain   ὦ παῖ Seidler: ὦ παῖ παῖ codd.: παῖ παῖ Hermann 1026 ἰὼ semel codd. recc., bis cett. (etiam Λ)   δαῖμον] δαίμων Seidler

ΤΡΑΧΙΝΙΑΙ

ἰὼ ἰὼ Παλλάc, τόδε μ' αὖ λωβᾶται. ἰὼ παῖ,
τὸν φύτορ' οἰκτίραc, ἀνεπίφθονον εἴρυcον
  ἔγχοc,
παῖcον ἐμᾶc ὑπὸ κληδόc· ἀκοῦ δ' ἄχοc, ᾧ μ'
  ἐχόλωcεν   1035
cὰ μάτηρ ἄθεοc, τὰν ὧδ' ἐπίδοιμι πεcοῦcαν
αὔτωc, ὧδ' αὔτωc, ὥc μ' ὤλεcεν. ὦ γλυκὺc
  Ἅιδαc,   1040
⟨ἒ ἔ.⟩
ὦ Διὸc αὐθαίμων,
εὔναcον εὔναcόν μ'
ὠκυπέτᾳ μόρῳ τὸν μέλεον φθίcαc.

Χο. κλύουc' ἔφριξα τάcδε cυμφοράc, φίλαι,
  ἄνακτοc, οἵαιc οἷοc ὢν ἐλαύνεται.   1045
Ηρ. ὦ πολλὰ δὴ καὶ θερμά, καὶ λόγῳ κακά,
  καὶ χερcὶ καὶ νώτοιcι μοχθήcαc ἐγώ·
  κοὔπω τοιοῦτον οὔτ' ἄκοιτιc ἡ Διὸc
  προὔθηκεν οὔθ' ὁ cτυγνὸc Εὐρυcθεὺc ἐμοὶ
  οἷον τόδ' ἡ δολῶπιc Οἰνέωc κόρη   1050
  καθῆψεν ὤμοιc τοῖc ἐμοῖc Ἐρινύων
  ὑφαντὸν ἀμφίβληcτρον, ᾧ διόλλυμαι.
  πλευραῖcι γὰρ προcμαχθὲν ἐκ μὲν ἐcχάταc
  βέβρωκε cάρκαc, πλεύμονόc τ' ἀρτηρίαc
  ῥοφεῖ ξυνοικοῦν· ἐκ δὲ χλωρὸν αἷμά μου   1055

1031 ἰὼ bis Bergk, semel codd.   1034 φύτορ' Dindorf: φύcαντ'
codd.   εἴρυcον] εἴρυcαι Blaydes   1035 ἐμᾶc] ἡμᾶc l
1036 ᾧ] ὅ L   ἐχόληcεν Lγρ   1037 τὰν Seidler: ἂν codd.
1040 ὦ γλυκὺc Ἅιδαc huc traiecit Seidler: post 1041 αὐθαίμων praebent
codd.   1041 ⟨ἒ ἔ⟩ suppl. Dain   1042 μ' huc transp. Erfurdt: post
prius εὔναcον praebent Laz: om. t   1044 τάcδε cυμφοράc] τάcδε
-ᾶc L   1045 οἵαιc zt: οἷαc La   1046 καὶ λόγῳ κακά codd.;
'dictu gravia' Cicero, Tusc. Disp. 2. 20: κοὐ λόγῳ κακά Bothe: καὶ λόγῳ καλά
Jackson   1047 χερcὶ] χειρὶ a   1051 Ἐρινύων L: Ἐρινν- cett.
1054 πλεύμονοc L, Λ s.l.: πνεύμονοc L s.l., Λzt: πνεύμοναc K: πλεύμοναc
a: πλευμόνων Süvern

45

ΣΟΦΟΚΛΕΟΥΣ

πέπωκεν ἤδη, καὶ διέφθαρμαι δέμας
τὸ πᾶν, ἀφράστῳ τῇδε χειρωθεὶς πέδῃ.
κοὐ ταῦτα λόγχῃ πεδιάς, οὔθ' ὁ γηγενὴς
στρατὸς Γιγάντων, οὔτε θήρειος βία,
οὔθ' Ἑλλάς, οὔτ' ἄγλωσσος, οὔθ' ὅσην ἐγὼ   1060
γαῖαν καθαίρων ἱκόμην, ἔδρασέ πω·
γυνὴ δέ, θῆλυς οὖσα κἄνανδρος φύσιν,
μόνη με δὴ καθεῖλε φασγάνου δίχα.
ὦ παῖ, γενοῦ μοι παῖς ἐτήτυμος γεγώς,
καὶ μὴ τὸ μητρὸς ὄνομα πρεσβεύσῃς πλέον.   1065
δός μοι χεροῖν σαῖν αὐτὸς ἐξ οἴκου λαβὼν
ἐς χεῖρα τὴν τεκοῦσαν, ὡς εἰδῶ σάφα
εἰ τοὐμὸν ἀλγεῖς μᾶλλον ἢ κείνης ὁρῶν
λωβητὸν εἶδος ἐν δίκῃ κακούμενον.
ἴθ', ὦ τέκνον, τόλμησον· οἴκτιρόν τέ με   1070
πολλοῖσιν οἰκτρόν, ὅστις ὥστε παρθένος
βέβρυχα κλαίων, καὶ τόδ' οὐδ' ἂν εἷς ποτε
τόνδ' ἄνδρα φαίη πρόσθ' ἰδεῖν δεδρακότα,
ἀλλ' ἀστένακτος αἰὲν εἱχόμην κακοῖς.
νῦν δ' ἐκ τοιούτου θῆλυς ηὕρημαι τάλας.   1075
καὶ νῦν προσελθὼν στῆθι πλησίον πατρός,
σκέψαι δ' ὁποίας ταῦτα συμφορᾶς ὕπο
πέπονθα· δείξω γὰρ τάδ' ἐκ καλυμμάτων.
ἰδού, θεᾶσθε πάντες ἄθλιον δέμας,
ὁρᾶτε τὸν δύστηνον, ὡς οἰκτρῶς ἔχω.   1080
αἰαῖ, ὦ τάλας,

1056 διέφθαρμαι] -αρται K: 'extabuit' Cicero   1060 ὅσην] ὅσων Blaydes: 'gens' Cicero   1062 θῆλυς οὖσα] θῆλυν σχοῦσα Reiske   κἄνανδρος Tournier: κοὐκ ἀνδρὸς codd.   1065 πρεσβεύσῃς] -σῃ K: 'superet' Cicero   1067 ἐς] εἰς a   εἰδῶ] ἴδω Nauck: 'cernam' Cicero   1069 om. Cicero   1070 οἴκτιρον edd.: οἴκτειρον codd.   τέ με] τ' ἐμέ Nauck   1071 ὥστε] ὥς τις L   1074 εἱχόμην Meineke: ἑσπόμην codd.: εἰπόμην sch. ad Aj. 318: ἑσπώμην Jackson   1075 ηὕρημαι Dindorf: εὔ- codd.   1077 δ'] θ' Nauck   1080 δύστηνον] δύστανον L in linea   1081 alterum αἰαῖ Lz: ἒ ἒ at

46

ΤΡΑΧΙΝΙΑΙ

αἰαῖ.
ἔθαλψέ μ' ἄτης cπαcμὸς ἀρτίως ὅδ' αὖ,
διῆξε πλευρῶν, οὐδ' ἀγύμναcτόν μ' ἐᾶν
ἔοικεν ἡ τάλαινα διάβοροc νόcοc.
ὦναξ Ἀΐδη, δέξαι μ',   1085
ὦ Διὸc ἀκτίc, παῖcον.
ἔνcειcον, ὦναξ, ἐγκατάcκηψον βέλοc,
πάτερ, κεραυνοῦ. δαίνυται γὰρ αὖ πάλιν,
ἤνθηκεν, ἐξώρμηκεν. ὦ χέρεc χέρεc,
ὦ νῶτα καὶ cτέρν', ὦ φίλοι βραχίονεc,   1090
ὑμεῖc ἐκεῖνοι δὴ καθέcταθ', οἵ ποτε
Νεμέαc ἔνοικον, βουκόλων ἀλάcτορα,
λέοντ', ἄπλατον θρέμμα κἀπροcήγορον,
βίᾳ κατειργάcαcθε, Λερναίαν θ' ὕδραν,
διφυᾶ τ' ἄμεικτον ἱπποβάμονα cτρατὸν   1095
θηρῶν, ὑβριcτήν, ἄνομον, ὑπέροχον βίαν,
Ἐρυμάνθιόν τε θῆρα, τόν θ' ὑπὸ χθονὸc
Ἄιδου τρίκρανον cκύλακ', ἀπρόcμαχον τέραc,
δεινῆc Ἐχίδνηc θρέμμα, τόν τε χρυcέων
δράκοντα μήλων φύλακ' ἐπ' ἐcχάτοιc τόποιc.   1100
ἄλλων τε μόχθων μυρίων ἐγευcάμην,
κοὐδεὶc τροπαῖ' ἔcτηcε τῶν ἐμῶν χερῶν.
νῦν δ' ὧδ' ἄναρθροc καὶ κατερρακωμένοc
τυφλῆc ὑπ' ἄτηc ἐκπεπόρθημαι τάλαc,
ὁ τῆc ἀρίcτηc μητρὸc ὠνομαcμένοc,   1105
ὁ τοῦ κατ' ἄcτρα Ζηνὸc αὐδηθεὶc γόνοc.
ἀλλ' εὖ γέ τοι τόδ' ἴcτε, κἂν τὸ μηδὲν ὦ,
κἂν μηδὲν ἕρπω, τήν γε δράcαcαν τάδε

1082 ἔθαλψέ μ' K, coni. Hermann: ἔθαλψεν cett.   1085 μ' t: με cett.   1089 ἐξώρμηκεν] ἐξώγκηκεν Dawe: ἐξώργηκεν West: ἀνεκάχλαcεν gl. apud at, sch. L   1091 ἐκεῖνοι azt et lm. sch. L: δὲ κεῖνοι L   1092 ἀλάcτορα] ληΐcτορα Blaydes   1093 ἄπλατον La: ἄπλαcτον Zgt: ἄπληcτον Zo   1095 διφυᾶ Dindorf: -ῆ codd. ἄμεικτον edd.: ἄμικτον codd.   1096 ὑπέροχον S. Clarke, Bentley: ὑπείρ- codd.   βίαν La: βίᾳ zt   1099 τὸν] τῶν t   1102 τροπαῖ' L: τρόπαι' cett.

47

ΣΟΦΟΚΛΕΟΥΣ

  χειρώσομαι κἀκ τῶνδε. προσμόλοι μόνον,
  ἵν' ἐκδιδαχθῇ πᾶσιν ἀγγέλλειν ὅτι   1110
  καὶ ζῶν κακούς γε καὶ θανὼν ἐτεισάμην.
Χο. ὦ τλῆμον Ἑλλάς, πένθος οἷον εἰσορῶ ⟨c'⟩
  ἕξουσαν, ἀνδρὸς τοῦδέ γ' εἰ σφαλεῖς' ἔςῃ.
Υλ. ἐπεὶ παρέσχες ἀντιφωνῆσαι, πάτερ,
  σιγὴν παρασχὼν κλῦθί μου νοσῶν ὅμως.   1115
  αἰτήσομαι γάρ σ' ὧν δίκαια τυγχάνειν.
  δός μοι σεαυτόν, μὴ τοιοῦτον ὡς δάκνῃ
  θυμῷ δύσοργος. οὐ γὰρ ἂν γνοίης ἐν οἷς
  χαίρειν προθυμῇ κἂν ὅτοις ἀλγεῖς μάτην.
Ηρ. εἰπὼν ὃ χρῄζεις λῆξον· ὡς ἐγὼ νοσῶν   1120
  οὐδὲν ξυνίημ' ὧν σὺ ποικίλλεις πάλαι.
Υλ. τῆς μητρὸς ἥκω τῆς ἐμῆς φράσων ἐν οἷς
  νῦν ἔστ' ἐν οἷς θ' ἥμαρτεν οὐχ ἑκουσία.
Ηρ. ὦ παγκάκιστε, καὶ παρεμνήσω γὰρ αὖ
  τῆς πατροφόντου μητρός, ὡς κλύειν ἐμέ;   1125
Υλ. ἔχει γὰρ οὕτως ὥστε μὴ σιγᾶν πρέπειν.
Ηρ. οὐ δῆτα τοῖς γε πρόσθεν ἡμαρτημένοις.
Υλ. ἀλλ' οὐδὲ μὲν δὴ τοῖς γ' ἐφ' ἡμέραν ἐρεῖς.
Ηρ. λέγ', εὐλαβοῦ δὲ μὴ φανῇς κακὸς γεγώς.
Υλ. λέγω. τέθνηκεν ἀρτίως νεοσφαγής.   1130
Ηρ. πρὸς τοῦ; τέρας τοι διὰ κακῶν ἐθέσπισας.
Υλ. αὐτὴ πρὸς αὑτῆς, οὐδενὸς πρὸς ἐκτόπου.
Ηρ. οἴμοι· πρὶν ὡς χρῆν σφ' ἐξ ἐμῆς θανεῖν χερός;
Υλ. κἂν σοῦ στραφείη θυμός, εἰ τὸ πᾶν μάθοις.
Ηρ. δεινοῦ λόγου κατῆρξας· εἰπὲ δ' ᾗ νοεῖς.   1135
Υλ. ἅπαν τὸ χρῆμ' ἥμαρτε χρηστὰ μωμένη.

1112 εἰσορῶ ⟨c'⟩ nos: εἰσορῶ codd.: αὖ c' ὁρῶ Blaydes
1113 σφαλεῖς' ἔςῃ Meineke: σφαλήσεται codd.   1114 παρέσχες]
παρείκεις Wecklein: παρίῃς Heimsoeth   1117 τοιοῦτον Mudge:
τοσοῦτον codd.   1123 ἔστ' ἐν Harleianus 5743 (coni. Blaydes): ἐστιν
cett.   οἷς] ὡς Nauck   1131 διὰ κακῶν] δαιμόνιον Herwerden
1132 αὑτῆς L: αὐ- cett.   1134 σοῦ Schaefer: σου codd.
1136 post χρῆμ' sunt qui interpungant   μωμένη P.Oxy. 1805, K, coni.
Heath: μνωμένη cett.

48

ΤΡΑΧΙΝΙΑΙ

Ηρ. χρῆcτ', ὦ κάκιcτε, πατέρα còν κτείναcα δρᾷ;
Υλ. cτέργημα γὰρ δοκοῦcα προcβαλεῖν céθεν
ἀπήμπλαχ', ὡc προcεῖδε τοὺc ἔνδον γάμουc.
Ηρ. καὶ τίc τοcοῦτοc φαρμακεὺc Τραχινίων; 1140
Υλ. Νέccοc πάλαι Κένταυροc ἐξέπειcέ νιν
τοιῷδε φίλτρῳ τὸν còν ἐκμῆναι πόθον.
Ηρ. ἰοὺ ἰοὺ δύcτηνοc, οἴχομαι τάλαc.
ὄλωλ' ὄλωλα, φέγγοc οὐκέτ' ἔcτι μοι.
οἴμοι, φρονῶ δὴ ξυμφορᾶc ἵν' ἔcταμεν. 1145
ἴθ', ὦ τέκνον· πατὴρ γὰρ οὐκέτ' ἔcτι coι·
κάλει τὸ πᾶν μοι cπέρμα cῶν ὁμαιμόνων,
κάλει δὲ τὴν τάλαιναν Ἀλκμήνην, Διὸc
μάτην ἄκοιτιν, ὡc τελευταίαν ἐμοῦ
φήμην πύθηcθε θεcφάτων ὅc' οἶδ' ἐγώ. 1150
Υλ. ἀλλ' οὔτε μήτηρ ἐνθάδ', ἀλλ' ἐπακτίᾳ
Τίρυνθι cυμβέβηκεν ὥcτ' ἔχειν ἕδραν,
παίδων τε τοὺc μὲν ξυλλαβοῦc' αὐτὴ τρέφει,
τοὺc δ' ἂν τὸ Θήβηc ἄcτυ ναίονταc μάθοιc·
ἡμεῖc δ' ὅcοι πάρεcμεν, εἴ τι χρή, πάτερ, 1155
πράccειν, κλυόντεc ἐξυπηρετήcομεν.
Ηρ. cὺ δ' οὖν ἄκουε τοὔργον· ἐξήκειc δ' ἵνα
φανεῖc ὁποῖοc ὢν ἀνὴρ ἐμὸc καλῇ.
ἐμοὶ γὰρ ἦν πρόφαντον ἐκ πατρὸc πάλαι,
πρὸc τῶν πνεόντων μηδενὸc θανεῖν ποτε, 1160
ἀλλ' ὅcτιc Ἅιδου φθίμενοc οἰκήτωρ πέλοι.

1137 κτείναcα δρᾷ] κτείναc' ἕδρα Blaydes: an κτείνουcα δρᾷ?
1138 cτέργημα] cτέργηθρα Nauck   προcβαλεῖν] προcλαβεῖν K
1141 Νέccοc az: Νέcοc Lt   1150 ὅc'] ὅcc' L: ⟨θ'⟩ ὅc' Dawe
1151 οὔτε] οὔ γε z   1153 τε Reiske: δὲ codd.   1155 δ' ὅcοι] δέ coι Nauck, Stinton   1156 del. Nauck, tuetur Stinton   πράccειν Brunck: πράττειν codd.   κλυόντεc West: κλύ- codd.: an κλυόντεc ⟨δ'⟩?
1157 δ' οὖν Lat: νῦν z, Τγρ: νυν Blaydes   τοὔργον] τοὔποc Nauck
1158 φανεῖc Harleianus 5743: φανῇc cett.   1160 πρὸc τῶν πνεόντων] τῶν ἐμπνεόντων Erfurdt, servato ὕπο   θανεῖν ποτε Musgrave: θανεῖν ὕπο codd.: θανεῖν ποτ' ἂν Dobree   1161 πέλοι v.l. ap. L et z: πέλει cett.

49

ΣΟΦΟΚΛΕΟΥΣ

ὅδ' οὖν ὁ θὴρ Κένταυρος, ὡς τὸ θεῖον ἦν
πρόφαντον, οὕτω ζῶντά μ' ἔκτεινεν θανών.
φανῶ δ' ἐγὼ τούτοισι συμβαίνοντ' ἴσα
μαντεῖα καινά, τοῖς πάλαι ξυνήγορα, 1165
ἃ τῶν ὀρείων καὶ χαμαικοιτῶν ἐγὼ
Σελλῶν ἐσελθὼν ἄλσος ἐξεγραψάμην
πρὸς τῆς πατρῴας καὶ πολυγλώσσου δρυός,
ἥ μοι χρόνῳ τῷ ζῶντι καὶ παρόντι νῦν
ἔφασκε μόχθων τῶν ἐφεστώτων ἐμοὶ 1170
λύσιν τελεῖσθαι· κἀδόκουν πράξειν καλῶς.
τὸ δ' ἦν ἄρ' οὐδὲν ἄλλο πλὴν θανεῖν ἐμέ·
τοῖς γὰρ θανοῦσι μόχθος οὐ προσγίγνεται.
ταῦτ' οὖν ἐπειδὴ λαμπρὰ συμβαίνει, τέκνον,
δεῖ σ' αὖ γενέσθαι τῷδε τἀνδρὶ σύμμαχον, 1175
καὶ μὴ 'πιμεῖναι τοὐμὸν ὀξῦναι στόμα,
ἀλλ' αὐτὸν εἰκαθόντα συμπράσσειν, νόμον
κάλλιστον ἐξευρόντα, πειθαρχεῖν πατρί.

Υλ. ἀλλ', ὦ πάτερ, ταρβῶ μὲν ἐς λόγου στάσιν
τοιάνδ' ἐπελθών, πείσομαι δ' ἅ σοι δοκεῖ. 1180
Ηρ. ἔμβαλλε χεῖρα δεξιὰν πρώτιστά μοι.
Υλ. ὡς πρὸς τί πίστιν τήνδ' ἄγαν ἐπιστρέφεις;
Ηρ. οὐ θᾶσσον οἴσεις μηδ' ἀπιστήσεις ἐμοί;
Υλ. ἰδού, προτείνω, κοὐδὲν ἀντειρήσεται.
Ηρ. ὄμνυ Διός νυν τοῦ με φύσαντος κάρα. 1185
Υλ. ἦ μὴν τί δράσειν; καὶ τόδ' ἐξειπεῖν σε δεῖ.

1163 ἔκτεινεν a: -νε L: ἔκτανε zt   1164 συμβαίνοντ' ἴσα] συμβαίνοντά σοι Wunder   1165 del. Dobree, Nauck   1167 Σελλῶν] Ἑλλῶν γρ ap. sch. L   ἐσελθὼν AY: εἰσ- LUZg: προσ- Zot   ἐξεγραψάμην Elmsley et Dobree: εἰσεγραψάμην codd.   1172 τὸ δ' L^ac K: τόδ' cett.   1173 del. Axt   1176 ὀξῦναι] ὠξύνθαι Herwerden   1177 εἰκαθόντα hoc accentu KA^ac: proparoxytone cett.   1180 ἐπελθών] ἐπελθεῖν noluit recipere Jebb   1182 post ἄγαν add. γ' t: ἄγαν ⟨μ'⟩ Hermann   1183 ἀπιστήσεις L s.l., aZg: -σῃς Lt: ἀπειθήσεις Zo: προστήσεις Lγρ   1186 ἐξειπεῖν σε δεῖ Heimsoeth (possis etiam σ' ἔδει): ἐξειρήσεται codd.

50

ΤΡΑΧΙΝΙΑΙ

Ηρ. ἦ μὴν ἐμοὶ τὸ λεχθὲν ἔργον ἐκτελεῖν.
Υλ. ὄμνυμ᾽ ἔγωγε, Ζῆν᾽ ἔχων ἐπώμοτον.
Ηρ. εἰ δ᾽ ἐκτὸς ἔλθοις, πημονὰς εὔχου λαβεῖν.
Υλ. οὐ μὴ λάβω· δράcω γάρ· εὔχομαι δ᾽ ὅμωc.   1190
Ηρ. οἶcθ᾽ οὖν τὸν Οἴτηc Ζηνὸc ὑψίcτου πάγον;
Υλ. οἶδ᾽, ὡc θυτήρ γε πολλὰ δὴ cταθεὶc ἄνω.
Ηρ. ἐνταῦθά νυν χρὴ τοὐμὸν ἐξάραντά cε
    cῶμ᾽ αὐτόχειρα καὶ ξὺν οἷc χρῄζειc φίλων,
    πολλὴν μὲν ὕλην τῆc βαθυρρίζου δρυὸc   1195
    κείραντα, πολλὸν δ᾽ ἄρcεν᾽ ἐκτεμόνθ᾽ ὁμοῦ
    ἄγριον ἔλαιον, cῶμα τοὐμὸν ἐμβαλεῖν,
    καὶ πευκίνηc λαβόντα λαμπάδοc cέλαc
    πρῆcαι. γόου δὲ μηδὲν εἰcίδω δάκρυ,
    ἀλλ᾽ ἀcτένακτοc κἀδάκρυτοc, εἴπερ εἶ   1200
    τοῦδ᾽ ἀνδρόc, ἔρξον· εἰ δὲ μή, μενῶ c᾽ ἐγὼ
    καὶ νέρθεν ὢν ἀραῖοc εἰcαεὶ βαρύc.
Υλ. οἴμοι, πάτερ, τί εἶπαc; οἷά μ᾽ εἴργαcαι.
Ηρ. ὁποῖα δραcτέ᾽ ἐcτίν· εἰ δὲ μή, πατρὸc
    ἄλλου γενοῦ του μηδ᾽ ἐμὸc κληθῇc ἔτι.   1205
Υλ. οἴμοι μάλ᾽ αὖθιc, οἷά μ᾽ ἐκκαλῇ, πάτερ,
    φονέα γενέcθαι καὶ παλαμναῖον cέθεν.
Ηρ. οὐ δῆτ᾽ ἔγωγ᾽, ἀλλ᾽ ὧν ἔχω παιώνιον
    καὶ μοῦνον ἰατῆρα τῶν ἐμῶν κακῶν.
Υλ. καὶ πῶc ὑπαίθων cῶμ᾽ ἂν ἰῴμην τὸ cόν;   1210
Ηρ. ἀλλ᾽ εἰ φοβῇ πρὸc τοῦτο, τἆλλα γ᾽ ἔργαcαι.
Υλ. φορᾶc γέ τοι φθόνηcιc οὐ γενήcεται.
Ηρ. ἦ καὶ πυρᾶc πλήρωμα τῆc εἰρημένηc;
Υλ. ὅcον γ᾽ ἂν αὐτὸc μὴ ποτιψαύων χεροῖν·

1191 Οἴτηc] -η Musgrave   ὑψίcτου Wakefield: ὕψιcτον codd.
1193 νυν t: νῦν cett.   1197 ἔλαιον] ἐλαιὸν L   1199 εἰcίδω
Jackson: εἰcίτω codd.   1201 ἔρξον LZot: ἔ- cett.   1203 τί lZg:
τίν᾽ a: τί μ᾽ t: τοῖ᾽ Zo: ποῖ᾽ Hense   εἴργαcαι] ἐργάcῃ Blaydes
1209 τῶν ἐμῶν] δυcτήνων Blaydes: an τῶν πάντων?   1211 πρὸc]
τι Herwerden   γ᾽ az: μ᾽ Lt   1214 ποτιψαύων La: ποτε ψαύω zt
(ψαύων s.l. in T, quod coniecit Hartung): τι προcψαύων Wunder

51

ΣΟΦΟΚΛΕΟΥΣ

	τὰ δ' ἄλλα πράξω κοὐ καμῇ τοὐμὸν μέρος.	1215
Ηρ.	ἀλλ' ἀρκέσει καὶ ταῦτα· πρόσνειμαι δέ μοι	
	χάριν βραχεῖαν πρὸς μακροῖς ἄλλοις διδούς.	
Υλ.	εἰ καὶ μακρὰ κάρτ' ἐστίν, ἐργασθήσεται.	
Ηρ.	τὴν Εὐρυτείαν οἶσθα δῆτα παρθένον;	
Υλ.	Ἰόλην ἔλεξας, ὥς γ' ἐπεικάζειν ἐμέ.	1220
Ηρ.	ἔγνως. τοσοῦτον δή ς' ἐπισκήπτω, τέκνον·	
	ταύτην, ἐμοῦ θανόντος, εἴπερ εὐσεβεῖν	
	βούλῃ, πατρῴων ὁρκίων μεμνημένος,	
	προσθοῦ δάμαρτα, μηδ' ἀπιστήςῃς πατρί·	
	μηδ' ἄλλος ἀνδρῶν τοῖς ἐμοῖς πλευροῖς	
	ὁμοῦ	1225
	κλιθεῖσαν αὐτὴν ἀντὶ σοῦ λάβῃ ποτέ,	
	ἀλλ' αὐτός, ὦ παῖ, τοῦτο κήδευσον λέχος.	
	πείθου· τὸ γάρ τοι μεγάλα πιστεύσαντ' ἐμοὶ	
	ςμικροῖς ἀπιστεῖν τὴν πάρος συγχεῖ χάριν.	
Υλ.	οἴμοι. τὸ μὲν νοσοῦντι θυμοῦςθαι κακόν,	1230
	τὸ δ' ὧδ' ὁρᾶν φρονοῦντα τίς ποτ' ἂν φέροι;	
Ηρ.	ὡς ἐργασείων οὐδὲν ὧν λέγω θροεῖς.	
Υλ.	τίς γάρ ποθ', ᾗ μοι μητρὶ μὲν θανεῖν μόνη	
	μεταίτιος, σοὶ δ' αὖθις ὡς ἔχεις ἔχειν,	
	τίς ταῦτ' ἄν, ὅστις μὴ 'ξ ἀλαστόρων νοσοῖ,	1235
	ἕλοιτο; κρεῖσσον κἀμέ γ', ὦ πάτερ, θανεῖν	
	ἢ τοῖσιν ἐχθίστοισι συνναίειν ὁμοῦ.	
Ηρ.	ἀνὴρ ὅδ' ὡς ἔοικεν οὐ νεμεῖν ἐμοὶ	
	φθίνοντι μοῖραν· ἀλλά τοι θεῶν ἀρὰ	
	μενεῖ σ' ἀπιστήσαντα τοῖς ἐμοῖς λόγοις.	1240

1217 μακροῖς ἄλλοις] μακραῖς ἄλλαις Blaydes   1220 ὥς γ' Schaefer: ὥστ' codd.   ἐπεικάζειν Lat: ἀπ- z   1224 προσθοῦ Dindorf: paroxytone codd.   1226 λάβῃ Elmsley: -οι codd.   1228 πείθου] πιθοῦ Brunck   1229 ςμικροῖς] ςμικρόν ς' Blaydes   1231 ὧδ' ὁρᾶν] ὧδε δρᾶν Groddeck   1234 δ' Schaefer: τ' codd.   1235 ταῦτ'] τήνδ' Fröhlich   νοσοῖ LaZg: -εῖ KZot   1236 ἕλοιτο La: αἱροῖτο z et fort. t   1237 τοῖσιν] τοῖςί γ' Dawe   1238 ἀνὴρ Hermann: ἀ- codd.   νεμεῖν Brunck: νέμειν codd.

52

ΤΡΑΧΙΝΙΑΙ

Υλ. οἴμοι, τάχ᾽, ὡς ἔοικας, ὡς νοσεῖς φανεῖς.
Ηρ. cὺ γάρ μ᾽ ἀπ᾽ εὐνασθέντος ἐκκινεῖς κακοῦ.
Υλ. δείλαιος, ὡς ἐς πολλὰ τἀπορεῖν ἔχω.
Ηρ. οὐ γὰρ δικαιοῖς τοῦ φυτεύσαντος κλύειν.
Υλ. ἀλλ᾽ ἐκδιδαχθῶ δῆτα δυσσεβεῖν, πάτερ; 1245
Ηρ. οὐ δυσσέβεια, τοὐμὸν εἰ τέρψεις κέαρ.
Υλ. πράσσειν ἄνωγας οὖν με πανδίκως τάδε;
Ηρ. ἔγωγε· τούτων μάρτυρας καλῶ θεούς.
Υλ. τοιγὰρ ποήσω, κοὐκ ἀπώσομαι, τὸ cὸν
θεοῖσι δεικνὺς ἔργον. οὐ γὰρ ἄν ποτε 1250
κακὸς φανείην σοί γε πιστεύσας, πάτερ.
Ηρ. καλῶς τελευτᾷς, κἀπὶ τοῖσδε τὴν χάριν
ταχεῖαν, ὦ παῖ, πρόσθες, ὡς πρὶν ἐμπεσεῖν
σπαραγμὸν ἤ τιν᾽ οἶστρον ἐς πυράν με θῇς.
ἄγ᾽ ἐγκονεῖτ᾽, αἴρεσθε. παῦλά τοι κακῶν 1255
αὕτη, τελευτὴ τοῦδε τἀνδρὸς ὑστάτη.
Υλ. ἀλλ᾽ οὐδὲν εἴργει σοὶ τελειοῦσθαι τάδε,
ἐπεὶ κελεύεις κἀξαναγκάζεις, πάτερ.

Ηρ. ἄγε νυν, πρὶν τήνδ᾽ ἀνακινῆσαι
νόσον, ὦ ψυχὴ σκληρά, χάλυβος 1260
λιθοκόλλητον στόμιον παρέχουσ᾽,
ἀνάπαυε βοήν, ὡς ἐπίχαρτον
τελέουσ᾽ ἀεκούσιον ἔργον.
Υλ. αἴρετ᾽, ὀπαδοί, μεγάλην μὲν ἐμοὶ
τούτων θέμενοι συγγνωμοσύνην, 1265

1241 οἴμοι **az**: ὤμοι L   φανεῖς Axt: φράσεις codd.: φανεῖν Hermann
1243 τἀπορεῖν] γ᾽ ἐπαπορεῖν **t**   1249 τὸ cὸν] cὸν ὄν Heimsoeth: τὸ δρᾶν Blaydes, ⟨cὸν⟩ ante θεοῖσι addito   1250 ἔργον] τοὔργον Dobree   1254 με θῇς] μεθείς L^ac, μεθῇς L^pc   1257–78 del. Dawe, 1259–78 Hartung et olim Bergk, 1264–78 Bergk postea   1259 νυν **t**: νῦν cett.   ἀνακινῆσαι] -κινεῖσθαι Blaydes   1260 σκληρά] -οῦ Nauck: -ὸν Blaydes   1263 τελέουσ᾽ L. Dindorf: τελέως codd.
1264–74 Hyllo tribuunt **Kzt**, personae nota carent **La**

53

ΣΟΦΟΚΛΕΟΥΣ
μεγάλην δὲ θεῶν ἀγνωμοσύνην
εἰδότες ἔργων τῶν πρασσομένων,
οἳ φύσαντες καὶ κληζόμενοι
πατέρες τοιαῦτ' ἐφορῶσι πάθη.
τὰ μὲν οὖν μέλλοντ' οὐδεὶς ἐφορᾷ,   1270
τὰ δὲ νῦν ἑστῶτ' οἰκτρὰ μὲν ἡμῖν,
αἰσχρὰ δ' ἐκείνοις,
χαλεπώτατα δ' οὖν ἀνδρῶν πάντων
τῷ τήνδ' ἄτην ὑπέχοντι.
λείπου μηδὲ cύ, παρθέν', ἀπ' οἴκων,   1275
μεγάλους μὲν ἰδοῦςα νέους θανάτους,
πολλὰ δὲ πήματα ⟨καὶ⟩ καινοπαθῆ,
κοὐδὲν τούτων ὅ τι μὴ Ζεύς.

1266 δέ] τε L   1270–8 choro tribuit Bergk   1270 ἐφορᾷ]
ἀφ- Wakefield: προ- Hartung   1273 πάντων UY: ἁπάντων lzt
1275–8 Hyllo continuant ZgT, choro tribuunt P.Oxy. 3688, KTa: partim choro
partim Hyllo cett.   1275 ἀπ' Laz: ἐπ' Lγρ et sch., t
1276 μεγάλους] μελέους Subkoff   1277 suppl. Bentley   καινοπαθῆ L s.l., cett.: -παγῆ l, s.l. in a et T

54

COMMENTARY

PROLOGUE (1-93)

The play begins with a scene whose closest parallel is Euripides' *Andromache*, where the prologue speech (by Andromache herself) is succeeded by a dialogue between Andromache and a θεράπαινα. The majority of S's surviving tragedies open with a dialogue that conveys essential information to the audience (*Electra* is a little different, commencing with two long *rheseis* that serve the same function as the shorter exchanges of dialogue just mentioned). The prologue of *Trachiniae* is unique in its preference for a more formal exposition conveyed in a long set speech which has reminded most scholars of the characteristic Euripidean prologue (for an early specimen of the comparison see Porson's *Praelectio in Euripidem* (*Adversaria*, p. 10)). But the similarities in technique can be (often have been) exaggerated: see H. Erbse, *Studien zum Prolog der Euripideischen Tragödie* (Berlin 1984), 292–3, for a recent and welcome reminder of some essential differences in approach between the present scene and the opening of most Euripidean dramas. In particular, whereas a prologue of Euripides will set out with the greatest clarity 'the scene, the characters and their relationship and antecedents, and the state of affairs as the play begins' (to quote Barrett on the *Hippolytus*' opening), S's aim here is not so much to set before us facts of this sort but to convey Deianeira's emotional mood and her particular state of dependence upon her husband (Leo, *Der Monolog im Drama: Ein Beitrag zur griechisch-römischen Poetik* (Abh. Ges. Wiss. Göttingen, phil.-hist. Kl., NS 10. 5; 1908), 13, long ago stressed that S 'die monologische Rede... nur für gesteigerten Affect zuläßt'). The Nurse's opening words at 49 ff. supply (as Leo, p. 14, observed) much more in the way of practical information for the audience than does Deianeira's *rhesis*.

1 ff. D's speech opens with a rhetorical mode of emphasis whereby the speaker's rejection of a traditional viewpoint focuses attention on the speaker's own divergent opinion. For examples of such a *refutatio sententiae* see Eur. *Suppl.* 195 ff. ἄλλοισι δὴ 'πόνης' ἁμιλληθεὶς λόγωι | τοιῶιδ'· ἔλεξε γάρ τις ὡc τὰ χείρονα | πλείω

COMMENTARY

βροτοῖcίν ἐcτι τῶν ἀμεινόνων· | ἐγὼ δὲ τούτοιc ἀντίαν γνώμην ἔχω, Aesch. *Ag.* 750 ff. παλαίφατοc δ' ἐν βροτοῖc γέρων λόγοc | τέτυκται, μέγαν τελεcθέντα φωτὸc ὄλβον | τεκνοῦcθαι μηδ' ἄπαιδα θνῄcκειν, | ἐκ δ' ἀγαθᾶc τύχαc γένει | βλαcτάνειν ἀκόρεcτον οἰζύν. | δίχα δ' ἄλλων μονόφρων εἰμί. Formally similar (though it encompasses *confirmation*, not rejection, of a traditional view) is Eur. *Hcld.* 1 ff. πάλαι ποτ' ἐcτὶ τοῦτ' ἐμοί δεδογμένον· | ὁ μὲν δίκαιοc τοῖc πέλαc πέφυκ' ἀνήρ, | ὁ δ' ἐc τὸ κέρδοc λῆμ' ἔχων ἀνειμένον | πόλει τ' ἄχρηcτοc καὶ cυναλλάccειν βαρύc, | αὑτῶι δ' ἄριcτοc· οἶδα δ' οὐ λόγωι μαθών. | ἐγὼ γάρ κτλ. The device is discussed by Arist. *Rhet.* 1395ᵃ18 ff. δεῖ δὲ τὰc γνώμαc λέγειν καὶ παρὰ τὰ δεδημοcιευμένα (λέγω δὲ δεδημοcιευμένα οἷον τὸ γνῶθι cεαυτὸν καὶ μηδὲν ἄγαν) ὅταν ἢ τὸ ἦθοc φαίνεcθαι μέλληι βέλτιον, ἢ παθητικῶc εἰρημένη κτλ. For modern discussions with further instances see Easterling, *PCPS* 20 (1974), 42–3, Stinton, ibid. 22 (1976), 71 ff. (The technique has some formal resemblances to another rhetorical device, the priamel, for which see on 498 ff. below). The present employment of the device has an added, tragic, point: 'one of the major ironies of the play is that [D] has much greater unhappiness to come; in the end the "old saying" is indeed justified' (Easterling, op. cit. 43). See further (on the structure of the argument in these lines) H. Friis Johansen, *General Reflection in Tragic Rhesis: A Study of Form* (Copenhagen 1959), 145–6.

1. **μέν:** Greek tragic prologues often open with μέν: see Fraenkel on Aesch. *Ag.* 1 for the details. S's other extant tragedies begin either thus (*Ajax*, *Philoctetes*) or with a vocative. **λόγοc ... ἔcτ' ... ἀνθρώπων:** for this sort of formula see Pind. *Nem.* 9. 6 ἔcτι δέ τιc λόγοc ἀνθρώπων, Eur. *Hel.* 18 ἔcτιν δὲ δὴ λόγοc τιc and Kannicht ad loc. (Kannicht thinks this Euripidean instance a smoke-screen for introducing καινοτομία). It should be contrasted with apparently analogous specimens like *Ant.* 829 ὡc φάτιc ἀνδρῶν, which are idiomatic in the context of mythological *exempla* (cf. N. Zagagi, *Tradition and Originality in Plautus* (Hypomnemata 62; 1980), 37 n. 79, 40 n. 86), or Theocr. *Id.* 15. 107 ἀνθρώπων ὡc μῦθοc, which are 'a common qualification of statements concerning matters outside the speaker's personal knowledge' (Gow ad loc.). Eriphus fr. 1. 1 KA λόγοc γάρ ἐcτ' ἀρχαῖοc οὐ κακῶc ἔχων parodies our verse. **λόγοc ...**

56

LINES 1-2

ἀρχαῖος: for the idea of an 'old' word see Aesch. *Ag.* 750–1 γέρων λόγος with Fraenkel ad loc., Eur. *Her.* 26 γέρων ... λόγος with Bond ad loc.: the παλαιὸς λόγος of Cratinus fr. 182. 1–2 KA and Plato *Leg.* 715E should also be quoted, and cf. Pind. *Ol.* 7. 54 ἀνθρώπων παλαιαὶ ῥήςιες, Eur. frr. 25, 333, 508 παλαιὸς αἶνος, Nicander *Ther.* 343 ὠγύγιος μῦθος. Cf. C. W. Müller, *Rh. Mus.* 128 (1985), 133 n. 68. **ἀρχαῖος ... φανείς:** 'φανείς is attributive and primarily linked with ἀρχαῖος, "which arose of old"' (Moorhouse, p. 205); in prose πάλαι φανείς. Cf. *Ant.* 593–4 ἀρχαῖα ... | ... πίπτοντ', Bruhn, *Anhang*, § 8. Not (*pace* Schwyzer, *Gr. Gr.* ii. 255) a periphrastic construction with ἔςτι ... φανείς equivalent to πέφανται. Cf. J. Aarts, *Periphrastica* (Amsterdam 1965), 29 n. 4, for pleonastic participles of the type we have here. For φανείς used of a λόγος cf. *Ant.* 621 ἔπος πέφανται, *OT* 848 φανέν γε τοὔπος. **ἀνθρώπων:** comparison with Pind. *Nem.* 9. 6 (cited above) shows that this word has been postponed in order to allow greater emphasis to ἀρχαῖος (compare too Archilochus fr. 174. 1 W αἶνός τις ἀνθρώπων ὅδε, Cratinus fr. 246. 1 KA ὡς μὲν ἀνθρώπων λόγος; cf. Alc. fr. 339 LP ὡς λόγος ἐκ πατέρων ὄρωρε, Pind. *Ol.* 7. 54 (cited above)). The displacement, together with the proximity of φανείς (and perhaps a belief in the periphrastic construction), encouraged the corruption ἀνθρώποις in Cramer's *Anecdota*.

1–2. **ἀνθρώπων ... βροτῶν:** for the collocation cf. Aesch. *Pers.* 706 ἀνθρώπεια δ' ἄν τοι πήματ' ἄν τύχοι βροτοῖς.

2. **αἰῶν':** 'lifetime', the existence of an individual person; for discussions of its meaning see Fraenkel on Aesch. *Ag.* 105–6, Johansen and Whittle on Aesch. *Suppl.* 46, Braswell on Pind. *Pyth.* 4. 186 (d), R. B. Onians, *Origins of European Thought* (Cambridge 1954), general index, s.v. *aiōn*, Burkert, *Eranos Jahrbuch* 51 (1982), 346–7 and n. 31. **ἐκμάθοις:** but third-person ἐκμάθοι might be defended as the *difficilior lectio*, with τις to be supplied from the context (it would be pedantic to claim that 2–3's τις and τωι strictly have a different reference); see, however, W. Kraus, *WS* 20 (1986), 87–8; for potential opt. + ἄν including 'a range of futures, and also present ... in general statement' see Moorhouse, p. 230, G. L. Cooper, *Zur syntaktischen Theorie und Textkritik der attischen Autoren* (Zurich 1971), 39. Here 'cannot find out': see below, on 5. See Addenda.

πρὶν ἄν βροτῶν is merely a reversion from VRZg to the *simplex ordo*

COMMENTARY

(cf. M. L. West, *Textual Criticism and Editorial Technique* (Stuttgart 1973), 22 n. 16), perhaps with an eye to the easier supplying of τις for ἐκμάθοι.

2–3. πρὶν ἂν | θάνηι: R's θάνει is an example of the frequent confusion of -ει(c)/-ηι(c): see Dover on Ar. *Nub.* 296. And 'the πρίν-clause relates to what will certainly take place: hence the opt. θάνοι cannot be supported as being potential' (Moorhouse, p. 297).

3. A mild example of the elliptical stylistic device discussed and illustrated by G. Kiefner, *Die Versparung* (Wiesbaden 1964), 41: here a τωι is to be supplied mentally before χρηcτóc. For the repeated τις ... τωι of the same indefinite person see Eur. *Hec.* 1178–9, *Or.* 1218–19. For the *gnome* 'call no man happy before he dies' see Fraenkel on Aesch. *Ag.* 928–9, Stevens on Eur. *Andr.* 101, etc. The sentiment is as proverbial as γνῶθι cεαυτόν, μηδὲν ἄγαν, to quote the two examples of τὰ δεδημοcιευμένα given by Arist. *Rhet.* (cited above on 1 ff.).

4. ἐγὼ δέ: D's divergent viewpoint is here stressed: cf. the same phrase at Eur. *Suppl.* 198, δίχα δ᾽ ἄλλων μονόφρων εἰμί at Aesch. *Ag.* 755 (passages quoted in full above, on 1 ff.), and cf. on 1062 below.

D. Korzeniewski, *Griechische Metrik* (Darmstadt 1968), 56 n. 63, notes this line as the solitary exception to the rule that the second longum of an iambic trimeter in tragedy is never resolved if the third longum is occupied by a monosyllable.

5. ἔξοιδ᾽: for the prefix ἐκ-, here signifying 'thoroughly', see Wilamowitz on Eur. *Her.* 155; E. Tsitsoni, *Untersuchungen der EK-Verbal-Komposita bei Sophokles* (Diss. Munich 1963), 33; Renehan, *Studies on Greek Texts* (Hypomnemata 43; 1976), 24 ff. Cf. ἐκμάθοι in line 2 (see n. ad. loc.).

6 ff. ἥτις ... ἔcχον: 'being one who had' (Moorhouse, p. 265, in his discussion of generalizing ὅcτις). For further instances of ὅcτις thus used in detailed proof of a statement see Johansen, *General Reflection in Tragic Rhesis*, p. 126 n. 80. For other passages wherein 'the enunciation of a universal truth at the beginning of a poem or other discourse' leads 'to a particular illustration' see West on Hes. *Op.* 11–46. **ἔτ᾽ ἐν:** ἐνὶ VRa: for such scribal attempts to fill out the metre cf. *PV* 520 (οὐκέτ᾽ ἂν LcLhKQF (*in ras.*): οὐκ ἂν οὖν *vel* οὐκ ἂν *fere rell.*). ἐνί is an impossible makeshift since 'ἐνί equivalent to ἐν does not occur in drama' (Fraenkel on Aesch. *Ag.* 78; for ἐνί as equivalent to ἔνεcτι see Page on the same passage) and ἐνὶ Πλ- would provide in iambic tri-

LINES 2-10

meters an instance of 'two consonants [with] the power of lengthening a preceding short syllable which is not contained within the same word. It has been generally held since Porson that this, the regular practice of the early Ionian writers, was inadmissible in Attic Tragedy at least from the time of Aeschylus onwards' (D. L. Page, *A New Chapter in the History of Greek Tragedy* (Cambridge 1951), 24; cf. Barrett on Eur. *Hipp.* 760 (lyric exceptions to this rule)), Hutchinson on Aesch. *ScT* 1055–6. Vitus Winshemius' ἔτ' ἐν, approved by Erfurdt (cf. *Sophoclea*, p. 150), seems supported by the famous lines from Sophocles' *Tereus* (fr. 583. 3 ff.): αἴ νέαι μὲν ἐν πατρὸς | ἥδιστον, οἶμαι, ζῶμεν ἀνθρώπων βίον. | . . . | ὅταν δ' ἐς ἥβην ἐξικώμεθα κτλ. By contrast, D's woes begin earlier. Of other corrections Margoliouth's ναίουσα πρός provides inadequate sense, while Jernstedt's ναίοντος puts emphasis upon the wrong person. Zieliński (p. 524 n. 9 = p. 309 n. 1 of the repr.) observes the subtle manner in which D's identity is established near the start of the *rhesis*. **νυμφείων . . . ὄτλον:** I read ὄκνον with the majority of the sources. Fear concerning 'bridals' (for νυμφεῖα with this meaning see Barrett on Eur. *Hipp.* 552, Bühler on Moschus' *Europa* 159–60). Hermann objected to ὄκνος with the epithet ἄλγιστον, but *Ant.* 857–8 ἀλγεινοτάτας . . . μερίμνας, Pind. *Nem.* 1. 48 ἄτλατον δέος seem adequate analogies, and an anticipation of the fear motif in this speech (cf. 24, 28 etc.) is welcome. The *v.l.* ὄτλον possibly derives from the similar phrase at Aesch. *ScT* 18 παιδείας ὄτλον | (cf. Kraus, *WS* 99 (1986), 88–9); for a defence of it see *Sophoclea*, p. 150.

8. **ἄλγιστον . . . εἴ τις:** for the strengthening of a superlative by the appending of the phrase εἴ τις (ἄλλος) see H. Thesleff, *Studies on Intensification in Early and Classical Greek* (Helsinki 1954), 190.

9. **μνηστήρ:** on the meaning of this Homeric noun (and μνάομαι) see P. Thieme, *Zeitschr. für vergl. Sprachforsch.* 94 (1980), 124 ff., esp. p. 137. The γάρ is idiomatic in introductions of a narrative section within a *rhesis*: see 155, 475, 680, 1159 below, and for other instances *Aj.* 285, *El.* 681, Aesch. *Pers.* 355, *ScT* 42, *Ag.* 650. Compare 900 n.

10. **ἐν τρισὶν μορφαῖσιν:** water-spirits and the like (Thetis, Proteus, Nereus, etc.) often resort to metamorphosis, in keeping with the changeable nature of their element: see Frazer in the Loeb Apollodorus ii. 67–8 n. 6, and appendix 10 (pp. 383 ff.), M. Ninck, *Die Bedeutung des Wassers im Kult und Leben der Alten* (*Philol.* suppl. 14; 1921), 138 ff. But, as H. P. Isler observes (*Acheloos* (Berne 1970), 11), all other retellings of

COMMENTARY

the story, both in literature (see Isler, p. 193 n. 4) and art, present the metamorphoses as defensive stratagems in the fight with Heracles, not voluntary exhibitions of prowess, and this is what the analogies with Thetis etc. would suggest as the original form of the myth. According to Philostr. *Imag.* 4. 2 (397–8 K), ἄλλος δὲ ἄλλοτε δοκῶν ὑπὸ τοῖς ὁρωμένοις εἴδεσιν ἐκπλήξειν ἡγεῖται τὸν Οἰνέα.

11. ἐναργής: in view of the passage of Philostratus just quoted, Jebb may be right to detect a 'sense of awe' in the adjective; for the representation of rivers as bulls see Eur. *Or.* 1378 Ὠκεανὸς ταυρόκρανος, *Ion* 1261 ὦ ταυρόμορφον ὄμμα Κηφισοῦ with Owen ad loc., and the metaphorical use of κέρας for the 'branch' of a river (see West on Hes. *Th.* 789). In art Achelous is often represented as a bull with human face: see Isler (last n.), C. Weiss, *Griechische Flußgottheiten in vorhellenistischen Zeit* (Beitr. zur Archäol. 17; 1984), 59 ff.

11 ff. Compare the fourfold ἄλλοτε used to convey the metamorphoses of Periclymenus at Hes. fr. 33A 14–17 MW, the threefold ἄλλοτε used of Nemesis' shape-changing at *Cypria* fr. 7. 8 ff. Davies.

11–12. αἰόλος | δράκων: for this epithet as used of snakes see Davies on Stes. S15.ii.5. Achelous' metamorphosis into a snake is represented in a stylized manner by some visual depictions of his fight with Heracles: see e.g. the gem illustrated as pl. XXII 291 in Isler (cited above on 10).

12–13. A real dilemma is presented by the variants here, one not to be resolved (with Hermann) by recourse to the notion of author's variants (against the notion of that phenomenon here see Van der Valk, *Researches on the Text and Scholia of the* Iliad ii (Leiden 1964), 598 ff.).[1] Philostratus confirms that Strabo's variant here is not fortuitous and Empedocles B 61. 2–3 DK ((πολλὰ μὲν ἀμφιπρόσωπα)... | βουγενῆ ἀνδρόπρωιρα... | ἀνδροφυῆ βούκρανα) serves to remind us that the two relevant epithets are old, poetic, and synonymous. (Incidentally, the entry in Hesych. s.v. βούπρωιρον (i. 340 Latte), σημαίνει δὲ καὶ τὴν βουπρόσωπον, is not (*pace* Latte ad loc. and Kannicht–Snell on *TrGF* (adesp.) fr. 587B) a tragic fragment, but an allusion to our passage.) -πρωιρος perhaps has liturgical connotations (so Fraenkel on Aesch. *Ag.* 235), but even after the prolix discussion by Van der Valk, ii. 602 ff., it is hard to see a significant difference between

---

[1] On the phenomenon as a whole see e.g. West, *Textual Criticism and Editorial Technique* pp. 15–16, Dover, *ICS* 2 (1977), 154 ff. = *The Greeks and their Legacy*, pp. 214 ff. On Hermann's particular theory see Eicken-Iselin (cited below on 455) p. vii and n. 2.

LINES 10-18

the meanings of the two variants. Certainly βούκρανoc is not to be limited (with Mazon, followed by Kamerbeek) to the back of the head. It occurs in later prose writers (e.g. Plut. *Mor.* 358 D (*Is. et Os.* 19): Isis' cow-headed helmet). The evidence of art does not help us, since it usually depicts Achelous either as a bull with a human face (see above, on 11), the exact opposite of what is here implied, or as a centaur-like figure with bull's horns, which is again difficult to reconcile with ἀνδρείωι κύτει or τύπωι. A small group of artefacts, most notably a coin from Metapontum (*LIMC* i/1. 75 (p. 18): a good illustration in *Megale Hellas* (Credito Italiano), 135, fig. 76), shows Achelous as a human figure (and head) with bull's horns, but even this does not precisely match our passage (whatever its exact reading): for, as Isler points out (p. 12), a Minotaur-like monster, with bull's head, seems implied by our lines. The only possible ground for rational choice might be that κύτοc (our earliest attestation in Alcman fr. 17. 1 P) is a slightly rarer word than τύποc (for whose association with adjectives like ἀνδρεῖοc, γυναικεῖοc (or the equivalent gen.) see Pearson, *CR* 26 (1912), 211; cf. besides ἐκβουτυποῦται (of Io) at fr. 268A. 37), hence, perhaps, *difficilior lectio*.

13. δαcκίου γενειάδοc: for the phrase cf. Aesch. *Pers.* 316 δάcκιον γενειάδα.

14. Cf. Ov. *Met.* 1. 266 'barba gravis nimbis, canis fluit unda capillis', Philostr. (cited on 12–13) γενειὰc ἀμφιλαφὴc πηγαί τε ναμάτων ἐκπλημμυροῦcαι τοῦ γενείου. For ποτόν used of the water of springs and streams see Gow on Theocr. *Id.* 13. 46.

15. προcδεδεγμένη: for the 'intensive' perf. with pres. sense cf. Moorhouse, p. 211. Cf. Homeric ποτιδέγμενοc and cf. τὸν ὃν προcμένουc᾽ ἀκοίταν at 525 below.

17. ἐμπελαcθῆναι: the simplex and compound forms of this verb frequently convey sexual connotations: see Johansen and Whittle on Aesch. *Suppl.* 300. It regularly takes the genitive (Bruhn, *Anhang*, § 35).

18 ff. Visual depictions of the story often portray *Heracles* as the aggressor and Deianeira as expressing anguish and sorrow at the worsting of *Achelous* (see Isler, p. 12).

18. For the general idea here ('late but welcome') cf. Eur. *Hel.* 1232 χρόνια . . ., ἀλλ᾽ ὅμωc etc.; contrast 'welcome but late' at 201 below. **ἀcμένηι δέ μοι:** for predic. dat. ἄcμενοc with this meaning cf. LSJ s.v., Bruhn, *Anhang*, § 46.

COMMENTARY

19. Cf. Eur. fr. 2. 15–16 Austin Ζεὺc δ' ἐc Ἀλκμήνηc λέχοc | πεcὼν τὸ κλεινὸν Ἡρακλέουc cπείρει δέμαc and Harder ad loc. for other passages where the hero is associated with the adjective κλεινόc.

20. ἀγῶνα ... μάχηc: cf. Eur. *Hcld.* 798, *Andr.* 725; Fraenkel on Aesch. *Ag.* 1378 for the same or similar phrases; for the metaphorical use of ἀγών to refer to a battle see N. Reed, *CP* 70 (1975), 275 and n. 7; for the principle of 'Synonyma in attribuitivem Verhältnis verbunden' see Bruhn, *Anhang*, § 205; cf. U. Hübner, *Philol.* 124 (1980), 185 n. 58.

21. ἐκλύεταί με: 'delivered me'; for this meaning with the middle see Johansen and Whittle on Aesch. *Suppl.* 1065. The present tense (after 19's ἦλθε) conveys the lasting nature of the effect (Moorhouse, p. 184).

22–3. ἦν | θακῶν: see W. Dietrich, *Glotta* 51 (1973), 202, for the meaning of this and similar periphrases; on the superiority of θακῶν to θωκῶν see Björck, *Das Alpha impurum und die tragische Kunstsprache* (Uppsala 1950), 239; for the resumption of ὅcτιc with ὅδε cf. *Ant.* 464.

24. ἤμην: ἤμην as Hellenistic κοινή form often intrudes into poetic texts under cover of similar-looking words: see Kannicht on Eur. *Hel.* 931.

25. Deleted by Dobree (*Adversaria*, ed. Wagner (1883), iv. 35) together with 24 as tautologous after 23's ἀταρβήc, by Radermacher because of its word-play and use of ποτε as 'sinnstörendes Versfüllsel', and by Kranz (*Jhsb. d. Philol. Vereins zu Berlin* 47 (1921), 32 = *Stud. zur antik. Lit. und ihrem Nachw.*, 283) because it gives the wrong reason for D's fear, this line seems in fact guaranteed by 7–8 above and 465 below. Cf. Easterling, *G&R* 24 (1977), 121–2. For the position of ποτε at line-end with the meaning 'at last, sooner or later' see 297 below.

26. For similar associations of τιθέναι with adverb see Fraenkel on Aesch. *Ag.* 913, 1672–3, arguing in the latter place that τιθέναι καλῶc always has an expressed object. τέλοc here, then, will be the noun, not the adverb (so too Holwerda, *Mnem.* 16 (1963), 341–2). For further instances of the phrase καλῶc τιθέναι see Diggle, *CQ* 33 (1983), 350–1; on the use of the adjective ἀγώνιοc to refer to 'gods of battle' see N. Reed, *CP* 70 (1975), 275–6.

26–7. δή is 'normally used in such conditional clauses to emphasize a word repeated from the apodosis': Bond on Eur. *Her.* 41 κἄμ' (εἴ τι δὴ χρὴ κἄμ' ἐν ἀνδράcιν λέγειν). Our example, however, conveys an element of doubt; cf. *Il.* 3. 180 εἴ ποτ' ἔην γε (with Stinton, *PCPS* 22 (1976), 62–3), Vergil *Aen.* 7. 4 'si qua est ea gloria', etc.

27. λέχος γὰρ ... κριτόν: the particle explains the reservation just considered. λέχος ... κριτόν is most usually taken as an internal accusative dependent upon ξυστᾶς᾽, with the dative Ἡρακλεῖ attached both to κριτόν and to the participle. But in this context I feel it is likeliest to mean 'adjudged as wife to the victorious Heracles' (so M. L. Earle, *CR* 9 (1895), 200 = *Classical Papers*, p. 30). For κρίνω with the meaning 'assign as the result of a contest' see *Aj.* 443, Pind. *Pyth.* 8. 84.

28. ἐκ φόβου φόβον: 'one fear after another': for ἐκ in such repetitional phrases conveying 'the notion of succession, continuity' see Headlam on Herodas 5. 85. On the word-order see Bruhn, *Anhang*, § 164, and for locutions involving similar repetition (χεὶρ ἐκ χειρός etc.) see Gygli-Wyss, *Das nominale Polyptoton* (Göttingen 1966), 73 n. 3, 139 n. 2. For other tragic trimeters which similarly exploit word-end after fourth and fifth longum to achieve a staccato rhythm cf. Korzeniewski, *Griechische Metrik*, p. 51.

29. κείνου προκηραίνουσα: cf. Eur. *Hipp.* 223 τί ποτ᾽, ὦ τέκνον, τάδε κηραίνεις;, *Her.* 518 ποῖ ὄνειρα κηραίνους᾽ ὁρῶ; For the intransitive sense 'be harassed in mind' see Johansen and Whittle on Aesch. *Suppl.* 999.

29–30. εἰσάγει ... ἀπωθεῖ: Heracles is suggested as object of the two verbs here by Campbell, followed by M. L. Earle, *CR* 9 (1895), 200 = *Classical Papers*, p. 30. But the more popular interpretation, with πόνον their object as it is of the participle, is supported by *OT* 198 εἴ τι νὺξ ἀφῆι | τοῦτ᾽ ἐπ᾽ ἧμαρ ἔρχεται, *TrGF* (adesp.) fr. 7. 2–3 πόνωι πόνον | ἐκ νυκτὸς ἀλλάσσουσα τὸν καθ᾽ ἡμέραν, as well as by the language of 141ff. below. The picture of *Heracles* thrust forth by the dying night is pointless and distracting, and anticipates the image of 34–5. With νὺξ εἰσάγει πόνον compare the epic notion of Zeus *vel sim.* 'bringing on' (ἐπάγει) the day (see West on Hes. *Th.* 176). For night as a time of cares see below on 149. **διαδεδεγμένη:** probably absolute ('in succession') or with νυκτί understood (so that πόνον is connected with the main verbs alone: the picture of each night 'receiving the πόνος in succession' would be obscure and inappropriate).

31. κἀφύσαμεν δή: Denniston, *GP*^{2}, p. 254, is non-commital as to

COMMENTARY

whether καί and δή are best taken together in such passages. The word-division κἄφυσα μέν (zt) cannot be right since φύω is not used of the mother alone.

31 ff. A literal translation of this simile reveals a small but significant inconcinnity: Heracles' relation to his children is like that of a farmer to his remote holding—he sees them only when he sows and reaps. In other words, we have here an example of a simile in which the two constituent parts, *illustrans* and *illustrandum*, become fused or interwoven. For a good discussion of this type of image, with numerous specimens drawn from early Greek poetry,[2] see O. Smith, *Class. et Med.* 26 (1965), 52 ff., who deals with our instance on p. 63. In the present case the fusion is the easier because cπείρω is a common metaphor for human propagation (see below on 33). Cf. Aesch. *Suppl.* 223–4 ἐν ἁγνῶι δ' ἑσμὸς ὣς πελειάδων | ἵζεσθε κίρκων τῶν ὁμοπτέρων φόβωι, where the transference of *illustrans* to *illustrandum* represented by κίρκων τῶν ὁμοπτέρων is facilitated by the ambiguity of the verb ἵζεσθε, which can be used of birds (see Johansen and Whittle ad loc.). On the general principle of such 'pivotal' words, whose ambivalence smooths such transitions, see M. S. Silk, *Interaction in Poetic Imagery* (Cambridge 1974), *passim*. **ποτε** is hard to translate; the most attractive renderings ('from time to time', 'every now and then') are difficult to parallel (Dodds on Eur. *Bacch.* 922 argues for 'perhaps'). Earle, *CR* 9 (1895), 201– 2 = *Classical Papers*, p. 32, is probably right to correlate the word with νῦν δ' in 36 (cf. 88 and 90, 1091 and 1103, below): *in the past* he at least saw the children σπείρων . . . κἀξαμῶν; *now* he is quite absent. (νῦν δ' certainly contrasts the present anxiety with a more general set of past worries (ἄθλων τῶνδ'), but since these past worries include Heracles' frequent absences the correlation may stand.)

32. γῄτης: characterized by Diggle, *CR* 19 (1969), 152, as 'a ἅπαξ redolent of the soil'. On the spelling see Wackernagel, *KZ* 27 (1885), 271 = *Kl. Schr.* i. 582.

33. σπείρων: metaphorical; see LSJ s.v. I. 2, Bond on Eur. *Hyps.* fr. 1 iii 25–6; cf. Braswell on Pind. *Pyth.* 4. 255 (b). **προσεῖδε:** a gnomic aorist idiomatic within the context of the simile; we should otherwise expect an imperfect for this repeated action of Heracles.

[2] Add the particularly interesting specimen in *Il.* 22. 26 (Ἀχιλῆα) παμφαίνονθ' ὥς τ' ἀστέρ' ἐπεσσύμενον πεδίοιο, badly misunderstood by D. J. Lee, *The Similes of the* Iliad *and the* Odyssey *Compared* (Melbourne 1964), 11.

LINES 31-42

34. εἰc δόμουc: for this phrase as signifying '(send/go) home' in tragedy see Fraenkel on Aesch. *Ag.* 1657.

35. λατρεύοντά τωι: D may be reluctant to name Eurystheus (mentioned only once by name in this play, at 1049), who is anyway dramatically irrelevant, like the equally anonymous Ceyx alluded to in 40.

36-7. ἡνίκ' ... ἐνταῦθα δή: for this sequence (whereby a word meaning 'when' is followed by ἐνταῦθα or εἶτα (δή)) see Headlam on Herodas 3. 33.

36. ὑπερτελήc: for the meaning of this word and its cognates see Fraenkel on Aesch. *Ag.* 286. **ἔφυ:** for the idiomatic replacement of ἦν with this synonym see Bruhn, *Anhang*, § 231; cf. West, *BICS* 26 (1979), 115.

37. ταρβήcαc' ἔχω: the periphrastic cχῆμα Cοφοκλεῖον: see Moorhouse, pp. 206-7.

38. ἔκτα: the identical form at Eur. *Her.* 423-4. Cf. cυγκατακτάc at *Aj.* 230 and for other tragic instances of the verb's epic athematic aorist see Sideras, *Aeschylus Homericus*, p. 106. **Ἰφίτου βίαν:** for tragedians' use of the epic periphrasis βία + genitive see Sideras, *Aeschylus Homericus*, pp. 252-3; cf. L. Bergson, *Rh. Mus.* 102 (1959), 36.[3]

39. ἐν Τραχῖνι τῆιδ': the only instance, in a Sophoclean prologue, of this type of a deictic pronoun attached to a geographical name for purposes of local indication. Euripides is fond of the device, especially in his prologues: see *Hipp.* 12 τῆcδε γῆc Τροζηνίαc and Barrett ad loc., Kassel, *ZPE* 21 (1976), 35. Not so S and Aeschylus, who rarely open their plays with the Euripidean type of monologue. The significance of the present reference to place is not particularly Euripidean: 'Die Bezeichnung des Ortes ... gestaltet sie [Deianeira] zu einem weiteren Argument für ihr Unglück' (Schwinge, p. 35).

40-1. ὅπου | βέβηκεν: cf. *Phil.* 256 μηδαμοῦ διῆλθε, *OC* 52 (χῶροc ...) ἐν ὧι βεβήκαμεν, Eur. *IT* 1285 ποῦ κυρεῖ βεβώc;, KG ii/1. 545 for the appearance of 'where' for the expected 'whither'. Brunck's ὅποι is therefore needless (like Elmsley's ποῖ in *IT*).

41-2. For metaphorical ὠδίc see Johansen and Whittle on Aesch. *Suppl.* 770. Cf. ὠδίνουcα at 325 below.

42. Cf. *Aj.* 972-3 ἀλλ' ἐμοὶ | λιπὼν ἀνίαc καὶ γόουc διοίχεται

[3] Our passage is overlooked by Maehler on Bacch. 5. 181 when he claims that S does not so use βία + gen. (see too 1059 below, *Phil.* 314, 321, 592).

65

COMMENTARY

(Schneidewin, *Philol.* 4 (1849), 474, took that passage to be an interpolation derived from the present lines; cf. next n.). For the choice between αὐτοῦ or αὑτοῦ see *Sophoclea*, p. 151. **προϲβαλών:** cf. Aesch. *Pers.* 781 οὐ κακὸν τοϲόνδε προϲέβαλον πόλει.

43 ff. 44–8 were deleted as an actor's interpolation by Wunder and Tycho von Wilamowitz: their case is revived and strengthened by M. D. Reeve, *GRBS* 11 (1970), 283 ff., who also dispenses with line 43 (rightly if deletion is to be accepted: D's speech then ends not with a new point abruptly left hanging in the air, but with a sentiment that echoes, as we saw on 42, the close of Tecmessa's final speech in *Aj.* 971 ff.). Their main complaint (lesser anomalies will be considered below) concerns dramatic technique: the δέλτοϲ is ominously connected, both here and at 155 ff., with a period of fifteen months; but only in the latter passage is it made clear that death or repose will directly follow that period. However, as Kranz appreciated (*Jhsb. d. Philol. Vereins zu Berlin* 47 (1921), 34 ff. = *Stud. zur antik. Lit. und ihrem Nachw.*, pp. 285 ff.), there is no inconsistency here: rather a masterly revelation of detail as and when appropriate. The crucial information is allowed to leak out slowly and at dramatically effective stages of the play: not so much a matter of creating suspense (for attacks on this notion see Reeve, art. cit., 285) as of progressive, climactic revelation of the truth, a technique already exemplified in Homer—e.g. the *Iliad*'s handling of the prophecy concerning Achilles' death (see Schwinge, pp. 103 ff.) or the *Odyssey* on Agamemnon's murder (cf. H. L. Lorimer, *Homer and the Monuments* (London 1950), 516 ff.)—and paralleled from drama, for instance, in the *PV* (the gradual emergence of Prometheus' secret about Zeus' overthrow) and the *OC* (the significance of the grove as Oedipus' place of rest). Complaints that the Nurse speaks as if D's *rhesis* had ended at 42, and that nothing is said of the δέλτοϲ in 76 ff. (cf. Nauck's objections), display an excessively realistic approach to the conventions of Greek drama.

43. ϲχεδὸν δ' ἐπίϲταμαι: for the understatement cf. Ar. *Plut.* 860 ϲχεδὸν τὸ πρᾶγμα γιγνώϲκειν δοκῶ.

44–5. δέκα ... πρὸϲ ἄλλοιϲ πέντ': a rather unusual way of ordering numerals; more familiar is the type of construction exemplified in τρίτον ἐπὶ δέκα (see Fraenkel on Aesch. *Ag.* 1605). Wackernagel, *Binz Festschr.* (1935), 35 = *Kl. Schr.* i. 238 n. 2, observes the uniqueness of the 'präpositioneller Anschluß der Zehn'.

LINES 42-49

46. The κἄςτιν τι δεινὸν πῆμα that is the paradosis sits rather oddly after 43's cχεδὸν δ' ἐπίcταμαί τι πῆμ' ἔχοντά νιν, and Jebb's distinction between the surmise of 43 and the stronger certainty of the present line is hard to justify dramatically or rationally (cf. Reeve (cited on 43 ff.), p. 285 n. 3). After πῆμ' two lines above, an original χρῆμα would easily be corrupted (so Wilamowitz*, approved by Kranz, *Jhsb. d. Philol. Vereins zu Berlin* 47 (1921), 34 = *Stud. zur antik. Lit. und ihrem Nachw.*, 285; cf. *Phil.* 1265 κακὸν τὸ χρῆμα, Plato *Gorg.* 485 B πικρόν τί μοι δοκεῖ χρῆμα εἶναι). Note that πημονῆc ἄτερ in 48 need not be (as Schwinge, p. 96 n. 2, supposes) a guarantee of δεινὸν πῆμα: it might be a further source of corruption.

47. ἔcτειχε: the imperfect tense is striking (cf. KG ii/1 143–5 on ἔλεγον where an aorist might be expected). **τήν:** another feature resolvable by localized emendation rather than wholesale deletion: on the use of the article for the relative in Aeschylus and S see Reeve (cited on 43 ff.), p. 285,[4] arguing that metrical necessity is the only relevant factor. A similar conclusion in Bergson, *Rh. Mus.* 102 (1959), 25, and Moorhouse, pp. 267–8. The former identifies as the only exceptions to this rule our passage and Aesch. *Suppl.* 265 τὰ δή, where Dindorf's ἃ δή is an easy change (see Johansen and Whittle ad loc.). For the latter, the only 'two cases where metre is not a factor' for S are again the present passage and OC 34–5 ἡμὶν αἴcιος | cκοπὸc προcήκεις τῶν ἀδηλούμεν φράcαι, where, however, the manuscripts are divided as to whether to interpret as τῶν ἀδηλούμεν or τῶν ἃ δηλούμεν (ὧν for τῶν Elmsley): see Reeve, p. 285 n. 7. The need to resort to slight emendation of our passage should be obvious; for the corruption of relative to article see Johansen and Whittle on Aesch. *Suppl.* 265, Diggle, *CR* 32 (1982), 130. τὴν ἐγὼ θάμ' in 'Electra's famous speech' (1144) may be not (as Reeve, p. 286) the source of interpolation, but rather an additional cause of corruption.

48. λαβεῖν: for the 'ingressive' aorist cf. Korzeniewski, *Gymnasium* 81 (1974), 240.

49. δέcποινα Δηιάνειρα: the first mention of the name of the speaker of the prologue (cf. Reeve (cited on 43 ff.), p. 287), though her identity has been clear since line 7 (see on 6 ff.). The θεράπαινα in the analogous scene from Euripides' *Andromache* (see start of the Commentary) addresses the heroine as δέcποιν' (line 56).

[4] On Euripides' practice see Diggle, *PCPS* 15 (1969), 58–9, *STE*, p. 75.

COMMENTARY

49 ff. πολλὰ μέν ... νῦν δ': for this sort of opening formula see 153–4 below, *Phil.* 1047–8 πόλλ' ἄν λέγειν ἔχοιμι... | ... νῦν δ' ἑνὸς κρατῶ λόγου, Cleon in Thuc. 3. 37. 1 πολλάκις μὲν ἤδη ἔγωγε καὶ ἄλλοτε ἔγνων ... μάλιστα δ' ἐν τῆι νῦν ἡμετέραι περὶ Μυτιληναίων μεταμελείαι, and the numerous examples gathered by Fraenkel, 'Eine Anfangsformel attischer Reden', *Glotta* 39 (1960), 1 ff. = *Kl. Beitr.* i. 505 ff. On the position of πολλὰ μέν cf. U. Hübner, *Philol.* 124 (1980), 183 n. 45.

50. πανδάκρυτ' ὀδύρματα: for S's fondness for combining 'abstract nouns in -ma and -mos with rare compound or privative adjectives' see Long, *Language and Thought*, p. 92.

50–1. ὀδύρματα ... ἔξοδον γοωμένην: for this type of double accusative (internal and external) see Johansen and Whittle on Aesch. *Suppl.* 230–1. On the use of the adj. Ἡράκλειος instead of the gen. see Wackernagel, *Mélanges... F. de Saussure*, p. 137 = *Kl. Schr.* ii. 1358. For other similar -ειος adjs. in Greek tragedy see 170, 260, 1219 below, and Bühler, *Zenobii Athoi Proverbia*, iv. 94. S uses γοάομαι again at 937 below and at *OT* 1249; for other tragic occurrences see Sideras, *Aeschylus Homericus*, p. 81.

52. νῦν δ': 'and now' (sc. that I see you lamenting again). This suggests the Nurse's presence during the opening *rhesis*: a contrast with the otherwise similar opening scene of Eur. *Andr.* (see start of Commentary), where the θεράπαινα enters at line 56.

52–3. εἰ δίκαιον: for the elaborately deferential introduction compare Eur. *El.* 300–1 λέγοιμ' ἄν, εἰ χρή (χρὴ δὲ πρὸς φίλον λέγειν), | τύχας βαρείας κτλ., *Hec.* 234 ff. εἰ δ' ἔστι τοῖς δούλοισι τοὺς ἐλευθέρους | μὴ λυπρὰ μηδὲ καρδίας δηκτήρια | ἐξιστορῆσαι,† σοὶ μὲν εἰρῆσθαι †χρεών, | ἡμᾶς δ' ἀκοῦσαι τοὺς ἐρωτῶντας τάδε. Note the elegant chiasmus of τοὺς ἐλευθέρους ... γνώμαισι δούλαις ... κἀμέ ... τὸ σόν. **γνώμαισι δούλαις:** Eur. *El.* 372 (εἶδον) γνώμην δὲ μεγάλην ἐν πένητι σώματι. **φράσαι τὸ σόν:** cf. Eur. *IA* 1167 ἦ 'μὲ χρὴ λέγειν τὰ σά, Soph. *El.* 577 ἐρῶ γὰρ καὶ τὸ σόν, *Aj.* 1313 ὅρα ... τὸ σόν. Not τόσον: tragedy uses τόσσος except in the phrase δὶς τόσα (*Aj.* 277 etc.) and the bare τόσα at Aesch. *Pers.* 786.

54. This and not κἀμὲ χρή in 53 is the apodosis to εἰ δίκαιον in 52 (cf. Eur. *Hec.* 234 ff., cited in the previous n.). Pearson's strong pause before this line and the consequent asyndeton (recently advocated again by

LINES 49-58

W. Kraus, *WS* 20 (1986), 90) produce an excessively abrupt (if not rude) effect. Jebb's semi-colon, also adopted by the OCT, is preferable (see *Sophoclea*, p. 151).

55. ἀνδρὸϲ κατὰ ζήτηϲιν: also in Eur. *Cycl.* 13-14 (ναυϲτολῶ | ϲέθεν κ. ζ.). For this use of κατά see Pearson on fr. 898. The other children of Heracles, it later transpires (1147-8), are actually far away, but here their mention adds urgency to the Nurse's suggestion.

57-8. Moorhouse, p. 248, offers two possible explanations of the double genitives here: 'πατρόϲ anticipates the subject of the inf. clause (instead of τοῦ πατέρα ... δοκεῖν); or else τοῦ ... δοκεῖν provides (after πατρόϲ) a second complement' for ὥραν. The latter seems likelier in view of the word-order. Cf. especially Alexis fr. 9. 6ff. τῶν δ' ὠνουμένων | προνοούμενοι τοῦ τὰϲ κεφαλὰϲ ὑγιεῖϲ ἔχειν | ἐκ κραιπάληϲ. On the double infinitives see KG ii/2 577 (β). νέμοι is more deferential towards Deianeira than the νέμει of Zo and requires understanding εἰκὸϲ ἂν εἴη.

58. Like Shakespeare's 'And in good time here comes the noble lord', a formula designed to smooth over the demands of dramatic economy. Σ's interpretation of the adjective here as being catachrestically re-etymologized to mean ἀρτίωϲ καὶ ἡρμοϲμένωϲ τῶι καιρῶι πορεύεται (the usual signification is 'of sound foot') is supported by the comparable formula of introduction at Aesch. *ScT* 372-3. ὅδ' αὐτὸϲ Οἰδίπου τόκοϲ | εἰϲ' ἀρτίκολλοϲ (-ον codd.: *corr.* Paley, *prob.* Fraenkel, *Sitzb. d. Bayer. Akad. d. Wiss., phil.-hist. Kl.* 3 (1957), 6 = *Kl. Beitr.* i. 276, Page (OCT)) ἀγγέλου λόγον μαθεῖν. For the force of ἀρτι- cf. *OT* 78-9 οἵδε τ' ἀρτίωϲ | Κρέοντα προϲϲτείχοντα ϲημαίνουϲί μοι, 1054; for -πουϲ cf. Eur. *Or.* 1549-50 ἀλλὰ μὴν καὶ τόνδε λεύϲϲω Μενέλεων δόμων πέλαϲ | ὀξύπουν, Ar. *Lys.* 326 μῶν ὑϲτερόπουϲ βοηθῶ; For such re-etymologizing see Campbell's *Essay on the Language of Sophocles* (vol. i of his commentary), 88ff., Fraenkel on Aesch. *Ag.* 149. **δόμοιϲ:** δόμουϲ codd., where the oddity of the pure accusative of 'motion towards' without preposition would have to be explained as analogous to the construction whereby ϲτείχω, ἔρχομαι, etc. take as direct obj. δόμον, δόμουϲ etc. (examples in Bers, pp. 81-2). Some emend by inserting a preposition: 'ϲ δόμουϲ Blaydes (but on the unlikeliness of prod-elision after -ει in S cf. L. Bergson, *Eranos* 51 (1953), 123-5, M. Platnauer, *CQ* 10 (1960), 141; cf. n. on 905 below), ἄρτι που

COMMENTARY

'cθρώιcκει Shilleto *ap.* Pretor's edition (Cambridge 1877) and Westcott *ap.* Jebb (but though more satisfactory as prodelision—see on 66 below—this removes the idiomatic ἀρτίπουc, above)). Or else, the accusative is removed: thus δόμων Bergk (cf. Eur. *Or.* 1549–50, above). But δόμοιc (dat. with ἐγγύc), proposed by Wakefield and accepted by the OCT, is the most plausible of this second class of conjectures, indeed the likeliest suggestion advanced (cf. *El.* 63, *Phil.* 496).

59. πρὸc καιρόν: for recent surveys of interpretations of this problematic word see J. R. Wilson, *Glotta* 58 (1980), 177 ff., W. H. Race, *TAPA* 111 (1981), 197 ff. (p. 205 deals with our instance).

60. τἀνδρί: for the zeugma (apparently misliked by those scribes who omitted τ' here) cf. in general Fehling, *Wiederholungsfiguren*, pp. 278 f.. S employs crasis of τῶι and ἄ only with this word: see 603, 748, 1175 below, *Aj.* 78; cf. Diggle, *ICS* 6 (1981), 85.

61 ff. Other Sophoclean scenes where 'an actor already present initiates dialogue after an announcement' are listed by D. J. Mastronarde, *Contact and Discontinuity: Some Conventions of Speech and Action on the Greek Tragic Stage* (Univ. Calif. Publications: Classical Studies, 21; Berkeley, Los Angeles, and London 1979), 20 n. 6 (cf. Taplin, *The Stagecraft of Aeschylus* (Oxford 1977), 397).

61. ὦ τέκνον, ὦ παῖ: *Phil.* 260, Eur. *Hec.* 172, *Tro.* 790 exhibit similar collocations. It and the use of ὦ rather than the unadorned voc. indicate emotion: see Moorhouse, p. 29; on the use of ἀγέννητοc here for ἀγεννήc (cf. ἀνάνδρωτοc for ἄνανδροc etc.) see Wilamowitz on Eur. *Her.* 290, Diggle on Eur. *Phaeth.* 263, Hopkinson on Callim. *h.* 6. 124.

62. μῦθοι καλῶc πίπτουcιν: for similar phrases see Johansen and Whittle on Aesch. *Suppl.* 91; the image derives from dicing (fr. 895 ἀεὶ γὰρ εὖ πίπτουcιν οἱ Διὸc κύβοι).

62–3. The same sentiment and antithesis occur in fr. 940 εἰ cῶμα δοῦλον, ἀλλ' ὁ νοῦc ἐλεύθεροc: see Pearson ad loc. and Kannicht on Eur. *Hel.* 726 ff. A slave makes a similar point in Menander fr. 722 Sandbach = *CGF* 297 Austin λαβέ με cύμβουλον πόνων. | μὴ καταφρονήcηιc οἰκέτου cυμβουλίαc . . . εἰ δ' ἡ τύχη τὸ cῶμα κατεδουλώcατο, | ὅ γε νοῦc ὑπάρχει τοῖc τρόποιc ἐλεύθεροc. On the pattern of generalization followed by specific instance (introduced by γάρ) see Johansen, *General Reflection in Tragic Rhesis*, p. 67 n. 47.

63. εἴρηκεν δ' ἐλεύθερον λόγον: a 'resultative perfect': see Aesch.

LINES 58-69

Suppl. 246 εἴρηκας ... λόγον, *PV* 821 εἰ δὲ πάντ' εἴρηκας, Johansen and Whittle on the first passage. ἐλεύθερον often features as a 'transferred epithet': see Pearson (last n.), Nisbet and Hubbard on Hor. *Odes* 1. 37. 1, etc.

64. δίδαξον ... διδακτά: for similar moves from verb to corresponding verbal adjective see Fehling, *Wiederholungsfiguren*, p. 268.

65-6. On this dramatically significant tendentious rephrasing of the Nurse's words at 56-7 'to create a sense of urgency' and to avoid an impression of Deianeira weakly parroting the Nurse's advice, see Easterling, *G&R* 24 (1977), 122-3. **cέ ... τὸ μὴ πυθέςθαι:** for the emphatic positioning of cέ cf. *Ant.* 710-11 ἀλλ' ἄνδρα, κεἴ τις ἦι ςοφός, τὸ μανθάνειν | πόλλ' αἰςχρὸν οὐδέν.

65. ἐξενωμένου: 'in exile' (see Barrett on Eur. *Hipp.* 1085).

66. ποῦ 'ςτιν: for the prodelision (or crasis if one writes ποὖςτιν) cf. Jebb on *Phil.* 16, Diggle, *STE*, p. 33. **φέρειν:** it is common in stichomythia for an infinitive to be syntactically dependent on a separate sentence (here 63 εἴρηκεν δ' ἐλεύθερον λόγον), and almost as common for uncomprehending scribes to alter to the third person the infinitive whose construction they do not understand: see Johansen and Whittle on Aesch. *Suppl.* 463 for examples of both tendencies.

68. The enclitic νιν does not usually follow a parenthetic vocative (as in **zt**). The oddity (in strictly realistic terms) that Hyllus has not previously revealed to Deianeira his knowledge of Heracles' whereabouts has several Sophoclean parallels (cf. Bain, *G&R* 26 (1979), 133 ff., on the most famous instance, from the *OT*). Perhaps it is mitigated by the extraordinary emphasis on the hearsay nature of the information Hyllus reveals (μύθοις (67), κλύεις (68), φαςί (70), κλύοι τις ἄν (71), ὡς ἐγὼ κλύω (72), ἀγγέλλεται (73), φαςίν (74)). This forestalls any premature easing of the tension about Heracles' whereabouts and safety, so that the atmosphere of uncertainty may continue through the parodos and be finally dispelled in the first episode. See Addenda.

69. For the year's enslavement to Omphale see on 252-3 below; for comparable cases of μέν *solitarium* 'where the speaker deliberately leaves the contrasting clauses to be mentally supplied' see Pearson, *CR* 38 (1924), 13. **ἐν μήκει χρόνου:** cf. Aesch. *Ag.* 610 ἐν μήκει χρόνου, *Suppl.* 57 λόγου ... ἐν μάκει, Plato *Leg.* 683 A ἐν χρόνου ... μήκεςιν.

COMMENTARY

70. Λυδῆι γυναικί: the dramatically irrelevant Omphale is mentioned as anonymously as Eurystheus (35) or Ceyx (40). For a brief summary of the sources and details of this legend see Kost on Musaeus' *Hero and Leander* 150–1; cf. H. Herter in *Victor Burr Festschrift*, pp. 38 ff. = *Kl. Schr.* 543 ff. **λάτριν:** see Wilamowitz on Eur. *Her.* 823.

71. A pungent irony, since D herself is shortly to achieve an even more remarkable feat, the killing (not merely the enslavement) of Heracles at a woman's hand. The theme of servitude to a female also prepares us for the role of Iole (cf. 489). K. Walter's τλαίη for κλύοι removes a thematically important reference to hearsay (see on 68) and inserts a mention of endurance that is irrelevant to D's character.

73. Cf. Aesch. *Ag.* 630–1 πότερα γὰρ αὐτοῦ ζῶντος ἢ τεθνηκότος | φάτις πρὸς ἄλλων ναυτικῶν ἐκλῄζετο;

74. For the equivalence of χώρα, χθών, *vel sim.* and πόλις see e.g. Eur. *Hcld.* 85 and Davies on Stes. fr. 263.

76–7. There is disagreement over the exact signification of the imperfect in passages such as this. Some suppose its implication to be that 'the consequence of the act persists, and so is durative' (Moorhouse, p. 192; so too, for instance, W. B. Sedgwick, *CQ* 34 (1940), 118: the tablets 'were left behind'). Others suggest that the imperfect can be used where the aorist would be expected (e.g. Wackernagel, *Vorles. über Syntax*² (Basel 1926–8), i. 182–3, Broadhead on Aesch. *Pers.* 478–9) purely for metrical convenience. Scholars often cite in favour of the latter interpretation *Il.* 2. 106–7 Ἀτρεὺς δὲ θνῄσκων ἔλιπεν πολύαρνι Θυέστηι· | αὐτὰρ ὁ αὖτε Θυέστ᾽ Ἀγαμέμνονι λεῖπε φορῆναι (of the family sceptre which Agamemnon still wields: but cf. H. Koller, *Mus. Helv.* 8 (1951), 92, against Wackernagel's approach to this passage). See further on 234–5 below.

77. χρείας: so O. Hense, *Studien zu Sophokles* (Leipzig 1880), 3–4. The paradosis is χώρας, changed to ὥρας by Dronke (*ap.* Bergk, *NJhb* 61 (1851), 245) to bring this reference into line with 44 ff. The flexibility of the oracle (cf. Tycho von Wilamowitz, pp. 119–20 n. 1, Appendix A below) renders this unnecessary; besides, ὥρα is not equivalent to καιρός (not even at Eur. *Bacch.* 723–4). Dobree (*Adversaria*, ed. Wagner, iv. 36), anticipating Dronke's desire for a consistent oracle ('in 77 exspectares πείρας, ὁδοῦ, ἀγῶνος ut 159, vel sim.'), and finding 79–80 intolerable even for Euripides, considered attributing 76–81 and 166–8 to an interpolator. Again the acceptance of a dramatically flexible oracle renders the first part of this expedient unnecessary. (The problem of 166–8 is more complex (see ad loc.).) If change is required, Hense's χρείας ('in the hour of need': cf. *Aj.* 740, *OT* 1442–3, etc.) supplies a favourite word of Sophocles.

78. τὰ ποῖα: for ποῖος with the article in questioning a statement thus cf. Bruhn, *Anhang*, § 84. For the line as a whole cf. Eur. *Phoen.* 707 τὰ ποῖα ταῦτα; τὸν λόγον γὰρ ἀγνοῶ.

79–80. ἢ ... ἤ: the disjunctives are idiomatic given the oracular context; cf. Hdt. 7. 220 = 100 PW ὑμῖν δ' ὦ Cπάρτης οἰκήτορες εὐρυχόροιο, | ἢ μέγα ἄςτυ ἐρικυδὲς ὑπ' ἀνδράςι Περςεΐδῃςι | πέρςεται, ἢ τὸ μὲν οὐχί, ἀφ' Ἡρακλέους δὲ γενέθλης | πενθήςει βαςιλῆ φθίμενον Λακεδαίμονος οὖρος and 166 below. On the dramatic effect of the change from the open 'either ... or' offered here to the closed inevitability of 'both ... and' in the oracle at 1164ff. see D. A. Hester, *Antichthon* 13 (1979) 12–13, and Appendix A below. οἱ (sc. Ἡρακλεῖ), recently readvocated by Kraus, *WS* 20 (1986), 90, would necessitate a harsh change of subject between μέλλει (understand χώρα from 77's χώρας) and ἄρας and ἔχειν, which patently refer to Heracles' activities.

80–1. For the emphatic redundancy expressive of duration cf. *Phil.* 1103ff. ὃς ἤ|δη μετ' οὐδενὸς ὕςτερον | ἀνδρῶν εἰςοπίςω τάλας | ... ὀλοῦμαι, Aesch. *Eum.* 763 τὸ λοιπὸν εἰς ἅπαντα πλειςτήρη χρόνον; cf. also τὸν ἀεὶ χρόνον ἤματα πάντα at *Iliup.* fr. dub. 5 Davies (oracular, like the Sophoclean instance here considered). The phrase εἰς τὸ ὕςτερον does not recur in S but we find ἐς ὕςτερον at *Ant.* 1194. Hermann's ὡς τὸν ὕςτατον, approved by Wilamowitz*, is therefore unnecessary. (The notion that the paradosis τὸν ὕςτερον can be justified as an elliptical form of εἰς τὸν ὕςτερον χρόνον (cf. Plato *Protag.* 353 D etc.) has long been exploded: *El.* 1075 and *OC* 1584, alleged instances of τὸν ἀεί (χρόνον), are both corrupt; *OC* 1701 is irrelevant.)

81. Cf. *OC* 1619 τὸ λοιπὸν ἤδη τὸν βίον διάξετον, and the phrase τὸ λοιπὸν ἤδη at 168, 921, below; cf. also Men. *Asp.* 6 ἤδη τὸ λοιπὸν καταβιώςεςθαί τινι, Plato *Apol.* 41 C ἤδη τὸν λοιπὸν χρόνον. **βίοτον εὐαίων':** cf. Eur. *Suppl.* 960 δυςαίων ... βίος and Collard ad loc.

82. For metaphorical ῥοπή see LSJ s.v. 2.

COMMENTARY

83. cεcώμεθa: the correct spelling; see Fraenkel on Aesch. *Ag.* 618, Sandbach on Men. *Sic.* 121.

84. Deleted by Bentley. Tragic interpolations often insinuate themselves by means of an initial ἤ: see the examples cited by Wilamowitz, *Analecta Euripidea* (Berlin 1875), 205 ff. (for the presumed motive behind the present instance see Page, *Actors' Interpolations in Greek Tragedy* (Oxford 1934), 90, 96). The intrusive line here interrupts the neat antithesis that will otherwise close this short speech in a very Sophoclean manner (cf. Reeve, *GRBS* 11 (1970), 289). R. Renehan's observation (*Greek Textual Criticism* (Harvard 1969), 33–4) that ἐξόλλυμι is met with several times in Euripides—it is totally in keeping with his fondness for compound verbs—never in S or Aeschylus, perhaps as not suiting their 'high tragic diction', clinches the case.

85. βίον cώcαντοc: for tragic equivalence of βίος and ψυχή see Johansen and Whittle on Aesch. *Suppl.* 937. **ᾗ οἰχόμεcθα:** for synizesis of ᾗ see Denniston on Eur. *El.* 1097 ff. It is common before οὐκ. Deletion of this line (proposed by Vauvilliers and also Wunder as an alternative to Bentley's damnation of 84) destroys the characteristically Sophoclean antithesis referred to above (on 84).

86. 'Wenn in einer Tragödie eine Person ἀλλ' εἶμι sagt, so verläßt sie nach wenigen Versen die Bühne' (Fraenkel, *Zu den Phoenissen des Euripides* (Sitzb. d. Bayer. Akad. d. Wiss., phil.-hist. Kl. 1; 1963), 29–30, citing examples). For an apparent exception that actually proves the rule see on 389 below. See further Diggle on Eur. *Phaeth.* 266.

87. βάξιν: for this word applied to oracles cf. *PV* 663. For its role as merely emphasizing the genitive upon which it depends see Long, *Language and Thought*, p. 103 n. 142. **κατῄδη:** on the spelling see Dover's note on Ar. *Nub.* 329, Alpers, *Das attizistische Lexikon des Oros* (Berlin 1981), 225–6. **παρῇ:** for the correctness of Dindorf's conjecture (*Ad Soph. Trag. Annotationes* (Oxford 1836), 239) see Barrett on Eur. *Hipp.* 700.

88 ff. ἀλλ'... νῦν δ': νῦν δ'... νῦν δ' codd., but the repetition of νῦν δ' over so short a space and with such different meanings ('as it was ... but now') has inspired disquiet over the text's integrity. For examples of such repetition see Jackson, *MS*, p. 243, D. Bain, *BICS* 24 (1977), 106–7, and (further bibliography) Sier on Aesch. *Cho.* 354 f. (p. 122 n. 12). Housman in his review of Pearson (*CR* 39 (1925),

LINES 83-91

78 = *Classical Papers*, iii. 1096 and n. 1) quoted *Aj.* 852–3[5] ἀλλ' οὐδὲν ἔργον ταῦτα θρηνεῖςθαι μάτην· | ἀλλ' ἀρκτέον τὸ πρᾶγμα cὺν τάχει τινί. See also 1075–6 below νῦν δ' ἐκ τοιούτου θῆλυς ηὕρημαι τάλας. | καὶ νῦν προςελθὼν ςτῆθι πληςίον πατρός, *El.* 1334–5. But the scribal eye might easily have allowed its copying of -δ'ὁ ξυν(ήθης) at 88 to be influenced by νῦν δ' ὡς ξυν(ίημ') in the next line but one (for this sort of error by anticipation cf. Jackson, *MS*, p. 224, Diggle, *PCPS* 18 (1972), 38, Sier on Aesch. *Cho.* p. 42, S. L. Radt, *The Importance of the Context* (Amsterdam 1988), 5 ff.). 'We must therefore transpose, excise or emend 88–9', to quote Stinton, p. 125, who considers each approach and concludes with a preference for Campbell's combination of two earlier emendations: πρὶν δ' (Wakefield) ὁ ξυνήθης πότμος οὐκ εἴα (Vauvilliers) κτλ. Brunck's ἀλλ' (preferred by the OCT) may seem to eliminate one repetition at the expense of another, but for ἀλλ' εἶμι in 86 as a set phrase see ad loc. (Stinton says nothing of Dindorf's proposal to delete 90–1 (*Ad Soph. Trag. Annot.*, p. 239—as opposed to Hermann's deletion of 88–9), approved by Dawe. Such a deletion makes Hyllus' parting words excessively sanguine for the dramatic context (one of doubt and foreboding).) An apt argument against the deletion of 88–9 (Hermann, Dindorf *olim*) is that (as Korzeniewski, *Rh. Mus.* 105 (1962), 149 n. 29, and Stinton, p. 125, observe) the two lines are echoed in the parodos (119 ff.).

88. ξυνήθης πότμος: cf. Dawe on *OT* 1082–3.

89. The prefix in προταρβεῖν should be mentally extended to δειμαίνειν: for a bibliography of studies of 'the habit of following a compound verb with a simple verb in which the force of the compound is maintained' see Diggle, *GRBS* 14 (1973), 265 n. 64, and *STE*, p. 18;[6] cf. Moorhouse, p. 95.

90–1. τὸ μὴ ... πυθέσθαι: as Page observes on Aesch. *Ag.* 1169 ff., 'Moorhouse, [*CQ* 34 (1940), 70 ff.] shows that all four dramatists have *unemendable* examples of μή for μὴ οὐ; there is therefore no linguistic necessity to insert the οὐ in emendable examples, though ... such insertion *might* be right', especially when the manuscripts vary (see Barrett on Eur. *Hipp.* 658). Cf. 226, 742 below.

[5] Lines not affected by the probability (on which see West, *BICS* 25 (1978), 113 ff.) that the following lines (854–8) are interpolated.

[6] Add G. Dunkel, *Zeitschr. für vergl. Sprachforsch.* 92 (1978), 14 ff. (Indo-European precedents).

COMMENTARY

93. ἐπεὶ πυθοίτο: for the omission of τιc here see Fraenkel on Aesch. *Ag.* 71. **κέρδος ἐμπολᾶι:** cf. *Phil.* 303 ἐξεμπολήcει κέρδοc, *Ant.* 1037 κερδαίνετ' ἐμπολᾶτε τἀπὸ Cάρδεων | ἤλεκτρον.

It is not perfectly clear whether D exits with Hyllus and the Nurse. For tragedies where a character stays on stage while the chorus sing see Griffith, *Authenticity of PV*, p. 124; Taplin, *Stagecraft*, pp. 248, 263, like Griffith, thinks we have a further example here: see also on 141 below.

PARODOS (94–140)

94–102 = 103–11 *first strophe and antistrophe*

94/103	∪ −∪− −∪∪−∪∪−	∪ e D (ia. hem.)
95/104	− −∪− − −∪∪−∪∪⌣ ᴴ ‖	− e − D
96/105	−∪∪−∪∪− −	D −
97/106	−∪− − −∪− −	e − e −
98/107	−∪∪−∪∪−	D
99/108	− −∪− − −∪∪−∪∪− ᴴ ‖	− e − D
100/109	− −∪− − −∪−	− e − e
101/110	− −∪− − −∪−	− e − e
102/111	− −∪− − −∪−⌣ ‖	− e − e −

For other purely dactylo-epitrite strophes in tragedy ('not particularly common') see Griffith, *Authenticity of PV*, p. 41. On the division in 94 ~ 103 cf. West, *GM*, p. 134 n. 144.

112–21 = 112–31 *second strophe and antistrophe*

112/122	−∪∪−∪∪− ⌣	D ⌣
113/123	−∪∪−∪∪− −	D −
114/124	−∪∪−∪∪− −	D −
115/125	−∪∪−∪∪−ᴴ ‖	D
116/126	−−∪−−∪∪−	chor. dim. B
117/127	∪−∪−−∪∪−	chor. dim. B
118/128	∪⌢∪−−∪∪−	chor. dim. B
119/129	−∪∪−∪−∪−	chor. dim. A
120/130	−∪∪−∪−∪−	chor. dim. A
121/131	−∪∪−∪−− ‖|	chor. dim. A cat. (aristoph.)

76

LINE 93

For this less strictly dactylo-epitrite strophe cf. Griffith *Authenticity of PV*, p. 45 (ibid. 265 for parallels to the rare contraction (– ⏑ ⏑ – ⏑ ⏑) at 114; ibid. 307 n. 106 for the comparative rarity of 116 ff.'s aeolics in *Tr.*, *OT*, and *El.*, their comparative frequency in *Ant.*, *Phil.*, and *OC*). On the responsion 112 ~ 122 cf. West, *GM*, p. 135.

132–40 *epode*

(1)	⏑ – ⏑ – – ⏑ –	ia. dim. sync. (ia. cr.)
(2)	– ⏑ – ⏑ – ⏑ –	lec. (cr. ia.)
(3)	⏑ – ⏑ – ⏑ – ⏑ –	ia. dim.
(4)	⏑ – ⏑ – ⏑ – ⏑ –	ia. dim.
(5)	– – ⏑ – ⏑ – – ᴴ ‖	ia. dim. cat.
(6)	⏑ – ⏑ – ⏑ – ⏑ – ⏑ – ⏑ –	ia. trim.
(7)	⏑ – ⏑ – – ⏑ – ⏑ – ⌣ ‖	ia. trim. sync. cat.
(8)	⏑ – – – ⏑ – ⏑ – ⌣ ‖	ia. trim. sync. cat.

For this epode I have numbered the lines internally to the stanza (i.e. from 1 to 8) to avoid confusion: the OCT's continuous numeration (like that in all modern texts of the play) is at odds with the actual number of lines because it derives from a time when the colometry was different (cf. Barrett, ed. Eur. *Hipp.*, p. 94).

The ode opens with an appeal to the all-seeing sun: for other tragic choruses that take the form of prayers to deities see Kranz, *Stasimon*, pp. 187–8. Several features of the parodos can be paralleled from other passages of poetry that draw upon motifs and formulae employed in hymnic contexts. On the style of the ode see in particular D. Korzeniewski, 'Zum Verhältnis von Wort und Metrum in sophokleischen Chorliedern', *Rh. Mus.* 105 (1962), 148 ff. ≙ *Griechische Metrik*, pp. 166–7, who draws upon the important collection of hymnal features in Norden's famous *Agnostos Theos*. He also usefully collects (p. 149 n. 29) the various correspondences between prologue and parodos of this play. Diggle on Eur. *Phaeth.* 63 remarks of that play's parodos: 'Several other tragedies begin in darkness. There is usually an early reference to (often apostrophe of) the arriving dawn or sun or the departing night'. The present instance is similar enough to Diggle's examples to be added to them (cf. Zieliński, p. 523 n. 7 = p. 307 n. 2).

COMMENTARY

94 ff. ὅν ... Ἅλιον αἰτῶ: what Norden (*Agnostos Theos*, pp. 168 ff.) calls 'der Relativstil der Prädikation' is, of course, very common in appeals to a god; but the relative usually follows the god's name, and that is usually in the vocative: so e.g. Soph. *Ant.* 781–2 *Ἔρως ἀνίκατε μάχαν, Ἔρως, ὃς κτλ.*, Eur. *Hipp.* 525–6 *Ἔρως, Ἔρως, ὁ κατ' ὀμμάτων cτάζεις πόθον*, and numerous other examples in Norden, loc. cit. Especially relevant is *Il.* 3. 277 *ἠέλιος θ' ὃς πάντ' ἐφορᾷς καὶ πάντ' ἐπακούεις*; see further Nisbet–Hubbard, on Hor. *Odes 1*, pp. 32–3, 127, 150. In the present instance the relative comes first and there is hyperbaton. Compare Aesch. *Cho.* 799 *οἵ τ' ἔςωθε δωμάτων | πλουτογαθῆ μυχὸν ἐνίζετε | ... cύμφρονες θεοί*, Anacreon 357. 1 ff. Ρ *ὦναξ, ὦι ... cυμπαίζουςιν*. For other poetic invocations to a god where the name comes after some or all of his attributes see T. E. V. Pearce, *CQ* 18 (1968), 339–40. See Addenda.

94–5. ὅν ... νύξ ... τίκτει: the very kernel of this elaborate structure is reminiscent of the hymnic allusions to a god's parentage in *HH Herm.* 1 ff. *Ἑρμῆν ὕμνει, Μοῦσα, ... ὃν τέκε Μαῖα*, Alcaeus fr. 308 LP *χαῖρε, Κυλλάνας ὁ μέδεις, ςὲ γάρ μοι | θῦμος ὕμνην, τὸν κορύφαιςιν †αὐγαῖς† | Μαῖα γέννατο Κρονίδᾳ κτλ.*, H. Orph. 30. 6 *Διὸς καὶ Φερςεφονείης ἀρρήτοις λέκτροιςι τεκνωθείς*, etc. But it would be misleading to compare such simple, almost naïve devices with the complex and sophisticated adaptation we find in the present parodos. The main differences are: (1) the sun's birth from night is metaphorical and recurs perpetually (for the underlying idea see Fraenkel on Aesch. *Ag.* 279 *τῆς νῦν τεκούςης φῶς τόδ' εὐφρόνης*); (2) the inner core here is elaborated almost out of recognition by the addition of adjectives (epithet and participles) and the carefully balanced chiasmus of participles and verbs in *ἐναριζομένα τίκτει κατευνάζει τε φλογιζόμενον*; (3) the assonance of *-ιζομένα ... -ιζόμενον* further elaborates and dignifies the style.

94. αἰόλα: 'Star-spangled' (Jebb's rendering, followed by LSJ): cf. Critias, *TrGF* i (43) fr. 4. 4–5 Sn. *νὺξ αἰολόχρως ἄκριτός τ' ἄστρων | ὄχλος* (= Eur. fr. 593. 4), H. Orph. 78. 4 (as corrected by Maas, *Rh. Mus.* 97 (1954), 378 = *Kl. Schr.* 109–10), *PV* 24 *ποικιλείμων νύξ*, Ar. *Thesm.* 1067–8 *ἀςτεροειδέα νῶτα ... | αἰθέρος ἱεράς*; for the idea of the sun rising from and sinking into the night see Johansen and Whittle on Aesch. *Suppl.* 769. **ἐναριζομένα:** an epic word rarely found in tragedy: see Sideras, *Aeschylus Homericus*, p. 85. In the present passage it probably signifies 'stripped of her armour', a metaphorical allusion to the night's being robbed of her light by the sun: cf. N. J. Richardson, *PCPS* 21 (1975), 69.

95. κατευνάζει: the simplex is used by S (in a similarly metaphorical sense) at 1005 below. For the hymnic ἀναδίπλωcιc see the repetition of Eros' name in *Ant*. 781–2, and by Eur. at *Hipp*. 525–6 (see 94 ff. n.). Cf. in general Norden, *Agnostos Theos*, p. 169 n. 1, his note on Verg. *Aen*. 6. 46, and his *Aus altrömischen Priesterbüchern* (Lund 1939), 233 n. 2; also Fehling, *Wiederholungsfiguren*, p. 169. The accusative here is followed by the vocative at 99 (ὤ ... φλεγέθων); cf. *OT* 158 πρῶτα cὲ κεκλόμενος, θύγατερ Διός, ἄμβροτ' Ἀθάνα.

96. αἰτῶ: the first-person verb is idiomatic in such requests for a particular service from the god invoked. Cf. Sappho 1. 2 LP παῖ Δίος δολόπλοκε, λίccoμαί cε, Anacr. 348. 1 and 357. 6 P γουνοῦμαι c(ε) and in general Fraenkel, *Philol*. 86 (1931), 4–5 = *Kl. Beitr*. i. 356–7 and Nisbet–Hubbard on Hor. *Odes* 1. 32. 1.

97–8. τοῦτο, καρῦξαι ... πόθι: 'I ask you this, to proclaim' or 'I ask you to tell me this, where ...' For the underlying picture cf. Aesch. *Ag*. 632–4, where the herald claims that only the sun is capable of stating whether Menelaus (like Heracles here) is alive or dead: οὐκ οἶδεν οὐδεὶς ὥcτ' ἀπαγγεῖλαι τορῶc | πλὴν τοῦ τρέφοντοc Ἡλίου χθονὸc φύcιν. Note also *HH Dem*. 69 ff. cὺ γὰρ δὴ πᾶcαν ἐπὶ χθόνα καὶ κατὰ πόντον | αἰθέρος ἐκ δίηc καταδέρκεαι ἀκτίνεccι, | νημερτέωc μοι ἔνιcπε φίλον τέκοc εἴ που ὄπωπαc, *Aj*. 845 ff. cὺ δ' ὦ τὸν αἰπὺν οὐρανὸν διφρηλατῶν | Ἥλιε, πατρῴαν τὴν ἐμὴν ὅταν χθόνα | ἴδηιc, ἐπιcχὼν χρυcόνωτον ἡνίαν | ἄγγειλον ἄταc τὰc ἐμὰc μόρον τ' ἐμὸν | γέροντι πατρὶ τῆι τε δυcτήνωι τροφῶι, and K. J. Dover, *ΗΛΙΟΣ ΚΗΡΥΞ*, in *Miscellanea Tragica* (Kamerbeek Festschrift), 49 ff. = *Greek and the Greeks*, pp. 186 ff. Dover argues for the meaning 'make a proclamation, asking where', which has convinced the editors of the OCT (cf. *Sophoclea*, p. 152), but the verb with this nuance means 'proclaim as a criminal' (or conqueror): cf. LSJ s.v. II.2, Gow–Page on Meleager *AP* 5. 177.1 = *HE* 4190, and the picture of Heracles as missing child is absurdly at odds with the grandiloquent apostrophe to the sun. We want the signification 'declare, tell' (LSJ s.v. III.2), as in the passage cited above from *Agamemnon*; cf. 45 above, ἀκήρυκτος μένει, and in general Stinton, *CQ* 36 (1986), 337 ff. **τὸν ... Ἀλκμήνας:** the circumstances of

COMMENTARY

Heracles' conception make this an expedient sobriquet: for comparable epic references to Heracles via his mother see West on Hes. *Th.* 526. -μηνα(-) is the form of the name found in the lyric portions of tragedy: see 644 below and Braswell on Pind. *Pyth.* 4. 172 (a). Either παῖc or the second μοι is metrically superfluous (see on 107 below). καρῦξαι τὸν Ἀλκμήναc πόθι μοι πόθι παῖc ναίει ποτ' would be an example of 'the trajection of the antecedent noun to the subordinate clause while the attribute remains in the main clause' illustrated by Diggle on Eur. *Phaeth.* 62 (cf. Stinton, p. 127; *Sophoclea*, p. 152); alternatively, for the frequency with which pronouns like μοι are erroneously repeated cf. Stinton, loc. cit. Schneidewin's deletion of μοι and further emendation of ΠΑΙC to ΓΑC (approved by Dawe) presuppose a more complex series of corruptions, but that is no decisive argument against it: πόθι γᾶc might be taken as an echo of ποῦ ... χθονόc (68). I prefer this approach.

99–100. ναίει ... Ποντιάc αὐλῶναc: for this verb used of the sea and water cf. Bowra, *CQ* 6 (1956), 5 = *On Greek Margins*, p. 79.

99. ὦ ... φλεγέθων: what Norden (*Agnostos Theos*, pp. 166 ff.) calls 'der Partizipialstil der Prädikation': cf. Pind. *Ol.* 2. 13 ὦ Κρόνιε παῖ Ῥέαc, ἕδοc Ὀλύμπου νέμων, *OT* 902–3 ὦ κρατύνων ... Ζεῦ, πάντ' ἀνάccων, and Norden's other examples. **λαμπρᾶι cτεροπᾶι:** cf. LSJ s.v. cτεροπή 2, 'generally of dazzling light, gleam, χαλκοῦ cτεροπή *Il.* 11. 83. *Od.* 4. 72 ... of the sun' (as here). Aesch. *Ag.* 676–7 εἰ δ' οὖν τιc ἀκτὶc ἡλίου νιν ἱcτορεῖ κτλ., Eur. *Hcld.* 748 ff. Γᾶ καὶ παννύχιοc cελάνα καὶ λαμπρόταται θεοῦ | φαεcιμβρότου (Musgrave: -οι) αὐγαί, | ἀγγελίαν μοι ἐνέγκαι· | ἰαχήcατε δ' οὐρανῶι.

100. A very difficult problem. Lloyd-Jones's interpretation (*CQ* 4 (1954), 91) has not convinced everyone (cf. id., *CR* 31 (1981), 171), but I still find it the most plausible advanced: Ποντίαc αὐλῶναc are to be identified with the straits of the Black Sea in the east, and 101 διccαῖcιν ἀπείροιc κλιθείc pictures Heracles 'leaning against the two continents', the Pillars of Hercules in the far west. In a stanza that opens with an extravagant address to the very sun, we should not be too concerned with the realism or propriety behind the picture. Cf. the fantasy element in the account of the ravening Argive host in the *Antigone*'s parodos. Of other recent attempts to explain this passage, West's idea that the hero is conceived as resting or feasting between

LINES 98-102

labours (*BICS* 26 (1979), 110) and Dawe's emendation διccὰc ἀν' ἀπείρουc cυθείc (*Studies* iii. 79–80) are both well disposed of by Stinton, *CQ* 36 (1986), 340. His defence here of his own conjecture διccαῖc ἐν ἀπείροιc κρυφείc (originally advanced in *JHS* 96 (1976), 129) is less convincing, as is his further criticism (pp. 340–1) of Lloyd-Jones. An east–west disjunction would suit not only the labours of Heracles but also the daily path of the sun (for comparable references to eastern and western limits see Barrett on Eur. *Hipp.* 3 ff.).

102. This line constitutes an intensifying repetition of the initial appeal to the sun at the start of the strophe; the device is characteristically Sophoclean: see Kranz, *Stasimon*, pp. 179–80. **εἴπ':** the imperative is yet another regular feature of this type of prayer, especially in the train of a verb of beseeching (here αἰτῶ). Cf. Sappho 1. 5 LP (λίccομαί cε) ... τυίδ' ἐλθ', and any number of appeals to the Muse(s): μῆνιν ἄειδε, ἄνδρα μοι ἔννεπε, etc. See in general Nisbet–Hubbard on Hor. *Odes* 1. 32. 1. **ὦ κρατιcτεύων κατ' ὄμμα:** at first this looks like a mere restatement of 'der Partizipialstil der Prädikation' exemplified in line 99's ὦ ... φλεγέθων. But Jebb well brings out the point behind the present phrase with his rendering 'thou who seest as none else can', and Korzeniewski's article (p. 150) rightly identifies this as an example of what Norden (*Agnostos Theos*, p. 221) calls 'dynamische Prädikationsart', whereby the appeal to the god is justified by some such appended explanation as δύναcαι δέ or *namque potes* (see further West on Hes. *Th.* 420). So here: 'I call upon you, for (you can tell me Heracles' whereabouts, since) your sight is the best.' Cf. *Il.* 3. 277 ἠέλιός θ' ὃc πάντ' ἐφορᾶιc, *Od.* 11. 109 ἠελίου, ὃc πάντ' ἐφορᾶι. **κατ' ὄμμα:** '(pre-eminent) in power of sight' (to be added to the examples of 'κατά + ACC. used in a variety of locative senses' given by Moorhouse, pp. 115–16). Contrast *Ant.* 760, where κατ' ὄμματ' = 'before the eyes of'. For the sun as the eye of the day *vel sim.* (an ancient and widespread notion) see e.g. Cook, *Zeus*, i. 196–7, O. Weinreich, *Hess. Blätt. für Volkskunde*, 8 (1909), 169 n. 1 = *Ausg. Schr.* i. 7 n. 1, L. Malten, *Die Sprache des menschlichen Antlitzes im frühen Griechentum* (Berlin 1961), 39 ff., A. Dihle in *Platonismus und Christentum* (H. Dörrie Festschrift; Münster 1983), 88. For the common picture of the deity who sees all things on earth cf. R. Pettazzoni, *The All-knowing God*, (trans. H. J. Rose 1956), *passim*; cf. J. Griffin, *CQ* 28 (1978), 1 ff. ≃ *Homer on Life and Death* (Oxford 1980), 179 ff. For its

COMMENTARY

application to the sun see *Il.* 3. 277 (cited above on 94 ff.), *Od.* 8. 270–1, *HH Dem.* 69 ff., and Dover (cited above on 97–8), 49 = *Greek and the Greeks*, p. 186.

103. ποθουμέναι ... φρενί: for S's use of the middle where one would expect the active see Pearson on fr. 858. 2. For the continuation of the thought from one stanza to another via the particle γάρ see Kranz, *Stasimon*, pp. 180–1.

103 ff. For πυνθάνομαι + acc. + inf. cf. Aesch. *Cho.* 839–40 νέαν φάτιν δὲ πεύθομαι λέγειν τινὰς | ξένους μολόντας οὐδαμῶς ἐφίμερον. Tragic choruses often thus motivate their entry by claiming to have heard of the suffering of a main character: *Aj.* 141 ff., Eur. *Hipp.* 130–1, etc. (cf. Leo, *Der Monolog*, p. 10, observing that S's choruses never do this in the obvious way, at the *start* of the parodos).

104. ἀμφινεικῆ: 'Disputed by two lovers' (i.e. Achelous and Heracles). Paley's rendering is supported by 527 below, and defended against Jebb's scepticism by Fraenkel on Aesch. *Ag.* 686, where we find the similar phrase τὰν ἀμφινεικῆ Ἑλέναν. **ἀεί:** for this word's tendency in S 'to forsake (positionally) verbs and cling to nominal elements' see J. H. Kells, *CR* 11 (1961), 189 n. 1. The verb here is τρύχεσθαι in remote line 110.

105. οἷά τιν' ἄθλιον ὄρνιν: the epithet suggests that this bird is the nightingale (so e.g. Radermacher ad loc., R. Oehler, *Mythologische Exempla in der älteren gr. Dichtung* (Aarhaus 1925), 92), the image of sorrowful lament (cf. Kannicht on Eur. *Hel.* 1107 ff.). Cf. 963 below. For the τις idiomatic in such similes see Vahlen, *Opusc. Acad.* ii. 181–2.

106–7. ἀδάκρυτον: for the proleptic adjective cf. Aesch. *Ag.* 1247 εὔφημον, ὦ τάλαινα, κοίμησον στόμα, *Ant.* 1186–7 κλῇθρ' ἀνασπαστοῦ πύλης | χαλῶσα, 881–2 τὸν δ' ἐμὸν πότμον ἀδάκρυτον | οὐδεὶς φίλων στενάζει; cf. *OC* 1200 τῶν σῶν ἀδέρκτων ὀμμάτων and Braswell on Pind. *Pyth.* 4. 276 (c). Dawe's reinterpretation of the paradosis' ἀδακρύτων (*Studies* iii. 80) is adopted by the OCT, disputed by Braswell as cited.

107. For the connection between πόθος and eyes see Barrett on Eur. *Hipp.* 525–6, West on Hes. *Th.* 910. In spite of Korzeniewski (p. 152 n. 43 ≏ p. 168 n. 64), O. Schröder's ἀλλ⟨ά⟩ is impossible given the period-end: see Stinton, pp. 125 ff.

108. ἀνδρὸς ... ὁδοῦ: for the two genitives here cf. πατρὸς | ... τοῦ καλῶς πράσσειν δοκεῖν at 56–7 above and Bond on Eur. *Her.*

LINES 102-112

162 for the general principle of two genitives in an appositional phrase. Long, *Language and Thought*, pp. 92–3 and n. 105, argues that the resultant hyperbaton favours taking εὔμναϲτον with δεῖμα rather than as an epithet transferred to ἀνδρόϲ. **δεῖμα τρέφουϲαν:** Casaubon's correction is confirmed by ἐκ φόβου φόβον τρέφω·at 28 above. On S's fondness for unusual metaphorical uses of τρέφω cf. C. Moussy, *Recherches sur τρέφω et les verbes grecs signifiant 'nourrir'* (Paris 1969), 70 ff.

109–10. εὐναῖϲ ... τρύχεϲθαι: cf. Herodas 1. 22 τρύχουϲα κοίτην and Wilamowitz on Eur. *Her.* 722, Harder on Eur. *Archel.* fr. 20. 2 for the various meanings of ἐνθύμιοϲ. **ἀνανδρώτοιϲι:** a typical Sophoclean doublet for ἀνάνδροιϲι: see Kaibel on *El.* 1063 and cf. 61 n.

110–11. κακὰν | δύϲτανον ... αἶϲαν: cf. Eur. *Hipp.* 162–3 κακὰ δύϲτανοϲ ἀμηχανία (unless, *pace* Barrett on that passage, in the present place δύϲτανοϲ be referred to Deianeira).

112 ff. On this and S's two other storm similes (*Ant.* 582 ff., *OC* 1240 ff.) see W. Elliger, *Die Darstellung der Landschaft in der gr. Dichtung* (Berlin 1975), 241–2. For 'elaborate Homeric similes' as 'usually confined to the lyrical passages of tragedy' see O. Smith, *Class. et Med.* 26 (1965), 55 n. 133; on the grammatical structure cf. C. J. Ruijgh, *Autour de τε épique* (Amsterdam 1971), 994, who notes the oddity of the use of potential optative dependent on ὥϲτε and equivalent to the gnomic aorist ἀνήρ εἶδεν or to ἀνὴρ ἰδεῖν δύναται, conveying a repeated and permanent situation.[7] Also strange is the position of ἄν outside its usual location (cf. Stinton, *JHS* 97 (1977), 128 n. 11, 135 nn. 34, 36; on Aesch. *Ag.* 933 see Fraenkel on 931 ff.; on Aesch. *Suppl.* 447 Johansen and Whittle ad loc.) as second or third in sentence or colon, or next to the verb. Perhaps (as Stinton suggests, followed by Burton, p. 46 n. 15) the hyperbaton πολλὰ ... κύματ(α) leads to the phrase itself and everything it encloses being treated as one word. **ἄν:** not ἐν: except in the case of questions (Moorhouse, p. 229) optative without ἄν in tragedy must stress the idea of possibility (Garvie on Aesch. *Cho.* 591–3); alleged exceptions are easily emended (see KG ii/1. 226) and the locative dative is sufficient without preposition (compare Latin phrases like *mari magno*: cf. Jocelyn on Ennius fr. XVII. 43–4). The pure optative can hardly be defended as an epicism (cf. Wackernagel,

[7] At *Od.* 9. 384 ὡϲ ὅτε τιϲ τρυπῶι δόρυ νήϊον ἀνήρ there may be a sort of parallel if we do really have ὡϲ + opt. (Wilamowitz*).

COMMENTARY

Vorles. über Syntax, i. 236), and Erfurdt's ἴδηι for ἴδοι provides an epic subjunctive of comparison equally without parallel in Attic.

116. οὕτω δέ: correlative with ὥϲτε in line 112; the δέ is apodotic (cf. Denniston, *GP*², pp. 179–80, examples of 'comparative parataxis'). **Καδμογενῆ:** 'Theban' rather than 'descendant of Cadmus': cf. patronymics like Ἐρεχθεῖδαι, Πριαμίδαι, and see in general C. Macleod, *Maia* 25 (1973), 268 n. 5 ≈ *JHS* 102 (1982), 125 = *Collected Essays*, p. 21 n. 6.

117. τρέφει, τὸ δ' αὔξει: the paradosis is retained by the OCT editors (cf. *Sophoclea*, p. 154), but for a recent approval of Reiske's simple change to ϲτρέφει see A. S. McDevitt, *Eranos* 81 (1983), 7 ff. τὸ μέν must be understood before the verb by a common ellipse (see Denniston, *GP*², p. 166, Stinton, p. 126).

118. Cf. Aesch. *ScT* 758 κακῶν δ' ὥϲπερ θάλαϲϲα κῦμ' ἄγει and (for ὥϲπερ introducing a metaphor) Solon fr. 37. 9 W ἐγὼ δὲ τούτων ὥϲπερ ἐν μεταιχμίωι | ὅροc κατέϲτην.

119 ff. ἀλλά ... ἐρύκει: the difficulty of ἀλλά (noted, for instance, by Stinton, p. 130 n. 41: what is the point of *contrast* between these lines and the preceding simile?) may be mitigated if we accept Triclinius' optative ἐρύκοι at the end of the strophe, as recommended by J. T. Hooker, *Eranos* 75 (1977), 71–2; see Bühler on Moschus' *Europa* 27 for this type of ἀλλά 'als Einleitung eines Wunsches am Ende einer Rede', and cf. W. H. Race, *GRBS* 23 (1982), 11.

120. ἀναμπλάκητον: ἀπλάκητον Hesychius (i. 211 Latte) in alluding to this line. Parallels for the corruption of αμπλ to απλ are given by Johansen and Whittle on Aesch. *Suppl.* 230.

122. ὧν ἐπιμεμφομένας: for the technique of beginning a new stanza with a relative that refers back to an antecedent in the preceding stanza see 647 below, and in general Johansen and Whittle on Aesch. *Suppl.* 49. What is referred back to in the present case is Heracles' troubles and D's distress thereat. The relative is in the genitive because governed by ἀντία δ' οἴϲω, which is treated as equivalent in this respect to ἀντιάομαι (see next n.). L's ἐπιμεμφομένας is a preferable interpretation to ἐπιμεμφομένα ϲ' (the verb usually takes the dative of the person blamed). See Addenda.

122–3. For a full discussion of the meanings of the manuscripts' ἀδεία and Musgrave's αἰδοῖα see Stinton, pp. 131–2, who concludes that we should preserve the former but make it dependent upon ἐρῶ in ellipse

LINES 112-127

(rather than upon an understood εἰμί, as the majority of scholars had hitherto interpreted the paradosis). The sense thus produced ('I shall oppose you, though in a manner agreeable to you') seems to him the only one which ἡδύc could bear in this context. The rare ellipse of ἐρῶ (rather than the familiar one of the copula) is perhaps justifiable by supposing we need to supply a verb of speaking *ex opposito* to ἀντία δ' οἴcω (cf. on 168 below).

124 ff. The consolatory section of this ode is marked off by ring-composition: the opening phrases are echoed at 136–7. The *consolatio* which Achilles offers to Priam in *Il.* 24 is similarly enclosed in a ring: οὐ γάρ τιc πρῆξιc πέλεται κρυεροῖο γόοιο (524) ~ οὐ γάρ τι πρήξειc ἀκαχήμενοc υἷοc ἑῆοc (550).

125 ff. The contrast here expressed between mortals and gods, the latter of whom are powerful and free from care, and deliberately inflict woes upon the former, is common in the context of a *consolatio*: cf. *Il.* 24. 525–6 ὡc γὰρ ἐπεκλώcαντο θεοὶ δειλοῖcι βροτοῖcι, | ζώειν ἀχνυμένοιc· αὐτοὶ δέ τ' ἀκηδέεc εἰcί with Macleod ad loc., and R. Kassel, *Untersuchungen zur gr. und röm. Konsolationsliteratur* (Zetemata 18; 1958), 54–5.

126 ff. οὐδ' ... **ἐπέβαλε θνατοῖc:** 'not . . . (to other mortals than you) either' (cf. Denniston, *GP*[2], p. 195, and Stinton, *CQ* 29 (1979), 260 n. 32). Cf. 280 below; underlying this expression is the common consolatory idea 'you are not the only one to suffer thus': cf. Kassel, op. cit. (last n.), p. 80, Harder on Eur. *Cresphont.* fr. 72. 1. For the verb cf. Eur. *Med.* 1115 (λύπην) ... θνητοῖcι θεοὺc ἐπιβάλλειν.

127. The reference to Zeus' power is idiomatic in the consolatory context: cf. *Od.* 4. 236–7 θεὸc ἄλλοτε ἄλλωι | Ζεὺc ἀγαθόν τε κακόν τε διδοῖ· δύναται γὰρ ἅπαντα, 6. 188–9 Ζεὺc δ' αὐτὸc νέμει ὄλβον Ὀλύμπιοc ἀνθρώποιcιν, | ἐcθλοῖc' ἠδὲ κακοῖcιν, ὅπωc ἐθέληιcιν, ἑκάcτωι, Soph. *El.* 173 ff. θάρcει μοι, θάρcει, | τέκνον· ἔτι μέγαc οὐρανῶι | Ζεύc, ὃc ἐφορᾶι πάντα καὶ κρατύνει, fr. 684. 4–5 καὶ τόνδ' (sc. Ἔρωτα) ἀπείργειν οὐδ' ὁ παγκρατὴc cθένει | Ζεύc. Cornutus, *Theol. Graec. Compend.*, pp. 7–8 Lang, derives the name Κρόνοc ἀπὸ τοῦ κραίνειν, and several modern scholars (see Pohlenz, *NeueJhb.* 1 (1916), 557 n. 2) detect an etymological play here too. For comparable Sophoclean word-play see L. P. Rank, *Etymologiseering en verwante verschijnselen bij Homerus* (Assen 1951), 24 n. 82.

COMMENTARY

127–8. βαcιλεύc ... Κρονίδαc: cf. Alcaeus' Κρονίδαιc βαcιλεύc (frr. 38 A, 9, 296 A. 3, 387 LP), and for βαcιλεύc applied to Zeus see Davies on *Thebais* fr. 3. 4 (*The Theban Epics* (Göttingen 1991)). The epic Κρονίδηc is very rare in tragedy (only here in S): see Roux on Eur. *Bacch*. 95.

129 ff. For a collection of passages that refer to the common concept of a cycle in human affairs see Kassel, *ZPE* 36 (1979), 15 ff. (add the present instance); cf. Renehan, *CP* 80 (1985), 147. This is another characteristic of consolations: see Kassel, *Konsolationsliteratur*, pp. 66, 74, 93–4; on the coupling of πῆμα and χαρά cf. Eur. *Tro*. 542 ἐπὶ δὲ πόνωι καὶ χαρᾶι, [Eur.] fr. 174. 2 N² πολλάκι τὸ λυποῦν ὕcτερον χαρὰν ἄγει. On the verb's derivation (whether from κυκλέω or κυκλόω) see Kassel's article, pp. 18–19. With πῆμα and χαρά nominative we have an example of intransitive or absolute (sc. πόδα) verb not paralleled until Plutarch (*Mor*. 160 F δελφῖνεc ... κυκλοῦντεc); for S's use of normally transitive verbs in an intransitive sense see Campbell, *Essay on the Language of S*., p. 88: but the present verb's denominative status (i.e. its derivation from κύκλοc) may render it a special case. With K's χαράν (conjectured by Hermann, approved by Nauck), adopted by the editors of the OCT, we will have κέλευθοι as subject of transitive κυκλοῦν (so e.g. Campbell, *Paralipomena*, p. 160) and a fusing of *illustrans* and *illustrandum* ('the image blends with the thing signified and simile is passing into metaphor', as Campbell expresses it) of the type illustrated on 31 ff. above. For the tmesis in ἐπὶ ... κυκλοῦcιν cf. Pind. *Ol*. 2. 37 ἐπί τι καὶ πῆμ' ἄγει.

130–1. Ἄρκτου cτροφάδεc κέλευθοι: cf. fr. 432. 11 Ἄρκτου cτροφάc with Pearson ad loc.; for the verb cτρέφομαι used of the course of heavenly bodies see Gow on Theocr. *Id*. 24. 11–12.

132 ff. A paratactic comparison introduced by γάρ (see on 144 ff. below) with οὔτε ... οὔτε equivalent to 'just as ... so' (cf. Denniston, *GP*², p. 515). **κῆρεc:** Jebb translates as 'calamities'; for passages in tragedy where the word bears this or a similar meaning see Diggle in *Dionysiaca* (Page Festschrift; Cambridge 1978), 161.

134 ff. Understand τῶι μέν with βέβακε (see above on 117); the epic ἄφαρ occurs four times in this play (529, 821, 958), twice in the rest of extant Greek tragedy (Aesch. *Pers*. 469, Eur. *IT* 1274).

134. βέβακε: 'is gone': on the perfect βέβηκα as 'a stronger equivalent

LINES 127-140

of εἰμί "be"' see Moorhouse, p. 198. Here, by contrast, 'the completion of the act leads to the present absence of the subject'.

136: Either the two infinitives are the subject of ἐπέρχεται (which they can be in spite of the absence of the definite article: see Fraenkel on Aesch. *Ag.* 584) or they are epexegetic and the verb's subject is supplied from what precedes. **ϲτέρεϲθαι:** here not so much 'to be deprived or robbed' (LSJ) as 'to lose' (see Maehler on Bacch. 1. 78).

137. ἅ: accusative of respect with reference to the preceding general statement; ὅ Wilamowitz*, unnecessarily. ἅ is not to be correlated with the following τάδ' (see Stevens on Eur. *Andr.* 650 ἦν χρῆν ϲ' ἐλαύνειν τήνδ' for the extreme rarity of such a construction) nor to be interpreted as feminine singular picking up (a probably illicit) ἐπιμεμφομένα ϲ' in remote 122 (Dale, *MATC* i. 24).

137-8. ἐλπίϲιν ... ἴϲχειν: probably locative dative: cf. Bers, pp. 89-90.

139. ἐπεί: for the word's use to introduce 'a question whose inescapable or probable answer serves to confirm or justify what has just been said' see Johansen and Whittle on Aesch. *Suppl.* 330.

139-40. For the notion 'that a god is under a moral obligation to protect and gratify his human progeny' see Johansen and Whittle on Aesch. *Suppl.* 168 ff. In view of the frequency of phrases like Διὸϲ δ' ἐτελείετο βουλή the notion of a Ζεὺϲ ἄβουλοϲ is strikingly paradoxical. As the sequel will show, however, Zeus' actual plan for his son is very different from what merely mortal knowledge can guess at: cf. 1266-9 *infra*.

FIRST EPISODE (141-204)

By means of a characteristic Sophoclean doublet (cf. the double burial of Polyneices in the *Antigone*, Teucer's encounter with first Menelaus and then Agamemnon in the *Ajax*, Electra's similar debate with Chrysothemis and then Clytemnestra) D is twice brought the news of Heracles' safe return, and the second occasion has the nature of a climax. Tycho von Wilamowitz, who saw this clearly (p. 148), also saw that the present instance is much more complex, since the second receipt of the joyful news is soon soured when the truth about Iole emerges. But this too is part of a characteristically Sophoclean dramatic device: the premature ode of choral rejoicing which acts as foil to the succeeding gloom (cf. 633 ff. below, *Aj.* 693 ff.; *Ant.* 1115 ff.; *OT* 1086 ff.) is thereby motivated (see in

COMMENTARY

general Kranz, *Stasimon*, pp. 213–14). For these devices to operate successfully the poet must take care not to emphasize the role of Heracles in the first of the two episodes: otherwise D would learn the truth from the messenger before the chorus can express their joy and before Lichas can deceive his mistress as to Heracles' reasons for sacking Oechalia. (This lying tale itself acts as foil to the true account that follows.) These crucial considerations determine the content of the exchange between the messenger and D at 180 ff. and explain why, after the emphatic announcement of Heracles' safety at the opening, the conversation is rather artificially confined to the activities of Lichas.

141 ff. For this type of transition from choral ode to episode, wherein a speaker's opening words draw attention to the content of the preceding ode, Kranz, *Stasimon*, pp. 203–4, compares *OT* 216 ff.

141. πεπυσμένη ... πάρει: cf. the chorus's own πυνθάνομαι earlier on (line 103). ὡς ἐπεικάσαι hardly excludes D's presence at that point, as Tycho von Wilamowitz (p. 125) over-logically assumes: cf. Schwinge, p. 37 n. 1. For the singular used by an actor to address the chorus at the end of their song see M. Kaimio, *The Chorus of Greek Drama within the Light of the Person and Number Used* (Soc. scient. Fenn. comm. hum. lit. 46; Helsinki 1970), 212 ff. **ὡς ἀπεικάσαι:** read ἐπεικάσαι. Hermann's conjecture is confirmed by 1220 ὥς γ' ἐπεικάζειν ἐμέ. ἀπεικάσαι signifies 'copy' (fr. 154. 2) or 'judge and compare' (Eur. *Or.* 1298, of one voice with another: but Willink ad loc. conjectures there and here (with Wunder) ὡς σάφ' εἰκάσαι; cf. the confusion of manuscripts at *OC* 16: ὡς ἀφεικάσαι **l** *in lin.*, ὡς σάφ' εἰκάσαι **a**, ὡς ἀπεικάσαι **l** *sub lin.*) In Hdt. 9. 32 the manuscripts are split between ὡς ἀπ- and ἐπεικάσαι (at Hdt. 1. 34 we have ὡς εἰκάσαι). For the confusion of ἀπο- and ἐπι- see below on 843–4.

142. θυμοφθορῶ: cf. ἄχος θυμοφθόρον in *Od.* 4. 716, and on the image in general M. L. West, *Philol.* 108 (1964), 171–2 and on Hes. *Op.* 799.

143. For analogies to the anacoluthon here, the sort 'in which the speaker makes a break in his line of argument', see Pearson, *CQ* 24 (1930), 162. **μήτ' ... δ':** cf. Denniston, *GP*², p. 511. On the thought expressed cf. Eur. *Suppl.* 580 γνώσηι σὺ πάσχων· νῦν δ' ἔτ' εἶ νεανίας. **ἄπειρος εἶ:** the Greeks believed in shared experience as a source of fellow feeling (see Johansen and Whittle on Aesch. *Suppl.* 215) and in the

LINES 141-150

happiness of youth as largely due to ignorance of good or ill (see D. E. Gerber, *GRBS* 16 (1975), 267). Cf. *Aj.* 552–3 and the contrast of youth's ἄνοια with later wisdom in fr. 583. 5–6.

144 ff. See Merkelbach, *Philol.* 101 (1957), 25 ff., on the traditional picture of 'Der Nymphengarten', H. Thesleff, *Gnomosyne* (W. Marg Festschrift; Munich 1981), 31 ff., on that of the *locus amoenus*; Bühler, *Zenobii Athoi Proverbia*, iv. 213 ff., on the proverb οὔθ' ὕεται οὔθ' ἡλιοῦται·... ἐπὶ τῶν ἔξω πάςης φροντίδος ἑςτώτων. Note too that Achilles is compared to a sapling in *Il.* 18. 56–7 ὁ δ' ἀνέδραμεν ἔρνεϊ ἶςος· | τὸν μὲν ἐγὼ θρέψαςα, φυτὸν ὣς γουνῶι ἀλωῆς). It has yet to be properly appreciated that technically and formally our lines, like the passage in *Od.* 6. 162 ff. (Odysseus compares Nausicaa to a palm-tree), constitute a paratactic comparison. On the frequency of these in this type of speech see Johansen, *General Reflection in Tragic Rhesis*, pp. 16 ff. (he fails to recognize the present specimen). Of the examples he cites, several (like our own) are introduced by γάρ: note especially Aesch. *ScT* 602 ff.; also Soph. fr. 683. 1 ff. οὐ γάρ ποτ' ἄν γένοιτ' ἄν ἀςφαλὴς πόλις κτλ. (on which see Diggle, Eur. *Phaeth.*, p. 125 n. 1). Cf. the use of ἐπεί to introduce a paratactic simile at Aesch. *Ag.* 393, Pind. *Ol.* 2. 98, etc.

144. See Moorhouse, pp. 257–8: 'τὸ νεάζον is not purely abstract "youth", as is seen by its coupling with βόςκεται and the further physical references to the effects of heat, rain etc.; it is closer to a collective "what is young".' For νέος *vel sim.* of vegetation see Johansen and Whittle on Aesch. *Suppl.* 105. For metaphorical βόςκεται cf. Anacr. 417. 5 λειμῶνας... βοςκέαι, *Aj.* 558 κούφοις πνεύμαςιν βόςκου; for the verb's position within an enclosing phrase (ἐν τοιοῖςδε... χώροιςιν) see Fraenkel on Aesch. *Ag.* 964.

144–50. for a recent treatment of this passage see Stinton, *Papers of the Liverpool Latin Seminar* 5 (1985), 412 ff. Several objections can be brought against the paradosis: (1) τοιοῖςδε sits oddly in this context: it would be otiose and unidiomatic as a means of introducing the simile (for whose paratactic nature see above on 144 ff.). Any reference back (to 143) would be exceedingly harsh and elliptical (contrast e.g. *Aj.* 148, where τοιούςδε λόγους is perfectly appropriate in a backward reference). One looks for a relative to follow it but as the text stands one looks in vain. (2) χώροιςιν αὐτοῦ is eccentric and hard to parallel precisely, as re-emerges from Dawe's recent examination of the passage

COMMENTARY

(*Studies* iii. 80). It is hardly to be defended by the much more explicit point behind Cat. 62. 39 'ut flos in saeptis *secretus* nascitur hortis' or by citing Pind. *Pyth.* 4. 263 ff., where we find a felled oak ἐὸν ἐρημώcαιcα χῶρον (a tree's 'place' is much more easily conceived than the vague and indefinite realms of 'what is young'); (3) κλονεῖ is an appropriate verb for ὄμβροc and πνεύματα, not so for θάλποc, since it means 'to set in violent or tumultuous motion, to agitate'. Of these objections (3) might perhaps be met by referring to such examples of zeugma as Aesch. *Suppl.* 1006–7 πρὸc ταῦτα μὴ πάθωμεν ὧν πολὺc πόνοc | πολὺc δὲ πόντοc οὕνεκ' ἠρόθη δορί (see further Stinton, art. cit. 413); (1) and (2) are still troublesome, however. But Dawe's wholesale deletion of the passage (loc. cit.) has rightly met with no approval.

The most popular and attractive emendation is Pearson's χώροιc ἵν' αὐαίνει νιν (χώροιcιν οὐ κάει νιν was already suggested by Moriz Schmidt, *Bull. de l' acad. impér. St Pétersb.* 26 (1880), 180f.), which seems to meet all requirements and furthermore restores a characteristic touch, since the *locus amoenus* is traditionally well watered: Sappho 2. 5–6 ἐν δ' ὕδωρ ψῦχρον κελαδεῖ δι' ὔcδων | μαλίνων, Ibyc. 286. 1 ff. αἵ τε Κυδώνιαι | μηλίδεc ἀρδομέναι ῥοᾶν | ἐκ ποταμῶν, Cat. 61. 23 ff. (the myrtle's branches nurtured 'roscido... umore'), Longus 2. 3 πηγαῖc τριcὶ κατάρρυτοc, Eur. *Hipp.* 78 Αἰδὼc δὲ ποταμίαιcι κηπεύει δρόcοιc. The use of νιν would be perfectly legitimate (see Schwyzer, *Gr. Gr.* ii. 191 (a)), and χώροιc ἵν' positively idiomatic (cf. the analogous Herodotean phrases collected by Renehan, *HSCP* 89 (1985), 25, esp. Hdt. 4. 95. 3 ἥξουcι ἐc χῶρον τ⟨οι⟩οῦτον (corr. Renehan) ἵνα αἰεὶ περιεόντεc ἕξουcι τὰ πάντα ἀγαθά). For a Sophoclean parallel cf. *Phil.* 16ff. πέτρα | τοιάδ', ἵν' ἐν ψύχει μὲν ἡλίου διπλῆ | πάρεcτιν ἐνθάκηcιc. The resulting position of οὐ has been criticized (Stinton, art. cit. 414–15) but see 440. For other emendations see Stinton, pp. 415–16. For a defence of χώροιcιν αὐτοῦ see *Sophoclea*, p. 155, supposing a plant uprooted from its proper place to be the underlying image. See on 144 and 147.

θάλποc θεοῦ: θεόc *tout court* is frequently used of the sun: cf. LSJ s.v. I d, Diggle on Eur. *Phaeth.* 6. The absence of heat and glare from such idyllic landscapes is often indicated by the presence of shade: Sappho 2. 6–7 βρόδοιcι δὲ παῖc ὁ χῶροc | ἐcκίαcτ', Ibyc. 286. 4–5 αἵ τ' οἰνανθίδεc | αὐξόμεναι cκιεροῖcιν ὕφ' ἕρνεcιν, Cat. 62. 39ff.

LINES 144-149

'flos... quem... educat umbra' (*coni*. Garrod, *prob*. Merkelbach art. cit. (on 144 ff.), 28 n. 2: imber *codd*., but see next n.). Cf. Odysseus' hiding-place in *Od*. 5. 479 ff. οὔτε ποτ' ἠέλιος φαέθων ἀκτῖcιν ἔβαλλεν κτλ. Bühler, op. cit. (on 144 ff.), 214–15.

146. οὐδ' ὄμβροc: another feature traditionally banished from the *locus amoenus*: *Od*. 4. 566 οὐ νιφετός, οὔτ' ἄρ χειμὼν πολὺς οὔτε ποτ' ὄμβρος, 6. 43–4 οὔτε ποτ' ὄμβρωι | δεύεται, cf. 5. 480 (of Odysseus' thicket) οὔτ' ὄμβρος περάαcκε διαμπερές, Bühler, loc. cit. (last n.). **οὐδὲ πνευμάτων οὐδέν:** not windy blasts (*Od*. 6. 43 οὔτ' ἀνέμοιcι τινάccεται, cf. 5. 478 τοὺς μὲν (sc. θάμνους) ἄρ' οὔτ' ἀνέμων διάη μένος ὑγρὸν ἀέντων; in Ibycus 286. 6 ff. Θρηίκιος Βορέας ἀίccων παρὰ Κύπριδος disturbs the poet and the preceding picture of the Παρθένων κῆπος) but gentle breezes characterize the *locus amoenus*: *Od*. 4. 567–8 αἰεὶ ζεφύροιο λιγὺ πνείοντος ἀῆταc | Ὠκεανὸς ἀνίηcιν ἀναψύχειν ἀνθρώπους, Cat. 62. 39 ff. 'flos... quem mulcent aurae'. The idealized picture of Athens at *OC* 675 ff. τὰν ἄβατον θεοῦ | φυλλάδα μυριόκαρπον ἀνήλιον | ἀνήνεμόν τε πάντων | χειμώνων is compared by V. Di Benedetto, *Ann. d. Scuola Normale Sup. di Pisa* 9. 3 (1979), 947. **κλονεῖ** is a Sophoclean verb unused by Aeschylus or Euripides; see Pfeiffer, *Sitzb. d. Bayer. Akad. d. Wiss., phil.-hist. Abt*. 2 (1938), 47.

147. For the string of negatives followed by ἀλλά (i.e. a positive description preceded by a negative one) cf. *Od*. 4. 566–7, 6. 43–4 (similar *loci amoeni*), Soph. fr. 314. 156 ff., Aesch. *TrGF* iii, fr. 196. 3–4 Radt, Bühler on Mosch. *Europa* 80 ff.; cf. Denniston, *GP*[2], p. xliv, Davies, *Prometheus* 13 (1987), 265 ff. **ἡδοναῖς:** more appropriate to young girls than to plants. For this frequent 'mutual penetration of the comparison and the thing compared' and the process whereby the 'image... assimilates elements characteristic of the thing compared' see Fraenkel on Aesch. *Ag*. 966, 1011, 1182. Cf. on 31 ff. above. For the word ἄμοχθος see Harder's note on Eur. *Archel*. fr. 14. 2.

148. ἐc τοῦθ', ἕωc τιc: with these words we move from the comparison to the reality. No explicit signal of the fact is given (contrast Aesch. *ScT* 609 οὕτως, *Od*. 6. 166, 168 ὣc δ' αὕτωc... ὥc). Cf. Ibyc. 286. ἡδοναῖς at 147, however (see n.), anticipated the move. **ἀντὶ παρθένου γυνή:** for the contrast of these two words see West on Hes. *Th*. 513, Bühler on Mosch. *Europa* 165–6.

149. κληθῆι: the verb is used with no implication of doubt: cf. *Phil*. 430

COMMENTARY

αὐδᾶcθαι νεκρόν and the Latin usage discussed by Housman on Manil. 4. 314. **ἐν νυκτί:** 'at night-time': a general reference. For the wedding night to be meant, μιᾶι would have to be present (cf. fr. 583. 11–12 καὶ ταῦτ' ἐπειδὰν εὐφρόνη ζεύξηι μία, | χρεὼν ἐπαινεῖν καὶ δοκεῖν καλῶc ἔχειν, Eur. Tro. 665–6 λέγουcιν ὡc μί' εὐφρόνη χαλᾶι | τὸ δυcμενὲc γυναικὸc εἰc ἀνδρὸc λέχοc) and line 150 deleted (see ad loc.). The phrase either goes with λάβηι or adjectivally with φροντίδων μέροc (cf. OC 586 ἀλλ' ἐν βραχεῖ δὴ τήνδε μ' ἐξαιτῆι χάριν for such an adjectival use of a prepositional phrase, and cf. Schwyzer, Gr. Gr. ii. 415). **φροντίδων μέροc:** φροντίδεc = 'anxieties', as in fr. 949. 2 and Eur. IA 646, etc.; for their connection with night (cf. 30–1 above) see the Gyges fragment (TrGF (adesp.) fr. 664. 25–6) ἐν δεμνίωι δὲ φροντίcιν cτροφωμένηι, | νὺξ ἦν ἀτέρμων ἐξ ἀυπνίαc ἐμοί, Ar. Eq. 1290 ἐννυχίαιcι φροντίcι, Anon. Epigr. 134. 2 Page (FGE 1613) νυκτῶν φροντίδεc ἑcπέριοι, Menand. Misum. 1 ff., Epitr. 252 ff. For their connection with children (as in 150) cf. Antiphon B 49 DK φέρε δὴ καὶ παῖδεc γενέcθωcαν· φροντίδων ἤδη πάντα πλέα (cf. Ter. Adelph. 866–7 'nati filii: alia cura') καὶ ἐξοίχεται τὸ νεοτήcιον cκίρτημα ἐκ τῆc γνώμηc.

150. Deleted as inconsistent with an interpretation of ἐν νυκτί in 149 as the wedding night by Dindorf (Ad Soph. Trag. Annotationes, p. 243), M. L. Earle (CR 7 (1893), 450 = Classical Papers, pp. 26–7), and Kranz (Jhsb. d. Philol. Vereins zu Berlin 47 (1921), 32–3 = Stud. zur antik. Lit. und ihrem Nachwirken, pp. 283–4). So it is, but that is no argument for excision. (Wilamowitz* approved the deletion, comparing for form and motive the interpolation at Eur. Med. 246 ἢ πρὸc φίλον τιν' ἢ πρὸc ἥλικα τραπείc (see Page ad loc.), but 149 tells against it.)

151–2. For the generalizing masculine participle used by a female speaker see El. 771 οὐδὲ γὰρ κακῶc | πάcχοντι μῖcοc ὢν τέκηι προcγίγνεται, and for a full discussion of masculine forms used by and for females Moorhouse, pp. 12–13; cf. Renehan, CP 80 (1985), 168; Langholf, Hermes 105 (1977), 290 ff.; H. Petersmann, Die Sprache 25 (1979), 151.

152. κακοῖcιν οἷc: 'for κακὰ οἷc: or the alternative is, οἷc as indirect interrogative with inversion of οἷc κακοῖcιν' (Moorhouse, p. 270).

153–4. πάθη ... πρόcθεν: for the opening formula see on 49 ff. above, and cf. W. H. Race, The Classical Priamel from Homer to Boethius (Mnem. suppl. 74; 1982), 112 n. 194. πάθη echoes πάθημα τοὐμόν in

142 (cf. παθοῦca in 143). κλαίομαι takes an accusative object at Aesch. Ag. 1096 κλαιόμενα ... cφαγάc (see Fraenkel ad loc.). For the. perfective aorist ('I have bewailed') see 201, 1135 below; Moorhouse, p. 195. **μὲν οὖν δή:** a unique collocation of particles (cf. Aj. 873 τί οὖν δή). δή here perhaps = ἤδη: cf. KG ii/2. 124–5.

154–5. ἓν δ' ... ἐξερῶ: cf. Eur. Hipp. 715 ἓν δὲ ... ἐρῶ, Aj. 1140 ἕν coι φράcω, and for examples of the pattern whereby a sentence begins with a ἕν which is then elucidated by a further sentence with explanatory γάρ (or in asyndeton) see Barrett on the first passage.

155. See on 531 ff. below.

156. ἀπ' οἴκων ... ἐν δόμοιc: for the distinction see Aj. 63 ff., OT 637, El. 1308, and below on 689.

157–8. ἐγγεγραμμένην | ξυνθήμαθ': for the verb see Knox, YCS 22 (1972), 255 = Word and Action p. 284; for the internal accusative see Moorhouse, p. 39, Diggle, STE p. 81. The noun probably refers to the writing down of the oracle (cf. 1167), as Jebb thought, comparing the famous Homeric cήματα λυγρά (Il. 6. 168). For anachronistic references to writing in the Attic tragedians see Easterling, JHS 105 (1985), 3 ff. (p. 4 on our line). Pearson's revival (CR 39 (1925), 2) of Pretor's notion (in his edition, Cambridge 1877) that the reference is to a will was unfortunate: as Tycho von Wilamowitz saw (p. 126), the repeated εἶπε of 161–2 makes it clear that Heracles' 'will' was purely verbal.

158–9. οὕτω: Tournier's conjecture would have to refer forward to 163, which is rather awkward given the distracting presence of 161–2 in between; οὔπω (recently defended by Kraus, WS 20 (1986), 91) would be the emphatic non-temporal use (LSJ s.v. 2; Dawe, The Collation and Investigation of Manuscripts of Aeschylus (Cambridge 1964), 123; West on Hes. Th. 560 denies the existence of this idiom, but see Verdenius, Mnem. 24 (1971), 4). It must be said, however, that the sequence οὔ ... ποτέ ... οὔπω would be unique (as Pearson stressed (CR 39 (1925), 2), citing OT 491 ff. οὔτε πάροιθέν | ποτ' ἔγωγ' οὔτε τανῦν πω | ἔμαθον for 'the normal combination'. But the OCT reads πωc).

159. ἀγῶναc ἐξιών: cf. 505 πάμπληκτα παγκόνιτά τ' ἐξῆλθον ἄεθλ' ἀγώνων, Thuc. 1. 15. 2 ἐκδήμουc cτρατείαc ... οὐκ ἐξῇιcαν οἱ Ἕλληνεc, Aj. 290 ἀφορμαῖc πεῖραν for similar cognate accusatives. Cf. Bers, p. 69.

161. ὡc ἔτ' οὐκ ὤν: for the word-order cf. OT 24 ἔτ' οὐχ οἶά τε, Phil. 1217 ἔτ' οὐδέν εἰμι.

COMMENTARY

161–2. εἶπε μὲν ... εἶπε δ': for the anaphora cf. *OC* 610 φθίνει μὲν ... φθίνει δέ with Jebb ad loc., Diggle, *STE* p. 55.

162. χρείη: for misdivisions of this optative similar to those offered by the MSS here see 166 below and *OT* 555, *OC* 268, *Ant.* 884, *PV* 213. On the optative of oratio obliqua see Schwyzer, *Gr. Gr.* ii. 332 (*b*); for an analogous point of Attic law cf. Isaeus 2. 9, on which see Harrison, *Law of Athens*, i. *Family and Property* (Oxford 1968), 47.

163. μοῖραν ... διαίρετον: 'for other examples of S. treating three termination adjs. as if they had only two' see Dawe, *Studies* iii. 105.

164–5. ἡνίκ' ἄν ... ἀπείη: Dawes's elimination of ἄν (*Misc. Crit.*[2], p. 573) is not essential, though most editors accept it. Moorhouse, p. 297, argues that 'justification might be found for ἄν in such cases as ours', if 'there is a potential sense which the speaker wishes to stress' (here the uncertainty that Heracles would be away so long). See further G. L. Cooper, *Zur syntaktischen Theorie und Textkritik der attischen Autoren* (Zurich 1971), 33–4 and note on 687 below.

166–8. These lines were deleted by Dobree cited on 77 above: 'hic ubi omnia pessima ominatur, inepta sunt ista 167–8, neque audivisse videtur Chorus 823–842' (he also found the three lines 'frigid'); he was followed by Nauck and Wecklein. Dobree supposed the τοιαῦτ' of 169 a sufficient reference (cf. τοιαύτην ... | δέλτον in 46–7 above), though Wunder by contrast thought that very word guaranteed the suspect lines. Equally two-edged is the argument that the construction of 164 presupposes 166–8 or that the oracular disjunction ἤ ... ἤ (166–7) recalls that of 79–80. A wish to clarify the construction of 164 might have prompted the interpolation and 79–80 might have inspired its content. By the time lines 1159 ff. are spoken, the open form of the oracle given at 76 ff. has changed to an inevitable and closed form for reasons of dramatic technique (see Appendix A). Whether the present passage is to be associated with the former or the latter lines is difficult to decide, because evaluation of its tone and effect depends precisely on whether 166–8 are deleted or not. Bergk's deletion of 169–70 as superfluous is considered below on 170.

167. ὑπεκδραμόντα: ὑπερδρ- (Burges) might seem to be supported by Aesch. *Pers.* 96 ff. παράγει | βροτὸν εἰς ἄρκυας Ἄτα, | τόθεν οὐκ ἔστιν ὑπὲρ (ὑπεκ I[γρ]) ... φυγεῖν, but cf. Eur. *Andr.* 414 ἦν δ' ὑπεκδράμηις μόρον and Holwerda, *Mnem.* 16 (1963), 350.

168. τὸ λοιπὸν ἤδη: 'from that time on': for the phrase's use in

LINES 161-172

solemn utterances see 921 below, Men. *Aspis* 5-6, Stevens on Eur. *Andr.* 1258. ζῆν ... βίωι: for this type of paronomasia see Schwyzer, *Gr. Gr.* ii. 166 (3); cf. 544 below. The infinitive ζῆν depends on an ἐξείη to be supplied *e contrario* from the χρείη of 166: on this species of ellipse in general see KG ii/2. 566-7.

169. ἔφραζε: for the imperfect see Holzinger on Ar. *Plut.* 42. τοιαῦτα is the subject and ἐκτελευτᾶcθαι the infinitive of the accusative and infinitive construction governed by this verb.

170. ἐκτελευτᾶcθαι: for this verb as used in prophetic contexts see Pind. *Pyth.* 4. 19, 12. 28-9. Numerous examples of phrases like τελευτὴ πόνων (Eur. *Her.* 427), τέρμα κακῶν, and the like are assembled by Diggle, *PCPS* 22 (1976), 44. They support Campbell's interpretation of πόνων as dependent on an ἐκ- of the infinitive (so too Pearson, *CR* 39 (1925), 2): 'such was the end and issue of his labours'. See too *Sophoclea*, p. 156, mentioning the further possibility of θείμαρμένα for εἱμαρμένα in 169. For the adjective Ἡράκλειοc see above on 50-1. Wunder wished to delete this line, as did Bergk (cf. on 166-8 above), but (even without the considerations raised by West on Hes. *Th.* 22, on poetic self-address in the third person) the audience is unlikely to have paused to consider the propriety of H applying this epithet to his own labours.

171. φηγόν: Zeus' tree at Dodona is called a δρῦc at 1168, but 'the discrepancy is only apparent ... for δρῦc is a generic term including φηγόc': Lloyd on Hdt. 2. 55, to whose lists of passages alluding to the tree in the two ways mentioned add both lines from our play. Lloyd gives a good account of Zeus' oak at Dodona.

172. On the worship and oracle of Zeus at Dodona see Lloyd (last n.); on the Peliae/Peliades of Dodona see L. Bodson, *ΙΕΡΑ ΖΩΙΑ: Contribution à l'étude de la place de l'animal dans la religion grecque ancienne* (Brussels and Liège 1978), 101 ff., Lloyd on Hdt. 2. 55, Harder's note on Eur. *Archel.* fr. 1. 21-2; for comparable examples of cult personnel or worshippers bearing the names of animals see C. Sourvinou-Inwood, *CQ* 29 (1979), 240 n. 49. Ancient authors differ as to the precise number of priestesses involved: see Lloyd, loc. cit.

173. τῶνδε ναμέρτεια: the genitive conveys both 'truth' and 'fulfilment' of: cf. Eur. *Hipp.* 9 δείξω δὲ μύθων τῶνδ' ἀλήθειαν τάχα, Hdt. 3. 64. 1 ἡ ἀληθείη τῶν τε λόγων καὶ τοῦ ἐνυπνίου. On the noun see Björck, *Das Alpha impurum*, pp. 128-9, on the form ibid. 230

COMMENTARY

(for other ἅπαξ nouns in -εια see Hutchinson on Aesch. *ScT* 515), on its connotations W. Luther, *Wahrheit und Lüge* (Leipzig 1935), 33 ff., Long, *Language and Thought*, p. 57. **cυμβαίνει:** the meaning 'congruere' (see Kannicht on Eur. *Hel.* 36 ff.) seems more appropriate here (as at 1164 below) than 'turned out' (the verb's meaning at 1174, Thuc. 2. 17. 2, etc.).

174. ὡc: O. Hense wrote ὧι for ὡc (*Studien zu Sophokles* 40–1), irritated by the ambiguity between ὡc causal and consecutive (for the latter see below on 590–1), especially so close to another ὡc (171; cf. ὧcθ' in 175). ὡc occurs at least twice in six words at 394–5, however, and no real ambiguity is involved: modal ὡc ('in the manner in which it is destined to be accomplished') gives adequate sense here.

175 ff. Compare and contrast Clytemnestra's hypocritical protestations at Aesch. *Ag.* 889 ff.

175–6. ἐκπηδᾶν ... φόβωι ... ταρβοῦcαν: the noun goes with the participle, not with the infinitive: cf. Eur. *Her.* 971 οἱ δὲ ταρβοῦντεc φόβωι | ὤρουον ἄλλοc ἄλλοc', and for the pleonasm see further *Phil.* 225 ὄκνωι | δείcαντεc, *OC* 1625 φόβωι δείcανταc.

177. Originally omitted by L because of homoioteleuton with the preceding line (ἐcτερημένην ~ χρὴ μένειν): see Aesch. *ScT* 195 and Hutchinson ad loc. for further instances of this type of omission.

178–9. A garlanded figure (Creon) is similarly descried at a distance in *OT* 78 ff. In the present passage, the chorus prescribe silence on his impending entry, a characteristic Sophoclean device (see Bain, *Actors and Audience* (Oxford 1977), 80 n. 3). **καταcτεφῆ:** for garlanded messengers in tragedy see Fraenkel on Aesch. *Ag.* 493–4, who supposes 'The sole reason for the garland is the victory and the triumphant homecoming ... announced.' Cf. Chaeremon, *TrGF* i (71) fr. 11 Sn. **cτεφάνουc ... εὐφημίαc | κήρυκαc. χάριν:** the reading of KR is accepted in the OCT. The previous note suggests a connection between καταcτεφῆ and πρὸc χαρὰν λόγων ('garlanded ... in view of his pleasant tidings'). For πρόc with this nuance ('in accordance with', 'in view of': LSJ s.v. C III. 5) cf. Eur. *Hipp.* 701 πρὸc τὰc τύχαc γὰρ τὰc φρέναc κεκτήμεθα. For confusion of χάριc and χαρά in MSS see Bond on Eur. *Hyps.* fr. 64. 61. Certainly 'garlanded ... in order to speak' would be less pointed, indeed wrongly pointed. But perhaps we should not divorce καταcτεφῆ from the immediately following cτείχονθ' ('coming garlanded'), which phrase would then fit either πρὸc χαρὰν λόγων ('coming garlanded in view of his pleasant tidings') or πρὸc χάριν λόγων ('coming garlanded in order to communicate the pleasant tidings implied by the garlands').

181. ὄκνου ϲε λύϲω: for comparable images see Diggle, *STE*, p. 17.
Ἀλκμήνης τόκον: see on 19 above.
182–3. An effective tricolon crescendo.
183. ἀπαρχάϲ: cf. 240 below.
184. τίν'... τόνδε: for the collocation τίϲ ὅδε see Diggle, *STE*, p. 42. The hyperbaton here expresses excitement.
186. ἥξειν: for the infinitive dependent on the λόγον of 184 cf. on φέρειν at line 66 above. **ϲὺν κράτει νικηφόρωι:** κράτοϲ and νίκη are often thus juxtaposed: see Johansen and Whittle on Aesch. *Suppl.* 951.
187. The καί is expressive of surprise: see 1140 below and Denniston, *GP²*, p. 310; τοῦ is to be understood before ξένων τοό (for the *Versparung* see above on 3). For R's confusion of ΤΟΥ and ΠΟΥ cf. Pearson on fr. 522. 1. (ποῦ is the wrong question in this context.)
188. βουθερεῖ λειμῶνι: cf. Hesych. s.v. βουθερεῖ (i. 337 Latte): ἐν ὧι βόες θέρουϲ ὧραι νέμονται. This interpretation is supported (with reference to modern Trachis) by G. Rougemont, *Rev. Phil.* 57 (1983), 285 ff. Other -θερήϲ compounds derive from the verb θέρω meaning 'to heat, to warm': cf. Aesch. *Suppl.* 70 Νειλοθερῆ παρειάν 'Nile-heated' (i.e. sun-tanned), where, however, Bothe conjectured εἰλοθερῆ (cf. *Od.* 7. 123 θειλόπεδον codd.: εἰλο- Toup, Bekker, von der Mühll). The implied derivation from the two nouns βοῦϲ and θέροϲ ('meadow of the summer-oxen') produces a compound paralleled by λειμῶνα βούχιλον at Aesch. *Suppl.* 540; cf. *Aj.* 143 τὸν ἱππομανῆ λειμῶν'. Derivation from βοῦϲ and the verb θερίζω 'to crop' is unnecessary. Wecklein's βουθόρωι was decorously translated 'in which oxen jump about' by Jebb, but the sense it actually provides is distracting ('in which oxen mate'), and furthermore Aesch. *Suppl.* 301 has 'the only compound in -θόροϲ attested in pre-Hellenistic literature' (Johansen and Whittle ad loc.). **πρὸϲ πολλούϲ:** Hermann's emendation of πρόϲπολοϲ is palmary: the paradosis supplies a noun that is inadequate without a genitive (so Tycho von Wilamowitz, p. 137) and anyway inaccurate (see on 453 below). The multitude restored by conjecture is dramatically significant: cf. 351 ff., 371 ff., 423–4, 456. Such passages amply establish this conjecture's superiority over the πρὸ πόλεωϲ of Radermacher.

COMMENTARY

189. κλυών: not present (κλύων) but aorist (κλυών), as Lloyd-Jones saw (*CQ* 4 (1954), 93 n. 2), citing Fraenkel on Aesch. *Ag.* 680. See now West, *BICS* 31 (1984), 172 ff., on the whole principle involved.

189–90. For the dramatic considerations that determine this otherwise cumbersome and uneconomic procedure see above, p. 88. In 189 Jebb prefers the interpretation of *TOYΔ* as τοῦδ' (with explanatory asyndeton).

190. cοι: Brunck's slight change produces a neater balance with πρὸc cοῦ at the start of the next line: 'having given the news first *to* you, I should get a reward *from* you.'

191. Cf. *OT* 232 τὸ γὰρ | κέρδοc τελῶ 'γὼ χἠ χάριc προcκείcεται. The messenger's traditional eagerness for reward is offered as the rationalization for an anticipating of Lichas' news that is actually rooted in the demands of dramatic technique: see above, p. 87.

192. εἴπερ εὐτυχεῖ: most naturally taken as a reference to Lichas; but the meaning of *his* 'good fortune' is obscure (unless εὖ is equivalent to οὐ κακῶc and the phrase means (euphemistically) 'if he has met with no accident'). There is no parallel for impersonal εὐτυχεῖ ('things go well') or for the direct identification of slave's and master's fortunes (though the inverse proposition is stated at Eur. *Med.* 54–5 χρηcτοῖcι δούλοιc ξυμφορὰ τὰ δεcποτῶν | κακῶc πίτνοντα καὶ φρενῶν ἀνθάπτεται). Lichas' later opening remark εὖ μὲν ἵγμεθ'... | ... ἄνδρα γὰρ καλῶc | πράccοντ' κτλ. (229 ff.) best explains the verb (εὐτυχὴc ἴκοιτο at *OC* 308 is different, being elaborately explained by its context). It has been suggested (cf. Lloyd-Jones, *CQ* 4 (1954), 94) that αὐτόc here means 'the master' (see Dover on Ar. *Nub.* 219) and is misunderstood by the messenger; but any direct mention of Heracles at this point would be dramatically inept: after the initial reference to him at 185 he must fade out, as it were; otherwise D will discover the truth about his passion for Iole too soon (see above). *Sophoclea*, p. 156, quotes *Aj.* 339–43, 'where Tecmessa's misunderstanding of [Ajax's] words is quite explicit'; but it is precisely the explicitness that distinguishes that scene from ours.

193. οὐκ εὐμαρείαι χρώμενοc πολλῆι: for 'the tragic idiom of answering a πῶc question with a nom. partcp. instead of a finite verb where sense and syntax permit' see Johansen and Whittle on Aesch. *Suppl.* 341. Our line is also an exemplification of the principle that 'a tragic *rhesis* may start with a sentence whose verb has to be supplied

98

from the preceding context, if that sentence contains the answer to a question or to a command' (the same scholars on *Suppl.* 468). On the meaning of εὐμάρεια and related words see D. L. Page, *Sappho and Alcaeus* (Oxford 1955), 228.

194–5. κύκλωι ... περιστάc: Paley's conjecture seems confirmed by Aesch. fr. 379. 2 Radt κύκλωι περίcτητ᾽, Eur. *Bacch.* 1106 περιcτᾶcαι κύκλωι, Hdt. 1.43.1, *Aj.* 723–4 αὐτὸν ἐν κύκλωι | ... ἀμφέcτηcαν, Eur. *Andr.* 1136–7 περιcταδὸν | κύκλωι. Aesch. *Cho.* 983 κύκλωι παραcταδόν (περιcταδόν Paley) is hardly a counter-example. On the confusion of περι(-) and παρα(-) in manuscripts see Cobet, *Var. Lect.*, pp. 278–9.

195. κρίνει: here and at 314 and 388 below (cf. *Aj.* 586, *Ant.* 399) the simplex = ἀνακρίνειν, just as at 382, 397, and 404 below ἱcτορεῖν = ἀντιcτορεῖν.

196. A notorious crux. See Stinton, pp. 132–3, for detailed analysis of previous attempts to solve the problem (add J. H. Kells, *CR* 2 (1962), 111: ὃ γὰρ ποθῶν ἕκαcτοc ἐκμαθεῖν θέλοι) and the suggested solution (already in J. Král, *Listy filologické* 6 (1897), 7) τοῦ γὰρ, ποθῶν ἕκαcτοc ἐκμαθεῖν, θέλων οὐκ ἂν μεθεῖτο. Since Stinton wrote, Moorhouse, pp. 111, 149, 258, has tried to reassert the interpretation of τὸ ποθοῦν as = 'feeling of desire' (cf. esp. *Phil.* 675).

198. οὐχ ἑκὼν ἑκουcίοιc: for this type of rhetorical juxtaposition of the same or similar words in different cases/number/gender, see *Od.* 5. 155 παρ᾽ οὐκ ἐθέλων ἐθελούcηι, Eur. *Hipp.* 319 οὐχ ἑκοῦcαν οὐχ ἑκών, *Andr.* 738 παρὼν δὲ πρὸc παρόνταc, Aesch. *Ag.* 1339 τοῖcι θανοῦcι θανών (cf. Seaford on Eur. *Cycl.* 258, Fehling, *Wiederholungs-figuren*, pp. 231, 282–3, Gygli-Wyss, *Das nominale Polyptoton*, pp. 124, 128–9). In the examples quoted, the same *participle* is varied, which is what the paradosis supplies for our line (ἑκὼν ἑκοῦcι). Nauck's ἑκουcίοιc for ἑκοῦcι δέ supplies a variation of the sort we find in *Phil.* 617–18 ἑκούcιον λαβών, | εἰ μὴ θέλοι δ᾽, ἄκοντα (juxtaposition of slightly different forms of the word). Not every feature of the paradosis is objectionable and in need of healing: on the omission of the balancing μέν see Denniston, *GP*[2], p. 165, and for the emphatically antithetical δέ at line-end without preceding μέν cf. Ar. *Nub.* 1462. The OCT editors, however, are worried by the use of predicate ἑκών when that word is used adverbially (cf. *Sophoclea*, p. 156), and follow Nauck.

COMMENTARY

199. The messenger, contrary to audience expectation, remains mysteriously on stage and then fatally intervenes at 335: on the dramatic technique see Taplin, p. 89 and n. 2. This entails, interestingly enough, that (given the consequent presence of three actors on stage) Iole (e.g. at 320) is unable to respond to D's invitations to speak, being a κωφὸν πρόcωπον.

200 ff. For similar expressions of thanks to the gods at a moment of good fortune as presented in drama see Jocelyn, *The Tragedies of Ennius* (Cambridge 1967), 310.

200. For the hyperbaton of the relative cf. Eur. *Alc.* 198 οὔποθ' οὗ λελήcεται, *Med.* 332 τῶνδ' ὃc αἴτιοc κακῶν, Nauck, *Euripideische Studien* ii (Mem. St Petersb. 8. 2; 1862), p. 4; on the idiomatic description of 'Sakrallandschaft' by adjectives with privative ἀ- see Elliger, *Die Darstellung der Landschaft in der gr. Dichtung*, p. 241 n. 68; cf. Eur. *Hipp.* 73–4. For Zeus' connection with Mt. Oeta see 1191 below, Cook, *Zeus*, ii/2. 903 n. 2.

201. For the thought ('though favourable, yet slow') see Tarrant on Sen. *Ag.* 403a; for the postponement of ἀλλά see Denniston *GP*², p. 13. **cὺν χρόνωι:** 'after a long time', as in *Aj.* 306; the dative can bear the same meaning without the preposition or with an adjective: see Moorhouse, p. 92.

202–3. For the corresponsive τε... τε with anaphora see Johansen and Whittle on Aesch. *Suppl.* 219; for the tone produced by the combination of vocative and article and imperative here and elsewhere see Wackernagel, 'Über einige antike Anredeformen' (1912), 9 = *Kl. Schr.* ii. 976.

203–4. ὄμμ': on the image here see D. Bremer, *Licht und Dunkel in der frühgr. Dichtung* (Bonn 1976), 382 n. 161, A. Dihle in *Platonismus und Christentum* (H. Dörrie Festschrift; Mainz 1983), 88.

CHORAL SONG (205–224)

205	⌒∪– ∪–∪ ‖	lec.
206	∪–∪– ⌒∪–	ia. dim. sync.
207	∪–∪– ∪–∪– ∪–∪–	ia. trim.
208	∪–– –∪– ∪––	ia. trim. sync. cat.
209	∪–– –∪–	ia. dim. sync.
210	∪–∪– –∪–	ia. dim. sync.

LINES 199–206

211	$-\smile\cup- \ -\cup-$	+ ia. dim. sync.
212	$\cup-\cup- \ \cup-\cup-\smile\|$	ia. dim.
213–14	$-\cup\cup-\cup\cup-\cup\cup-\cup\cup-\cup\cup-$	dact. hexam. cat.
215	$-\cup-\cup--$	ithyph.
216	$-\cup\cup-\cup-\cup-$	chor. dim. A
217	$\cup-\cup- \ \cup-\cup- \ \cup-\cup\smile\|$	ia. trim.
218	$\cup-\cup\smile \ --$	ia. dim. sync. (ia. sp.)
219a	$--$	sp. (or exclamation *extra metrum*)
219b	$\cup-\cup- \ \cup-\cup-$	ia. dim.
220	$\cup-\cup- \ \cup-\smile\|$	ia. dim. cat.
222	$\cup-\cup- \ --$	ia. dim. sync. (ia. sp.)
223	$\smile\cup- \ \cup-\cup-$	lec.
224a	$\cup-\cup- \ \cup--$	ia. dim. cat.
224b	$\cup-\cup- \ \cup--\|\|$	ia. dim. cat.

Instead of the expected first stasimon, S presents us with an astrophic chorus positioned between iambic scenes (see Griffith, *Authenticity of PV*, p. 321 n. 119). For literary allusions to the use of a double chorus of young men and women (the former here only *imagined* as in the vicinity), especially in the context of the worship of Apollo and Artemis, see Nisbet–Hubbard on Horace *Odes* I. 21. Light is cast on several of the prayer-formulae that feature here by Norden, *Aus altrömischen Priesterbüchern*, pp. 200–1. The textual and metrical problems that encumber these lines are numerous and great: see the recent treatment by Stinton, *Papers of the Liverpool Latin Seminar* 5 (1985), 416 ff.

205 ff. A reference to the actual chorus on the Attic stage: cf. Wilamowitz, ed. Eur. *Her.* iii. 149, Kranz, *Stasimon*, pp. 182–3.

206 ff. The reference is to a shout of joy, as at Aesch. *Ag.* 587 ἀνωλόλυξα μὲν πάλαι χαρᾶς ὕπο: cf. Fraenkel on Aesch. *Ag.* 594, L. Deubner, 'Ololyge und Verwandtes', *Abh. d. Preuß. Ak. d. Wiss.* 1 (1941), 1 ff., esp. 10–11 = *Kl. Schr.*, pp. 609 ff., esp. pp. 616–17.

205–6. ἀνολολυξάτω: 'An injunction is needed here, and the third-person imperative ... is favoured by the Σ εὐχὰς ποιείτω': Stinton, art. cit. 417, who considers and convincingly rejects other readings and conjectures. **ἐφεστίοις ἀλαλαγαῖς:** the noun is supported by Σ

COMMENTARY

Pind. *Ol.* 7. 68 (i. 216 Dr.) ἡ γὰρ ἀλαλαγὴ κυρίως ἐπὶ τῆς τῶν πολεμίων cυμβολῆc γίνεται· εἶτ' οὖν λέγεται καὶ ἐπὶ τῶν ἐκβακχευμάτων, as well as Eur. *Phoen.* 335–6 cὺν ἀλαλαγαῖcι δ' αἰὲν αἰαγμάτων | cκότια κρύπτεται, where the manuscripts are divided between ἀλαλαῖcι and ἀλαλαγαῖcι. Radermacher's ἐφεcτίοιcιν ἀλαλαϊc is excellent sense but metrically dubious (Parker, *CQ* 18 (1968), 241–2, shows that split resolution is to be avoided if possible). **δόμοc:** Burges's emendation of δόμοιc. On this interpretation (favoured, for instance, by Stinton, art. cit. 417, and the OCT) the noun will go with ὁ μελλόνυμφοc and the allusion will be to the imminent reunion of Deianeira and Heracles: the house which witnesses this reunion is about to witness their marriage renewed. Those who (like the present writer) find this reference rather strained may prefer to retain the locative dative δόμοιc and follow Erfurdt in writing ἁ μελλόνυμφοc, a collective self-reference to the young women who constitute the chorus (see above, p. 101). With the form μελλόνυμφοc (also at *Ant.* 633) compare μελλόγαμοc (*Ant.* 628; Theocr. *Id.* 22. 140), μελλόποcιc (fr. 1068). Erfurdt's correction—supported by Musgrave—may be confirmed by Σ's ὁ πᾶc οἶκοc if that is intended to gloss ἁ μελλόνυμφοc δόμοc and ἐν δὲ κοινόc κτλ. Stinton, art. cit. 417–18, lists and criticizes other conjectures. (I find his insistence that 'μελλόνυμφοc should mean not "of marriageable age" but "about to be married"' excessively captious.) LSJ take μελλόνυμφοc with κλαγγά, which is difficult given the intervening ἐν δὲ κοινὸc ἀρcένων.

207. ἐν δέ: 'and besides': for such a phrase in the context of a deity's invocation see Ov. *Met.* 4. 28–9 'clamor iuvenilis et una | femineae voces'; cf. Pind. fr. 70B. 10ff., where ἐν δέ occurs thrice of given items in a celebration, Stinton, *JHS* 97 (1977), 141.

208. ἴτω κλαγγά: for ἴτω used of cries (βοά, ἀοιδά, and the like) see Pearson on fr. 490, Diggle on Eur. *Phaeth.* 101 (cf. Fraenkel, *Beob. zu Aristoph.*, pp. 96–7): many of these instances occur in the context of references to marriage (e.g. *Phaeth.* 101 ἴτω τελεία γάμων ἀοιδά).

κλαγγά: almost invariably of animal sounds (see Davies on Stes. fr. 209. i. 5), but cf. Aesch. *Ag.* 1152, 156.

208–9. The accusative is governed by ἴτω κλαγγά, as if that phrase were equivalent to ὑμνεῖτε *vel sim.* 'In elevated language ... a periphrasis, consisting of a vb. and direct object' can 'itself be regarded as equivalent

LINES 205-214

to a transitive vb. and govern in turn an additional acc.': so Renehan, *Studies in Greek Texts* (Hypomnemata 43; 1976), 51-2, giving examples of this construction, 'especially common in encomiastic and "hymnal" contexts', and including the present intransitive instance. Cf. Moorhouse, p. 37, on the 'accusative as secondary complement of a verbal phrase', and, for further bibliography, Diggle, *STE*, p. 58. **τὸν εὐφαρέτραν Ἀπόλλω:** the epithet is used thrice of Apollo in Pindar (*Pyth.* 9. 26, *Paean* 6. 111, fr. 148 Sn.). On the rightness of Dindorf's correction of the manuscripts' Ἀπόλλωνα see Stinton, *BICS* 22 (1975), 90. **προστάταν:** cf. *El.* 637 Φοῖβε προστατήριε, LSJ s.v. προστατήριος II; used of Apollo merely to mean 'defender', or perhaps as referring to his image in front of houses (see Fraenkel on Aesch. *Ag.* 1081, Sandbach on Men. *Dysc.* 659, Diggle, *STE*, p. 34).

210-11. παιᾶνα παι|ᾶν᾽ ἀνάγετε: cf. Eur. *Phoen.* 1350 ἀνάγετ᾽ ἀνάγετε κωκυτόν, both for the equivalence of ἀνάγω to ἀναβάλλω (also exhibited in Lasus fr. 702. 2 P μελιβόαν ὕμνον ἀναγνέων; cf. Pind. *Is.* 6. 62 ἀνὰ δ᾽ ἄγαγον ἐς φάος οἵαν μοῖραν ὕμνων, Eur. *El.* 126 ἄναγε πολύδακρυν ἀδονάν; Borthwick, *CR* 21 (1971), 318-19) and for the repetition which is idiomatic in the context of ritual cries or the expression of religious excitement (see Dodds on Eur. *Bacch.* 107 and n. on 96 above). For the comparable use of the verb παιανίζω with feminine subject see Gerber, *ZPE* 49 (1982), 5. **ὦ παρθένοι:** for this type of choral self-address combined with second-person plural imperative see Kaimio, *The Chorus of Greek Drama within the Light of the Person and Number Used*, p. 122.

213-14. Ὀρτυγίαν: on this obscure cult-title see Farnell, *Cults of the Greek States*, ii. 558-9 n. 4, 562 n. 25. **ἐλαφαβόλον:** an epithet rare in Greek literature, though used widely as a cult-title: see Page, *Sappho and Alcaeus*, p. 263; Bruchmann, *Epitheta Deorum*, p. 45; Farnell, *Cults of the Greek States*, ii. 561-2. **ἀμφίπυρον:** for Artemis' torch cf. *OT* 204 ff., Eur. *IT* 21, Ennius trag. fr. xv. 30 Jocelyn. In Athens Artemis was identified in cult with Hecate and given the epithets πυρφόρος and φωσφόρος (cf. Preller–Robert, *Gr. Myth.* i. 321, 323 n. 4, Johansen and Whittle on Aesch. *Suppl.* 676). ἀμφίπυρος is used of Dionysus at Eur. *Ion* 716, where, as here, it must mean 'with a flame in either hand': cf. Ar. *Ran.* 1361-2, where Hecate is described as δίπυρους ἀνέχουσα | λαμπάδας (Artemis has just been mentioned). The accumulation of epithets is hymnic: Page, op. cit., p. 17.

COMMENTARY

215. γείτονάϲ τε Νύμφαϲ: on the notion of deities as 'neighbours' see J. S. Rusten, *HSCP* 87 (1983), 291 and n. 11.

216. αἴρομαι: '-αι cannot be elided in tragedy' (Platnauer on Eur. *IT* 679; cf. Diggle, *PCPS* 20 (1974), 27, *CR* 34 (1984), 67), and Lloyd-Jones's conjecture (*CR* 31 (1981), 171) may well be the best solution. (D. Sansone, *GGA* 234 (1982), 40, cites other potential instances of such elision as ἀείρομ' from tragedy, but none is textually secure.) **ἀπώϲομαι:** the future here is closely akin to those found in certain types of prayer (see Norden, op. cit.) and certain passages in choral lyric where the chorus announce their intention of doing what they actually are doing by virtue of making the announcement (cf. W. J. Slater, *CQ* 19 (1969), 86ff.; M. Treu. *Gymnasium* 72 (1965), 445–6).

217. τὸν αὐλόν: on the nature of this instrument and its role in Greek literature and art see e.g. D. Paquette, *L'Instrument de musique dans la céramique de la Grèce antique* (Paris 1984), ch. 1, Lloyd on Hdt. 2. 60. It was especially linked with Dionysiac revels (Pearson on Eur. *Phoen.* 789ff.). **ἀναταράϲϲει:** see Sier on Aesch. *Cho.* 331.

219. κιccόc: for the ivy's connection with Dionysus see Dodds's notes on Eur. *Bacch.* 81 and 1054–5.

219–20. Βακχίαν ... ἅμιλλαν: for the internal accusative as governed by ὑποϲτρέφων cf. *El.* 493 ἐπέβα ... ἁμιλλήμαθ', Eur. *Hel.* 356 πελάϲω ... ἅμιλλαν, and cf. Lloyd-Jones, *YCS* 22 (1972), 265.

221. ἰὼ ἰώ: for the circumstances in which ἰώ is used in tragedy cf. Pfeiffer, *Sitzb. d. Bayer. Akad. d. Wiss., phil.-hist. Abt.* 2 (1938), 11–12. For the 'sacral *geminatio*' see Nisbet–Hubbard on Hor. *Odes* 2. 19. 7.

222. ἴδε ἴδ': for the excited repetition see above on 210–11. For the hiatus 'after exclamations, urgent imperatives and the like' see West, *GM*, p. 15 n. 24. But for the *first* ἴδε to stand in hiatus is suspicious, and Schroeder's ἰδοῦ ἴδ' may be right (ἴδ' ἴδε Wilamowitz (preceded by Schütz) in *Griechische Verskunst* (Berlin, 1921), p. 528).

223. ἀντίπρωιρα: for similar metaphors see Denniston on Eur. *El.* 846. The last few words of this astrophic lyric announce an approaching entry: on the technique see Taplin, *Stagecraft*, p. 174.

LINES 215-228

SECOND EPISODE (225-496)

On strictly realistic grounds it is odd to find D asking Lichas whether her husband is still living (233) when the messenger has already told her he is (182) and the chorus has just performed an astrophic lyric inspired by joy at that news.[8] Tycho von Wilamowitz noted this oddity (p. 146) and explained it in terms of S's concern not to have the formal announcement of Heracles' safe return weakened in any way by the preliminary and unofficial report which the anonymous messenger brings. One must also remember that the information about Heracles' activity can only now be brought to the fore so that D may be deceived by Lichas and then told the truth by the messenger (see above, p. 88). D's question must therefore be posed again. For the way in which ancient dramatists will repeat information on two separate occasions regardless of realism's demands see W. G. Arnott, *WS* 16 (1982), 131 ff.

225-6. The positive ὁρῶ is stressed through being followed by a negative phrase conveying the same idea: cf. 235 below. Positive and negative are regularly linked by a particle in such circumstances: see the examples cited by Stevens on Eur. *Andr.* 96; cf. Fehling, *Wiederholungsfiguren*, pp. 272-3. Dawe's οὐδάμ᾽ for οὐδέ μ᾽ (*Studies* iii. 82) is therefore unidiomatic. For the construction with accusative of the whole and part cf. *El.* 147 ἐμέ γ᾽ ... ἄραρεν φρένας, fr. 171. 2 τὴν ῥῖνά μ᾽ εὐθὺς ψηλαφᾷ, Diggle, *CQ* 40 (1990), p. 102 n. 4. As subject of παρῆλθε understand τάδε (from 223). See further Kraus, *WS* 20 (1986), 92.

226. 'A στόλος is a company of persons characterised externally in some particular way and moving or having moved to a certain place for a definite purpose' (Johansen and Whittle on Aesch. *Suppl.* 2). **μή**: against Hermann's conjecture μὴ οὐ see on 90-1 above.

227 ff. On the initiation of dialogue here see on 61 ff. above.

227-8. χαίρειν ... χαρτόν: one of those instances listed by Fraenkel on Aesch. *Ag.* 251 ff. of cases where 'although χαῖρε had long ago crystallized into a formula of greeting, it still sometimes conveyed the original meaning'. For similar poetic variations of the formula see Headlam on Aesch. *Ag.* 577. The tradition is divided between φέρεις

---

[8] One is reminded of the notorious problem in Aesch. *Ag.* 355 ff. where a first stasimon that opens with the chorus celebrating the news of Troy's capture ends with it doubting that very report.

COMMENTARY

and φέρει: the switch within a conditional or relative clause from third person to second person represented by τὸν κήρυκα ... εἰ ... φέρεις can be paralleled (see Johansen and Whittle on Aesch. *Suppl.* 27) and is *difficilior lectio*. For greetings in the third person conveying an effect of formality see Kraus, *WS* 20 (1986), 92 n. 9. For the notion of a tale that brings joy see Collard on Eur. *Suppl.* 647 ff.

229. ἀλλ' εὖ μέν: for the messenger's insistence on opening his news with a word of good omen cf. *OT* 86–7: (Οἰ.) τίν' ἡμῖν ἥκεις τοῦ θεοῦ φήμην φέρων; | (Κρ.) ἐςθλήν. ἀλλ': not so much a reply 'to the doubt expressed in χαρτὸν εἴ τι καὶ φέρει' (Jebb) as 'a sympathetic reaction to the previous speaker's words or actions: "Well"' (Denniston, *GP*[2], p. 19). For the anaphora of εὖ see Fehling, *Wiederholungsfiguren*, pp. 197–8. The special point behind εὖ προςφωνούμεθα is noted by Headlam on Aesch. *Ag.* 351 ff., who observes that verbs like προςφωνεῖν, προςειπεῖν do not usually require an additional εὖ to produce the requisite meaning. The present passage is one of the places where μέν ... δέ is virtually equivalent to *ut ... ita*: cf. Dawe, *Studies* i. 146. Attempts to tamper with the mood of the second verb (e.g. προςφωνοίμεθα F. W. Schmidt, προςφωνώμεθα Schneider) destroy S's carefully contrived balance (cf. now W. Kraus, *WS* 20 (1986), 92–3).

230. γύναι: see Wackernagel, 'Über einige antike Anredeformen' (1912), 25–6 = *Kl. Schr.* ii. 992–3, on this form of address; for the emphatic genitive see on 87 above.

232. ὦ φίλτατ' is a phrase often used in tragedy in addressing a messenger who has brought good news or news that affords some sort of relief: see D. B. Gregor, *CR* 7 (1957), 14–15, who ingeniously suggests that the absence of any such phrase at 187 is indicative of D's incredulity. A more likely explanation is that S intends the second announcement of Heracles' safe return as a climax (see above, p. 105).

πρῶθ' ἃ πρῶτα: for the repetition cf. Fehling, *Wiederholungsfiguren*, pp. 200–1; for the plural cf. on διδακτά at 64 above.

234–5. Moorhouse (p. 192) adds a further dimension to the controversy over imperfect λείπω (see above on 76–7) by ingeniously suggesting for the example we find here 'an *attractio temporis*: the durative aspect of the past state of Heracles' health (expressed in the participles) passes over into ἔλειπον'. He compares *Od.* 11. 86 (of the dead Anticleia) τὴν ζωὴν κατέλειπον ἰὼν εἰς Ἴλιον ἱρήν. A likelier explanation might be that imperfect λείπω is used of events where the verb's subject would possibly or probably return, while the aorist signifies the finality of desertion, forsaking, leaving a legacy on dying, etc.

235. For the second time (cf. 181 ff. above) we find a tricolon crescendo employed to convey the crucial news of Heracles' safe return. ζῶντα καὶ θάλλοντα ~ Eur. IA 1225 ζώσάν τε καὶ θάλλουcαν; cf. Aesch. Ag. 677 καὶ ζῶντα καὶ βλέποντα with Fraenkel ad loc. on the 'strengthening double phrase', Eur. fr. 898. 13 N² ζῆι τε καὶ θάλλει. For similar examples of the idiom whereby, in order to stress existence, two verbs are used, the first general (ζῆν, πνεῖν, vel sim.), the second specific (βλέπειν, θάλλειν, vel sim.), see A. Henrichs, Cron. Ercol. 6 (1976), 17 n. 16. **κοὐ νόcωι βαρύν:** Schwinge, pp. 57–8, detects an irony here, since Heracles *is* suffering a νόcοc in the sense of his love for Iole (see on 443 below).

236. **πατρώιαc, εἴτε βαρβάρου:** since D has long since been told that Heracles is in the vicinity of Oechalia (74–5), it might be argued that this cannot be a literally meant question: rather it is a 'polar expression' for 'where on earth is he?' (for the general phenomenon involved see e.g. Kannicht on Eur. Hel. 229 ff.). But perhaps the poet and/or his audience have by now forgotten the earlier scene and are only interested in the sort of question an anxious wife would be likely to ask; for the ellipse of εἴτε before πατρώιαc cf. OT 517, Denniston GP², pp. 507–8; cf. on 3 above.

237–8. Cf. 752 ff. and n. on 752–3 for the ἀκτή τιc . . . ἔνθα formula. **Εὐβοιίc:** for the form see Wackernagel, GN (1914), 109 = Kl. Schr. ii. 1166. On the construction with ὁρίζω here and at 754 see Kannicht on Eur. Hel. 1670 ff.

238. **τέλη . . . ἔγκαρπα:** cf. El. 635 (θύμαθ') . . . | πάγκαρπ', fr. 398. 3 ἐνῆν δὲ παγκάρπεια cυμμιγὴc ὁλαῖc κτλ. **Κηναίωι Διί:** for Zeus of Mt. Cenaeon and the sacrifices which Heracles makes to him see Cook, Zeus, ii/2. 902 n. 2.

239. See Diggle, CQ 22 (1972), 242 (and PCPS 20 (1974), 3 and n. 3) for the asymmetrical 'linking of participle and prepositional phrase as its equivalent'. **εὐκταῖα:** 'prayers (rather than 'votive offerings'), as εὐχαῖc at 240 confirms: cf. Aesch. fr. 78A. 11–12 Radt εὐκταῖα . . . καλλίγραπτον εὐχάν, Suppl. 631–2, Hesych. s.v. εὐκταῖον· τὸ κατ' εὐχὴν . . . ἀποδιδόμενον. **ἢ 'πο μαντείαc:** for other examples of prodelided ἀπο(-) in Greek drama see Platnauer, CQ 10 (1960), 142.

COMMENTARY

For this type of martial vow see W. K. Pritchett, *The Greek State at War* iii (Berkeley 1979), 231–2.

241. γυναικῶν ὧν ὁραῖc: cf. Men. *Asp.* 36–7 τῶν τ' αἰχ]μαλώτων τοῦτον ὃν ὁραῖc πληcίον [ὄχλον. For our passage's attraction of the relative from accusative to genitive see Moorhouse, p. 269. **ὁραῖc ἐν ὄμμαcιν:** for the pleonastic emphasis see 997–8 below, *Ant.* 764 ἐν ὀφθαλμοῖc ὁρῶν, and the numerous examples cited by Johansen and Whittle on Aesch. *Suppl.* 716; cf. Moorhouse, p. 107.

242. For the phrase οὗτοc/αὕτη τίc see Diggle, *STE*, p. 43. The hyperbaton here well conveys amazement and perhaps pity; compare the inversion ὅδε τιc discussed by Diggle, loc. cit., which throws emphasis on the demonstrative.

243. ξυμφοραί: West's ξυμφορᾶc (ablatival genitive) (*BICS* 26 (1979), 110), is unnecessary: 'κλέπτειν and its compounds are used of any kind of action which involves deceit, and the meanings are multifarious' (Denniston on Eur. *El.* 364). Here 'mislead' *vel sim.*; cf. 437 below.

247. Expressive hyperbaton (see on 647 below); cf. *Aj.* 646 ὁ μακρὸc κἀναρίθμητοc χρόνοc. **βεβώc:** 'as βέβηκε can have the meaning "be, be at rest (in a place)"... so βεβώc is used here (and not as equivalent to οἰχόμενοc, as Campbell on *Tr.* 41) with special emphasis on the fixed state': Moorhouse, p. 205. **ἡμερῶν ἀνήριθμον:** for the genitive cf. *El.* 232 ἀνάριθμοc... θρήνων and Kaibel ad loc.

248. As in the preceding line, another instance of expressive hyperbaton involving χρόνοc: cf. *Aj.* 311 τὸν μὲν ἧcτο πλεῖcτον ἄφθογγοc χρόνον. For other Sophoclean instances of separation of article from noun, all of which 'occur in narrative and involve proper names or a standard phrase', see Hutchinson on Aesch. *ScT* 298 ff.

249. κατείχεθ': presumably passive ('was held back') rather than intransitive (cf. Richardson on *HHDem.* 126). **ὡc φηc' αὐτόc:** cf. ὡc αὐτὸc λέγει in 253 and 252–3 n.

249–50. οὐκ... ἀλλ': cf. on 225–6.

250. τῶι λόγωι: Margoliouth's emendation (*Studia Scenica* (London 1883), 27) makes better sense of the prefix of προcεῖναι in 251.

251. γύναι: see on 230 above. **Ζεὺc... πράκτωρ:** cf. κοὐδὲν τούτων ὅ τι μὴ Ζεύc at 1278. The noun πράκτωρ is used of Aphrodite at 861 below; on the absence of ἄν from the present passage see KG ii/2. 426 (1).

LINES 239-258

252-3. Deleted by Wunder (followed by Reeve, *GRBS* 14 (1973), 166) on the ground of repetition (κεῖνος ... πραθείς ~ ἐμποληθείς (250); ὡς αὐτὸς λέγει ~ ὥς φης' αὐτός (249); Ὀμφάλη τῆι βαρβάρωι | ἐνιαυτὸν ἐξέπλησεν ~ τὸν μὲν παρελθόντ' ἄροτον ἐν μήκει χρόνου | Λυδῆι γυναικὶ φασί νιν λάτριν πονεῖν (69-70)). Reeve supposes that the two lines were meant to replace 248-51 as 'a more explicit version', and originally began οὔκ, ἀλλὰ πραθείς ... But the repetition of 'as Heracles himself says' is highly effective, set in the mouth of a servant who wishes to stress that events potentially discreditable to his master are fully admitted by that master. There is a further interesting contrast with lines 255 ff. of his speech, where Lichas invents details to which his master would not admit. If we take δέ in 252 to be equivalent to γάρ and to open the narrative proper after the introduction (cf. 475 below, Denniston, *GP*², pp. 170-1, Pfeiffer, *Sitzb. d. Bayer. Akad. d. Wiss., phil.-hist. Kl.* 6 (1958), 19 = *Sophokles* (Wege der Forschung 95; 1967), 476), the repetition of the concept 'sold' is hardly offensive, and the two lines do not merely repeat the picture of slavery to a foreign queen, but add the name Omphale.

253. ἐνιαυτὸν ἐξέπλησεν: cf. Ion of Chios, *TrGF* i (19) fr. 21 Sn. ἐναυσίαν γὰρ δεῖ με τὴν ὀρτὴν ἄγειν.

254. ἐδήχθη: cf. such phrases as λύπηι καρδίαν δηχθήσομαι (Eur. *Alc.* 1100; cf. Fraenkel, *Beob. zu Aristoph.*, p. 18, Rau, *Paratragodia*, p. 185). **τοὔνειδος λαβών:** cf. ζημίαν λαβεῖν in fr. 807.

255. For an oath as 'an additional sanction to the bare word' see Pearson on fr. 472. 1.

256. ἀγχιστῆρα: for comparable nominal forms see Ernst Fraenkel, *Nomina Agentis* (Strasburg 1910), ii. 14.

257. ξὺν παιδὶ καὶ γυναικί: since Eurytus had several children (cf. 266 below), 'with wife and child' must be taken as a collective singular (so Moorhouse, p. 1). For the set phrase cf. *Od.* 9. 199 οὕνεκά μιν σὺν παιδὶ περισχόμεθ' ἠδὲ γυναικί.

258. κοὐχ ἡλίωσε τοὔπος: cf. *Il.* 16. 737 οὐδ' ἁλίωσε βέλος. **ἁγνός** 'is a vague term, which requires qualification from its context to describe purity from a specific taint' (R. Parker, *Miasma: Pollution and Purification in Early Greek Religion* (Oxford 1983), 147). The present passage obviously refers to purification from the blood-guilt incurred by the murder of Iphitus, though in all later accounts (see Parker, p. 382) that purification *precedes* the sale to Omphale.

COMMENTARY

259. cτρατὸν λαβὼν ἐπακτόν: on the adjective see Kassel–Austin on Ar. fr. 375. **ἔρχεται πόλιν:** for the direct accusative after a verb of motion see Schwyzer, *Gr. Gr.* ii. 68 and (more specifically on πόλιν/ πόλεις thus treated) Bers, p. 81.

259–60. πόλιν | τὴν Εὐρυτείαν. τόνδε: for this sort of ellipse see *Il.* 9. 382 αἵ θ' ἑκατόμπυλοί εἰcι, διηκόcιοι δ' ἀν' ἑκάcτας (πύλας), Soph. *El.* 589 καὶ παιδοποιεῖc· τοὺς δὲ πρόcθεν (παῖδας); for further examples and discussion see Wilamowitz on Eur. *Her.* 262, Bond on *Her.* 157, Diggle on *Phaeth.* 113–14, Courtney on Juv. 14. 241–2. On the adjective cf. 51 above.

260 ff. As will later emerge, the following details represent a lying attempt on Lichas' part to conceal his master's infatuation for Iole. For the likelihood that S has invented them see Davies, *CQ* 34 (1984), 480 ff., *SIFC* 7 (1989), 7 ff.

260–1. μεταίτιον | μόνον βροτῶν: cf. 1233–4 μόνη | μεταίτιος: these two passages naturally gave rise to the notion that μεταίτιος could be equivalent to αἴτιος, a notion that Fraenkel on Aesch. *Ag.* 811 memorably combats. In the present passage, the appended genitive helps us to identify the other party as none other than Zeus (cf. 251 above).

261. τοῦδ' ... πάθους: cf. 256 above. The presence of the article there, its absence here, serve to confirm L. Bergson's view (*Rh. Mus.* 102 (1959), 29–30) that the use of the article in tragedy is often a function of polymorphism.

262. ὅς: here a relative introduces a mythical narrative, as regularly in the epinicia of Pindar and at 562 ff. below. **ἐλθόντ' ἐς δόμους ἐφέcτιον:** cf. *Rhes.* 201 ἐλθὼν δ' ἐς δόμους ἐφέcτιος, and for the general use of ἐφέcτιος predicatively to verbs of motion (or staying) in epic and tragedy see Fraenkel on Aesch. *Ag.* 851. The adjective is frequently combined with the noun δόμοι (cf. LSJ s.v. ἐφέcτιος; Dawe, *The Collation and Investigation of Manuscripts of Aeschylus*, p. 181).

263–4. πολλὰ μέν ... πολλὰ δ': for other instances of this popular type of anaphora with identical forms of πολύς see Johansen and Whittle on Aesch. *Suppl.* 1006, Fehling, *Wiederholungsfiguren*, pp. 199 ff.

264. 'πολλὰ ἐφύβριcε καὶ λόγωι καὶ ἔργωι: post φρενί scil. supprimitur verbum ex opposito ἐπερρόθηcε supplendum' Dobree (*Adversaria*, ed. Wagner, iv. 36) (cf. Stevens on Eur. *Andr.* 1096).

ἀτηρᾶι φρενί: cf. *Ant.* 603 (for a recent attempt to take the first five words there together cf. Winnington-Ingram, *BICS* 26 (1979), 8), and for a general consideration of the phrase J. Stallmach, *Ate* (Beitr. z. kl. Phil. 18; 1968), 48 ff.

265. ἄφυκτ'... βέλη: cf. *Phil.* 105 ἰούς γ' ἀφύκτους.

266. For tragedy's employment of the epic idiom ὅc as possessive see Sideras, *Aeschylus Homericus*, p. 130. **κρίcιν:** for the word's near equivalence to ἀγών in the sense 'trial of skill' see Braswell on Pind. *Pyth.* 4. 253 (c). On Heracles' archery contest with the sons of Eurytus see above p. xxxvi.

267. φωνεῖ: if right, the verb (taken with λέγων in 265) constitutes another instance of the type of pleonasm discussed on 346 below. For the unaugmented form at the start of a line within a messenger-speech see on 904.

267 ff. This puzzling crux is analysed and earlier attempts to heal it are listed by Stinton, pp. 133–4. Jebb ad loc. defends ὡc, but by the time of the third edition of his commentary on *Antigone* he preferred (in his note on 186 ἀντὶ τῆc cωτηρίαc) ἀνδρὸc ἀντ' ἐλευθέρου ('a slave, and not a free man (as he ought to be)'). Cf. *Aj.* 1020 δοῦλοc λόγοιcιν ἀντ' ἐλευθέρου φανείc, and 148 above. For the now generally recognized impossibility of the genitive of agent in S see Moorhouse, p. 76, and for the frequent interpolation of ὡc in manuscripts see Pearson on fr. 873. 1.[9] For other rhetorical juxtapositions of the Greek words for slave and free see Com. fr. adesp. 210 (iii. 448 Kock); cf. Kock's n. ad loc., adding to his parallels now Eur. *Alcmeon* (?) (*P.Oxy.* 3215. fr. 1. 11) and *Antig.* (*P.Oxy.* 3317. 10) ἐγώ c' ἔθηκα] δοῦλον ὄντ' ἐλεύθερον and διαλέ]γηι μοι δοῦλοc ὢν ἐλε[υθέρωc.

268. δείπνοιc: plural for singular (with reference to the plurality of courses): see Braswell on Pind. *Pyth.* 4. 31(a). **ὠινωμένοc:** for the scribal omission of the augment see Kassel–Austin on Cratinus fr. 504.

269. Dawe objects to the sentence ending with αὐτόν, but *El.* 535 is analogy enough. **ὧν ἔχων χόλον:** for S's use of a causal genitive after verbs expressing anger see Pearson on fr. 697 (contrast the construction at 274 below). The genitive is often (as here with χόλον) supported by a noun.

271. κλειτύν: for the form see Wackernagel, *Spr. Unt. zu Hom.* pp. 74–5,

[9] For an amusing modern instance of ὡc displacing the correct reading cf. *PCPS* 27 (1981), 95 n. 23.

COMMENTARY

L. Threatte, *Grammar of Attic Inscriptions* (Berlin 1980), i. 192. Manuscripts regularly corrupt to κλιτ- (Eur. *Cycl.* 50, *Hipp.* 227, etc.). Cf. *Od.* 21. 22–3 (Ἴφιτος) ἵππους διζήμενος, αἵ οἱ ὄλοντο | δώδεκα θήλειαι, ὑπὸ δ' ἡμίονοι ταλαεργοί, above, p. xxviii.

272–3. For a similar disjunction see Cat. 62. 15 'nos alio mentes, alio divisimus aures'; cf. Theogn. 87 μή μ' ἔπεσιν μὲν στέργε, νόον δ' ἔχε καὶ φρένας ἄλληι, and for other Greek equivalents of our idiom 'to have one's mind somewhere' Diggle on Eur. *Phaeth.* 265 (add [Plato] *Theages* 129c ἄλλοσε τὸν νοῦν ἔχοντα, quoted by Jebb on our passage).

273. The insertion of a verb between preposition + adjective and (second adjective +) noun is easily paralleled: cf. 1242 σὺ γάρ μ' ἀπ' εὐνασθέντος ἐκκινεῖς κακοῦ and the numerous examples cited by Fraenkel on Aesch. *Ag.* 964. For the wall or tower from which Iphitus is regularly described as pushed see Pherecydes *FGrH* 3 F 82ᴮ. **πυργώδους:** for the form and meaning of the word see M. J. O'Brien, *CQ* 35 (1985), 267–8.

274–5. The simple genitive of cause of anger is often thus re-enforced by a preposition: see Schwyzer, *Gr. Gr.* ii. 134 (δ). On 275's word-order see Sier on Aesch. *Cho.* 783 f.

276. πρατόν νιν ἐξέπεμψεν: this phrase closes the circle of ring-composition opened at 251–2 above (Ζεύς . . . κεῖνος δὲ πραθείς). Zeus is responsible for Heracles' sale to Omphale in Pherecydes *FGrH* 3 F 82ʙ. **οὐδ' ἠνέσχετο:** echoed by οὐ στέργουσιν at 280; cf. Eur. *Her.* 1318–19 ἀλλ' οἰκοῦς' ὅμως | Ὄλυμπον ἠνέσχοντό θ' ἡμαρτηκότες, 1341–2 ἐγὼ δὲ τοὺς θεοὺς οὔτε λέκτρ' ἃ μὴ θέμις | στέργειν νομίζω.

280. οὐ στέργουσιν: for the litotes see Johansen and Whittle on Aesch. *Suppl.* 273. **οὐδὲ δαίμονες:** 'the gods don't like hybris either', any more than do mortals: see 126 above for οὐδέ thus used. The line was deleted by van Deventer, but the sentiment expressed is important for the drama's themes, though this should not be over-simplified (sensitive remarks in Easterling, *BICS* 15 (1968), 61–2).

281. ὑπερχλίοντες: Σ glosses as ὑπερεντρυφήσαντες (τρυφή is the regular glossing equivalent of χλιδή: see Headlam on Aesch. *Ag.* 1445 ff.) The compound occurs only here (cf. Aesch. *Cho.* 137 χλίω, *Suppl.* 914 ἐγχλίω). Its present tense is to be explained in terms of morphology. Note the seamless transition from the ὕβρις of Heracles to that of his victims.

LINES 271-295

282. Ἅιδου ... οἰκήτορες: cf. Ἅιδου φθίμενος οἰκήτωρ at 1161 below, *Aj.* 517 Ἅιδου θανασίμους οἰκήτορας.

283. πόλις δὲ δούλη: for passages in tragedy where a πόλις is conceived as a slave see Harder on Eur. *Archel.* fr. 35. 1; for the 'reverse attraction' in τάσδε δ' ἅσπερ εἰσορᾶις see KG ii/2. 413 (4). Blaydes's δούλη 'σθ'· αἵδε is therefore unnecessary (the prodelision is legitimate: see 295).

284. εὑροῦσαι: one of a number of passages where the verb is better translated 'get' than 'find': further examples and discussion in R. M. Frazer, *Mnem.* 29 (1976), 182-3. Cf. on 1177-8 below.

285-6. For the combination τε ... δέ (especially common with personal pronouns, as here) see on 143 above.

287. αὐτὸν δ' ἐκεῖνον: on this set phrase see Janko, *CQ* 35 (1985), 20 ff., especially p. 26 on passages (like the present) where enclitics, particles, etc. separate the two words constituting the phrase. **ἁγνὰ θύματα:** see J. Casabona, *Recherches sur le vocabulaire des sacrifices en grec* (Aix-en-Provence 1966), 305, on the probable meaning of this phrase (H shows himself ἁγνός by fulfilling his oath (240 above) to Zeus).

288. τῆς ἁλώσεως: 'in return for the capture': genitive of exchange (cf. Eur. *Med.* 534-5; *Rhes.* 467-8, etc.). Cf. on 737 below.

289. φρόνει νιν ὡς ἥξοντα: 'know that he will come': Moorhouse, pp. 306-7, cites 1145 below and *Aj.* 942 (σοὶ μὲν δοκεῖν ταῦτ' ἔστ', ἐμοὶ δ' ἄγαν φρονεῖν) for this meaning of φρονέω. Cf. Pearson on fr. 91. The νιν is redundant after 287's emphatically placed αὐτὸν δ' ἐκεῖνον at the start of the line, but cf. *OT* 246 ff. κατεύχομαι δὲ τὸν δεδρακότ'... κακὸν κακῶς νιν ἄμορον ἐκτρῖψαι βίον.

291. Cf. the chorus at 223-4 τάδ' ἀντίπρωιρα δή σοι | βλέπειν πάρεστ' ἐναργῆ |, of the earlier good news. κυρῶ + personal dative is an idiom confined to Sophocles (here and at *OC* 1290): cf. Johansen and Whittle on Aesch. *Suppl.* 787-8 for an analysis of various uses of this verb + dative in the tragedians.

294. πανδίκωι φρενί: 'with all my heart': cf. on 611 below; for tragic use of φρενί adverbially as a locative dative see Johansen and Whittle on Aesch. *Suppl.* 606.

295. πολλή 'στ' ἀνάγκη: for prodelided ἐστι in S see Johansen and Whittle on Aesch. *Suppl.* 718; cf. on 381 and 905 below. **τῆιδε τοῦτο:** sc. τῆι πράξει ... τὸ ἐμὲ χαίρειν: with the resulting ellipse

113

COMMENTARY

and juxtaposition cf. Aesch. *Ag.* 1330 καὶ ταῦτ' ἐκείνων μᾶλλον οἰκτίρω πολύ. The verse was doubted by Wunder, as contributing nothing beyond what has gone before.

296 ff. For rejoicing at a city's sack followed by fear of consequences for the victor cf. Aesch. *Ag.* 338 ff.

296. τοῖcιν: Dawe's small change to τοῖcί γ' (*Studies* iii. 83), provided one accepts his assurance that 'Deianeira is drawing a very fine distinction between her own rejoicing πανδίκωι φρενί and those who are guided by prudence', economically sharpens the sense here. But Kraus, *WS* 20 (1986), 93–4, shows good grounds for supposing that D alludes to herself with the phrase τοῖcιν εὖ cκοπουμένοιc.

297. For this construction with accusative after verb of fearing see *Phil.* 493–4, Eur. *Med.* 37, KG ii/2. 579 ff.

298 ff. D's argument here (a specific justification of the generalization uttered in 296–7, introduced idiomatically by γάρ) is well analysed by Johansen, *General Reflection in Tragic Rhesis*, pp. 66–7.

298. For the locative dative in this construction cf. *Phil.* 965 ἐμοὶ μὲν οἶκτος δεινὸς ἐμπέπτωκέ τις, Hdt. 3. 14. 11 Καμβύσηι ἐcελθεῖν οἰκτόν τινα, 6. 138. 3 καί cφι βουλομένοιcι δεινόν τι ἐcέδυνε, Verdenius, *Mnem.* 28 (1975), 418.

298–9. For the hyperbaton created by ἐμοὶ ... ὁρώcηι with another verb (εἰcέβη) intervening see Gow on Theocr. *Epigr.* 21. 1.

300. ἀοίκουc ἀπάτοράc τ': for similar groups of adjectives in privative α- see Johansen and Whittle on Aesch. *Suppl.* 143, Fehling, *Wiederholungsfiguren*, pp. 238–9.

301–2. ἐξ ἐλευθέρων ἴcωc | ἀνδρῶν: on the word-order here cf. *Phil.* 180–1 πρωτογόνων ἴcωc | οἴκων and in general J. Nuchelmans, *Miscellanea Tragica* (Kamerbeek Festschrift; Amsterdam 1976), 243 ff. The two verses were deleted by Nauck and Hense. In defence of the seemingly illogical πρὶν μὲν ἦcαν, Zieliński (p. 587 n. 6 = pp. 340–1 n. 1) compared Eur. *Her.* 443–4 τοὺc τοῦ μεγάλου δή ποτε παῖδαc | τὸ πρὶν Ἡρακλέουc and *Tro.* 581 τέκεα :: πρίν ποτ' ἦμεν.

303–4. For the apotropaic appeal to Zeus cf. Aesch. *ScT* 255 ὦ παγκρατὲc Ζεῦ, τρέψον εἰc ἐχθροὺc βέλος. **τροπαῖε:** a cult-title of Zeus: see *Ant.* 143, Eur. *El.* 671, *Hcld.* 867, Men. *CGF* fr. 148. 45 Austin. For **μή ποτ'** thus used cf. Eur. *Phoen.* 190 ff. μήποτε τάνδ' ... δουλοcύναν τλαίην. For the ἀποπομπή see Eur. *Hipp.* 528–9

("Ερως) μή μοί ποτε cὺν κακῶι φανείης | μηδ' ἄρρυθμος ἔλθοις, and in general Fraenkel on Aesch. Ag. 1573 and Horace, pp. 410–11. In the present case the negatived εἰcίδοιμι is idiomatic: cf. Aesch. Ag. 472 ff. μήτ' εἴην πτολιπόρθης, | μήτ' οὖν αὐτὸς ἁλοὺς (ἁλόνθ' Margoliouth) ὑπ' ἄλλωι βίον κατίδοιμι (κατέδοιμι Valckenaer),[10] ScT 220 ff. μηδ' ἐπίδοιμι τάνδ' | ἀστυδρομουμέναν πόλιν καὶ στράτευμ' | ἁπτόμενον πυρὶ δαΐωι.

304. **πρὸς τοὐμὸν οὕτω cπέρμα:** for the insertion of οὕτω in this position see Fraenkel on Aesch. Ag. 964; for cπέρμα of a mother's child cf. Aesch. Suppl. 141 cπέρμα cεμνᾶς ματρός.

305. Plausibly deleted by G. H. Müller, Emendat. et Interpr. Soph. (1878), p. 63, as an otiose and enfeebling expansion of 303–4, which in themselves are equivalent to 'may I die before I see such a dreadful thing' (cf. Il. 6. 464–5, 24. 244 ff. with Macleod ad loc., Aesch. Ag. 1537 ff.). There is no such anti-climax in the otherwise similar passage at Aesch. ScT 219–20 μήποτ' ἐμὸν κατ' αἰῶνα λίποι θεῶν | ἅδε πανάγυρις, μήδ' ἐπίδοιμι κτλ. τι is 'euphemistic for something disastrous' (Stevens on Eur. Andr. 1072). **τῆcδε ... ζώcης:** the special tragic use of ὅδε for the first person: see Moorhouse, p. 155. One is to understand εἰcίδοιμί cε δράcαντα after this phrase: on this class of ellipse see KG ii/2. 574–5.

306. This line closes the ring opened at 297 ff. (δέδοικα τάσδ' ὁρωμένη ~ ταρβεῖν ... ἐμοί ... οἶκτος ... ταύτας ὁρώσηι). On this method of structuring the argument cf. Johansen, General Reflection in Tragic Rhesis, p. 67.

307 ff. Iole's silence here seems to be modelled on Cassandra's in Aesch. Ag. (cf. S. G. Kapsomenos, Sophokles' Trachinierinnen und ihr Vorbild (Athens 1963), 68 ff.) though Cassandra, unlike Iole here (see on 218), is not a κωφὸν πρόσωπον. For an extremely sensitive analysis of the episode and its production see Mastronarde, Contact and Discontinuity, pp. 76–7.

308. On the form τεκνοῦς(ς)α see the important remarks of V. Schmidt in Kyklos (Keydell Festschrift; Berlin 1978), 38 ff. **πρὸς ... φύcιν:** for the meaning of φύcις here ('appearance', 'outward form') cf. OT 740–1 τὸν δὲ Λάιον φύcιν | τίν' εἶχε φράζε, J. W. Beardslee jun., The Use of ΦΥΣΙΣ in Fifth-Century Greek Literature (Chicago 1918),

[10] Prob. Lloyd-Jones, CQ 12 (1962), 193 n. 1, CR 26 (1976), 7; Hermann deemed the conjecture 'inventistissimus'.

COMMENTARY

24–5 and n. 4; C. E. Hajistephanou, *The Use of ΦΥΣΙΣ and its Cognates in Greek Tragedy with Special Reference to Character Drawing* (Nicosia 1975), 51–2. On γάρ (following a question as to identity or origin) see S. Radt, *Mnem.* 29 (1976), 257. See Addenda.

309. πάντων ἄπειρος τῶνδε: cf. 143 ἄπειρος εἶ of the chorus, ignorant as yet of the sorrows of married life. This is the interpretation of our phrase presupposed by Σ: but it does not do justice to the problem created by the μέν . . . δέ construction ('you seem to have no experience of married life, but rather to be of noble birth'), where the contrast seems incoherent. It has been suggested to me that πάντων . . . τῶνδε might have a more general reference and τῶνδ' might be genuinely deictic ('all of these abject circumstances', with an eye to the wretched chain of prisoners).

311. For 'the periphrasis with pred. arthrous participle' represented by the first phrase here see Aesch. *Suppl.* 571–2 τίς ἦν ὁ θέλξας and Johansen and Whittle ad loc. For the set phrase ὁ φιτύσας πατήρ see Bruhn, *Anhang*, § 210.

312. ὤικτισα: the aorist of instantaneous emotion: see Barrett on Eur. *Hipp.* 614: 'the speaker, in voicing a sudden emotion, thinks of the moment (just past) of the access of that emotion'; also Denniston on Eur. *El.* 215, Moorhouse, pp. 195–6.

314–15. Lichas' shifty reply reveals a guilty conscience.

314. κρίνοις: for the meaning see on 195 above.

315. τῶν ἐκεῖθεν: cf. 601 ταῖς ἔςωθεν and *Ant.* 1070 τῶν κάτωθεν for the superfluous -θεν suffix. **οὐκ ἐν ὑςτάτοις:** for the litotes here compare *Il.* 15. 11 ἐπεὶ οὔ νιν ἀφαυρότατος βάλ' Ἀχαιῶν.

316. For other instances of μή introducing a question in tragedy see Diggle, *ICS* 2 (1977), 117; cf. Moorhouse, p. 324. Generalizing plural followed by specifying singular is a quite common device: cf. Eur. *Hipp.* 49ff. τοὺς ἐμοὺς ἐχθρούς . . . τόνδε παῖδα Θηςέως and Johansen and Whittle on Aesch. *Suppl.* 164–5. This type of plural is often used of lords and masters: see *OT* 1095 ὡς ἐπίηρα φέροντα τοῖς ἐμοῖς τυράννοις and Bruhn, *Anhang*, § 3. III. Various emendations have been offered for this line, and Εὐρύτου was taken as a gloss by Dobree (*Adversaria*, ed. Wagner, iv. 36) since after 257 and 266 D can hardly need to pose this question again. However, the line is not a literal request for information ('Did Eurytus have any children?') but an emotional exclamation ('A child of Eurytus!'). Cf. Aesch. *Ag.* 1344

LINES 308-327

cîγα· τίc πληγὴν αὐτεῖ καιρίωc οὐταcμένοc; (cf. K. J. Dover, *Greek Word Order* (Cambridge, 1960), 12 n. 1) and below on 892.

317. μακράν: see Fraenkel on Aesch. *Ag.* 916 for this type of feminine adjective without a noun.

319. ἥκιcτα: a possible colloquialism: see Stevens, *Colloquial Expressions in Euripides* (Hermes Einzelschr. 38; 1976), 14. **τοὖμον ἔργον:** ἔργον + genitive or with the possessive adjective is a common idiom: see Rossi in Ed. Fraenkel, *Due seminari romani* (Rome 1977), 45.

320. ἀλλά: probably emphatic of ἐκ cαυτῆc (not of ἡμῖν: i.e. as opposed to Lichas), which means 'from your own lips', i.e. unprompted: cf. ἀπὸ cαυτῆc, as illustrated by Headlam on Herodas 6. 4. (For the announcement of names as a necessary preliminary to hospitality cf. Ar. *Av.* 644 ff.) On ἡμῖν/ὑμῖν (common in S, alien to Aesch. and Eur.) see Johansen and Whittle on Aesch. *Suppl.* 959.

321. ξυμφορά: the banalizing emendation ξυμφορόν coί μ' removes a dramatically significant exaggeration (with tragically ironic overtones): cf. Hdt. 1.216.3 cυμφορὴν ποιεύμενοι ὅτι οὐκ ἵκετο ἐc τὸ τυθῆναι. **μὴ εἰδέναι:** for synizesis of μη_εἰ(-) in tragedy (usually involving the verb εἰδέναι) see Denniston on Eur. *El.* 961, Fraenkel on Aesch. *Ag.* 1196f.

322-3. For the word-order cf. *Phil.* 1253 οὔ τἄρα ... μαχούμεθα; numerous passages cited by Fraenkel, *Beob. zu Aristoph.* p. 107; for the use of οὐ (δαμά) rather than μή here see Moorhouse, p. 324, and for οὔ τἄρα here as one of a number of instances where the phrase is equivalent to τοι in threats or warnings see J. C. B. Lowe, *Glotta* 51 (1973), 54-5.

323. διήcει γλῶccαν: cf. *El.* 596 πᾶcαν ἵηc γλῶccαν, where the noun is equivalent to φωνή, as in fr. 929. 3. διοίcει for διήcει is a simple οι/η confusion. The existence of the idiom φέρω γλῶccαν provides no justification for διαφέρω γλῶccαν.

324. προὔφηνεν: for προφαίνω used thus of *speech* see 1159 below, and L. S. Wilson in *Greek Poetry and Philosophy* (Woodbury Festschrift; Chico, Calif. 1984), 331. Cf. 1 λόγοc ... φανείc. **οὔτε μεῖζον' οὔτ' ἐλάccονα:** although μικρὸν/μέγα/μεῖζον λέγειν vel sim. can mean 'speak quietly, loudly, louder' (cf. Bain, *Actors and Audience*, p. 82 n. 1), this phrase is merely a 'polar expression' meaning 'she said nothing at all' (cf. on 236).

325. ὠδίνουcα: for the metaphor see on 41-2 above.

327. διήνεμον: the epic ἠνεμόεccαν. Zieliński (p. 537 n. 9 = p. 325

COMMENTARY

n. 4) and Kamerbeek prefer to follow Hermann in accepting Σ's less ornamental interpretation ἔρημον, and cite Aesch. *Ag.* 818–19 καπνῶι δ' ἁλοῦca νῦν ἔτ' εὔcημοc πόλιc· | ἄτηc θύελλαι ζῶcι.

328. The various ways of making sense of *AYTH(I)Γ* are analysed by Stinton, p. 135. His third interpretation ('her situation is bad in itself, but deserves sympathy') is surely the best and (in spite of Stinton himself) does provide the desired contrast (between the intrinsic badness of the situation and the claim to sympathy it confers): 'a bad situation but still there is comfort in the fact that we are sympathetic.' See further *Sophoclea*, p. 158. **cυγγνώμην ἔχει:** cf. Thuc. 3. 44. 2 ἔχοντάc τι ξυγγνώμηc.

329. πορευέcθω cτέγαc: see Bers, p. 82, for similar cases of accusative cτέγαc dependent on a verb of motion and for similar instances of 'terminal accusative' involving words meaning 'house'.

330–1. πρὸc κακοῖc | τοῖc οὖcιν: cf. Pearson on fr. 259. 2, H. J. Rose, *CQ* 27 (1933), 54, for the equivalence of τοῖc οὖcιν to τοῖc παροῦcιν: ἅλιc γὰρ ἡ παροῦcα in 332 thus echoes the present sentiment.

331. ἄλλην ... λύπην: the λύπην ... λύπην offered (or presupposed) by most manuscripts is that common phenomenon, an error of anticipation: see on 88 ff. above.

335. ἀμμείναc': sc. χώρει (from 333's χωρῶμεν)? But perhaps the participle goes just as well with the τιθῶ which ends l. 334.

336–7. μάθηιc ... ἐκμάθηιc: for other passages where the simplex verb is followed by the compound as an 'intensifying device' see Renehan, *Studies in Greek Texts*, pp. 22 ff. esp. p. 23.

336. ἄνευ τῶνδ': after this categorical exclusion of the captives, it is decidedly odd that D should still be asking at 342–3 whether she is to call them back. Deletion has therefore been proposed (Hense, *Stud. z. Soph.*, pp. 77 ff., would exclude 336, omitting τ' in 337; Reeve, *GRBS* 14 (1973), 166–7, would also cut out 338). But Mastronarde, *Contact and Discontinuity*, pp. 31–2, ingeniously suggests that with her address to the departing figures D 'breaks contact with those remaining outdoors'. These details are intended largely for the audience, and D's dramatically significant ignorance is stressed by the repeated injunction (334) to leave the captives out of it. Cf. Eur. *IA* 829 ff. Objections have also been levelled at the line's language: οὕcτιναc γ' (τ'?) is not very satisfactory, but we can always prefer cφ' (Barrett *ap.* Reeve, art. cit.

167 n. 47: for the corruption cf. Diggle, *STE*, p. 59); rather than further evidence of interpolation (Reeve), this seems a case where emendation again solves the problem (cf. on 43 ff. above). On the interlinear hiatus see Appendix B.

338. The paradosis has been variously interpreted: πάντα has been taken as an accusative of respect ('I have in all regards understanding of these things': so e.g. Bruhn, *Anhang*, § 62. I. 1; but τούτων ... πάντων more naturally expresses this); or as a direct object of the periphrasis ἔχω ... ἐπιστήμην treated as equivalent to ἐπίσταμαι (see above on 208–9; but then we would expect ταῦτα ... πάντα, not τούτων ... πάντα). The postponement of γάρ to third place in the sentence is also odd (though perhaps defensible as a further colloquialism (cf. on 319 above): Handley on Men. *Dysc.* 66 ff. cites more extreme instances from 'the conversational style of later comedy', and see now K. J. Dover, *CQ* 35 (1985), 339–40 = *Greek and the Greeks*, pp. 61–2). In view of these difficulties the line was deleted by Nauck, Blaydes, and Reeve (art.cit. (last n.), p. 167), but effectively emended by Jackson, *MS*, p. 130: cf. the phrase πάντ' ἐπίστασαι λόγον at 484 below (Reeve's objection (p. 167 n. 48) that this makes Lichas say 'I know, for I know' ignores the rhetorical variation (cf. the Odyssean line γιγνώσκω, φρονέω· τά γε δὴ νοέοντι κελεύεις (16. 136; 17. 193, 281))). On the proneness to corruption of such parentheses see, apart from the context of Jackson's discussion (pp. 127 ff.), Diggle, *CQ* 30 (1980), 416. On the legitimacy of parentheses 'separating a verb or other governing word from its noun' see the same scholar, *STE*, p. 116. The messenger's 'fussy self-importance' (to quote Jackson) is dramatically effective. See further *Sophoclea*, pp. 158–9.

339. τοῦ: for the causal genitive cf. *OT* 697–8 δίδαξον κἄμ', ἄναξ, ὅτου ποτὲ | μῆνιν τοςήνδε πράγματος ςτήςας ἔχεις, *Phil.* 327–8 τίνος γὰρ ὧδε τὸν μέγαν | χόλον κατ' αὐτῶν ἐγκαλῶν ἐλήλυθας; **με τήνδ' ἐφίσταςαι βάςιν:** Porson on Eur. *Phoen.* 1373 suggested τοῦ καὶ τήνδ' ἐφίσταςαι βάςιν; an alternative is ὑφίςταςαι '"subsistis", metaphora a venatione ducta' (Dobree, *Adversaria*, ed. Wagner, iv. 36: for confusion of ἐπ(-) and ὑπ(-) see on 356 below). But for the construction with double accusative where the second accusative is etymologically different from the verb see Schwyzer, *Gr. Gr.* ii. 79(β). Pearson illustrated βάςιν by citing (*CR* 26

COMMENTARY

(1912), 210) *Aj.* 42 τήνδ' ἐπεμπίπτει βάcιν, fr. 314. 174 [⏑]φίcτω
... βάcιν, Eur. *Hcld.* 802 ἐκβὰc πόδα.

340 ff. On the present technique of the brief delaying comment (often introduced, as here, by ἄκουε/ἄκουcον) see Mastronarde, *Contact and Discontinuity*, p. 37. The exhortation emphasizes the messenger's eventual reply to D.

340. cταθεῖc': equivalent to ἐπιcταθεῖc' (see Denniston on Eur. *El.* 403), as cταίη at 655 below is equivalent to ἐπιcταίη.

342. αὖθιc πάλιν: for the pleonasm in S see αὖ πάλιν at 1088 below, and in general Dawe, *Studies* i. 232.

343. ἢ 'μοί: rather ἤ μοι: on the correct accentuation see Schwyzer, *Gr. Gr.* ii. 187 (1), with the reservations expressed by Diggle, *CR* 32 (1982), p. 134 n. 4.

343-4. This allusion to the chorus's presence is interesting and unusual in Greek tragedy: cf. Bain, *Actors and Audience*, p. 59 n. 1: 'Presumably Sophocles felt it implausible for the conversation to proceed unless the man admitted that he was prepared to speak in front of the chorus.' Bain goes on to remark his uncertainty 'that in a similar situation Euripides would have felt such a procedure necessary'. For other Sophoclean attempts to gloss over non-naturalistic conventions cf. 1114-15 below (Hyllus seeming to apologize for Heracles' massive *rhesis*) or *OC* 1096 ff. (the 'unnatural' silence of the κωφὸν πρόcωπον Ismene during her and Antigone's reunion with Oedipus mitigated by dual and plural verbs at e.g. 1102 and 1104, and Theseus' inaccurate reference to τὰ τῶνδ' ἔπη (1141)). See Addenda.

345. For καὶ δή with present or perfect in response to a definite command see Denniston, *GP*², p. 251; the καί before ὁ λόγοc is presumably emphatic rather than connective, since asyndeton often follows καὶ δή thus used.

346-7. For the non-deictic ὅδε see Kannicht on Eur. *Hel.* 324 ff. **ἔλεξεν ... | φωνεῖ:** for the two verbs thus pleonastically used cf. Eur. *Cycl.* 210, 259, Hdt. 2. 22.

347. φωνεῖ δίκηc ἐc ὀρθόν: cf. Eur. *Phoen.* 1210 τοῦτ' εἰc ὕποπτον εἶπαc, Soph. fr. 612 εἰc ὀρθὸν φρονεῖν, and for other instances of adverbial εἰc ὀρθόν Pearson on the second passage. The notion of ὀρθὴ δίκη is rare in early Greek literature: cf. *Bacch.* 14. 23, Pind. *Pyth.* 11. 9, Hdt. 1. 96. 3. εὐθεῖα δίκη is more common: cf. D. Müller,

LINES 339-358

Handwerk und Sprache (Beitr. zur kl. Phil. 51; 1974, 42ff.).
φωνεῖ (present) after the aorist of ἔλεξεν conveys continuing effect (cf. on 21 ἐκλύεται).

350. **ἀγνοία μ' ἔχει:** 'abstract nouns which are used in periphrasis as the subject of a copula or object of an auxiliary verb often close the fifth foot of the iambic trimeter': Long, *Language and Thought*, p. 59, citing this and other examples. The μέν contrasts with what precedes: cf. Hes. *Op.* 37 and Denniston, *GP*², pp. 377-8. For ἀγνοίᾳ see Hutchinson on Aesch. *ScT* 402.

352. **πολλῶν παρόντων μαρτύρων:** cf. Men. *Asp.* 354 παρόντων μαρτύρων τρισχιλίων. Cf. 188 πρὸς πολλοὺς θροεῖ.

353-4. The same syllepsis (for more general instances see Johansen and Whittle on Aesch. *Suppl.* 70) in *Il.* 11. 328 ἐλέτην δίφρον τε καὶ ἀνέρε, Pind. *Ol.* 1. 88 ἕλεν δ' Οἰνομάου βίαν παρθένον τε ξύνευνον. **ὑψίπυργον Οἰχαλίαν:** cf. 859-60 ἀπ' αἰπεινᾶς... Οἰχαλίας.

355. **θέλξειεν:** often used of Eros' activity: see Barrett on Eur. *Hipp.* 1274ff., Kost on Musaeus, *Hero and Leander* 147. **αἰχμάσαι:** on the word's meaning and occurrences see Sideras, *Aeschylus Homericus*, p. 76.

356. On the signification of the manuscripts' prepositions here see Moorhouse, p. 112: ἐπί 'cannot be taken in a local sense with a sing. personal name (as it can with the pl. Λυδοῖς): hence, if the reading is right, it would mean "in the power of O." and it might then be neater to give the same meaning to ἐπὶ Λυδοῖς'. But Herwerden's change to ὑπ' Ὀμφ. is very easy (for the corruption presupposed see Diggle, *STE*, p. 40).

356-7. **πόνων | λατρεύματα:** cf. 829-30 ἐπίπονον | ἔχοι θανὼν λατρείαν; for the genitive cf. *PV* 900.

357. **ὁ ῥιπτὸς Ἰφίτου μόρος:** cf. V. Bers, *Enallage and Greek Style* (*Mnem.* suppl. 29; 1974), 60, who approves Jebb's interpretation of the phrase as a species of *enallage*, and his citation of *Ant.* 36 φόνον... δημόλευστον. Cf. the death of Astyanax (*Il.* 24. 735; *Il. Parv.* fr. 20. 4 Davies).

358. **ὅν** refers back to Ἔρως (354) despite the intervening μόρος (357); according to the manuscripts, ἥν in 997 refers back to κρηπίς (992), not λώβαν (996), but Wunder's transposition (see ad loc.) removes that analogy. In 708 ἧς... ὕπερ refers back to ἐμοί despite the intervening εὔνοιαν, but there the emphatic form of the pronoun and its position allow παρέσχ' εὔνοιαν to be treated as a post-positive unit,

COMMENTARY

which again makes a difference. **παρώcαc:** 'thrusting aside' (cf. Eur. *Andr.* 30).

359. For the 'circumstantial' ἡνίκα cf. A. Rijksbaron, *Temporal and Causal Conjunctions in Ancient Greek* (Amsterdam 1976), 137–8. Similarly, **ἔπειθε** registers as an 'eyewitness imperfect' (cf. *Ant.* 231 and Moorhouse, p. 189).

360. κρύφιον ... λέχοc: as D. Korzeniewski points out (*Hermes* 103 (1975), 377), λέχοc means a legitimate and regular union unless a characterizing epithet is added, as here (at Eur. *El.* 1089–90 ἐπηνέγκω λέχει | τἀλλότρια, μιcθοῦ τοὺc γάμουc ὠνουμένη and Pind. *Pyth.* 11. 24–5 ἢ ἑτέρωι λέχεϊ δαμαζομέναν | ἔννυχοι πάραγον κοῖται the context clarifies the meaning). For κρύφιος of an illegitimate liaison (as opposed to wedded union) see Kost on Musaeus, *Hero and Leander* 1. The meaning 'spouse' (cf. 27 above, *Aj.* 211–12, etc.) is less likely. For the postponed position of ὡc cf. Braswell on Pind. *Pyth.* 4. 7 (b) (discussing the general effect as emphasizing 'somewhat the words placed before the conjunction'). **ἔχοι:** ἔχηι L, but the optative is more idiomatic: see Moorhouse, p. 286.

361. W. Kraus (*WS* 20 (1986), 94) would delete θ' to produce the sense 'preparing a trivial accusation as his justification (for war)'.

362 ff. These lines provide several difficulties: (1) the subject of the verbs ἐπιcτρατεύει (362) and εἶπε (363) either (*a*) changes harshly from Heracles to Lichas or (*b*) stays the same so that Heracles is given a pointless and otiose remark; (2) the anticipation of 377 ff.'s revelation of Iole as daughter of Eurytus at 364 is unmotivated and far too casual; (3) the role of the definite article in τὸν Εὔρυτον τῶνδ' (though not in τὸν Εὔρυτον τόνδ') is unidiomatic (as Dawe, *Studies* iii. 84, first observed). Few approaches remove all of these problems (e.g. Dobree's deletion of 362–3 as tautologous (*Adversaria*, ed. Wagner, iv. 35; so too Wunder) does nothing to solve (2), which is also left untouched by the damnation of τὸν Εὔρυτον as an intrusive gloss (Dawe loc. cit.: cf. Dobree's treatment of 316 above)). Hartung's detection of an 'internal interpolation' from τὴν ταύτηc to πατέρα does economically sweep away all difficulties and the type of interpolation presupposed is not so rare as Dawe (loc. cit.) supposes (cf. Jachmann, 'Binneninterpolation', *Nachrichten von d. Gesellsch. d. Wiss. z. Göttingen, phil.-hist. Kl.* 1. 7 (1936), 123ff., 9 (1936), 185ff. = *Textgeschichtliche Studien*, pp. 528ff.

LINES 358-377

365-6. δόμουc | ἐc τούcδε πέμπων: the paradosis would have to be defended as an extension of the Attic idiom exemplified at 533 whereby ὡc can take the accusative of persons: the licence might be justified in view of the meaning 'household, family' which δόμοc can bear in tragedy (cf. LSJ s.v. II). ὡc is frequently interpolated in manuscripts, however (see above on 266), so that Brunck's ἐc is very attractive.

367. οὐδ' ... μηδέ: the use of μηδέ after a negative statement is perfectly in order: see Fraenkel on Aesch. *Ag.* 1498.

368. ἐντεθέρμανται: on the figurative use of θερμαίνω see Headlam on Herodas 1. 20. The present verb is ἅπαξ, but for ἐν- as a preverb rendering the verb perfective see Stinton *ap.* Lloyd-Jones in *Dionysiaca* (Page Festschrift), p. 50. ἐκτεθέρμανται would be a more regular word, and for the corruption which this emendation by Dindorf (and Herwerden) presupposes see e.g. ἔντοcθεν codd., ἔκτοcθεν P.Berol. 17073 at Theocr. *Id.* 1. 32,[11] and n. on 677 below.

369. δηλῶcαι τὸ πᾶν: 'to show all, the whole story': for τὸ πᾶν with this meaning cf. 876 and 1136, and W. H. Race, *California Studies in Classical Antiquity* 12 (1979), 253-6, 265 n. 5.

371 ff. Cf. on 188 above.

371-2. πρὸc μέcηι ... | ἀγορᾶι: one would expect (as in 423) ἐν μέcηι Τραχινίων | ἀγορᾶι; Aesch. *ScT* 210 νεὼc καμούcηc ποντίωι πρὸc (v.l. ἐν) κύματι is no very reassuring parallel (see Hutchinson ad loc.). For 'πρόc c. dat. of location, without attachment to the verb (or anything else)' see Aesch. *Ag.* 995 (quotation from Page ad loc.).

372-3. cυνεξήκουον: for the vivid 'eyewitness' imperfect see above on 359. **ἐξελέγχειν:** on the meaning see *Sophoclea*, p. 87.

374. τὸ δ' ὀρθὸν ἐξείρηχ': 'I have spoken the truth': for ὀρθόc with the meaning 'true' see Pearson on fr. 351. 2.

375. ποῦ ποτ' εἰμὶ πράγματοc: for similar locutions (e.g. *OT* 413 ἵν' εἶ κακοῦ) see Diggle, *Dionysiaca* (Page Festschrift), p. 176 n. 23, *STE*, p. 35. Cf. ποῖ γνώμηc πέcω at 705 and ξυμφορᾶc ἵν' ἕcταμεν at 1145 below.

376-7. For the language and sentiment here compare the paratragic passage at Men. *Sam.* 516-17 ἀλλ' ἐγὼ πρὸc τοῖcιν ἄλλοιc τὴν τὰ

[11] Cf. *Chroniques d'Égypte* 100 (1975), 192. Note too Aesch. *Ag.* 17 (ἐντέμνων: ἐκτέμνων FG), Lycophr. 498.

COMMENTARY

δείν' εἰργασμένην | εἰσεδεξάμην μελάθροις τοῖς ἐμοῖς. In contrast to that passage's aorist, our verse and the corresponding 537 employ the 'resultative' perfect (cf. Moorhouse, pp. 199–200): D has received Iole into her home and there she is. For the present passage's pattern of 'a noun accompanied by the interrogative pronoun ... further modified ... by an adjective' see D. Sansone, *AC* 52 (1983), 231.

378. πέφυκεν = ἔστιν (cf. on 36 above); for ἐπάγω as 'bring in above me' cf. Aesch. *Ag.* 1446–7 ἐμοὶ δ' ἐπήγαγεν | εὐνῆς παροψώνημα τῆς ἐμῆς χλιδῆς, *Aj.* 1295 ff. ἐφ' ἧι | λαβὼν ἐπακτὸν ἄνδρ' ὁ φιτύσας πατὴρ | ἐφῆκεν ἐλλοῖς ἰχθύσιν διαφθοράν. The reference is to Lichas' delivery of Iole. Likewise διώμνυτο refers to Lichas' reply to D's question at 318–19.

379. ἥ: this is a frustratingly ambiguous word: (1) ἥ (is she nameless or famous); (2) ἥ (is she nameless, she who is outstanding); (3) ἥ (is she nameless? To be sure she is outstanding ...). All these interpretations presuppose that D is the speaker of the line. But (3) is also compatible with the possibility that the line constitutes the opening words of the messenger's reply, and indeed the collocation ἦ κάρτα is frequent in replies to questions of this type. Wilamowitz (*Hermes* 59 (1924), 251–2 = *Kl. Schr.* iv. 345–6) preferred the alternative attribution of this line to D and conjectured ἦν κ. (of Iole). Kraus (*WS* 20 (1986), 95) prefers (2); cf. Pearson, *CR* 39 (1925), 3. **λαμπρά:** on the meaning of this word in this type of context see Schadewaldt, *WS* 79 (1966), 77 = *Hellas und Hesp.*² i. 493, Bremer, *Licht und Dunkel in der frühgr. Dichtung*, p. 275 n. 95. Cf. 1174 below. **καὶ κατ' ὄμμα καὶ φύσιν:** for καί ... καί as equivalent to *ut ... ita* see on 229 above; **ὄμμα:** 'beauty' or 'appearance': cf. *OT* 81, *El.* 903; Aesch. *Suppl.* 496 μορφῆς δ' οὐχ ὁμόστολος φύσις. Against the conjectures ὄνομα for ὄμμα (Fröhlich) and πέφηνεν for πέφυκεν (Dawe, *Studies* iii. 85) see Kraus, *WS* 20 (1986), 95.

380 ff. For a detailed comparison of the stichomythia here with that at *OT* 1117 ff. see W. Jens, *Die Stichomythie in der frühen gr. Tragödie* (Zetemata 11; 1955), 75 ff.

380. γένεσιν: an 'ornate alternative for γένος' (cf. *Phil.* 31 οἴκησις for οἶκος and perhaps *Aj.* 70 πρόσοψις for πρόσωπον), according to A. A. Long, *Mus. Helv.* 21 (1964), 230 (cf. id., *Language and Thought*, p. 41 n. 48). Note too ἐνθάκησις at *Phil.* 18. **ποτέ:** read as enclitic

LINES 376-383

ποτε, to be taken with the participle οὖca, not the accented form going with the next line's ’καλεῖτο (see E. Harrison, *CR* 55 (1941), 23); an example of what Renehan, *Studies in Greek Texts*, pp. 41–2, has called '"nostalgic" use of ποτε to denote a former happy state': further instances in Headlam on Herodas 6. 54. Others (e.g. the OCT) have preferred to take the word as a mere filler inserted once some such original as Blaydes's cπορά had dropped out: see further *Sophoclea*, p. 159. The lacuna placed by Radermacher and Dawe after this line is unnecessary, the μέν solitarium being perfectly idiomatic (see Denniston, *GP*[2], p. 380: 'the Messenger meant, I think, to add further details: Jebb, less probably, takes this as equivalent to π.μ.ο.γ.E., Ἰόλη δὲ καλουμένη').

381. Ἰόλη ’καλεῖτο: an unaugmented verb outside of a messenger-speech is an implausible entity (see on 904 below). The verb here must have suffered aphaeresis or prodelision of its syllabic augment after -η. For examples of this phenomenon after -η in Greek tragedy see L. Bergson, *Eranos* 51 (1953), 123. It is commoner in S than in either Aeschylus or Euripides, particularly (as here) when the syllabic augment is involved (see Platnauer, *CQ* 10 (1960), 140, 143). On the imperfect tense Wilamowitz (art. cit. (379 n.), 252 = p. 346) commented: 'man nicht vergessen soll, daß der Sklave keinen eigenen Namen hat; der Herr kann ihn rufen, wie er will.' But in spite of its sensitivity this view is probably wrong and it is more likely that we have an instance of the (admittedly debated) use of ὀνομάζω in the imperfect of a single act: cf. *Naupact.* fr. 1 Davies τὴν δὲ μεθ' ὁπλοτάτην Ἐριώπην ἐξονόμαζεν, | Ἀλκιμάχην δὲ πατήρ τε καὶ Ἄδμητος καλέεcκεν. **τῆc:** on the article used for the relative see above on 47.

382. δῆθεν οὐδὲν ἱcτορῶν: a reference back to 317 καὶ γὰρ οὐδ' ἀνιcτόρουν μακράν. Dawe's dissatisfaction over the position of δῆθεν (*Studies* iii. 85) is unnecessary. Apart from *PV* 986, quoted by Dawe himself, cf. such passages as Eur. *Or.* 1119 ἔcιμεν ἐc οἴκουc δῆθεν ὡc θανούμενοι for the particle's use to stress what follows.

383. ὄλοιντο: on this formulaic imprecation ('a curse on') see Moorhouse, p. 232. Dobree was right to see a generalized reference to Lichas, not to Heracles. On the optative -οιντο see Wackernagel, *Spr. Unt zu Homer*, p. 252.[12] **μή τι πάντεc:** cf. Eur. *Alc.* 210 οὐ γάρ τι πάντεc,

---

[12] Delete *Tr.* 905 from his examples (see ad loc.).

COMMENTARY

Ion 1035 μή ⟨τι add. Wakefield⟩ πᾶcι. 'The clemency is foolish', objected Jackson in *CQ* 6 (1912), 162–3, but the phrase (though perhaps originating in a superstitious reverence for the power of curses) is not meant to be analysed logically: it is a rhetorical device for isolating and emphasizing the victims of the curse. Jackson also misliked the article's position in τὰ δὲ | λαθραῖ᾿, but cf. 92–3 τό γ᾿ εὖ | πράccειν, 742–3 τὸ γὰρ | φανθέν, *OC* 265–6 τό γε | cῶμ᾿ and Denniston, *CQ* 30 (1936), 76.

384. μὴ πρέπονθ᾿: for the idiomatic plural participle here see Fraenkel on Aesch. *Ag.* 1395–6. On the choice between πρέπονθ᾿ αὑτῶι and πρέποντ᾿ αὐτῶι see Kraus, *WS* 20 (1986), 95–6.

389. ἀλλ᾿ εἶμι: this example of the phrase seems to contradict the generalization of Fraenkel quoted on 86 above, but as Fraenkel himself observes, Lichas' unexpected entry delays the exit of D that these two words prepare us for. **ἀπὸ γνώμηc:** 'away from (i.e. without) good judgement' (cf. Homeric ἀπὸ δόξηc (*Il.* 10. 324 etc., *Od.* 11. 344 etc.)). In the light of Aesch. *Eum.* 674–5, Eur. *Ion* 1312–13, and several prose passages, E. Viketos, *Hermes* 113 (1985), 494–5, argues that the phrase ἀπὸ γνώμηc would normally mean 'with good judgement' (cf. S. N. Mouraviev, *Glotta* 51 (1973), 72: 'not without reason (i.e. knowledge of what you say)') and that here we should consequently read καὶ γὰρ οὖν (for οὐκ) ἀπὸ γνώμηc λέγειc. D. Sansone, *CQ* 37 (1987), 227, cites οὐκ ἀπὸ γνώμηc at Paus. 7. 1. 4 with the meaning 'not contrary to the wishes of', but cf. Viketos, *Hermes* 118 (1990), 128.

390. 'Am I to wait?' For messengers' use of plural for singular in S see Moorhouse, p. 8.

391. Cf. Eur. *Andr.* 562 μυρίων ὑπ᾿ ἀγγέλων.

392. For the contrast cf. Aesch. *Cho.* 838 ἥκω μὲν οὐκ ἄκλητοc ἀλλ᾿ ὑπάγγελοc. The same dramatic economy dictates Lichas' reappearance here as dictated Hyllus' entry above (line 58).

393. For this mode of address see on 230 above.

394. εἰcοραῖc: Wakefield's emendation ὡc ὁρᾶιc is easily made (cf. above on 365–6) but, given the near equivalence in meaning of εἰcοράιc to ὁρᾶιc (cf. *El.* 997) and the legitimacy of parenthetic ὁρᾶιc, it may be unnecessary. (On the insignificant repetition of ὡc which it introduces see n. on 174 above.)

396. κἀννεώcαcθαι: for the apocope see KB i/1. 180. The corruption to καὶ νεώcαcθαι was caused by 'the combination of crasis and an unfamiliar word': see Johansen and Whittle on Aesch. *Suppl.* 235, giving parallel cases. See Addenda.

399. ἴϲτω μέγαϲ Ζεύϲ: cf. *Ant.* 184 ἴϲτω Ζεὺϲ ὁ πάνθ' ὁρῶν ἀεί, *OC* 522 θεὸϲ ἴϲτω.

400. ἣν ἥκειϲ ἄγων: cf. Ar. fr. 469. 2 KA ἥκειν ἄγων.

401. Εὐβοιίϲ: for similar feminine ethnica see on 237–8 above.

402 ff. The anonymous messenger intervenes before D's interrogation can proceed very far. D's failure to speak until 436 has been taken as a sign of immature dramatic technique, but see ad loc. and above, p. xviii n. 4.

402. For rude or peremptory use of οὗτοϲ in this sort of question see Johansen and Whittle on Aesch. *Suppl.* 911, Wackernagel, 'Über einige antike Anredeformen' (1912), 9 n. 1 = *Kl. Schr.* ii. 976–7 n. 1. *OT* 1121 οὗτοϲ ... δεῦρό μοι φώνει βλέπων, and Men. *Sam.* 312 οὗτοϲ, βλέπε δεῦρο are notable examples.

403. On the emphatic positioning of cύ here cf. G. Thomson, *CQ* 33 (1939), 149; ἐρωτήϲαϲ ἔχειϲ is equivalent to ἠρώτηκαϲ, just as 412 ποικίλαϲ ἔχειϲ is equivalent to πεποίκιλκαϲ; in both cases the non-periphrastic form is in fact relatively late: cf. W. J. Aerts, *Periphrastica* (Amsterdam 1965), 138–9.

405. Lichas misunderstands the preceding question as a literal request for information.

405 ff. For comparable cases of single τε connecting 'indications of the different relations of one person' see Johansen and Whittle on Aesch. *Suppl.* 42, who discuss the implications of such passages for Elmsley's canon. The present instance creates an effective tricolon crescendo.

409. δίκαια γάρ: for the plural cf. 495–6 κενὸν γὰρ οὐ δίκαιά ϲε | χωρεῖν, 1116 αἰτήϲομαι γάρ ϲ' ὧν δίκαια τυγχάνειν), Davies on Stes. fr. 244 P. For the technique whereby a verse is broken up by the interposing of an expression of agreement see Kaibel on *El.* 1322.

411. μὴ δίκαιοϲ ὤν: cf. οὐ δίκαιοϲ at 348 above.

412. ποικίλαϲ ἔχειϲ: on the metaphorical use of ποικίλλω here see D. Müller, *Handwerk und Sprache* (Beitr. zur kl. Phil. 51; 1974), 14; on the periphrasis see above on 403.

414. ἦ: in favour of Elmsley's emendation see Barrett on Eur. *Hipp.* 700, especially his conclusion: 'ἦν was unwelcome in the 5th cent. even when metrically convenient, so that we may safely deny it in indifferent positions, viz. before a consonant and at line-end. Probably A. and S. never used it at all.' On the combination of imperfect verb with present participle (as in OT 1368 κρείccων γὰρ ἦcθα μηκέτ' ὢν ἢ ζῶν τυφλόc) see Schwyzer, Gr. Gr. ii. 393 (3).

416. Cf. Eur. Suppl. 567 (also to a herald) λέγ' εἴ τι βούληι· καὶ γὰρ οὐ cιγηλὸc εἶ. Diggle on Eur. Phaeth. 46 lists similar requests.

417. ἣν ἔπεμψας ἐς δόμους: 'whom you accompanied into the palace': see on 571 below.

418. For this technique of breaking off a probing question in mid-line, leaving the rest of the line to be filled by the response, see Kaibel on El. 1322. On δήπου ('no doubt') as a possible colloquialism see Stevens, CQ 39 (1945), 101.

419. The present tense baffles (φωνεῖ at 347 is no parallel: see ad loc.). Implausible emendations are assembled by Jackson, MS, p. 129, whose own lively οὔκουν cὺ ταύτην—⟨μ⟩ή μ' ὑπ' ἀγνοίας ὅρα—| Ἰόλην κτλ. lacks the conviction of his similar effort at 338 above. For ὑπ' ἀγνοίας = 'through ignorance' see Aesch. Suppl. 499 and Johansen and Whittle ad loc.: but Jebb was right to observe here that 'there is perhaps no instance in which [ὑπό + gen.] refers distinctly to the mental or moral circumstances (as distinct from motives) of the agent'. See further Sophoclea, pp. 159–60.

420. The periphrasis is equivalent to Ἰόλην ταύτην εἶναι ἣν Εὔρυτος ἔσπειρε: cf. D. Holwerda, Commentatio de vocis quae est ΦΥΣΙΣ vi atque usu (Groningen 1955), 110.

421. For the double question cf. Homeric τίς πόθεν εἰς ἀνδρῶν, and for tragic analogies cf. Diggle, STE, p. 98.

422. For West's aorist infinitive here and at 425 see on 189. Bothe's πάρα is a clever correction presupposing an easy corruption. But there is the danger that it will eliminate a characteristic instance of the use of παρών to produce emphasis; for examples of this idiom see 431 below, von der Mühll, Mus. Helv. 19 (1962), 202 ff. = Ausg. kl. Schr., pp. 286ff., citing e.g. Ant. 1112 αὐτός τ' ἔδησα καὶ παρὼν ἐκλύσομαι.

423. πολλοῖσιν ἀστῶν: understand ἐν (π.α.) from 421's ἐν ἀνθρώποισιν.

423–4. See on 188 above.

425. Tragic manuscripts provide us with ναί extra metrum in several places: see Stevens on Eur. Andr. 242. Whether they derive from poet or scribe is often a moot point. Dindorf's proposed deletion of the present instance is considered sympathetically by Diggle, STE, p. 56 n. 1, who

LINES 414-436

observes that the γε that follows this particular ναί is hard to parallel. Kraus's defence of ναί (*WS* 20 (1986), 96), invoking Lichas' psychology, does not convince.

426. δόκηcιν εἰπεῖν: 'state mere opinion (not knowledge)': see Headlam on Aesch. *Ag.* 287, Kannicht on Eur. *Hel.* 119.

427. ποίαν δόκηcιν: for ποῖοc used to pick up and criticize a word or notion in a preceding line, especially during the course of a cross-examination, see Bond on Eur. *Her.* 518, Diggle, *STE*, pp. 50–1, Stevens, *Colloquial Expressions in Euripides*, pp. 38–9. Wilamowitz on the *Heracles* line supposed that the idiom was meant to characterize the messenger as plebeian (a view disputed by Vahlen, *Opusc. Acad.* ii. 439).

429. ἐγὼ δάμαρτα: another indignant repetition of a speaker's word; the repeated word must, in such passages, be in the same case as the original occurrence (see Diggle, *STE*, p. 50), but the verb is usually omitted (see Headlam on Herodas 5. 4). On δάμαρ in tragedy see Stevens on Eur. *Andr.* 4. It most often signifies 'lawfully wedded wife', and Stevens suggests there may be 'a special point' here 'in using of Iole a word that should properly have been used only of Deianeira'.

429–30. φίλη | δέcποινα: cf. the same character's ὦ φίλη δέcποιν' at 472, and *Ant.* 1192 (messenger to queen Eurydice).

431. παρών: for the emphatic participle see on 422 above. For 'imperfect παρών see Bond on Eur. *Hyps.* fr. 60. 35, KG ii/1. 200.

433. ὁ τῆcδ' ἔρωc φανείc: cf. Men *Sam.* 334 τὸν φανέντ' αὐτῶι γάμον.

435. ληρεῖν: nowhere else used by the three tragedians (or any other tragic poet), hence such conjectures as Heimsoeth's νοcοῦντ' ἐλέγχειν. But given the numerous colloquial features of this scene (see on 402, 427, 429, etc.), the vulgar ἅπαξ effectively conveys Lichas' emphatic contempt for the messenger. (Against Heath's νοcοῦντα see Kraus, *WS* 20 (1986), 96–7.) **cώφρονοc:** the non-moral sense of the word (see Pearson on fr. 896).

436 ff. Note the striking change of tone and style (from the near-colloquial brawling of Lichas and the herald to elevated and dignified rhetoric) represented by D's *rhesis* here; on the question of whether it represents a deception-speech see on 531 ff.

436. πρόc cε τοῦ: for the position of cε here see Eur. *Med.* 324 μή, πρόc cε γονάτων, *IT* 1068 ἀλλὰ πρόc cε δεξιᾶc, Wackernagel, *IF* 1 (1892), 360–1 = *Kl. Schr.* i. 28–9, Barrett on Eur. *Hipp.* 503–4.

COMMENTARY

437. ἐκκλέψηιϲ λόγον: for κλέπτειν and its compounds as used of any kind of action which involves deceit see on 243 above. The present instance means 'conceal'.

439. For the use of οὐ rather than μή see Moorhouse, p. 324.

439–40. Either a generalized reference to Heracles' constitutional infidelity ('man is not intended by nature to take pleasure in the same things always') or an allusion to the consolation offered by the chorus at 129 ff. ('rejoicing does not, by nature, belong to the same people always'). The former interpretation fits the present (as opposed to an earlier) scene better, and is supported by the following sentence in asyndeton, which will then be explanatory of our lines' cryptic generalization.

441–2. For the related picture of Eros as a wrestler see E. J. Kenney, *CQ* 9 (1959), 244, N. Zagagi, *Tradition and Originality in Plautus* (Hypomnemata 62; 1980), 60. In spite of Denniston–Page on Aesch. *Ag.* 1206, that is a far more common motif than Eros as boxer, for which, however, Anacreon 396. 2 P ὡϲ δὴ πρὸϲ Ἔρωτα πυκταλίζω is an obvious and close parallel. As for the exact pointing and interpretation of our passage, see Fraenkel on Aesch. *Ag.* 1316 (who claims that to take ἐϲ χεῖραϲ with ἀντανίϲταται (so Jebb, Radermacher, etc.) 'seems decidedly forced and makes the structure of the sentence clumsy'). For the structure of the lines as thus construed cf. Eur. *Her.* 869 ἀμπνοὰϲ δ' οὐ ϲωφρονίζει, ταῦροϲ ὣϲ ἐϲ ἐμβολήν, *Or.* 44–5 ποτὲ δὲ δεμνίων ἀπὸ | πηδαῖ δρομαῖοϲ, πῶλοϲ ὣϲ ὑπὸ ζυγοῦ, and the other passages cited by Fraenkel, esp. *Aj.* 651 βαφῆι ϲίδηροϲ ὥϲ (cf. Fraenkel, *Mus. Helv.* 24 (1967), 79); Aesch. *Ag.* 1316 itself differs from these, which exhibit 'preposition + noun, with a verb easily supplied from the context' (Page ad loc.)). **οὐ καλῶϲ φρονεῖ:** equivalent to κακῶϲ φρονεῖ, i.e. (see Page on Eur. *Med.* 250) meaning 'is a fool'.

443. For this common picture of Eros as ruler of gods and men see below on 497; on love conceived as a disease see below, 491, 544, etc., and on the theme of disease in this and other Sophoclean plays P. Biggs, *CP* 61 (1966), 223 ff., Winnington-Ingram, *BICS* 26 (1979), 5.

444. If genuine, the line is structurally comparable with *Aj.* 650, where a maxim applicable to all mankind is then applied by the speaker to himself (κἀγὼ γάρ: cf. 677's ἡμεῖϲ δέ): for comparisons of the *Ajax*'s *Trugrede* with D's present *rhesis* see on 531 ff. But 444 was deleted by Wunder (and Zieliński, p. 532 = pp. 318–19), followed by Reeve (*GRBS* 14 (1973), 167), probably rightly. Not all Wunder's arguments are valid, but the clear implications of καὶ θεῶν in 443 hardly need to be spelt out with κἀμοῦ γε, and πῶς δ' οὐ χἀτέρας οἵας γ' ἐμοῦ (for the epic-type attraction of the relative clause without verb see Chantraine, *Grammaire homérique* ii (Paris 1958), 237, and Moorhouse, p. 269) is pointlessly distracting, whether it be referred to a generalizing plurality of women or more specifically to Iole herself (whose feelings for Heracles are quite beside the point, dramatically irrelevant to plot and theme alike in the austere and selective world of Greek tragedy: cf. Fraenkel on *Aj.* 900 ff. (*Due seminari romani*, p. 31)). Stinton, pp. 135–6, has a sensitive defence of the line, which he seeks to justify by reference to 461–2 below. But the argument that 'the subject of ἐντακείη' there 'is most naturally Iole' is a circular one which will only convince those who already believe in the authenticity of 444. Vv. 459–60 (note especially 459 χἀτέρας) may have inspired the insertion. For this type of interpolation in general (πρὸς cαφήνειαν τῶν λεγομένων) see Fraenkel on Aesch. *Ag.* 1226.

445. Denniston, *GP*², p. 514 (iv), defends τ' ἀνδρί (as against Schaefer's γ' ἀνδρί) with largely Platonic parallels, but cites no poetic analogy, and the symmetry thus produced between τὠμῶι ... ἀνδρί and τῆιδε τῆι γυναικί seems unnecessary. For love conceived as a disease see on 443 above.

446. τὠμῶι γ' ἀνδρὶ ... μεμπτός εἰμι: the dative construction as with μέμφομαι (cf. 470 below); cf. Moorhouse, p. 171, Renehan, *HSCP* 87 (1983), 23. Moorhouse thinks that 'the use of μεμπτός εἰμι stead of the simple vb. suggests a persistent attitude of reproach'. **κάρτα μαίνομαι:** equivalent to the generalizing οὐ καλῶς φρονεῖ of 442.

447. μεταιτίαι: see on 260–1 above.

449–50. μαθών | ... μάθησιν: with the elaborate periphrasis cf. 711 below.

451. αὐτὸς αὐτόν: on the αὑτὸς αὑτόν of most manuscripts and the linguistic principle involved see Fraenkel on Aesch. *Ag.* 836.

452. λέγεςθαι: the OCT's emendation of γενέςθαι provides a neater antithesis: 'you want to be *called* good, but will be *perceived* as base.' **ὀφθήςηι κακός:** cf. *OT* 509–10 καὶ cοφὸς ὤφθη | βαcάνωι θ' ἡδύπολις. See Addenda.

453–4. On the sentiment cf. K. J. Dover, *Greek Popular Morality in the Time of Plato and Aristotle* (Oxford 1974), 115.

COMMENTARY

453. ἐλευθέρωι: it is important that Lichas is presented as no slave but a figure of some importance (cf. Schmid, *GGL* i/2. 377 n. 5). For the relatively respectful manner in which he is addressed by D throughout this scene see Fraenkel on *Aj.* 791 (*Due seminari romani*, p. 27).

454. κῆρ: 'disgrace' (see on 132 ff. above).

455–6. The OCT's app. crit. mentions a proposal to delete these two lines (E. Eicken-Iselin, *Interpretationen und Untersuchungen zum Aufbau der sophokleischen Rheseis* (diss. Basle 1942), 156 n. 1, cf. 205). They may not seem to add a great deal, but πολλοί in the second is an important motif: see on 188 above.

458. τὸ μὴ πυθέςθαι, τοῦτο: for the neuter resuming a preceding verbal phrase see Johansen and Whittle on Aesch. *Suppl.* 708. Contrast 819–20 below. With the whole line cf. *OT* 1067 τὰ λῶιςτα τοίνυν ταῦτά μ' ἀλγύνει πάλαι.

459–60. χἀτέρας | πλείςτας ... εἷς: for other examples of this juxtaposition of antithetical words signifying 'one' and 'many' see Fraenkel on Aesch. *Ag.* 1455.[13] Here, as part of a mixed construction, the superlative adjective is emphasized by the addition of εἷς (see Moorhouse, p. 174, for other examples of this), but so is χἀτέρας: cf. Bruhn, *Anhang*, § 181.

460. ἔγημε: for γαμῶ of the sort of casual union here presupposed see LSJ s.v. I. 2; **δή:** on the late positioning of the particle see Stinton, *JHS* 97 (1977), 133 (cf. Denniston, *GP*², pp. 227–8).

462. ἥδε τ' οὐδ' ἄν: understand (with Campbell) ἐνέγκαιτο: for similar ellipses of the negative optative see *Ant.* 321, *El.* 364–5, *Phil.* 115; cf. KG ii/2. 572.

463. ἐντακείη τῶι φιλεῖν: for the metaphor cf. Plato *Symp.* 192E ςυντακεὶς τῶι ἐρωμένωι, and cf. ἐντεθέρμανται πόθωι (of Heracles) at 368 above; for the absence of the arthrous infinitive from tragedy except after ἐν see Johansen and Whittle on Aesch. *Suppl.* 802–3. The subject of the verb must be Heracles (see above on 444): 'D. cares not whether Iole loves Heracles but whether Heracles loves Iole' (Lloyd-Jones, *CR* 33 (1983), 172). E. Harrison could 'offer no palliation of' the interlinear hiatus between this and the following line (*CR* 57 (1943), 62), but Lloyd-Jones suggests ἔγωγ' to me as an obvious remedy. See Appendix B and 1112–13 n.

[13] Cf. the type of juxtaposition exemplified by πάντων εἷς (see Wankel on Dem. 18. 143, Diggle, *STE*, p. 48, Gygli-Wyss, *Das nominale Polyptoton*, p. 145).

LINES 453-479

463 ff. For ὅτι here see Moorhouse, p. 301: 'this ὅτι-clause can be seen as standing in the same relation as an accus. of respect, with ὅτι in its substantivising role: "I pitied her with regard to the fact that her beauty bought her to ruin".' Cf. on 25 above.

464. ὤικτιρα δὴ μάλιστα: cf. Eur. Hel. 563 Ἑλένηι c' ὁμοίαν δὴ μάλιcτ' εἶδον and Denniston, GP², p. 228, for other passages where δή 'precedes the emphatic word'.

467. κἀδούλωcεν: for Oechalia's enslaved state see 283 above.

467-8. ἀλλὰ ταῦτα μὲν | ῥείτω κατ' οὖρον: cf. Od. 15. 523 ἀλλὰ τά γε Ζεὺc οἶδεν; for the resigned tone behind the phrase, and for the image ἴτω κατ' οὖρον (Aesch. ScT 690), cf. Arist. HA 535^{a}19, 541^{a}27, 560^{b}13. 'Well, let wind and wave take that' is T. B. L. Webster's lively rendering (in Greek Poetry and Life (Murray Festschrift; Oxford 1936), 169).

468-9. For Sophocles' tendency to end a long speech with this sort of antithesis see 819-20 below and Reeve, GRBS 11 (1970), 288-9. The lines are, of course, a rhetorical means of obtaining emphasis by contrast, not an analysable statement about personal morality.

470. πείθου: πιθοῦ Dindorf, probably without cause (see Fraenkel on Aesch. Ag. 1054).

472 ff. ἐπεί . . . γάρ: for this sort of reduplication (more usually γὰρ . . . γάρ) see G. Zuntz, Rh. Mus. 94 (1951), 341. But 475's γάρ is also idiomatic as introducing a narrative near the start of a messenger-speech: see Braswell on Pind. Pyth. 4. 70 (a).

473. θνητὴν φρονοῦcαν θνητά: cf. fr. 590. 1 θνητὰ φρονεῖν χρὴ θνητὴν φύcιν with Pearson ad loc. and Gygli-Wyss, Das nominale Polyptoton, p. 103 n. 3, for this principle as enunciated in Greek literature.

476-7. For the idea of love as a force or emanation proceeding from outside see Pearson on frr. 474.4, 874.

477. τῆcδ' οὕνεχ': cf. Hes. fr. 26. 32 MW (above, p. xxvi); similar phrases are used in early Greek literature to convey Helen's responsibility for the sack of Troy (cf. Davies, Hermes 114 (1986), 260 n. 15).

πολύφθοροc: for the 'passive' meaning cf. El. 10, and for the prolepsis see 240 above.

478. See on 163 above.

479. δεῖ . . . λέγειν: for similar 'intrusion[s] cutting a sentence in half' and introduced by γάρ see Fraenkel on Aesch. Ag. 800. **πρὸc**

133

COMMENTARY

κείνου: 'from the standpoint' or 'in the interest' of Heracles. For other passages where πρός exhibits the same ambiguity see Johansen and Whittle on Aesch. *Suppl.* 531.

483. ἥμαρτον ... ἁμαρτίαν: for this sort of word-play cf. Men. *Dysc.* 303 εἰ τοῦτ' ἀδίκημ' εἴρηκας, ἠδίκηκ' ἴϲωϲ and Callim. *Epigr.* 42. 6–7 Pf. = HE 1080 εἰ μὲν ἑκών, Ἀρχῖν', ἐπεκώμαϲα, ... εἰ τοῦτ' ἐϲτ' ἀδίκημ', ἀδικέω. **τι τῶνδ':** so Dawe (*Studies* iii. 86), followed by the OCT (cf. *Sophoclea*, p. 160). For the demonstrative's attraction to the gender of the predicate offered by the paradosis τι τήνδ' cf. *OC* 88 ταύτην (not τοῦτο) ἔλεξε παῦλαν and Jebb ad loc., Kraus, *WS* 20 (1986), 97.

484. πάντ' ἐπίϲταϲαι λόγον: for similar phrases involving πάντα λόγον see Fraenkel on Aesch. *Ag.* 599.

485. ϲὴν ... χάριν: cf. Simias *Pelekus* 8 ϲὰν χάριν.

486. ϲτέργε: 'put up with' Iole. With this worldly-wise advice cf. the sentiments at Eur. *Andr.* 213–14 χρὴ γὰρ γυναῖκα, κἂν κακῶι πόϲει δοθῆι, | ϲτέργειν, ἅμιλλάν τ' οὐκ ἔχειν φρονήματοϲ.

487–8. ἐμπέδωϲ: ἐμπέδουϲ Nauck. On ὡϲ see *Sophoclea*, p. 205.

488–9. Other examples of this sort of antithesis in Johansen and Whittle on Aesch. *Suppl.* 1014–15.

489. ἔφυ: see on 36 above.

490 ff. For the plural verb coupled with masculine participle used by a female speaker see Moorhouse, pp. 9–10, who compares *Ant.* 925–6 εἰ μὲν οὖν τάδ' ἐϲτιν ἐν θεοῖϲ καλά, | παθόντεϲ ἂν ξυγγνοῖμεν ἡμαρτηκότεϲ, *El.* 399 πεϲούμεθ', εἰ χρή, πατρὶ τιμωρούμενοι, and concludes that all three passages seem to share 'a common note of boldness and resolution'. On the general principle cf. Renehan, *CP* 80 (1985), 168. αἱρ- often occurs as variant for future or aorist ἀρ-: see Johansen and Whittle on Aesch. *Suppl.* 342.

491. νόϲον γ' ἐπακτόν: cf. Eur. *Hipp.* 318 with Barrett ad loc., and the note on 378 above.

492. θεοῖϲι δυϲμαχοῦντεϲ: the plurals give the impression of mortals fighting gods (cf. Johansen and Whittle on Aesch. *Suppl.* 439), but presumably stand for singular and refer to Eros or Aphrodite (cf. Cat. 68. 75–6 'inceptam frustra, nondum cum sanguine sacro | hostia caelestis pacificasset eros', where Nisbet, *PCPS* 24 (1978), 101, takes 'eros' as 'a sinister euphemism for Venus'), thus returning us to the image of 441–2 (boxing against Eros).

LINES 479–(530)

493. λόγων τ' ἐπιστολάς: a defining genitive: cf. 356–7 πόνων | λατρεύματ', 506 ἄεθλ' ἀγώνων; note the tragic idiom τοὺς λόγους φέρειν = 'to bring a message' (cf. Jackson, *MS*, p. 154).

494. ἀντὶ δώρων δῶρα: see Gygli-Wyss, *Das nominale Polyptoton*, p. 86, on this and similar phrases involving repetition and conveying the basic notion of 'good returned for good'. **δῶρα ... προσαρμόσαι:** for the various meanings of this verb in simplex and compound forms see Wilamowitz on Eur. *Her.* 179: here merely 'bestow' (though some have detected a sinister irony foreshadowing the literal 'fastening' of the shirt to Heracles).

495. δίκαια: for the plural see above on 409.

496. στόλωι: for the word's meaning see above on 226. The messenger 'should go unobtrusively at 496, just as he stayed unobtrusively at 199' (Taplin, p. 91).

FIRST STASIMON (497–530)
497–506 = 507–16 *strophe and antistrophe*

497/507–8	∪∪−∪∪−∪∪−∪∪− ⏒−∪−	anap.-ia.
498/509	−∪− −ₕ ‖	e —
499–500/510	∪∪−∪∪−∪∪−∪∪− ∪−∪⌣ₕ ‖	anap.-ia.
501/511	−∪∪−∪∪− −	D —
502/512	−∪− − −∪∪−∪∪− −	e — D —
503/513	−∪∪−∪∪− −	D —
504/514	∪∪−∪∪−∪∪−∪∪−	anap.
505/515	∪−− −∪− ∪−∪−	ia. trim. sync.
506/516	−∪∪−∪−⌣ ‖	+ aristoph.

For a metrical analysis of the ode as a whole see Dale, *MATC* i. (*Dactylo-Epitrite*), 27. On the relationship between 497–500 and the dactylo-epitrites that follow see Griffith, *Authenticity of PV*, pp. 44–5 (cf. p. 43). For the aristophanean at 506 see ibid. 59.

517–30 *epode*

517	∪−∪∪−∪−	tel.
518	−∪∪−	chor.
519	−−−∪∪−∪∪−− ‖	dact. tetram.

135

COMMENTARY

520	— —∪— — —∪∪—∪∪—	—e—D
521	—∪∪— ∪	d¹ ∪
522	—∪∪—∪∪— —‖	D—
523	—— —∪— —	sp. cr. anc.
524	—— —∪— —ₕ‖	sp. cr. anc.
525	—∪∪— —∪—∪——	chor. + ithyph.
526	∪—∪— —∪— ∪——	ia. trim. sync. cat.
527	∪—∪— —∪— ∪——	ia. trim. sync. cat.
528	∪—∪— ∪—⟨∪—⟩	ia. dim.
529	—∪—∪∪—∪—‖	glyc.
530	—∪—∪∪——‖	pher.

'The Epode takes a further step away' from dactylo-epitrite (Dale, loc. cit.). On 520–2 see Griffith, op. cit. 41: 'Both Sophocles and Euripides have numerous stanzas in which individual dact.-ep. periods occur only briefly, usually in the form of the "iambelegos" × — ∪ — × — ∪ ∪ — ∪ ∪ —, though the rest of the stanza is of a different metrical nature' (he cites instances). For the syncopated iambic metra at 523 ff. see ibid. 264, and for the aeolic 'dicolon' clausula to iambic produced by the correction *βέβαχ'* at 529–30 ibid. 39. (He observes that 'there are not many parallels', and Dale, loc. cit., hesitates to accept the emendation 'in view of our total uncertainty about words and metre in 528' (see ad loc.).) The emendation is Dobree's (*Adversaria* iv. 37).

Comparison with prologue. It often happens in Greek tragedy that a choral passage is succeeded by a scene in iambic trimeters which treats the same material in a different manner: the lyric in an excited and emotional way, the spoken trimeters in a calmer and more rational mode (e.g. Aesch. *Ag.* 1072 ff. (the Cassandra scene), *Cho.* 306 ff., Soph. *Aj.* 331 ff., *Ant.* 802 ff.). For further discussion and bibliography see Kannicht on Eur. *Hel.* 252 ff. (add L. H. G. Greenwood, *Aspects of Euripidean Tragedy* (Cambridge 1953), 131 ff.). Here, however, the sequence is reversed (cf. the prologue and parodos of the *OT*) and the two treatments are separated by a large number of lines. But that the two scenes do unmistakably correspond is clear from the following analysis:

(1) *general subject-matter*: the battle of Heracles and Achelous for Deianeira;
(2) *rhetorical structure*: the battle is in each passage introduced by a

LINES (497-530)

generalization which serves to emphasize the concrete exemplification that follows;

(3) *phraseology*:

15 τοιόνδ' ἐγὼ μνηςτῆρα προςδεδεγμένη ~ 525 τὸν ὃν προςμένουϲ' ἀκοίταν
19 κλεινὸϲ ἦλθε Ζηνὸϲ Ἀλκμήνηϲ τε παῖϲ ~ 510ff. ὁ δὲ βακχίαϲ ἄπο ἦλθε... Θήβαϲ... παῖϲ Διόϲ
24 ἐγὼ γὰρ ἤμην ~ 523ff. ἁ δ' ἧϲτο.

Scholars have sometimes used the term 'ballad' of this stasimon's lyric narration (Kranz, *Stasimon*, pp. 254ff., Reinhardt, p. 253 (English trans., p. 242), Burton, p. 55, etc.). Such a label is not very enlightening. There are numerous features which remind us of Pindar (see on 497, 505, etc.). Note too the abundance of Homeric words (504 ἀμφίγυοι and 523 εὐῶπιϲ are ἅπαξ in tragedy). Another common comparison is with the technique of visual art: 'the scene and the combatants are presented ... with the clarity of a work of art' (Burton, p. 55). Here too the differences are perhaps as striking as the similarities, as we can observe by examining specific instances of analogous scenes. For recent treatments of the artistic tradition concerning Heracles' battle with Nereus or Triton see P. Brize, *Die Geryoneis des Stesichoros und die frühe gr. Kunst* (Beitr. für Arch. 12; 1980), 66ff., and R. Glynn, *AJA* 85 (1981), 121ff.

The first stasimon opens with a grandiose generalization about the way the world is constituted: the device is characteristic of S: cf. *Ant.* 332 πολλὰ τὰ δεινά κτλ. and in general Kranz, *Stasimon*, p. 191. The idea that Love (Aphrodite or, more usually, Eros[14]) has power over gods and men is very common in Greek literature: see the passages cited by Stinton, p. 135 n. 58, adding fr. 684. 1 ff. ἔρωϲ γὰρ ἄνδραϲ οὐ μόνουϲ ἐπέρχεται, | οὐδ' αὖ γυναῖκαϲ, ἀλλὰ καὶ θεῶν ἄνω | ψυχὰϲ ταράϲϲει (cf. Aristophon fr. 11. 3 KA (of Eros and the gods) ἐτάραττε κἀκείνουϲ (sc. as well as mortals)), Hes. *Th.* 120ff. Ἔροϲ... | ... πάντων τε θεῶν πάντων τ' ἀνθρώπων | δάμναται ἐν ϲτήθεϲϲι νόον καὶ ἐπίφρονα βουλήν, Eur. fr. 136 N² (the famous line from the *Andromeda*) ὦ θεῶν τύραννε κἀνθρώπων Ἔρωϲ, and Anacreon (?) 505

[14] The two are often indistinguishable in early Greek literature and thought (see e.g. Easterling, *PCPS* 20 (1974), 41). Notice the smooth transition from one to the other in Eur. *Hipp.* 1268ff. ϲὺ τὰν θεῶν ἄκαμπτον φρένα καὶ βροτῶν | ἄγειϲ, Κύπρι, ϲὺν δ' ὁ ποικιλόπτεροϲ ἀμφιβαλὼν | ὠκυτάτωι πτερῶι κτλ.

COMMENTARY

(d) P = fr. anacr. vet. 1 West Ἔρωτα... | μέλομαι... |... | ὅδε καὶ θεῶν δυνάϲτηϲ· | ὅδε καὶ βροτοὺϲ δαμάζει. See too on 500 below. The picture has already been prefigured at 443–4 above.

Choruses of Greek tragedy often extol the might of Love: see especially *Ant.* 781 ff. and Eur. *Hipp.* 525 ff. (where, significantly, Heracles' lust for Iole serves as a *paradeigma* at 545 ff.). Sophocles' interest in the emotion is attested by frr. 149, 932, as well as the fragments cited below. Cf. Plato *Rep.* 329 c = *TrGF* iv, T N 80[A] Radt, and in general J. de Romilly, 'L'excuse de l'invincible amour dans la tragédie grecque' in *Miscellanea Tragica* (Kamerbeek Festschrift), pp. 309 ff.

497. μέγα ... ἀεί: the various interpretations advanced for these two phrases are conveniently assembled and analysed by Stinton, pp. 136 ff. He rightly excludes most of them as foisting an impossible meaning upon ϲθένοϲ or ἐκφέρεται (cf. Dawe's app. crit. ad loc.: 'quid velit ἐκφ. vix liquet') and finds Brunck's 'invictum ubique est Veneris robur' with μέγα τι ϲθένοϲ in apposition to ἁ Κύπριϲ and νίκαϲ accusative plural somewhat less promising than the sense produced by Wakefield's punctuation: 'Mighty strength is Cypris; she ever bears away victories.' (Wakefield himself unnecessarily went one step further to conjecture ἐκφέρεται νικῶϲ': 'Cypris is extolled as victorious.') For the emphatic τιϲ cf. *Aj.* 1266 and such generalizations as Alcman's ἔϲτι τιϲ θεῶν τίϲιϲ (see West on Hes. *Op.* 11–46). This is surely right: it provides an appropriately Pindaric opening generalization, terse and effective (the absence of the copula from the first phrase is particularly Pindaric: ἄριϲτον μὲν ὕδωρ). A similar conclusion is reached by F. Ferarri, *Ricerche sul testo di Sofocle* (Pisa 1983), 43–4. Stinton might have compared, for sense, structure, rhythm, and asyndeton, Anacreon (?) 505 (d) P = fr. anacr. vet. 1 West (of Eros: quoted in the introduction to the ode above) ὅδε καὶ θεῶν δυνάϲτηϲ· | ὅδε καὶ βροτοὺϲ δαμάζει. The agonistic imagery in our passage takes up the references to boxing with Eros[15] in 441–2 and θεοῖϲι δυϲμαχοῦντεϲ at 492. See also *Ant.* 781 Ἔρωϲ ἀνίκατε μάχαν and 779–800. For praise of the might of love see Men. fr. 383 Koerte Ἔρωϲ δὲ τῶν θεῶν | ἰϲχὺν ἔχων πλείϲτην, Eur. fr. 898. 6 N² ἔργωι δὲ δείξω τὸ ϲθένοϲ τὸ τῆϲ θεοῦ (Ἀφροδίτηϲ).

---

[15] For the interchangeability of Aphrodite and Eros see p. 137 n. 14.

LINES (517)-500

498 ff. After the opening *gnome* on the power of love we find the rhetorical device known as the priamel whereby 'a series of three (occasionally more) paratactic statements of similar form serves to emphasize the last' (West on Hes. *Op.* 435–6). There is a large scholarly literature on the priamel or *praeambulum*: recent instances, rich in bibliography, are Nisbet–Hubbard, *Horace Odes 1*, pp. 1ff.; A. Henrichs, *HSCP* 83 (1979), 207–8; W. H. Race, *The Classical Priamel from Homer to Boethius* (*Mnem.* suppl. 74; 1982), *passim*. In the present case, the amours of the gods[16] are passed over and act as 'foil' to the human dimension, which achieves a particular prominence by reason of this rhetorical structure (and by the use of ἀλλ', τάνδ', and ἄρ': see ad locc.). The three brothers between whom the universe has been divided (*Il.* 15. 190) aptly sum up love's universality (cf. fr. 941. 9ff. εἰcέρχεται μὲν (sc. Κύπρις) ἰχθύων πλωτῶι γένει, | ἔνεςτι δ' ἐν χέρcου (χέρcου δ' ἔνεcτιν ἐν Nauck) τετραcκελεῖ γονῆι, | νωμᾶι δ' ἐν οἰωνοῖcι τοὐκείνης πτερόν). In other words, we have here, on a more elaborate and splendid level, the thought expressed by D herself at 443 οὗτος (sc. Ἔρως) γὰρ ἄρχει καὶ θεῶν ὅπως θέλει.

499–500. παρέβαν: for 'der "emphatische", eine momentane Handlung im Augenblick ihrer sprachlichen Fixierung als schon "vergangen" bezeichnende Aorist' see Kannicht on Eur. *Hel.* 330; cf. Moorhouse, pp. 195–6. **οὐ λέγω:** the *praeteritio* is idiomatic in this type of priamel: cf. Tyrtaeus 12. 1–2 W οὔτ' ἂν μνηςαίμην οὔτ' ἐν λόγωι ἄνδρα τιθείην κτλ. Similarly Archilochus 114. 1ff. W οὐ φιλέω... οὐδὲ... οὐδ'... | ἀλλά and the instances of ἐχθαίρω discussed by Henrichs, loc. cit. (last n.). In the Archilochean example, as here, the negatives are followed by an ἀλλά that serves to emphasize the climax. For other specimens of 'οὐκ—ἀλλά Priameln' see U. Schmid, *Die Priamel der Werte im Griechischen von Homer bis Paulus* (Wiesbaden 1964), 35ff., 146. **ἀπάτας εν:** the omission of the temporal augment occurs c. 6 times in S: see Austin and Reeve, *Maia* 22 (1970), 4 (cf. 514 below); the verb here perhaps recalls particularly the *Iliad*'s Διὸς ἀπάτη (cf. West on Hes. *Th.* 205–6, 224), but the amours of Zeus were, of course, legion (the scholarly equivalent of a Leporello Catalogue of his seductions is thoughtfully supplied by Hans Schwabl

---

[16] This is what τὰ τῶν θεῶν means here, not (as LSJ s.v. ὁ, ἡ, τό BII2 (p. 1195)) 'that which is ordained by the gods' (for which see, e.g., Eur. *Phoen.* 352).

COMMENTARY

in *RE Suppl.* xv. 1225 ff.). For the idea that even Zeus is subject to the power of love see fr. 684. 4–5 καὶ τόνδ' ("Ερωτα) ἀπείργειν οὐδ' ὁ παγκρατὴς cθένει | Ζεύς κτλ., 941. 15ff. Διὸς τυραννεῖ πλευμόνων; there are non-tragic examples in Bühler on Moschus' *Europa* 76, and Page on *AP* 5. 100 (*Further Greek Epigrams*, p. 312).

501. Ἀιδαν: Hades hardly compares with his brothers as a great lover, but his abduction of Persephone is the archetypal instance of rape in Greek literature, and his mention is part of the cosmic whole (above, on 498 ff.). Cf. fr. 941. 3 ἔcτιν μὲν Ἅιδης (sc. Κύπρις). For the epithet cf. *OC* 1558–9 ἐννυχίων ἄναξ Ἀιδωνεῦ.

502. Ποcειδάωνα: 'Neptunus fratri par in amore Iovi', says Propertius tendentiously (2. 26. 46). Even more unexpected is Nonnus' γυναιμανέων Κυανοχαίτης (*Dion.* 8. 235). But the Hesiodic Κατάλογος Γυναικῶν lists many of his sexual conquests (see Merkelbach–West's edition of the Hesiodic fragments, *Index Nominum* s.v. Ποcειδάων: the form here, then, 'epic' rather than (as Jebb) 'Homeric'), and Poseidon frequently features in myth as a progenitor of monsters. For a full list of his 'Geliebte' see Ernst Wüst in *RE* 22 (1953), 462 ff. **τινάκτορα γαίας:** with this phrase as applied to Poseidon cf. *PV* 924–5 θαλαccίαν τε γῆς τινάκτειραν ... | τρίαιναν, αἰχμὴν τὴν Ποcειδῶνος, Nonn. *Dion.* 21. 155 χθονὸς ... τινάκτορα κυανοχαίτην, and compare the picture in *Il.* 20. 57–8 Ποcειδάων ἐτίναξεν | γαῖαν.

503. ἀλλ': for the emphatic function of this particle at the climax of a priamel see Bundy, *Studia Pindarica* i (Univ. Calif. Publ. 2; 1962), 36 (describing Pind. *Is.* 1. 14 as a 'cap introduced by the conventional ἀλλά marking [preceding lines] as focussing foil') and n. 3, where he lists other Pindaric instances in which ἀλλά 'dismisses the foil' (cf. *Stud. Pind.* i. 22 and n. 50: 'ἀλλά ... frequently signal[s] a climax'; Race op. cit. (on 498 ff.), 14 n. 39 etc.). **τάνδ':** for non-deictic ὅδε of this kind see above on 346–7. Here it is emphatic: like ἀλλ(ά) and ἄρ(α) before and after, and the following question, it marks the rhetorical transition to the climax of the priamel, the consequences of love on the mortal level. For similar uses of ὅδε or οὗτος in a priamel see e.g. *Il.* 2. 274, *Od.* 4. 242, 7. 243; Race, *The Classical Priamel*, p. 15 n. 47, pp. 33–4, etc. **ἄρ':** belongs to the category which Denniston, *GP*[2], p. 33, defines as 'primary use, expressing a lively feeling of interest' (*not* to be treated, as by Denniston himself, p. 40, as the sole and solitary example of ἄρα

LINES 499-506

in a question 'preceding the interrogative'; perhaps he was misled by the alleged analogy with the epic question at *Il.* 1. 8 τίς τ' ἄρ ςφωε θεῶν ἔριδι ξυνέηκε μάχεςθαι;).

504. **ἀμφίγυοι**: in Homer (*Il.* 4. 674 etc.; cf. *Lexikon d. frühgr. Epos* s.v.) the word is always used of an ἔγχος, usually in the dat. pl. According to ΣΑ *Il.* 13. 147 (iii. 429 Erbse), οἱ μέν, ἐπεὶ ἀμφοτέραις ταῖς χερςὶ διερείδοντες χρῶνται, οἱ δὲ ἀπὸ τοῦ γυ⟨ι⟩ῶςαι, ὅτι βλάπτει ἀμφοτέρωθεν. οἱ δὲ μεταφορικῶς ἀπὸ τῶν γυίων, ὅτι ἑκατέρωθεν ἄκρον ἔχει. γυῖα γὰρ τὰ ἄκρα. For modern explanations of the word see Chantraine, *Dict. Ét.* s.v., and in particular H. Humbach, in *Studi linguistici in onore di Vittore Pisani* (Brescia 1969), ii. 569 ff. (p. 574 deals with our passage). The scholion on the present line offers four explanations of the word: (1) ἀντίπαλοι ('antagonist, rival'); (2) ἰςχυροὶ ἐν τοῖς γυίοις μαχεςάμενοι χερςὶν καὶ ποςίν (so LSJ); (3) ἀμφότεροι τεθεωρημένοι; (4) ἄμφω παρωξυμμένοι (an attempt to reconcile this Sophoclean with the Iliadic usage: sharpened → provoked?). (2), the most popular solution, entails a catachrestic usage involving a picture of 'balanced strength on both sides' (Burton, p. 56); (4) is supported by Humbach, loc. cit.: 'das Wort bei S. zu "beide scharf" im Sinne von "beide kampfeslustig" umgedeutet ist.' **κατέβαν**: cf. LSJ s.v. καταβαίνω I. 3 ('go down into the scene of contest'). On the epic third-person plural form see Barrett on Eur. *Hipp.* 1247–8, L. Bergson, *Rh. Mus.* 102 (1959), 15. **πρὸ γάμων**: equivalent to ὑπὲρ γάμων, as at Eur. *Hel.* 1477. Add that instance to those given by Jebb in his notes on the present passage and on Soph. *El.* 495 ff. as exemplifying the equivalence of πρό to ὑπέρ. As Jebb observes in the latter note, πρὸ γάμων here must signify '*For* the marriage (not "before it", which would ... be pointless).' For other examples of the equivalence of πρό to ὑπέρ (or περί) see Schwyzer, *Gr. Gr.* ii. 506 (1), adding Eur. *Hcld.* 622.

505–6. **πάμπληκτα παγκόνιτά τ'**: such intensifying παν- prefixes often occur in pairs: cf. Aesch. *ScT* 296 πανδημεὶ πανομιλεί, Soph. *El.* 851 πανςύρτωι παμμήνωι, and in general Fehling, *Wiederholungsfiguren*, p. 247. **ἐξῆλθον**: for this verb in an agonistic context cf. *El.* 687 (Orestes εἰςῆλθε and) νίκης ἔχων ἐξῆλθε πάντιμον γέρας. For its construction with an accusative cf. 159 above. **ἄεθλ' ἀγώνων**: cf. 20 ἀγῶνα ... μάχης; also *Phil.* 507 δυςοίςτων πόνων ἄθλα. ἀγών = 'contest' (the usual Pindaric meaning). The

141

COMMENTARY

technique whereby the poet answers the question he himself has just asked is often compared to the epic (*Il.* 1. 8–9 (cited on 503), 5. 703 ff., 11. 299 ff., 16. 692 ff.). But it is equally Pindaric (cf. the opening of *Ol.* 2, also e.g. *Ol.* 10. 60 ff., *Pyth.* 4. 70 ff.), which would be more to the point here in view of the epinician opening of the present ode (note too Bacch. 19. 15 ff.). The only tragic parallel is Aesch. *Suppl.* 571 ff., according to Johansen and Whittle on that passage, but cf. Kranz, *Stasimon*, pp. 155–6. Race, *The Classical Priamel*, pp. 14 n. 43, 87 ff., etc., observes the frequency of rhetorical questions at the climax of priamels (see especially Aesch. *Ag.* 1017 ff., *Cho.* 594–5).

507 ff. Sophocles here conveys the style of a herald's proclamation at athletic games which regularly supplied the name and city of the contestants: cf. *El.* 693–4 Ἀργεῖος μὲν ἀνακαλούμενος, | ὄνομα δ' Ὀρέστης, Pind. *Pyth.* 1. 30 ff. (Αἴτνας ... ὄρος) τοῦ μὲν ἐπωνυμίαν | κλεινὸς οἰκιστὴρ ἐκύδανεν πόλιν | γείτονα Πυθιάδος δ' ἐν δρόμωι κᾶρυξ ἀνέειπέ νιν ἀγγέλλων Ἱέρωνος ὑπὲρ καλλινίκου (cf. Timotheus fr. 802 P κᾶρυξ | εἶπε· νικαῖ Τιμόθεος | Μιλήςιος, Philodem. περὶ κακιῶν p. 25 Jensen (explained by Wilamowitz, *Sappho und Sim.* (Berlin 1913), 146 n. 2) of musical contests). Note the chiasmus.

507–8. ποταμοῦ ϲθένος: Moorhouse's rendering (p. 53), 'mighty river god, awful image of a horned bull', well conveys the sense; for the epic periphrasis as concentrating 'attention on a particular quality' see Long, *Language and Thought*, pp. 101–2. The same scholar takes φάϲμα ταύρου ('in appearance a bull')[17] as 'very close to the Homeric type' represented by ϲθένος, ἴς vel sim. and genitive (cf. KG ii/1. 280). **ὑψίκερω:** the 'normal' gen. as opposed to the 'lyric' -κέρατος: see Kannicht on Eur. *Hel.* 381–2. **τετραόρου:** only here meaning 'four-legged' (perhaps re-etymologized from ἀείρω 'raise' (cf. πεδ-/μετ-/ ἤορος): so Zieliński, p. 528 n. 3 = pp. 313–14 n. 3; cf. Schuursma, p. 66). The monster's identity is kept to the end like a riddle: see on 1092, 1093, 1095 below.

510–11. Βακχίας ἄπο | ἦλθε ... Θήβας: Heracles has not just 'arrived' from Thebes but 'is from' that city in the sense indicated above

---

[17] But there may be an additional connotation of monstrousness, as with Latin *facies*: cf. Verg. *Aen.* 8. 298 (of Hercules) 'nec te ullae facies, non terruit ipse Typhoeus'; ibid. 194 'Caci facies'. See Eur. fr. 82. 23–4 Austin ταύρον ... φάϲμα and Lloyd-Jones, *YCS* 22 (1972), 266.

142

LINES 505–516

on 507 ff. The hiatus in ἄπο and the preposition's placing between epithet (Βακχίας) and noun (Θήβας) entail a pause in sense before ἦλθε, which is thus dissociated from the preceding ἄπο: 'the other, from Bacchic Thebes, came...': see Stinton, p. 126, and CQ 27 (1977), 63; the point was already made by Zieliński, p. 528 n. 3 = p. 313 n. 3.

512 ff. 'Observe how misty and dreamlike the battle is' (G. Murray, *Greek Studies* (Oxford 1946), 116); the 'vague outlines of the differing attributes of the contenders ... are suggested rather than described exactly' (J. T. Hooker, *Maia* 31 (1979), 245).

511. παλίντονα: on the epithet, its occurrences in Homer, and its meaning see Kirk, *Heraclitus: The Cosmic Fragments* (Cambridge 1954), 213–14, Sideras, *Aeschylus Homericus*, pp. 69–70.

512. For the bow and club as traditional weapons of Heracles in literature and art see Davies on Stes. fr. 229 P. One would naturally suppose that Heracles is here envisaged as holding the club in his right hand, the spear in his left, and having the bow slung around his shoulders. See further below on 517. Artistic depictions, of course, have to make up their minds about such practicalities: cf. Glynn, *AJA* 85 (1981), 126, and 128–9 (on Heracles' weapons in the fight against Nereus or Triton).

513. παῖς Διός: the phrase is often used of Heracles (see Davies's note on Stes. fr. 185 P = S 17. 9). For the emphatic postponement cf. e.g. Eur. *Hipp.* 532. **ἀολλεῖς:** only here of two people: S employs the word καταχρηστικῶς as Σ ad loc. observes; he uses the adjective elsewhere only at *Phil.* 1469: cf. fr. 1017. On ἀολλήδην in Mosch. *Europa* 49 see Bühler ad loc.

514. ἴσαν ἐς μέσον: 'For ἐς μέσον used of combatants advancing to meet each other' see Diggle, *GRBS* 14 (1973), 265.

515. εὔλεκτρος: used again of Κύπρις at *AP* 5. 245. 8, as is εὐλέχης at *APl.* 4. 182. 1. Cf. *Ant.* 795–6 νικᾶι δ' ἐναργὴς βλεφάρων | ἵμερος εὐλέκτρου | νύμφας.

516. ῥαβδονόμει: the verb occurs only here, and ῥαβδονόμος is post-classical. We know of ῥαβδοῦχοι from Ar. *Pax* 734, Thuc. 5. 50. 4, Plato *Protag.* 338 A, and later we hear of ῥαβδοφόροι who were in charge of religious festivals and games, to quote an inscription from Messenia, *IG* v¹. 1390. 41–2 (AD 91/2), ὅπως εὐσχημόνως καὶ εὐτάκτως ὑπὸ τῶν παραγεγενημένων πάντα γίνηται. For the ῥάβδος as 'the judge's normal badge of office' see Dodds on Plato *Gorgias* 526 C 6. For its deterrent use at athletic contests note in

COMMENTARY

particular the famous anecdote at Hdt. 8. 59 ὦ Θεμιcτόκλεεc, ἐν τοῖcι ἀγῶcι οἱ προεξανιcτάμενοι ῥαπίζονται. Innumerable vase-paintings of athletic events (especially, but not exclusively, boxing (and wrestling)) include an umpire holding his forked staff: see e.g. H. A. Harris, *Greek Athletes and Athletics* (London 1964), pls. 4B, 8, and most of 13–21, or the same scholar's *Sport in Greece and Rome* (London 1972), pls. 5, 17, 20, etc. For a ῥαβδονόμοc conceived as present at a mythical wrestling-match see the depiction of Peleus' bout with Atalanta on the black-figure neck amphora now in Munich (Antikensamml. 1541: *LIMC* s.v. Atalanta F 68 (ii/1. 945)). Athena overlooks Heracles wrestling various adversaries (especially Antaeus or Achelous himself: see below, on 517) on numerous vases, and holding her spear she does rather resemble a ῥαβδονόμοc. But the inspiration for Aphrodite in this role is Sophocles' entirely, her appearance as umpire utterly unexpected (a fact re-enforced by the change from 497–8's picture of Aphrodite as victor). Cf. Fraenkel on Aesch. *Ag.* 437ff., with their image of χρυcαμοιβὸc Ἄρηc cωμάτων: 'it is characteristic of Aeschylus that in order to heighten the effect of terrible happenings he ... borrow[s] his imagery ... from the familiar processes of everyday life.'

517ff. On the structure of the first part of the epode see Long, *Language and Thought*, p. 76: 'the fight is expressed impersonally, as a series of short alternate actions ... Each stage of the contest is described by verbal nouns limited by an adj. or defining gen. ... The use of nouns instead of verbs has an abrupt effect which harmonizes admirably with the events described.'

517–18. τότ' ἦν ... ἦν δέ: 'In anaphora, with verbs at least, μέν is more commonly omitted' (Diggle, *STE*, p. 55, with examples from tragedy on p. 56; for non-tragic instances see Fehling, *Wiederholungsfiguren*, pp. 207–8). χερόc is singular because 'multiple parts of the body can be thus represented in poetical use' (Moorhouse, p. 1). Jebb's 'then was there clatter of fists and clang of bow' partly conveys the 'alliterative and onomatopoeic effect' of the Greek original remarked on by e.g. Burton, p. 56. But as a translation it is lacking: since the combatants are already fighting hand to hand at the start of the epode, it would be needlessly confusing if we were then to envisage Heracles as withdrawing to use the bow. It is likelier that we are meant to think of the rattle of the arrows in the quiver as it clatters about Heracles'

LINES 516-520

shoulders (compare the memorable description of Apollo in *Il.* 1.46 ἔκλαγξαν δ' ἄρ' ὀϊστοὶ ἐπ' ὤμων χωομένοιο). The quiver is certainly positioned around Heracles' shoulders on the black-figure hydria (Brit. Mus. 228, 313: *ABV*² 370. 122) which depicts his combat with Achelous, but there, since he is clasping Achelous' horns with both hands, he has no club or spear. For other instances of πάταγος in tragedy see Rau, *Paratragodia*, p. 39.

519. ταυρείων ... κεράτων: literary sources (especially Ov. *Met.* 9. 8) have Heracles win by breaking off one of Achelous' horns; visual depictions often show Heracles grasping one horn (see on 18 ff. above). Compare Theseus' treatment of the Cretan bull (Callim. *Suppl. Hell.* 288. 1, with Lloyd-Jones and Parsons ad loc.). **κεράτων:** the usual tragic scansion (see Diggle, *PCPS* 20 (1974), 22 n. 2).

520. ἦν ... ἦν: for the so-called *schema Pindaricum* whereby a singular verb (especially ἦν and ἔστι) is followed by plural subject see West on Hes. *Th.* 321, Richardson on *HH Dem.* 279, Johansen and Whittle on Aesch. *Suppl.* 714-15. Burton (p. 56) observes the effect produced by having 'the four clauses [at the start of the epode] each introduced by the most naked of verbs (ἦν)'. The opening epithet is problematical: Pearson suggested ἀμφίπλικτοι[18] (for the corruption cf. Theocr. *Id.* 18. 8 περιπλέκτοις ASU, -πλίκτοις Tr.), the only one of his emendations which Wilamowitz (*Deutsche Litztg.* 45 (1924), 2317 = *Kl. Schr.* i. 463) deemed 'richtig und hübsch', one of the three conjectures placed in the text of Sophocles that Housman (*CR* 39 (1925), 77 = *Classical Papers*, iii. 1094) commended as 'evidently true'. Both paradosis and conjecture would be ἅπαξ and the choice between them is a choice between a word meaning 'interwoven' (ἀμφίπλεκτοι) and a word meaning 'straddling' (ἀμφίπλικτοι) as applied to the undefined wrestling-trick known as κλῖμαξ. Let us consider the two possibilities: (1) ἀμφίπλεκτος: LSJ defines as 'intertwined' and gives no other attestation (the verb ἀμφιπλέκω occurs in Euripides but not in S); (2) ἀμφίπλικτος (cf. LSJ s.v.): derived from the verb ἀμφιπλίσσω ('straddle': ἅπαξ in Pollux s.v. 2. 172). πλίσσω, πλίγμα and their cognates are discussed by Cobet, *Variae Lectiones*, pp. 135-6, who does not, however, cite our passage in his treatment of the corruptions such words have suffered. Hesych. s.v. πλίγμα derives the word ἀπὸ τῶν

[18] He was actually anticipated by Headlam (*JHS* 22 (1902), 214 n. 11). Wilamowitz's ἀμφίπληκτοι (*Gr. Versk.* (Berlin 1921), 529) is eccentric.

COMMENTARY

κυλιομένων καὶ παλαιόντων ὅταν περιβάντες (Cobet, loc. cit.: παραβάντες) τοῖς σκέλεσι κατέχωσιν. Other late lexicographical definitions of the verb or the derivative nouns are handily assembled in the app. crit. of Sophocles *TrGF* iv, fr. 596 (p. 447). That fragment uses the ἅπαξ word ἀμφιπλίξ of snakes coiling themselves around a chariot-wheel's axle. M. Poliakoff, *Studies in the Terminology of the Greek Combat Sports* (Beitr. zur kl. Phil. 146; 1982) 75 ff., considers ἀμφίπλικτος and its cognates, stressing (p. 85) the broad range of their usage, which is what makes decision in the present place so difficult.

κλίμακες: the ancient testimonia on this wrestling trick are usefully assembled and discussed by E. N. Gardiner, *JHS* 26 (1906), 15 ff., who concludes (following Hermann) that 'κλιμακίζειν means to jump on to an opponent's back knotting one's legs and arms about him, to make, as it were, a ladder of him'. Cf. Poliakoff, op. cit. 172, and in *Combat Sports in the Ancient World: Competition, Violence and Culture* (New Haven 1987), 51; Kassel–Austin on Ar. fr. 50. See Addenda.

522. πλήγματα: 'the guttural sound adds harshness to the violent sense' (Long, *Language and Thought*, p. 38). **στόνος ἀμφοῖν:** edd. appropriately cite Cic. *Tusc. Disp.* 2. 23. 56 on the psychological benefits of this tactic in boxing: '(pugiles) etiam cum feriunt adversarium in iactandis caestibus ingemescunt, non quod doleant animove succumbant, sed quia profundenda voce omne corpus intenditur venitque plaga vehementior.'

523 ff. The strife of the two combatants reaches a climax of noise and energy. S then abruptly breaks off and transfers us to the object of their passion, awaiting in silent resignation the outcome of their strife. The change in content is re-enforced by a corresponding change of metre (from dactylic to iambic) and language (harshly onomatopoeic adjectives and nouns give way to gentler and more ornamental epithets, vowels replace consonants). The result is extraordinarily moving. (A different but perhaps comparable effect is produced at *Il.* 16. 765 ff. (on which see Adam Parry's Introduction to his father Milman Parry's *Collected Papers* (*The Making of Homeric Verse* (Oxford 1971, p. liii)), where Trojans and Greeks fight over the corpse of Cebriones and (774 ff.) πολλὰ δὲ χερμάδια μεγάλ' ἀσπίδας ἐστυφέλιξαν | μαρναμένων ἀμφ' αὐτόν· ὁ δ' ἐν στροφάλιγγι κονίης | κεῖτο μέγας μεγαλωστί, λελασμένος ἱπποσυνάων. For other Greek legends employing the motif of a duel over a woman see J. Th.

LINES 520-526

Kakridis, *Homer Revisited* (Lund 1971), 33–4, who notes that the woman concerned is regularly envisaged as present: 'this... responds to a primeval necessity of man that the thing for whose sake he is going to strive, often at the peril of his life, should be visible to him, so that he might estimate its value.'

523. ἁβρά: on the connotations of this adjective see Verdenius, *Mnem.* 15 (1962), 392.

524. τηλαυγεῖ παρ' ὄχθωι: cf. Nonn. *Dion.* 43. 12 ff. εἴκτο δὲ Δηιανείρηι, | ἥ ποτε νυμφιδίοιο περιβρομέοντος ἀγῶνος | ἤθελεν Ἡρακλῆα καὶ ἀσταθέος ποταμοῖο | ἵστατο δειμαίνουσα βοοκραίρους ὑμεναίους. 'The opinion of any other reader is equally valuable, even if he lacks the qualification of having composed forty-eight books of semi-accentual hexameters on the career of Dionysus' (Jackson, *MS*, p. 18, on a different problem), but Nonnus does seem to envisage D as watching the fight from the river-bank, and ὄχθος can mean, simply, 'eminence, bank, hill' (LSJ s.v.; see further Fraenkel on Aesch. *Ag.* 1161).

525. ἧστο: the hiatus before this verb encourages us to take it with what follows rather than what precedes: 'sat waiting for her bridegroom' (cf. Stinton, *CQ* 27 (1977), 63, and as cited above on 510–11). **τὸν ὃν... ἀκοίταν:** for the 'possessive' ὅς see 266 above; **προσμένους':** see on 15 above.

526. ἐγὼ δὲ... φράζω: for this phrase in Pindaric lyric as concluding a mythical narrative see Burton, pp. 57–8; cf. Kranz, *Rh. Mus.* 104 (1961), 37 = *Stud. zur antik. Lit. und ihrem Nachw.*, p. 52. μάτηρ has long been thought senseless (the latest attempt at defence by A. S. McDevitt, *Hermes* 110 (1982), 245 ff., does not convince any more than earlier ones). It is futile to compare Soph. *El.* 233–4 ἀλλ' οὖν εὐνοίαι γ' αὐδῶ | μάτηρ ὡσεί τις πιστά, for there the chorus *is* old enough to be the mother of Electra and thus address her, whereas in our play D is old enough to be the chorus' mother (see especially 146 ff.). Kamerbeek's rendering 'as my mother told it to me' is rightly rejected by Page (*Gnomon* 32 (1960), 318: 'we know and care nothing about the mothers of the chorus'). Σ ad loc. gives a paraphrase (ἐγὼ παρεῖσα τὰ πολλὰ τὰ τέλη λέγω τῶν πραγμάτων) quite irreconcilable with the paradosis. Numerous emendations have been proposed (many are listed in Jebb's Appendix). The least unsatisfactory is surely Zieliński's (pp. 528–9, n. 5 = p. 315 n. 1) θατήρ, which picks up lines 22–3 of the prologue

COMMENTARY

ἀλλ' ὅcτιc ἦν | θακῶν ἀταρβὴc τῆc θέαc, ὅδ' ἂν λέγοι); for other correspondences between the prologue and the first stasimon see above, introduction to the ode. For the type of corruption presupposed see below on 555–6. θατήρ is cited by Hesych. s.v. as meaning θεατάc, which may imply that he found it in choral lyric. Wilamowitz's objection (*Griechische Verskunst* (Berlin 1921), 530) that 'die Endung auf -ηρ würde der Athener statt θεατήc nimmer brauchen' seems refuted by ἀγροτήρ at Eur. *El.* 463: cf. Breitenbach, *Untersuchungen zur Sprache der Euripideischen Lyrik* (Stuttgart 1934), 30. Johansen and Whittle on Aesch. *Suppl.* 182 talk of 'Aeschylus' tendency (shared to some degree by the younger tragedians) to use a derivate in -τήρ instead of one in -τηc/-τήc'. **οἷα:** here alone equivalent to ὡc not merely in meaning but in position, following the relevant word (cf. above on 360).

527. τὸ δ'... ὄμμα νύμφαc: on the effect of the reference to D's 'face or the quality of the face' see the sensitive remarks of Long, *Language and Thought*, pp. 101–2, 102 nn. 135–6. It may hark back to 25 τὸ κάλλοc. On the word-order (article, adjective, noun, second dependent noun in genitive, second adjective for first noun) see Moorhouse, p. 153. **ἀμφινείκητον:** cf. 104 above, Aesch. *Ag.* 686 τὰν ἀμφινεικῆ θ' Ἑλέναν and Fraenkel ad loc., who says of our passage 'it is obvious from 507 ff. that the strife of the two opponents [Heracles and Achelous] is meant'.

528. ἐλεινόν: Porson's correction of the manuscripts' uncontracted form (cf. Porson, *Euripidis Tragoediae*[3], ed. J. Scholefield (Cambridge 1851), 3–4), which is epic, Ionic, and the usual κοινή. These facts explain its regular ousting of the Attic form in dramatic texts even at the expense of metre: see Sandbach on Men. *Dysc.* 297. Kraus (*WS* 20 (1986), 97–9) was wrong to defend the paradosis as an epicism. **ἀμμένει:** Wilamowitz (*Gr. Versk.*, pp. 529–30) notes the effective change to the historic present; metre shows (cf. P. Gildersleeves, *JHS* 105 (1985), 154–5) that ⟨∪ –⟩ has dropped out after ἀμμένει (on the absence of the metron ∪ – ∪ – ∪ – from contexts other than dochmiac cf. Hutchinson on Aesch. *ScT* 766–7). H. Gleditsch, *Die Cantica der Sophokleischen Tragödien*[2] (Vienna 1883), 255, preferred τέλοc to his original suggestion of λάχοc (not used, as he observes, by S). τέλοc was also proposed by Wilamowitz in 1921 (*Gr. Versk.*, p. 529) and λάχοc by Dawe in his edition. More recently, P. Gildersleeves (art. cit. 155) has proposed λέχοc, detecting a further echo of the prologue

(27–8 λέχος γὰρ Ἡρακλεῖ κριτὸν | ξυστᾶς ἀεί τιν' ἐκ φόβου φόβον τρέφω). λέχος might, indeed, be described as ἐλεινόν, especially by a chorus claiming to speak 'as a spectator'.

529. ἄφαρ βέβαχ': 'is gone at once': resultative perfect (see on the identical phrase at 133–4 above). **ὥστε πόρτις ἐρήμα:** young girls are compared to heifers as regards *speed* in *HH Dem.* 174ff. αἱ δ' ὥς τ'... ἢ πόρτιες... ὥς αἱ... ἤιξαν. For more general comparisons of young girls to delicate creatures such as does or fawns see Dodds on Eur. *Bacch.* 873ff., Nisbet–Hubbard on Horace *Odes* 1. 23. 1, Maehler on Bacch. 13. 87. For the pathetic detail of the mother within such comparisons see Anacr. 408 P ἀγανῶς οἷά τε νεβρὸν νεοθηλέα | γαλαθηνὸν ὅς τ' ἐν ὕληι κεροέσσης | ἀπολειφθεὶς ἀπὸ μητρὸς ἐπτοήθη, Hor. *Odes* 1. 23. 1ff. 'vitas inuleo me similis, Chloe, | quaerenti pavidam montibus aviis | matrem', and perhaps Anacr. 346. 3ff. P ὦ καλλιπρό[c]ωπε παίδ[ων·] | καί ςε δοκεῖ μὲν ἐ[ν δό]μοιςι[ν] | πυκινῶς ἔχουςα [μήτηρ suppl. complures] ἀτιτάλλειν. For the mother's role outside the simile in the reality represented cf. Catullus 62. 20ff. 'Hespere ... | qui natam possis complexu avellere matris, | complexu matris retinentem avellere natam | et iuveni ardenti castam donare puellam'.

SECOND EPISODE (531–632)

531ff. The apparent discrepancy between D's speech here and at 436ff. has long been observed and variously explained. Reinhardt compared the '*Trugrede*' at *Aj.* 646ff. (cf. on 445), but this has failed to convince most scholars. If D's *rhesis* at 436ff. is not, in fact, a deception speech, what is its dramatic function? The question is well posed and answered by D. A. Hester, *Antichthon* 14 (1980), 1ff., who points out that the etymology of Deianeira's name (see F. Errandonea, *Mnem.* 55 (1927), 145ff.) suggests she was originally conceived in the myth as a wicked husband-murderer in the same mould as Clytemnestra. It is clear from the start of the present play that S is presenting her as drawn along quite different lines. And he seems to go a step further in suggesting that even when D is attacked at the central core of her existence, her marriage, she will not actively resist. But the suggestion is deliberately misleading. She emerges, in fact, as the one monster powerful enough

COMMENTARY

to destroy Heracles. This paradox is characteristically Sophoclean: D kills the man who means more to her than any other creature, just as Antigone, who struggles to preserve the glory of her family, contributes to its further downfall, Oedipus, having saved Thebes from the Sphinx, all but ruins it by bringing the plague down on it, and the cunning Odysseus stupidly brings his plan for Philoctetes' return to nothing. A similar argument (independently advanced and on partly independent grounds) in March, *The Creative Poet*, pp. 66 ff.

531 ff. ἦμος ... τῆμος: the latter is the only attested instance in Attic literature of the epic word (for a list of 'Homeric Words as Tragic Hapax Legomena' see Renehan, *Studies in Greek Texts*, pp. 27 ff. (with Addenda, including this instance, on p. 165)). The correlatives are here used in a very unepic manner, however; Homer and Hesiod employ them to indicate the time of day or year at which a given event occurs: some natural phenomenon (dawn, sunset, etc.) or (more rarely) some item of human behaviour (e.g. the preparation of the midday meal) which recurs regularly at a fixed time is cited to fix the event's position within the day or year (for more detail see Davies on Stesichorus 185 P = S 7. 1).

531-2. ~ 601 ἕως cὺ ταῖc ἔcωθεν ἠγορῶ ξεναῖc. According to Jebb, 'the verb θροεῖ seems to imply that their voices could be heard within, and that therefore [D] felt safe from sudden interruption'. Rather 'θροεῖν in der Tragödie [ist] nur edlerer Ausdruck für λέγειν' (Kaibel on *El.* 853).

532. ὡc ἐπ' ἐξόδωι: 'with his departure in view, with a view to departing': cf. Moorhouse, p. 113, for this use of ἐπί.

533. θυραῖος ἦλθον: see on 163 above.

534-5. τὰ μὲν ... τὰ δ': this particular combination is attested elsewhere in tragedy only at Eur. *Hel.* 261.

534. χερcὶν ἀτεχνηcάμην: on this metaphorical usage see D. Müller, *Handwerk und Sprache*, p. 12 n. 12.

536. κόρην γάρ, οἶμαι δ' οὐκέτ': cf. Eur. *IA* 460ff. τὴν δ' αὖ τάλαιναν παρθένον· τί παρθένον; | Ἅιδης νιν, ὡς ἔοικε, νυμφεύcει τάχα. The rhetorical device in these passages is characterized thus by Fraenkel, *Horace*, p. 194: 'a passionate utterance is after the first phrase interrupted by the speaker himself, who is carried away by the feeling that what he has been saying is wrong because it is not true or only partially true and in any case does not go to the root of his grief.'

LINES 531-539

He gives further examples at p. 194 n. 1. **ἐζευγμένην:** see Barrett on Eur. *Hipp.* 545–6 for 'the common metaphor of yoke = marriage or other sexual union'; also Nisbet–Hubbard, *Horace Odes 2*, pp. 78 ff., especially p. 80, R. Seaford, *JHS* 107 (1987), 111. The messenger called Iole a κόρη at 352; see further Theocr. *Id.* 27. 66 γυνὴ . . . οὐκέτι κώρα.

537 ff. Long, *Language and Thought*, pp. 118–19, has good remarks on the imagery here: D's 'language, superficially resigned, reveals beneath the surface undercurrents of conflict which grow in intensity as her speech proceeds'.

537–8. παρεcδέδεγμαι . . . ἐμπόλημα: cf. D's description of Iole at 376–7 τίν' ἐcδέδεγμαι πημονὴν ὑπόcτεγον | λαθραῖον; This has led some scholars to suppose that παρ-ecδέδεγμαι here = ἐcδέδεγμαι λαθραῖον there. Jebb's objection to this ('Deianeira was the victim not agent of the fraud') is inept and over-logical but παρα(-) with the suggestion of secrecy cannot be paralleled from classical Greek (though cf. 226 φρουρὰν παρῆλθε), and a likelier picture is of 'one piece of cargo too many, through the dictates of the ship's owner, so that the ship sinks' (cf. Zieliński, pp. 515–16 n. 11 = p. 299 n. 2).

538. Cf. *Ant.* 1063 ὡc μὴ 'μπολήcων ἴcθι τὴν ἐμὴν φρένα. For the abstract noun 'in apposition to a personal subject as . . . a peculiarly Sophoclean idiom' see Long, *Language and Thought*, p. 120 and n. 26). In his note on Aesch. *Ag.* 1447 εὐνῆc παροψώνημα τῆc ἐμῆc χλιδῆc (χλιδῆι Musgrave) Fraenkel compared our λωβητὸν . . . φρενόc. 'Anyone who has studied in detail the manner in which Sophocles draws on Aeschylean material can have no doubt that here the younger poet, dealing with a similar situation, had in mind the crowning line of Clytemnestra's speech: not only is παροψώνημα echoed in ἐμπόλημα (a rare word), but, more important, the rhythmical character of the two lines in their entirety is very similar and so are their endings.' For a further parallel between the eternal triangles of Agamemnon, Clytemnestra, Cassandra and Heracles, Deianeira, Iole see on 539 ff.

539 ff. On the image here see in particular Long, *CR* 13 (1963), 128–9 (summarized in *Language and Thought*, pp. 119–20), where Kamerbeek's remarkably confused and misleading note ad loc. is corrected. Long rightly advocates a concrete passive sense for ὑπαγκάλιcμα here, which stands in poignant opposition to δύ' οὖcαι as the subject

COMMENTARY

of the intransitive μίμνομεν: 'and now we wait, a pair to be embraced under one blanket.' The singular ὑπαγκάλιcμα ('one object of embrace') forms what Long calls 'a pathetic contrast with δύ' οὔcαι', and this contrast between singular and plural obviates the need for an explicit ἕν before ὑπαγκάλιcμα. Similarly Campbell ad loc. ('The sense of μιᾶc is continued: i.e. μ. ὑ. χ. ἓν ὑπαγκάλιcμα'). There is a series of similarities between our passage as thus understood and Eur. *El.* 1032 ff.:

El.	*Tr.*
ἀλλ' ἦλθ' ἔχων μοι μαινάδ' ἔνθεον κόρην	
λέκτροιc τ' ἐπειcέφρηκε, καὶ νύμφα δύο	καὶ νῦν δύ' οὔcαι μίμνομεν μιᾶc ὑπὸ
ἐν τοῖcιν αὐτοῖc δώμαcιν[19] κατείχομεν.	χλαίνηc ὑπαγκάλιcμα.

For χλαῖνα in descriptions of the *gaudia Veneris* see Pearson on fr. 483. 2. Add the Cologne epode of Archilochus 44–5 μαλθακῆι δ[ὲ μιν | χλαί]νηι καλύψαc, Eur. fr. 603. 4 N², Hieronymus of Rhodes fr. 35 Wehrli = Soph. *TrGF* iv ᴛ ɴ Radt (p. 61), Longus 3. 24, Petron. *Sat.* 11. For the force of μία cf. Theocr. *Id.* 18. 19 ὑπὸ τὰν μίαν . . . χλαῖναν, Asclepiades *AP* 5. 169. 3 = *HE* 814 f. ὁπόταν κρύψηι μία τοὺc φιλέ-ονταc | χλαῖνα, and see in general G. Arrigoni, 'Amore sotto il manto e iniziazione nuziale', *QUCC* 15 (1983), 7 ff., citing the evidence of vase-painting as well as literature.

540 ff. τοιάδ' . . . οἰκουρί': hyperbaton of τοιόcδε and its noun (as in Aesch. *Ag.* 156–7 τοιάδε . . . μόρcιμα). For such hyperbaton see Fraenkel, *Iktus und Akzent* (Berlin 1928), 321 n. 3.

541–2. ἡμῖν has been taken as going with πιcτόc and ἀγαθόc (cf. Men. fr. 16 Koerte ὁ χρηcτὸc ἡμῖν μοιχόc), or with καλούμενοc (Jebb favours this interpretation). That it goes in fact with ἀντέπεμψε in the following line has been shown as likely by Fraenkel, *Beob. zu Aristoph.*, pp. 65 ff., especially p. 67, who quotes *El.* 1372–3 οὐκ ἂν μακρῶν ἔθ' ἡμῖν οὐδὲν ἂν λόγων, | Πυλάδη, τόδ' εἴη τοὔργον, Aesch. *Eum.* 636–7 ἀνδρὸc μὲν ὑμῖν οὗτοc εἴρηται μόροc | τοῦ παν-τοcέμνου, and numerous comic and prose passages, to illustrate the tendency of ἡμῖν and ὑμῖν to occupy second place in a sentence, even at the price of a considerable segregation from the word with which they grammatically belong. For comparable irony cf. *OT* 385–6

[19] cτρώμαcιν *tempt.* Zieliński (pp. 515–16 n. 11 = p. 298 n. 2), but the word is not Tragic. κατείχομεν L: κατείχ' ὁμοῦ Dawes, *prob.* Diggle.

LINES 539-547

ταύτης Κρέων ὁ πιcτόc, οὐξ ἀρχῆς φίλος, | λάθραι μ' ὑπελθών and Austin on Men. *Asp.* 75; the definite article seems to be idiomatic in such contexts (cf. Page on Eur. *Med.* 207, Barrett on *Hipp.* 589–90).

542. οἰκούρι': 'reward (given by the husband to his wife) for keeping the house': Fraenkel's definition, given in the course of a discussion of this and cognate words (in his note on Aesch. *Ag.* 1625 ff.). Eur. *Her.* 1373 μακρὰς διαντλοῦς' ἐν δόμοις οἰκουρίας was taken to be the model for our passage by Wilamowitz ad loc.

543. ἐπίcταμαι: cf. *Ant.* 686 οὔτ' ἂν δυναίμην μήτ' ἐπιcταίμην λέγειν. ἐπίcταμαι bears the same meaning at *Il.* 16. 142 as Σ ad loc. (iv. 195 Erbse) observes, quoting Soph. *TrGF* iv, fr. 903 οὐ πώποθ' ὑμᾶς cυμβαλεῖν ἐπίcταμαι as another example. See further Barrett on Eur. *Hipp.* 996 and Pearson, *CQ* 22 (1928), 179; cf. Martial's 'non norunt haec monumenta mori' (10. 2. 12).

544. νοcοῦντι: for the 'disease of love' metaphor see on 443 above. Moorhouse, p. 89 is divided as to whether τῆιδε ... νόcωι should be regarded as comitative or a means of avoiding a cognate accusative (awkward after the internal accusative πολλά). *PV* 384 ἔα με τῆιδε τῆι νόcωι νοcεῖν suggests we may have here a means of stressing the metaphorical nature of the disease.

545. τὸ δ' αὖ: emphatic positioning of the infinite (re-enforced by αὖ); for the articular infinitive where the simple infinitive would have sufficed see Pearson on fr. 149. 9. 'ὁμοῦ coupled with a cύν compound' is an 'idiomatic pleonasm': see Diggle, *STE*, p. 39. **τίc ἂν γυνή:** the question is kept back until the infinitive phrase has established the theme: cf. 1231 below, and in general Moorhouse, p. 247, for this principle of word-order.

547. On the more flexible meaning required here for ἥβη see Pearson on fr. 786.

547 ff. The actual wording of these sentiments is problematic (see, in particular, Pearson, *CR* 39 (1925), 4). The sequence of thought would be considerably clearer if we had ὁρῶ γὰρ ἥβην τῆς (or τῆι) μὲν ἔρπουcαν πρόcω, | τῆς (or τῆι) δὲ φθίνουcαν· ὧν (sc. τῆς μὲν) ἀφαρπάζειν φιλεῖ | ὀφθαλμὸς ἄνθος τῆς, δ' κτλ. In this reconstruction τῆς μὲν ... τῆς δέ is due to Blaydes (τῆι μὲν ... τῆι δέ Musgrave) and τῆς δέ in 549 to Nauck. The assimilation of endings is a common form of corruption (see e.g. West, *Textual Criticism and Editorial Technique*, pp. 23–4). For the idiomatic omission of τῆς μέν

153

COMMENTARY

before τῆc δέ see Denniston, *GP*², p. 166, Stinton, p. 129, above on 117. Zippmann's correlative ὧν δ'... τῶνδ' (with one and the same woman liked in her youth but shunned when old), accepted by the OCT (cf. *Sophoclea*, p. 162), is less attractive since an explicit indication of the shift from young to aged is really needed for this alternative to work. **ἀφαρπάζειν ... ἄνθοc:** cf. Mimn. fr. 1. 4 W ἥβηc ἄνθεα ... ἁρπαλέα. Gentili–Prato ad loc. (p. 51), West on Hes. *Th.* 988, and Braswell on Pind. *Pyth.* 4. 158 (b) cite other examples of the 'flower of youth' metaphor; this is often found in sexual contexts with some such verb as (ἀπο-)δρέπειν fulfilling the function of ἀφαρπάζειν here: see Johansen and Whittle on Aesch. *Suppl.* 663 ff. **ὀφθαλμόc:** love is regularly located in the eye in Greek poetry: see Barrett on Eur. *Hipp.* 525 ff., West on Hes. *Th.* 910, Kost on Musaeus *Hero and Leander* 90, etc. For the violently mixed metaphor whereby the ὀφθαλμόc appears to have a foot, cf. Eur. *Med.* 1244 ff.[20] ἄγ', ὦ τάλαινα χείρ ἐμή, λαβὲ ξίφοc, | λάβ', ἕρπε πρὸc βαλβῖδα λυπηρὰν βίου, | καὶ μὴ κακίcθηιc μηδ' ἀναμνηcθῆιc τέκνων, | ὡc φίλταθ', ὡc ἔτικτεc, ἀλλὰ τήνδε γε | λαθοῦ βραχεῖαν ἡμέραν παίδων cέθεν, | κἄπειτα θρήνει. In other words, there as here, the poet's mind returns to the owner of the bodily part (a transition easier in the present instance if we read ὑπεκτρέπει (not -ειν) in 549). Cf. 1260 below.

550. ταῦτ': adverbial accusative referring back to the explanation just given, not introducing the μή clause: Moorhouse, pp. 41–2.

550–1. πόcιc ... ἐμόc: Dawe, *Studies* iii. 87, complains that 'the distinction ... between a respectable husband, πόcιc, and a less respectable lover, ἀνήρ is by no means always valid. πόcιc means "lover" at Eur. *Or.* 561, and ἀνήρ means "husband" in our present play at e.g. v. 150.' He is thus led to conjecture τῆc νεωτέραc δ' ἄρ' ἦν, a suggestion rightly stigmatized by West (2), p. 524 (cf. (1), p. 366), as 'grammatically impossible'. Dawe's remarks about the interchangeability of ἀνήρ and πόcιc on certain occasions are correct as far as they go (he might have cited Andromache's address to Hector's corpse at *Il.* 24. 725, where Hector is apostrophized as ἄνερ, and cf. now Braswell on Pind. *Pyth.* 4. 87 (d)), but here the two words are rhetorically juxtaposed, and as West ((2), p. 524), says, 'the antithesis, though lacking a parallel, is

---

[20] Though here the tendency of χείρ to stand for the whole person (see on 898 below) makes a difference.

guaranteed by the structure of the phrases'. Fehling, *Wiederholungsfiguren*, p. 301, puts it very well: 'πόcιc und ἀνήρ sind synonym, aber der kleine Unterschied der Assoziation, der beim einen mehr an den legalen, beim andern mehr an den physischen Aspekt denken läßt, ermöglicht die überraschende Antithese.' Cf. G. P. Shipp, *Antichthon* 11 (1977), 3 (arguing that πόcιc is 'the old word [used] to express Deianeira's legal position against Iole's sexual relationship to Heracles, the two aspects of wifedom being divided thus between the two women'), and Kaibel on *El.* 1220–1. A future indicative would be grammatically possible after μή, but in the present context would provide an inappropriate tone of certainty.

552–3. An allusion back to D's remarks at 438 ff. (especially 483 οὐ γὰρ γυναικὶ τοὺc λόγουc ἐρεῖc κακῆι and 441–2 Ἔρωτι μὲν γὰρ ὅcτιc κτλ.) and 543–4 ἐγὼ δὲ θυμοῦcθαι μὲν οὐκ ἐπίcταμαι κτλ.

553–4. ἧι δ' ἔχω ... τῆιδ' ... φράcω: wrongly explained by Moorhouse, p. 271, as an example of attraction by the adverbial antecedent: 'we should normally expect τῆιδε to refer to the mode (not the contents) of telling. But here the word occurs by attraction for τόδε: "'I shall tell you this, in what way" ... thereby "replacing a pronominal with an adverbial function".' However, although the relative is frequently attracted thus to the demonstrative (cf. 701–2 ἐκ δὲ γῆc ὅθεν | προὔκειτ᾽), the reverse is not the case, and Moorhouse's alleged parallel, *OC* 1226 κεῖθεν ὅθεν, is easily emended away (cf. *Sophoclea* p. 251). A likelier explanation is to hand if we examine the idiom represented by Platonic τῆιδε λέγω (cf. 1135 ἧι νοεῖc, *OC* 1300 ταύτηι κλύω). Cf. Wackernagel, *Vorlesungen über Syntax*, i. 55. But the question cannot be entirely divorced from the following problem.

554. λυτήριον λύπημα: Stinton defends the paradosis (pp. 138–9) as referring to the pain D feels at using deceit: the phrase is taken as an oxymoron (already interpreted thus by Scholefield (ed. Porson's *Euripidis Tragoediae priores quatuor*, p. 406 n. δ (comparing φίλον ἄχθοc at Eur. *Her.* 637, but see Bond, ad loc. for the true meaning of that phrase)). Lloyd-Jones, however (*Sophoclea*, p. 162), more convincingly interprets the phrase in the light of the common tragic metaphor ἄκοc τομαῖον (Aesch. *Cho.* 539) *vel sim.* (see his remarks in *Dionysiaca* (Page Festschrift), pp. 48 ff.). Such a remedy by excision is naturally painful but can also be conceived as bringing release: cf.

COMMENTARY

Aesch. *Suppl.* 268 ἄκη τομαῖα καὶ λυτήρια, Eur. *Melanippe Sapiens* (Page, *Lit. Pap. (Poetry)*, 14. 17) ἄκη πόνων... καὶ λυτήρια. So here D's remedy for Heracles' affliction can thus be painful, but will also bring release (see further on 1021 below). The emendations advanced (κήλημα (cf. 575 below) Hermann, τέχνημα Blaydes, *prob.* Wilamowitz*, νόημα Campbell, λώφημα Jebb (a word not found in tragedy, though the equivalent verb is)) presuppose corruption due to 'the subconscious repetition of a letter or two, copied or soon to be copied' (Jackson, *MS*, pp. 223–4) citing numerous examples, e.g. line 700 of our play and Ar. *Eq.* 768 διαπριcθείην διατμηθείην for διαπριcθείην κατατμηθείην). Cf. Radt, *The Importance of the Context*, pp. 5 ff. But none of them convinces. Perhaps λυτήριόν τι πημονῆc (conjectured by E. Ziel, *De asyndeto apud Sophoclem* (Progr. Gymnas. Celle 1847), 7) is superior, since it also removes the problematic τῆιδ' (see last n.). τι would drop out before π (see on 944 below); πημονῆc becomes λύπημα by dittography after λυτήριον; and τῆιδ' would be introduced from ἧι δ' immediately above.

555 ff. ἦν μοι... τοῦτ' (578): one is reminded, perhaps, of the ἀκτή τιc... ἔνθα formula in 237 and 752–3 (see my note on the latter). For the much rarer use of the idiom as applied to an object see Eur. *Suppl.* 1197ff. ἔcτιν τρίπουc cοι (~ ἦν μοι... δῶρον)... | ὅν (~ *Tr.* 557 ὅ)... (1201) ἐν τῶιδε (~ τοῦτ').

555. παλαιὸν δῶρον: 'παλαιόc ("old", in the sense of "having existed since long ago") is often used of a period of time continuing from long ago up to the present' (Barrett on Eur. *Hipp.* 907–8; see further Denniston on Eur. *El.* 1). Cf. 1141–2 Νέccοc πάλαι Κένταυροc ἐξέπειcέ νιν | τοιῶιδε φίλτρωι. **παλαιὸν δῶρον... ποτέ:** the words belong together rhetorically: cf. *Il.* 7. 89–90 ἀνδρὸc μὲν τόδε cῆμα πάλαι κατατεθνηῶτοc | ὅν ποτ' ἀριcτεύοντα κατέκτανε φαίδιμοc Ἕκτωρ.

555–6. ἀρχαίου... θηρόc: Jebb's sensitive and thoughtful explanation of ἀρχαίου ('this emphasis on the past is natural in one who is looking back sadly to days of her youth' etc.: cf. Eur. *Cycl.* 435) for once seems over-sensitive and far-fetched, forced and unconvincing. It is likelier that we have here a corruption of the sort analysed and illustrated by Fraenkel (ed. Aesch. *Ag.* iii. 655 n. 1; cf. *JRS* 56 (1966), 145 n. 9), wherein 'two elements are combined, a mechanical error, arising from the literal similarity of two words, and a mental error, the writer's

LINES 554-560

thought straying to some word suggested by the context'. In the present case ἀρχαίου will have arisen under the influence of παλαιόν one word before. Wakefield's ἀγρίου is a plausible restoration of the original sense: cf. Eur. *Her.* 364-5 ἀγρίων | Κενταύρων, Ov. *Met.* 12. 219 'saevorum saevissime Centaurorum'. Cf. below on 1096.

556. χαλκέωι: on the metrically guaranteed uncontracted form of the adjective here (contrast 683 χαλκῆc) see Bergson, *Rh. Mus.* 102 (1959), 16 ff., arguing for metrical convenience as the criterion for its use in tragedy.

557-8. δαcυcτέρνου ... Νέccου: for shaggy centaurs see *Il.* 2. 743 φῆραc ... λαχνήενταc, *HH Herm.* 224 (*pace* Jebb here, Cometes at Ov. *Met.* 12. 284 is the name of a lapith, not a centaur); G. S. Kirk, *Myth: Its Meaning and Functions* (Cambridge 1971), 160; for the anastrophe of παρά see Wackernagel, *Kl. Schr.* ii. 1084 n. 2.

559. ὅc: for the relative introducing a narrative see above on 262.

559-60. τὸν ... ποταμὸν ... βροτοὺc ... 'πόρευε: 'ferried men over the river': for the accusative of extent (place) see Eur. *Alc.* 442 ff. γυναῖκ' ἀρίcταν | λίμναν Ἀχεροντίαν πορεύcαc, Moorhouse, p. 44.

560. μιcθοῦ 'πόρευε: is this an unaugmented verb, or has its initial vowel suffered prodelision of syllabic augment? Unaugmented verbs are rare in tragedy outside of messenger-speeches (see on 904 below). The present *rhesis* is certainly akin in a stylistic sense to a messenger-speech, but in such messenger speeches 'the augment is ordinarily omitted only at the beginning of a line' (Dodds on Eur. *Bacch.* 1134 γυμνοῦντο δέ |, one of the very few seemingly intractable exceptions to the rule). For a list of other apparent exceptions (*Tr.* 767 should not be included: see ad loc.) see Dodds's note (cf. L. Bergson, *Eranos* 51 (1953), 124). As Dodds implies, Aesch. *Pers.* 313 ἐκ μιᾶc πέcον | is from a passage deleted by Paley on quite independent grounds (see Broadhead's supplementary note ad loc.). And Eur. *Alc.* 839 and *OC* 1506 are not only 'doubly suspect as not being narrative', to quote Dodds again, but also easily emended (the latter from θῆκε τῆcδε to τῆcδ' ἔθηκε (Heath), the former from Ἠλεκτρύωνοc γείνατ' to ἐγείνατ' Ἠλεκτρύωνοc (Gaisford)). Prodelision or aphaeresis is the likeliest answer here, then, as at 381 (see ad loc.). For examples of the phenomenon after -ου see Bergson, op. cit. 123. **χερcίν:** 'arms'

COMMENTARY

(contrast the meaning 'hands' at 565, 566, and 573 below). **πομπίμοις:** see on 571 ἔπεμψ'.

562-3. Dawe, like Nauck before him, mistrusts the phrase and actually obelizes πατρῷον, and Wecklein (followed by Zieliński, p. 529 n. 5 = p. 315 n. 1) placed a lacuna after 562; but, as Dobree saw (*Adversaria*, ed. Wagner, iv. 37), the internal accusative is perfectly idiomatic (cf. Moorhouse, p. 40, rendering the present instance as '"I went... on my father's sending" (i.e. "sent by him")': cf. 155-6 ὁδὸν ... | ὡρμᾶτ', 159 ἀγῶνας ἐξιών, etc. Oeneus is shown as present at Nessus' death on various vase-paintings (cf. F. Brommer, *Herakles*, 11 (Darmstadt 1984), 48 ff.), but this is merely a feature of the common device of 'telescoping' or combining several scenes in one.

563. εὖνις: the first instance of the meaning 'wife' in Greek (Eur. *Or.* 929 is unlikely to be earlier). In *BICS* 33 (1986), 101-2, D. Armstrong argues for an ambiguity here between this and the word's earlier meaning 'bereft, deprived' ('πατρός understood... from πατρῷον') to emphasize D's lack of a proper wedding, and pick up the theme of desolation from 530.

564. Not for the last time a choice between rarities confronts us: HN is the paradosis: do we interpret it as a first person-singular reference to D herself, followed by ἐν in prodelision (ἦ 'ν: so Cobet) or as a third-person-singular reference to Nessus followed by a locative dative: ἦν μέσωι πόρωι? Nessus as the carrier of D would more naturally be the object of the reference, and this intuition may be backed up by something more concrete. According to E. Harrison, *CR* 56 (1942), 8, 'a clear instance of prodelision after such an ἦ is in all our tragedies not to be found' (for examples of prodelided ἐν in Greek drama, including cases after different types of (-)η, see Platnauer, *CQ* 10 (1960), 143, who includes our instance without reference to Harrison).[21] It seems likely that a locative dative, not unlike some of the instances cited by Moorhouse, p. 87, is what faces us here. See Addenda.

565. ματαίαις χερσίν: 'rash' with a connotation of lewdness: see esp. Eur. *El.* 1064 (of Clytemnestra and Helen) ἄμφω ματαίω, Aesch. *Suppl.* 762 ματαίων ἀνοσίων τε κνωδάλων (cf. ibid. 229), Den-

---

[21] If those scholars are right who deny the existence of *any* reliable instance of prodelided ἐν in tragedy (cf. Pfeiffer, *Sitzb. d. Bayer. Akad. d. Wiss., phil.-hist. Kl.* 6 (1958), 13 = *Sophokles* (Wege der Forschung 95; 1967), 470 n. 13) the case against ἦ 'ν here is even stronger. But see Diggle, *STE* p. 33 for the likeliest instances.

niston on the first. (For μάται meaning 'lustfulness' see Johansen and Whittle on Aesch. *Suppl.* 820. (ψαύω too can be used 'de inhonesta tactione': see Gow and Page on Philodemus *AP* 12. 173. 3 = *GP* 3256, J. N. Adams, *The Latin Sexual Vocabulary* (London 1982), 185–6.

566. ἐπιςτρέψας: What is the verb's object? Did Heracles turn his bow or himself against Nessus? The former interpretation seems supported by such metaphorical usages as Theognis 213 θυμέ, φίλους κατὰ πάντας ἐπίστρεφε ποικίλον ἦθος, 1083 οὕτω χρὴ τόν γ' ἐςθλὸν ἐπιςτρέψαντα νόημα, as well as the close proximity of χερςίν here. March, *The Creative Poet*, pp. 49 ff., ingeniously argues that 'from all the known representations of the Nessus episode ... before the classical period, it must be concluded that in this earlier age Nessus' death does not seem to have been caused by a distant arrow-shot, and thus that there seems to have been no connection between the death of Nessus and the later death of Heracles' (p. 56). That connection, she thinks, is S's invention.

567. πλεύμονας: on the variant πνευ- here and at 1054 see V. Di Benedetto, *Maia* 20 (1968), 160–1; cf. Gow on Theocr. *Id.* 25. 237, Hunter on Eubulus fr. 24 (= fr. 23 KA). See Addenda.

571. For πέμπω meaning 'escort, accompany' in tragedy (as at 417 above) see e.g. Diggle, *ICS* 2 (1977), 112.

572 ff. A notorious crux, not least because there are so many conditions to be fulfilled before any solution can hope to be called definitive. We require an approach that will make good sense of ἧι and θρέμμα, which will provide a suitable subject for the verb ἔβαψεν, and will establish a coherent relationship between μελαγχ. ... ἰ. and θρ. Λερν. ὕδρ. Few candidates indeed, manage to meet these requirements.

The Σ's once popular idea that θρέμμα ... ὕδρας can be a periphrasis for the hydra along the lines of 509 φάςμα ταύρου (cf. the transmitted φάςματι ὕδρας in 837) has been convincingly challenged by Long in *GRBS* 8 (1967), 275 ff. (cf. *Language and Thought*, p. 103), the most helpful of recent attempts to solve the problems of this passage. In spite of Moorhouse, p. 53, comparing *Ant.* 472 τὸ γέννημα τῆς παιδός ('the offspring which is the maiden': cf. παῖδες Τρώων, Renehan, *Greek Lexicographical Notes* i. (Hypomnemata 45; 1975), 156–7) and *El.* 758 ςῶμα δειλαίας ςποδοῦ ('the body which is (reduced to) sad dust'), I share the widespread scepticism about the

COMMENTARY

notion that our phrase is equivalent to 'the creature, the Lernaean hydra'.

Wunder achieved the sense 'si cruorem sumpseris de ea parte vulneris mei in quam venenatam sagittae cuspidem Hercules demersit' by emending to produce the locative genitive μελαγχόλου ... ἰοῦ; by taking θρέμμα as equivalent to αἷμα; by supplying Heracles as subject of ἔβαψεν; and by giving ἔβαψεν the sense it bears at *Aj.* 95 ἔβαψας ἔγχος εὖ πρὸς Ἀργείων cτρατῶι, Eur. *Phoen.* 1577–8 φάcγανον εἴcω cαρκὸc ἔβαψεν (*v.l.*), or *PV* 863 δίθηκτον ἐν cφαγαῖcι βάψαcα ξίφοc (listed by LSJ s.v. βάπτω Ib 'of slaughter in Trag.'). This final feature is perhaps the most objectionable part of Wunder's approach, but this meaning for our instance of the verb has recently been recommended once more by M. L. West, *BICS* 26 (1979), 111, without mention of Wunder, but with the gratuitous assertion that 'surely we are bound to take the verb in the same way' as in the passages just cited. Surely, on the contrary, when we encounter the verb in this context we are bound to think of the famous story of Heracles' literal dipping of his arrows into the hydra's gall (a story familiar as early as Stesichorus' *Geryoneis* (see S 15, ii. 4 ff.)) and soon acquiring a near-proverbial status: cf. Eur. *Her.* 1187–8 μαινομένωι πιτύλωι πλαγχθεὶc | ἑκατογκεφάλου βαφαῖc ὕδραc, Zenob. *Cent.* 6. 26 τοὺc οἰcτοὺc τῆι χολῆι ... βάψαι). This literal dipping is a quite separate action from the slaughtering of the hydra, and Sophocles would hardly have confounded the two deeds by using the verb in the unusual way required by West and Wunder, even if (what is uncertain) βάπτω could thus be used of an arrow in the same way as it is of sword or spear.

As we have seen, Wunder's approach requires that we take θρέμμα as equivalent to αἷμα—which is extraordinary enough. West avoids this difficulty by supposing θρ. Λερν. ὕδρ. to be in apposition to the χολήν implicit in μελαγχόλουc. For such an ellipse he compares 259–60 πόλιν | τὴν Εὐρυτείαν· τόνδε γάρ and the two passages cited ad loc. But though this idiom is in fact more common than West allows (see the bibliography in my note ad loc.), none of his examples, nor any others one might quote, presents us with an understood word in apposition to an extant word or phrase, and such a construction I find very strained. The supplying of Heracles as subject for ἔβαψεν (not impossible, but perhaps a little awkward) is favoured not

LINE 572

only by Wunder and West but by Long as cited above. West supposes Long's interpretation to entail an unparalleled construction of βάπτω with double accusative, whereby Heracles dips his arrows (ἰούς) with venom (ἰόν). But he rightly approves of Long's identification of the θρέμμα with the hydra's poison (cf. 572 ἀμφίθρεπτον), and for τρέφω 'used of anything growing or solidifying', especially within the body (e.g. a foetus), see West on Hes. *Th.* 192. We may retain the advantages of this particular part of Long's interpretation, and evade the above-mentioned difficulty of construction (and, indeed, all other difficulties noted so far) if we combine it with Dobree's conjecture[22] μελαγχόλος ... ἰός (*Adversaria*, ed. Wagner, iv. 37), originally conceived in the context of the implausible rendering of θρέμμα as periphrastic, but perfectly at home in its new environment. Would ἰός mean 'arrow', as Dobree intended, or 'poison'? In view of the accompanying epithet μελάγχολος the difference between the two renderings is hardly very great. The noun will be in apposition to θρέμμα (ἰός as 'poison' would suit this better) and subject of ἔβαψεν, with 'blood' the (understood) object supplied from ςφαγῶν in 573.

West had earlier complained of Long's treatment that he could find no 'parallel for making θρέμμα the subject [of ἔβαψεν] so that the poison βάπτει the arrows'. The complaint seems a little unreasonable in its original context, and no longer applies to our solution, where arrows are not the object of βάπτει. Accepting Dobree's emendation, we will have in these lines a literary device of the type discussed by I. Wærn, ΓΗΣ ΟΣΤΕΑ: *The Kenning in Pre-Christian Greek Poetry* (Uppsala 1951), 30, 49–50. Sometimes 'artistic kennings' (to use Wærn's terminology) take the form of a γρῖφος followed by its explanation as answer follows riddle: cf. e.g. Pind. *Isth.* 6. 50 ἀρχὸν οἰωνῶν ... αἰετόν, *PV* 1021–2 Διὸς ... | πτηνὸς κύων, δαφοινὸς αἰετός, Soph. fr. 726 ὦ πρῷρα λοιβῆς Ἑστία, though as Wærn (p. 50) observes, 'the oldest usage is that of the normal word followed by a kenning'; cf. Pind. *Pyth.* 1. 6 αἰετός ... ἀρχὸς οἰωνῶν, or Soph. fr. 884 ὁ ςκηπτροβάμων αἰετός, κύων Διός. Our passage would fall within the first category; for θρέμμα in such a kenning-like context see 1093 and 1099 below.

ᾗ: rightly interpreted by Dobree ('ubi: circa eam partem cuspidis

[22] So too Hermann etc. Dobree only asked 'vide an legendum μελάγχολος ... ἰός', and ended by preferring the vulgate.

161

COMMENTARY

qua'). Dawe's bafflement and consequent advocacy of Page's ὧι (*Studies* iii. 88; cf. Wakefield's ἧι for ὧι at 924 of our play) are both unjustified. **μελάγχολος:** the only example of the word thus used; cf. 717 below.

575–6. τῆς Ἡρακλείας: for the -ειος adjective see on 51 above.

576–7. The μή + indicative construction here is problematic: see Moorhouse, p. 323, suggesting either 'a blending of the notions of result and purpose' (by analogy with final clauses introduced by ἔνθα μή or ὅπου μή: see on 800 below) or the type of μή 'used in strong asseveration or oath (*KG* ii/2. 183 (4) (ζ)'. In addition to this there is a mixture of two types of expression οὕτινα cτέρξει ἀντὶ coῦ and οὕτινα cτέρξει coῦ πλέον: see Bruhn, Anhang, § 180, for examples. Schwinge, p. 100, detects a sinister irony in these dying words: as a result of the poison Heracles certainly will be prevented from loving any woman more than his wife.

577. γυναῖκα κεῖνος: for the choice between this and γυναῖκ᾽ ἐκεῖνος: see Barrett on Eur. *Hipp.* 319ff.

578–9. These two lines close the ring opened at 555–6 and enclosing the narrative of Nessus' death.

580. ἔβαψα: a sinister repetition of 573's ἔβαψεν (however interpreted) is here detected by M. R. Halleran, *CP* 83 (1988), 129ff. Both actions lead to death, the first Nessus', the latter Heracles'. **προσβαλοῦσ᾽:** for the legitimacy of the manuscripts' aorist participle against Radermacher's προσβάλλουσ᾽ see Barrett on Eur. *Hipp.* 289ff., esp. p. 214: 'when ... a part. refers to the same action as an aor. leading verb ... that part. is naturally also aor.' Cf. Moorhouse, p. 212. For προσβάλλω as the *vox propria* for the application of medicine *vel sim.* see Headlam on Herodas 3. 85.

581. Dawe's κεῦ for καί (*Studies* iii. 89) is definitely wrong: D is here very uncertain as to the rightness of her action (the chorus later have to reassure her twice: 588–9, 592–3), a dramatically vital point. For πεπείρανται τάδε = 'this is all ready' cf. *Od.* 12. 37 ταῦτα μὲν οὕτω πάντα πεπείρανται.

582–3. Cf. Eur. *Hipp.* 413–14 μισῶ δὲ καὶ τὰς σώφρονας μὲν ἐν λόγοις, | λάθραι δὲ τόλμας οὐ καλὰς κεκτημένας (Phaedra attacking bold-faced adulteresses).

584. φίλτροις ... ὑπερβαλώμεθα: see Harder on Eur. *Cresphont.* fr. 71. 4–5 for this construction of ὑπερβάλλω + dative. **ἐάν πως**

LINES 572-591

τήνδ' ὑπερβαλώμεθα: Jebb well terms this an 'elliptical expression of a hope or aim': see Diggle, *Dionysiaca* (Page Festschrift), p. 168, for other examples of the idiom. (Wilamowitz* preferred to place a full stop after Ἡρακλεῖ, taking ἐάν πως as an absolute construction.)

585. Deleted by Wunder as an expansion and clarification of 584 (on this type of interpolation see on 444 above). θέλκτρον (equivalent to θελκτήριον) only here (though conjectured at Ap. Rhod. 1. 515); cf. 575 above. ἐφ' Ἡρακλεῖ: for ἐπί used of the effects of magical devices cf. Theocr. *Id.* 2. 23.

586. μεμηχάνηται: the verb is used by S alone of the three tragedians: see Pfeiffer, *Sitzb. d. Bayer. Akad. d. Wiss., phil.-hist. Abt.* 2 (1938), 45; εἴ τι μή: 'unless indeed': for the phrase as expressing an afterthought see Headlam on Herodas 2. 101, for the word-order Fraenkel on Aesch. *Ag.* 1308.

587. πεπαύσομαι: for the use of the future perfect alongside perfects (586, 589) see Moorhouse, p. 202.

589. παρ' ἡμῖν: 'in my judgement', as at Eur. *El.* 1015, *Hel.* 881, etc. S and Aeschylus employ both singular and plural when the chorus-leader engages in such self-reference, Euripides only the singular: see Kaimio, *The Chorus of Greek Drama within the Light of the Person and Number Used*, p. 161 and n. 1.

590-1. The syntax here has been taken in three different ways: (1) with ὡς as causal: but this produces an odd ἔχει; (2) with ὡς equivalent to ὅτι and correlative to οὕτως ('my ground for confidence is this, namely that'): which presupposes a rather verbose Deianeira (unless this is an attempt realistically to represent nervous hesitancy); (3) with ὡς equivalent to ὥστε ('my confidence is such, that there is appearance of success': cf. 1126 ἔχει γὰρ οὕτως ὥστε)—so Goodwin, *Syntax... of the Greek Verb* (London 1889), 233, Moorhouse, p. 312, etc. 'There was metrical advantage [in using ὡς for ὥστε] available if the following word began with a consonant; and it is in these circumstances (and only these) that Aeschylus and S. use ὡς for ὥστε', says Diggle, *STE*, pp. 8-9, in the course of an enquiry which establishes that 'Euripides declined to use that advantage'. In a footnote (p. 9 n. 1) he observes that 'there are thirteen instances in Aeschylus ... four in S.' The other three Sophoclean examples are 1125 ὡς κλύειν ἐμέ, *OT* 84 ξύμμετρος γὰρ ὡς κλύειν, *Ant.* 292 ὡς στέργειν ἐμέ. On line 174 of the present play see ad loc. τὸ ... δοκεῖν = 'the possibility of seeming':

COMMENTARY

for similar abstracts see Long, *Language and Thought*, p. 72 n. 34. The same scholar (ibid. 135) comments on 'the language of experimental science' which seems to colour this part of the scene: proof (πίcτιc) ... conjecture (δοκεῖν) ... testing (πεῖρα). See on 593. For the delayed position of the responsive γε see Denniston, *GP*[2], p. 133 (iv).

592. ἀλλ' εἰδέναι χρὴ δρῶcαν: Solmsen, *AJP* 106 (1985), 490ff. (independently following the same track as W. Kraus, *WS* 20 (1986), 99–100), argues that at this crucial turning-point of the drama the chorus do not *encourage* D but *warn* her, a warning interrupted by Lichas' entry and then forgotten until it is too late. For criticism of this interpretation see *Sophoclea*, p. 163.

593. γνῶμα: on this word see Long, *Language and Thought*, p. 39: 'not an alternative to γνώμη as in Aesch. (*Ag.* 1352) and Eur. (*Hcld.* 407), but ... the "test" of D's love-charm, which cannot be made without experiment.'

594–5. Another dramatically economic entry (cf. on 58 and 178–9 above). For τόνδε in entry formulas cf. Diggle, *ZPE* 24 (1977), 291.

595. θυραῖον ἤδη: for ἤδη as an 'entry formula' cf. Eur. *Suppl.* 981 and Collard ad loc.

596. μόνον: this word often functions in various types of asyndeton: see Johansen and Whittle on Aesch. *Suppl.* 1012. On its meaning here ('provided that', 'wenn nur') cf. D. Tabachovitz, *Homerische εἰ-Sätze* (Lund 1951), 43.

596–7. For cτέγω of metaphorical concealment see Diggle, *STE*, pp. 73–4. **αἰcχύνηι:** for this type of dative with the verb πίπτω see Schwyzer, *Gr. Gr.* ii. 156 (*b*).

601. ταῖc ἔcωθεν ... ξέναιc: for similar references in Greek drama to those 'within the palace' see Harder's note on Eur. *Archel.* fr. 19. 10. Here the remark takes up κατ' οἶκον at 532 above. **ἔcωθεν:** for S's use of adverbs in -θεν to indicate 'place where' see 938 πλευρόθεν and Bruhn, *Anhang*, § 28. **ἠγορῶ:** a unique form (but similarly unique is ηὔγμην at 610). Dawe's lacuna after this line (*Studies* iii. 89–90) is as unnecessary as Nauck's deletion of the line itself, provided we see the parenthetic function of 601.

602. ταναϋφῆ: in the sequence ΤΟΝΔΕΤΑΝΑΥΦΗ the letters ΤΑΝ might easily slip out leaving an ignorant scribe to supply the wrong letters plus a γ' to make up the metre.

604 ff. For the construction of ὅπωc and future see Moorhouse, p. 308.

LINES 590-613

605. χροΐ: for the word's equivalence to 'body' in tragedy see Johansen and Whittle on Aesch. *Suppl.* 790.

608. φανερὸς ἐμφανῶς: an effective juxtaposition, with which we may compare 613 καινῶι καινόν. There is no need to emend the manuscripts' ἐμφανῶς: for other examples of synonymous words varied by a switch from adjective to adverb cf. Gygli-Wyss, *Das nominale Polyptoton*, p. 40 n. 1. **cταθεὶc:** cf. Eur. *Or.* 365 ἐμφανῶς, καταςταθείς.

610. ηὔγμην: on this interesting form cf. fr. 730f. 16 ηὖκτ', *Thebais* fr. 3. 3 εὖκτο and Davies's note on the latter (*The Theban Epics* (Göttingen 1991)). It is either a genuine archaism (an athematic imperfect or aorist form[23] of a usually thematic verb) or (as O. Szemerényi, *Syncope in Greek and Indo-European* (Naples 1964), 176 n. 4) 'a poetic venture not a precious survival'. Regularly but wrongly taken as pluperfect (e.g. Moorhouse, p. 201; 'though an aorist would have been possible, the use of the perfect stem shows the continuing effect of the vow'). In fact the pluperfect would have no conceivable force or point (Kamerbeek's citation of Aesch. *Ag.* 963 πολλῶν πατηςμὸν δ' εἰμάτων ἂν ηὐξάμην is clearly irrelevant).

611. πανδίκως: association of this with ηὔγμην rather than κλύοιμι seems urged by 293-4 πῶς δ' οὐκ ἐγὼ χαίροιμ' ἄν, ἀνδρὸς εὐτυχῆ | κλύουσα πρᾶξιν τήνδε, πανδίκωι φρενί; (note the hyperbaton in both cases on this interpretation). But association with ςτελεῖν is suggested by the paratactic and explanatory function of καὶ φανεῖν κτλ. which this third interpretation produces. On the meaning of the adverb ('by all means': πάντως, παντὶ τρόπωι) see Hutchinson on Aesch. *ScT* 171; cf. 1247 below.

613. θυτῆρα: the same word at 659 and 1192 below; not in Euripides. For its meaning see J. Casabona, *Recherches sur le vocabulaire des sacrifices en grec* (Aix-en-Provence 1964), 145. **καινῶι καινόν:** for further instances of what Jebb calls the 'collective emphasis' produced by such duplication, see Denniston on Eur. *El.* 337, Diggle on *Phaeth.* 94; Gygli-Wyss, *Das nominale Polyptoton*, p. 139 n. 4. For duplication of καινός in particular see Collard on Eur. *Suppl.* 593. Note the chiasmus and hyperbaton that characterize our line's use of the device. For ἐν used of the wearing of clothes see Bond on Eur. *Her.* 677, Diggle, *STE*, p. 60. πέπλωμα is regularly used for πέπλος in tragedy: see Eur. *Suppl.* 97

[23] On athematic forms in general see L. R. Palmer, *The Greek Language* (London 1980), 294.

COMMENTARY

and Collard ad loc.; for similar doublets see Long, *Language and Thought*, p. 45. On the word-order see Diggle, *ICS* 2 (1977), 110.

614–15. The manuscripts here present us with an oddly suspended locative cφραγῖδοc ἕρκει and a strange use of ὄμμα θήcεται ('Heracles will set it before his own eye'?). Billerbeck's εὐμαθὲc ... ἕρκει, 'easily recognized by reason of the bezel', is an obvious correction, with cφραγῖδοc epexegetic genitive (Bruhn, *Anhang*, § 31). On the technical meaning of cφραγῖδοc ἕρκει here see J. Boardman, *Greek Gems and Finger Rings* (London 1970), 429. For the seal as guarantee of authenticity see J. Kroll, *Theognis-Interpretationen* (*Philol.* suppl. 29. 1; 1936), 53 and n. 132. For ἀποίcειc M. L. West conjectures ἅμ' οἴcειc (*BICS* 31 (1984), 182), misliking the sense provided by the preverb ἀπ- and finding the reference of τῶνδ' 'rather loose'. But it alludes to the vow mentioned in the previous lines (for the plural where one might expect the singular see below on 1248 τούτων), and LSJ s.v. ἀποφέρω I.1 provides adequate parallels to the sense required; cf. Moorhouse, p. 101.

616–17. For the warning against officiousness in a messenger, Fraenkel (*Horace*, p. 351) compares Hor. *Epist.* 1. 13. 4–5 'ne studio nostri pecces odiumque libellis | sedulus importes opera vehemente minister'. The whole epistle deals with this theme.

616. φύλαccε ... νόμον: cf. νόμος φυ[λάττεται in the papyrus fr. of comedy published by Kannicht (*Praestant Interna* (U. Hausmann Festschrift; Tübingen 1982), 374–5) (νόμος φυ[λακτέος suppl. K. Gaiser, *ZPE* 51 (1983), 40) and such technical terms as νομοφύλαξ etc.

618. (φύλαccε) | ὅπωc ἄν: for this type of construction cf. (with Diggle, *Dionysiaca* (Page Festschrift), p. 167) *El.* 1402–3 φρουρήcουc' ὅπως | Αἴγιcθος ... μὴ λάθηι, Eur. *Hel.* 742–3 φρουρεῖν ὅπωc ἄν ... | ἐκ βαρβάρων cωθῶμεν. Moorhouse, p. 228, prefers either to understand ἐπιμελοῦ *vel sim.* from the context (on the ground (p. 290) that φύλαccε 'is followed by a *negatived* clause (since it indicates what is to be guarded *against*)') or to take the clause independently.

619. ἐξ ἁπλῆc διπλῆ: for the effective rhetorical juxtaposition see on 613 above; for the significance of ἐξ cf. 284.

620. For Hermes' role as patron of heralds cf. H. Herter, *Rh. Mus.* 119 (1976), 208 ff., esp. p. 209 n. 62.

LINES 613-628

621. οὔ τι μή: cf. OC 450, fr. 208. 9.
622. On μὴ οὐ here see Moorhouse, CQ 34 (1940), 75, Barrett on Eur. *Hipp.* 658 (cf. on 90 above).
623. ἔχεις seems to have intruded itself into the text because of ἔχει in the same part of the preceding verse. Either Wakefield's θέλεις or Wunder's λέγεις is preferable. **ἐφαρμόςαι:** cf. 494 προςαρμόςαι.
624. cτείχοις ἂν ἤδη: ἤδη = forthwith (see Gow–Page on Leonidas *AP* 7. 478. 5 = *HE* 2425).
626. For τε καί used thus in an answer cf. OC 113, Eur. *Alc.* 420–1. **φράcω cεcωμένα:** cf. Men. fr. 286. 3–4 τὸν υἱὸν εὐτυχοῦντα καὶ cεcωμένον | πρῶτος λέγω coι, Sic. 121 φράςῃι cεcωμένους. On the spelling see above on 83. See Addenda.
628. Prima facie the manuscripts' reading would seem to labour under one general and two rather more specific disadvantages: (1) the sense offered seems tautologous: 'you know having seen my reception of Iole, how I received Iole in friendly fashion'; (2a) αὐτήν is emphatic when it should not be; (2b) the αὐτήν θ᾽ of L has the further difficulty of a τε which implies an extension of the sense or a contrast that is not easily produced. Hermann sought to counter (2a) by rendering 'vel hanc', but for this sense we require τήνδε to follow. Jebb tried to meet (2a) by arguing that the whole clause αὐτήν ... φίλως depends on οἶςθα and the emphasis falls on φίλως. But Ellendt–Genthe s.v. αὐτός acc. (p. 107) provides no parallel for such a sentence with the pronoun standing first in a subordinate clause of this kind. We must therefore resort to emendation.

Some remedies are easily dismissed: deletion of 628 (advocated by Nauck and Wecklein) is unattractive since 629 is most naturally interpreted as presupposing some form of 628. The positioning of a lacuna after 629 (Zieliński, p. 590 n. 11 = p. 344 n. 1) seems unduly drastic: its proposer could himself find little to put in the allegedly missing line. The replacement of αὐτήν with αὐτός (tentatively advanced by Bergk and approved by Dawe with the modifications of a comma after ξένης and cφ᾽ after ὡς in the following line) places an excessive and inappropriate stress on the reactions of Lichas. What we are interested in is Deianeira and Iole, not the herald, but Koechly's αὐτή θ᾽ (ZA 9 (1842), 763) retains a problematic connective (see (2b) above). Therefore αὐτή cφ᾽ ὡς ἐδεξάμην φίλως (Radermacher) or αὐτὴν ὡς ἐδεξάμην φίλα (Wunder) supply the most appropriate sense. This

COMMENTARY

remedy may be thought to deal adequately with objection (1) by elaborating upon the more general statement contained in τὰ τῆc ξένηc . . . | προcδέγματ'. The latter noun, however, is ἅπαξ and Hermann's προcφθέγματ' removes it and the last hint of tautology. For the corruption presupposed see above on 554.

629. ἐκπλαγῆναι τοὐμὸν . . . κέαρ: the verb is usually applied to the θέαρ, ξυμόc, *vel sim.* to describe the effects of love; cf. Eur. *Med.* 8 ἔρωτι θυμὸν ἐκπλαγεῖc' Ἰάcονοc, with Page ad loc.

631. λέγοιc ἄν: for ἄν with optative denoting 'a mild expression of fear' see Moorhouse, p. 291. **τὸν πόθον τὸν ἐξ ἐμοῦ:** cf. *Ant.* 95 τὴν ἐξ ἐμοῦ δυcβουλίαν, and for other instances of 'nominalized prepositions' see Schwyzer, *Gr. Gr.* ii. 416; cf. Long, *Language and Thought*, p. 108 n. 155.

632. τἀκεῖθεν εἰ ποθούμεθα: on this type of plural for singular (to convey the speaker's modesty) cf. F. Slotty, 'Der sogenannte Pluralis modestiae', *IF* 44 (1926), 155 ff., A. G. Katsouris, *Rh. Mus.* 120 (1977), 232–3. τἀκεῖθεν is an appropriately vague way of referring to Heracles in this context (Schneidewin's κἀκεῖθεν would marginally reduce the modesty and vagueness).

SECOND STASIMON (633–662)
633–9 = 640–6 *first strophe and antistrophe*

633–4/640–1	⏓–∪∪–∪– ∪–∪– ∪–∪–	tel. + ia. dim.
635/642	––∪∪–∪∪–∪–∪––	enop.
636/643	–∪∪–––	dodrans dragged
637/644	⏓–∪∪–––∪–	chor.-ia. enneasyll.
638–9/645–6	––––∪∪– ∪–∪– ∪–– |||	chor. heptasyll. + ia. dim. cat.

633–5 are hard to analyse precisely: see Griffith, *Authenticity of PV*, pp. 44–5, for some partial parallels. 635–6 provide an instance of the isolated dactylo-epitrite period exemplified on 520–2 above.

647–54 = 655–62 *second strophe and antistrophe*

647/655	∪∪–∪∪–∪––⏒ ||	enop.
648/656	∪∪–∪∪–∪–∪––	enop.
649/657	⏓–∪⏓ ∪⌒∪–	ia. dim.
650/658	∪–∪– ∪–∪– ∪––	ia. trim. cat.

LINES 628-636

651/659	−∪− ∪−∪−	ia. dim. sync.
652/660	⏒−∪− ∪−∪⏓ ‖	ia. dim.
653/661	− − − − − −	2 mol.
654/662	−∪− ⌒∪− −∪−‖	3 cr.

For the rarity of the aeolics at 647–8 see on 116 ff. above. For the relationship between 647–8 and the following iambics see Griffith, op. cit. 44–5. 653 is strangely heavy but there is a close parallel for such a sequence (as the penultimate line of an iambic strophe) at Aesch. *ScT* 770.

For a sensitive study of the ode's relevance to the themes of the play and its further appropriateness as a joyous welcome home to the triumphant hero see Stinton, *Papers of the Liverpool Latin Seminar* 5 (1985), 403 ff.

633 ff. For similar apostrophes to a landscape in Greek tragedy see Kranz, *Stasimon*, pp. 191–2. 'There is a good deal of local reference in the three triumphal odes which precede the catastrophe in *Ant.*, *OT*, and *Trach.*' (Bond on Eur. *Her.* 781 ff., itself full of similar local references).

633. ναύλοχα: either an adjective with λουτρά, like πετραῖα and θερμά (ναύλοχος 'affording safe anchorage for ships') or a substantive like λουτρά and πάγους (ναύλοχον 'haven, harbour'). The latter would not be paralleled until Plut. *Mor.* 984 B, and the Suda s.v. ναύλοχον, though for Sophocles' tendency to use adjectives as substantives see Campbell's *Essay on the Language of Sophocles*, p. 36 f. (deleting from his examples *OT* 1411, where θαλάσσιον does not signify 'the sea', but belongs to the construction με ... θαλάσσιον ἐκρίψατ').

634. θερμὰ λουτρά: for Heracles' connection with hot springs see J. H. Croon, *The Herdsman of the Dead* (Utrecht 1952), 6 ff.

635. μέσσαν | Μηλίδα πὰρ λίμναν: either 'the innermost part of the Malian mere' (Jebb, Stinton, loc. cit.) or 'by the Malian mere between' with reference to the hills that surround it.

636. Μηλίδα ... λίμναν: cf. Björck, *Das Alpha impurum*, p. 239, on the form Μηλίδα. παρά or πάρ? The choice is between two rarities, resolution in a choriamb or apocope. As regards the latter, there is no secure example of πάρ for παρά in the lyrics of S or Euripides, though there are a handful of very plausible candidates in Aeschylus, esp. *Suppl.* 1048 παρβατός (Askew: παραβατάς): see Johansen and

COMMENTARY

Whittle ad loc. for the other likely Aeschylean instances. The alternative is to suppose that we have here an instance of resolution of the second longum of a choriamb: for parallels see Diggle, *PCPS* 20 (1974), p. 26 n. 5.

637. χρυcαλακάτου ... κόραc. Wilamowitz (*Gr. Versk.*, p. 531) wrote Κόραc and supposed a reference to the daughter of Demeter (for Κόρη *tout court* as referring to her see Headlam on Herodas 1. 32). But χρυcηλάκατος is an epithet in epic for Artemis (on its occurrences and meaning see W. D. Meier, *Die epische Formel im pseudohesiodeischen Frauenkatalog* (Diss. Zurich 1976), 28–9, esp. p. 29 n. 2),[24] a goddess who is also traditionally associated with marshes and meres (for epithets such as λιμενοcκόπος used of this goddess see Bruchmann, *Epitheta Deorum*, p. 48; for her general connection with lagoons and the like Barrett on Eur. *Hipp.* 148 ff.) and thus appropriately mentioned after the waters of the Malian marsh. She is often conceived of as a κούρη (cf. Bruchmann, op. cit. 47). No temple to her is attested in the relevant locale (the nearest being at Brauron in Euboea: cf. Burkert, *Gr. Relig.* 236 (Engl. trans., p. 151), Stinton op. cit. 405), but this may be the result of chance. No more is any temple to Kore-Persephone known of. A temple of Δημήτηρ Ἀμφικτυονίc at Anthela, meeting-place of the Amphictyonic Council, might be alleged to fit Ἑλλάνων ἀγοραί in the next line. But Demeter is not Persephone, and it seems unlikely that we have here an instance of the esoteric 'construction by which one member of a pair may be put for both, or even for the other member' (see Nisbet–Hubbard, *Horaces Odes 1*, pp. 211–12). Artemis, then, is the deity referred to.

639. κλέονται: Musgrave's elimination of the manuscripts' metrically intrusive α seems the likeliest remedy here. Whether we accept it or καλεῦνται (Hermann) we will have the general type of idiom in which 'ἔνθα *x* is called' = 'ἔνθα is *x* (as it is called)': see Barrett on Eur. *Hipp.* 121–2 (cf. W. Kroll, *Rh. Mus.* 52 (1897), 579 n. 2), Kassel–Austin on Cratinus fr. 7, Gow on Theocr. *Id.* 1. 7, D. Tabachovitz, *Eranos* 58 (1960), 9 ff.

640–1. ὁ καλλιβόας ... αὐλός: cf. Ar. *Av.* 682, *lyr. fr. adesp.* 947B. 2 P, with H. W. Smyth ad loc. (*Greek Melic Poets* (London 1900), 326)

---

[24] For its other appearances in literature see Maehler on Bacch. 11. 38. For a general study of the word see O. S. Due, *Class. et Med.* 26 (1965), 1 ff. (p. 9 n. 28 on our passage).

LINES 636-644

and Stinton, op. cit. 405. **ὑμὶν:** this minor reinterpretation of the paradosis is proposed by K. Itsumi, *BICS* 37 (1990), on the ground that in dicola starting with an enoplion no division occurs after the anceps when that anceps is long. Cf. on 320.

642. ἀχῶν: the manuscripts' superfluous *ἰ-* is to be removed: ἰάχων cannot respond to Ὀίτας in this enoplion-type colon,[25] and synizesis (ἰ̄άχων ~ Ὀίτας) would be unparalleled (cf. West, *GM*, pp. 12ff.). On the frequency with which ἀχά is corrupted to ἰαχά see Page on Eur. *Med.* 149, Barrett on Eur. *Hipp.* 584–8.

643. ἀντίλυρον: Σ's gloss ἰσόλυρον ('like that of the lyre') is preferable to LSJ's and Stinton's (op. cit. 405) 'responsive to the lyre': for ἀντι- words with the required nuance ('Gegenstück, Entsprechung') see Schwyzer, *Gr. Gr.* ii. 442. For the general picture cf. the opening of Pind. *Pyth.* 1 and Kranz, *Sokrates* 7 (1919), 252 ff. = *Studien zur antiken Lit. und ihrem Nachwirken*, pp. 261 ff. For the combination of αὐλός (641) and lyre cf. *lyr. fr. adesp.* 947B2 P πολύχορδος αὐλός, with H. W. Smyth ad loc. (cited on 640–1) Hor. *Epod.* 9. 5 'sonante mixtum tibiis carmen lyra', Stinton, op. cit. 405.

644. Διὸς Ἀλκμήνας κόρος: Triclinius' omission of the manuscripts' τε is the simplest expedient for restoring metre. For the double genitive construction without connecting particle Jebb compares Aesch. *Suppl.* 314 ὁ Δῖος πόρτις ... βοός (where, as Jebb himself and Johansen and Whittle ad loc. observe, Δῖος is an adjective) and [Eur.] *Rhes.* 386–7 ὁ Στρυμόνιος πῶλος ἀοιδοῦ Μούσης where ἀοιδοῦ too may be adjectival (and, if substantival, is in apposition to Μούσης). In Jebb's remaining parallel, Pind. *Ol.* 2. 13 ὦ Κρόνιε παῖ Ῥέας, we again have an adjective with genitival force, not a genuine genitive. For the wider principle of the same noun qualified by two genitives see Shackleton Bailey on Prop. 4. 1. 103 (*Propertiana* (Cambridge 1956), 223). Cf. 1191 below. For the form Ἀλκμήνας see on 97 above. We

---

[25] Apparent exceptions to this rule are easily disposed of: at *OT* 174 ἰηίων καμάτων ἀνέχουσι γυναῖκες ~ 185 λυγρῶν πόνων ἱκτῆρες ἐπιστενάχουσιν read ἱκετῆρες (O); at ibid. 1096 ἰήιε Φοῖβε, coί ~ 1109 Νυμφᾶν Ἑλικωνιάδων (A^pc, *rell.*) read Ἑλικωνίδων (A^ac, quod coni. Porson) or ἑλικωπίδων (Wilamowitz). At *Ant.* 584 οἷς γὰρ ἂν ςεισθῆι ~ 595 πήματα φθιμένων read φθιτῶν (Hermann); at *OC* 1563 (παγκευ)θῆ κάτω νεκύων (complures codd.) πλάκα ~ 1574 Ταρτάρου, κατεύχομαι read νεκρῶν (Triclinius).

COMMENTARY

find a scribe's insertion of epic κοῦρος for κόρος in A: cf. Denniston on Eur. *El.* 117, Jackson, *MS*, pp. 27 ff. See Addenda.

645. cοῦται: both paradosis and correction present what would be a ἅπαξ in this part of the verb. The form presented by Elmsley's emendation (supported by Blomfield) is a little better paralleled than that of the manuscripts, though the choice is a nicely balanced one. (A similar dilemma faces us in Callim. fr. 239 *Suppl. Hell.* (Antinoop. pap. 113 fr. 1b) 10, where the traces are ambiguous between cοῦτο or cεῦτο: see A. W. Bulloch, *CQ* 20 (1970), 272 and n. 1.) cοῦνται in Aesch. *Pers.* 25 and cοῦcθε in *ScT* 31, for example, support Elmsley here[26] (further examples from tragedy in Johansen and Whittle on Aesch. *Suppl.* 836). On cοῦται as implying cοϝοομαι see Wackernagel, *Spr. Unt. zu Hom.*, pp. 3 ff., 174, Schulze, *Kl. Schr.*, pp. 378–9. Schwyzer, *Gr. Gr.* i. 679, takes cεῦται to be correct and treats it as an athematic present (cεύομαι certainly has athematic aorists[27] (ἐccύμην, ἔccυτο) side by side with the thematic variety (cεύατο, ἐccεύατο)). For further discussion see J. Narten *ap. Pratidānam: Indian, Iranian and Indo-European Studies Presented to F. B. J. Kuiper on his 60th Birthday* (The Hague and Paris 1968), 18–19, preferring (p. 16 n. 50) Elmsley's cοῦται. **πάcαc ἀρετᾶc:** cf. *Aj.* 436 πρὸc οἶκον ἦλθε πᾶcαν εὔκλειαν φέρων.

647. ὃν ἀπόπτολιν εἴχομεν: for the relative at the start of a stanza picking up a reference in the previous stanza see on 122 above. I cannot accept such explanations of ἀπόπτολιν εἴχομεν as Σ's ὃν ἐκτὸc εἴχομεν τῆc πόλεωc, Campbell's 'i.e. ὃc ἦν ἀπόπτολιc ἡμῖν', or Jebb's 'whom we had absent', both meant as equivalent to 'whose absence we endured'. Where is the parallel for such a use of ἔχω in the context of absence rather than proximity? Paley joined εἴχομεν and ἀμμένουcαι: cf. Eur. *Tro.* 317 τὸν θανόντα πατέρα πατρίδα τε | φίλαν καταcτένουc' ἔχειc for a parallel to the alleged construction of ἔχω and present participle as a periphrastic construction. The idiom of ἔχω and *aorist* participle as equivalent to perfect is particularly Sophoclean (*Ant.* 22, *OC* 1140, line 37 above: further examples and discussion in Moorhouse, pp. 206–7, who takes our particular passage as 'a rare periphrasis "for whom we kept on waiting", with the meaning of duration stressed'). I do not see why Jebb found the analogous present

---

[26] cτεῦ(ν)ται in Aesch. *Pers.* 49 a counter-example.
[27] On athematic forms in general see above, p. 165 n. 23.

participle 'inadmissible' here; the gap between the phrase's constituent parts can be justified as 'expressive hyperbaton' (see below on πάντα).

πάντα: on the problems posed by this highly ambiguous word see Stinton, *Papers of the Liverpool Latin Seminar* 5 (1985), 419–20. Since (see Schwyzer, *Gr. Gr.* i. 550, Barrett on Eur. *Hipp.* 563) παντα in manuscripts often conveys (and may, indeed, be the correct form of) the adverbial πάνται with long final syllable, there are three conceivable interpretations of the paradosis in the present place: πάντα may be (1) adverbial neuter plural, to be taken with the preceding ἀπόπτολιν; (2) accusative singular masculine to be taken with χρόνον in line 649, stressing length of time; (3) adverbial πάντᾱ, to be taken with ἀπόπτολιν in line 647 or ἀμμένουσαι in line 649. Of these possibilities the first may be dismissed as abruptly as we please on formal grounds of style, for πάντα as adverbial neuter plural regularly stands between definite article and governed adjective, as in ὁ πάντ' ἄναλκις (*El.* 301: further Sophoclean examples in Bruhn, *Anhang*, § 62 I.2; on the general idiom see Lobeck on *Aj.* 1415 (cf. Maas, *Berl. phil. Woch.* (1912), 1427 = *Kl. Schr.*, p. 52)). For (2) the only analogy cited by LSJ s.v. πᾶc C 'to mark an exact number' would be Hes. *Th.* 803 ἐννέα πάντ' ἔτεα (its other instances, like *Il.* 19. 247 δέκα πάντα τάλαντα are not strictly comparable, not relating to time). Cf. *OT* 1136–7 τρεῖc ὅλουc | ἐξ ἦρος εἰς ἀρκτοῦρον ἐκμήνουc χρόνουc ('three full seasons'). The distance between πάντα and χρόνον might be excused as 'expressive hyperbaton': cf. the twenty-two words that keep apart οὐ πολὺν and χρόνον at Ar. *Ran.* 707/712 and note the comments of Rhys Roberts, *Dionysius of Halicarnassus on Literary Composition* (London 1910), 340f., and Fraenkel, *Beob. zu Aristoph.*, pp. 136–7, who cites less extreme parallels and suspects there parody of elevated choral lyric. Whether such a hyperbaton emphasizes, or distracts attention from, the oddness of the reference to twelve months (as opposed to the *fifteen* months and twelve *years* of other passages: see Appendix A) it is difficult to judge. *Brevis in longo* without pause at this very early stage in the stanza is an undesirable aspect of this interpretation, however (cf. Stinton, op. cit. 419–20). As for (3), the first option, the combining of πάντᾱ and ἀπόπτολιν, is decidedly undesirable, not so much because of the illogicality of 'absolutely lost to the city' (a point characteristically stressed by Dawe, *Studies* iii. 90: but perhaps the emotional tone might excuse this) but because πάντᾱ usually signifies 'everywhere',

COMMENTARY

not 'totally' (cf. Stinton op. cit. 419). The second possibility, πάντā . . . ἀμμένουcαι, would have to be explained as a development by analogy from the Homeric παντῆι παπταίνων (Od. 12. 233 etc.: other instances in Headlam's note on Herodas 1. 39). The verb 'to wait' might not seem to lend itself to such a collocation quite so naturally as a verb meaning 'to look' or 'stare', but cf. OC 122 προcπεύθου πανταχᾶι and Stinton, op. cit. 420.

We have yet to consider the word πελάγιον, which clearly belongs to the complex of ideas (even if it is the final word, perhaps expressively delayed) and has received no satisfactory treatment from any other of the interpretations of πάντα thus far considered. Dawe (loc. cit.), observing that 'πελάγιοc means only "at sea"', suggests βάντα for πάντα on the ground that 'βάντα helps both ἀπόπτολιν and πελάγιον'. But if we were to take πάντα δυοκαιδεκάμηνον ἀμμένουcαι χρόνον πελάγιον as a single coherent word-group, and if πάντα . . . ἀμμένουcαι . . . πελάγιον could mean 'waiting for Heracles, staring everywhere out to sea for him', Dawe's change, slight though it is, would be unnecessary, and the *brevis in longo* at so early a point in the stanza again avoided.

649. ἴδριεc: this adjective usually takes the genitive, but for the accusative in lyric see OC 525, *Inachus* fr. 269A. 31 and Carden ad loc. (p. 63).

650. ἁ δέ οἱ: the hiatus before ϝοι (for which cf. Maas, GM, § 133) occurs within Attic literature only in melic and anapaesto-dactylic metres: see Wackernagel, *Spr. Unt. zu Hom.*, p. 269. Likewise, οἱ's equivalence to non-reflexive αὐτῶι is a rarity confined to the lyric portions of Attic literature (Moorhouse, p. 142), and the dative's equivalence to the genitive seems unique to tragedy: so Johansen and Whittle on Aesch. *Suppl.* 278, rightly characterizing our phrase as 'epically-coloured'. The definite article, however, is not an epic feature (introducing a noun), since it forms part of the adjectival phrase that follows: see Moorhouse, p. 141.

650. τάλαιναν: so Dindorf, but the emendation of τάλαινα is necessary neither on metrical grounds (if τάλαινα stands at the end of line 650 its final α will be *brevis in longo* with period-end: cf. Stinton, op. cit. 421) nor on stylistic ones. Changes of case in rhetorical repetitions of this general kind do, of course, occur (e.g. *Il.* 22. 480 Ἠετίωνος, ὅ μ' ἔτρεφε τυτθὸν ἐοῦcαν δύcμοροc αἰνόμορον, Eur. *Hec.* 156

LINES 647-654

δειλαία δειλαίου γήρωc, Ant. 1266 νέοc νέωι ξὺν μόρωι; further examples in Gygli-Wiss, *Das nominale Polyptoton*, p. 125 and nn. 4–5). But when, as here, it is a matter of a second adjective being varied and *intensified* (cf. Empedocl. B 141 DK δειλοί, πάνδειλοι, Aesch. *Pers.* 986 κακὰ πρόκακα; further examples in Fehling, *Wiederholungsfiguren*, p. 176) no such change seems required. Lloyd-Jones's tentative τάλαιν' ἆ δυcτάλαινα might seem preferable, given the reference to Deianeira in Bacch. Dith. 16. 30 ἆ δύcμοροc, ἆ τάλαιν' οἷον ἐμήcατο (cf. Stinton, op. cit. 421). But the pathetic exclamation ἆ does not feature in tragedy. (In *OT* 1147 ἆ, μὴ κόλαζε and *Phil.* 1300 ἆ μηδαμῶc... μή 'φηιc βέλοc the tone is different; at *TrGF* (adesp.) fr. 626. 21 Sn. ὁρᾶιc γ' ἄρ', ἆ (γὰρ ὤ;) δέcπο[ινα, as Snell remarks ad loc., ἆ is 'valde suspectum'; at *Ant.* 5, for ὁποῖον Lloyd-Jones conjectures ἆ, ποῖον.) **οἰcτρηθείc:** of the effects of love: see Headlam on Herodas 1. 57, Kost on Musaeus, *Hero and Leander* 134. But αὖ cτρωθείc (Musgrave) provides better sense (after the sack of Oechalia, Ares may reasonably be described as 'laid to rest again').

654. On the metrical problems posed by this line see Stinton, op. cit. 421–2. The manuscripts' ἐξέλυc' ἐπίπονον ἀμέραν (– ∪ – ∪ ∪ ∪ ∪ – ∪ –) is implausible metre. Pearson conjectured ἐξέλυcεν, producing a doubly resolved cretic and split resolution (on the latter see L. P. E. Parker, *CQ* 18 (1968), 241 ff.; there is an instance at 657–8 below), a phenomenon rare enough not to be introduced by emendation. Besides, the accusatives of the paradosis are not healed by this approach, though they seem as dubious as the metre. For ἐκλύω + accusative of the thing from which release comes scholars have cited *OT* 35–6 ὅc γ' ἐξέλυcαc ἄcτυ Καδμεῖον μολὼν | cκληρᾶc ἀοιδοῦ δαcμὸν ὃν παρείχομεν (but there δαcμόν could be attracted to the case of the following relative in order to avoid ambiguity with the two preceding genitives, and Herwerden proposed replacing ὅν with ἧι) and Eur. *Phoen.* 695 καίτοι ποδῶν cῶν μόχθον ἐκλύει παρών (but there too the neighbouring genitive makes a difference). Erfurdt's correction to genitive plural makes for good metre internally speaking (the corresponding part of the antistrophe is corrupt) by eliminating the rare dochmiac with resolved initial anceps. For Ares as subject of this verb cf. *Aj.* 706 ἔλυcεν αἰνὸν ἄχοc ἀπ' ὀμμάτων Ἄρηc, for the phrase ἐπίπονοι ἀμέραι cf. Homeric δούλιον ἦμαρ and Pearson on Eur. *Phoen.* 540. Heracles is more naturally understood object of a

COMMENTARY

reference to release from πόνοc, though the stanza did open by picturing the chorus's own anxiety.

655. ἀφίκοιτ' ἀφίκοιτο: for the ἀναδίπλωcιc as idiomatic in contexts of prayer see such repeated imperatives as ὕcον ὕcον, ὦ φίλε Ζεῦ (*Carm. pop.* 854 P), δέξαι με κωμάcδοντα, δέξαι (Alcaeus fr. 374 LP), and in general Fehling, *Wiederholungsfiguren*, pp. 169–70, 177–8; cf. Kranz, *Stasimon*, p. 231. Repetition often accompanies what Dodds on Eur. *Bacch.* 107 calls 'ritual cries or the natural expression of religious exaltation'.

656–7. ὄχημα: usually employed of a wagon or chariot, but for its application to a ship see *PV* 468 ναυτίλων ὀχήματα, Eur. *IT* 410 νάιον ὄχημα, Wærn, *ΓΗΣ ΟΣΤΕΑ*, p. 56. Johansen and Whittle on Aesch. *Suppl.* 32 explain the phenomena by supposing in cases such as the present 'a reversion to primary meaning, "holder" (ἔχειν)' for ὄχημα and ὄχοc, a meaning modified by the accompanying adjective. The addition of a second genitival substantive to this noun-and-adjective construction creates a type of 'enallage': for a bibliography of discussions of this device see Diggle, *GRBS* 14 (1973), 261, to which add now V. Bers, *Enallage and Greek Style* (*Mnem.* suppl.; 1974), who deals with our passage on p. 34. For 'the use of an appositional genitive where a modifying adjective might seem more natural' see Braswell on Pind. *Pyth.* 4. 271 (e). **ἀνύcειε:** for this verb's 'absolute' use cf. Usener, *Rh. Mus.* 29 (1874), 27 n. 2 = *Kl. Schr.* iii. 385 n. 8. ἑcτία is sometimes equivalent to βωμόc: see Diggle, *STE*, pp. 33–4. **ἀμείψαc:** 'leaving', as in *Phil.* 1262, Eur. *El.* 750.

659. κλῄζεται θυτήρ: sc. ὤν; cf. Eur. *Hel.* 132 θανὼν δὲ κλῄζεται, 126 ἀφανήc... κλῄζεται. On the noun θυτήρ see on 613 above.

660. μόλοι πανάμεροc: Mudge's slight change is generally preferred, and as interpreted by most scholars the paradosis can make no sense at all. This is because πανάμεροc has been almost universally taken as the Doric form of πανήμεροc ('all day long'), and the chorus are hardly likely to crown their prayer for Heracles' speedy homecoming by requesting a lengthy return for that hero! Grammar aids common sense here, since obviously the aorist tense of μόλοι conveys the sense 'arrive', not 'be travelling'. The least objectionable approach along these lines is Pearson's (*CR* 39 (1925), 4), which would have πανάμεροc mean 'in the fullness of time', i.e. 'after an interval

LINES 654-661

comprising all the days' which Heracles named (cf. 44–5, 164 ff., 648). But this is to place an impossible meaning upon the adjective (equally impossible is the idea of W. Theiler, *Mus. Helv.* 7 (1950), 106 = *Untersuchungen zur antiken Literatur*, p. 71, that it can mean 'today' ('heute')). Σ ad loc., however, glosses the word as εὐμενής, and B. Forssman, *Untersuchungen zur Sprache Pindars* (Wiesbaden 1966), 41 ff., esp. p. 43, finds the rendering 'all-gentle' perfectly plausible in this place and the hyper-Dorism tolerable. One is reminded of such cletic addresses as Anacr. 357. 6–7 εὐμενὴς | ἔλθ' ἡμῖν, Plato *Leg.* 712 B ἵλεως εὐμενής τε ἡμῖν ἔλθοι (further instances in Nisbet–Hubbard on Horace *Odes* 1. 19. 16: cf. Gow on Theocr. *Id.* 15. 143 for analogous examples of ἵλαος εἴης or ἴσθι; for Latin see Ov. *Met.* 4. 31 'placatus mitisque... adsis' with Bömer ad loc.). Similar epithets were used in prayers to heroes: cf. Aesch. *Ag.* 516 and Denniston–Page ad loc. This is not to deny that Mudge's πανίμερος (active: 'full of love') would be perfectly appropriate: for eloquent approbation of it see Stinton, op. cit. 422 ff.

661 ff. There are five main difficulties here which are admirably summarized by Stinton, op. cit. 424 ff.: (1) internal metre (the uncertainty regarding 654 exacerbates this); (2) the responsion of cυγκραθείς ~ ἐξέλυς' (but Stinton's treatment shows that – – – ~ – ∪ – can perhaps be defended); (3) προφάcει (a reading of A. A. Nikitias, *Zur Bedeutung von ΠΡΟΦΑΣΙΣ in der altgr. Lit.* (Akad. d. Wiss. und der Lit. Mainz 4 (1976), 15 n. 44[28] confirms one's initial impression that the dative here cannot mean 'prescription' or 'prompting' ('excuse' or 'pretext' being its usual sense); (4) πειθοῦc and its superfluous definite article; (5) παγχρίcτωι and its want of the definite article. On (3)–(5) Stinton himself plausibly argues for the slight change of προφάcει to παρφάcει ('beguilement'), which was advocated by Paley and Pretor. Then, building on further suggestions of Pretor and Pearson, he suggests for the whole phrase cυγκραθεὶς θηρὸς ἐπὶ παρφάcει ('united in love through the beast's beguilement of Persuasion'). On his own admission this belongs to the realm of 'guesswork ... and the passage must remain a crux'.

---

[28] For further bibliography on the meaning of the noun πρόφαcιc see L. S. Wilson in *Greek Poetry and Philosophy* (Woodbury Festschrift), p. 319 n. 1.

COMMENTARY

THIRD EPISODE (663–820)

666. ἀθυμῶ δ' εἰ φανήcομαι: for the *vereor ne* construction cf. Eur. *Andr.* 61 φόβωι μέν, εἴ τις δεσποτῶν αἰcθήcεται, Xen. *Cyr.* 6. 1. 17 ὃ δ' ἴcωc ἄν τινεc ὑμῶν φοβηθεῖεν, εἰ δεήcει (Eur. *Med.* 184–5 φόβοc εἰ πείcω | δέcποιναν ἐμήν = *vereor ut*).

667. ἀπ' ἐλπίδοc καλῆc: 'contrary to' (cf. *El.* 1127–8 ὡc ⟨c'⟩ ἀπ' ἐλπίδων | οὐχ ὦνπερ ἐξέπεμπον εἰcεδεξάμην) or 'starting from, as a result of' (*Aj.* 1078, *Ant.* 1078). Cf. Ar. fr. 597. 2–3 ΚΑ καλῆc ἀπ' ἐλπίδοc | cφαλέντα.

668. οὐ δή τι: cf. *Phil.* 900 οὐ δή cε, *Ant.* 381, *OT* 1472 οὐ δή που. The τι which distinguishes our passage is likeliest to be the object of an ἐκπράξαc' understood from 667 κακὸν . . . ἐκπραξαc'. **τῶν cῶν Ἡρακλεῖ δωρημάτων:** on the 'pregnant' dative here see Kannicht on Eur. *Hel.* 1548, Gow on Theocr. *Id.* 28. 2. For the word-order cf. e.g. Eur. *IT* 387 τὰ Ταντάλου θεοῖcιν ἑcτιάματα, Ar. *Nub.* 305 οὐρανίοιc τε θεοῖc δωρήματα. Cf. 872 below.

669. μάλιcτά γ': for this as a possible colloquialism in answers see Stevens, *Colloquial Expressions in Euripides*, p. 16. For omission of the pronoun after ὥcτε see Headlam on Herodas 3. 49.

669–70. προθυμίαν . . . ἔργου . . . λαβεῖν: cf. Aesch. *Suppl.* 178 προμηθίαν λαβών, 955 θράcοc λαβοῦcαι, Eur. *Hec.* 795 λαβὼν προμηθίαν. **προθυμίαν ἄδηλον ἔργου:** for the 'transferred epithet' see 817–18 ὄγκον . . . ὀνόματοc . . . | μητρῶιον and Bruhn, *Anhang*, § 10. II.

671. δίδαξον, εἰ διδακτόν: see on 64 above.

672. ἄν cannot do service for ἤν/ἐάν in tragedy, and the corruption of ἤν to ἄν must be presupposed.

673. βαλεῖν. παθεῖν is senseless (a bad conjecture based on μαθεῖν), so if we restrict ourselves to the available lections, we have to make a choice between λαβεῖν and μαθεῖν.[29] For a construction involving θαῦμα and λαβεῖν we may remind ourselves that in Greek a man may seize wonder or some comparable emotion, or the emotion may seize him. The former is exemplified[30] by *Aj.* 345 αἰδῶ . . . λάβοι, *El.* 897 ἔcχον θαῦμα, *OC* 729–30 εἰληφόταc | φόβον, Eur. *Suppl.* 1050 ὀργὴν λάβοιc ἄν, Eur. *IT* 949 οἳ δ' ἔcχον αἰδῶ, the latter by

[29] μαθεῖν is a *v.l.* entered by the same hand as the scribe of L's.
[30] On 801 εἰ δ' οἶκτον ἴcχειc see note ad loc.

LINES 666-675

Ar. Av. 511 μ' ἐλάμβανε θαῦμα: Homeric εἷλε θάμβος (see Kost on Musaeus, *Hero and Leander* 96). ὑμᾶς, either as conjectured by Blaydes for ὑμῖν or supplied mentally out of a retained ὑμῖν, could therefore be subject or object, and the construction equivalent to ὥσθ' ὑμᾶς θαυμάζειν, provided that οἷον were thus equivalent to ὥστε. But it is not so equivalent. λαβεῖν is therefore to be rejected (and explained as a corruption imported from the end of line 670) and μαθεῖν is to be preferred: how is it to be related to οἷον ... ὑμῖν? Apparent parallels for οἷον + dative + consecutive infinitive with relative pronoun governed by verb are few, but in Thuc. 6. 12. 2 we find καὶ τὸ πρᾶγμα μέγα εἶναι καὶ μὴ οἷον νεωτέρωι βουλεύσασθαί τε καὶ ὀξέως μεταχειρίσαι. Here, however, οἷον could be governed by βουλεύσασθαι. In Ar. *Plut.* 349 ποῖός τις (sc. χρησμός); — οἷος ... | ἢν μὲν κατορθώσωμεν, εὖ πράττειν ἀεί the interruption of the stichomythia makes all the difference. The most plausible solution is for μαθεῖν to be taken as an epexegetic infinitive (cf. μαθεῖν at 694 below and D. Korzeniewski, *Hermes* 103 (1975), 376). We must understand not the usual ἔστι but ἔσται. This slightly rarer form of ellipse is rendered easier by the preceding ἢν φράσω protasis. Compare 56–7 above, where νέμοι implies an ellipse of εἴη. Whether we suppose ὑμῖν belongs to φράσω or this implied ἔσται makes no difference at all, for in either case we must mentally supply a second ὑμῖν from the explicit one. Others may prefer to treat the final infinitive as totally corrupt and replace it with e.g. πορεῖν or the βαλεῖν printed in the OCT and supported at *Sophoclea*, p. 165. (For θαῦμα ... βαλεῖν cf. *Phil.* 67 λύπην ... βαλεῖς, and for λαβεῖν as a corruption of βαλεῖν see on 810 below.)

γυναῖκες: for other similar plural addresses to the chorus as a whole in response to a remark by the chorus-leader see Kaimio, *The Chorus of Greek Drama within the Light of the Person and Number Used*, p. 212.

674. ἐνδυτῆρα: ἅπαξ λεγόμενον: cf. ἐνδυτήριος (also ἅπαξ) at fr. 526; for the word-order cf. *Phil.* 393 τὸν μέγαν Πακτωλὸν εὔχρυσον, Bruhn, *Anhang*, § 166.

675. ἔχριον: the *vox propria* for D's operation, both in this play (e.g. 689) and elsewhere: see Lobel, *Oxy. Pap.* 28 (1962), 15, Gow on Theocr. *Id.* 11. 2. **ἀργῆς οἰὸς εὐείρωι πόκωι**: the manuscripts uniformly exhibit the reading ἀργῆτ' (cf. Aesch. *Eum.* 45 ἀργῆτι μαλλῶι), an

COMMENTARY

impossible elided dative, not accusative, and the use of two adjectives for πόκος causes the second (εὐείρωι) to ring very weak at the end of the line. Bergk's ἀργῆς (for the assimilation of endings presupposed see on 547 ff. above) presents an epithet used catachrestically.

677. τῶν ἔνδον: this is the reading of all the manuscripts: Jebb obligingly glosses as '(devoured by) nothing in the house (such as fire, or a corrosive substance' (what?)), and Zieliński (p. 605 n. 23 = p. 361 n. 3) as 'by nobody (cf. 934) in the house'—this ignores διάβορον—both renderings unconvincing and distracting. It is more likely that the correct reading is ἐκτός and that we have one of those instances where the scribe has, almost literally, written black for white (on such 'polar errors' see e.g. Housman on Manilius 5. 463, C. Kopff, *AJP* 96 (1975), 117 ff., W. W. Briggs, ibid. 104 (1983), 268 ff.). 'Devoured by no external agent but eaten up by itself' makes an excellently pointed remark (cf. 1132 below). The correction was proposed by Herwerden in *Exercitationes Criticae* (1862), 125. For a likely instance of the reverse corruption see *El.* 382 χθονὸς τῆςδ' ἐκτός, where ἐντός was plausibly conjectured by Schenkl (cf. on 368). See Addenda.

678. ψῆι: the intransitive usage here has troubled some scholars (ψηκτόν (from ψήχω 'crumble') was conjectured for καὶ ψῆι by Wecklein); it cannot be divorced entirely from the next crux. Soph. fr. 371. 3 λίμνας ἐφ' ὑψηλαῖς ϲπιλάδεϲϲι) shows us the proper meaning of ϲπιλάϲ[31] (a pointed rock or crag: cf. Apion fr. 125 Neitzel) and confirms that this object has no more place in Deianeira's household than the corrosive substance of Jebb's fancy. The meaning of κατά here is also odd in spite of Moorhouse's defence (p. 115). Of palaeographically motivated emendations the most ingenious is doubtless West's πτιλάδος (from *πτιλάς, analogous in formation to φυλλάς ((2), p. 526)). But unattested words are not to be introduced by conjecture; nor is the sense ('crumbled from its downy surface inwards') very apposite. The likeliest solution is Jebb's, that an original κατ' ἄκρας ϲπόδιον was replaced by the paradosis (Jebb thinks that the letters after ϲπ- were effaced and replaced by a rare substantive that happens to begin with ϲπ-. Misunderstanding of the construction with adverbial κατ' ἄκρας (glossed as δι' ὅλου, παντελῶς by Suda s.v.) could be another source of error.

[31] Also introduced (by a very uncertain conjecture of Wieseler's) into the text at *Ant.* 966.

LINES 675-686

680. ὧν | ὁ θήρ με ... προυδιδάξατο: for the relative extending beyond the 'Kolonanfang' see Fraenkel, *Kl. Beitr.* i. 113-14.

680-1. πονῶν | πλευράν: for the ambiguity here as to whether the accusative is internal or one of respect see Moorhouse, p. 43.

681. γλωχῖνι προυδιδάξατο: for the meaning of γλωχίc see *Lexikon d. frühgr. Epos* s.v.; as for the verb, the force of the middle is obscure: see Bers, p. 116 n. 42.

682. οὐδέν: but the sequence of letters is better interpreted as masculine οὐδέν᾽, as Wakefield and then Herwerden (*Lucubrationes Sophocleae* (Leiden 1887), 12) saw.

683. χαλκῆc: for the use of bronze (and other metals) to record inscriptions see G. Zuntz, *Persephone* (Oxford 1971), 278-9. ἐκ δέλτου γραφήν: a very common metaphor in Greek tragedy: cf. *PV* 789 ἐγγράφου cὺ μνήμοcιν δέλτοιc φρενῶν, fr. 597 θοῦ δ᾽ ἐν φρενὸc δέλτοιcι τοὺc ἐμοὺc λόγουc, and see Pfeiffer, *History of Classical Scholarship* (Oxford 1968), i. 26, Johansen and Whittle on Aesch. *Suppl.* 179, Sier on *Cho.* 450.

684. Deleted by Wunder as unbearably otiose and repetitious. The line might originate out of an attempt to provide a more obvious construction for the infinitive cώιζειν in 686, actually dependent on προυδιδάξατο in remote 681 (for interpolations of this sort πρὸc cαφήνειαν τῶν λεγομένων see on 444 above). The repetition in τοιαῦτ᾽ ἔδρων|κἄδρων τοιαῦτα cuts both ways. Interpolations often seem to have been patched together out of words in the immediate vicinity (see on 696), and if the line is removed one more easily perceives that 685-6 gives the context of the instructions mentioned in 681-2. On the other hand the chiasmus might be defended on stylistic grounds (Jebb thought it denoted urgency) and Lloyd-Jones *ap.* Stinton, p. 139, compared 'the insistence on detail in the performance of a ritual that we find elsewhere in tragedy' (e.g. Aesch. *Pers.* 607ff., *OC* 469ff.). Zieliński (p. 606 n. 25 = p. 362 n. 1) compared *El.* 288 τοιάδ᾽ ἐξονειδίζει ... 293 τάδ᾽ ἐξυβρίζει. Stinton himself detects a tragic irony 'in that D's very exactness ensures that the Centaur's cunning has its full, deadly effect'. The καί ... καί would be equivalent to *ut ... ita* (see on 229 above).

686 ff. Note how these significant details were not mentioned in D's initial account of Nessus' remarks (569ff.). They are kept back until their significance is dramatically crucial.

COMMENTARY

686. (ἀκτῖνος ...) | θερμῆc ἄθικτον: for the principle of alpha privative governing the genitive cf. 691 below, *El.* 36, *OC* 677–8, Aesch. *Eum.* 704 κερδῶν ἄθικτον.

687. The question of the legitimacy of ἕως ἄν with the optative here is discussed by Moorhouse, p. 297, who concludes that 'the use of ἄν with opt. instead of simple opt. to replace subj. with ἄν must be regarded as dubious' unless D is trying to stress the potentiality in, the lack of compulsion behind, her use of the unguent. See further G. L. Cooper, *Zur syntaktischen Theorie und Textkritik der attischen Autoren* (Zurich 1971), 33–4. Cf. above on 162. On **ἁρμόcαιμι** see on 623 above.

689. κατ' οἶκον ἐν δόμοιc: the duplication has been taken as indicative of corruption (Dindorf's ἔνδυτον would presuppose the mode of corruption discussed on 555 above), but see Diggle on Eur. *Phaeth.* 56, who translates our line 'in the house, in the women's quarters', and cites instances where δόμοι = rooms and as such are distinguished from a less extensive word meaning 'home' (δῶμα etc.) by the present type of juxtaposition. Similarly Moorhouse, p. 4: '"at home" ... "in my apartments" (i.e. the γυναικωνῖτιc).'

690. μαλλῶι: see J. A. C. Greppin, *Glotta* 59 (1981), 70 ff., on the precise meaning of this noun.

691. ἀλαμπὲc ἡλίου: ~ 686 (ἀκτῖνος ...) | θερμῆc ἄθικτον: see note ad loc.

693. δέρκομαι φάτιν: on the 'synaesthesia' here see C. P. Segal, *ICS* 2 (1977), 91–2 (cf. Verdenius, *Mnem.* 25 (1972), 243). Blaydes's θέαν may therefore be dispensed with.

694. ἀξύμβλητον ἀνθρώπωι μαθεῖν: cf. Aesch. *Suppl.* 90 πόροι κατιδεῖν ἄφραcτοι for the idiom whereby the infinitive re-enforces the sense of the accompanying adjective. For the epexegetic infinitive see above on 673.

696. Dobree (*Adversaria*, ed. Wagner, iv. 35) found this verse 'suspectus ob constructionem nisi legas φλόγα | ἀκτῖνος ἡλιῶτιν'. Even with this expedient the contents of the line are entirely otiose; the contrast between 695's casual τυγχάνω ῥίψαcά πωc and 696's specific ἐc μέcην φλόγα odd; the use of φλόξ *tout court* of the sun's rays unparalleled (cf. Renehan, *HSCP* 87 (1983), 20. Hence for φλόγα G. Wolff conjectured πλάκα). Most of the words in this line could have been cobbled together from 674–5 as part of an attempt to explain κάταγμα (for this mode of interpolation πρὸc cαφήνειαν τῶν λεγομένων see on 444 above).

697. ὡc: here meaning 'while' (cf. Moorhouse, p. 296).

698. ῥεῖ ... καὶ κατέψηκται: the former verb present, the latter a perfect conveying instantaneous result.

699. μορφῆι μάλιστ' εἰκαcτόν: μάλιστα is idiomatic in this type of comparison: see Sappho fr. 115 LP τίωι c', ὦ φίλε γάμβρε, καλῶc εἰκάcδω; | ὄρπακι βραδίνωι cε μάλιcτ' εἰκάcδω, and the Aristophanic passages cited by Fraenkel, *Plautinisches in Plautus*, p. 172 ≃ *Elementi plautini in Plauto*, p. 163 (cf. the latter's Addenda, p. 422).

699–700. πρίονοc | ἐκβρώμαθ': rightly interpreted by Long, *Language and Thought*, p. 98, as a poeticism for παραπρίcματα ('sawdust', on which see Müller, *Handwerk und Sprache*, p. 40) meant 'to elevate a simile drawn from everyday life'. Dawe's small correction (*Studies* iii. 91) neatly improves the sense (for ἂν (ἃ + ἄν) cf. *Aj.* 1085); for the corruption *ΕΚβρώματ' ΕΚβλέψειαc* in L and other MSS see above on 554. **ἐν τομῆι ξύλου:** for this 'local-temporal force' of ἐν see Fraenkel on Aesch. *Ag.* 1288. See Addenda.

701–2. ἐκ δὲ γῆc, ὅθεν | προὔκειτ': for the attraction of the relative adverb (ὅθεν for ἧι) to the antecedent genitive see *OC* 1226–7 βῆναι κεῖθεν ὅθεν περ ἥ|κει: cf. Wackernagel, *Vorles. über Syntax* i. 55), *Sophoclea* p. 251 (cf. p. 55).

702. θρομβώδειc: for a consideration of this and other -ώδηc adjectives in S see M. J. O'Brien, *CQ* 35 (1985), 269 n. 20.

703–4. Cf. Argentarius *AP* 9. 87. 3–4 = *GP* 1413–14 ἄμπελοc ἔνθα | ἀντέλλει γλαυκῶν cύcκιοc ἐκ πετάλων, Maccius *AP* 9. 249. 1 = *GP* 2524 εὐπέταλον γλαυκὰν ἀναδενδράδα τάνδε. On the precise meaning of γλαυκόc here see P. G. Maxwell-Stuart, *Studies in Greek Colour Terminology* i (*Mnem.* suppl. 65; 1981), 104.

705. οὐκ ἔχω ... ποῖ γνώμηc πέcω: for this and parallel idioms see Diggle, *STE*, p. 35. **τάλαινα:** for τάλαc used thus as an exclamation without the definite article and as the subject of a verb see Headlam on Herodas 3. 5.

706. ἔργον ... ἐξειργαcμένην: for similar examples of this *figura etymologica* see Rau, *Paratragodia*, p. 165. For the construction with the accusative used of a speaker looking at his or her case from without 'to give a certain objectivity' Jebb ad loc. cited *El.* 470–1 πικρὰν | δοκῶ

COMMENTARY

με πεῖραν τήνδε τολμήςειν ἔτι and *Aj.* 606–7 κακὰν ἐλπίδ' ἔχων | ἔτι μέ ποτ' ἀνύςειν τὸν ἀπότροπον ἀΐδηλον Ἅιδαν from tragedy. Add *PV* 268–9 οὐ μήν τι ποιναῖς γ' ᾠιόμην τοίαιςί με | κατιςχνανεῖςθαι.

707. Wakefield's θνήιςκειν (for θνήιςκων) removes what some see as an awkward jingle (θνήιςκων ... ἔθνηιςκ'), others as significant repetition.

709. ἀποφθῖςαι: see Wackernagel, *Spr. Unt. zu Homer*, p. 237; cf. 1043 below.

710 ff. For the theme of 'late-learning' in this play (and the *OT*) see R. B. Rutherford, *JHS* 102 (1982), 148–9, with bibliography p. 149 n. 21. Cf. 934 ὄψ' ἐκδιδαχθείς.

711. μάθηςιν ἄρνυμαι: an emphatic periphrasis for μανθάνω (cf. Long, *Language and Thought*, p. 88 and n. 88).

712. On εἴ τι μή see on 586 above; on the attraction whereby ψεύδω and its synonyms are cast in the future tense (because the statement will be verified in the future) see Radt in *ΣΧΟΛΙΑ* (Holwerda Festschrift; Groningen, 1986), 111.

713. ἐξαποφθερῶ: for ἐξαπο- compound verbs in S see Pfeiffer, *Sitzb. d. Bayer. Akad. d. Wiss., phil.-hist. Kl.* 6 (1958), 21 = *Sophokles* (Wege der Forschung 95; 1967), 478–9.

714–15. θεὸν | Χείρωνα: as the offspring of Cronus and the nymph Phillyra (see *Titanom.* fr. 6 Davies): cf. the phrase φὴρ θεῖος at Pind. *Pyth.* 4. 119, and for other passages which treat him as a god *PV* 1027, Lucian *De mort.* 26; cf. M. Vogel, *Der Kentaur mit der Kithara* i (Bonn 1978), 27, B. C. Dietrich, *Death, Fate and the Gods* (London 1965), 40 n. 1.

715. χὤνπερ: Wakefield's emendation (for the corruption cf. Dawe, *Studies* i. 198) removes the anomaly of χὥςαπερ with its unmetrical fifth-foot anapaest (avoided by Wunder's deletion of ἄν). χὥςπερ ἄν with the sense 'provided that, as soon as' is not classical Greek, and synizesis of καὶ ἕως (χέως) is impossible (contrast ἕως(περ) ἄν at *Aj.* 1117, *Phil.* 1330, *OC* 1361, etc.).

716. τοῦδ' ὅδε: for the direct juxtaposition of these pronouns cf. Eur. *Cycl.* 30 τάςδε, τῶιδε. Easterling, *Hermes* 101 (1973), 20, approves Jebb's notion that 'the reiterated pronoun really marks the stress of the inductive argument'. But Meineke's τοῦδε δή is an easy change which makes for greater clarity (*Analecta Sophoclea* (Berlin 1863), 297).

LINES 706-730

718. δόξηι γοῦν ἐμῆι: for other examples of the rhetorical device whereby the speaker answers a question he or she has just posed see Vahlen, *Opusc. Acad.* i. 210.

719. δέδοκται: 'my mind is made up': for the first time in the play the hitherto indecisive D assumes the stance and tone of a resolute Sophoclean hero: cf. *Phil.* 1277 and B. Knox, *The Heroic Temper* (Berkeley and Los Angeles 1966), 10–11.

720. ταύτῆι cὺν ὁρμῆι: ὀργῆι would mean 'under the same state of mind', with cύν instrumental or circumstantial: see Moorhouse, p. 126. Moorhouse himself, like most editors, prefers ὁρμῆι, but for ὁρμή as a gloss or variant for ὀργή stemming from Byzantine scribes' ignorance that the latter can mean more than merely 'anger' see West on Hes. *Op.* 304 and in *BICS* 26 (1979), 112 (add Eur. *Suppl.* 1050). There may not, in fact, be such a great difference in meaning between the two words. ὁρμή is usually supposed to mean something like 'impetus' here ('impulse of fate' Moorhouse, loc. cit.): cf. *Ant.* 135 μαινομέναι ξὺν ὁρμᾶι of a warrior's mad rush. But φρενὸς ὁρμῆς at Hes. fr. 204. 120 MW suggests that the word might mean 'attitude' here too. **cυνθανεῖν ἅμα:** for the pleonasm see on 545 (ξυνοικεῖν . . . ὁμοῦ).

721. For the sentiment cf. *Aj.* 479, *El.* 989. For the heroic rejection of 'intolerable' conditions see Knox, *The Heroic Temper*, p. 41.

724. For the association of ἐλπίς and τύχη see fr. 201. 1–2 πῶς οὖν μάχωμαι θνητὸς ὢν θείαι τύχηι; | ὅπου τὸ δεινόν, ἐλπὶς οὐδὲν ὠφελεῖ.

725. On the absence of regular caesura from this line see Diggle, *CR* 32 (1982), 130. On the 'abstract' μή cf. KG ii/2. 201–2.

726. ἐλπίς, ἥτις καί: emphatic καί after a relative pronoun (usually ὅστις) is a common idiom: see Kannicht on Eur. *Hel.* 1200. **προξενεῖ:** 'causes, brings about': cf. *OT* 1482–3, Xen. *Apol. Socr.* 6. 5. 14. The original image was that of a πρόξενος who 'brings about' something by means of his influence.

727–8. This common maxim is illustrated by Pearson on fr. 665; for ὀργὴ πέπειρα cf. Ar. *Vesp.* 646 τὴν γὰρ ἐμὴν ὀργὴν πεπᾶναι, Xen. *Cyr.* 4. 5. 21 πεπαίνειν ὀργήν.

728. τῆς: for the articular form of the relative see on 47 above.

730. οἴκοι βαρύ: Wakefield's emendation of the manuscripts' οἴκοις; for the metaphorical troubles 'at home' cf. Hdt. 7. 152. 2 οἰκήια κακά.

185

COMMENTARY

731. For πλείων with a redundant article as characteristic of S see Platnauer on Eur. *IT* 1233; cf. τὸν πλείω χρόνον at Ar. *Ran.* 160, Dinarch. 1. 77, etc.

732. παιδὶ τῶι cαυτῆc: for the emphatic position of παιδί cf. *Aj.* 101 παῖc ὁ τοῦ Λαερτίου, Bruhn, *Anhang*, § 165.

733. μαcτὴρ πατρόc: cf. *OC* 455–6 ἐμοῦ | μαcτῆρα. See further on this rare word Roux on Eur. *Bacch.* 985 ff.

734 ff. The conventional pessimistic proem from a messenger or other bringer of news is often, as here, greeted with the question τί δ' ἔcτιν; See Mastronarde, *Contact and Discontinuity*, p. 69 n. 55. For the more general pattern of statement–question–more specific statement–demand for details cf. S. P. Mills, *Class. Journ.* 76 (1980), 132.

735. εἶναι ζῶcαν: on the tragic pleonasm (ζῶν ἔcτι = ζῆι) see Rau, *Paratragodia*, p. 104. **cεcωμένην:** for the spelling see on 83 above.

737. Genitive of exchange: see Schwyzer, *Gr. Gr.* ii. 127 (2), Diggle, *CQ* 34 (1984), 63 n. 67.

738. τί δ' ἔcτιν ... πρόc γ' ἐμοῦ cτυγούμενον: for the elaborately rotund expression cf. Aerts, *Periphrastica*, 34–5, and *Sophoclea*, p. 166 (scouting the πρόc γε cοῦ of Campe (and Viketos, *LCM* 13/5 (1988), 79)).

739–40. τὸν δ' ἐμὸν ... | πατέρα: for δ' cf. *OC* 1275 ὦ cπέρματ' ἀνδρὸc τοῦδ', ἐμαὶ δ' ὁμαίμονεc; cf. B. Haiden, *Mnem.* 42 (1989), 472 on λέγω here.

742. μή: against Nauck's μὴ οὐ see on 90 above.

742–3. For examples of this common motif see Pearson on fr. 860, R. Kassel, *Untersuchungen zur gr. und röm. Konsolationsliteratur* (Zetemata 18; 1958), 91. The closely proximate ἄνs are due to the tendency, 'when ἄν is repeated', for one ἄν to be 'placed beside the verb, the other at the second place of the sentence or colon, or as near as possible to it' (Page on Eur. *Med.* 250). See esp. Fraenkel, 'Kolon und Satz II', *Nach. Gött. Ges. d. Wiss., phil.-hist. Kl.* (1933), 321 ff. = *Kl. Beitr.* i. 96 ff.

744. μαθών: P.Oxy.'s παρών is a mere unconscious repetition of the preceding παρ': see Jackson, *MS*, p. 224; for the position of παρ' here, sandwiched between two dependent words, see Bruhn, *Anhang*, § 162.

745. ἄζηλον: cf. 284 above.

746–7. Emphatic hyperbaton combined with an interweaving of the AbAb pattern.

747. δεδορκὼc κοὐ ... κλυών: another common polarity: see Page on Eur. *Med.* 652, Collard on Eur. *Suppl.* 684ff., Diggle *GRBS* 14 (1973), 262 n. 60 and *STE*, p. 18. For the aorist participle κλυών see on 189 above.

749. An introductory line ('let me tell you what happened...') often thus opens such a *rhesis*: see Kaibel on *El.* 947. For an excellent stylistic characterization of Hyllus' *rhesis* ('essentially a messenger-speech' with 'a high style of description') see Long, *Language and Thought*, p. 97.

750ff. ὅθ' εἷρπε ... ἀκτή τις ... ἐστιν: the inconcinnity is matched by a formally similar description at Eur. *Hipp.* 1198–9 ἐπεὶ δ' ... | ἀκτή τις ἔςτι. Contrast e.g. Eur. *El.* 774ff. ἐπεὶ μελάθρων τῶνδ' ἀπήραμεν πόδα, | ἐςβάντες ἦιμεν δίκροτον εἰς ἁμαξιτὸν | ἔνθ' ἦν ὁ καινὸς τῶν Μυκηναίων ἄναξ.

752–3. ἀκτή τις ... | ... ἐστιν, ἔνθα: Eur. *Hipp.* 1199 takes up ἀκτή τις ἔςτι with ἔνθεν at 1201. See too ibid. 125ff. Ὠκεανοῦ τις ὕδωρ ςτάζουςα πέτρα λέγεται ... τόθι and Barrett ad loc. for similar asyndetic phrases; cf. Latin *est locus* ... (cf. Nisbet, *CR* 21 (1971), 63, G. Williams, *Tradition and Originality in Roman Poetry* (Oxford 1968), 640ff.).

754. ὁρίζει: present because the dedication was in the past, but the effect remains (cf. on 21 above); or merely the vivid present so common in messenger-speeches.

755. οὗ: for the demonstrative after a strong pause see Barrett on Eur. *Hipp.* 125ff. **ἐςεῖδον, ἄςμενος πόθωι:** cf. Eur. *Ion* 1437 ὦ φιλτάτη μοι μῆτερ, ἄςμενός ς' ἰδών.

756. πολυθύτους ... ςφαγάς: for this sort of *figura etymologica* cf. Aesch. *Pers.* 153–4 προςφθόγγοις ... μύθοιςι, *Suppl.* 736 περίφοβον ... τάρβος, and cf. 760–1 ταυροκτονεῖ ... βοῦς below.

757. οἰκεῖος: the epithet was deemed 'unbestimmt und vage und nach ἀπ' οἴκων nur lästig' by Hense, *Studien zu Sophokles*, p. 152, who proposed ὠκύπους (used by S, in the same position within the line, at *El.* 699; cf. *OC* 1093). F. W. Schmidt's οὐ κενός (cf. 495) is an alternative solution. Others prefer to detect a deliberate word-play intended to stress the monstrousness of a death deriving from Heracles' own house and home.

758. τὸ ςὸν φέρων δώρημα: for Hyllus' emphasis on D's guilt see 759 ὡς ςὺ προὐξεφίεςο, 773 Λίχαν, τὸν οὐδὲν αἴτιον τοῦ ςοῦ κακοῦ, 775–6 τὸ ςὸν μόνης | δώρημ', etc.

COMMENTARY

759. προὐξεφίεcο: the verb is ἅπαξ, but cf. προὐδιδάξατο at 681 of Nessus' instructions to D, and for other Sophoclean verbs compounded with two prepositions and similarly ἅπαξ cf. B. Knox, *Gnomon* 40 (1968), 759 = *Word and Action*, p. 181; for the legitimacy of the imperfect with this and analogous verbs cf. W. B. Sedgwick, *CQ* 34 (1940), 119.

760–1. ταυροκτονεῖ ... βοῦc: the same verb is used absolutely at Aesch. *ScT* 276 (*del.* Ritschl, *prob.* Hutchinson); for the *figura etymologica* whereby (as in *El.* 190 οἰκονομῶ θαλάμους) 'the verb is compounded with a noun similar in sense to its object' cf. Diggle, *CR* 18 (1968), 2, Bruhn, *Anhang*, § 52; cf. on 756 above; for the denominative verb in -έω here and at *Aj.* 549 (πωλοδαμνεῖν) as representing 'einen Streben nach gewähltem Ausdruck' see Wifstrand, *Eranos* 44 (1946), 244–5.

762. For the trimeter 'beginning with a resolved anceps followed by a longum created by "positional lengthening"' see Johansen and Whittle, *Symb. Osl.* 50 (1975), 22; **cυμμιγῆ βοcκήματα:** on the combination of adjective and noun here and at 770 ὀδαγμὸς ἀντίςπαςτος see on 50 above.

763–4. ἴλεωι φρενὶ ... κατηύχετο: for the adverbial dative cf. Aesch. *Ag.* 895 ἀπενθήτωι φρενὶ λέγοιμ' ἄν. Meineke's κατήρχετο is attractive: κατάρχομαι refers to the cutting of a hair from the victim's forehead and the throwing of it into the fire (cf. Pease on Verg. *Aen.* 4. 698); for κατάρχομαι used absolutely see Kassel–Austin on Athenio fr. 1. 40. On κατεύχομαι and κατάρχομαι see further Stinton, *JHS* 97 (1977), 151, Denniston on Eur. *El.* 791 ff.

765. cεμνῶν ὀργίων: for cεμνός of rites and rituals see Pearson on fr. 804, Richardson on *HH Dem.* 273, 478. **ἐδαίετο:** this epic word is found only here in S, once or twice in Aeschylus and Euripides: cf. Sideras, *Aeschylus Homericus*, p. 82.

766. δρυός: if a reference to pine (which is what the epithet πιείρας would suggest), an instance of the generic use of δρῦς (see on 171 above and cf. Seaford on Eur. *Cycl.* 383, Braswell on Pind. *Pyth.* 4. 264 (c), Renehan, *CP* 80 (1985), 153).

767. ἱδρὼς ἀνῄει χρωτί: cf. *Il.* 13. 705 = 23. 507: πολὺς δ' ἀνεκήκιεν ἱδρώς. **προcπτύccεται:** Musgrave's small correction will introduce a perfectly acceptable historic present and remove an undesirable instance of an unaugmented verb: undesirable because

188

LINES 759-770

although Hyllus' *rhesis* can be characterized as a 'messenger-speech' (see on 749 above) and unaugmented verbs are at home in such a context (see on 904 below), the augment is ordinarily omitted only at the beginning of a line (see on 560 above). προςπτύccεται at line-end and as historic present in *Ant.* 1237 (messenger-speech).

768. ἀρτίκολλος: 'close-glued, clinging close' (LSJ etc.) seems a likelier meaning (in spite of ἀρτίχριστον at 687) than Dobree's (*Adversaria*, ed. Wagner (1883), iv. 38) 'quasi a fabro *recens* fuisset adglutinata'. **ὥστε τέκτονος:** read (Herwerden) ὥς ἐκ τέκτονος. The paradosis would have to mean 'as if belonging to a τέκτων' (Kannicht on Eur. *Hel.* 1162 compares Aesch. *Eum.* 627-8 οὔ τι θουρίοις | τόξοις ἐκηβόλοισιν ὥστ' Ἀμαζόνος, Eur. *Hcld.* 423 οὐ γὰρ τυραννίδ' ὥστε βαρβάρων ἔχω, as well as the *Helen* passage itself: τείχεα δὲ φλογερός, ὥστε Διός, ἐπέςυτο φλόξ). The paradosis is not to be explained by resort to an impossible genitive of the agent (cf. on 267 ff. above), and Hermann's interpretation 'like the work of a sculptor' may be vivid enough (one thinks of the way in which the contours of the body show through the garment in such contemporary sculptures as the birth of Athena on the east pediment of the Parthenon, or Aphrodite's emergence from the waves on the Ludovisi throne) but hardly suggests a unique crisis. Similarly, the idea of a sweaty artisan's cloak sticking to him (Zijderveld, *Mnem.* 3 (1936), 175-6, West, (1), 366 n. 9) supplies a merely familiar idea instead of a characteristic blend of the sinister and the mundane (cf. Fraenkel on Aesch. *Ag.* 437 ff., quoted on 516 above). The pointing required by Herwerden is προςπτύccεται πλευραῖςιν, ἀρτίκολλος ὥς ἐκ τέκτονος (cf. on 441-2), while Zijderveld and West's approach (followed by the OCT) entails postponing the comma until χιτών. See Addenda.

769. ὀςτέων: on the legitimacy of the uncontracted form in tragedy see L. Bergson, *Rh. Mus.* 102 (1959), 19.

769-70. ὀδαγμός is the reading of the manuscripts and Σ. ἀδαγμός is attributed to Sophocles by Photius s.v. See Theodoridis' edition of Photius ad loc. (i. 39), and for the meaning of ἀδαγμός see Long, *Language and Thought*, pp. 133-4 (cf. ibid. 21 for a list of comparable abstract nouns ending in -ός and denoting violent action). On ὀδαγμός cf. Chantraine's *Dictionnaire étymologique de la langue grecque* s.v. and Kassel–Austin on Ar. fr. 416.

770. φοίνιος: on the principle of equitable distribution of epithets to

COMMENTARY

nouns involved in Pierson's φοίνιος for φοινίας see Diggle, *STE*, pp. 48–9: Pierson, edn. of Moeris (1830), 38.

770–1. Dawe (*Studies* iii. 92) finds 'the irony of describing what is actually poison of a hateful monster as being like poison of a hateful monster ... so elementary and frigid' that he posits a lacuna after 771 and prefers to interpret ὡς as 'when' or emend it to ὅς ⟨σφ'⟩: for the corruption presupposed see on 336 above). But we may rather have here another specimen of the mixture of *illustrans* and *illustrandum* discussed on 31 ff. above: 'then the poison of the hateful ἔχιδνα began to feast as it were' (for the dramatic economy involved in Hyllus' knowing of the poison see on 934 below); for the appropriateness here of the image of the ἔχιδνα (a creature that kills its mate during intercourse) see E. K. Borthwick, *CR* 17 (1967), 250–1. Heracles as object of ἐδαίνυτο can be supplied as easily here as at 1088 below.

772–3. 'βόηϲε: for the prodelision after -η see above on 381; the verb means here 'called for Lichas'. For 'the general ancient practice of adapting the content of the cry to the construction of the sentence' see Fraenkel on Aesch. *Ag.* 48 ff. **Λίχαν:** cf. Aesch. *TrGF* iii. fr. 25E 13–14 Radt τύμβον ἀθ[λίου Λίχα.

775–6. τὸ ϲὸν μόνης | δώρημ': for the juxtaposition of possessive adjective and genitive adjective in apposition cf. *OC* 344 τἀμὰ δυϲτήνου κακά and, in general, Braswell on Pind. *Pyth.* 4. 175 (e), Schwyzer, *Gr. Gr.* ii. 177 (γ). Cf. on 1068 below.

777. ὡς: *ut primum*: for this meaning cf. Fraenkel on Aesch. *Ag.* 306 ff.

778. ϲπαραγμός: on the meaning of this term here and at 1254 see Long, *Language and Thought*, p. 134. **πλευμόνων ἀνθήψατο:** for the general idea of the lungs as a vital seat see Gow–Page on Antip. Thess. *AP* 9. 309. 3–4 = *GP* 421–2; the phrase πλευμόνων τ' ἀνθάψεται | Ταρτηϲϲία μύραινα at Ar. *Ran.* 474 (parodic: see Rau, *Paratragodia*, p. 117) is similar; for other instances of the verb see Page on Eur. *Med.* 55.

779. μάρψας ποδός νιν: 'seizing him by the foot': see Moorhouse, p. 62, for cases where 'a genitive is used of the part of the body with which contact is made, coupled with an accusative of the whole'. Compare ῥίπτω in such passages as *Il.* 1. 591, *Il. Parv.* fr. 20. 4 Davies, Sositheus *TrGF* i. 99. fr. 5. 1 Sn.; cf. Eur. *Cycl.* 400 τένοντος ἁρπάσας ἄκρου ποδός.

780. ἀμφίκλυστον ἐκ πόντου πέτραν: the adjectival placing of ἐκ πόντου (for ἐκ with this meaning ('projecting from') see Johansen and Whittle on Aesch. *Suppl.* 720): cf. Aesch. *TrGF* iii. fr. 25E. 13–14 Radt Εὐβοῖδα καμπὴν ἀμφὶ Κηναίου Διὸς | ἀκτὴν κατ' αὐτὸν τύμβον κτλ. (of Lichas).

781–2. The closest analogy to the language of these lines is to be found in a fragment of Euripides' *Theseus* (384 N²): κάρα τε γάρ cου cυγχέω κόμαιc ὁμοῦ, whose bloodthirsty violence has led D. F. Sutton (*Hermes* 106 (1978), 49) to conclude that the play in question must have been satyric.[32] κόμης seems distinctly odd in our passage, even so, though it is sometimes defended as a vivid detail. The singular is permissible for hair of the head (cf. *Il.* 1. 197, Archil. fr. 31 W, Anacr. fr. 347. 1. 1), but, much more important, it is difficult to see how the participle διαcπαρέντοc can coherently be applied to both μέcου | κρατόc and αἵματοc (an inconcinnity veiled by Jebb's rendering 'as the skull was dashed to splinters and blood scattered therewith'). The lines have been supposed corrupt, but none of the emendations advanced is at all persuasive (e.g. ὁμοῦ διαcπαρέντοc αἵματοc θόλου: Schmidt, as cited above on 144–50, pp. 176 ff.). Perhaps, then, the lines are spurious. It is true that Homer's *Iliad* contains accounts of wounds that are both gruesomely bloodthirsty and physiologically dubious (see the remarks of W. H. Friedrich, *Verwundung und Tod in der Ilias* (Göttingen 1956), 11 ff.). On the other hand, the lines may constitute a gory concession to an audience's degenerate taste by some actor (a not very helpful *terminus ad quem* is provided by Apollodorus of Athens (born c.180 BC), who quotes the two lines (*FGrH* 244 F 246)). Deletion was suggested by Meineke, *Beitr. z. philol. Krit. der Antigone* (Berlin 1861), 42, approved by Bernhardy, *Grundriß der gr. Lit.*[3] ii. (1880), 376: cf. Dawe's deletion of the end of the *Ajax* for reasons including (*Studies* i. 174) the physiological oddity of the description of Ajax's corpse at 1411 ff. ἔτι γὰρ θερμαὶ | cύριγγεc ἄνω φυcῶcι μέλαν | μένοc) and West's of *OT* 1278–9 (*BICS* 25 (1978), 121) as 'clumsy and tasteless lines... an obvious interpolation in the interests of goriness, like *Aj*. 918 ff.' (φυcῶντ' ἄνω πρὸc ῥῖναc ἔκ τε φοινίαc | πληγῆc μελανθὲν αἷμ' κτλ.: *del.* Nauck). S's 'characteristic over-statement in matters of physical horror' (Dawe, *PCPS* 14 (1968), 13, writing before he deleted *Aj*. 1411 ff.) may not, after all, be to blame.

---

[32] It is 'impossible to match the explicit bloody-mindedness (*sic*) of these threats with anything in a tragedy.'

COMMENTARY

781. ἐκραίνει: cf. Eur. *Cycl.* 401–2 παίων πρὸc ὀξὺν cτόνυχα πετραίου λίθου | ἐγκέφαλον ἐξέρρανε. The parallel reminds us that the Greeks regarded the brain (ἐγκέφαλοc) as a type of μυελόc: for the equivalence of the two words see Lloyd-Jones in *Dionysiaca* (Page Festschrift), p. 51, adding to his evidence Apollodorus of Athens, loc. cit. (last n.), who quoted our passage in support of his thesis that οἱ παλαιοί did not use the word ἐγκέφαλοc. The fragment from Euripides' *Theseus* mentioned above (384 N²) more frankly states ῥανῶ τε πεδόc· ἐγκέφαλον.

782. αἵματοc θ' ὁμοῦ: cf. the fragment of the *Theseus* once again: κάρα τε γάρ cου cυγχέω κόμαιc ὁμοῦ, | . . . ὀμμάτων δ' ἄπο | αἱμοcταγῆ πρηcτῆρε ῥεύcονται κάτω.

783. ἀνηυφήμηcεν: 'mit höchster Kühnheit nennt Soph. . . . das Ausstoßen eines Weherufs beim Opfer, also eine βλαcφημία, ἀνευφημεῖν οἰμωγῆι' (Wilamowitz on Eur. *Her.* 1185, in a discussion of this verb and its compounds). On similar Aeschylean exploitations of 'a blasphemous paradox' see Fraenkel on Aesch. *Ag.* 645; cf. D. Clay, *Philol.* 110 (1966), 129–30. Cf. Amfortas' 'zu diesen Amt [a sacred office] verdammt zu sein' in Wagner's *Parsifal*, Act I.

786. πεδόνδε: an epic ἅπαξ in tragedy; for comparable epicisms, likewise unattested elsewhere in tragedy, see Aesch. *Suppl.* 33 πόντονδ', 886 ἅλαδ' (*coni.*), 1018 ἄcτυδ' (*coni.*).

787–8. Diogenes Laertius in his quotation of these lines provides several variants. δάκνων for βοῶν is easily dispensed with, since Diogenes introduces his quotation thus: ὁ Ἡρακλῆc καταβιβρωcκόμενοc ὑπὸ τοῦ χιτῶνοc βοᾶι, and has clearly adjusted Sophocles' phrasing accordingly. δάκνων has quite inappropriate overtones of Stoic endurance (see below on 976). **βοῶν, ἰύζων:** for other examples of participles in asyndeton at the start of a line see Kannicht on Eur. *Hel.* 930. On the tragic pleonasm involved see Renehan, *CP* 80 (1985), 148. **ἰύζων:** see Sideras, *Aeschylus Homericus*, p. 88. **ὄρειοι πρῶνεc:** on this combination of adjective and noun see Gow–Page on *AP* 9. 328. 2 = *HE* 1438.

789. τάλαc: see on 705 above.

791. δυcπάρευνον λέκτρον: cf. Aesch. *Suppl.* 67 δυcμάτοροc κότου, 394 γάμου δύcφρονοc, 1063 γάμον δυcάνορα, *Ag.* 1319 δυcδάμαρτοc ἀντ' ἀνδρόc. On the unmetrical λέχοc of ZoZp see Dawe, *Studies* i. 249. **ἐνδατούμενοc:** the original meaning of

LINES 781-803

ἐνδατεῖcθαι was 'allot, distribute', and how it comes to mean 'revile' here, and 'celebrate' in Aesch. fr. 350 Radt (see Radt's note on line 1; cf. LSJ s.v. 2 (a)) is uncertain: cf. Lesky in *Studi in onore di G. Funaioli* (1955), 169 = *Ges. Schr.* 237-8 (suggesting λόγουc ἐνδατεῖcθαι περί as an intermediate stage), Hutchinson on Aesch. *ScT* 577-8. The Σ^γε ἐμματ- is to be explained by the interchangeability of MM and NΔ in manuscripts: see Jackson, *MS*, p. 121.

792. ταλαίνηc: not the usual pathetic sense (as e.g. at 789 and 878 of this play), but with the meaning 'heartless': see Denniston on Eur. *El.* 1171, J. R. Wilson, *AJP* 92 (1971), 300 n. 23, D. Bain, *Antichthon* 18 (1984), 34.

794-5. διάcτροφον | ὀφθαλμόν: for rolling eyes as symptomatic of madness or frenzy see e.g. Dodds on Eur. *Bacch.* 1122-3, Bond on Eur. *Her.* 930 ff.

796. καλεῖ: the verb is often equivalent to κελεύω vel sim.: see Kannicht on Eur. *Hel.* 1560. The tense is historic present (see on 767 above). The speech's content is a frightening index of the hero's egotism.

798. θανόντι cυνθανεῖν: for similar phrases see Collard on Eur. *Suppl.* 1006-7, and for the juxtaposition of simplex and compound verbs see Fehling, *Wiederholungsfiguren*, pp. 254 ff. The verbs are regularly in the same tense, so Herwerden's θνήιcκοντι here is unnecessary.

799. μάλιcτα: short for 'this is what I most desire': for this type of ellipse with μάλιcτα see Schwyzer, *Gr. Gr.* ii. 414 (d). **μέν με θέc:** this provides a better contrast with ἆρον ('lift me up and set me down') than would μέθεc, pace Wunder. For the line-end in three monosyllables (to which Radermacher objected) there are numerous parallels (e.g. from our play alone 462 οὐδ' ἂν εἰ, and, if the elision makes a difference, *Aj.* 1015 ὡc τὰ cά, 1108 μὴ cὺ φῆc, 1313 καὶ τὸ cόν).

801. εἰ δ'... ἀλλά: requests mentioning what the speaker most desires (μάλιcτα) are often followed by a reference to the next-best thing ('but if... at least'): see KG ii/2. 485-6. **οἶκτον ἴcχειc:** Jebb raised the possibility of οἶκτοc ἴcχει c' (already canvassed by Kuiper) only to dismiss it as 'needless'; but it may be thought to supply a clearer antithesis to the following ἀλλά μ'... πόρθμευcον. Cf. 673 n.

802. The plan for a private death anticipates Deianeira's secluded suicide.

803 ff. ἐπιcκήψαντοc ... cφε ... βρυχώμενον: for the lack of concord (arising from the emphasis placed on the initial genitive participle) see Moorhouse, p. 77.

COMMENTARY

805. cπαcμοῖcι: cf. Long, *Language and Thought*, pp. 20–1, on this and other Sophoclean -μός nouns 'denot[ing] violent action'.

806. ἐcόψεcθ': Reinhardt's idea (*Sophokles*, p. 225 n. (English trans., p. 244)) that this verb is addressed to the audience is effectively rebutted by D. Bain, *BICS* 34 (1987), 5: it is the chorus that Hyllus here speaks to. Cf. on 1080.

807. τοιαῦτα: for this summarizing formula at the end of a tragic *rhesis* see Pfeiffer, *Sitzb. d. Bayer. Akad. d. Wiss., phil.-hist. Kl.* 6 (1958), 26 = *Sophokles* (Wege der Forschung 95; 1967), 483–4.

807–8. βουλεύcαc' ... δρῶc': for the common antithesis of planning and devising see Barrett on Eur. *Hipp.* 649–50.

808–9. Δίκη ... Ἐρινύc τ': for the frequent connection of these two deities cf. Aesch. *Ag.* 1432–3, 1535–6, and Fraenkel on the latter.

809. Stinton, p. 140 (cf. Kraus, *WS* 20 (1986), 101–2), exposed the difficulties of the traditional text here (as traditionally interpreted) but later approved Dawe's Ἐρινῦc (*Studies* iii. 93). Both scholars (like F. Ferrari, *Studi sul testo di Sofocle* (Pisa 1983), 44–5) suppose that ἐπεύχομαι coming after a brief prayer, means 'I pray'. But Lloyd-Jones (in *Sophoclea*, p. 167) argues for the common meaning 'exult' (cf. *Il.* 5. 119, 11. 431; *Od.* 22. 411, Archil. fr. 134 W, Aesch. *Ag.* 1394, etc.). This would in itself obviate the difficulties which impressed Stinton.

810. προὔβαλεc: corrupted to προὔλαβεc in **lt**. For this sort of corruption (the reversal of three letters) in the Laurentian manuscript see Housman, *Journal of Philol.* 20 (1892), 40 = *Classical Papers* i. 220. It must, however, be admitted that an exact parallel for θέμιν προβάλλω and dative is hard to find (cf. LSJ s.v. προβάλλω II b 3). Jebb's citations of *Aj.* 830 and Aesch. *Eum.* 215 are nothing to the point, nor is Plato *Phaedr.* 241 E (quoted by Campbell, *Paralipomena*, p. 178) or Eur. fr. 82. 6 Austin εἰ μὲν ἀνδρὶ προὔβαλον δέμαc | τοὐμόν, (quoted by Lloyd-Jones, *Sophoclea*, pp. 167–8). Wunder's ἔριν for θέμιν (note θέμιc in the identical part of the preceding line), approved by Reeve, *GRBS* 11 (1970), 283–4 n. 2 (for the corruption involved see Jackson, *MS*, pp. 223 ff. ('unconscious repetitions by the copyist'), for the idiom cf. *Il.* 11. 529, and compare the construction ἐμβάλλω νεῖκόc τινι (LSJ s.v. ἐμβάλλω I. 3)) does not, perhaps, convey the right sense (what is the 'quarrel' or 'rivalry' between mother and son here?).

811. Cf. Eur. *Alc.* 151 γυνή τ' ἀρίcτη τῶν ὑφ' ἡλίωι. For sinisterly silent exits in S see Rau, *Paratragodia*, p. 152. The present instance is misunderstood by those present, like Jocasta's at *OT* 1076 ff.

814. Cf. fr. 928. 2 ἡ γὰρ cιωπὴ τὠγκαλοῦντι cύμμαχοc.

815–16. οὖροc ... | αὐτῆι γένοιτ' ... καλόc: the effective hyperbaton is well defended (as against the banalizing καλῶc) by J. H. Kells, *CR* 12 (1962), 111–12.

817–18. On the rhetorical point here conveyed ('a mother in name but not in deed') cf. M. Griffith, *HSCP* 82 (1978), 83 ff., esp. p. 86 n. 12.

819. ἑρπέτω χαίρουcα: equivalent to 'good riddance!': cf. Stevens, *Colloqial Expressions in Euripides*, p. 26.

819–20. For substantival τήνδ' resuming τὴν τέρψιν see Johansen and Whittle on Aesch. *Suppl.* 708. As they point out, the more frequent construction is for a neuter to resume a verbal phrase, as at 458 above. **τέρψιν ... λάβοι:** the noun is here used sarcastically for the opposite of its normal meaning, and the verb is indeed usually employed of enduring some evil (LSJ s.v. AII.1): [Eur.] *Med.* 43 cυμφορὰν λάβηι, *Hel.* 200 θάνατον ἔλαβε, etc., though cf. fr. 636. 1 χάρμα λάβοιc. Perhaps τέρψιc picks up χαίρουcα two words before, as if it meant 'let her go rejoicing': cf. on 227–8 above. Hyllus' speech ends with an effective antithesis (see on 468–9 above).

THIRD STASIMON (821–861)

821–30 = 831–40 *first strophe and antistrophe*

821/831	⏑ –⏑– – –⏑⏑–⏑⏑–	⏑e — D
822/832	– –⏑⏑–⏑⏑– –	— D —
823/833	–⏑– ⏑ –⏑– –ₕ ‖	e ⏑ e —
824/834	⏑◠⏑◠ ⏑◠⏑– ⏑–⏑–	ia. trim.
825/835	–◠⏑◠ ⏑◠⏑– ⏑–⏑–	ia. trim.
826a/836a	–⏑⏑–⏑–⏑ ‖	aristoph.
826b/836b	–⏑––	tr.
827/837	–⏑⏑⏑–––	?
828/838	–⏑⏑⏑–––	?
829/839	⏑◠◠⏑⏑	doch.
830/840	⏑–⏑– ⏑–⏐ ‖	ia. dim. cat.

'The most difficult linguistically of all the lyrics in the play' (Burton, p. 65), this is also the most metrically complex. For the '"impure", partly

COMMENTARY

dactylo-epitritic strophic pair' at 821 ff. ~ 831 ff. cf. Griffith, *Authenticity of PV*, pp. 40–1. On 827–8 and 837–8 see below on 846–7.

841–50 = 852–61 *second strophe and antistrophe*

841/852	−−−−−∪∪−	chor. dim. B
842a/853a	∪∪−∪∪−∪∪−∪	enop.
842b/853b	∪−∪− ∪−−	ia. dim. cat.
843/854	−∪−∪∪−⏓	pher.
844/855	⏑∪−∪∪−∪−	glyc.
845/856	⏓−∪− ⏑∪−∪∪−∪⏓‖	ia. + glyc.
846/857	−∪∪∪−⏓−ᴴ‖	?
847/858	−∪∪−−−	?
848/859	−−∪∪−−−ᴴ‖	chor. dim. (tel. 'dragged')
849/860	−−∪∪−−∪∪−−∪∪−	chor. trim.
850/861	−∪∪−−−‖‖	chor. dim. (aristoph. 'dragged')

Metrical complexity and textual corruption make interpretation of the first half of the second strophic pair very problematic. I follow the OCT's division (cf. *Sophoclea*, p. 168) of 842 ff. ~ 853 ff. (842a μεγάλαν προcορῶcα δόμοιcι, 842b–843 βλάβαν νέων ἀίccου-|cαν γάμων τὰ μὲν αὐτά), which presupposes Triclinius' δόμοιcι in 842 and Jebb's supplements in 852 ff. (see ad locc.). 846–7 are particularly difficult to analyse. See West, *GM*, p. 120, who very tentatively suggests that 846 could be regarded as two cretics (the second dragged in 857) or as a dochmius Kaibelianus, with 'what follows ... derived from it by successive mutations'. The metrical kinship with dochmiacs was observed by Maas, *GM*, § 129, in extenuation of the corruption at 846–7 (ἤ που ὀλοὰ ... ἤ που ἀδινῶν). 'The only parallel in drama for correption in the sequence ⏑ ∪ ⏑' is Ar. *Nub.* 512–13 (ἀνθρώπωι ὅτι): so Dover ad loc. See Addenda.

821. ἴδ': for the choral use of the imperative ('you-form') and in particular its combination with 822's ἡμῖν (the 'we-form') see Norden, *Aus altrömischen Priesterbüchern*, pp. 196 ff. For the self-address with voc. pl. cf. 212 above, Aesch. *ScT* 852 ὦ φίλαι, etc. **προcέμειξεν:** 'has approached': cf. LSJ s.v. II.1, Verdenius on Pind. *Isthm.* 2. 29. **ἄφαρ:** see on 134 ff. above.

LINES 821–827

822. θεοπρόπον: on this epic word (which recurs in tragedy only at *PV* 659) see Sideras, *Aeschylus Homericus*, p. 26.

823. παλαιφάτου: the Σ^γρ presumably originates from a supralinear gloss. Cf. Aesch. *Cho.* 32–3 τορὸς γὰρ [Φοῖβος] ὀρθόθριξ δόμων | ὀνειρόμαντις, and Sier on Aesch. *Cho.* 614.

824. ὅ τ' (or ὅτ') **ἔλακεν:** *vox propria* of oracles (*Ant.* 1094, Aesch. *Ag.* 1426, etc.). Here the subject is not so much τοὔπος in 822 as ὁ θεός implicit in τὸ θεοπρόπον. **τελεόμηνος:** usually of children born after the normal period of pregnancy (Arist. *HA* 585ᵃ20). According to F. Sommer, *Zur Geschichte der gr. Nominalkomposita* (Abh. d. Bayer. Ak. d. Wiss., phil.-hist. Kl. 27; 1948), 56, the word here 'ist an sich ein nüchternes Gebilde ... poetisch nur seine Verbindung mit ἄροτος'. **ἐκφέροι:** the verb is regularly intransitive ('issue, come to fulfilment'), as in *OC* 1424 ὁραῖς τὰ τοῦδε ... ὡς ἐς ὀρθὸν ἐκφέρει[33] μαντεύμαθ' (cf. LSJ s.v. V.2). Cf. χρόνος ἐξήκει of prophecies (*OT* 1011, *Phil.* 199). A transitive usage here would require an object (ἔπος supplied from 822's τοὔπος?). τελεόμηνον ... δωδέκατον ἄροτον was conjectured by Bergk. See Addenda.

825. δωδέκατος ἄροτος: the chorus's sudden and unexpected knowledge as to the precise period of time specified by the oracle is logically indefensible (cf. Schwinge, p. 97 n. 2) but dramatically necessary (see Appendix A) to produce the required impression of inescapable destiny. **ἄροτος:** 'season' in 69 above. **ἀναδοχάν:** Jebb, followed by LSJ, renders 'series, succession', the only instance of this meaning (the regular signification of διαδοχή) for this noun. The rendering 'submission' is suggested by the verb ἀναδέχομαι.

826. αὐτόπαιδι: cf. Sem. 7. 12 W αὐτομήτορα, Risch, *IF* 59 (1949), 271 = *Kl. Schr.*, p. 88. **ὀρθῶς:** cf. ἐς ὀρθόν of oracles' fulfilment in *OC* 1424 (cited on 824 ἐκφέροι).

827. κατουρίζει: the verb is a ἅπαξ and we have only analogy to help us decide whether its meaning here is transitive (with τοὔπος or ὁ θεός as subject) or intransitive. Unfortunately these analogies are themselves ambiguous: the simplex verb in *OT* 694 ff. ὅς γ' ἐμὰν γᾶν φίλαν ἐν πόνοις | ἀλύουσαν κατ' ὀρθὸν οὔρισας is transitive indeed, but of the two instances of ἐπουρίζω, in Ar. *Thesm.* 1226 ff. τρέχε νυν κατὰ τάχος ἐς κόρακας ἐπουρίσας it would be all too

---

[33] ἐκφέρεις Tyrwhitt.

COMMENTARY

easy to insert c(ε) as object of ἐπουρίϲαϲ in front of ἐπουρίϲαϲ and in Epicr. fr. 9. 3–4 KA τὴν νέαν δ' ἐπουρίϲαϲ | πλήρωϲον the accusative may be the object of both verbs or merely of πλήρωϲον. ἔπουροϲ has an active sense in 954.

828ff. The chorus's enlightenment as to the oracle's content and true meaning is as realistically inexplicable but as dramatically satisfying as its awareness of the time specified by the oracle (see on 825).

828. ὁ μὴ λεύϲϲων: for the equivalence of seeing and living cf. Aesch. *Ag.* 677 ζῶντα καὶ βλέποντα and Fraenkel ad loc., LSJ s.v. βλέπω III.2, W. Deonna, *Le Symbolisme de l'œil* (Paris 1965), 303 ff., esp. p. 309.

829. ἔτι ποτ' ἔτ' ἐπίπονον: an extraordinary combination of short syllables and short words (contrast the responding line 840). For the idea that the dead are free from toil see 1173 below.

831. φονίαι νεφέλαι: a very difficult metaphor to fathom. Let us start with the obvious meaning of νεφέλη: 'cloud'. The word has a wide range of metaphorical meanings in Greek. See e.g. Eur. *Med.* 108 νέφοϲ οἰμωγῆϲ, *Her.* 1140 ϲτεναγμῶν ... νέφοϲ, and Wilamowitz and Bond on the latter (on the former cf. Diggle, *CQ* 34 (1984), 53). But the general context and perhaps the proximity of the verb χρίω might lead us in the direction of the rendering offered by LSJ s.v. νεφέλη I.2 (metaph.) 'i.e. with his blood' cf. κελαινεφὲϲ αἷμα'. In Homer νεφέλη has a rich store of metaphorical connotations with death: see e.g. *Il.* 20. 417–18 νεφέλη δέ μιν ἀμφεκάλυψε | κυανέη and in general Bremer, *Licht und Dunkel in der frühgr. Dichtung*, index s.v. νεφέλη and νέφοϲ. The word is a favourite metaphor of Pindar (e.g. *Nem.* 9. 38 φόνου ... νεφέλαν, *Isthm.* 7 (6). 27 ἐν ταύται νεφέλαι αἵματοϲ). Or can νεφέλη here mean 'net', a sense it bears, for instance, in Ar. *Av.* 194, 528, Callim. *Aetia* fr. 75. 37, Satyrius, *AP* 6. 11. 2 = *Further Greek Epigrams* (Page) 324; cf. LSJ s.v. III 'fine bird net', Page on *AP* 6. 11. 2 (*Further Greek Epigrams*, p. 88)? That it can was first suggested by Wakefield (also by Dobree); this is strongly advocated by T. C. W. Stinton, *PCPS* 21 (1975), 90 ff., esp. pp. 92–3, opposed by Page in his review of Kamerbeek (*Gnomon* 32 (1960), 318). The netimagery would certainly fit in with a number of other passages in this play where Heracles' fate at the hands of his wife is compared to that of Agamemnon at Clytemnestra's, especially in terms of the deadly robe (cf. 1052 below, Aesch. *Ag.* 1580–1, and in general Kapsomenos, *Sophokles' Trachinierinnen und ihr Vorbild*, pp. 39 ff.). For the corruption

LINES 827-834

of νεφέλαι to νεφέλαν in Zo cf. E. L. B. Meurig-Davies, CR 63 (1949), 49.

832. ἀνάγκα: for the term's various connotations see Dover, *JHS* 93 (1973), 65 = *Greek and the Greeks*, p. 145. On our passage see in particular H. Schreckenberg, *Ananke: Untersuchungen zur Geschichte des Wortgebrauchs* (Zetemata 36; 1964), 2. Here the abstract stands for the more concrete 'poison' (cf. Hutchinson on Aesch. *ScT* 429).

833. πλευρά: governed by χρίει, or an internal accusative to προστακέντος; note the repetition προστακέντος . . . προστετακώς (836), which is 'characteristic of S's choral odes' (J. H. Kells, *CR* 11 (1961), 190 n. 1, citing examples).

834. τέκετο . . . ἔτεκε: thus the paradosis. The change from middle to active presented by this reading is hard to justify (that the active describes the mother's role, the middle the father's, is often true but there are numerous exceptions (cf., e.g., in close proximity *Il.* 2. 728 τὸν ἔτεκεν Ῥήνη, 742 τὸν . . . τέκετο . . . Ἱπποδαμεία: see in general A. Hoekstra, *Epic Verse before Homer* (Amsterdam 1981), 72 ff.). In the light of the similarly metaphorical ἐτεκ' ἔτεκε μεγάλαν . . . ἅδε νύμφα . . . Ἐρινύν at 893 ff. we are entitled to ask why the change of voice exhibited by the manuscripts occurs. Lloyd-Jones (*Sophoclea*, p. 168) suggests that (as at *OT* 1215 and *OC* 618) τέκετο could bear the general meaning 'originate'. (τεκνοῦσθαι is used of procreation in general rather than of actual parenthood at Eur. *Med.* 574 and fr. 317. 3 N[2]; note also *IT* 1262 Χθὼν ἐτεκνώσατο). In that case the hydra would be pictured as the parent of the poison on the shirt but death as its originator in a wider and more general sense. But such a distinction seems hard to parallel. On the other hand, since the same person usually bears *and* rears (naturally enough) when a literal usage of the relevant verbs is in a question (see e.g. *Od.* 2. 131 ἥ μ' ἔτεχ', ἥ μ' ἔθρεψε) we must also demand what the present metaphor gains by the variation which ἔτρεφε (Lobeck on *Aj*. 706) imports.. In fact such variation is very common in rhetorical structures of this kind. See e.g. *El.* 197 δόλος ἦν ὁ φράσας, ἔρος ὁ κτείνας, Eur. *Phoen.* 1576 ἂν ἔλαχ' Ἅιδας, ὦπασε δ' Ἄρης, Diggle on Eur. *Phaeth*. 99. It is particularly common in the case of the two verbs and concepts involved in our passage. M. L. West, *ZPE* 45 (1982), 7 n. 14, quotes *Il.* 2. 548 ὃν (sc. Ἐρεχθῆα) ποτ' Ἀθήνη θρέψε Διὸς θυγάτηρ, τέκε δὲ ζείδωρος ἄρουρα, Ibyc. 288 P Εὐρύαλε γλαυκέων χαρίτων

COMMENTARY

θάλος ... cὲ μὲν Κύπρις | ἅ τ' ἀγανοβλέφαρος Πειθὼ ...
θρέψαν, [Arion] 939. 9ff. P δελφῖνες, ἔναλα θρέμματα |
κουρᾶν Νηρεΐδων θεᾶν, | οὓς (West: ἃς) ἐγείνατ' Ἀμφιτρίτα
(further examples of coupling of the two verbs in C. Moussy, *Recherches
sur* τρέφω *et les verbes grecs signifiant 'nourrir'* (Paris 1969), 58–9).
τέκετο θάνατος: what Dodds on Eur. *Bacch.* 987ff. calls 'the conventional suggestion that inhuman conduct implies inhuman origin':
cf. *Il.* 16. 34–5 γλαυκὴ δέ cε τίκτε θάλαccα | πέτραι τ' ἠλίβατοι
ὅτι τοι νόος ἐcτὶν ἀπηνής. Compare further the remarks of West,
comm. on Hes. *Th.*, p. 34: 'when the Greek, in poem or proverb, wishes
to say that two things are significantly connected he ... says ... that
they are blood-relations' (see further ibid. n. 1, Handley on Men. *Dysc.*
88 ff.). A fairly close parallel to the present passage is Eur. *Tro.* 766 ff.
(Helen addressed by Hecuba) ὦ Τυνδάρειον ἔρνος, οὔποτ' εἶ
Διός, | πολλῶν δὲ πατέρων φημί c' ἐκπεφυκέναι, | Ἀλάcτορος
μὲν πρῶτον, εἶτα δὲ Φθόνου, | Φόνου τε Θανάτου θ' ὅcα τε γῆ
τρέφει κακά. Much the same metaphorical point can be made by
reference to rearing: see Vetta on Theogn. 1231. For αἰόλος used of
snakes see on 11–12 above.

835. The paradosis presents us with a choice between two undesirable
anomalies: either normal scansion of ἀέλιον and abnormal responsion
with 825 (ᾱ̆ε̆λῐο̆ν ~ -ο̆c ᾰ̆ρο̆το̆c) or normal responsion and abnormal
(indeed unique)[34] scansion of ἀέλιον (ᾰ̆ε̆λῐο̆ν ~ -ο̆c ᾰ̆ρο̆το̆c). Both
can be avoided by Seidler's (and Seebass's) transposition of ἀέλιον to
follow ἕτερον (so too Zieliński, p. 601 n. 15 = p. 357 n. 1), a course
rightly approved by West ((2), p. 526). Σ's πῶc ἂν ἕτερον ἥλιον ἢ
τανῦν ἴδοι is suggestive in this context. We may dispense, then, with
Wilamowitz's* πῶc ἄλιον ὅδ' ἂν ἕτερον.

836 ff. φάcματι is usually supposed corrupt (in this context it would
have to mean 'what appears as a hydra' (cf. 509 φάcμα ταυροῦ) and
what Heracles is here regarded as glued to can by no stretch of the
imagination be called hydra-shaped). The hydra is now dead, though
its venom lives on and can still wreak havoc—invisibly. Emendations
aiming at palaeographical plausibility (that is, involving a noun ending
in -μα) are listed by Jebb in his appendix on this passage. To them may
be added Pearson's ingenious νήματι (*CR* 39 (1925), 4), which takes its

---

[34] Eur. *Med.* 1252 (ἀελίου codd.: ἁλίου Hermann) is no counter-example.

LINES 834-838

inspiration from Wunder's νάματι. Hesych. s.v. νῆμα· ὕδωρ, ὕφαςμα is evidence of confusion between νῆμα ('thread', from the verb νέω (cf. LSJ s.v. B) 'spin') and νᾶμα ('stream', from the verb νάω 'flow'). Either νάματι or νήματι could have been ousted from Sophocles' text by a gloss ὑφάςματι, which might then have been curtailed to φάςματι by a scribe more interested in procuring metre than sense. The difficulty here is that neither word quite produces the required meaning, νάματι signifying 'stream' rather than 'venom' (cf. Wilamowitz on Eur. *Her.* 625), νήματι 'thread' rather than 'robe'. From the point of view of sense Blaydes's θρέμματι revived by A. A. Long, *GRBS* 8 (1967), 277, has more to commend it: it could be interpreted as harking back to 834's ἔτρεφε δ' αἰόλος δράκων (if Lobeck's emendation there is correct: see ad loc.).

Breaking away from the presumption that φάςματι must be corrupt, Lloyd-Jones (*YCS* 22 (1972), 265-6) has suggested that δεινοτάτωι is the guilty word, and should be replaced by δεινοτέρωι: H is envisaged by the chorus as now 'glued to a shape (φάςματι) more deadly than the hydra'. Comparatives and superlatives are certainly corrupted in manuscripts with great frequency (cf. Fraenkel, *Sitz. d. Bayer. Akad. d. Wiss., phil.-hist.* (1957), 48 n. 137 = *Kl. Beitr.* i. 316 n. 1, *Horace*, p. 20 n. 4). Lloyd-Jones's own alleged parallels for φάςμα as applicable to the shirt of Nessus hardly convince; but *El.* 197ff. may provide a better analogy: in that play the chorus describe the death of Agamemnon in the following terms: δόλος ἦν ὁ φράςας, ἔρος ὁ κτείνας (cf. *Tr.* 834), | δεινὰν δεινῶς προφυτεύςαντες | μορφάν. The vague word μορφά there, like φάςμα here, could have a sinister and uncanny connotation. δεινοτέρωι ὕδρας would constitute a 'mythological hyperbole' of the type discussed by Zagagi, *Tradition and Originality in Plautus*, pp. 15 ff., and *CQ* 36 (1986), 267 (cf. on 1046ff. below). See Addenda.

838 ff. The corresponding section of the strophe makes perfect sense with no addition, and the present passage can be made to yield the required metre by the deletion of Νέςςου. That (see on 828) might be alleged to be exactly the sort of glossing phrase that gets added to the text to explain a vague reference such as μελαγχαίτα. The question is, does the present passage make adequate sense without it, or is it the case, as Dawe's app. crit. alleges ad loc., that 'μελαγχαίτα nomen desiderat'. μελαγχαίτης is an epithet for the centaur Mimas in [Hes.] *Scut.* 186

COMMENTARY

and the name of a centaur in Diod. 4. 12. 7 and on the François Vase (for the possibility that it is a proper name in the 'Hesiodic' passage too see West, *CQ* 11 (1961), 140). On the basis of these occurrences can μελαγχαίτης here stand for the centaur Nessus in the way that χρυcοκόμης can stand for Apollo, κυανοχαίτης for Poseidon, without the need to add either deity's name? It may be objected (1) that the number of occasions on which μελαγχαίτης is used of a centaur would have to be far more numerous; (2) that to allude thus to a centaur is rather perverse, since 'black-haired' is by no means so obvious a way of referring to him or of encapsulating his vital characteristics as is 'golden-haired' for Apollo or 'sable-locked' for Poseidon. On the other hand Κενταύρου (831) at the start of the stanza might be thought sufficient to keep that notion to the fore of our minds, and κέντρ' at the stanza's end (840) may be another reminder (for the derivation of Κεντ-αῦροc from κεντέω in the sexual sense and αὔρα, presupposed by Pind. *Pyth.* 2. 44–5, cf. von der Mühll, *Mus. Helv.* 25 (1968), 227ff. = *Ausg. kl. Schr.* 245–6). T. C. W. Stinton, *PCPS* 21 (1975), 91, thinks μελαγχαίτα here is deliberately ambiguous as between the centaur and death (cf. *HH Dem.* 347 Ἄιδη κυανοχαῖτα, Eur. *Alc.* 439 Ἀίδαc ὁ μελαγχαίταc θεόc, *OT* 29–30 μέλαc δ' | Ἅιδης, *Epigr.* 1046B. 84 (Kaibel), Σ ad 856 below μέλαc ... ὁ θάνατοc, and my note ad loc.)[35] and detects a further reference to the corresponding situation in Aesch. *Ag.* (cf. on 831 above). If Νέccου is deleted (with Dindorf), we need not follow that scholar in also damning θ' ὕπο, words which are not so easily excluded as a gloss whose origin is obvious. Hermann read ὑπόφονα δολόμυθα (for θ' ὕπο φόνια δολιόμυθα), which gives responsion with 829 (θ' will then have been added to avoid the hiatus seemingly produced by Νέccου ὑπο-).

840. ἐπιζέcαντα: for other examples of this verb in tragedy see Rau, *Paratragodia*, p. 39 n. 50.

841. ὦν ... ἄοκνοc: the manuscripts' ἄοκνον would have to mean 'unhesitatingly, swiftly' (i.e. it would be adverbial, not (as Jebb) an epithet of βλάβαν in the next line (for personified βλάβη cf. on 843 below)), and this provides bad sense, since Deianeira did hesitate before her fatal decision. Besides, ἄοκνον entails a coupling of ὦν to

---

[35] See too Eur. *Hec.* 1105–6 τὸν ἐc Ἅιδα (Dindorf: ἀΐδα *fere codd.*: -δαν *v.l.*) | μελάγχρωτα πορθμόν (the *v.l.* advocated by Johansen and Whittle on Aesch. *Suppl.* 154–5).

the distant τὰ μὲν... τὰ δέ of 843–5, which is decidedly awkward. Musgrave's ὧν... ἄοκνος, on the contrary, provides perfect sense ('quorum... secura'), with an idiomatic backward reference at the start of the stanza (see on 122 above) and a no less idiomatic late introduction of D towards the end of the choral ode (cf. 523, 650).

842. δόμοιϲι: on Triclinius' reading here see the metrical scheme.

842–3. ἀΐϲϲουϲαν: βλάβη is more readily personified than marriages: cf. *Ant.* 1104.

843–4. αὐτὰ | προϲέβαλεν: the paradosis cannot be right as regards both οὔτι and προϲέβαλεν (which Σ ad loc. glosses with οὐκ ἔγνω, οὐ ϲυνῆκεν, foisting an unparalleled meaning upon the verb (hardly justified by Kamerbeek's citation of προϲέχειν τι = προϲέχειν τὸν νοῦν τινι), as does Campbell's no more tolerable rendering 'help to bring to pass'). Blaydes's αὐτὰ προϲέβαλεν is very much to the point: Deianeira herself applied the charm cf. 580–1 χιτῶνα τόνδ᾽ ἔβαψα, προϲβαλοῦϲ᾽ ὅϲα | ζῶν κεῖνοϲ εἶπε and note ad loc., 1138–9 ϲτέργημα γὰρ δοκοῦϲα προϲβαλεῖν ϲέθεν | ἀπήμιλαχ᾽ (Wunder, by contrast, kept οὔτι and emended the verb to προϲέλαβεν ('hanc quidem non adscivit'), i.e. of the two βλάβαι available (to be supplied from the βλάβαν of 842), to share her husband with another woman or to use the charm, she did not adopt the former and now bewails the latter. For the required sense of προϲλαμβάνω ('take to oneself') cf. *OC* 378–9 προϲλαμβάνει | κῆδόϲ τε καινὸν καὶ ξυναϲπιϲτὰϲ φίλουϲ and Eur. *Med.* 885 κῆδοϲ ... προϲλαβών, both in marital contexts. For the type of corruption presupposed see on 810 above). **ἀπ᾽:** the ἀπό/ἐπί confusion is very common (see Johansen and Whittle on Aesch. *Suppl.* 909); for another instance see 855 below. Wunder's οὐλίαιϲι and Dale's οὐλομέναιϲ (*MATC* i. 31) are not required by the metre).

846. ὀλοά: on the 'passive' sense here and at *Pers.* 962 see Schuursma, p. 50; feminine singular adjective or neuter plural adverb; cf. *Il.* 23. 10 ὀλοοῖο... γόοιο.

847–8. χλωρὰν ... ἄχναν: 'fresh, warm' (cf. on 1055 below): used of tears in Dioscorides *AP* 7. 31. 4 = *HE* 1578 etc.

848. τέγγει δακρύων ἄχναν: for this verb with a cognate accusative see Verdenius, *Miscellanea Tragica* (Kamerbeek Festschrift), p. 461; on the different meanings of ἄχνη see Pearson on fr. 45.

849. δολίαν: of Nessus' trickery: cf. 839–40 δολόμυθα.

COMMENTARY

850. ἄταν: another important word kept back to the end of the stanza (see on 895 below). For its close connection with μοῖρα (mentioned in the previous line) cf. Eur. *Med.* 986 ff. τοῖον εἰς ἕρκος πεσεῖται | καὶ μοῖραν θανάτου δύστανος· ἄταν δ' | οὐκ ὑπεκφεύξεται and J. Stallmach, *Ate* (Beitr. z. kl. Phil. 18; 1968), 51.

851. παγὰ δακρύων: for the 'flood of tears' metaphor see Bond on Eur. *Her.* 449–50, Kassel on Men. *Sic.* 219. On the asyndeton see next n.

852. ὦ πόποι: a Homeric exclamation (cf. Sideras, *Aeschylus Homericus*, p. 98) which occurs at *OT* 167 and in Aeschylus (*Pers.* 731, 852, *Eum.* 145) but is shunned by Euripides. Kranz, *Stasimon*, p. 197, lists other choral odes whose final antistrophe is marked off in some way from the preceding stanzas, usually by means of an initial exclamation, here by initial asyndeton followed by exclamation.

854 ff. The corruption here is very serious and certainty as to the original wording unattainable. Presumably the general sense was that of 1058 ff., that D has brought Heracles to a pitch of suffering which his worst enemies failed to achieve against him. The ἀνάρςιοι here will be the giants, beasts, and the like more fully enumerated there: cf. Eur. *Her.* 852 f. ἀνέςτηςεν μόνος | τιμὰς πιτνούςας ἀνοςίων ἀνδρῶν ὕπο. Jebb's supplements, placed in the text by the editors of the OCT, are not totally secure, but they provide suitable sense and metre (see the metrical scheme), and (in the case of ⟨ὑπ'⟩ οὔπω) a plausible *corruptelae ratio*.

855. For the confusion of ἀπο(-) and ἐπι(-) see above on 843–4. **οἰκτίςαι:** consecutive epexegetic infinitive.

856. κελαινὰ λόγχα: Σ ad loc. explains the colour epithet by stating μέλας ... ὁ θάνατος. 'The primary reference is presumably to the colour of the metal (μέλας ςίδηρος, Hes. *Op.* 151), but both words have also the sinister associations of Lat. "ater", Eng. "dark", which may have been felt in all these passages' (Dodds on Eur. *Bacch.* 628). See further Wilamowitz on Eur. *Her.* 780 κελαινὸν ἅρμα,[36] Stanford on *Aj.* 231, Kannicht on Eur. *Hel.* 1656. **λόγχα προμάχου δορός:** for λόγχη/-αι dependent on the genitive of δόρυ see Eur. *Hel.* 1152 λόγχαιςί τ' ἀλκαίου δορός and Kannicht ad loc.

857. θοὰν νύμφαν ἄγαγες: θοᾶι Musgrave, but θοάν could be predicative with ἄγαγες: cf. Eur. *Hipp.* 550 ζεύξας'... δρομάδα ναΐδ'

---

[36] Though Wilamowitz regards our passage as 'verdorben'.

LINES 850-863

ὅπωc (also of Heracles' abduction of Iole): do both passages draw on a lost source (e.g. the Οἰχαλίαc ἅλωcιc)? Oehler, *Mythologische Exempla in der älteren gr. Dichtung*, p. 89 n. 1, observes that in both passages Iole is identified by her place of origin (νύμφαν ... ἀπ' ... Οἰχαλίαc ~ οἴκων ... ἀπ' Εὐρυτίων ... ναῖδ'), not her name.

858–9. αἰπεινᾶc ... Οἰχαλίαc: cf. 354 ὑψίπυργον Οἰχαλίαν.

861. πράκτωρ: again a weighty word kept back to the end: the title was used of Zeus in 251, of Aphrodite here.

CHORUS AND NURSE (862–895)

863–78: iambic trimeters except 862 (ἰώ μοι), 865 (τί φημί;), and 868 (ξύνεc δέ).

880	⏑ – – ⏑ –	doch.
881	– – ⏑ – – – ⏑ ⟨– ⏒ – ⏑ –⟩	ia. trim.
882	– – ⏑ – ⏑ – ⏑ –	ia. dim.
883	– – – ⏑ ⏑ – ⏑ –	glyc.
884	⏑ – ⏑ – ⏑ – ⏑ ⏕	ia. dim.
885	– ⏑ ⏑ – ⏑ ⏑ ⏕ ‖	hem. (or – ⏑ ⏑ – ⏑ ⏕ doch.)
886	⏑ ⏑ – ⏑ ⏑ – ⏑ ⏑ – ⏑	enop.
887	– ⏑ – ⏑ – –	ia. dim. sync. cat. (cr. + bacch.)
888	⏑ – ⏑ – ⏑ – ⏑ – ⏑ – ⏑ –	ia. trim.
889	⏑ – ⏑ – – – ⏑ – ⏑ – ⏑ –	ia. trim.
890	⏑ – – ⏑ – ⏑	2 bacch.
891	– – ⏑ – – – ⏑ – – – ⏑ ⏑	ia. trim.
892	⏑ – – ⏑ – –	2 bacch.
893	⏕ ⏕ ⏕ ⏑ –	doch.
894	⏑ ⏑ – ⏑ – ⏑ – –	anacr.
895	⏑ – ⏑ – ⏑ – ⏑ ‖‖	ia. dim. cat.

862. Meineke not unreasonably introduces an exclamation for the Nurse to clarify the chorus' anguished reaction (*Analecta Sophoclea* (1863), 300).

863 ff. Unlike the OCT, some scholars (e.g. Pearson) envisage a change of speakers here: for the technique whereby a stasimon is followed by three single voices expressing anxiety and uncertainty cf. Eur. *Her.* 815 ff., where the trimeters are likewise interrupted.

COMMENTARY

863. πότερον ἐγὼ μάταιος: cf. fr. 58 μάτην ἀλυκτῶ, Eur. *El.* 747 δοκῶ κενή. **μάταιος:** used of the female chorus: see on 163 above.

864. δι' οἴκων: 'a cry arising *in* the house': for διά as implying merely 'motion or presence within an area' see Moorhouse, p. 102.

865. τί φημι; φῶμεν Nauck, but for the singular see Kaimio, *The Chorus of Greek Drama within the Light of the Person and Number Used*, pp. 65 ff. On the interjection here (and at *OT* 1471) see Moorhouse, p. 159, rightly preferring 'What do I say it is?' (with reference to a mysterious noise in each case) to 'Do I speak sense?' (presupposing an unlikely equivalence of φημί and λέγω: contrast *OT* 1475 λέγω τί;). For comparable 'interrogative exclamations' in tragedy see Fraenkel on Aesch. *Ag.* 1216.

866–7. ἠχεῖ ... κωκυτόν: an easy extension of the principle of the internal accusative, with κωκυτόν replacing the expected ἀχάν: see Moorhouse, pp. 39–40, LSJ s.v. ἠχέω II. **οὐκ ἄσημον:** cf. Eur. *El.* 749 τάδ' οὐκ ἄσημα πνεύματ'.

868–9. ξύνες δὲ | τήνδ': for similar 'imperatival exclamations' see Fraenkel on Aesch. *Ag.* 1216. The present instance differs from e.g. *Ichn.* 132 ἄκουε δή by having a subordinate clause attached.

869. Choricius of Gaza 1. 93 may supply the correct emendation here: for the consequent κατηφὴς καὶ cυνωφρυωμένη cf. Eur. *Alc.* 777 cτυγνῶι προcώπωι καὶ cυνωφρυωμένωι. κατηφής is well attested, M. Schmidt's ἀγηθής (anticipated by Herwerden, *Exerc. Crit.* (1862), 126) not at all (though conjectured at fr. 583. 10 in a phrase variously transmitted as ἀήθη or ἀληθῆ δώμαθ': see Radt ad loc. for details) even if supported by analogous forms such as εὐγηθής (Eur. *Her.* 792).

871–2. The familiar tragic motif of the ἀρχὴ κακῶν (cf. Kannicht on Eur. *Hel.* 229 ff.).

871. παῖδες ... ἡμίν: such plurals are always used in such amoebaea when the conversation begins with the arrival of one of the participants: see Kaimio, *The Chorus of Greek Drama within the Light of the Person and Number Used*, p. 231.

872. δῶρον Ἡρακλεῖ τὸ πόμπιμον: Zieliński (cited on 874 ff.) objected that the Nurse knows nothing of this gift, but for comparable dramatic economy see 934 below and note ad loc.; for the postponement of the articular verbal adjective see Bruhn, *Anhang*, § 161. For the

LINES 863-874

'passive' use of πόμπιμος here and at Eur. *Hipp.* 579 cf. Schuursma, p. 51.

873. Cf. Eur. *Her.* 530 γύναι, τί καινὸν ἦλθε δώμασιν χρέος; But καινοποιηθέν in our passage is otherwise a late prose word (LSJ s.v.).

874 ff. 'Characters of low social standing (except the Phrygian in the *Orestes*) are never given lines in sung metres, but are given instead anapaests, like the Nurse in the *Hippolytus*, or hexameters like the Old Man in the *Trachiniae* [below, lines 976 ff.]' (Maas, *GM*, § 76). In *Zeitschr. für das Gymnasialwesen* 65 (1911), 253 = *Kl. Schr.*, pp. 47–8, the same scholar observed that the apparent contradiction of this aesthetically based rule at 886–7 can be removed if the phrase cτονόεντοc ἐν τομᾶι cιδάρου is sung by the chorus, not the Nurse. Building on these observations, L. J. D. Henderson, *Maia* 28 (1976), 24, proposed further slight modifications of the paradosis which not only preserve the rule but eliminate other quite independent difficulties.

This is one way of proceeding with the problems to hand. An alternative approach applies large-scale remedies. A. M. Dale, in her review of Dain (*CR* 6 (1956), 106), pointedly referred to 'the confusion of the kommos *Tr.* 876–95, where question and answer continually elude each other', and her massive reordering of this passage in *MATC* i. 32 has been partially approved by D. J. Mastronarde, *Contact and Discontinuity*, p. 120, on the ground that there is no 'dramatic point' to the manuscripts' presentation. However, the technique allows 'the news of Deianeira's death' to be 'revealed gradually, point by point, in a prolonged series of statement and counter-statement', as M. Alexiou, *The Ritual Lament in Greek Tradition* (Cambridge 1974), 137, puts it; she further observes that 'this technique of catechistic questions is an integral part of the structure of many tragic laments'. Zieliński (p. 593 n. 16 = p. 347 n. 1) boldly deleted 871–9 (and 891 and 898 ff. into the bargain) as a large-scale interpolation intended to replace the lyrics at 882–3 (he compared the aim of the interpolation at Eur. *Hipp.* 871–3, which seems designed as substitute for 866 ff.: see Barrett's note on the former, but cf. Mastronarde, *Phoenix* 32 (1978), 127 n. 95). The lines thus removed certainly labour under a number of individual oddities of expression (see ad locc.). (When Bernard Knox writes in defence of [Eur.] *IA* 1–163 (*YCS* 22 (1972), 258–9 = *Word and Action*, p. 287) 'if the occurrence of a word which is found elsewhere only in prose is to be reckoned as a count against authenticity one trembles to think of the

COMMENTARY

fate of e.g. Sophocles, *Trachiniae* 873–91', he overlooks Zieliński's treatment of just that passage.) See Addenda.

874–5. 'This is one of those proverb-like turns of phrase which a homely speaker would use in the desire to be impressive'—so Jebb, implausibly attributing to S an interest in the psychology of a very minor character. The solemn euphemism is more relevant to Deianeira's status and importance in the drama than to the station in life of the speaker. The form of the statement, with its riddling and paradoxical negative phrase ἐξ ἀκινήτου ποδός, is stylistically akin to a certain type of kenning (see on 1051–2 below). On the concept of death as a journey see Gow–Page on Mnasalces *AP* 7. 194. 1 = *HE* 2651–2 (cf. Gow, *CR* 6 (1956), 92) and Lattimore, *Themes in Greek and Latin Epitaphs* (Urbana, Ill. 1942), 169.

875. ἐξ ἀκινήτου ποδός: cf. Theocr. *Id.* 7. 6–7 Βούριναν ὅς ἐκ ποδὸς ἄνυε κράναν κτλ.; for phrases employing ἐκ in a similar manner cf. *El.* 455 ἐξ ὑπερτέρας χερός, *OT* 528 ἐξ ὀμμάτων δ' ὀρθῶν τε κἀπ' ὀρθῆς φρενός, Bruhn, *Anhang*, § 68.1; cf. Diggle, *GRBS* 14 (1973), 249, Dawe, *The Collation and Investigation of Manuscripts of Aeschylus*, p. 185; the whole line was denounced by Zieliński as 'der fatalste Vers im ganzen Sophokles' (as cited above on 874 ff.).

876. οὐ δή ποθ': a characteristically Sophoclean collocation: see Denniston, *GP*[2], p. 223. Dover's deletion of this line (*ap.* Dawe[2]) is as inappropriate as most of the small-scale tamperings that try to remove repetition in this passage (see p. 207). **πάντ' ἀκήκοας:** distinguish from πάντ' ἀκήκοας λόγον = *dixi* (*Aj.* 480; cf. *Phil.* 1240).

877. τέθνηκεν ἡ τάλαινα: for the chorus's incredulous response to an announcement of death cf. *OC* 1583 ὄλωλε γὰρ δύστηνος. Our line is deleted by R. H. Allison, *Eranos* 81 (1983), 59 ff., who is offended by the triple statement of Deianeira's death within seven lines; but see above, p. 207, and note on 876.

878. τάλαιν' ὀλέθρου: so Blaydes. The paradosis is τάλαιν' ὀλεθρία, and Zieliński (as cited on 874 ff.); declared the second of these epithets as applied to Deianeira 'sinnlos'; for 'the rare personal sense "belonging to death"' which ὀλέθριος can bear see West, *BICS* 26 (1979), 115. Whether this applies here is less certain, and Blaydes may well have been right.

879. On the difficulties here see Henderson (as cited on 874 ff.), pp. 23–4 (and recall that Zieliński deleted 871–9). Hermann's remedy (pre-

LINES 874-888

supposing dittography) still leaves us with an unconvincing πρός γε πρᾶξιν (for πρός = 'with regard to' see Headlam on Aesch. *Ag.* 835), which may be removed by Nauck's cχετλιώτατ' ἐξέπραξεν or Henderson's own cχετλιώταθ' ἅπερ ἔπραξεν. For cχέτλιος with the required meaning ('foolhardy', 'rash') cf. J. R. Wilson, *AJP* 92 (1971), 294 n. 8.

880. γύναι: used by females addressing another woman (as in *HH Dem.* 213, 225 etc.). For γύναι as a form of address see 193 above.

881. διηίcτωcεν: the verb 'is found nowhere except as a conjecture of Grenfell and Hunt at Pindar *Paean* 6. 96 (rejected by Bowra and not recorded by Snell)' (Knox, as cited on 874 ff.). Henderson suggests the supplement ⟨ἀμφήκει ξίφει⟩ after this verb in order to give the Nurse a complete iambic trimeter and explain how (at 882) the chorus know D used an αἰχμά. Lloyd-Jones (*Sophoclea*, pp. 169–70), arguing that the emphatic tone of 891 suggests that line to be the first specific mention of D's suicide, prefers to fill out 881 as ⟨τ⟩αὐτὴν διηίcτωcεν ⟨ἄμφηκες ξίφος⟩, which will leave open until 891 the possibility that D (like Abimelech, Cassius, or Nero) got someone to stab her. But Zieliński deletes 891 (see above).

884 ff. ἐμήcατο ... ἀνύcαcα: equivalent to ἐμήcατο καὶ ἄνυcε: see Page on Gaetulicus *AP* 7. 71. 3–4 (*Further Greek Epigrams*, p. 56) for similar constructions, and cf. Gow, *CQ* 1 (1951), 115, on 'this idiom, in which verb and participle as it were change places'.

885. πρὸς θανάτωι θάνατον: for this sort of phrase (πρὸς κακοῖc κακά vel sim.) cf. Gygli-Wyss, *Das nominale Polyptoton*, p. 75 n. 3 (cf. p. 139 n. 2).

886. Cf. Anacreon fr. 347. 7 τλῆμον[.]c τομῆι cιδήρου; for our passage's instrumental ἐν cf. *Ant.* 1003 cπῶντας ἐν χηλαῖcιν.

888. 'μάταιος, when used in the voc., combines pity and reproach in varied proportions' (Gow on Theocr. *Id.* 15. 4); the word therefore seems perfectly appropriate here and there is no call to follow Conington, who suggested μαῖα ('a familiar and affectionate form of address to old women-servants (nurse or house-keeper)': Dale, ed. Eur. *Alc.*, p. 85). Dawe (*Studies* iii. 93), followed by the OCT, prefers the exclamatory neuter plural—ὦ μάταια—on grounds of both sense and metre; the second argument has more weight since a bacchius in the second metron of the trimeter would be unusual. For ὦ followed by neuter plural cf. Aesch. *Ag.* 1214 ἰού, ἰού, ὦ ὦ κακά. See Addenda.

COMMENTARY

889. πληcία παραcτάτιc: for other such references in tragedy to proximity to murder or death cf. Kaibel on *El.* 920.

890. τίc ἧνεν; Wunder's emendation for τίc ἧν; πῶc; (Dawe prints Page's τίc ἧνε;), but apart from the objection that, as West ((2), p. 525) observes, this would most naturally mean 'Who was seeing it through?', the chorus have long since been told that Deianeira killed herself and cannot still be asking[37] a literal question of this sort. The same difficulty meets West's interpretation (loc. cit.) of the paradosis as meaning τίc ἧν (sc. ὁ δράcαc); Wunder supposed that τίc ἧν; would have to refer back to the question of the last line but one: 'what was the deed of violence?', and this is surely right (though he himself emended). **φέρ᾽ εἰπέ:** on the phrase see Stevens, *Colloquial Expressions in Euripides*, p. 42.

891. αὐτὴ πρὸc αὑτῆc: the same phrase, of the same act of suicide, at 1132 below. For similarly emphatic (and postponed) announcements of suicide cf. *OT* 1237 (the same phrase), *Aj.* 906, *Ant.* 1177 (αὐτοc πρὸc αὑτοῦ). **χειροποιεῖται** recurs only in late prose (cf. Knox (as cited on 874ff.), p. 259 = p. 287 and n. 53).

892. τί φωνεῖc; the OCT (see above on 881) so orders the text that D's suicide is only clearly revealed in 891. If we reject this approach, the chorus have learnt the truth some time ago, so that τί φωνεῖc; cannot be a genuine question indicative of surprise. Even given the OCT's arrangement, we may still conclude that these two words are not so much a question as an exclamation of horror: 'What dreadful news you bring!' Collard on Eur. *Suppl.* 1064 discusses a similar use of τί φῄc in stichomythia as 'an exclamation following a clear statement'. Cf. Mastronarde, *Contact and Discontinuity*, p. 12. For analogous uses of τί questions, not as literal requests for information but as emotional reactions, see K. J. Dover, *Maia* 15 (1963), 25 = *Greek and the Greeks*, p. 305; cf. above on 316. See Addenda.

893 ff. A. M. Dale, in *Greek Poetry and Life* (Murray Festschrift), 188–9 = *Collected Papers*, p. 7 (cf. *MATC* i. 32), rejects ἔτεκεν ἔτεκε μεγάλαν | ἁ νέορτοc ἅδε νύμφα | δόμοιc (Wilamowitz, *Gr. Versk.* p. 609, following Nauck), which presents us with a dimeter (two

---

[37] Wunder had already combined τίc ἧνεν with the ejection of πῶc. Since he also remembered to change 881's αὐτὴν διηιcτωcεν to ἄτη νιν ἥίcτωcεν his approach is at least free from the second of the criticisms that can be levelled against the remedy preferred by Dawe and Page, as is the OCT's treatment.

210

LINES 889-899

cretics) plus trochaic dimeter, since 'a division into cola which makes an iambic metron ... follow upon an acatalectic trochaic – ∪ – –, without even a grammatical pause, is surely an intolerable violation of the "principle of alternation"' (cf. Maas, *GM*, § 43). Her own interpretation follows Schroeder and Pearson in emending 893 to ἔτεκ' ἔτεκε μεγάλαν ἁ | νέορτος ἅδε νύμφα | δόμοισι τοῖσδ' Ἐρινύν, an iambic dimeter followed by two ia. dim. catalectic as 'twin clausulae'. Against this, T. C. W. Stinton, *BICS* 22 (1975), 107 n. 27, objects to the 'impossible form of cretic' in 893 (∪ ∪ cr. ∪ ∪ + ∪ ∪ cr.). He prefers (p. 96) ἔτεκεν ἔτεκε μεγάλαν | ἁ νέορτος ἅδε νύμ|φα δόμοις τοῖσδ' Ἐρινύν, where the successive bicipites in the opening ∪ ∪ cr. ∪ ∪ + ∪ ∪ cr. are likewise odd. A likelier solution was advanced by L. P. E. Parker *ap.* Easterling's commentary (p. 186): ἔτεκεν ἔτεκεν μεγάλαν | νέορτος ἅδε, comparing for the fully resolved cretic *OT* 208. But the editors of the OCT prefer Schroeder's ἔτεκ' ἔτεκε and then μεγάλαν | ἀνέορτος ἅδε, comparing (cf. *Sophoclea*, p. 170) *Ant.* 611 ~ 622 for the rare solitary anacreontic.

893. ἔτεκε: for τίκτω of the begetting of evil see Eur. fr. 732N² ῥώμη ... τίκτει βλάβην, Aesch. *Suppl.* 498 θράσος τέκηι φόβον. Cf. above on 834.

894. ἀνέορτος: ἁ νέορτος is the reading of Σ, but ἀνέορτος is preferred by Wilamowitz* (and Lloyd-Jones *ap.* Stinton, loc. cit., p. 96, and in *Sophoclea*, p. 170). Cf. Eur. *El.* 310 for the adjective.

895. Ἐρινύν: for the postponement of the fatal word see Fraenkel on Aesch. *Ag.* 681 ff., Sier on Aesch. *Cho.* 652.

FOURTH EPISODE (896-946)

896. ἄγαν γε: see Bond on Eur. *Her.* 1414 for the meaning 'very much so'.

896-7. πλησία | ἔλευσσες: πλησίον coni. Lobeck, but cf. *El.* 640 παρούσης τῆσδε πλησίας, Harrison, *CR* 55 (1941), 25. 'Apod. aor. with ἄν: ἔλευσσες is durative "if you had been observing", and the aor. is not in classical use' (Moorhouse, p. 280). For the idea that seeing a sorrowful deed increases one's feelings of pity cf. *El.* 761 ff. (at the end of the Paedagogus' deception-speech).

898-9. The two lines were deleted by Hermann. The repetition need not

COMMENTARY

be offensive, however, provided our approach is not excessively realistic (cf. above, p. 207) but rather directed to formal criteria. For the double use of material, first in lyrics, then in the calmer context of iambic trimeters, see above, headnote to first stasimon (497ff.). For narrative introduced by a single line see above on 749.

898. χεὶρ γυναικεία: for this 'metonymic use of χείρ for the whole person' see Johansen and Whittle on Aesch. *Suppl.* 604. For the adjective in -ειος instead of the genitive noun see on 51 above. **κτίcαι:** the only instance of the verb in LSJ s.v. (6) with the meaning 'perpetrate a deed'.

899. δεινῶc γε: (sc. κτίcαι from 898): cf. *El.* 805 δεινῶc δακρῦcαι.

900. ἐπεὶ παρῆλθε: ἐπεὶ γὰρ ἦλθε Schaefer, and ἐπεὶ γάρ is indeed a regular formula of introduction to the main narrative of a messenger speech (cf. on 9 and 475 above); see Eur. *Alc.* 158, *IA* 1543, *Rhes.* 762; cf. *OT* 1241 ὅπως γὰρ ὀργῆι χρωμένη παρῆλθ' ἔcω | θυρῶνος, *Ant.* 407 ὅπως γὰρ ἥκομεν, *OC* 1587 ὡς μὲν γάρ. But for the commencement of a narrative in asyndeton after an introductory line ('if you want to find out, listen to me') see 749–50, where the asyndetic clause, as here, is relative (ὅθ'); cf. 555ff. above. Elsewhere (and particularly in Euripides) a messenger-speech can begin thus in asyndeton without any introductory line (e.g. Eur. *Med.* 1136–7 ἐπεὶ τέκνων cῶν ἦλθε δίπτυχος γονὴ | cὺν πατρί, καὶ παρῆλθε νυμφικοὺς δόμους; for other examples see Ritchie, *The Authenticity of the Rhesus of Euripides* (Cambridge 1964), 253). Contrast ἐπεὶ δ' ἀφίκτο at the start of the messenger's main narrative at *OC* 1590. *OT* 1241 and Eur. *Med.* 1137 (cited above) further remind us that παρῆλθε is the *mot juste* for entering the palace (cf. also *El.* 1337, Eur. *Hipp.* 108, etc.).

901–3. Deleted by Wunder, followed by e.g. Tycho, pp. 157ff., and Kranz, *Jhsb. d. Philol. Vereins zu Berlin* 47 (1921), 33 = *Stud. zur antik. Lit. und ihrem Nachwirken*, p. 284; 901–2 are convincingly defended by Winnington-Ingram, *BICS* 16 (1969), 44ff., esp. 46, on the grounds that 'δέμνια sets a theme in operation and suggests a course of action to Deianeira. It reminds her ... of the imminent return of Heracles and leads to her action at 915–16 ...' Furthermore, 'it is necessary that Hyllus should still be [in the palace] when the Nurse goes to fetch him (927f.); and he is therefore given something to do which will at once detain him ... and keep him out of Deianeira's way'. Line 903, however, remains difficult: see ad loc.

901. εἶδε: cf. Verg. Aen. 4. 648–9: 'postquam Iliacas vestes notumque cubile | conspexit' (sc. Dido). **κοῖλα δέμνια:** the epithet has been called into doubt and is difficult to parallel precisely, but is adequately justified by Hermann as an appropriate way of describing the slack sort of bier (with a hollow in the middle) required for the ailing Heracles' transport.

902. ἄψορρον: the epic word (cf. Sideras, *Aeschylus Homericus*, p. 51) is frequently used by S, never by Euripides; *PV* 1021 uses it adverbially, as here and at e.g. *El.* 53.

903. Both the place where and the reason why D conceals herself are obscure and unexplained as the text stands, and Meineke may have been right to delete this line (cf. on 901 ff.), whose statement about D hiding herself away contradicts the immediately following account of her actions. **ἐcίδοι:** on the optative see the discussion by Moorhouse, p. 275, who rejects Jebb's interpretation of it as deliberative (as if dependent on οὐκ οἶδεν, οὐκ ἔχει που: but this is hard to supply from κρύψαc' ἑαυτήν), and the possibility of an epic-style final relative clause (cf. *Od.* 15. 458: ἄγγελον ἧκαν ὅς ἀγγείλειε) justified by the passage's occurrence in a *rhesis*, in favour of a construction analogous to ἵνα: 'what more natural than that S. should innovate and give ἔνθα (already used with the fut. in local/final sense) the same opt. construction?' Cf. ὅπωc ... ἀντώιη above.

904 ff. The general similarities between this passage and the farewell which Alcestis bids her house in Euripides' play (152 ff.) have long been recognized and discussed (see Schwinge, pp. 42 ff., esp. 62 ff., Kapsomenos, *Sophokles' Trachinierinnen und ihr Vorbild*, pp. 20 ff.), most recently by Lesky, *Miscellanea Tragica* (Kamerbeek Festschrift), pp. 213 ff. D's farewell to the characteristic features of the life she has led is that of a typical Sophoclean hero or heroine: cf. Heracles' words at 1089 ff. and cf. Schwinge, p. 61 n. 4. Note too Schwinge's explanation of the central point in the whole episode (p. 63): 'Durch die Abschiedsszene ... wird er darüber unterrichtet, daß D. nicht etwa aus Trotz, Verzweiflung, Haß gegen Herakles oder eigenem Schuldbewußtsein—die Tragödie höbe sich selbst damit auf—ihr Leben beendete, sondern ihrem Wesen treu blieb, ihr Schicksal annahm und gerade dadurch die Liebe zu Herakles bewahrte.' Cf. my remarks above, p. 149.

904. βρυχᾶτο: this verb, positioned at the start of the line, like

COMMENTARY

φρούρουν at 915 below, φορεῖθ᾽ at *El.* 715, etc. (see on 767) is of the unaugmented epic type characteristic of a messenger-speech (cf. Page on Eur. *Med.* 1141, L. Bergson, *Eranos* 51 (1953), 121 ff., and *Rh. Mus.* 102 (1959), 9 ff., Collard's commentary on Eur. *Suppl.*, ii. 275).
βωμοῖϲι προϲπίπτουϲ᾽: cf. Eur. *Alc.* 170–1 πάνταϲ δὲ βωμοὺϲ οἳ κατ᾽ Ἀδμήτου δόμουϲ | προϲῆλθε.

905. γένοιντ᾽ ἐρῆμοι: Nauck's slight change of the paradosis γένοιτ᾽ ἐρήμη has won general approval (see especially Jebb's eloquent approbation: 'She is saying *farewell* to the surroundings of happier days)', but can be excluded on a technicality: **κλαιε:** interpretation of *ΚΛΑΙΕ* as a verb suffering aphaeresis or prodelision of its syllabic augment rather than an anomalous unaugmented verb in the middle of a line (cf. on 767 above) is advocated by Bergson (cited in the last n.), p. 123 (cf. on 381 above). This is surely right. But whereas prodelision after the manuscripts' -η is perfectly in order (again see on 381), the same phenomenon following Nauck's -οι would be a good deal less certain. Platnauer, *CQ* 10 (1960), 142, denies that ε is ever prodelided after -οι in Greek drama, except when 'the exclamation οἵ causes the prodelision of the epsilon of ἐγώ'. The only (dubious) cases cited by Bergson, pp. 123–4, are two passages from Aesch. *Pers.* (310 | κυκώμενοι (v.l. νικώμενοι) κύριccον and 490 ἔνθα δὴ πλεῖϲτοι θάνον). Broadhead ad loc. classes the first as 'omission of syllabic augment', and our earliest extant Greek tragedy with its plethora of Homeric features (on its relatively vast number of unaugmented verbs see Sideras, *Aeschylus Homericus*, pp. 258–9) is no automatic guide concerning augment or prodelision as to what is proper in later plays. Note, at all events, that Blaydes conjectured ἔνθα πλεῖϲτοι δὴ 'θάνον at 490 and that several emendations have been produced which remove the anomaly of κύριccον in 310 (see Dawe, *Repertory of Conjectures on Aeschylus* (Leiden 1965), 47). Jebb's 'Those words could certainly mean, "that she had become desolate"—nor is the plaint less natural because death is so near' is an adequate explanation of the paradosis.

905–6. ὀργάνων ... | ... οἷϲ ἐχρῆτο: for the attached clause cf. (with Kells, *CR* 11 (1961), 194–5) *OT* 1476–7 τὴν παροῦcαν τέρψιν, ᾗ ϲ᾽ εἶχεν πάλαι. **ὅτου ψαύϲειεν:** on the optative with the relative pronoun see Schwyzer, *Gr. Gr.* ii. 336.

907–11: deleted by Wecklein (approved by A. M. Dale, *CR* 6 (1956), 106) as an intrusion from a different context. But they fit remarkably well

LINES 904-916

here, with the exception of 911, which is corrupt or spurious (see ad loc.).

908. For confusion of ΤΟΥ and ΠΟΥ see above on 187. For δέμας + genitive in the tragedians (a mainly Euripidean device) see Harder on Eur. *Archel.* fr. 1. 16.

910. Cf. Anacr. 346 fr. i. 14 P δαίμον' αἰτιωμένην. In such passages δαίμων in the singular represents 'the divine agent responsible for a man's good or ill fortune at any given time' (West on Hes. *Op.* 122–3). For ἀνακαλεῖcθαι used to implore deities see Burkert, *CQ* 20 (1970), 5. This line is omitted in Y[ac] because of homoioteleuton: see on 177 above.

911. Both ἄπαιδας and οὐσίας in this line seem doubtful, the latter more so: οὐσία in the concrete sense here required ('possessions, property, wealth') seems impossible: see Kannicht on Eur. *Hel.* 1253, who points out that high poetry (unlike comedy or prose authors) avoids such a concrete meaning for the word—only Euripides (in the *Helen* and fr. 354 N[2]) breaks this rule, and he is careful to add a word or phrase of explanation to his two exceptional uses. On *Her.* 337 see Wilamowitz and Bond ad loc. (the latter observing that there 'the meaning of οὐσία becomes tinged ... with its philosophical sense "reality"' especially in view of ὄνομα in the next line). Pearson's οἰκίας is an undesirable conjecture because (as M. D. Reeve, *GRBS* 13 (1972), 260 n. 36 observes) the word is otherwise absent from poetry. If Reiske's ἑστίας were correct, ἄπαιδας might refer to Hyllus' absence from the house due to his hatred of his mother. At any rate, the parallel created with Eur. *Alc.* 162 καὶ στᾶσα πρόσθεν ἑστίας κατηύξατο is attractive given the other verbal resemblances between the two passages (see above, p. 213). For ἑστία = 'altar' see 656–7 n. L. Dindorf (*Thes. Gr. L.* 5. 654[b]c) preferred to delete the line. If the 'illogical use of τὸ λοιπόν is a Sophoclean cliché' (Knox, *Gnomon* 40 (1968), 754 = *Word and Action*, p. 173), that might tell us where the interpolator got part of the line from (see too 921 below). See Addenda.

913. Cf. Eur. *Alc.* 175 θάλαμον ἐσπεσοῦσα καὶ λέχος; on the adjective Ἡράκλειος instead of the genitive see above on 51.

914. For the prolepsis of the adjective see 240 and 376 above, Bruhn, *Anhang*, § 9. On the unaugmented verb see on 904 βρυχᾶτο.

915–16. See on 51 above.

916. φάρη: 'Greek garments, being mostly rectangular pieces of stuff,

COMMENTARY

can be used indifferently for bed-clothes or hangings' (Gow on Theocr. *Id.* 18. 18–19, with examples).

917–18. Cf. Eur. *Alc.* 175 (cited on 913), Verg. *Aen.* 4. 650 (of Dido) 'incubuitque toro' (cf. R. Heinze, *Vergils epische Technik*, 3rd edn. (Leipzig 1915), 137 n. 2). 'ἄνω is added because of the height of the bedstead', according to Broadhead on Aesch. *Pers.* 357 ff.

919. δακρύων ... νάματα: for the image of the 'flood of tears' see above on 851. **ῥήξαca ... νάματα:** this seems to be an extension of the idiom ῥήγνυμι φωνήν (*rumpere vocem*), for which cf. Collard on Eur. *Suppl.* 710ff. Jebb on our passage cited Plut. *Pericl.* 36 κλαυθμόν τε ῥῆξαι. Page on *AP* 7. 10. 6 ἔρρηξαν ... δάκρυα (*Further Greek Epigrams*, p. 336) added Dioscorides *AP* 7. 434. 3 = *HE* 1669 δάκρυα δ' οὐκ ἔρρηξε.

920–1. Cf. Eur. *Alc.* 177ff. ὦ λέκτρον, ἔνθα παρθένει' ἔλυc' ἐγὼ | ... | χαῖρ'. **νυμφεῖ' ἐμά:** 'bridal chambers': on the wide range of meanings the word can bear see Diggle on Eur. *Phaeth.* 231.

921. τὸ λοιπὸν ἤδη χαίρεθ': for the solemn formula see on 168 above.

922. κοίταιcι ταῖcδ': one MS' κοίτηιcι is unconvincingly explained by Bergson, *Rh. Mus.* 102 (1959), 11, as an attempt at euphonic variation. **εὐνάτριαν:** the latter word-form is preferable to εὐνήτριαν: Björck, *Das Alpha impurum*, p. 239: other instances of εὐνάτρια, εὐνάτωρ, and εὐνάτηρ are cited by Diggle, *CQ* 33 (1983), 347.

923. τοcαῦτα φωνήcαcα: for other examples of τοcαῦτα used in concluding a directly quoted speech see *Kölner Papyri*, vii/2 (1978), 24.

924–5. Explained by Stinton, pp. 141–2, with reference to Jacobsthal, *Greek Pins* (Oxford 1956), 109–10. His small change of μαcτῶν to μαcτῶι (p. 142) is attractive: cf. *Il.* 14. 180 χρυcείηιc δ' ἐνετῆιcι κατὰ cτῆθοc περονᾶτο. The OCT follows Schaefer in emending ὧι ... προὔκειτο to οὗ (ἧι Wakefield: cf. on 573).

926. ὠλένην: a word rarely used in tragedy, with the exception of Euripides (for details see Th. K. Stephanopoulos, *ZPE* 73 (1988), 218).

927. δρομαία βᾶc': on the form and sense of δρομαῖοc see Chantraine, *La Formation des noms* (Paris 1933), 48: 'δρ. ... s' oppose à εὐναῖοc dans le langage des chasseurs'); Fraenkel, *Glotta* 37 (1958), 287 and n. 3 = *Kl. Beitr.* i. 155–6 and n. 1.

928. τῆc τεχνωμένηc: for the genitive after a verb of saying see KG ii. 1. 363 (c); contrast the construction at 1122 below.

LINES 916-932

930–1. Cf. Verg. *Aen.* 4. 664 ff. '(illam)... | conlapsam aspiciunt comites, ensemque cruore | spumantem' (compared by Heinze, *Vergils epische Technik*, 3rd edn., p. 137 n. 2). On ἀμφιπλήξ cf. E. Coughanowr, *CQ* 34 (1984), 235; on the echo of the word in πεπληγμένην see Easterling, *Hermes* 101 (1973), 23. It is highly unusual for a tragic heroine to end her life with the sword: a noose is the more conventional suicide weapon for such (cf. Fraenkel, *Philol.* 87 (1932), 470 ff. = *Kl. Beitr.* i. 465 ff.), and Diod. 4. 39. 3 has D kill herself thus (ἀγχονῆι τὸν βίον κατέστρεψεν). Most of the counter-examples cited by Zieliński (p. 594 n. 19 = p. 349 n. 2) prove to be illusory: Eur. *El.* 688 παίσω κάρα γὰρ (γὰρ ἧπαρ Geel) τοὐμὸν ἀμφήκει ξίφει occurs in a passage deleted by Nauck (*prob.* Diggle), *Hel.* 301–2 σφαγαὶ δ' ἔχουσιν εὐγενές τι καὶ καλόν, | σμικρὸν δ' ὁ καιρὸς σάρκ' ἀπαλλάξαι βίου in a passage deleted by Hartung (*prob.* Kannicht). Both passages (like *Hel.* 353 ff. φόνιον αἰώρημα | διὰ δέρης ὀρέξομαι, | ἢ ξιφοκτόνον δίωγμα | λαιμορ⟨ρ⟩ύτου σφαγᾶς | αὐτοσίδαρον ἔσω πελάσω διὰ σαρκὸς ἅμιλλαν: Kannicht ad loc. observes the 'Exuberanz' of language and metre) are anyway prospective rather than descriptive. Eurydice certainly kills herself with a sword in *Ant.* 1315–16, but this is a special case, as we are told (ὅπως | παιδὸς τόδ' ἤισθετ' ὀξυκώκυτον πάθος): besides, Antigone's mode of suicide must not be repeated. Perhaps Euripides' first Phaedra killed herself with a sword, involving a special dramatic significance (see O. Zwierlein, *Senecas Phaedra und ihre Vorbilder* (Mainz 1987), 41 ff.). Jocasta does likewise at Eur. *Phoen.* 1455 ff. (a passage not mentioned by Zieliński), but this is motivated by the dramatic necessity of a suicide over the corpses of her two sons. So here the need to have D end her life symbolically on the marriage-bed partly explains the departure from the normal rule. There may be the further significance that 'Sophocles' most "feminine" character ... dies by the sword: that is a horrifyingly masculine way to die, and the shock of it reverberates through the play' (J. Gould, *JHS* 100 (1980), 57; cf. S. Wiersma, *Mnem.* 37 (1984), 25 ff.).

931. ὑφ' ἧπαρ: in the Greek language one strikes *to* the heart (*vel sim.*) rather than striking the heart: see Jackson, *MS*, p. 235. The symbolism of this part of the body is clear. A's ἐφ' provides a nice example of the frequent confusion of ὑπ- and ἐπ- (for which see above on 356).

932–5. Deleted by V. Jernstedt, approved by Zieliński (p. 595 n. 20 = p. 349 n. 3) and also by Radermacher, who calls them 'nach

COMMENTARY

'Inhalt und Form anstößigen Verse' and thinks them a sort of doublet of 936 ff. The latter they are not, especially since they add the detail of Hyllus' ὀψιμαθία, which is extremely important as a motif. On their content and form see below ad locc.

932. δ' ὁ παῖς: the metrically unnecessary article here and at 936 (δέ could have been used here, κἀνταῦθα there) support Bergson's thesis (*Rh. Mus.* 102 (1959), 29–30) that its occurrence in tragedy is often a matter of polymorphism. **τάλας:** see on 705 above.

933. ἐφάψειεν: the verb means *malum inferre alicui*: see Holwerda, *Mnem.* 16 (1963), 350.

934. ὄψ' ἐκδιδαχθείς: for the theme of 'late-learning' see on 710 ff. above. **τῶν κατ' οἶκον:** the verb takes the genitive by analogy with μανθάνω (Hyllus learns *from* the servants in the house): cf. *El.* 343 ἅπαντα γάρ coι τἀμὰ νουθετήματα | κείνης διδακτά, Schwyzer, *Gr. Gr.* ii. 119 (δ). To accept διδάσκεσθαί τινος but gag at διδαχθείς τινος seems eminently unreasonable. For such references to ill-defined persons 'in the house' see on 601 above. To complain (with some literal-minded critics) that the servants in the house were not in a position to inform Hyllus of the truth, least of all as to the centaur's role (935), is to misunderstand an economic device of literature: see e.g. Dodds on Eur. *Bacch.* 686 ff., Macleod on *Il.* 24. 203 ff., Mastronarde, *Phoenix* 32 (1978), 116 and n. 45. For a Shakespearian instance see *Hamlet* III. ii. 202 and the Arden editor ad loc. (p. 507).

935. The construction πρός + genitive has been found difficult but *OT* 1488 οἷον βιῶναι cφὼ πρὸς ἀνθρώπων χρέων is parallel enough.

937 ff. For the general picture cf. Verg. *Aen.* 4. 685 ff. 'sic fata gradus euaserat altos, | semianimemque sinu germanam amplexa fouebat | cum gemitu' (compared by Heinze, *Vergils epische Technik*, 3rd edn., p. 137 n. 2).

937. ἀμφί νιν: for this use of ἀμφί + accusative = 'concerning' (rare in tragedy) see Johansen and Whittle on Aesch. *Suppl.* 246; cf. Moorhouse, p. 97.

938. ἀμφιπίπτων στόμασιν: cf. Eur. *Alc.* 403 ποτὶ coῖcι πίτνων cτόμαcιν.

938–9. πλευρόθεν | πλευράν: for similarly closely juxtaposed repetitions of this word see Diggle, *PCPS* 28 (1982), 62; for examples of the more general stylistic feature involved (χεῖρα δὲ χειρί etc.) see Gygli-Wyss, *Das nominale Polyptoton*, p. 90 n. 5. πλευρόθεν is

218

interesting, since -όθεν adverbs usually derive from masculine and neuter nouns, -άθεν (here metrically impossible) being the form of adverbs derived from the feminine (cf. M. Lejeune, *Les Adverbes grecs en -θεν* (Bordeaux 1939)); the juxtaposition here is almost provocative in stressing the contravention of the norm.

940. αἰτίαι βάλοι κακῆι: cf. LSJ s.v. βάλλω AI.3 ('*metaph.*'), where it will be seen that one may pelt a victim with κακά, φθόνος, ψόγος, and the like. First proposed in *CR* 39 (1925), 5, Pearson's αἰτίαι ⟨'μ⟩βάλοι was one of his three Sophoclean conjectures that Housman found 'evidently true' (see above on 520). It has also been approved by Diggle, *STE*, p. 33 (where for '*C.R.* n.s. 22 (1972) 244 n. 3' read '*C.Q.*' etc.), in a discussion which shows that Platnauer's claim (*CQ* 10 (1960), 141) that tragedy can offer no certain instance of prodelision after -αι goes too far, and that prodelided prepositions or prepositional prefixes do occasionally occur after a dative termination -αι (for prodelided ἐν- ἐμ-, *vel sim.* in Greek drama see Platnauer, op. cit. 143). Pearson cited *OT* 656–7 μήποτ' ἐν αἰτίαι... βαλεῖν, Plato *Epist.* 7, 341 A βαλεῖν ἐν αἰτίαι τὸν δεικνύντα in support, but in these passages the verb is simplex not compound. For the scribal omission of vowels in synizesis or crasis presupposed by Pearson's emendation see below on 1046–7.

941–2. The manuscripts' βίου cannot possibly be retained if we are to render it 'livelihood', for Hyllus is a grown man and will not be deprived of this by his parents' deaths. The best expedient, if we must cling to the paradosis, is Hermann's punctuation and interpretation: 'bereft of the life of two, mother and father'. But this may well seem strained. Wakefield's βίον is best taken not as an accusative of length of time ('bereft of his father and mother for the period of his life'—a distinctly odd concept) but as an accusative of respect ('with his life made desolate by two, father and mother'—so e.g. Wunder and Jebb). Cf. esp. Eur. *Alc.* 396–7 προλιποῦσα δ' ἐμὸν βίον ὠρφάνισεν τλάμων. Our favoured emendation and interpretation can be judged independently of any choice between the manuscripts' ἐκ (of the agent: cf. *Ant.* 207 ἔκ γ' ἐμοῦ) and Nauck's further change to εἰς, which Lloyd-Jones (p. 171) thinks 'both removes an awkwardness and makes a point that is telling in the context'. This is surely right. For similar juxtapositions of numbers see Eur. *Hel.* 731–2 κρεῖccον γὰρ τόδ' ἢ δυοῖν κακοῖν | ἕν' ὄντα χρῆcθαι and Kannicht ad loc. Lloyd-Jones makes a similar emendation at *Aj.* 636 (ὃc ἐκ (εἰc Ll.-J.,

COMMENTARY

JHS (1956), 112, and *CR* 28 (1978), 218) πατρώιας ἥκων γενεᾶς κτλ. See further his remarks in *Sophoclea*, p. 171.

943. τοιαῦτα τἀνθάδ' ἐcτίν: cf. on 807 above for this concluding formula.

943 ff. The Nurse concludes with a γνώμη that appropriately takes our minds back to the similar γνώμη of Deianeira at the beginning of the play. For other such 'conclusive reflections' at the end of such a speech see Johansen, *General Reflection in Tragic Rhesis*, p. 152 n. 3. On the more specific issue of the τόποc 'man is a creature of the day' see Hermann Fränkel's famous study, *TAPA* 77 (1946), 131 ff. ≏ *Wege und Formen frühgr. Denkens*², pp. 23 ff., and more recently M. Dickie, *ICS* 1 (1976), 7 ff.

943. ὥcτ': the same word introduces a general concluding γνώμη at *OT* 857, [1528], Men. *Perikeirom*. 167 (cf. *Koneiazomenai* 18).

944. The majority of manuscripts have the unmetrical ἢ καὶ πλείους τις. Triclinius' πλέους is a crude attempt to restore metre without considering whether πλέους can ever stand for πλείους (the short form of πλείονας): the brisk answer is it cannot, only πλέονι for πλείονι being an acceptable licence. Of the numerous conjectures the best is ἢ κἀπὶ πλείους (West, *BICS* 26 (1979), 111), which admirably fits the context and content of the Nurse's γνώμη (see above, on 943 ff.) and supplies the requisite notion of futurity. ἐπί will go with δύο in the previous line too, of course: for 'the ellipse of the preposition with the first of two co-ordinated members' West compares *Ant.* 367 τοτὲ μὲν κακόν, ἄλλοτ' ἐπ' ἐσθλόν, *OT* 734 Δελφῶν κἀπὸ Δαυλίας, 761 ἀγροὺς ... κἀπὶ ποιμνίων νομάς, and KG ii/1. 550. See further for this idiom Wilamowitz on Eur. *Her.* 237, Bruhn, *Anhang*, § 199 ff.; cf. Diggle, *STE*, pp. 23–4 (ellipse of preposition in the second member of a negative disjunction). πι and τι often fall out thus before π in manuscripts: cf. Diggle, *STE*, p. 18 n. 1.

945. ἢ γ' αὔριον: in view of τὴν παροῦσαν ἡμέραν in 946 the present phrase implies the Attic formula ἡ αὔριον ἡμέρα (cf. D. M. Lewis, *CQ* 11 (1961), 63).

LINES 941-947

FOURTH STASIMON (947-970)

947–9 = 950–2 *first strophe and antistrophe*

947/950	⏑⏔⏑⏔ ⏑–⏑–	ia. dim.
948/951	⏑⏔⏑⏔ ⏑–⏑–	ia. dim.
949/952	–⏑⏑–⏑––– ‖	chor. dim. A.

The opening strophe and antistrophe, though short and simple in style and metre, exhibit considerable repetition and balance (947 πότερα πρότερον ἐπιςτένω, πότερα μέλεα περαιτέρω ~ 953 τάδε μὲν ἔχομεν ὁρᾶν δόμοιc κτλ.): see for instance Sier on Aesch. *Cho.* 22 ff. (p. 17), Fehling, *Wiederholungsfiguren*, pp. 170 ff., Alexiou, *The Ritual Lament in Greek Tradition*, pp. 131 ff.

953–61 = 962–70 *second strophe and antistrophe*

953–4/962–3	––⏑⏑–⏑– ⏕–⏑– ⏑–⏑–	tel. + ia. trim. cat.
	⏑––ᴴ ‖	
955/964	⏓–⏑– ⏑–⏑– ⏑–⏑–	ia. trim.
956/965	––⏑– ⏑–⏑–	ia. dim.
957/966	⏓–⏑⏑–⏑–⏑	enop.
958/967	–⏑– ⏑–⏑⌣ ‖	cr. + ia.
959/968	⏔–⏑⏑–––⏑⏑–	anap. dim.
960/969	⏓–⏑⏑–⏑–⌣	enop.
961/970	–⏑– ⏑–≈ ‖	ia. dim. syn. cat.
		(cr. + bacch.)

Unless Hermann's φθίμενον (for θανόντα) is accepted at 969–70, those lines' responsion with 960–1 is hard to explain or parallel (cf. Griffith, *Authenticity of PV*, p. 45). The loose responsion with anaclasis offered by the paradosis is, indeed, ranked by West, *GM*, p. 117, along with various freedoms of responsion in aeolic presented by the manuscripts of Euripides. But not all of these are textually certain, and Sophocles is a different case.

947 ff. The run of short syllables and the alliteration of π create what following Webster (*Introduction to Sophocles* (Oxford 1936), 161 n. 7) we may characterize as an 'anxious stammer'. This passage should surely be added to those listed by Fraenkel on Aesch. *Ag.* 268 to illustrate

221

COMMENTARY

repeated π as conveying 'breathless excitement'. For other examples of the parechesis of πότεροc πρότεροc see Bruhn, *Anhang*, § 242; on the more general principle of parechesis of this sort in drama see Jocelyn, *The Tragedies of Ennius*, p. 211. For the preliminary 'which disaster shall I mourn first?' cf. [Aesch.] *ScT* 825 ff. πότερον χαίρω κἀπολολύξω | πόλεωc ἀcινεῖ cωτῆρι ⟨   ⟩ | ἢ τοὺc μογεροὺc καὶ δυcδαίμοναc | ἀτέκνουc κλαύcω κτλ.

948. The paradosis makes no sense (τέλεα περαιτέρω = 'more final'?). Musgrave's μέλεα is inescapable (cf. *Sophoclea*, p. 171).

950. δόμοιc: best interpreted as a locative dative (see Bers, p. 92 n. 14).

951. μένομεν: is preferable to Hermann's rather artificial μελόμεν(α) (sc. ἔcτι) = μέλει. Dawe combines Hermann's remedy with his own ἔτ(ι) for ἐπ(ί) (*Studies* iii. 94) because he supposes a 'sense of worry' is required. But this is abundantly supplied anyway with μένομεν ἐπ' ἐλπίcιν: Dawe complains that the last two words are 'unusual, since this kind of ἐπί normally denotes circumstances under which, or conditions on which, something happens, but here we have nothing to tell us whether the ἐλπίc is good or bad'. As if at this stage of the tragedy anyone can suppose the expectation would be of something good! ἐλπίc is given colour in Greek by its context: at line 136 the context provided an optimistic gloss but here the tone is decidedly grim. However, an exact parallel for ἐπί thus used with ἐλπίcιν is hard to find: Eur. *Her.* 804 is doubtful (see Bond ad loc.) and in Thuc. 6. 31.6 and Xen. *Mem.* 2. 1. 18 the meaning is 'on the basis of hope', as the discussion in *Sophoclea*, p. 172 reminds us. The OCT's adoption of Blaydes's ἐν ἐλπίcιν is therefore desirable. See Eur. *El.* 352 and *Or.* 785 (*coni.* Wecklein).

953 ff. For the desire for flight into the air as a means of escape from present evils see Barrett on Eur. *Hipp.* 732 ff., Renehan, *CP* 80 (1985), 163.

953–4. ἀνεμόεccά τιc ... αὔρα: cf. Eur. *Cycl.* 44 ὑπήνεμοc αὔρα with the remarks of Kassel (*Maia* 25 (1973), 100) and Seaford ad loc.

954. γένοιτ': Barrett (cited on 953 ff.) observes that 'γενοίμαν rather than εἴην is normal' in wishes of the kind just analysed 'where the speaker is thinking rather of the immediate (and perhaps temporary) change from his present state than of any continuance in the new one'. The same is true of the third person: cf. Anacr. 411A. 1 P ἀπό μοι θανεῖν γένοιτ'.

955 ff. On the partial interlacing (ABA) of the words here see Stinton, *PCPS* 21 (1975), 87.

956. Ζηνός: for other passages of tragedy where Διός has replaced Ζηνός in manuscripts see Dawe, *CP* 79 (1984), 63.

960. πρὸ δόμων: not adverbial πρό (Schwyzer, *Gr. Gr.* ii. 422; cf. Eur. *Hec.* 59) but (Moorhouse, p. 93) 'come to the house (so as to be before it)'.

961. θέαμα is Schenkl's emendation of the paradosis τι θαῦμα, but for that word's use of persons see Diggle, *STE*, p. 90 (adding *Od.* 11. 287, *Cypria* fr. 7. 1 Davies).

962 ff. In the last stanza we move (via 964's idiomatic γάρ, explaining what the chorus have seen to make them react in the way they do) from what is reported (960) about Heracles' condition to the reality of his approach. On 'entry announcement within an act-dividing song' in tragedy see above, 222 ff., and Taplin, *Stagecraft*, p. 174. On the responsion with 969–70 see the metrical scheme above.

962. ἀγχοῦ . . . κοὐ μακράν: for examples of the formula whereby a word meaning 'near' is strengthened by a following negative see Eur. *Hyps.* fr. 10. 3 and Bond ad loc. For the words' association with προυκλαιον cf. fr. 210. 38–9 ἀγχοῦ προςεῖπας (sc. τὸν δαίμονα)· οὐ γὰρ ἐκτὸς ἑςτὼς | ςύρει δὴ φύρδαν.

963. ὀξύφωνος ὡς ἀηδών: for other passages in tragedy involving comparison with a nightingale see R. Oehler, *Mythologische Exempla in der älteren gr. Dichtung* (Aarhus 1925), 92–3. The bird's ὠιδαί are ὀξύτονοι at *Aj.* 629 ff.

964 ff. The stress on Heracles' support by strangers is well explained by Winnington-Ingram, *BICS* 16 (1969), 45 ff.

964. ξένων . . . cτάcιc is Meineke's conjecture. The paradosis ξένων . . . βάcιc is equivalent to 'approaching strangers' (on the genitive of definition see Moorhouse, p. 53). ξένων coupled with ἐξόμιλος stresses their alien aspect. For a sensitive analysis of the phrase see Long, *Language and Thought*, p. 73. There seems no good reason for change. **ἅδε τις:** for examples of the collocation ὅδε/ἥδε τις see Diggle, *STE*, pp. 43–4. ἅδε for ἥδε was conjectured by Blaydes, and the restoration of Doric vocalization in this lyric stanza's trimeter is approved in *Sophoclea*, p. 172.

965. πᾶι δ᾽ αὖ φορεῖ νιν; πὰρ δὲ φορεῖ νιν coni. M. L. West, *BICS* 31 (1984), 183, arguing that αὖ is 'incomprehensible', and πᾶι little better, since the chorus can see the answer to their question and πᾶι should anyway mean 'by which route' not 'how'. With this

COMMENTARY

emendation, the manuscripts' Διός in the corresponding position within the second strophe (945) can stand. However, West's objections to the paradosis are misconceived: this is another of those questions (see on 892 above) which are not literal requests for information but rather equivalent to an emotional exclamation ('ah, here they come, carrying him!'). In such a context αὖ is idiomatic (see *Sophoclea*, p. 30). The apocope of παρά which West's emendation involves is not to be introduced by conjecture (see on 636 above).

966. βαρεῖαν . . . βάϲιν: on this phrase see Long, *Language and Thought*, pp. 73–4.

968. ἀναύδατοϲ: for this form of ἄναυδοϲ cf. Archias *AP* 7. 191. 5 = *GP* 3714.

969. φθίμενον: Hermann's correction of θανόντα (which poses a problematic freedom of responsion with 960) restores normality: see the metrical scheme.

969–70. Cf. *El.* 766–7 ὦ Ζεῦ, τί ταῦτα, πότερον εὐτυχῆ λέγω, | ἢ δεινὰ μέν, κέρδη δέ; On speculation as to possible alternative significances of a character's approach see Taplin, *Stagecraft*, pp. 297–8. On Hyllus' entry here, simultaneous with but separate from that of Heracles, see on 901–3, and Taplin, p. 177 and n. 1. Cf. J. Mattes, *Der Wahnsinn im gr. Mythos und in der Dichtung bis zum Drama des 5. Jhdts.* (Heidelberg 1970), 85 n. 44 on the exchange between Hyllus and the Old Man.

ANAPAESTIC–LYRIC EXCHANGE 971–1043

971–3. οἴμοι ἐγὼ ϲοῦ: ὤμοι is the older, epic form (see Renehan, *Greek Lexicographical Notes* i (Hypomnemata 45; 1975), 148). 'Woe is me for you': both first person nominative and the genitive of the person or thing for whom or which are idiomatic: cf. Eur. *El.* 1109 οἴμοι τάλαινα τῶν ἐμῶν βουλευμάτων, *Phoen.* 373 οἴμοι τῶν ἐμῶν ἐγὼ κακῶν, Renehan, *CP* 80 (1985), 174. The following part of the outburst is corrupt and needs emending. Of recent scholars, Jackson (*MS*, p. 225 n. 1) attempted πάτερ, ὤμοι ἐγὼ μέλεοϲ, τί πάθω; | ⟨τί πάθω;⟩ τί δέ μήϲομαι; οἴμοι (∪∪–∪∪–∪∪–∪∪– | ∪∪–∪∪–∪∪– –). A simpler remedy, again presupposing corruption under the influence of 971's ἐγὼ ϲοῦ, would be the transposition πάτερ, οἴμοι, ἐγὼ μέλεοϲ ϲοῦ· | τί πάθω; τί δὲ μήϲομαι; οἴμοι (∪∪–∪∪–∪∪– –| ∪∪–∪∪–∪∪– –), suggested by Dale (*CR* 6 (1956), 106) in her

LINES 965-977

review of Dain's edition. Cf. Eur. *IA* 1277 οἴ 'γὼ θανάτου ⟨τοῦ Heath⟩ coῦ μελέα (μελέα . . . coῦ Hartung) *Andr.* 513–14 ὤμοι μοι, τί πάθω, . . . | . . . μᾶτερ;, *OC* 216 ὤμοι ἐγὼ τί πάθω, τέκνον ἐμόν; **τί πάθω;** 'what can I do?': see Collard on Eur. *Suppl.* 256–7, Johansen and Whittle on Aesch. *Suppl.* 777; cf. Stevens, *Colloquial Expressions in Euripides*, pp. 57–8. **τί δὲ μήcομαι;** for 'fut. indic. and aor. subj. aligned in dubitative questions' see Johansen and Whittle, loc. cit. Contrast *ScT* 1057 τί πάθω; τί δὲ δρῶ; τί δὲ μήcωμαι;

974 ff. From here on, and especially in the great speech of Heracles at 1046 ff., the poison or disease attacking Heracles is characterized by expressions which treat it as a wild beast or an Erinys. Cf. the treatment of Philoctetes' νόcημα in his play as analysed by Long, *Language and Thought*, p. 79, and on the general similarities between the affliction of Heracles and that of Philoctetes in Sophocles' play of that name here and at 988 ff., 1004 ff., 1040 ff. cf. D. M. Jones, *CR* 63 (1949), 85. The *Trachiniae*'s scene is also reminiscent of Eur. *Her.* 1042 ff., where Amphitryon cautions the chorus (as here the old man warns Hyllus) not to rouse the slumbering Heracles. Attempts to decide which of the two playwrights was first to use these motifs (e.g. the suggestion that our play's anonymous old man is less 'integral' than Amphitryon, the hero's father, and therefore derivative from him) are dangerously subjective: see Bond on the Euripidean passage.

974–5. Cf. *OC* 1276–7 κινῆcαι πατρὸc | τὸ δυcπρόcοιcτον κἀπροcήγορον cτόμα and the other examples of metaphorical κινέω ('provoke, arouse') given by Diggle on Eur. *Phaeth.* 72. Cf. 980, 1242 below.

976. προπετής: is the adjective here literal (ἐπὶ πρόcωπον κοιμώμενοc Σ) or metaphorical (εἰc τὸν θάνατον προνενευκώc another Σ)? Cf. Eur. *Alc.* 909–11 πολιὰc ἐπὶ χαίταc | ἤδη προπετὴc ὤν | βιότου τε πόρcω, and 143 ἤδη προνωπής ἐcτι καὶ ψυχορραγεῖ.

976–7. ἴcχε δακὼν cτόμα cόν: for ἔχω cτόμα and similar locutions see Diggle, *STE*, p. 66 (add Men. *Sam.* 356). For biting the lip to fortify one's spirit see Dover on Ar. *Nub.* 1369, Th. K. Stephanopoulos, *ZPE* 75 (1988), 14.

977. The ἀντιλαβή within the anapaestic metron here and at 981 and 991 below is unique.[38]

[38] I do not count *IA* 2, 3, 149 from that play's suspect anapaestic prologue. On

COMMENTARY

978. οὐ μὴ 'ξεγερεῖc: on the οὐ μή construction here see Moorhouse, pp. 337–8, preferring an interpretation as prohibition to Pearson's question 'will you not see to it that you don't wake him?': this implies Elmsley's theory (on Eur. *Med.* 1151 (1120): cf. Hermann, *Opusc.* iii. 235 ff.) of mutually excluding negatives. A similar approach in e.g. D. Lightfoot, *Natural Logic and the Greek Moods* (Amsterdam 1975), 76: (οὐ μή + subjunctive or future indicative) 'an emphatic future denial, which may sometimes be best translated as a command'. For the line as a whole compare fr. 201g ἄπελθε· κινεῖc ὕπνον ἰατρὸν νόcου, for sleep as the soother of pain see Pearson on fr. 197 = 201g. See Addenda.

979 ff. κἀκκινήcειc ... νόcον: cf. 1242.

980–1. φοιτάδα ... νόcον: for φοιτᾶν and derivative words applied to states of madness and frenzy see Mattes, *Der Wahnsinn im gr. Mythos und in der Dichtung*, p. 107.

982. For the cut here and at 995 (⌣̅ – ⌣ ⌣ | – ⌣ ⌣ – –) cf. L. P. E. Parker, *CQ* 8 (1958), 84. **ἐμμέμονεν φρήν:** cf. *Il.* 16. 435 διχθὰ δέ μοι κραδίη μέμονεν φρεcὶν κτλ., Eur. *IT* 655 δίδυμα μέμονε φρήν.

983 ff. Heracles' first words on stage are addressed to himself, he is oblivious of the presence of others. For a detailed analysis of H's switches from *Selbstgespräch* to less introverted utterance and back cf. Leo, *Der Monolog*, p. 11.

984. τοῖcι: equivalent to τίcι (cf. *Od.* 10. 110 and Schwyzer, *Gr. Gr.* i. 616). H. Müller conjectured τέοιcι.

984 ff. Cf. *Od.* 13. 200 (= 6. 119) ὤ μοι ἐγώ, τέων αὖτε βροτῶν ἐc γαῖαν ἱκάνω; (Odysseus' lament on arriving at Ithaca). On the dramatic significance of Heracles' ignorance here see Winnington-Ingram, *BICS* 16 (1969), 45–6. It is all the more striking if the drama's status as a *nostos* play (see Easterling, *ICS* 6 (1981), 57) has led us to expect a climax in the form of a prayer to his native land from the returning traveller (for examples of such prayers in drama see Fraenkel on Aesch. *Ag.* 503). **ποῖ γᾶc:** for partitive genitive with ποῖ see *OT* 1309, Eur. *Her.* 74, and probably Aesch. *Suppl.* 777–8 (see Johansen and Whittle ad loc.).

985. For this specialized use of κεῖμαι cf. *Il.* 2. 721 (of Philoctetes) ἐν νήcωι κεῖτο κρατέρ' ἄλγεα πάcχων, *Od.* 5. 13 ἐν νήcωι the three instances that have been alleged from the *Rhesus* see A. Ritchie, *The Authenticity of the* Rhesus *of Euripides* (Cambridge 1964), 290 ff.

LINES 978-989

κεῖται; with the following phrase cf. 959 ἐν δυcαπαλλάκτοιc ὀδύναιc. For the technique whereby two syllables overrun the end of the anapaestic metron see Fraenkel on Aesch. *Ag.* 52.

986 ff. These lines have several features in common stylistically with the agonies of Hippolytus in Euripides' play (1347 ff.); see W. Schadewaldt, *Monolog und Selbstgespräch: Untersuchungen zur Formgeschichte der griechischen Tragödie* (Berlin 1926), 164–5, esp. p. 165 n. 1; Schwinge, pp. 21 ff.; Stinton, pp. 142 ff.

987. ἃ δ' αὖ μιαρά: for the metaphorical use of μιαρόc cf. R. Parker, *Miasma* (Oxford 1983), 5 (often of 'bestial' behaviour). **βρύκει:** cf. esp. βρύκομαι at *Phil.* 745 (see on 974 ff. above); for the metaphorical use of βρύκω see Gow and Page on Erucius *AP* 9. 233. 3 = *GP* 2252. **αὖ** is idiomatic in the description of a renewed onset of madness or frenzied pain: cf. *PV* 878–9 ὑπό μ' αὖ cφάκελοc καὶ φρενοπλῆγεc | μανίαι θάλπουc' and in general Mattes, *Der Wahnsinn im gr. Mythos und in der Dichtung*, p. 77 n. 12.

988. Moorhouse, p. 202, approves Cobet's ἐξῄδηcθ' (*Mnem.* 5 (1856), 263 = *Novae Lect.*, p. 215): for the corruption presupposed cf. Ar. *Nub.* 329 (ᾔδειc codd.: ᾔδηcθ' Blaydes); on the spelling cf. on 87 above: '"did you fully understand how much better it was (not to wake him)?" with the implication that it was not so understood ... what is questioned is the *depth* of Hyllus' appreciation of the situation (note the preverb ἐξ-).' Wilamowitz (on Eur. *Her.* 617): ἆρ' ἐξῄδηcθα 'ist von dem Scholiasten mit ἆρ' ἔγνωc ... ganz richtig erklärt und darf nicht zerstört werden'. Wecklein's ἆρ' ἐξῄδη c', however, with its self-righteous tone, is convincingly commended by Lloyd-Jones, *CR* 31 (1981), 171, and in *Sophoclea*, p. 173, though we need not accept[39] his view that the old man is a doctor (so too already Zieliński, p. 614 n. 47 = p. 370 n. 1 etc.). For the force of ἆρ' see Denniston, *GP*[2], p. 46 (3).

989. κεύθειν: for the absolute use see Pearson on fr. 79. Note the contrast in tense between the continuous silence here and the momentary scattering of sleep in cκεδάcαι: see Moorhouse, p. 208.

989 ff. Cf. Alcm. 3. 1. 7 P ὕπνον ἀ]πὸ γλεφάρων cκεδ[α]cεῖ γλυκύν (what is poured, as in e.g. *Od.* 2. 395, 11. 245, Pind. *Pyth.* 1. 10–11, Ar. *Vesp.* 7, can be scattered; so perhaps can what is seated: cf. A. W. Bulloch, *CQ* 20 (1970), 270 n. 2). For other examples of the scattering

---
[39] Compare Diggle's dismissal (*CR* 32 (1982), 13) of Burton's notion (p. 254) that the ξένοc of *OC* 36 ff. is a gardener.

COMMENTARY

of sleep see Headlam on Herodas 7. 7 ff.; cf. *H. Orph.* 78. 9 τὸν γλυκὺν ὕπνον ἀπὸ βλεφάρων ἀποϲείϲηιϲ. **ἀπὸ κρατὸϲ | βλεφάρων θ᾽**: cf. [Hes.] *Scut.* 7 ἀπὸ κρῆθεν βλεφάρων τ᾽ ἄπο.

991–2. For the indirect πῶϲ here see Austin and Reeve, *Maia* 22 (1970), 17.

992. For ϲτέργω and participle see Eur. *Hipp.* 458. φιλῶ, μιϲῶ, and similar verbs can also take the participle: see Holzinger on Ar. *Plut.* 645.

993 ff. For the reproachful address of a locale cf. *Aj.* 418, Eur. *Her.* 217. Leo, *Der Monolog*, p. 10, strangely denies that S's characters (in contrast to Aeschylus' or Euripides') address lands and gods thus in extant plays (he allows (ibid. n. 1) the counter-evidence of frr. like 384 ὦ Λῆμνε Χρύϲηϲ τ᾽ ἀγχιτέρμονεϲ πάγοι, 911 ὦ γῆ Φεραία κτλ.; see too *Aj.* 596).

994–6. The OCT adopts Wunder's transposition of these lines to after 998's ὄϲϲοιϲ, and its editors justify this procedure (which avoids the need to take 994–6 parenthetically) in *Sophoclea*, p. 173.

994. ἱερῶν οἵαν οἵων ... (χάριν): for the interlaced word-order (AbaB) see Diggle, *ICS* 2 (1977), 110; for other juxtapositions of οἷοϲ in different genders, cases, numbers, see Bruhn, *Anhang*, § 223. I, Gygli-Wyss, *Das nominale Polyptoton*, p. 125 n. 3. S is particularly fond of patterning the word thus (cf. 1044–5).

994–5. 'An mir' (Schwyzer, *Gr. Gr.* ii. 468), not (with Radermacher ad loc.) 'mir zugedacht'; cf. Hyllus' ἐπί μοι μελέωι | βάροϲ ἄπλετον· ἐμμέμονεν φρήν at 981–2.

995. See on 982 above.

996. οἵαν ... οἵαν: for the agonized repetition see 1008 ἀπολεῖϲ μ᾽, ἀπολεῖϲ, 1026 θρώιϲκει δ᾽ αὖ, θρώιϲκει. For the double accusative construction governed by ποιεῖϲθαι, τίθεϲθαι, *vel sim.* see Schwyzer, *Gr. Gr.* ii. 80 (δ).

997. ἦν: Dawe's dissatisfaction at the reference back to κρηπίϲ (993) leads him into conjecture (*Studies* iii. 94: see on 358 above): ἥ for ἦν.

997–8. προϲιδεῖν ... ὄϲϲοιϲ: see on 241 above. Blaydes's προϲιδών is needless.

999. μανίαϲ ἄνθοϲ: for the similarities between the ensuing scene and other scenes of literal madness in Greek tragedy see Mattes, *Der Wahnsinn im gr. Mythos und in der Dichtung*, p. 80. ἄνθοϲ here is equivalent to ἀκμή, the peak of a state (good or bad); cf. *Ant.* 959–60 οὕτω τᾶϲ μανίαϲ δεινὸν ἀποϲτάζει | ἀνθηρόν τε μένοϲ and 1089 below.

LINES 989-1003

Also Solon fr. 4. 35 W ἄτης ἄνθεα φυόμενα. (Soph. fr. 172 Radt ἄλυπον... | ... ἄνθος ἀνίας is not, *pace* Pearson ad loc., a further example: see Renehan, *Glotta* 50 (1972), 41 ≏ *Greek Lexicographical Notes* i. 32.)

1000–1. For the implied link between medicine and magical incantations cf. *Aj.* 581–2 οὐ πρὸς ἰατροῦ σοφοῦ | θρηνεῖν ἐπωιδὰς πρὸς τομῶντι πήματι, Pind. *Pyth.* 3. 54 μαλακαῖς ἐπαοιδαῖς, *Od.* 19. 455 ff. (on which cf. J. U. Powell, *Folk-Lore* 41 (1930), 104–1, S. Laser, *Medizin und Körperflege* (Archaeol. Hom. S; 1983), 117 and nn. 309–10). The omission of the definite article before ἀοιδός is idiomatic in this type of duplication: see Kiefner, *Die Versparung*, pp. 41–2. For χειροτέχνης as a medical term see *Concordance des œuvres hippocratiques* s.v. (5. 4690) and D. Müller, *Handwerk und Sprache* (Beitr. z. kl. Phil. 51; 1974), 13 (Barrett on Eur. *Hipp.* 1399, followed by the OCT, argues that this 'actual vernacular word' should be spelt χειροτέχνας in these lyric anapaests) and on ἱατορία cf. N. van Brock, *Recherches sur le vocabulaire médical du grec ancien* (Paris 1961), 66, Long, *Language and Thought*, p. 56 and n. 97.

1001–2. ἄταν... κατακηλήσει: on the precise meaning of the noun here see J. Stallmach, *Ate* (Beitr. z. kl. Phil. 18; 1968), 83. On the notion of medical magic revealed by the verb see previous n.

1003. The Greek here is difficult to parallel precisely. Bruhn, *Anhang*, § 247 (25), alleges the existence of an idiom 'πόρρωθεν ἰδεῖν im Sinne von nicht, nicht mehr sehen'. Similarly Mazon's note to his translation: 'le sens est: "ce serait là un miracle que je ne verrais sans doute jamais"' and Radermacher. But the alleged idiom is hardly established by passages like Eur. *Hipp.* 102 πρόσωθεν ἀσπάζομαι (see Barrett ad loc.), which are essentially different. Zieliński's interpretation (pp. 613–14 n. 46 = p. 370 n. 2) of πόρρωθεν as meaning 'aus uralter Zeit', 'from the distant past' (with reference to Asclepius) as in Eur. *Hipp.* 831 is rather obscure. **θαῦμ':** for this noun used of people see on 961 above.

HERACLES, HYLLUS, OLD MAN (1004–1043)
Strophe and antistrophe

1004a/1023a	– –	sp. or exclamation
		extra metrum
1004b/1023b	– ∪ ∪ – ∪ ⌣	doch.

COMMENTARY

1005a/1024	$-\cup\cup-\bar{\cup}\rightharpoondown\|$	doch.
1005b/1025	$-\cup\cup-\bar{\cup}-{}^H\|$	doch.
1006/1026	$\bar{\cup}\cup\cup---$	doch.
1007/1028	$--------$	anap. dim.
1008/1029	$\cup\cup-\underline{\underline{\cup}}-$	anap.
1009/1030	$\widetilde{\cup\cup}\widetilde{\cup}\cup\cup-\cup\rightharpoondown\|$	glyc.?
1010–14/1031–40	dactylic hexameters	
1015a/1041a	$--$	sp. or exclamation *extra metrum*
1015b–16/1041b–42	$-\cup\cup---\quad-\cup\cup-\cup-$	2 doch.
1017/1043	$-\cup\cup-\cup-\quad-\cup\cup-\bar{\cup}-\|\|$	2 doch.
1018–22	dactylic hexameters	

In the above, 1023a, 1004b, and 1041a are hypothetically supplied on the assumption that they have dropped out of the text. For hexameters in Attic tragedy see Jocelyn, *The Tragedies of Ennius*, p. 386, Radt, *TrGF* iv. 237, Maas, *GM*, § 85.

J. F. A. Seidler, *De versibus dochmiacis tragicorum Graecorum* (Leipzig 1811–12), 311 ff., proposed a complex rearrangement of these lines which for some time won general acceptance, particularly in the influential editions of Jebb and Pearson. It is still supported by J. Irigoin, *Théâtre et spectacle dans l'antiquité* (Actes du Colloque de Strasbourg, 5–7 novembre, 1981). But the vastly intricate interlacing response thus produced (far surpassing in complexity the interweaving of the stanzas in the κομμός at Aesch. *Cho.* 306 ff.) is quite without parallel, and relies for its existence upon a considerable number of emendations. Since a far more normal scheme of response can be produced by postulating no larger a number of corruptions and lacunae, it seems a reasonable principle to prefer the normal to the eccentric. This was the approach of A. H. Coxon, *CR* 61 (1947), 69 ff. (and, independently, of Dain and Mazon in their Budé text), whose treatment has been further refined and improved on by Lloyd-Jones, *YCS* 22 (1972), 267 ff. (cf. Stinton, p. 142), and *Sophoclea*, pp. 173–4, and now seems to have won general approval. Coxon's thesis can claim a sort of independent confirmation inasmuch as the metrical responsions postulated also exhibit verbal response (cf. Pfeiffer, *Sitzb. d. Bayer. Akad. d. Wiss., phil.-hist. Abt.* 2 (1938), 46).

LINES 1004-1010

1005. ἔᾱτέ μ᾽ ἔᾱτέ μέ ~ 1024 τᾶιδέ μέ, τᾶιδέ μέ: cf. Aesch. *Pers.* 1038 διαῑνε διαῑνε ~ 1046 ἔρεcc᾽ ἔρεccέ. Cf. the variation of quantity of the type δείλαιοc ... δειλαίαι (*Ant.* 1310–11) which 'of the tragedians only S appears to affect' (Renehan, *CP* 80 (1985), 150); for the enclitic με cf. 1008 below. **ἐᾶτέ με** = 'let go of me', according to Stinton (pp. 142–3), comparing Eur. *Hipp.* 1372 μέθετέ με, *Phil.* 816 ff. μέθες μέθες με ... μέθες ποτέ (cf. Neoptolemus' reply οὔ φημ᾽ ἐάcειν). The meaning 'let me sleep' is preferred by Lloyd-Jones (*Sophoclea*, p. 174), citing *Phil.* 768 and Eur. *Tro.* 466. See Addenda.

1005–6. See Stinton, pp. 142 ff., arguing that the available evidence shows εὐνά(ζ)ω and compounds to be invariably transitive (whether used literally or metaphorically): cf. εὔναcον εὐναcόν μ᾽ at 1041 below. Therefore either (*a*) εὐνάcαι here is optative and its subject has been displaced thus: ἐᾶτέ μ᾽ ἐᾶτέ με | δύcμορον· εὐνάcαι [ἐᾶτέ με δύcτανον εὐνάcαι] ⟨μ᾽⟩ | εὐνάcαι ⟨δαίμων⟩ (cf. *Ant.* 833 ἅι με δαίμων ὁμοιοτάταν κατευνάζει), providing further word-responsion (⟨δαίμων⟩ ~ 1026 δαίμον); or alternatively (*b*) Ellendt's εὐνᾶcθαι for εὐνάcαι is right. The latter is preferred by Lloyd-Jones in *Sophoclea*, p. 174.

1008. ἀπολεῖc μ᾽, ἀπολεῖc: on enclitic με's position here see above 1005; cf. Eur. *Andr.* 856 ὀλεῖ μ᾽ ὀλεῖ με; contrast Eur. *Hipp.* 1371 ὀδύνα μ᾽ ὀδύνα βαίνει.

1009. ἀνατέτροφαc: the perfect tense stresses the duration of the effect ('it is (and will always be) awake'); on the form see Wackernagel, 'Studien zum gr. Perfektum' (1904), 12 = *Kl. Schr.* ii. 1009. **μύcηι:** the verb is found elsewhere in drama only at fr. 774 (cf. Pfeiffer, *Sitzb. d. Bayer. Akad. d. Wiss., phil.-hist. Abt.* 2 (1938), 40) but for the metaphor of the sleeping disease cf. 1242 below. On the relative clause with subjunctive see Bers, p. 157.

1010 ff. The 'odd placing of syntactic pauses here' (ἅδ᾽ αὖθ᾽ ἕρπει· | πόθεν ἔcτ᾽ ὦ || Ἕλλανες πάντων ἀδικώτατοι ἀνέρεc | οἷc δή ||) is observed by West, *GM*, p. 128. For the employment of short, sharp clauses thus to convey the effects of frenzy or madness see Mattes, *Der Wahnsinn im gr. Mythos und in der Dichtung*, p. 81.

1010. ἧπταί μου, τοτοτοῖ: for this type of *Klangeffekt* used in tragedy to convey the picture of possession by madness, frenzy, and the like cf. Eur. *Hipp.* 1370–1 αἰαῖ αἰαῖ· | καὶ νῦν ὀδύνα μ᾽ ὀδύνα βαίνει, and in general Mattes (cited in previous n.), p. 81 n. 19. Such

COMMENTARY

exclamations are commonly corrupted in at least some manuscripts: see Headlam's *Herodas*, p. 154 n. 2. **ἄδ' αὖθ' ἕρπει:** the only Sophoclean instance of αὖτε, an epicism shunned by Euripides, more popular with Aeschylus: see Johansen and Whittle on Aesch. *Suppl.* 474. For the idiomatic nature of the word in referring to a new onset of madness or pain see on 987 above.

1010–11. πόθεν ἔστ' κτλ.: on the meaning of this question and its tone ('not a mere request for information ... but an expression of indignation') see Winnington-Ingram, *BICS* 16 (1969), 47 n. 12; also Mastronarde, *Contact and Discontinuity*, p. 16. **ὦ:** the exclamation introducing a vocative at line-end was taken as a sign of corruption by Wilamowitz, *Gr. Versk.*, p. 348 n. 2. More likely it is indicative of impassioned frenzy (see above on 1010ff.). Koechly (*ZA* 9 (1842), 787) conjectured Ἕλλανες πάντων, which is approved by Lloyd-Jones (*Sophoclea*, p. 175) and printed in the OCT. The paradosis Ἑλλάνων gives us a genitive difficult to interpret (Campbell took it as partitive) and the assimilation of endings the emendation presupposes is a common form of corruption (cf. on 547ff.).

1011. ἀνέρες: epic (like S here) uses this form for its metrical convenience: see Sideras, *Aeschylus Homericus*, p. 100. **οἷς:** the antecedent to the relative here must be Ἕλλανες: see Winnington-Ingram (cited in the previous n.).

1012. πολλὰ ... ἐν πόντωι ... καθαίρων: cf. Eur. *Her.* 225 ποντίων καθαρμάτων, ibid. 400ff. ποντίας θ' ἁλὸς μυχοὺς | εἰσέβαινε κτλ. **ἐν πόντωι ... κατά τε δρία:** cf. Pind. *Nem.* 1. 63–4 (Heracles' labours) ὅσσους μὲν ἐν χέρσωι κτανών, | ὅσσους δὲ πόντωι θῆρας. **κατά τε δρία πάντα:** see Barrett's edn. of Eur. *Hipp.*, pp. 310, 435, on the legitimacy of this scansion in tragedy. As for the sense conveyed, cf. Eur. *Her.* cited above. For the sequence with τε following μέν here see Hutchinson on Aesch. *ScT* 922ff., Kranz, *Stasimon*, p. 305.

1014. For the position of the negatives here (at the start of the clause and then before the verb) see Fraenkel on Aesch. *Ag.* 1634–5, Moorhouse, p. 336. **ἔγχος** = 'weapon' (see Pearson on fr. 781). **οὔ ποτε τρέψει:** Zo's ἐπιτρέψει would have to be taken as Sophoclean *abusio* of the usual meaning ('entrust'). There is no parallel for the alleged construction of ἀποτρέψω ἐπί + dative by analogy with ἀποβλέπω εἰς. (On the confusion between ἀπο(-) and ἐπι(-) evinced by the manuscripts

LINES 1010-1023

see on 843-4 above.) οὔ ποτε τρέψει ('non aliquando convertet') is the most convincing conjecture so far (cf. *Sophoclea*, p. 175).

1015 ff. With these agonized instructions to end the speaker's pain (and life) cf. *Phil.* 747 ff. πρὸς θεῶν, πρόχειρον εἴ τί coι, τέκνον, πάρα | ξίφος χεροῖν, πάταξον εἰς ἄκρον πόδα· | ἀπάμηςον ὡς τάχιςτα· μὴ φείςηι βίου (βίαι Burges).

1016. Dawe's alteration of κρᾶτα to χρῶτα (*Studies* iii. 94-5) has won the approval of West ((1), p. 366) and (with reservations) D. Bain, *Masters, Servants and Orders in Greek Tragedy* (Manchester 1981), 23 n. 1; his grounds do not bear investigation, however. Against his incredulity at decapitation as a means of suicide see Bain, loc. cit., and the sensible remarks of P. Gildersleeves, *JHS* 105 (1985), 155. Heracles seems to recur to this request ten lines or so later: cf. 1035 παῖςον ἐμᾶς ὑπὸ κληιδός. Dawe's complaint (accepted by Bain) that the form of the question is ludicrous is no more acceptable: on questions that are really exclamations see above on 892.

1017. Lloyd-Jones, *YCS* 22 (1972), 269-70, suggests interpreting these lines as οὐδ' ἀπαράξαι ⟨μου⟩ κρᾶτα βίου θέλει | ⟨–∪∪–⟩ μολὼν τοῦ στυγεροῦ, with παυσίπονος or λυσίπονος in the lacuna to govern the genitive βίου ('putting an end to the pains of life'): cf. the scholion's paraphrase ἐλευθερῶσαι τοῦ μοχθηροῦ βίου. This is approved by Stinton, p. 145 n. 89. Wakefield's βίαι, then, is unnecessary, indeed otiose (cf. *Sophoclea*, p. 175).

1018-19. Examples of the formula μεῖζον ἢ κατ' ἄνθρωπον or ἄνδρα are collected by Headlam on Herodas 4. 69.

1019-20. This hopeless crux is analysed by Stinton, pp. 144-5. Like Heracles it cannot be healed.

1021. λαθίπονον δ' ὀδύναν: Musgrave suggested λαθίπονον δ' ὀδυνᾶν ... βίοτον ('a life which makes him forget his pains') but ὀδύναν need not be changed (cf. Stinton, p. 145): see on 1017 above.
οὔτ' ἔνδοθεν οὔτε θύραθεν: for this type of polar expression see Ed. Fraenkel, *Plautinisches im Plautus*, p. 11 ≏ *Elementi plautini in Plauto* p. 10 and n. 4 and on Aesch. *Ag.* 961.

1022. τοιαῦτα νέμει Ζεύς: for Zeus as the subject of this and similar verbs see B. Borecký, *Survivals of some Tribal Ideas in Classical Greek* (Prague 1965), 81.

1023 ff. For an analysis of the impassioned exclamations here see Schadewaldt, *Monolog und Selbstgespräch*, p. 70.

COMMENTARY

1026. ἰὼ δαῖμον: some scholars (see e.g. Schadewaldt (cited in previous n.), p. 71 n. 2) take this as a mere cry of pain (cf. 1112), not an appeal for help; others take it as a genuine apostrophe like 1031 ἰὼ ἰὼ Παλλάς: cf. Hutchinson on Aesch. *ScT* 481, arguing that ἰώ + vocative in Aeschylus and S is always a proper address (cf. *OT* 1311 ἰὼ δαῖμον, ἵν' ἐξήλου). For continuation with δέ after such a vocative cf. Hes. *Op.* 213 ὦ Πέρςη, cὺ δ' ἄκουε, Fraenkel, *Beob. zu Aristoph.*, p. 96.

1027ff. θρώιςκει ... νόςος: cf. Eur. *Hipp.* 1351–2 διά μου κεφαλῆς ἄιccouc' ὀδύναι, | κατά τ' ἐγκέφαλον πηδᾶι cφάκελος. For this metaphor of leaping (down etc.) upon the victim, used of destructive agents, see B. C. Dietrich, *Death, Fate and the Gods* (London 1965), 145 n. 1. On the significance of αὖ see on 987 above.

1031. ἰὼ ἰὼ Παλλάς: the constant protector and helper of Heracles in literature (cf. West on Hes. *Th.* 318) and art (cf. G. Beckel, *Götterbeistand in d. Bildüberlieferung gr. Heldensagen* (Waldsassen 1961), 17–18). **τόδε μ' αὖ λωβᾶται:** when με and αὖ are juxtaposed, sometimes one sometimes the other yields its usual right to stand second in the sentence (cf. e.g. Ar. *Eq.* 336 οὐκ αὖ μ' ἐάcειc): for details see Fraenkel on Aesch. *Ag.* 1215–16.

1034. ἔγχος: see on 1014 above. Hyllus ignores the request here and at 1016 since its fulfilment would be unthinkable: see Bain, *Masters, Servants and Orders in Greek Tragedy*, p. 21.

1035. παῖcον ἐμᾶc ὑπὸ κληιδόc: like 1016 (see ad loc.), this is probably a request to be beheaded: κληῖc in *Il.* 5. 146, 579, 17. 309, 21. 117 seems to refer to the collar-bone. **μ' ἐχόλωcεν:** outside of Homer the only authors to use this verb in the active with aorist tense are Hes. *Th.* 568 and S here: see West on the Hesiodic passage, Wackernagel, *Spr. Unt. zu Homer*, p. 290.

1036. ἄθεος can be used merely as 'a generic term for wicked' (Stevens on Eur. *Andr.* 491); cf. W. Fahr, *ΘΕΟΥC NOMIZEIN: Zum Problem der Anfänge des Atheismus bei den Griechen* (Spudasmata 26; 1969), 16. **τὰν ὧδ' ἐπίδοιμι πεcοῦcαν:** for other instances of this *Racheformel* see Fraenkel, *Horace*, p. 29 n. 1 (additional examples in Headlam's note on Herodas 3. 97). For the legitimacy of such wishes within a relative clause see KG ii/2. 429 (5).

1040–1. For parallels to Seidler's effective transposition here see Jackson, *MS*, p. 230.

1040. ὦ γλυκὺς Ἅιδας: for other examples of ὦ followed by the

LINES 1026-1045

nominative ('address rather than exclamation') see Moorhouse, p. 25; cf. V. Schmidt, *Spr. Unt. zu Herondas* (Berlin 1968), 91–2. Prayers to a directly named Hades are rare in Greek literature (see on 1085 below); here the invocation is accompanied by the paradoxical propitiatory adjective γλυκύϲ (cf. *OC* 106 ἴτ' ὦ γλυκεῖαι παῖδεϲ ἀρχαίου Ϲκότου (of the Erinyes) and Wilamowitz on Men. *Epitr.* 143 (*Das Schiedsgericht*, pp. 52 f.), Schadewaldt, *Monolog und Selbstgespräch*, pp. 70–1). Since sleep is γλυκύϲ (Alcm. 3. 1. 7 P (cited above on 989 ff.) etc.) and H prays in the next line for metaphorical slumber (= death), the adjective is appropriate.

1042. Διὸϲ αὐθαίμων = 'one of Zeus' own blood': cf. *OC* 1078, where αὔθαιμοϲ means 'one of one's own blood' and the discussion of analogous words (αὐτάδελφοϲ, αὐτογενήϲ, etc.) by Johansen and Whittle on Aesch. *Suppl.* 8. For the coexistence of the forms αὐθαίμων/αὔθαιμοϲ cf. ὁμαίμων/ὅμαιμοϲ, ϲυναίμων/ϲύναιμοϲ. F. Sommer, *Zur Geschichte der gr. Nominalkomposita* (Abh. d. Bayer. Ak. d. Wiss., phil.-hist. Kl. 27; 1948), 85, compared αὐτόετεϲ in *Od.* 3. 322, Theophr. *Hist. plant.* 3. 7. 1; αὐτομήτωρ in Semon. 7. 12 W.

1043. ὠκυπέται μόρωι: noted by Johansen and Whittle on Aesch. *Suppl.* 734 as one of the few exceptions (together with *Ant.* 1215 and Aesch. *ScT* 65) to their rule that 'ὠκύϲ and its compounds normally denote an inherent property, not the quickness shown on a particular occasion, for which ταχύϲ is normally used'. **φθίϲαϲ:** see on 709 above.

FINAL EPISODE (1044-1258)

1044–5. The chorus's reaction to Heracles' frenzied raving both here and at 1112–13 is one of regret at the suffering and impending death of the great hero. No criticism or reproach is offered.

1044. ἔφριξα: for the aorist of sudden emotion cf. *Aj.* 693 ἔφριξ' ἔρωτι, περιχαρὴϲ δ' ἀνεπτάμαν, and see Barrett on Eur. *Hipp.* 614, Denniston on Eur. *El.* 215, Moorhouse, pp. 195–6. Contrast Aesch. *Suppl.* 346 πέφρικα λεύϲϲων, *PV* 695 πέφρικ' εἰϲιδοῦϲα, ibid. 540 φρίϲϲω.

1044–5. ϲυμφοράϲ ... οἵαιϲ ... ἐλαύνεται: cf. Eur. *Ion* 1619 f. ἐλαύνεται | ϲυμφοραῖϲ οἶκοϲ, *Andr.* 31 κακοῖϲ ... ἐλαύνομαι, *Alc.* 675–6, *Aj.* 275. On the juxtaposition οἵαιϲ οἶοϲ see above on

COMMENTARY

994. For such relatives as governed by a verb (κλύουϲ') cf. *El.* 751–2 ϲτρατὸϲ ... ἀνωτότουξε τὸν νεανίαν, | οἷ᾽ ἔργα δράϲαϲ, οἷα λαγχάνει κακά, KG ii/2. 101.

1046 ff. The opening lines introduce a theme that recurs throughout Heracles' great speech (1058 ff., 1101 ff.), in each case emphasized by a priamel: 'I, who have endured so much, am now destroyed—by a woman.' See Zagagi, *Tradition and Originality in Plautus*, pp. 42 ff., 55, 59, in her important discussion of the 'mythological hyperboles in monologues and speeches' of Greek and Roman drama. As she says, Heracles here 'belittles his past experiences in comparison with his present distress ... the passage falls into the category of that familiar pattern of thought in which the present occurrence on stage is declared to have surpassed former mythological events (even though these events were also personal experiences of Heracles)'. For the priamel framework (cf. on 499 above) in which this pattern of thought is expressed see on 1046, 1058, 1089 ff.

1046. ὦ πολλὰ δὴ κτλ.: cf. Eur. *Her.* 1250 ὁ πολλὰ δὴ τλὰϲ Ἡρακλῆϲ λέγει τάδε; (Theseus to Heracles) and Heracles' self-address at Eur. *Alc.* 837 ὦ πολλὰ τλᾶϲα καρδία καὶ χεὶρ ἐμή. In the present passage, however, πολλά is idiomatic in the context of a priamel formally similar to the famous instance at *Ant.* 332 ff.: 'many hardships have I suffered, but never [see on 1048] one such as this.' See W. H. Race, *The Classical Priamel from Homer to Boethius* (*Mnem.* suppl. 74; 1982), 92 (on our passage in particular), pp. 31–2, 81, 112 (on words like πολλά, μυρία at the start of a priamel). **θερμά:** Aesch. *ScT* 603 ff. ἢ γὰρ ξυνειϲβὰϲ πλοῖον εὐϲεβὴϲ ἀνὴρ | ναύτῃϲι θερμοῖϲ καὶ πανουργίαι τινὶ | ὄλωλεν ἀνδρῶν ϲὺν θεοπτύϲτωι γένει, *Eum.* 560 γελᾶι δὲ δαίμων ἐπ᾽ ἀνδρὶ θερμῶι, etc. display the usual pejorative sense of this adjective, though Antiphon 2. 4. 5 (θερμὸϲ καὶ ἀνδρεῖοϲ) looks like an approving use of the word, as does Ar. *Plut.* 415 θερμὸν ἔργον. Some scholars (e.g. Jebb) have wished to see such a use here. However, in the light of the whole passage's literary function, θερμά, like the following κακά, *must* be pejorative,[40] since Heracles is using past sufferings as a foil to his present agony which exceeds even

---

[40] καθάρματ᾽ οὐ ... | ... μοχθήϲαϲ (cf. Eur. *Her.* 225–6 ποντίων καθαρμάτων | χέρϲου τ᾽ ἀμοιβὰϲ ὧν ἐμόχθηϲεν χάριν) was proposed by B. Jaya Suriy, *CR* 24 (1974), 3, under the misapprehension that καὶ θερμὰ κοὐ (rather than καὶ θερμὰ καί) is the paradosis.

LINES 1044-1047

them: cf. Aesch. *Cho.* 631–2 κακῶν δὲ πρεσβεύεται τὸ Λήμνιον | λόγωι (followed by the statement that Clytemnestra's wickedness outdoes even that of the Lemnian women).

1046–7. According to Mazon ad loc. 'le καί qui précède n'a pas la même valeur que les autres καί des deux vers 1046–1047. Il signifie même et renforce l'expression' ('cruel even to relate': Lloyd-Jones in his review of the Budé text (*Gnomon* 28 (1956), 109)): for phrases like αἰςχρὸν καὶ λέγειν/λόγωι cf. Vahlen's edition of Aristotle's *Poetics*, 3rd edn. (Berlin 1885), Mantissa Adnotationis Grammaticae, p. 212. For κακά of H's labours cf. Eur. *Her.* 1411 ἔτλην κακά. But the change in meaning of καί is very harsh. Bothe's κοὐ λόγωι (for similar scribal omission of vowels in synizesis or crasis see Fraenkel, *Mus. Helv.* 24 (1967), 85)[41] may likewise seem deficient as an antithesis, though one might quote Aesch. *ScT* 845–6 ἦλθε δ᾽ αἰακτὰ πήματ᾽ οὐ λόγωι and the other passages cited by Headlam on Aesch. *Ag.* 1196 for λόγωι implying 'in word *only*'. However, as we shall shortly see, such denigration of tradition (λόγος) does not suit the general tenor of our passage. Jackson's καὶ λόγωι καλά (*MS*, pp. 218–19) presupposes a very common corruption (illustrated by Kannicht on Eur. *Hel.* 264 ff.).[42] One is loath to reject his eloquent translation of this ('wild work which the world called glorious') but the Greek does boil down to 'and fine in reputation'; also (more to the point) Heracles is not boasting here but lamenting (see above, p. 236). More appropriate, therefore, is Wunder's καὶ λόγων πέρα (dismissed as 'divination' by Jackson, loc. cit.). But, again, denigration of 'report' is undesirable. For, given the context's status (see above) as a mythological *exemplum*, λόγος here should bear the same meaning it has in other passages where it introduces the *exemplum* (see Zagagi (cited on 1046 ff.), pp. 37 n. 79, 40

---

[41] To the examples there cited Fraenkel later added in the margin of his copy of the offprint (now in the Ashmolean Library) our passage, Men. *Dysc.* 180 τὸ πρᾶγμα ⟨ἦν⟩ (sic suppl. Maas; ⟨γ᾽⟩ *complures*) and Soph. *Ant.* 33 (τοῖς μὴ εἰδόςιν codd.: τοῖςι μὴ εἰδόςιν Heath). See too *Ichn.* (fr. 314) 228: καιποδων Π, κὠπαδῶν Maas, *Deutsche Literaturzeitung* (1912), 2783–4 = *Kl. Schr.* 43, prob. Lehnus, *Anagennesis* 2 (1982), 71–2; cf. line 896 of our play.

[42] For modern examples see Wilamowitz's text of Eur. *Her.* 96 (καλῶν for κακῶν), Denniston's note on Eur. *El.* 1015, where line 589 of our play is cited as δοκεῖς παρ᾽ ἡμῖν οὐ βεβουλεῦςθαι καλῶς, and S. L. Schein, *The Iambic Trimeter in Aeschylus and Sophocles: A Study in Metrical Form* (Leiden 1979), 49.

COMMENTARY

n. 86). Compare in particular Aesch. *Cho.* 631–2 (from a passage that, like the present, combines *exemplum* with priamel form), cited in the previous n.

1048–9. Cf. the similar reference to Hera at Eur. *Her.* 1303 ff.; but the theme is not prominent in our play (nor is that of Eurystheus' persecution, that tyrant being named for the first and last time in the play at 1049).

1048. κοὔπω: see J. Blomqvist, *Das sogenannte KAI Adversativum* (Uppsala 1979), 49 n. 30. The present instance, like that at *Ant.* 332 πολλὰ τὰ δεινὰ κοὐδὲν ἀνθρώπου δεινότερον πέλει, marks a crucial stage in the progression of the priamel (see on 1046 above). Similarly idiomatic within the priamel is the occurrence of words like οὐδεπώποτε: see Race (cited on 1046), pp. 36–7 and n. 11. **ἄκοιτις ἡ Διός:** for the position of the definite article cf. on 732 above.

1050. For the use of οἷον within a priamel to emphasize a 'crowning example' see Race (cited on 1046), p. 34 and n. 6 (cf. p. 105 and n. 169 on ὅσον). **δολῶπις** is ἅπαξ: cf. εὐῶπις (also of Deianeira) at 523.

1051–2. Ἐρινύων | ὑφαντὸν ἀμφίβληστρον: cf. Aesch. *Ag.* 1580 ὑφαντοῖς ἐν πέπλοις Ἐρινύων, 1382 ἄπειρον ἀμφίβληστρον, *Cho.* 492 μέμνησο δ' ἀμφίβληστρον ὡς ἐκαίνισας, note on 831 above; for the force of Ἐρινύων cf. also *Aj.* 1034 ἆρ' οὐκ Ἐρινὺς τοῦτ' ἐχάλκευσε ξίφος; **ὑφαντόν:** Jebb perceptively observed that the occurrence of this adjective rather than πλεκτόν shows that what is referred to is not a real net but a robe metaphorically described as a net. In other words, we have a literary kenning whereby a noun used metaphorically is qualified by an adjective denying a quality of that noun in its literal sense to emphasize the noun's metaphorical status. Cf. Wærn, *ΓΗΣ ΟΣΤΕΑ*, p. 55: 'The Greek kenning often contains an oxymoron or a paradox.' The paradox is usually expressed by a negative adjective (e.g. πέδαις ἀχαλκεύτοισι of Clytemnestra's ἀμφίβληστρον in Aesch. *Cho.* 493; other examples in Wærn and in West on Hes. *Op.* 525), but it can be expressed, as here, positively. Jebb compared *PV* 1022 πτηνὸς κύων (of an eagle); see too ibid. 395 τετρασκελὴς οἰωνός, Aesch. *Ag.* 135 πτανοῖσιν κυσί, ibid. 1258 δίπους λέαινα, *Suppl.* 895 δίπους ὄφις, *ScT* 64 κῦμα χερσαῖον στρατοῦ, 206 ἱππικὰ πηδάλια, fr. 282 Radt κυσὶν ἀεροφοίτοις, 'Faith, he tonight hath boarded a Land Carract' (Shakespeare, *Othello*, 1. ii. 5, cited by Rose on *ScT* 64). See too such Homeric examples as ὑγρὰ

LINES 1045-1058

κέλευθα (Il. 1. 312, Od. 3. 71, etc.) or ἰχθυόεντα κέλευθα (Od. 3. 117).

1053. πλευραῖcι ... προcμαχθέν: cf. 767-7 προcπτύccεται | πλευραῖcιν ἀρτίκολλοc.

1054. πλεύμονόc τ' ἀρτηρίαc: on lungs as the vital seat see above on 778. The plural is more familiar but for singular cf. Plato *Tim.* 84D; on the variant πνευ- see above on 567. On the meaning of ἀρτηρία see Long, *Language and Thought*, p. 57 and n. 102.

1055-6. ῥοφεῖ ... πέπωκεν: cf. fr. 743 Radt αἱματορρόφοc (of the Erinys Tisiphone: see Pfeiffer, *WS* 79 (1966), 63 ff.). For the blood-drinking Erinys see Pearson on fr. 743. With the whole picture compare *El.* 784 ff. ἥδε γὰρ μείζων βλάβη (= Ἐρινύc: cf. *Ant.* 1104, Eur. *Ion* 520, etc.) | ξύνοικοc ἦν μοι, τοὐμὸν ἐκπίνουc᾽ ἀεὶ | ψυχῆc ἄκρατον αἷμα.

1055. ξυνοικοῦν: the verb is perfectly appropriate, indeed Sophoclean, in this context of personification (cf. K. J. Dover, *Aristophanic Comedy* (London 1972), 47-8, *El.* 784 ff. as cited above, *Phil.* 1168 ἄχθοc ὁ ξυνοικεῖ, *OC* 1237-8 γῆραc ἄφιλον, ἵνα πρόπαντα | κακὰ κακῶν ξυνοικεῖ, ibid. 1259 γέρων γέροντι cυγκατῴκηκεν πίνοc (see further Johansen and Whittle on Aesch. *Suppl.* 415)). Cf. too the medical use of the verb cυνεδρεύω (cf. LSJ s.v. III) of attendant symptoms. Dawe's complaint that the word is 'a dry, cold, tame, and unemotional statement of location' (*Studies* iii. 95) is totally misleading and his bafflement at 'the relationship in sense between ῥοφεῖ and ξυνοικοῦν' unnecessary. His conjecture is best left unspecified.

χλωρὸν αἷμα: see West on Hes. *Op.* 743 for this adjective's use of 'vigorous life without reference to colour'; also R. J. Edgeworth, *Glotta* 65 (1987), 137 n. 14 (and pp. 136-7 on Cicero's rendering of the phrase (*Tusc. Disp.* 2. 8) as 'decolorem sanguinem').

1057. ἀφράcτωι ... πέδηι: cf. Aesch. *Cho.* 493 πέδαιc γ᾽ ἀχαλκεύτοιcι θηρευθείc (cf. on 1052 above), 982 πέδαc τε χειροῖν καὶ ποδοῖν ξυνωρίδα (-ίδοc Hermann).

1058 ff. A similar list of adversaries whom Heracles has overcome occurs in a fragmentary papyrus (*TrGF* adesp. 653 (see the bibliography cited ad loc.)). There too the hero is probably the speaker.

1058. κοὐ: καί Wilamowitz*, but the long list of negatives at 1058 ff. (κοὐ ... οὔθ᾽ ... οὔτε ... οὔτ᾽ ... οὔθ᾽, cf. *TrGF* adesp. 653. 54 ff. ὃν οὐ λέοντεc εἶδον [| παίζ[ο]ντεc οὔτ᾽ ἀμει. [), leading up

239

COMMENTARY

to the mention of D at 1063 μόνη με δὴ καθεῖλε; cf. fr.adesp. 653. 56 γυνὴ καθεῖλε δυcκλ[ε(-)]), is very effective, and indeed perfectly idiomatic within the framework of a priamel: '*not* spears, *not* Giants, *not* ... *but* a mere woman: see Race, *The Classical Priamel*, pp. 92–3. **λόγχη:** collective for spearsmen, as in Eur. *Phoen.* 442; cf. Verdenius on Pind. *Ol.* 7. 19.

1059. cτρατὸc Γιγάντων: the Giants were often portrayed as soldiers in early literature and art: see West on Hes. *Th.* 186, F. Vian, *La Guerre des Géants* (Paris 1952), 186–7, 210ff. For γηγενής see Batr. 7 γηγενέων ἀνδρῶν μιμούμενοι ἔργα Γιγάντων. **θήρειος βία:** translated by Cicero as referring specifically to the Centaurs (*Tusc. Disp.* 2. 8 'non biformato impetu | Centaurus').

1060. οὔθ' Ἑλλάc: it is not necessary to supply γαῖα from 1061 (cf. Pearson on fr. 17). For Ἑλλάc as a noun on its own see e.g. 1112 below. **ἄγλωccoc:** here alone equivalent to βάρβαρος. Fraenkel on Aesch. *Ag.* 1050f. pertinently quotes from the *Daily Telegraph*, 8 May 1939, the observation that 'the Russian masses ... group together as "the dumb ones" ... those (Western foreigners) who cannot speak Russian'. **ὅcην:** Blaydes conjectured ὅcων, but for the attraction of the antecedent into the case of the relative see above on 283.

1061. γαῖαν καθαίρων: cf. Eur. *Her.* 225 ποντίων καθαρμάτων and above, 1012 κατά τε δρία πάντα καθαίρων. For the emphatic force within the priamel of the postponed πω at the end of this line see on κοὔπω at 1048 above.

1062. γυνὴ δέ: the adversative δέ is idiomatic when the priamel's foil is dismissed and its climactic point achieved (cf. on ἀλλ' at 503 above): cf. Sappho fr. 16. 4 and Race (cited on 1046), *passim*. **κἄνανδρος:** the impossibility of the paradosis is inadvertently revealed by Kamerbeek's defence of it: 'οὖcα stands zeugmatically (first with predicate, then with internal acc.) in such a way that in the second phrase it is equivalent to φῦcα'; Jackson (*MS*, pp. 70–1) says all that is needful (except that Tournier, *Rev. Phil.* 6 (1882), 142, anticipated his conjecture). His reconstruction of the process whereby the wrong negating syllable came to be added (γυνὴ δὲ θῆλυc οὖcα κἄνανδρος φύcιν → γυνὴ δὲ θῆλυc οὖcα κἀνδρός φύcιν → γυνὴ δὲ θῆλυc οὖcα κοὐκ ἀνδρὸς φύcιν) is completely convincing. For the juxtaposition of γυνὴ and θῆλυc cf. Eur. *Med.* 928 γυνή δὲ θῆλυ and Ar. *Lys.* 708 (paratragic: see Rau, *Paratragodia*, p. 199) κακῶν γυναικῶν ἔργα καὶ θήλεια φρήν. For γυνὴ δέ... | μόνη με δὴ καθεῖλε cf. TrGF adesp. 653. 56 γυνὴ καθεῖλε δυσκλ[ε(-).

1063. μόνη με δὴ καθεῖλε: this phrase represents the climax of the priamel commenced at 1058 (see ad loc.); for the frequency of words like μόνος, *solus* at such a climax see Race (cited on 1046), p. 33 n. 4, and for the ambiguity of μόνη in the present passage ('alone/only') ibid. 93 n. 142, 105 and n. 170.

1064. For this sort of rhetorical device to stress true parentage or filial status see M. Griffith, *HSCP* 82 (1978), 83 ff., esp. pp. 85 n. 8 and 86 n. 12 (add to his examples in the latter note *Aj.* 547 εἴπερ δικαίως ἔστ᾽ ἐμὸς τὰ πατρόθεν). We need not follow E. Harrison, *CQ* 7 (1913), 133–4[43] in detecting an allusion to the sinister etymology of Deianeira's name (see above on 531 ff.).

1066–7. χεροῖν caῖν... | ἐς χεῖρα: an effective repetition (though ranked by Jackson, *MS*, p. 222, among his 'unconscious repetitions by the poet': see, rather, Easterling, *Hermes* 101 (1973), 24).

1068–9. τοὐμὸν... ἢ κείνης... εἶδος: for the omission of the definite article in the second colon here see Moorhouse, p. 153. For the juxtaposition of adjective and genitive pronoun linked by connecting or disjunctive particle cf. OC 606 τἀμὰ κἀκείνων πικρά, Eur. *Phoen.* 474 τοὐμόν τε καὶ τοῦδ᾽, Braswell on Pind. *Pyth.* 4. 175 (e). Cf. on 775 above.

1070. ἴθ᾽, ὦ τέκνον: cf. *Phil.* 750 ἴθ᾽, ὦ παῖ in a very similar context (see above on 974 ff.). I am reminded that there is a significant pattern to Heracles' use of affectionate vocatives like τέκνον or παῖ when he is getting his own way: they disappear when (e.g. at 1238 below) Hyllus thwarts (or seems to thwart) him. Compare *Philoctetes* and its hero's addresses to Neoptolemus. **τόλμησον:** for the verb used thus in tragic appeals see Rau, *Paratragodia*, p. 151.

1070–1. Cf. Eur. *El.* 672 οἴκτιρέ γ᾽ ἡμᾶς· οἰκτρὰ γὰρ πεπόνθαμεν. **ὥστε παρθένος:** see R. P. Winnington-Ingram, *Sophocles: An Interpretation* (Cambridge 1980), 84–5: H 'feels pity only for himself and only in the extreme of agony and weakness, when he seeks from others the pity he has never shown... he is not only destroyed, but reduced to crying like a girl... he is reduced to woman's status (1075)'.

1072. βέβρυχα κλαίων: the paradoxical picture of the supreme hero

[43] So too (independently) L. P. Rank, *Etymologiseering en verwante verschijnselen bij Homerus* (Assen 1951), 143.

COMMENTARY

Heracles breaking down in tears is used by several authors to emphasize different events: see e.g. Bacch. 5. 155 ff. with Maehler ad loc., Gow on Theocr. *Id.* 24. 31, Wilamowitz on Eur. *Her.* 1353. On Greek attitudes to weeping in general and Sophocles' exploitation of the motif (here and elsewhere) 'to combine heroism with pathos' see Hutchinson on Aesch. *ScT* 656–7.

1074. ἀcτένακτοc: cf. Aesch. fr. 307. 2 Radt and Ar. *Eccl.* 464 (parodic incongruity: cf. Rau, *Paratragodia*, p. 15, Ussher ad loc.). **εἰχόμην:** the manuscripts' ἑcπόμην has been taken as *difficilior lectio* than the εἱπόμην of the *Ajax* scholion; but in whatever tense, the verb has no exact parallel (no more, at this date, does the metaphorical phrase in Jackson's ἑcπώμην κακοῖc (*MS*, p. 148), as he himself admits). Meineke's and Blaydes's εἰχόμην is a slight change and seems supported by *Aj.* 272 αὐτὸc μὲν ἥδεθ', οἵcιν εἴχετ' ἐν κακοῖc and Hdt. 1. 35. 1 ἀνὴρ cυμφορῆι ἐχόμενοc. Cf. *OT* 741: εἶχε codd., εἷρπε Schneidewin.

1075. Contrast Eur. *Her.* 1412 (Theseus to Heracles) εἴ c' ὄψεταί τιc θῆλυν ὄντ' οὐκ αἰνέcει.

1078. ἐκ καλυμμάτων: 'away from' (i.e. without) coverings: cf. Schwyzer, *Gr. Gr.* ii. 463 (1). The present phrase is not metaphorical but perfectly literal: H exposes his hideously maimed body, like Amfortas in Act III of *Parsifal*; cf. Schadewaldt, *Monolog und Selbstgespräch*, p. 82 n. 2.

1079. ἰδού, θεᾶcθε: see Wilamowitz on Eur. *Her.* 1131, citing this and other passages where the original meaning of ἰδού has virtually vanished, so that a second imperative meaning 'look' may follow (as in English 'lo and behold'); cf. Bond on Eur. *Her.* 867.

1079–80. Fraenkel, *Mus. Helv.* 24 (1967), 190 ff. (esp. pp. 191–2), and ibid. 25 (1968), 179–80, argued that these plurals are addressed not to the dramatically unimportant attendants who brought in H and are now irrelevant, but to an imagined audience, the world in general as it were. Cf. esp. *Aj.* 1028–9 cκέψαcθε, πρὸc θεῶν, τὴν τύχην δυοῖν βροτοῖν, Eur. *Andr.* 622–3 τοῦτο καὶ cκοπεῖτέ μοι, | μνηcτῆρεc (Σ ad loc. comments διαλέγεται δὲ πρὸc τὸ θέατρον), *Ion* 1090 ff. ὁρᾶθ' ὅcοι δυcκελάδοιcιν . . . ἀείδεθ' ὕμνοιc | ἀμέτερα λέχεα . . . ὅcον . . . κρατοῦμεν. D. Bain, 'Audience Address in Greek Tragedy', *CQ* 25 (1975), 13 ff., esp. p. 19, distinguishes such passages from the phenomenon of speech addressed *ad spectatores*, a phenomenon he convincingly denies to Attic tragedy (cf. Taplin, *JHS* 106 (1986), 166–7). Cf. above on 806.

1080. **τὸν δύστηνον, ὡς οἰκτρῶς ἔχω:** for the transition from the third to the first person cf. Bruhn, *Anhang*, § 183.

1081 ff. On the 'extraordinary lyric outburst in trimeters' here and below see Kaibel on *El.* 1160, Stinton, *JHS* 97 (1977), 130.

1082. **ἔθαλψέ:** cf. *PV* 879–80 ὑπό μ' αὖ cφάκελος καὶ φρενοπλῆγες | μανίαι θάλπουc'. For ἄτη in the present passage see J. Stallmach, *Ate* (Beitr. zur kl. Phil. 18; 1968), 83. On the meaning and tone of our passage see Adam Parry, *BICS* 16 (1969), 112, Long, *Language and Thought*, p. 134. On the idiomatic αὖ see above on 987.

1083. **διῆιξε πλευρῶν:** cf. *Phil.* 743–4 ἀτταταῖ, διέρχεται, | διέρχεται. **ἀγύμναcτον:** for the adjective in this position within the trimeter see Kannicht on Eur. *Hel.* 533.

1084. **τάλαινα:** for τάλαc and other adjectives 'of commiseration or abuse' as 'applied not only to persons but to things' see Headlam on Heródas 3. 14.

1085–6. This 'isolated outburst amid iambic trimeters may be regarded as two tripodies or as three metra' (West, *GM*, p. 123 n. 110) within the anapaestic context. Cf. Stinton, *JHS* 97 (1977), 130.

1085. For the rarity in Greek literature of prayers to Hades (especially prayers that name the grim deity) see Harder on Eur. *Cresphont.* fr. 66. 56 ff.

1086. For passages in tragedy where characters wish for destruction by thunderbolt see Johansen and Whittle on Aesch. *Suppl.* 779–80.

1087. **βέλος:** for the thunderbolt conceived as an arrow cf. Renehan, *CP* 80 (1985), 169.

1088. **δαίνυται γὰρ αὖ πάλιν:** on the metaphor behind the verb here cf. 1054 βέβρωκε cάρκας; on the idiomatic αὖ see on 987 above; for the pleonastically appended πάλιν cf. on 342 above.

1089. **ἤνθηκεν:** 'it is at its height': see on 999 μανίας ἄνθος. Dawe's misconceptions (*Studies* iii. 95–6) as to the verb's meaning are effectively dispelled by West, *BICS* 26 (1979), 111–12. **ἐξώρμηκεν:** 'it has broken out' (LSJ), a meaning that dissatisfies both Dawe and West, loc. cit. (the latter unconvincingly suggests ἐξώργηκεν, a verb 'not otherwise attested before Plutarch'); but cf. 979 κἀκκινήcεις κἀναcτήcεις, 1259 πρὶν τήνδ' ἀνακινῆcαι | νόcον.

1089 ff. Near to death, Heracles invokes his physical strength as Ajax invoked his country (859 ff.). Here begins this great speech's third and

COMMENTARY

final priamel (cf. Race, *The Classical Priamel*, p. 93), leading to the climactic restatement of H's suffering at 1103 ff.

1089. ὦ χέρες, χέρες: cf. *TrGF* i (15) 2. 12–13 (from Neophron's *Medea*) ὦ χέρες, χέρες, | πρὸς οἷον ἔργον ἐξοπλιζόμεθα, *Phil.* 1004–5 ὦ χεῖρες, οἷα πάσχετ' ἐν χρείαι φίλης | νευρᾶς, Eur. *Alc.* 837 ὦ πολλὰ τλᾶσα καρδία καὶ χεὶρ ἐμή, and for other addresses of this sort to one's hands see Schadewaldt, *Monolog und Selbstgespräch*, p. 220, Rau, *Paratragodia*, p. 52, Jocelyn, *The Tragedies of Ennius*, p. 317, A. G. Katsouris, *Linguistic and Stylistic Characterisation: Tragedy and Menander* (Ioannina 1975), 158–9.

1091. ὑμεῖς ἐκεῖνοι ... οἵ ποτε: for ἐκεῖνος of past and distant events cf. *TrGF* i (97) 6. 3 ἦν γάρ ποτ' αἰὼν κεῖνος, *OC* 1195–6 cὺ δ' εἰς ἐκεῖνα, μὴ τὰ νῦν, ἀποςκόπει | ... πήματα. L has δὲ κεῖνοι, and Kranz interpreted as ὑμεῖς δ' ἐκεῖνοι, which can, perhaps, be defended as the normal Attic form (see Barrett on Eur. *Hipp.* 321). But with ἐκεῖνοι in asyndeton we get this anyway, and such is the reading of most of our sources. **ποτε:** cf. fr. 730. 16–17; the reference to the past prepares for the contrast with νῦν δ' at 1103, the priamel's climax: cf. Race, *The Classical Priamel*, pp. 36–7.

1092. The Nemean lion is regularly represented as the first of Heracles' labours (see Maehler on Bacch. 9. 9), and is therefore mentioned here first. βουκόλων ἀλάστορα here, like μηλοδαΐκταν ... λέοντα at Bacch. 9. 6 ff. may represent (as Maehler suggests on the latter passage) an interpretation of Hes. *Th.* 330 ([the lion] ἐλεφαίρετο φῦλ' ἀνθρώπων) along the lines of Σ ad loc. ἐλεφαίρετο ἀντὶ τοῦ ἔβλαπτεν. Note how the riddling allusions of this line to 'the dweller in Nemea, the ravager of herdsmen' are followed in the next line by the solution to the riddle—'the lion': see on 574 above. The following appositional reference to the beast as a θρέμμα does, however, complicate the pattern.

1093. ἄπλατον ... κἀπροσήγορον: for similar use of privative ἀ- in emphatic litotes applied to an opponent of Heracles see 1095–6 ἄμεικτον ... στρατόν and ἄνομον, and Bond on Eur. *Her.* 393 Ἀμφαναίας οἰκήτορ' ἄμεικτον (of Cycnus). On ἄπλατος see Verdenius, *Mnem.* 21 (1968), 140–1 **θρέμμα:** cf. fr. 387 ἄπλατον ἀξύμβλητον ἐξεθρεψάμην: the noun is appended here (in a kenning-like phrase) to the clear statement λέοντ' in a way that reminds us of its appearance at 574 above (see ad loc.).

LINES 1089-1100

1094. The hydra is often mentioned second in lists of Heracles' labours: on the story as a whole see Bond on Eur. *Her.* 419–22.

1095. Here and at 1098 a monstrous enemy of Heracles is referred to by means of a γρῖφοc. Cf. Renehan, *CP* 80 (1985), 156, on similar references in Eur. *Her.* **διφυᾶ:** for διφυήc of centaurs cf. Pherecydes *FGrH* 3 F 50 Κρόνοc ἀπεικαcθεὶc ἵππωι ἐμίγη τῆι Φιλυρᾶι . . . καὶ διὰ τοῦτο διφυὴc ὁ Χείρων (cf. Apollod. 1. 9). Compare Latin *bimembris* used of Centaurs at Verg. *Aen.* 8. 293 etc.; the form is Attic: see *Phil.* 1014.

1095–6. ἱπποβάμονα cτρατὸν | θηρῶν: cf. Eur. *IA* 1059 θίαcοc . . . ἱπποβάταc Κενταύρων. ἱπποβάμων, as at Aesch. *Suppl.* 284 (see Johansen and Whittle ad loc.), must mean 'moving like horses' (cf. Schuursma, pp. 30–1).

1096. ὑβριcτήν, ἄνομον: Typhoeus is δεινόν θ' ὑβριcτήν τ' ἄνομόν τε at Hes. *Th.* 307, the Centaurs a τετραcκελὲc ὕβριcμα at Eur. *Her.* 181; cf. J. Taillardat, *Les Images d'Aristophane: Études de langue et de style* (Paris 1962), 239 and n. 5.

1097. Ἐρυμάνθιόν τε θῆρα: the earliest extant literary reference to this particular labour: see Gow and Page on Callim. *Epigr.* 34 Pf. = *HE* 1151.

1098. For other references to Cerberus in tragedy see Bond on Eur. *Her.* 612 and 1277. On the possible reluctance of much early poetry to mention him by name see Renehan, *CP* 80 (1985), 144–5. For τέραc used of monsters see Calame on Alcman fr. 146 P (p. 502). **τρίκρανον:** for the various traditions as to the number of Cerberus' heads see West on Hes. *Th.* 312.

1098 ff. See G. Stephan, *Die Ausdruckskraft der caesura media im iambischen Trimeter der attischen Tragödie* (Beitr. zur kl. Phil. 126; 1981), 64.

1098–9. Cf. Bacch. 5. 62 υἱὸν ἀπλάτοι' Ἐχίδναc. This family tree is first attested by Hes. *Th.* 310.

1099–1100. On the characteristically Sophoclean word-order here see F. Sommer, *Zur Geschichte der gr. Nominalkomposita* (Abh. d. Bayer. Akad. d. Wiss., phil.-hist. Kl. 27; 1948), 89. On the uncontracted **χρυcέων** see Bergson, *Rh. Mus.* 102 (1959), 16 ff. (cf. above on 556).

1100. ἐπ' ἐcχάτοιc τόποιc: for this traditionally remote labour of Heracles to gain the apples of the Hesperides see Bond on Eur. *Her.* 394 ff.; for the phrase cf. fr. 956 of the Φοίβου κῆποc . . . πάντ' ἐπ' ἔcχατα χθονόc (where a lost verb of motion must have governed ἐπί).

COMMENTARY

1101. **μόχθων μυρίων:** words like μυρία and πολλά are idiomatic within priamels such as the present passage (see on 1046 above). For the actual phrasing here cf. Eur. *Her.* 1353 ἀτὰρ πόνων δὴ μυρίων ἐγευcάμην. Presumably a conscious borrowing (as e.g. Bond on the Euripidean passage presumes). But by whom? Reinhardt, *Sophokles* p. 259 (English trans., p. 247), finds Euripides' employment more artificial, but such subjective impressions are not very helpful (see above, p. xviii). For the phrase cf. also *TrGF* (adesp.) 653.51 μόχθοιc μυ[ρίοιc and Harder on Eur. *Archel.* fr. 10; for the metaphor in **ἐγευcάμην** cf. Moschus *Meg.*(4) 12 τόcων... ἐγεύcατο... κηδέων.

1102. For the phrase τροπαῖον/-αια ἱcτάναι/-αcθαι see Rau, *Paratragodia*, p. 49; for the genitive cf. Eur. *Andr.* 694 τροπαῖα πολεμίων, Andoc. 1.47. In the present passage **ἐμῶν χερῶν** = 'deeds of strength' but is also a reminder of 1089's apostrophe to H's χέρεc.

1103. For νῦν δ' as marking the climax of a priamel see Race (cited on 1046), p. 32 and n. 2, pp. 36, 38, 75, 93. ὧδ' has equally idiomatic force in this context: see on 503 τἀνδ'. **ἄναρθροc:** cf. Eur. *Or.* 228 ἄναρθρός εἰμι κἀcθενῶ μέλη. **κατερρακωμένοc:** cf. *PV* 1023 (of Prometheus' treatment by the eagle) cώματοc μέγα ῥάκοc, 'The hag and hungry goblin / That into rags would rend ye' (from the start of the 17th-cent. poem *Tom O'Bedlam*).

1104. **τυφλῆc ὑπ' ἄτηc:** 'by hidden, invisible *atē*': for this meaning see Bond on Eur. *Her.* 199 τυφλοῖc... τοξεύμαcι, Gow and Page on Serapion *AP* 7.400.2 = *GP* 3405. **ἐκπεπόρθημαι:** cf. *Aj.* 896 διαπεπόρθημαι.

1105–6. For comparable rhetorical repetitions of the definite article see Lloyd-Jones, *SIFC* 35 (1965), 215–16, Austin on Men. *Sam.* 211–12. **αὐδηθείc:** the verb here not with its Homeric meaning but merely 'speak, say': cf. A. H. M. Kessels, *Mnem.* 28 (1975), 65 n. 8; the αὐθηδήc of A provides a nice scribal spoonerism: cf. Jackson, *MS*, p. 208 n. 1.

1107. **εὖ γέ τοι τόδ' ἴcτε:** a common minatory formula in Attic drama: see Fraenkel on *Aj.* 1308 (*Due seminari romani*, p. 37). **κἂν τὸ μηδὲν ὦ:** on this set phrase see Moorhouse, *CQ* 25 (1965), 35.

1108. **κἂν μηδὲν ἕρπω:** ἕρπων (Ellendt) is more stylish, and would easily have been corrupted after 1107's κἂν... ὦ.

1109. **χειρώcομαι κἀκ τῶνδε:** 'I shall destroy her even in my present state of health': so translated by Diggle, *GRBS* 14 (1973), 249, who cites other examples of ἐκ with this nuance (e.g. Eur. *Hcld*. 148 ἐξ ἀμηχάνων 'in a desperate situation'); cf. Bruhn, *Anhang*, § 68. III.

1109–10. προcμόλοι μόνον: for the position of μόνον after the imperatival verb see Pearson on fr. 478. For the effectiveness of the following subjunctive of will (rather than the optative of wish) see Moorhouse, p. 287: it 'expresses [Heracles'] strong feeling and will that it should be so'.

1110. ἀγγέλλειν: for 'the curious idiom whereby the victim of an exemplary punishment is said to proclaim the danger of committing the offence that has incurred it' Lloyd-Jones refers me to Pind. *Pyth*. 2. 21, Plato *Gorg*. 525 c, Verg. *Aen*. 6. 618–19.

1111. καὶ ζῶν ... καὶ θανών: one of the two terms qualified by a καί ... καί construction is often more important than the other: cf. Aesch. *Suppl*. 515 cύ καὶ λέγων ⟨μ'⟩ εὔφραινε καὶ πράccων φρένα, where, as in the present instance, it is the latter term that is more important, and the participles create a hyperbaton. Examples where the former term is more important in Johansen and Whittle on the Aeschylean passage. **καὶ ... καί:** 'as in life, so in death'—for the equivalence to *ut ... ita* see on 229 above. Cf. Eur. *Hcld*. 320.

1112. εἰcορῶ ⟨c'⟩ |: on the use of this compound verb for mental vision see Gow on Theocr. *Id*. 8. 11. Lloyd-Jones's εἰcορῶ ⟨c'⟩ (for elision at the end of a trimeter see West, *GM*, 83–4) clarifies the syntax and eliminates the interlinear hiatus (see E. Harrison, *CR* 57 (1943), 62): for the corruption see on 336 above.

1112–13. Cf. Eur. *Her*. 877–8 μέλεος Ἑλλάc, ἆ τὸν εὐεργέταν | ἀποβαλεῖc, *Hipp*. 1459–60 ὦ κλείν' Ἀθηνῶν Παλλάδος θ' ὁρίcματα | οἵου ϲτερήϲεϲθ' ἀνδρόc. The paradosis ϲφαλήϲεται would indicate that we have exclamation not vocative ('ein Ausruf und nicht eine Anrede': Kaibel on *El*. 1127; cf. on 1026n.). For this cf. Eur. *IT* 1106ff. ὦ πολλαὶ δακρύων λιβάδες, | αἳ ... ἔπεϲον κτλ. Meineke's ϲφαλείc' ἔϲηι (*Analecta Sophoclea* (1863), 308) provides the more predictable vocative, and is readvocated in *Sophoclea*, pp. 176–7.

1114–15. It is at last possible for a character on stage to communicate with Heracles: on his previous lack of contact with the other figures see Mastronarde, *Contact and Discontinuity*, p. 75 (though cf. 1031ff.).

1114. παρέϲχες: 'allowed': the same meaning in Theocr. *Id*. 21. 3. That only three words separate this verb from παραϲχών in precisely the same position in the next line is bound to create doubts as to the

COMMENTARY

integrity of one or the other (παρείκεις conjectured here by Wecklein, παρὸν cχεῖν in 1115 by Pearson), but perhaps unjustly: see on 88 above and cf. 1269f. below (ἐφορῶcι ... ἐφορᾶι).

1115. κλῦθί μου: taken by Johansen and Whittle (on Aesch. *Suppl.* 348) as one of the earliest examples of the phrase's use in addressing equals or inferiors (in early poetry it is employed in cletic hymns to address gods or heroes). But Heracles is neither the equal of nor inferior to Hyllus, and the verb may still have a deferential tone reflecting at least Heracles' heroic status (and possibly (see p. xx) his impending divinity). **νοcῶν ὅμωc:** the ὅμωc is idiomatic as a means of emphasizing the preceding concessive participle: Schwyzer, *Gr. Gr.* ii. 389 (ζ).

1116. δίκαια: for the plural see on 409 above.

1117. δόc μοι cεαυτόν: on this phrase see Headlam on Herodas 1.62, Stevens, *CQ* 39 (1945), 104.

1117–18. τοιοῦτον: τοcοῦτον is the paradosis but Mudge's emendation offers better sense. Campbell's interpretation of ὡc as introducing a final clause is ruled out by word-order ('ὡc should then precede μή' (Jebb): Campbell retorted (*Paralip.*, p. 191) that at *Phil.* 492 etc. relatives 'are postponed for the sake of emphasis'). **δύcοργοc:** the nominative after δόc μοι cεαυτόν is perfectly proper: for comparable attractions into the nominative of a word standing at the end see Stinton, *JHS* 96 (1976), 127. (Or δύcοργοc might be the subject of δάκνηι.) Cf. *Aj.* 1017, *Phil.* 377, and W. Muri, *Mus. Helv.* 4 (1947), 275 = *Gr. Studien*, p. 198, on this word's meaning.

1118–19. ἐν οἷc | χαίρειν: cf. the phrase ἐν θαλίηιc τέρπεcθαι (for which see West on Hes. *Th.* 65).

1119. κἀν ὅτοιc ἀλγεῖc: for the ἐν of 'attendant circumstances' see Gow and Page on Antip. Thess. *AP* 9. 72. 1–2 = *GP* 609–10.

1121. ξυνίημ': L's spelling ξυνείημ' is a common mode of rendering ι *productum* (see Jackson, *MS*, p. 145); on the metaphorical use of ποικίλλω see Müller, *Handwerk und Sprache*, 14–15. For πάλαι employed of immediately preceding events see Dawe, *Studies* i. 208 n. 1, iii. 119.

1122. ἥκω φράcων: on the periphrastic construction (ἥκω + future participle) see W. Dietrich, *Glotta* 51 (1973), 219.

1122–3. τῆc μητρὸc ... φράcων ... οἷc θ' ἥμαρτεν: in such constructions 'the genitive almost always depends, not on the verb [of saying or thinking], but on an accusative (nominative in the case of a passive or intransitive verb) or subordinate clause', if Denniston on Eur. *El.* 228 is to be believed; see *contra* Moorhouse, pp. 73–4, arguing that 'there is no syntactic connection between' the two relative clauses (ἐν οἷc and οἷc θ') and τῆc μητρόc here, which 'must be linked with φράcων' (similarly Bruhn, *Anhang*, § 37, Schwyzer, *Gr. Gr.* ii. 132 (β)); but if (with the OCT) we accept the Harleianus' ἔcτ' ἐν, a syntactic connection is inescapable. ὥc θ' for οἷc θ' Nauck: but for the *Versparung* see on 423 above.

1125. τῆc πατροφόντου μητρόc: cf. Eur. *Or.* 193 πατροφόντου ματρόc (Clytemnestra) and (for the κατάχρηcιc involved in both passages) Schuursma, p. 143. **ὡc κλύειν ἐμέ:** for ὡc as equivalent to ὥcτε see above on 590.

1127–8. See Mastronarde, *Contact and Discontinuity*, pp. 86–7, on the difficulty of construing the exchange between father and son here. He is right to prefer an interpretation whereby Hyllus 'deliberately ignores his father's anger and shifts the terms of the discussion': right also to find the implied antithesis in 1128 'still ... a serious problem'. Zieliński (pp. 619–20 n. 4 = p. 377 n. 2) deleted the two lines (as interpolated to clarify 1126?).

1128. ἀλλ' οὐδὲ μὲν δή: for this collocation of particles as rejecting an alternative see Pearson on fr. 162. 1. **τοῖc γ' ἐφ' ἡμέραν ἐρεῖc:** the difficulty of interpreting this line is noted by Moorhouse, p. 114. His 'in view of the deeds of to-day' (not, given the context, 'the deeds done during the day', which τὰ ἐφ' ἡμέραν (πεπραγμένα) might more usually signify) is certainly preferable to the alternative '"for the day", i.e. to meet the needs of the day (not properly a temporal sense of the acc. or prep.)', which he also mentions. For the dative conveying the sense 'in the light of', cf. West, *Gnomon* 59 (1987), 195. See further on 1127–8 above.

1129–30. λέγ' ... | λέγω: for this sort of picking up of a word of command see below on 1179ff.; cf. (for mainly lyric and Euripidean instances) G. Zuntz, *An Inquiry into the Transmission of the Plays of Euripides* (Cambridge 1965), 235.

1130. ἀρτίωc νεοcφαγήc: with this pleonasm compare the same phrase at *Aj.* 898 and *Ant.* 1282–3 τέθνηκε ... | ... ἄρτι νεοτόμοιcι πλήγμαcιν.

1131. τέραc τοι διὰ κακῶν ἐθέcπιcαc: cf. Aesch. *Ag.* 1133ff.

249

COMMENTARY

·κακῶν γὰρ διαὶ | πολυεπεῖс τέχναι θεcπιῳδῶν | φόβον φέρουcιν μαθεῖν with Fraenkel's note. J. C. B. Lowe, *Glotta* 51 (1973), 43, compares Aesch. *Pers.* 245 δεινά τοι λέγειc.

1132. αὐτὴ πρὸc αὑτῆc: the same phrase for the same deed at 891 above.

1133. A wonderfully self-centred line with no trace of regret for D. **ἐξ ἐμῆc θανεῖν χερόc:** for similar phrases signifying 'death at the hand of' see Fraenkel on Aesch. *Ag.* 1495–6.

1134. coῦ cτραφείη θυμόc: for the image involved here see Johansen and Whittle on Aesch. *Suppl.* 623. **εἰ τὸ πᾶν μάθοιc:** 'if you could learn the whole story': see on 369 above.

1135. ἧι νοcεῖc: cf. 553–4 above.

1136. ἅπαν τὸ χρῆμ' ἥμαρτε: better with comma after χρῆμ' ('the whole thing is, she erred . . .'): see Stevens, *Colloquial Expressions in Euripides*, p. 21. **μωμένη:** see Sier on Aesch. *Cho.* 44 f.

1138. cτέργημα: a ἅπαξ (changed by Nauck to cτέργηθρα); for the force of προcβαλεῖν see on 844 above.

1139. τοὺc ἔνδον γάμουc: it is unlikely that γάμοc can mean 'bride': on Eur. *Andr.* 103–4 (γάμον internal accusative) see Stevens ad loc.; Eur. fr. 405. 1–2 τὴν εὐγένειαν, κἂν ἄμορφοc ἧι γάμοc, | τιμῶcι πολλοὶ προcλαβεῖν τέκνων χάριν does not entail this meaning for γάμοc. On the plural for singular see Ellendt–Genthe s.v. γάμοc.

1140. For the καί expressive of surprise cf. 187 above, Denniston, GP^2, p. 310.

1141–2 ~ 555–6 ἦν μοι παλαιὸν δῶρον . . . ποτὲ | θηρόc. **τὸν cὸν ἐκμῆναι πόθον:** for other examples of ἐκμαίνω used transitively see Page on Alcaeus fr. 42. 4–5 (*Sappho and Alcaeus* (Oxford 1955), 276).

1143 ff. These three lines in asyndeton strikingly convey H's amazement, and stress the turning-point reached.

1143. ἰοὺ ἰοὺ δύcτηνοc κτλ.: cf. *OT* 1182 ἰοὺ ἰού· τὰ πάντ' ἂν ἐξήκοι cαφῆ (at a like moment of revelation: see R. B. Rutherford, *JHS* 102 (1982), 148–9). For similar exclamations evoked by the fulfilment of a prophecy see Eur. *Cycl.* 696 αἰαῖ· παλαιὸc χρηcμὸc ἐκπεραίνεται and the other examples cited by Rau, *Paratragodia*, p. 171.

1144. φέγγοc: for this word meaning 'the light of day' see Braswell on Pind. *Pyth.* 4. 111 (c); cf. on 828 above.

LINES 1131-1156

1145. φρονῶ: that this verb here and at *Aj.* 942 and *OC* 1741 means 'know, understand' (a meaning it did not possess before S) is argued by Verdenius, *Mnem.* 28 (1975), 190. **ξυμφορᾶс ἵν' ἔсταμεν:** see on 375 above.

1147. ὁμαιμόνων: used here since the genitive plural of ὅμαιμος would not scan: see Johansen and Whittle, *Symb. Osl.* 50 (1975), 26.

1148-9. Ἀλκμήνην, Διὸς | μάτην ἄκοιτιν: cf. Eur. *Her.* 339 ὦ Ζεῦ, μάτην ἄρ' ὁμόγαμόν с' ἐκτηсάμην.

1149-50. τὴν τελευταίαν | ... φήμην ... θεсφάτων: for the popular folk-tale motif of the dying man inspired to prophecy see Shakespeare, *King Richard II* II. 1. 31 ff., where John of Gaunt says 'Methinks I am a prophet new inspired, | And thus expiring do foretell ...', and in general T. H. Gaster, *Myth, Legend and Custom in the Old Testament* (London 1969), 214-15.

1151. ἀλλ' ... ἀλλ': for this type of correspondence see Bruhn, *Anhang*, § 188.

1151-2. ἐπακτίαι | Τίρυνθι: see G. P. Shipp, *Studies in Mycenaean and Homeric Greek* (Melbourne 1961), 42, for this phrase as falling 'outside any normal pattern' inasmuch as the locative dative of such a proper noun is only legitimate *without* adjective or participle. For a local sense cf. Eur. *IT* 452-3 κἂν γὰρ ὀνείροιсι сυνείην δόμοιс πόλει τε πατρώιαι. However, if we take Τίρυνθι as equivalent to Τιρυνθίοιс (cf. *OC* 616 καὶ ταῖсι Θήβαιс εἰ τανῦν εὐημερεῖ) the difficulty is mitigated.

1155-6. Nauck's emendation and deletion were approved by Jachmann ('Binneninterpolationen II', *Nachrichten von d. Gesellsch. d. Wiss. z. Göttingen, phil.-hist. Kl.* I. 9 (1936), 190-1 = *Textgesch. Stud.*, pp. 555-6) and Reeve (*GRBS* 14 (1973), 167-8), the emendation but not the deletion by Stinton, p. 145, observing that εἴ τι χρή *per se* could not mean 'if anything is needed', and repunctuating after πάρεсμεν. Lloyd-Jones (*Sophoclea*, p. 177) suggests the further modification of ⟨δ'⟩ after κλυόντες. Certainly, as Jachmann argues, this phrase is most dramatically effective if referred to Hyllus alone. The manuscripts' δ' ὅсοι must therefore be corrected as Nauck enjoins. For the force of the verb here cf. 397 ἀλλ' εἴ τι χρῄζεις ἱсτορεῖν, πάρειμ' ἐγώ. **πράссειν:** the manuscripts' πράττειν was taken as a further sign of interpolation by Jachmann; but cf. Reeve, p. 168 n. 48, for other examples of this and similar corruptions.

COMMENTARY

1156. The play's only three-word trimeter (there are seventeen in all in S's extant plays: cf. Stanford, *CR* 54 (1940), 9). **κλυόντες:** for the aorist participle see on 189. **ἐξυπηρετήςομεν:** elsewhere only in prose (cf. LSJ s.v.). See Addenda.

1157. τοὔργον: the same meaning as in *Aj.* 536 ἔργον.

1158. φανεῖς: for this verb with personal subject see Bond on Eur. *Her.* 811.

1159. On the 'narrative γάρ' see above on lines 9 and 475. **πρόφαντον:** see on 324 above.

1160 ff. For the motif of the dead killing the living see (in Greek tragedy) Aesch. *Cho.* 886 τὸν ζῶντα καίνειν τοὺς τεθνηκότας λέγω, *Aj.* 1026–7 εἶδες ὡς χρόνωι | ἔμελλέ ς᾽ Ἕκτωρ καὶ θανὼν ἀποφθίςειν; *Ant.* 871, *El.* 808, and (on the idea in general) Stith Thompson, *Motif-Index of Folk-Literature* E266. The idea's un-Homeric nature is observed by Kaibel on *El.* 807.

1160. The paradosis (πρὸς τῶν πνεόντων μηδενὸς θανεῖν ὕπο) is usually emended to remove one of the prepositions. Moorhouse (p. 130) protests that 'the use of two prepp. with the same *regimen* cannot be ruled out as impermissible' and quotes Johansen, *General Reflection in Tragic Rhesis*, p. 272, to the effect that ὑπό 'implies a more direct participation in the act of killing' than πρός; he concludes that 'the combination would give a wider meaning than either πρός or ὑπό alone, and the universality is appropriate in the context'. But of Moorhouse's two Sophoclean parallels *OT* 949 πρὸς τῆς τύχης ὄλωλεν οὐδὲ τοῦδ᾽ ὕπο is not precisely analogous and *Phil.* 554 ἀμφί ςοῦ ᾽νέκα[44] is too easily emended (ἀμφὶ ςοῦ νέα Auratus). μή with infinitive 'indicates strong assurance (here certainty) about what is to happen, and is so found after phrases of oracular response' (Moorhouse, p. 327); for the aorist infinitive (instead of future) in the report of a prophecy cf. Ar. *Vesp.* 160 ὁ γὰρ θεὸς | μαντευομένωι μοὔχρηςεν ἐν Δελφοῖς ποτε | ὅταν τις ἐκφύγηι μ᾽, ἀποσκλῆναι τότε). On the omitted ἄν (supplied by Dobree's θανεῖν ποτ᾽ ἄν) cf. E. Crespo, *Glotta* 62 (1984), 13. See Addenda.

1161. Ἅιδου **φθίμενος οἰκήτωρ:** for the emphatic tautology cf. Aesch. *Suppl.* 228 ἐν Ἅιδου θανών and Johansen and Whittle ad loc. Ἅιδου ... οἰκήτορες at 282 above gives the more normal phrasing.

[44] Thus the paradosis (ἀμφὶ ςοῦ ᾽νέκα AUY, ἀμφὶς εἵνεκα G, ἀμφὶς οὕνεκα R, ἀμφὶς ὃν G^rc, ἀμφὶ ς᾽ οὕνεκα rell.).

LINES 1156-1169

1163. ζῶντά μ' ἔκτεινεν θανών: cf. *Ant.* 871 θανὼν ἔτ᾽ οὖσαν κατήναρές με, *El.* 808 Ὀρέστα φίλταθ᾽, ὥς μ᾽ ἀπώλεσας θανών, Aesch. *Cho.* 886, cited on 1160 ff.

1164–5. cυμβαίνοντ'... μαντεῖα: cf. Ar. *Eq.* 220 χρησμοί τε cυμβαίνουcι καὶ τὸ Πυθικόν and the phrasing at 1174 below.

1165. Deleted by Dobree on the grounds that there is some inconsistency in describing as καινά oracles earlier (157, 825) referred to as 'old', and because the content here presupposed for the different set of old oracles is anything but congruous with what we can elsewhere infer of the content of the oracles here called 'new'. Nauck was impressed, but in fact the extreme flexibility of the play's references to the oracle will explain the inconsistencies of content (see Appendix A), and the present scene's emphasis on the ineluctable nature of Fate requires not only this different content but also a plurality of oracles pointing to the same outcome. See further Kranz, *Jhsb. d. Phil. Vereins zu Berlin* 47 (1921), 37 = *Studien zur antiken Literatur und ihrem Nachwirken*, pp. 287–8.

1166 ff. For the probable mode of consulting the oracle at Dodona see Lloyd on Hdt. 2. 57, who suggests that the noises made by the oak and doves were interpreted by the Ϲελλοί (see next n.).

1166–7. χαμαικοιτῶν... Ϲελλῶν: on the Ϲελλοί or Ἑλλοί, priests who lay naked on the ground and abstained from washing their feet, see Lloyd's note on Hdt. 2. 55 and Erbse's on Σ *Il.* 16. 234. On the amplificatory phrases in 1166 and the following lines ('calculated to inspire awe') cf. Long, *Language and Thought*, p. 87 n. 84.

1167. ἐξεγραψάμην: Elmsley followed by Dobree (*Adversaria*, ed. Wagner, iv. 35) suggested this; their conjecture is usually confined to the app. crit. but it provides better sense than εἰcεγραψάμην (what is the meaning of the preverb?). Cf. Ar. *Av.* 982 (χρησμὸς) ὃν ἐγὼ παρά τ᾽ Ἀπόλλωνος ἐξεγραψάμην: the same verb was surely used in our own passage. For confusion between εἰc and ἐξ in the manuscripts of Greek tragedy see Diggle, *STE*, p. 116. The middle here and in the Aristophanic passage indicates that the consulter of the oracle had the answer written out for him: cf. Bowra, *Philol.* 103 (1959), 160 = *On Greek Margins*, p. 102. For the anachronism see on 157–8.

1168. δρυός: compatible with 171's reference to a φηγός (see ad loc.).

1169. For the underlying idea cf. *OC* 7–8 χρόνος ξυνὼν | μακρός and Norden, *Die Geburt des Kindes* (Leipzig and Berlin 1931), 44 and n. 3;

COMMENTARY

'be it man or god, as he grows old, χρόνος itself grows old' (Fraenkel's edn. of Aesch. *Ag.*, 2. 63). Cf. Bruhn, *Anhang*, §257.

1170–1. μόχθων . . . λύcιν: for similar expressions cf. Vetta on Theogn. 1385, H. D. Broadhead, *CQ* 9 (1959), 316. With μόχθων τῶν ἐφεcτώτων cf. the tragic phrase τῶν παρεcτώτων κακῶν (cf. Diggle, *STE*, p. 108).

1171. λύcιν τελεῖcθαι: future middle form with passive meaning, common in tragedy: see Johansen and Whittle on Aesch. *Suppl.* 516. On the effect of the impersonal expression here see Long, *Language and Thought*, pp. 87–8.

1171–2. Reinhardt (*Sophokles*, p. 71; English trans., pp. 61–2) compares Hdt. 3. 64 (of Cambyses) ὁ μὲν δὴ . . . ἐδόκεε . . . τὸ δὲ χρηcτήριον ἔλεγε ἄρα. For the force of ἄρα see too Hdt. 3. 63. 3 οὐκ ἐνῆν ἄρα τὸ μέλλον γίνεcθαι ἀποτρέπειν. (The similarity with Hdt. is not fortuitous: 'among the Sophoclean plays the most Herodotean is *Trach.* with its emphasis on life stories stretching over considerable periods of time and on the interconnection of separate individual destinies' (H. R. Immerwahr, *Cambridge History of Class. Lit.* i (Greek), p. 433.[45]) As for the tense appropriate in such contexts, 'the imperfect is used because, although the speaker is talking of the actual state of affairs as it now appears to him, he is more struck by the fact that it was so before, when it seemed otherwise' (West on Hes. *Op.* 11). Cf. *TrGF* 2 (adesp.) fr. 374 = *TrGF* 1. 88, fr. 3 ὦ τλῆμον ἀρετή· λόγος ἄρ' ἦcθ', ἐγὼ δέ cε | ὡς ἔργον ἤcκουν, cὺ δ' ἄρ' ἐδούλευες τύχηι.

1173. For the general idea that the dead are free from misery and toil see Johansen and Whittle on Aesch. *Suppl.* 802–3. For the expression of that idea through 'the combination of a masc. aor. part. form of θνήιcκειν designating death as an occurrence, not as an established condition, with a verb in the pres. or pfct. describing the condition of the person(s) to whom death occurs or has occurred' see ibid. Axt deleted this line as an unnecessary gloss on 1172: the audience would probably not have needed so explicit a reminder of the familiar saw. Lines 828–30 (at the start of the third stasimon) do provide such a reminder, but that could be the source of the interpolation: for a similar double-edged argument relating to interpolation see above on 166–8.

[45] On the more general issue of the relationship between S and Herodotus see Schwinge, *Die Stellung der Trachinierinnen im Werk des Sophokles*, p. 101 n. 3.

1174. Cf. *OT* 1182 τὰ πάντ' ἂν ἐξήκοι cαφῆ (at a similar moment of revelation: see on 1143 above). On the meaning of λαμπρόc here see Schadewaldt, *WS* 79 (1966), 77 = *Hell. und Hesp.* i. 493.

1177. εἰκαθόντα: for this 'absolute' use of εἴκειν see Johansen and Whittle on Aesch. *Suppl.* 202.

1177-8. In other contexts ἐξευρίcκω is idiomatic of the discovery of laws *vel sim.* (see e.g. K. Thraede, *Rh. Mus.* 105 (1962), 161 ff.), but here, as with εὑροῦcαι at 284 above, the verb is better taken as equivalent to 'have' or 'get' (and translated (in view of the aorist aspect) e.g. 'realizing the excellence of this law'). This 'weaker' sense is particularly Sophoclean: cf. LSJ s.v. εὑρίcκω IV. Greeks often asked themselves τί τὸ κάλλιcτον; and answered with an infinitive (cf. fr. 356 κάλλιcτόν ἐcτι τοὖνδικον πεφυκέναι, and in general Fraenkel on Aesch. *Ag.* 899 ff.).

1179 ff. For a detailed stylistic analysis of the stichomythia here (especially the repetition of words) see Schwinge, pp. 85 ff.

1179. cτάcιν: the word at *OT* 634 would suggest some such rendering as 'debate' for λόγου cτάcιν.

1181. For the clasping of the right hand as a pledge of good faith see Dover on Ar. *Nub.* 81.

1182. For other instances of (ὡc) πρὸc τί; = 'with what purpose?' either complete in itself (as here) or requiring something to be understood from the previous line see Pearson, *CQ* 24 (1930), 156.

1183. οὐ θᾶccον οἴcειc: cf. Men. *Sam.* 678-9 οὐκ εἰcδραμὼν | θᾶττον ἐξοίcειc ἅ φημι; On the μή following οὐ here see Moorhouse, p. 338 who suggests that 'the first question with οὐ equals an order, the second adds a further negative μή to οὐ and this produces a prohibition instead of an order' (cf. Bruhn, *Anhang*, § 159 II). Cf. esp. *Aj.* 75, Callim. fr. 194. 98-9 Pf.

1184. ἰδού: the word is idiomatic in response to a demand: see Denniston on Eur. *El.* 566, Stevens, *Colloquial Expressions in Euripides*, p. 35.

1186. Cf. Mastronarde, *Contact and Discontinuity*, p. 49 n. 52, for stichomythic exchanges like the present where 'the first question adds an interrogative element to the previous line'.

1186-7. ἦ μήν: for the Attic construction whereby these particles and infinitive introduce a 'feierliche Versprechen' (as here) see A. Citron, *Semantische Untersuchung zu* cπένδεcθαι — cπένδειν — εὔχεcθαι (Winterthur 1965), 18. **ἐξειπεῖν cε δεῖ:** Heimsoeth's conjecture

COMMENTARY

provides far more vivid sense ('swear... to do what? This too you must clearly state') than the ἐξειρήcεται of the paradosis, which is distractingly vague and allusive ('this too will (or 'will this too...?') be clearly stated'). ἀντειρήcεται at the end of 1184 will have been the source of the corruption.

1188. Ζῆν' ἔχων ἐπώμοτον: for the double accusative cf. LSJ s.v. ἔχω I. 13, T. F. Higham, *CQ* 26 (1932), 113; for the adjective see 427 above.

1189. This sort of eliciting (by the person who exacts the oath) of the naming of the penalty is a common feature of stichomythia: see Barrett's edn. of Eur. *Hipp.*, p. 19.

1190. The line is effectively broken up into three parts.

1191. οἶcθ' οὖν: for the Euripidean device of starting a stichomythia with this question—answered (as here) by οἶδα—see *Bacch.* 462 and Dodds ad loc.[46] Mastronarde, *Contact and Discontinuity*, p. 44, suggests that S 'creates a deliberate parallelism when he has Heracles terminate browbeating stichomythic passages' with the question οἶcθα here and at 1219. On the general technique see further Mastronarde, p. 43 nn. 23–4. **τὸν Οἴτης Ζηνὸς... πάγον:** for the construction whereby a locale is specified by two genitives, one defining or partitive-local (Οἴτης), the other possessive or pertinentive (Ζηνός), see *Phil.* 489 τὰ Χαλκώδοντος Εὐβοίας cταθμά, Eur. *Cycl.* 293–4 ἡ ... Coυνίου | δίας Ἀθάνας... πέτρα, Hyps. fr. 1 iv 21 (p. 29 Bond) ἐν Διὸς λειμῶνι Νεμεάδος χθον[ός, ibid. 24–5 τίνος τάδ' ἀνδρῶν μηλοβοςκὰ δώματ[α] | Φλειουντίας γῆς... νομίζεται. (on *Hipp.* 1459 see Barrett ad loc.), Pind. *Pyth.* 4. 56 Νείλοιο πρὸς πίον τέμενος Κρονίδα (see Braswell ad loc.), Wilamowitz on Eur. *Her.* 170. Ζηνὸς πάγος (like Ἥρας πάγος in fr. 248. 3) is modelled on Ἄρειος πάγος. **ὑψίcτου:** on this epithet of Zeus see Cook, *Zeus* ii/2. 876ff., Nock, *Harv. Theol. Rev.* 29 (1936), 56ff. = *Essays on Religion and the Ancient World* i. 416ff. (esp. p. 60 = p. 420, arguing that the present instance's context implies a literal mountain height rather than the more usual signification 'supreme').

1192. For θυτήρ see on 613 above, for cταθείς cf. 608 above.

1193. ἐνταῦθα: questions initiated by the formula οἶcθα (1191) are

---
[46] Our passage is overlooked by Kannicht (edn. of Eur. *Hel.*, ii. 101) in his discussion of the device.

often followed by a demonstrative pronoun or adverb of this sort: see Mastronarde, *Contact and Discontinuity*, p. 43.

1195–8. Deleted by Wunder as an actor's interpolation inspired by a misreading of 1213 πυρᾶc . . . τῆc εἰρημένηc as meaning 'the pyre whose construction I have described' rather than 'the pyre I have ordered on Mt. Oeta (1191)': the construction was duly added to the text. What aroused Wunder's suspicions were the repetition of cῶμα in ἐξάραντά cε cώμ' . . . cῶμα τοὐμὸν ἐμβαλεῖν, the definite article used of the oak in 1195, the phrase ὕλην δρυόc to signify oak-wood, the redundancy of κείραντα and ἐκτεμόνθ' in 1196, and the empty bombast of 1198. He might have added the interlinear hiatus at 1196–7 (see Appendix B). Scholars have not been very impressed by this catalogue of sins: the most disturbing (the repetition of cῶμα) might be explained as S's way of hinting at H's apotheosis by stressing the hero's body (as opposed to his soul), a dichotomy exploited by some authors who describe the apotheosis: see Stinton in *Papers Given at a Colloquium . . . in Honour of R. P. Winnington-Ingram* (London 1987), 1 ff.

1195. πολλὴν μέν: cf. on 49 ff. above.

1196. πολλὸν δ': for this rare Ionicism as Sophoclean see Pfeiffer, *Sitzb. d. Bayer. Akad. d. Wiss., phil.-hist. Abt.* 2 (1938), 31 n. 3. On the 'male' olive see Platt, *CQ* 4 (1910), 164–5.

1197. ἄγρicν ἔλαιον: cf. Pind. fr. 46 Sn. for the phrase, which later contracted to ἀγριέλαιοc (cf. Risch, *IF* 59 (1949), 257 = *Kl. Schr.*, p. 74). Four of the five complete Attic vase-paintings of Heracles on the pyre show olive-trees nearby: see Boardman in *Studien zur Mythologie und Vasenmalerei* (Schauenburg Festschrift), pp. 127 ff.

1199 ff. A paradoxical forbidding (cf. *OC* 1751 ff.) of the traditional ritual mourning and lamentation expected for a great hero. If in fact H is not really going to die (see p. xx) this detail will have an extra point.

1199. μηδὲν εἰcίδω δάκρυ: the paradosis εἰcίτω is certainly suspicious (cf. Jackson, *MS*, p. 158). In particular, the use of εἰcέρχεcθαι of the approach of emotions (fear etc.) to an individual (cf. on 298 above) may not be thought an adequate analogy. Jackson lists earlier attempts at emendation (e.g. Blaydes's ἐξίτω: for the corruption presupposed see on 1167 above) and himself proposed εἰcίδω: for the first-person subjunctive cf. 802 μηδ' αὐτοῦ θάνω, *OC* 174 μὴ δῆτ' ἀδικηθῶ (cf. Eur. *Tro.* 170 ff.), *Il.* 1. 26 μή cε . . . κιχείω, 21. 475 μή cευ . . .

COMMENTARY

ἀκούcω. For 'the minatory undertone' Jackson cites the last passage in particular. Other parallels are cited by Broadhead, *Tragica* (Christchurch, New Zealand 1968), 105, whose own ἱέcθω does not convince. **γόου ... δάκρυ:** for the explanatory genitive cf. *TrGF* (adesp.) 664. 24 αἰcχύνηc βοήν and Snell ad loc.

1200. ἀcτένακτοc: see on 1074 above.

1201. εἰ δὲ μή: 'this formula often introduces an ominous prediction ... conditional on a prayer or request not being fulfilled' (Johansen and Whittle on Aesch. *Suppl.* 154, citing examples).

1202. ἀραῖοc: 'of a person (living or dead) whose curse weighs heavy on another' (Barrett on Eur. *Hipp.* 1415). Cf. Rohde, *Psyche*, 9th edn., 264–5 = Eng. trans. p. 210 n. 148, Sier on Aesch. *Cho.* 326.

1203. τί εἶπαc; for phrases in Sophocles (and the tragedians in general) where such hiatus after τί is allowed see Johansen and Whittle on Aesch. *Suppl.* 306. **οἷά μ' εἴργαcαι:** for this and similar exclamations in tragedy (τί μ' ἠργάcω; etc.) see Rau, *Paratragodia*, pp. 50, 63.

1204–5. On the opening formula here see on 1201 above; for the motif 'true son of mine' and its opposite see on 1064 above.

1206. The pattern of exclamation followed by a οἷον or οἷα equivalent to ὡc is a common one: see *OT* 1317 οἴμοι μάλ' αὖθιc, οἷον εἰcέδυ κτλ.; *Aj.* 367 οἴμοι γέλωτοc, οἷον ὑβρίcθην ἄρα, and in general Fraenkel, *Studien zur Textgesch. u. Textkritik* (Jachmann Festschrift), p. 15 = *Kl. Beitr.* i. 433–4.

1207. φονέα ... καὶ παλαμναῖον: for this placing together of synonymous or nearly synonymous words as a stylistic feature see Vahlen, *Opusc. Acad.* ii. 302–3. See Addenda.

1208. οὐ δῆτ' ἔγωγ': for this formula cf. Bruhn, *Anhang*, § 197. III. **ὤν:** given φονέα and παλαμναῖον in 1207 we expect the parallel plain accusatives παιώνιον and ἰατῆρα here: Winnington-Ingram's ὥc c' (*BICS* 16 (1969), 47: ὥc iam Hermann) is less welcome, therefore.

1209–10. Cf. Eur. *Hipp.* 1373 καί μοι θάνατοc παιὰν ἔλθοι. Inevitably we are reminded of the notion of death as the final healer, for which cf. Aesch. fr. 255 Radt ὦ θάνατε παιάν ... | μόνοc γὰρ εἶ cὺ τῶν ἀνηκέcτων κακῶν | ἰατρόc (cf. fr. 132c. 6), Soph. fr. 698 Radt ἀλλ' ἔcθ' ὁ θάνατοc λοῖcθοc ἰατρὸc νόcων with Pearson ad loc., Aesch. *Suppl.* 802–3 with Johansen and Whittle ad loc. On the form ἰατῆρα see van Brock, *Recherches sur le vocabulaire médical du grec ancien*, pp. 13–14.

LINES 1199-1222

1212. φθόνηcιc: only here; cf. Long, *Language and Thought*, p. 80 (cf. pp. 34, 164), who argues that the abstract expression here and (with πλήρωμα) in the next line is meant to dignify the essentially mundane questions of transporting H's body and preparing the pyre; the same scholar lists (p. 67 n. 22) Sophoclean instances of 'the use of abstract nouns as a means of amplification'. For the combination of particles **γέ τοι** ('at all events, all I can say is . . .') see Pearson on Eur. *Phoen.* 730.

1213. πλήρωμα: the only parallel for this use is Eur. *Tro.* 824 (in a similarly periphrastic expression) Ζηνὸc ἔχειc κυλίκων πλήρωμα. Cf. previous n.

1214. ποτιψαύων: cf. Aesch. *Eum.* 79 ποτὶ πτόλιν for the only other example in tragic trimeters of the epic and Doric form.

1216. ἀρκέcει καὶ ταῦτα: see J. H. Quincey, *JHS* 86 (1966), 141, on this expression of satisfaction.

1216ff. H here moves on to the second of his demands. See J. K. Mac-Kinnon, 'Heracles' Intention in his Second Request of Hyllus: *Trach.* 1216–1251', *CQ* 21 (1971), 33 ff. (an important study).

1219. τὴν Εὐρυτείαν . . . παρθένον: on the adjective with genitival force see Davies on Stes. fr. 209 i 2 P (on the -ειοc adjective in particular see on 51 above). For 'unmarried young girl' rather than 'virgin' as the meaning of παρθένοc see Wilamowitz and Bond on Eur. *Her.* 834. **οἶcθα:** see above on 1191.

1220. ΩCΓ or ΩCT? See Moorhouse, p. 243: 'if ὡc is read, the addition of the subject ἐμέ is paralleled by Hdt. 2. 125. 6: ὡc ἐμὲ εὖ μεμνῆcθαι etc. (KG ii. 2. 509). But', he continues, 'parallels for ὥcτε are available (Hdt. 2. 10. 1: ὥcτε εἶναι . . . "if it is possible . . .", Plat. *Phaedr.* 230b ὥcτε γε . . . τεκμήραcθαι), and it would not seem impossible in S. for ὥcτε to have this function of ὡc' (he compares tragedy's usurpation of epic ὥcτε as relative adverb meaning ὡc (see 1071 above etc.). **ἐπεικάζειν:** for the verb's meaning see on 141 above.

1221 ff. For the pattern of a word such as τοcοῦτον (or τοcόνδε, τόδε, *vel sim.*) followed by a verb of commanding, followed by an imperative in asyndeton, see Barrett on Eur. *Hipp.* 712. In the present case hyperbaton of ταύτην (1222) and προcθοῦ δάμαρτα (1224) creates effective suspense.

1222. ταύτην: the demonstrative here is idiomatic as a sequel to the

COMMENTARY

οἶcθα formula of 1219 (see above on 1193) and implies nothing as to Iole's presence or absence from the stage. **εὐcεβεῖν:** for a handy thumb-nail sketch of this word's history and significance see J. Kroll, *Theognis-Interpretationen*, pp. 215 ff. n. 141 (though on Aesch. *Ag.* 338 see Fraenkel ad loc.).

1224. προcθοῦ δάμαρτα: on the meaning of this phrase see Mac-Kinnon (cited on 1216 ff.), p. 37; though δάμαρ usually refers to a legitimate wife (see on 429 above) it is used of a less formal relationship at e.g. Eur. *Tro.* 658 ff. (Andromache speaking) ἐπεὶ γὰρ ᾑρέθην, | Ἀχιλλέωc με παῖc ἐβουλήθη λαβεῖν | δάμαρτα. Likewise, προcθοῦ may have the meaning 'associate yourself with' (cf. *OC* 404).

1225 ff. μηδ' ἄλλοc ... ἀλλ' αὐτόc: note the emphatic contrast. For the attitude to Iole implied here see MacKinnon (cited on 1216 ff.), p. 41: 'This is surely the speech not of a lover, but of a typical heroic warrior, who regards the preservation of his property ... as an integral and necessary component of his honourable status, and who sees his son to be, in this matter, an extension of himself.' **ὁμοῦ:** 'near', cf. Moorhouse, p. 133.

1227. κήδευcον λέχοc: on the phrase's significance see MacKinnon (cited on 1216 ff.), pp. 37–8. λέχοc is used of Tecmessa the concubine at *Aj.* 211 and may bear the same meaning here with direct reference to Iole, rather than being the equivalent of a cognate accusative.

1228. πείθου: on the superiority of this over πιθοῦ see on 470 above. **πιcτεύcαντ':** 'obeying' only here and at 1251 below: the antithesis with the negative form ἀπιcτεῖν in the succeeding line makes the meaning clear. On the general technique of the 'frame antithesis' see Johansen, *General Reflection in Tragic Rhesis*, p. 107 n. 20.

1230. τὸ μὲν νοcοῦντι θυμοῦcθαι κακόν: cf. 543–4 θυμοῦcθαι μὲν οὐκ ἐπίcταμαι | νοcοῦντι κείνωι πολλὰ τῆιδε τῆι νόcωι, and for the disease motif in this play see on 443 above.

1231. ὧδ' ὁρᾶν: Groddeck's emendation δρᾶν was approved by Wunder and, most recently and fully, by Winnington-Ingram, *BICS* 26 (1979), 4–5, as producing an effective contrast: 'what is excusable in a sick man to ask would be intolerable for a sane man to act upon.' The consequent shift of attention away from Heracles, however, is less desirable (cf. *Sophoclea*, p. 177). For the word-order (infinitive phrase first for emphasis) see on 545 above.

1232. Cf. *El.* 1025 ὡc οὐχὶ cυνδράcουcα νουθετεῖc τάδε (Electra to

Chrysothemis). On θροεῖc see on 531–2 above; on forms like ἐργαcείω, δραcείω cf. Wackernagel, *BPW* 12 (1892), 1112 = *Kl. Schr.* iii. 1605, and *KZ* 28 (1887), 142 = *Kl. Schr.* i. 624.

1233–4. μόνη | μεταίτιοc: for an explanation of the phrase see Fraenkel on Aesch. *Ag.* 811: 'Deianeira has taken her own life: she herself was primarily αἰτία τοῦ θανεῖν so that the person who, through being her rival, has driven her to death appears only as μεταίτιοc.' The same scholar disposes of the errors of Campbell (that Nessus is the other guilty party here) and Jebb (that Hyllus is tactlessly suggesting that Iole shares the blame with *Heracles*!) and the longer-standing misconception that μεταίτιοc can be equivalent to αἴτιοc (see on 260–1 above).

1234. ὡc ἔχειc ἔχειν: for examples of comparable figures in Greek and Latin drama see Jocelyn, *The Tragedies of Ennius*, p. 367 nn. 2–3; cf. H. W. Johnstone, *Glotta* 58 (1980), 58.

1235. On the concept of the ἀλάcτωρ see Fraenkel on Aesch. *Ag.* 1501. Fraenkel notes as particularly close to our passage Hippocr. περὶ ἱερῆc νούcου 1, and for comparable phrases indicative of possession by a god (often involving ἐκ + genitive) cf. Mattes, *Der Wahnsinn im gr. Mythos und in der Dichtung*, p. 42. On the more general issue of supernatural intervention in diseases which is here presupposed see G. E. R. Lloyd, *Magic, Reason and Experience* (Cambridge 1979), 29 and n. 98.

1237. τοῖcιν ἐχθίcτοιcι: on this type of plural for singular see Moorhouse, p. 7 (a class that 'avoids being too specific'); on the masculine for feminine see on 151–2 and 316. **cυνναίειν ὁμοῦ:** cf. 545 ξυνοικεῖν . . . ὁμοῦ and n. ad loc.

1238. An unusual employment of ὅδε with third-person verb referring to Hyllus, who is directly addressed in the next sentence (contrast the frequent tragic application of ὅδε to the first person: Moorhouse, p. 155). The striking device well conveys Heracles' indignant coldness towards his son: contrast 1070 above (see ad loc.) and cf. *Ant.* 740 (Creon of Haemon) ὅδ', ὡc ἔοικε, τῆι γυναικὶ cυμμαχεῖ, *OT* 1160 ἀνὴρ ὅδ', ὡc ἔοικεν, ἐc τριβὰc ἐλᾶι (cf. Headlam on Herodas 6. 27 αὕτη ἡ γυνή). In these passages ὡc ἔοικεν is truly parenthetical, whereas here it is part of a mixed construction, i.e. it also governs νεμεῖν. For examples of other similarly mixed constructions see Bruhn, *Anhang*, § 176, Gow on Theocr. *Id.* 12. 13 f., Dodds on Plato *Gorg.* 453 A 8.

COMMENTARY

1239–40. ἀρὰ | μενεῖ c': Radt suggests μένει, but cf. the similar language and sentiments at 1201–2 μενῶ c' ἐγὼ | καὶ νέρθεν ὢν ἀραῖος κτλ. With θεῶν ἀρά cf. θεῶν . . . ἐρινύν in the father's curse at *Thebais* fr. 2. 8 Davies.

1241. Difficult: for a consideration of the various interpretations advanced for the paradosis φράcειc see J. H. Kells, *CR* 12 (1962), 185–6, who thinks an ironical 'at any moment you will be telling [us] how you are suffering' (sc. as if your present actions did not make it abundantly clear what you suffer from), with a play on the significance of νόcοc (physical or mental sickness), is the likeliest meaning for the line. Axt's φανεῖc for φράcειc is readvocated in *Sophoclea*, p. 177, as helping to clarify the sense: 'you will be showing us how you are suffering (as if your actions did not make it clear).' But for the near equivalence of the two verbs see 324 and 1159 above.

1242. For the notion of rousing a sleeping sickness see on 974–5, 979 ff., and 1009 above.

1244. οὐ . . . δικαιοῖc: the 'transference of the negative from the subordinate inf. to the principal vb.' when the verb is one of saying or thinking etc. (οὐκ ἀξιῶ, οὐ δικαιῶ, etc.) is treated by A. C. Moorhouse, *Studies in the Greek Negatives* (Cardiff 1959), 129. But the negative *could* go with δικαιοῖc ('you don't choose to obey your father').

1245. ἀλλ' . . . δῆτα: cf. Denniston, *GP*[2], p. 274, Kassel–Austin on Crates fr. 16. 2.

1246. A line of massive egotism. **δυccέβεια:** cf. 1222–3 εἴπερ εὐcεβεῖν | βούληι.

1247. πανδίκωc: nothing is implied about the demand's justice (or lack of it): see on 611 above.

1248. τούτων: for the plural where sense requires the singular cf. Aesch. *ScT* 64–5 βοᾶι γὰρ κῦμα χερcαῖον cτρατοῦ | καὶ τῶνδε καιρόν κτλ., *Cho.* 1055–6 ποταίνιον γὰρ αἷμά cοι χεροῖν ἔτι· | ἐκ τῶνδέ τοι ταραγμὸc ἐc φρέναc πίτνει. Cf. on 614–15 above.

1249–50. τὸ cὸν | θεοῖcι δεικνὺc ἔργον: equivalent to θεοῖcι δεικνὺc τὸ ἔργον cὸν ὄν. For this type of construction (where the verb's object also contains its predicative complement) see J. H. Kells, *CR* 11 (1961), 193–4, *Philol.* 108 (1964), 72 ff.

1250–1. Hyllus' three-line speech brings this crucial stichomythia to a close. 'Heracles, in obedience to the will of Zeus, has reconstructed the

LINES 1239-1260

family from the ruins that he created, but Hyllus sees only the devastation' (C. E. Sorum, *GRBS* 19 (1978), 73); a very different interpretation by J. H. Kells, *CR* 12 (1962), 185–6 and n. 2.

1251. πιcτεύcac: cf. on 1228 above.

1252. καλῶc τελευτᾶιc: a variation of the idiom καλῶc λέγειc: see J. H. Quincey, *JHS* 86 (1966), 143.

1252 ff. On the construction here (τὴν χάριν . . . πρόcθεc, ὡc πρὶν ἐμπεcεῖν . . . ἐc πυράν με θῆιc) see T. Kalen, *Selbständige Finalsätze und imperativische Infinitive im Gr.* (Uppsala 1941), 30–1.

1253. ἐμπεcεῖν: cf. *Phil.* 699 εἴ τιc (sc. νόcοc) ἐμπέcοι, and for the verb's medical associations Miller, *TAPA* 75 (1944), 165.

1254. cπαραγμὸν ἤ τιν' οἶcτρον: on the term cπαραγμόν here see on 778 above; for cπαραγμόc of an onset of madness cf. Aesch. fr. 169 Radt; for οἶcτροc as a metaphor for madness or frenzy see Mattes, *Der Wahnsinn im gr. Mythos und in der Dichtung*, pp. 105, 110.

1255. ἄγ' ἐγκονεῖτ', αἴρεcθε: 'the singular ἄγε and not the plural ἄγετε is used in exhortations, even when a plural follows' (Diggle, *Gnomon* 47 (1975), 290, citing examples). **ἄγ' ἐγκονεῖτ':** cf. Ar. *Plut.* 255 ἴτ' ἐγκονεῖτ' (an iambic trimeter cannot begin with ἐγκονεῖτ(ε) or ἐγκονῶμεν: cf. Aj. 811 χωρῶμεν, ἐγκονῶμεν, Eur. *Hec.* 507 cπεύδωμεν, ἐγκονῶμεν). **παῦλα . . . κακῶν:** the first noun is found in S but not Aeschylus or Euripides (cf. Th. K. Stephanopoulos, *ZPE* 73 (1988), 231–2).

1256. τελευτὴ . . . ὑcτάτη: for τελευτή as the end of life see Braswell on Pind. *Pyth.* 4. 210 (d); for comparable pleonasms see ἐcχάτοιc τέρμαcιν at Eur. *Hcld.* 278–9, *Andr.* 1081. **τοῦδε τἀνδρόc:** equivalent to ἐμοῦ (see Denniston on Eur. *El.* 43).

1257 ff. Like the ends of many Sophoclean tragedies, that of the *Trachiniae* has been variously assailed and parcelled out to interpolators (cf. Eicken-Iselin (as cited on 455–6), p. 279 and n. 3; *Sophoclea*, p. 178), but the grounds for suspicion are inadequate.

ANAPAESTIC CODA (1269-1278)

1259. τήνδ' ἀνακινῆcαι | νόcον: cf. on 974–5 above.

1260 ff. ὦ ψυχή . . . ἀνάπαυε βοήν: for this sort of address to one's ψυχή, θυμόc, καρδία, *vel sim.* see Leo, *Der Monolog*, pp. 36, 96 ff. Its close kinship with several Homeric passages is perfectly consonant with

COMMENTARY

the character of Heracles. 1262's βοή shows that the speaker's thoughts have by then returned to the owner of the ψυχή (i.e. to the speaker himself). Cf. Archil. fr. 128. 2–3 W θύμε, προcβαλὼν ἐναντίον | cτέρνον, and cf. on 547 ff. above. **ψυχὴ cκληρά:** for this epithet used of the soul cf. *Aj.* 1361 cκληρὰν ... ψυχήν; for its likely tone in such self-address cf. Eur. *Alc.* 837 ὦ πολλὰ τλᾶcα καρδία,[47] *IT* 344 ὦ καρδία τάλαινα (cf. on 1084 above), *Or.* 466 ὦ τάλαινα καρδία ψυχή τ' ἐμή; cf. *Med.* 1056–7 μὴ δῆτα, θυμέ ... | ... ὦ τάλαν, and the parodic example in Anaxandrides fr. 5. 9 ὦ πονηρὰ καρδία; cf. Soph. fr. 757. 1–2 ὦ γλῶccα ... | πῶc δῆτα τλήcηι πρᾶγμ' ὑπεξελεῖν τόδε;

1260. χάλυβοc: χάλυψ is often applied thus to metals: see e.g. Hutchinson on Aesch. *ScT* 728, K. Thraede *RAC* s.v. 'Erfinder' (5. 1210).

1261. λιθοκόλλητον cτόμιον παρέχουc': F. K. Ball, *CR* 8 (1894), 197–8, and Lloyd-Jones, *CQ* 7 (1957), 14–15, have shown (as against Jebb) that the image here is of a bit set with stones whose function is 'to impose upon the agonized Heracles the painful constraint of a self-discipline that enforces silence' (Lloyd-Jones, p. 15). Dawe's προcέχουc' (*Studies* iii. 98) provides a more consistent picture within the *illustrans* ('applying the bit'): παρέχουc', however, works on the level of the *illustrandum* (the soul 'supplying' the courage characterized as a bit), and for the blending of the details appropriate to *illustrans* and *illustrandum* see on 31 ff. and 147 above.

1263. τελεοῦc': cf. 1257 τελειοῦcθαι. For verbs with similar epic forms in the lyrics of tragedy see Diggle on Eur. *Phaeth.* 236–7.

ἀεκούcιον: another uncontracted epic form: this recurs in tragedy only at Aesch. *Suppl.* 39 ἀεκόντων (again in anapaests).

1264. αἴρετ', ὀπαδοί: for similar injunctions to extras to remove a character see Bain, *Masters, Servants and Orders in Greek Tragedy*, p. 2 and p. 5 n. 13.

1265. cυγγνωμοcύνην: here alone in the whole of Greek literature, to produce impressively polysyllabic assonance and rhyme with the following ἀγνωμοcύνην. Compare Aesch. *Suppl.* 6 ff. δημηλαcίαν ... φυξανορίαν (both words also ἅπαξ), and for the general

---

[47] When Leo (p. 16) says of this Euripidean passage that there is nothing in Aeschylus or S to compare with its Homeric tone, he must be overlooking the present line.

264

LINES 1260-1275

phenomenon of rhyme at the end of consecutive anapaestic dimeters see Johansen and Whittle on Aesch. *Suppl.* 29 ff. (Aeschylean examples).

1266. θεῶν ἀγνωμοcύνην: for comparable tragic references to the folly of the gods (a feature more usually associated with Euripides) see Pearson, *CQ* 24 (1930), 159.

1267. πράccω is sometimes used of divine action: see Pearson on fr. 107. 6.

1268-9. S here exploits the common notion (see R. Pettazzoni, *The All-Knowing God*, trans. H. J. Rose (1956), *passim*, and J. Griffin, *CQ* 28 (1978), 1 ff. ≃ *Homer on Life and Death* (Oxford 1980), 179 ff.) of god or gods looking down in a calm and detached manner on the activity and suffering of mortals.

1268. The reference to parentage in the context of reproach from mortal to gods recalls *Od.* 20. 201 ff. Ζεῦ πάτερ, οὔ τιc cεῖο θεῶν ὀλοώτεροc ἄλλοc· | οὐκ ἐλεαίρειc ἄνδραc, ἐπὴν δὴ γείνεαι αὐτόc, | μιcγέμεναι κακότητι καὶ ἄλγεcι λευγαλέοιcιν. In the present passage, of course, the generalized reference hints particularly at Heracles. **κληιζόμενοι:** note particularly Eur. *Her.* 339-40 ὦ Ζεῦ, ... | μάτην ... παιδὸc κοινεῶν' ἐκλῄιζομεν.

1270. A familiar cliché (see e.g. Nisbet-Hubbard on Hor. *Odes* 1. 9. 13), here effectively worked in.

1271. τὰ δὲ νῦν ἑcτῶτ': cf. 1170 μόχθων τῶν ἐφεcτώτων and n. ad loc.

1271 ff. An impressive tricolon crescendo.

1273. δ' οὖν: the particles here convey the nuance 'but in truth' ('aber wirklich'): cf. Schwyzer, *Gr. Gr.* ii. 586.

1275. λείπου μηδὲ cύ: the extreme rarity in tragic anapaests of metra of this shape (— — — ∪ ∪) is observed by Diggle, *STE*, pp. 45-6, who lists five instances in Sophocles, three of them (including the present instance) removable by transposition (μηδὲ cὺ λείπου).

1275-8. For a recent discussion of the problems raised by these lines (Who speaks them? To whom are they addressed? What are the right readings in 1275?) see W. Kraus, *WS* 20 (1986), 102 ff.

1275. παρθέν': for a discussion of this person's identity see Easterling, *ICS* 6 (1981), 70-1. Campbell's anonymous 'girls of the household' (cf. 202 above) can quickly be dismissed (with Easterling, p. 71) as 'too shadowy' to be invoked at this important stage of the drama. The real choice is between Iole and the chorus. The former's absence from the

COMMENTARY

stage during Hyllus' stichomythia with his father may be inferred from the mode of reference to her at 1219–20, and this tells against her silent reappearance at any point following that reference, a reappearance that would be quite at odds with the text's failure to return her to any prominence. The chorus, then, seem the likeliest candidate, either addressed as παρθέν' by Hyllus or addressing themselves. There is no secure parallel for the singular self-address of the latter (plural is common: 821 ὦ παῖδες) or for the former, as is stressed by Kaimio, *The Chorus of Greek Drama within the Light of the Person and Number Used*, pp. 190–1. ἀπ' οἴκων: read ἐπ'. The inadequacy of ἀπ' is sufficiently exposed by Dawe (*Studies* iii. 98): λείπομαι ἀπό in *Il.* 9. 437 and 444 has the wrong connotation ('be left alone, away from'), and (as Easterling, p. 72, adds) the chorus's homes are irrelevant. ἐπ' will allow the meaning 'do not be left behind in the house', and the phrase may then be assimilated to the numerous passages where a chorus ends a play by proposing locomotion (see Easterling for examples). The chorus is to be imagined as processing towards Mt. Oeta as part of the funeral cortège. For the frequent confusion of ἀπο(-) and ἐπι(-) in manuscripts see on 843–4 above. οἶκος and οἶκτος are also easily confused (see e.g. Aesch. *Ag.* 134, Soph. *Ant.* 859, *El.* 92–3), but against the ἔτ' οἴκτων of Vauvilliers and Dawe (loc. cit.) Easterling (p. 72) cites the solemn instructions of Heracles at 1200, where abstention from mourning is enjoined. This, however, only concerns Hyllus: no rules were there laid down for the chorus.

1276–7. The careful balance of words here is noted by Easterling (cited in previous n.), p. 72, as telling against Subkoff's μελέους, advocated by Dawe (*Studies* iii. 98), who also suggests μεγάλου (cf. Eur. *Her.* 444). This labours under the further disadvantage that we do not wish to confine the death (even if θανάτους must be plural for singular: cf. Denniston on Eur. *El.* 484, Diggle, *ICS* 2 (1977), 113–14, Moorhouse, p. 6, Bers, pp. 41–2) to Heracles. On the metaphor implicit in the *v.l.* καινοπαγῆ see Müller, *Handwerk und Sprache*, p. 34.

1278. κοὐδὲν τούτων ὅ τι μὴ Ζεύc: the special use of ὅτι μή is observed by Moorhouse, p. 264, noting that 'elsewhere in literary texts ὅτι μή "except" is stereotyped as a conjunction, but here the pronominal sense of ὅτι is still apparent'. The phrase means 'Zeus is present in everything that has happened.' West, *BICS* 26 (1979), 112, approves Σ's notion that we must understand ἔπραξεν: 'the stark

LINES 1275-1278

presentation of a subject and object suffices to imply the most basic of subject-object relationships, "do"', and adds (p. 117 n. 18) 'fifth-century Greeks were capable of some strange identifications with Zeus or God... but they could not have said that the events of the *Tr.* were Zeus'. But the play is ending not with a philosophical speculation but a poetical statement: for parallels to it see Gow on Theocr. *Id.* 15. 8. *Il.* 13. 631–2 Ζεῦ πάτερ, ... | cέο δ' ἐκ τάδε πάντα τελεῖται, Aesch. *Ag.* 1485 ff. διαὶ Διὸς | παναιτίου πανεργέτα· | τί γὰρ βροτοῖc ἄνευ Διὸc τελεῖται; | τί τῶνδ' οὐ θεόκραντόν ἐcτιν; are examples of the sort of generalization we have here. Its sublimity recalls the Homeric Διὸc δ' ἐτελείετο βουλή.

APPENDIX A

The Flexibility of the Oracle in the *Trachiniae*

THAT the various references to an oracle in the play contain prima-facie inconsistencies has long been recognized. The relevant passages are:

(1) 44 ff. When Heracles left Deianeira *fifteen months* previously he bequeathed her an ominous δέλτος [Deianeira].

(2) 76 ff. When Heracles left Deianeira he bequeathed her oracles concerning Oechalia to the effect that he must either die or (after sacking Oechalia) win a happy existence [Deianeira].

(3) 155 ff. When Heracles left Deianeira he bequeathed her a δέλτος which revealed that after *fifteen months* he must either die or win repose [Deianeira].

(4) 820 ff. These lines refer to an oracle's prophecy that after *twelve years* Heracles' labours will end [the chorus].

(5) 1159 ff. An oracle of Zeus told Heracles that he was destined to be killed by someone already dead; a different oracle (from Zeus' shrine at Dodona) stated that Heracles would soon cease from his labours [Heracles].

Earlier scholars sought to remove these inconsistencies by emendation (e.g. Dronke's of 77) or deletion (e.g. Wunder's of 44–8, Dobree's of 76–81 and of 1165). More recently, it has been appreciated that the above passages rather exhibit a flexibility or fluidity that is extremely characteristic of Sophocles' dramatic technique. Tycho von Wilamowitz laid bare the contradictions with a ruthless clarity (pp. 119 ff.). W. Kranz, *Jahresberichte d. Philol. Vereins zu Berlin* 47 (1921), 32 ff. = *Studien zur antiken Literatur und ihrem Nachwirken*, pp. 283 ff., gave a much more sympathetic account of how the dramatic situation at each of the relevant stages of the play determines the content and presentation of the oracle. Thus, for instance, the open form of the oracle in (2) changes to closed inevitability in (5) because in the first passage S is concerned to build up tension and uncertainty, in the second to show acceptance of fate. Furthermore, dramatic technique becomes here the means of expressing a world-view:

THE ORACLE IN THE *TRACHINIAE*

the open alternatives suggestive of man's freedom to change his destiny are replaced by a revelation of the decision already made by the gods. This contrast between human and divine knowledge is perhaps the most important of all Sophoclean themes. On the role of the varying oracle in all this see further Schwinge, pp. 96 ff., D. A. Hester, *Antichthon* 13 (1979), 12–13, and (more generally) R. B. Rutherford, *JHS* 102 (1982), 148–9.

The obvious parallel for this extreme flexibility in Sophoclean dramatic technique is the oracle concerning Philoctetes' bow in the play of that name (cf. Tycho, pp. 275 ff., Schwinge, pp. 114 ff., Lloyd-Jones, *CQ* 22 (1972), 227 n. 1 = *Blood for the Ghosts*, p. 235 n. 42). Note also the wide fluctuations in the *Oedipus Coloneus* between the various accounts given as to the circumstances in which Oedipus left Thebes and cursed his sons (a particularly clear summary in Hester, *Antichthon* 18 (1984), 16–17).

APPENDIX B

Interlinear Hiatus in the *Trachiniae*

In his discussion of 'Interlinear Hiatus in Greek Tragic Trimeters' (*CR* 55 (1941), 22 ff.) E. Harrison made the interesting discovery that 'interlinear hiatus, not coincident with stop' (p. 23) was considerably more frequent in Sophocles' *Trachiniae* than in any other of his tragedies. This discovery may well have repercussions for the dating of our play (cf. Stinton, *CQ* 27 (1977), 67 ff., esp. p. 72, arguing that it constitutes 'evidence for chronological development, and ... an additional ground for regarding the *Tr.* as the earliest of Sophocles' extant plays'). It certainly has repercussions for its textual criticism, since, as Harrison expressed himself in a later article (*CR* 57 (1943), 63),[1] 'every instance [of interlinear hiatus in *Tr.*] should put us on the alert'. This generalization is indeed truer than Harrison himself seems to have realized. In his first article, having set apart seventeen examples of interlinear hiatus in *Trachiniae* not coincident with a stop, he explained ten to his own satisfaction as due to particular circumstances; in his second article he turned to the remaining seven, similarly explained away or regarded as corrupt five, but concluded in the light of the surviving two instances: 'even in this play a small residue of inexplicable hiatus persists' (p. 62). This may have been a premature verdict since one of the two passages he had in mind was 463–4 ἐπεί cφ' ἐγὼ | ᾤκτιρα δὴ μάλιcτα προcβλέψαc', where Harrison himself could 'offer no palliation' (p. 62: cf. p. 63: 'even in *Tr*. ... not every interlinear hiatus can be palliated') but Lloyd-Jones once suggested ἔγω ⟨γ'⟩ to me. The second (misreported as 1138–9) was 1196–7: πολλὸν δ' ἄρcεν' ἐκτεμόνθ' ὁμοῦ | ἄγριον ἔλαιον, where emendation is indeed difficult, but 1195–8 had been deleted by Wunder (see ad loc.). Whether these are cast-iron instances of irremediable hiatus may therefore be doubted.

It is also distinctly worrying that so many of Harrison's other instances of interlinear hiatus in *Trachiniae* have likewise been (or can be) emended or deleted *on quite independent grounds*. Of the other five, two he regarded

[1] This was posthumously published, which no doubt explains (at least partly) some of its inconcinnities and overlookings of the obvious.

INTERLINEAR HIATUS IN THE *TRACHINIAE*

as corrupt: in 1112–13 πένθος οἷον εἰςορῶ | ἕξουςαν ἀνδρὸς τοῦδέ γ' εἰ cφαλήcεται Harrison himself suggested cχήcουcαν (with some diffidence, feeling that even then 'the sentence does not command confidence' (p. 62)). The OCT prints εἰcορῶ ⟨c'⟩ | ἕξουcαν on the quite separate grounds that the sentence's construction is thereby clarified and ὦ τλῆμον Ἑλλάc unambiguously revealed as vocative (see ad loc.).

In 548–9 ἀφαρπάζειν φιλεῖ | ὀφθαλμὸς ἄνθος hiatus occurs in a notoriously difficult passage (see ad loc.). 'Some remedy which removes the hiatus may be right' thought Harrison (p. 61), and Nauck's φιλεῖ | τὸ κάλλος ἀνήρ certainly does that. Whether it be required on grounds of sense may be doubted, but the lines are so problematic that one would not like to see them used as irrefragable evidence for interlinear hiatus.

Of the remaining three examples, 934–5 ὄψ' ἐκδιδαχθεὶς τῶν κατ' οἶκον οὕνεκα | ἄκουcα κτλ., explained by Harrison (p. 62) as designed to emphasize ἄκουcα, is from a passage deleted by Jernstedt and Nauck (see ad loc.). Lines 277–8 ὁθούνεκ' αὐτὸν μοῦνον ἀνθρώπων δόλωι | ἔκτεινεν are similarly related by Harrison to 'the necessary stress on δόλωι which . . . may have been meant to be indicated by hiatus and pause' (p. 62).

Finally, at 761–2 ἀτὰρ τὰ πάνθ' ὁμοῦ | ἑκατὸν προcῆγε cυμμιγῆ βοcκήματα Harrison declared that τὰ πάνθ' ὁμοῦ (p. 62) was 'appositional and should be marked off by commas'. This seems reasonable, and the pause required adequately obviates the hiatus. Certainly, we can now see, more clearly than Harrison himself, that none of his potentially problematic cases provides a clear instance of 'inexplicable hiatus'.

Even the other few instances which Harrison had earlier explained away to his own satisfaction are more often than not suspect from quite independent sources of doubt. Thus, in *Tr.* 83–4 ἡνίκ' ἢ ceςώμεθα | ἢ πίπτομεν coῦ πατρὸς ἐξολωλότος '84 is spurious', as Harrison himself (p. 23) accepts (*del.* Bentley: see ad loc.). Lines 335–7 are a more complicated problem: ὅπωc | μάθηιc ἄνευ τῶνδ' οὕcτινάc γ' ἄγειc ἔcω, | ὧν τ' οὐδὲν εἰcήκουcαc ἐκμάθηιc ἃ δεῖ . . . Harrison (p. 23) reads οὕcτινάc τ' and explains this as an instance of 'hiatus between two clauses co-ordinated by a pair . . . of τε'. But 336 was deleted by Hense and Reeve, and this also involves omitting τ' in 337 (see ad loc.). Even those who keep 336 may prefer γ' (**a**) in it to τ' (Tr.: *om. cett.*), or Barrett's cφ' to both (again see ad loc.). Harrison's mode of explanation fails whatever approach we adopt.

APPENDIX B

In 252–3 'hiatus follows a self-contained participial clause', but the two lines were also deleted by Wunder (see ad loc.). In 896 the selfsame justification for hiatus is proposed by Harrison, but πληcίον for πληcία | ἔλευccεc (see ad loc.) removes it, and after 380 πατρὸc μὲν οὖcα γένεcιν Εὐρύτου ποτὲ | Ἰόλη κτλ. Radermacher posited a lacuna (see ad loc.), which again eliminates the phenomenon. Only for 919 δακρύων ῥήξαcα θερμὰ νάματα | ἔλεξεν κτλ. is there no obvious mode of excluding the hiatus.

In the next group of analogous explanations devised by Harrison, 943–4 exemplifies 'hiatus between two clauses co-ordinated by a single ἤ'. But the two partial analogies of 'hiatus between two clauses co-ordinated by a pair of ἤ' (83–4) or τε (336) have been destroyed above. Line 805 is a case where hiatus 'precedes the first of two clauses co-ordinated by a pair of ἤ' (cf. *Ant.* 38 εἴτε... εἴτε, 539 οὔτε... οὔτε). Last of all, in 1049 and 1067 hiatus 'precedes a dependent clause that has a finite verb'. The five cases just mentioned seem legitimate, legitimately explained, and otherwise untainted by the scent of corruption. But five is a small number of explicable examples of interlinear hiatus indubitably attested.

There is, of course, room for considerable doubt over several of the hiatus-eliminating deletions and conjectures mentioned above. But Harrison's main conclusions as to the rareness of this type of hiatus in *Trachiniae* emerge much strengthened from the present reinvestigation, in particular his contention that 'every instance... should put us on the alert'.

ADDENDA

Introduction

P. xvii n. 1: for the original German text of Schlegel's remarks here (*Vorlesungen über dramatische Kunst und Literatur*) see the critical edition by G. V. Amoretti (Bonn and Leipzig 1923), i. 92.

P. xix n. 5: for further consideration of the general topics of character and unity of action and their particular relevance to the *Trachiniae* see Malcolm Heath, *The Poetics of Greek Tragedy* (London 1987), 98 ff., etc.

Commentary

2. On αἰών see further G. Zuntz, 'Aion Gott des Römerreichs', *Abh. Heid. Akad. Wiss., phil.-hist. Kl.* (1989), 11–30. On ἐκμάθοι Diggle convinces me that I should have rejected this variant more decisively: ellipse of τις is legitimate when there is a participle to replace it (*El.* 697, fr. 951, *Aj.* 155; Aesch. *Ag.* 71, Hes. *Op.* 12, *Od.* 5. 400; cf. Fraenkel on *Ag.* 71, West on *Op.* 12, KG ii/1. 36) but not when a participle is absent (at Eur. *Or.* 908 cited by KG, Diggle reads ἡδύς τις (Musgrave) for ἡδὺς τοῖς λόγοις, φρονῶν κακῶς).

3. My parallels 'for the repeated τις . . . τωι of the same indefinite person' are vulnerable: Eur. *Or.* 1219 is deleted by Herwerden (see Willink ad loc.) and anyway, like *Hec.* 1178–9, involves a repetition in co-ordinated clauses not, as here, in clauses of different syntactical structure. For a much more striking repetition Diggle refers me to Eur. *Andr.* 733–4 ἔστι γάρ τις οὐ πρόσω | Σπάρτης πόλις τις, cf. Fraenkel, *Beob. zu Aristoph.*, pp. 89–91.

6 ff. Given the similarities between the prologues of *Tr.* and Eur. *Andr.* (see p. 55), v. 8 f. of the latter should be compared: ἥτις πόσιν μὲν "Εκτορ' ἐξ Ἀχιλλέως | θανόντ' ἐσεῖδον. On ἐνὶ Πλ- see further Denniston on Eur. *El.* 1058, West *GM*, p. 17 n. 32.

17. τῆςδε has inspired disquiet, as the conjectures of Wunder (τοῦδε) and Schneidewin (ταῖςδε (κοίταις)) attest. It might be defended as an extension of the idiom whereby ὅδε is used of something just

ADDENDA

mentioned to a case where the something (marriage to Achelous) is implied rather than mentioned directly.

38. One may add ἔκτα in Eur. *Hyps.* fr. 1. iv. 3 and ἔκταν in fr. 625 N² to Sideras's list.

40–1. βέβηκεν is here a stationary vb. (cf. my notes on 134 and 247 below) which constitutes the real argument against ποι (διῆλθε in *Phil.* 256 is hardly a parallel, therefore).

57. On the double infinitives see now G. K. H. Ley, *Hermes* 117 (1989), 498, who unnecessarily proposes νέμειν ... δοκοῖ.

68. Enclitic pronouns *can* follow a vocative when that vocative comes second in its sentence: see Barrett on Eur. *Hipp.* 327 (Diggle adds Eur. *Hcld.* 971 to his exx.).

88 ff. *Aj.* 853 (and thus the second ἀλλά) was deleted by Geel, *Mnem.* 2 (1853), 206 and Cobet, *Nov. Lect.*, p. 303. On *El.* 1334–5 see Stinton, *BICS* 32 (1985), 38.

94 ff. In citing Eur. *Hipp.* 525–6 I follow Barrett's text. Diggle's OCT prefers to adopt Paley's (Ἔρως) ὁ κατ' ὀμμάτων στάζων πόθον, which transforms the passage from an instance of 'der Relativstil' to one of 'der Partizipialstil der Prädikation' (see 99 n.).

112 ff. On ὥστε see further Diggle, *SIFC* 5 (1987), 169. On the locative dative in general see KG ii/1. 441–2, Moorhouse, pp. 86–7. The MSS of Eur. *Or.* 990 provide a parallel with πελάγεσι: for a discussion of that passage see Diggle, *The Textual Tradition of Euripides' Orestes* (Oxford, 1991) ad loc.

122. For the ellipse of definite (as opposed to indefinite) subject with participle represented by ἐπιμεμφομένας cf. Diggle, *PCPS* 28 (1982), 61.

154–5. As on 94 ff. I have followed Barrett's text of Eur. *Hipp.* which accepts Hadley's ἐρῶ (ἐγὼ codd.). Diggle's OCT prefers to obelize.

163. Further bibliography on three-termination adjs. treated as if they had only two in Diggle, *ICS* 2 (1977), 123.

167. Note also Eur. *Andr.* 338 ἦν ... μὴ θανεῖν ὑπεκδράμω.

178–9. For confusion of χάρις/χαρά see further Willink on Eur. *Or.* 159.

198–9. To the parallels cited add Eur. *Or.* 613 ἑκοῦσαν οὐκ ἄκουσαν (οὐχ ἑκοῦσαν Canter) and cf. Diggle, *Proceedings of the African Classical Associations* 12 (1973), 1.

218 (metrical analysis on p. 101). Diggle reminds me that my analysis of this line would entail resolution before syncopation (instances listed

ADDENDA

in *STE* pp. 18–21, 119). An alternative approach would analyse as ∪ – ⌣ | ∪ – – (for the resolved bacchius see Eur. *Tro.* 564 and possibly 319 ~ 535 (*STE* p. 19)).

210–11. *Phoen.* 1350 may be spurious (cf. Diggle, *CQ* 40 (1990), 117 n. 90). On ἀνάγω as equivalent to ἀναβάλλω see further Eur. *Tro.* 325, 332.

257. ἔτι (especially in its emphatically delayed positioning) requires comment: it is 'common in threats, prophecies, etc.' (Pearson on Eur. *Hel.* 57).

289. For further instances and discussion of redundant νιν or other pronoun see Page on Eur. *Med.* 1296, Fraenkel, *Beob. zu Aristoph.*, pp. 90–91 and 216, and Diggle, *Papyrologica Florentina* 7 (1980), 58; however, Wecklein's deletion of *OT* 246 ff. is approved by the OCT (cf. *Sophoclea*, p. 86) and this eliminates the parallel for redundant νιν here cited.

308. At *OT* 740–1 τὸν δὲ Λάιον φύειν | τίν' εἶχε φράζε the OCT in fact adopts Schneidewin's εἶρπε for εἶχε (rightly: see 1074 n.). The issue of the noun's meaning is not affected.

315. A closer analogy for the litotes is Eur. *Ion* 1115 μεθέξεις οὐκ ἐν ὑστάτοις κακοῦ.

343–4. It is true, indeed, that 'no intrigue in Greek tragedy can take place without the complicity of the Chorus; consequently it is a commonplace that a character should pledge them to secrecy' (Barrett on Eur. *Hipp.* 710–12). What we have at *Tr.* 343 ff., however, is not really describable as the preliminaries of an intrigue.

348. οὐ δίκαιος = 'unjust' in the sense of 'untruthful' (cf. vv. 410 ff.): see H. Fränkel, *Wege und Formen* (Munich 1955), 170 and n. 4.

396. See further Denniston on Eur. *El.* 868 (who overlooks 582), Collard on Eur. *Suppl.* 984–6, Jebb on Soph. *Ant.* 1275.

400. For φέρων, ἔχων, ἄγων as equivalent to 'with' see Stinton, *PCPS* 21 (1975), 85.

408. The duplication of τοῦτο here is striking: cf. Men. *Dysc.* 327 ff., 808 ff.; *Sam.* 461–2.

412. The opening πῶς μὴ δίκαιος, taking up the μὴ δίκαιος ὤν at the end of the previous speaker's contribution, is analogous to the 'indignant repetition of a previous speaker's word' discussed in 429 n.

429. A particularly close parallel to ἐγὼ δάμαρτα; is ἐγὼ σ' ἀδελφὸν τὸν ἐμόν; at Eur. *IT* 803.

ADDENDA

430. For the construction τόνδε τίc ποτ' ἐcτὶν ὁ ξένοc see 97–8 n.

452. Cf. Diggle's conjecture at Eur. *Suppl.* 913 and Broadhead's at Eur. *Alc.* 153 (λέγεcθαι for γενέcθαι) and cf. Jackson, *MS*, p. 42.

457. I should have commented on the characteristically Sophoclean *variatio* in δέδοικαc . . . ταρβεῖc. Cf. *Aj.* 458–9 μιcεῖ . . . ἔχθει. *OT* 54 ἄρξειc . . . κρατεῖc, *El.* 986–7 cυμπόνει . . . cύγκαμν', Bruhn, *Anhang*, §218.1.

520. For the *schema Pindaricum* see further Barrett on Eur. *Hipp.* 1255 (and Addenda, pp. 436 f.), West, *BICS* 28 (1981), 62 n. 6.

553–4. τῇδε was conjectured by F. W. Schmidt at Eur. *El.* 757 (for τήνδε): Diggle ad loc. compares Soph. *El.* 643 (ὧδ' ἄκουε) and *OC* 1300 (ταύτηι κλύω), but Reeve's deletion of the latter is accepted in the OCT.

564. Dindorf's ἤ here is rather more likely than my note allows, in view of the regularity with which MSS give ἤν for ἤ (cf. 414 n.).

567. Cf. Eur. *Or.* 277, where the MSS' πνευμόνων is defended against the conjecture πλ- by Bond on Eur. *Her.* 1093 but effectively assailed by Willink ad loc.

626. This note too blandly assumes the correctness of the paradosis in *OC* 113 and Eur. *Alc.* 420–1. In fact, in *OC* Nauck conjectured τοι καὶ for τε καί and in *Alc.* Diggle prints Nauck's τοι for the τε of BOV and the γε of LP. He tells me that he believes the text of *Rhes.* 219–20 is to be cured by a similar remedy: cωθήcομοί τοι (τε VLG: δε' O) καὶ κτανὼν 'Οδυccεώc | οἴcω κάρα coι. These passages differ from our line in being answers to commands (cf. Denniston, *GP*[2], p. 541), as do *Rhes.* 570–1 ὅρα . . . :: φυλάξομαί τοι (OLQ: τι Va), *Ion* 759–60 εἴφ' . . . :: εἰρήcεταί τοι; cf. *Phil.* 48 ἀλλ' ἔρχεταί τε (τοι Blaydes) καὶ φυλάξεται cτίβοc. In all these passages τοι would occupy, the first element of the second metrum and follow a verb ending in -μοι or -ται, as in *Aj.* 743 ἀλλ' οἴχεται τοι, Eur. *El.* 415 ἠcθήcεταί τοι καί . . . Diggle therefore suggests τοι καί for our passage too (comparing, for the corruption with following καί, Eur. *Alc.* 38; and elsewhere Soph. *Aj.* 268, *El.* 1469, Aesch. *Pers.* 795, *PV* 39; Eur. *Hipp.* 610, *Phoen.* 1327, fr. 335 N[2]).

644. For the double genitive cf. *Phil.* 489 cited in my note on 1191 and see further Page on Eur. *Med.* 49, Johansen and Whittle on Aesch. *Suppl.* 549. Doubts may still remain about the present instance, however (why did S not write τε παῖc for κόροc?), though Wecklein's ὁ γὰρ Διὸc ἀλκαῖοc κόροc is unattractive.

ADDENDA

647. On πάνται see further Diggle, *CQ* 33 (1983), p. 352 n. 58, 40 (1990), 114.

668. For οὐ δή τι cf. Eur. *El.* 57.

677. Schenkl's emendation of *El.* 382 in fact receives no mention at all either in the OCT or in *Sophoclea*; but a very strong case for it is made by R. Seaford, *JHS* 110 (1990), 79–80.

680. On the position of με here see Barrett's note on Eur. *Hipp.* 10–11.

699–700. Dawe's conjecture is approved by Diggle, *SIFC* 5 (1987), 169, on the ground that it eliminates a problematic instance of ὥcτε with finite vb. introducing a comparison in tragic iambics.

768. Should a certain class of critic object to the 'ugly jingle' in Herwerden's ὥc ἐκ τέκτονοc, Diggle refers me to his remarks in *PCPS* 15 (1969), 59 and *STE*, pp. 75–6; also Hopkinson on Callim. *h.* 6. 128, McKeown on Ov. *Am.* 2. 2. 52; L. P. Wilkinson, *Golden Latin Artistry* (Cambridge 1963), 28–9. Herwerden's conjecture is in *Exerc. Crit.* (1862), 128.

824. On ὅ τε see Diggle, *SIFC* 5 (1987), 172.

836 ff. *El.* 197 ff. is itself textually suspect (Wakefield transposed ἔροc and δόλοc and conjectured μομφάν for μορφάν) so caution is in order.

846–7 (metrical scheme on p. 196). For the rarity of correption in dochmiacs see Conomis, *Hermes* 92 (1964), 40, Stinton, *BICS* 22 (1975), 105 n. 22.

874 ff. (on the issue of 'large-scale remedies') and **892** (on 'questions as emotional reactions'). M. C. Stokes in *Owls to Athens* (Dover Festschrift; Oxford 1990), 17–18 is reluctant to interpret the chorus' τι φωνεῖc; at 892 as an 'emotional "question"', mainly because 'repetition of news after an initial surprised question is not normally followed by a further emotional "question".' Regarding Alexiou's reference to catechistic questions in tragic laments as of dubious relevance, he contemplates the deletion of 881–90 as an 'actor's doublet'. The suggestion is advanced in inevitable ignorance of the OCT's treatment of the passage, and in perhaps slightly less inevitable ignorance of Dale's re-ordering of the passage and Zieliński's alternative deletion of 871–9 (and 891 and 898 ff.) as a doublet.

888. For the 'bacchius in the second metron of the trimeter' see Stinton, *BICS* 22 (1975), 84 ff.

911. Perhaps the deletion should be extended to include the next two

ADDENDA

lines as well. This is suggested to me by Diggle, who finds the καί in κἀγώ at the start of 914 odd since the Nurse (as the text stands) is already the subject of the verb in 912–13. The content of these two lines could be inferred from 907. Both Pearson's conjecture and Reeve's objection to it pre-date the twentieth century by some considerable time, as is clear from the remarks of Meineke, *Analecta Sophoclea* (1863), 301.

941. At *OT* 656 Nauck's μήποτέ c' αἰτίαι is adopted by the OCT (cf. *Sophoclea*, p. 95) thus removing the strongest analogy for Pearson's conjecture here.

978. For 'οὐ μή + subjunctive or future indicative' as urgent imperative see also Barrett on Eur. *Hipp.* 212–14.

1003. I now think that the Greek here is an illogical but effective combination of two ideas: (*a*) if I saw that, it would be a wonder; (*b*) I would *never* (litotes: see esp. τηλόθεν at *Phil.* 454–5) see that.

1005. In fact (as Diggle reminds me) Euripides too employs the variation in quantity here discussed: see *Suppl.* 42 γεραιά γεραιῶν, *Phoen.* 881 νεκροὶ περὶ νέκροιc and Barrett, edn. of Eur. *Hipp.*, p. 370.

1007–9. On the illogical (but emotionally effective) sequence 'I want to die—you're killing me!—I want to die' which this passage shares with Eur. *Hipp.* 1347 ff. see Sommerstein, *BICS* 35 (1988), 41.

1156. I should have cited M. Marcovich, *Three-Word Trimeter in Greek Tragedy* (Beitr. zur kl. Phil. 158; 1984), esp. 53.

1160. On the two prepositions see further Willink on Eur. *Or.* 407.

1207. On the meaning of παλαμναῖοc see H. Tresp, *Die Fragmente der gr. Kunstschriftsteller* (Giessen 1914), 44.

INDEX OF GREEK WORDS

(for particles see General Index s.v.)

ἅ (pathetic exclamation) 650
ἀγγέλλω 1110
ἀγηθής 870
ἁγνός 258, 287
ἀγώνιος (of gods) 26
αἰών 2
ἀκτίς 697
ἀλάςτωρ 1235
ἀμφίγυος 504
ἀμφίπλεκτος/-ικτος 520
ἀμφίπυρος 214
ἀνευφημῶ 783
ἀνθῶ/ἄνθος 1089
ἀντίλυρος 643
ἀραῖος 1202
ἀργῆς 675
ἀρτίκολλος 768
ἀρτίπους 58
αὐθαίμων 1042
ἄφαρ 134

βάλλω/ἐμβάλλω 940
βάπτω 574
βασιλεύς (of gods) 127
βίος 941–2
βόσκομαι 144
βουθερής 188
βούκρανος/-πρωιρος 13
βρύκω 987

γάμος 1139
γείτων (of gods) 215
γύναι 230

διήνεμος 327
δρῦς 766

-ειος adjs. 51, 70
ἔκβρωμα 700
ἐκγράφομαι 1167
ἐκκλέπτω 437
ἐμπελάζω 12
ἐμπόλημα 533
ἐνδατοῦμαι 791
ἔξοιδα 5, 988
ἐξολλύμι 84
ἐξορμῶ 1089
ἐπεικάζω 141, 1220
ἐπεύχομαι 809
ἐπίσταμαι (= δύναμαι) 543
ἕρκος (bezel) 615
εὐνά(ζ)ω 1005
εὐνάτρια 918
εὑρίσκω/ἐξευρίσκω 284, 1177–8
ἐφεστίος 262
ἐφορῶ 1269
ἔχιδνα 771

ἠγορῶ 601
ἦμος 531
ηὔγμην 610

θαῦμα 1003
θερμός 1046
θρέμμα 574, 580
θροέω 531
θρώισκω 1027

INDEX OF GREEK WORDS

καταρρακόω 1103
κελαίνος 856
κληΐc 1035
κλύω 189, 1115
Κρονίδης 127
κτίζω 898

λείπω 76, 157, 266
λέχος 27, 360
ληρέω 435
λόγος 1

μαστήρ 733
μάταιος 888
μελαγχαίτης 839
μεταίτιος 260–1, 1234
μόνος 1063, 1109–10
μυρίος 1101

ναύλοχος/-ον 633
νεφέλη 831

ξυνοικέω 1055

ὀδαγμός/ἀδαγμός 770
ὅδε 39, 1238
ὄλεθρος/ὀλέθριος 878
ὀρμή/ὀργή 720
οὐδέ ('not … as well') 280
οὔπω (non-temporal) 158–9
οὐcία 911
ὀφθαλμός (of love) 549
ὄχημα 656

πανάμερος 660
πάντα 647
παρῆλθε 960
παρθένος 148, 1070–1, 1275
πελάγιος 647
πέπειρα 728
περονίς 925

πλεύμων 778
πόcιc 550
ποτέ 25, 31
πρό (= ὑπέρ) 504
προπετής 976
προστάτης 208

ῥαβδονομέω 516
ῥήγνυμι 919

Cελλοί 1167
cεcωμένος 83
cπείρω (metaph.) 33
cπιλάc 678
cτάcιc 964, 1179
cτόλος 226, 562
cτόμιον 1261
cυγγνωμοcύνη 1265

τάλας 792, 1084, 1148
τέκομαι 834
τελεόμηνος 824
τῆμος 533
τρέφω 107, 834
τροπαῖος 303

ὑπαγκάλιcμα 540
ὑπερ-/ὑπεκτρέχω 167
ὑφαντός 1052
ὕψιcτος 1191

φαίνω (of speech) 1, 1241
φέγγος 1143
φθόνηcιc 1212
φύcιc 308

χαρά/χάρις 179
χλωρός 1055
χρυcηλάκατος 638

ὡς (= ὥστε) 590

INDEX OF PASSAGES DISCUSSED

(a) SOPHOCLES

Aj. 852 ff.: 88 ff.
   972–3: 42
   1020: 267 ff.
   1026–7: 1160 ff.
Antig. 186: 267 ff.
   686: 543
   1315 f.: 930–1
El. 197 ff.: 835
   596: 322
   758: 572 ff.
   1032 ff.: 539 ff.
OC 35–6: 47
   1506: 560
OT 491 ff.: 158
fr. 172 Radt: 999

(b) OTHER AUTHORS

Aeschylus, *Ag.* 472 ff.: 303–4
   1344: 316
Cho. 886: 1160 ff.
ScT 372–3: 58
Suppl. 265: 47
   314: 644
Anacr. (?) 505(d) P = fr. Anacr. vet. 1 West: 497, 497 ff.
Antiphon B94 DK: 149
Aristophanes, *Av.* 982: 1167
   Thesm. 1226 ff.: 827
Apollodorus 2. 7. 7: pp. xxxiii f.

Bacchylides, *Dith.* 16: p. xxxii

Callimachus fr. 239 *Suppl. Hell.*: 645

Cornutus, *Theol. Graec. Compend.*, pp. 7–8 Lang: 127

Epicrates fr. 9. 3–4 KA: 827
Euripides, *Alc.* 152 ff.: 904 ff.
   837: 1089
   839: 560
El. 688: 930–1
   784 ff.: 1055–6
Hel. 353 ff.: 930–1
   1253: 911
Her. 337: 911
   1353: 1101
Hipp. 550: 857
   871–3: 874 ff.
   1198–9: 750 ff.
Med. 1244 ff.: 549
Phoen. 1455 ff.: 930–1
Tro. 317: 647
   766 ff.: 834
Phaedra: 930–1
fr. 354 N^2: 911
   384 N^2: 781–2
[Euripides], *Rhesus* 386–7: 644

Herodotus 2.255: 173, 1167
   3.64: 1171–2
   8.59: 516
Hesiod fr. 26. 31 ff. MW: p. xxvi
Homer, *Il.* 1. 105 ff.: p. xxi
   2. 106–7: 76
   22. 26: 31 ff.
ΣA *Il.* 13. 147: 504
Od. 7. 123: 144
   11.86: 234

INDEX OF PASSAGES DISCUSSED

Homer, *Od. (cont.)*:
   19. 455 ff.: 1000–1
   21. 22 f.: 271

Men. *Sam.* 516–17: 336

Pherecydes *FGrH* 3 F 50: 1095
Pind. *Ol.* 2. 13: 644

Theocr. *Id.* 1. 32: 368
Thuc. 6. 12. 2: 673
TrGF 1 (15) 2. 12–13: 1089
   2 (adesp.) fr. 374 = 1. 88 fr. 3: 1171–2
   (adesp.) fr. 587: 12–13

Verg. *Aen.* 4. 650: 917 ff.
   664 ff.: 930–1

GENERAL INDEX

Note that, as far as possible, related entries have been grouped together under the relevant (generalized) heading. Thus 'Aphrodite' and 'Zeus' both appear under 'Gods'; 'aorist' and 'perfect' under **'grammar/syntax'**, subsection 'verbs (tenses)'; and a multitude of phenomena under **'style'**.

accentuation 343, 380
Aeschylus:
  use of by S 307 ff., 538, 831
  compared with S 516, 526, 586, 1010, 1214
  contrasted with S 84, 146, 381, 589, 1255
anapaests, special features of 977, 1275
artefacts as illuminating texts, etc. pp. xxxiv ff., 11, 11–12, 12–13, 18 ff., 512, 516, 562–3
author's variants, possibility of existence discussed 12–13
characters:
  Deianeira pp. xvii ff., in Prologue p. 55; rhetorical appeal 436 ff., *Trugrede* (?) 531 ff., farewell to house 903 ff., suicide 930–1
  Heracles pp. xvii ff., weapons 512, self-address 993 ff., 1260, labours 1012, 1046 ff., tears 1072
  Hyllus, timely entrance of 58; *rhesis* of 749
  Iole p. xxvii; status as concubine not wife 1216 ff., 1227
  Lichas 'good fortune' of 192; not mere slave 453

Old Man, relationship to Amphitryon in Eur. *Her.* 974 ff.; not doctor 988
chorus:
  address, by self 202, 821, 865, 1275; by others 141, 673, 871, 1275
  advise or warn 592–3
  consolation offered by 124 ff.
  entrance motivated 103 ff.
  exit announced 1275
  presence artificially alluded to 343–4
  self-reference 589, 871
  singular vb. used of self 865
  sudden knowledge (for dramatic ends) 825, 828 ff.
corruptions, discussed 44 ff., 206, 526, 528, 545 ff., 554 f., 614–15, 623, 628, 677–8
  anticipation/repetition of letters/words 88 ff., 331, 554, 744
  assimilation of endings 547 ff.
  construction misunderstood 66
  crasis misunderstood 396
  hiatus abhorred 839
  homoioteleuton and omitted line 176–7

GENERAL INDEX

corruptions (*cont.*):
　intrusion of letter 639, 642
　lipography 944
　mechanical plus mental error
　　555–6
　misdivision of letters, words 162,
　　615
　parenthesis confuses 338
　'polar' error 368, 677, 756
　prefix confused: ἀπο-/ἐπι- 141;
　　ἐν-/ἐκ- 368, 677; παρα-/περι-
　　194–5; ὑπερ-/ὑπεκ- 167;
　　ὑπο-/ἐπι- 356
　reversal of letters 673, 844, 1105–6
　similar letters confused 2–3
　similar words confused 98, 162,
　　187, 445, 1074, 1199
　syllable omitted 120, 206
　synonym (unmetrical) ousts
　　original 956
　word from context ousts original
　　267 (ὡς), 380, 623, 1114, 1184
　word omitted, later replaced by
　　wrong one 602, 1062
cruces 196, 267 ff., 419–20, 661 ff.,
　854 ff., 1019–20

dramatic irony 1 ff., 71, 321, 576–7,
　684
dramatic technique, discussed
　p. xxiv f., 35, 43 ff., 58, 61 ff.,
　68, 70, 79–80, 141–204, 178–9,
　189–90, 199, 222, 225–456,
　236, 307 ff., 336, 340 ff., 343–4,
　389, 392, 402 ff., 531 ff., 592,
　686 ff., 811, 825, 828 ff., 934,
　962 ff., 969–70, 984 ff.,
　1114–15, 1127–8
anonymous references to dramat-
　ically insignificant figures 70

audience address denied 806,
　1079–80
characters of low social standing
　do not sing 874 ff.
economy (characters unrealistically
　know what audience knows)
　872, 934
timely entry 58

emendations, discussed/accepted 47,
　58, 71, 77, 88, 100, 105, 108,
　114, 117, 118 ff., 144 ff., 158–9,
　188, 190, 198, 250, 296, 321,
　338, 356, 389, 394, 452, 526,
　528, 562–3, 581, 615, 627–8,
　801, 835, 836 ff., 890, 1016,
　1017, 1021, 1155–6, 1160, 1208,
　1231
Euripides, compared with S 1 ff.,
　986 ff., 1101, 1125
　contrasted with S 84, 146, 381,
　586, 613, 902, 1010, 1256

gods:
　Apollo 208–9
　Aphrodite 492, 515–16, 860
　Artemis 214, 638
　Athena 1031
　Chiron (ranked as god) 714–15
　Eros 354; as boxer/wrestler 442;
　　assimilated to Aphrodite, p. 137
　　n. 14
　Hades 501, 1040, 1085
　Hermes 620
　Poseidon 502
　Zeus: generally 127, 139–40, 279,
　　500, 1022, 1278; associated
　　with: Cenaeum 238, Dodona
　　172, Oeta 200, 436, 1191,
　　epithets: ἀγώνιος 26,

GENERAL INDEX

τροπαῖος 303–4, ὕψιστος 1191
grammar/syntax:
NOUNS
cases
 nominative: attraction into 1117–18; + ὤ 1040
 vocative 202–3; or apostrophe 1026; 'ingratiating' 1070
 accusative: cognate 159, 848; double 339; of motion towards 58, 329; internal 157–8, 219–20, 866–7; of respect 137; of whole and part 225–6
 genitive: attraction of accusative into 241, of relative advb. into 701–2; double 56–7, 108, 644, 1191; of exchange 737; explanatory 1199; of learning 934; of part + accusative of body 779
 dative: locative 114, 298, 1151–2; 'pregnant' 668
 juxtaposition of different cases *see* 'polyptoton' (s.v. **'style'**)
gender
 masc. for fem. 151–2, 1237
 masc. participle used by fem. speaker 151–2, with pl. vb. 490 ff.
number
 plural: for singular 268, 390, 409, 492, 632, 1237, 1248; generalizing 316; of modesty 632
 singular for plural: collective 257, ἄγε in exhortation 1255
PREPOSITIONS
 ἀμφί + acc. 937
 ἐκ 875, 1078, 1109, 1133
 ἐν 207, 613
 ἐπί 532
 κατά + acc. 102

πρός + gen. 935
ὑπό 931, 1160
VERBS
middle, special uses 103, 1167, 1171
mood, optative in simile 112 ff.
tenses
 aorist: athematic 38, 610, 645; emphatic 499–502; gnomic 33; ingressive 48, 500; of sudden emotion 1044
 future: attraction into 712; + negative as 'emphatic denial' 978
 imperfect 76–7, 234–5 (λείπω), 381 (καλῶ); of sudden realization 1171–2
 perfect, of duration 1009; intensive 15; resultative 133–4
 present, historic 528, 767; use of, baffling 419
 contrast in juxtaposition of two different tenses 21, 698, 989
varia
 'mixed' construction 1238
 prefix of first vb. extended to second 89
 simplex equivalent to compound 195
 tmesis 129 ff.
 unaugmented vbs. 499–500, 514, 560

Herodotus, kinship with S 1171–2
iambic trimeter:
 repeats in calmer mood content of lyrics 497 ff., 898–9
 special features of 4, 28, 350, 725, 762, 888, 1098 ff., 1112
ideas/motifs
 blanket covers lovers 539 ff.

285

GENERAL INDEX

ideas/motifs (*cont.*):
  cycle in human affairs 129 ff.
  'dead' and 'blind' equivalent 828
  dead kill living 1160 ff., 1163
  death as healer 1209
  death as journey 874–5
  dying man prophesies 1150
  Erinys sucks blood 1054 ff.
  'eye' of day/sun 102
  eye and love 107, 549
  'late-learning' 710, 934
  love as disease 445
  love overpowers even gods/Zeus 497 ff., 500
  marriage as yoke 536
  medicine as magic 1001–2
  metamorphosis and water 10
  mind as writing tablet 683
  misunderstood oracle 1171–2
  night as time of worries 29, 149
  nightingale as symbol of woe 105, 963
  pain as monster 974 ff., 1027 ff.
  river as bull 12–13
  slaves speak truth/wisdom 62–3
  sleep 'scattered' 989 ff.
  time accompanies man 1169
  writing, anachronistic use of 157–8
  youth, happy because innocent 143 ff.
interpolations, discussed 25, 43–8, 84, 150, 252–3, 280, 295, 305, 356–7, 362 ff., 424, 444, 455–6, 584, 684, 696, 781–2, 874 ff., 901–3, 903, 907–9, 911, 932–4, 1156, 1165, 1173, 1250 ff., 1257 ff.
  beginning with ἦ 84
  Binneninterpolation 362 ff.
  'bloodthirsty' 781–2

close of play 1257 ff.
gloss introduced into text 823, 838
ναί inserted *extra metrum* 424
patched together from words in context 684, 911
πρὸς cαφήνειαν τῶν λεγομένων 444, 696
replace other lines 252–3, 871 ff.

morality 383, 453–4, 468–9; gods hate hybris 280

orthography:
  ἐλε(ε)ινός 528
  θακῶν/θωκῶν 23
  κατή(ι)δη 87
  κλ(ε)ιτύc 271–2
  πάρ/παρά 636
  πλεύμων/πνεύμων 567
  cεcωcμένοc 83
  crasis/prodelision 60, 66, 239, 295, 381, 560, 564, 772–3, 905, 940
  elision of -αι illicit 216; at end of iambic trimeter 1112; of syllabic augment 560, 904
  synizesis 85 (ἠ οἰ), 321 (μὴ εἰ), 715

paradosis, ambiguous 328, 379, 564, 1220
particles:
  general remarks 225–6, 626
  specific instances: ἀλλά 119 ff., 147, 229, 503, 801; γάρ 9, 27, 62–3, 132 ff., 144 ff., 252–3, 338, 472 ff., 900, 962 ff.; δέ 116, 198, 1062, = γάρ 252; δή 26–7, 668; καί 31, 187, 345, 1048; μέν 1, 69; μέν . . . δέ 229; τε . . . δέ 143; τε . . . τε 202–3

GENERAL INDEX

various collocations 153–4, 876–7, 1128
production 61 ff., 307 ff., 336, 389, 402 ff.; *see also* pp. xxxvii ff.
prosody:
  hiatus: after τι 1203; interlinear: Appendix B
  lengthening: before δρ- 1012; before πλ- 7
  punctuation 52 ff., 497, 768, 1136
  hiatus as form of 510–11, 525

religion:
  animal names for priestesses 172
  averting prayer (ἀποπομπή) 303 ff.
  martial vow 238–9
  oracles 86–9, Appendix A
  purification 258, 287
  sacrifice 764, 1195 ff.
  see also s.v. 'gods' and 'hymnic/prayer features' (s.v. **'style'**)

style
  alliteration 947 ff.
  anacoluthon 143
  anadiplosis (reduplicatio) 96, 221, 655
  anaphora 161–2, 263–4, 517–18, 550–1
  antithesis: emphatic 1228; juxtaposed 459–60
  apocope 636
  apostrophe 96 ff., 633 ff., 1026, 1079, 1089, 1112–13
  article (definite) 47, 78, 261, 540, 650, 932, 1068–9; repetition of 1105–6
  asyndeton 189–90, 439–40, 596, 787–8, 851, 900, 1221 ff.
  balance 229
  'blasphemous paradox' 783

catachresis (abusio) 58, 504, 513, 675, 1014, 1125
colloquialisms 319, 338, 408, 418, 421, 427, 429, 435, 669, 819, 890, 1136, 1184
'elevation' 380, 699, 1166–7, 1212
ellipse 117, 122–3, 134 ff., 168, 259–60, 264, 295, 305, 505–6, 547 ff., 584, 799; '*Versparung*' 3, 236, 423, 1122–3
emphasis/intensification 8, 320, 383, 403, 422, 431, 468–9, 505–6, 545, 613, 650, 694, 803 ff., 891, 1093, 1115, 1225 ff.
enallage 357, 656
epic features 94, 112 ff., 127–8, 531 ff., 650, 765, 786, 852, 902, 904, 1011, 1214, 1263
etymology/word-play 128, 168, 483, 706, 756, 757, 760–1
exclamation at prophecy's fulfilment 1143
exemplification of generalization 6, 9, 444
gnome 1, 3, 439–40, 497, 943 ff., 943
hiatus 650
hymnic/prayer-like features 94 ff., 102, 205 ff., 221, 222, 655 ff., 660; relative in: 94 ff.; repetition in: 94 ff., 95, 210–11, 221–2
hyperbaton 112 ff., 184, 200, 242, 247–8, 298, 540 ff., 646 ff., 746–7, 815–16, 1111, 1221 ff.
juxtaposition 775–6, 1062, 1068–9, 1207
kenning 572 ff. (p. 161), 874–5, 1051–2, 1093, 1095
litotes 43, 280, 315, 1093
locus amoenus 144 ff.
'mixed metaphor' 549
numerals, ordering of 44–5

GENERAL INDEX

style *(cont.)*:
onomatopoeia 517–18, 522
oxymoron 554, 1051–2
parechesis 947 ff.
periphrasis: βιά + gen. 38; μέγα τι cθένοc 497; cθένοc/φάcμα + gen. 507–8, 836 ff.; ἔχω + participle: aorist (cχῆμα Cοφοκλεῖον) 37, imperfect 646, present 646; θρέμμα 574; θακῶν ἦν 22–3; abstract nouns in 350; participial 311; verb + direct object governing accusative 420
'polar expressions' 236, 324, 747, 1021
polyptoton *vel sim.* 28, 198, 459, 473, 494, 608, 613, 650, 798, 885, 938–9, 994
priamel *(praeambulum)* 1 ff., 497 ff., 503, 1046 ff., 1103; *praeteritio* idiomatic within: 499–500
proleptic adj. 106–7
question answered by own asker 505–6, 718
question as exclamation 316, 865, 892, 965, 1010–11
Racheformel 1036
refutatio sententiae 1 ff.
relative: at start of stanza 122; attracted to genitive 701; attracts antecedent into own case 283, 1060; referring back 136, 358; definite article used for 47; idiomatic in prayers 94 ff.
repetition: intentional/rhetorical 300, 650, 707, 716, 833, 996, 1066–7, 1105–6, 1129–30, 1234; unintentional 88, 174, 1114

rhesis 1 ff., 141 ff., 193, 306, 749, 807; close of 42, 84, 468–9, 807, 819–20, 943 ff.; *est locus* formula within: 750 ff., 752–3; start of: 193, 749, 900
riddle 572 ff. (p. 161), 874–5, 1092
ring-composition 124 ff., 306
schema Pindaricum 520
similes 118; Homeric 112 ff.; *illustrans* and *illustrandum* fused within: 31 ff., 129, 147, 770–1, 1261–2; μάλιcτα idiomatic in 699; paratactic 132 ff., 144 ff.; problematic 768
Sophoclean features of: adjectives used for nouns 633; doublet, use of 109–10; etymology 128; Ionicism, use of 1196; κυρῶ + personal dative 291; metaphorical use of τρέφω 108; middle for active in vb. 103; noun (abstract) + rare adj. 50; noun (abstract) in apposition to personal subject 537–8; particles 876–7; positioning of ἀεί 104; repetition in odes 102, 833; three termination adjs. 163; word-order 1099–1100
stichomythia 380 ff., 1179 ff., 1186, 1189, 1191, 1250–1
syllepsis 353–4
'synaesthesia' 693
synonyms juxtaposed 1207
'transferred' epithet 63
tricolon 180, 234, 405 ff., 734
variation 1005; rhetorical, of vbs. 834
verbal pleonasm/redundancy 80–1, 175–6, 241, 267, 315, 346, 545, 731, 735, 738, 997–8, 1130, 1161, 1207, 1256

GENERAL INDEX

verbal responsion in lyrics p. 221,
p. 230
word-order 1, 2, 65–6, 112 ff.,
144–5, 161, 273, 301–2, 322–3,
338, 350, 360, 382, 436, 460,
464, 526, 541–2, 545, 611, 668,
674, 742, 780, 955 ff., 994,
995 ff., 1014, 1031, 1099–1100,
1117–18, 1221 ff., 1231
zeugma 144–56

variants discussed 1, 2, 7, 12–13, 121,
227–8, 673, 787–8, 1220, 1226